Lecture Notes in Computer Science 12199

Vincent G. Duffy (Ed.)

Digital Human Modeling and Applications in Health, Safety, Ergonomics and Risk Management

Human Communication, Organization and Work

11th International Conference, DHM 2020
Held as Part of the 22nd HCI International Conference, HCII 2020
Copenhagen, Denmark, July 19–24, 2020
Proceedings, Part II

 Springer

Editor
Vincent G. Duffy
Purdue University
West Lafayette, IN, USA

ISSN 0302-9743   ISSN 1611-3349 (electronic)
Lecture Notes in Computer Science
ISBN 978-3-030-49906-8   ISBN 978-3-030-49907-5 (eBook)
https://doi.org/10.1007/978-3-030-49907-5

LNCS Sublibrary: SL3 – Information Systems and Applications, incl. Internet/Web, and HCI

This Springer imprint is published by the registered company Springer Nature Switzerland AG
The registered company address is: Gewerbestrasse 11, 6330 Cham, Switzerland

Foreword

The 22nd International Conference on Human-Computer Interaction, HCI International 2020 (HCII 2020), was planned to be held at the AC Bella Sky Hotel and Bella Center, Copenhagen, Denmark, during July 19–24, 2020. Due to the COVID-19 coronavirus pandemic and the resolution of the Danish government not to allow events larger than 500 people to be hosted until September 1, 2020, HCII 2020 had to be held virtually. It incorporated the 21 thematic areas and affiliated conferences listed on the following page.

A total of 6,326 individuals from academia, research institutes, industry, and governmental agencies from 97 countries submitted contributions, and 1,439 papers and 238 posters were included in the conference proceedings. These contributions address the latest research and development efforts and highlight the human aspects of design and use of computing systems. The contributions thoroughly cover the entire field of human-computer interaction, addressing major advances in knowledge and effective use of computers in a variety of application areas. The volumes constituting the full set of the conference proceedings are listed in the following pages.

The HCI International (HCII) conference also offers the option of "late-breaking work" which applies both for papers and posters and the corresponding volume(s) of the proceedings will be published just after the conference. Full papers will be included in the "HCII 2020 - Late Breaking Papers" volume of the proceedings to be published in the Springer LNCS series, while poster extended abstracts will be included as short papers in the "HCII 2020 - Late Breaking Posters" volume to be published in the Springer CCIS series.

I would like to thank the program board chairs and the members of the program boards of all thematic areas and affiliated conferences for their contribution to the highest scientific quality and the overall success of the HCI International 2020 conference.

This conference would not have been possible without the continuous and unwavering support and advice of the founder, Conference General Chair Emeritus and Conference Scientific Advisor Prof. Gavriel Salvendy. For his outstanding efforts, I would like to express my appreciation to the communications chair and editor of HCI International News, Dr. Abbas Moallem.

July 2020   Constantine Stephanidis

HCI International 2020 Thematic Areas and Affiliated Conferences

Thematic areas:

- HCI 2020: Human-Computer Interaction
- HIMI 2020: Human Interface and the Management of Information

Affiliated conferences:

- EPCE: 17th International Conference on Engineering Psychology and Cognitive Ergonomics
- UAHCI: 14th International Conference on Universal Access in Human-Computer Interaction
- VAMR: 12th International Conference on Virtual, Augmented and Mixed Reality
- CCD: 12th International Conference on Cross-Cultural Design
- SCSM: 12th International Conference on Social Computing and Social Media
- AC: 14th International Conference on Augmented Cognition
- DHM: 11th International Conference on Digital Human Modeling and Applications in Health, Safety, Ergonomics and Risk Management
- DUXU: 9th International Conference on Design, User Experience and Usability
- DAPI: 8th International Conference on Distributed, Ambient and Pervasive Interactions
- HCIBGO: 7th International Conference on HCI in Business, Government and Organizations
- LCT: 7th International Conference on Learning and Collaboration Technologies
- ITAP: 6th International Conference on Human Aspects of IT for the Aged Population
- HCI-CPT: Second International Conference on HCI for Cybersecurity, Privacy and Trust
- HCI-Games: Second International Conference on HCI in Games
- MobiTAS: Second International Conference on HCI in Mobility, Transport and Automotive Systems
- AIS: Second International Conference on Adaptive Instructional Systems
- C&C: 8th International Conference on Culture and Computing
- MOBILE: First International Conference on Design, Operation and Evaluation of Mobile Communications
- AI-HCI: First International Conference on Artificial Intelligence in HCI

Conference Proceedings Volumes Full List

http://2020.hci.international/proceedings

11th International Conference on Digital Human Modeling and Applications in Health, Safety, Ergonomics and Risk Management (DHM 2020)

Program Board Chair: **Vincent G. Duffy, Purdue University, USA**

- Giuseppe Andreoni, Italy
- Mária Babicsné Horváth, Hungary
- Stephen Baek, USA
- André Calero Valdez, Germany
- Yaqin Cao, China
- Damien Chablat, France
- H. Onan Demirel, USA
- Yi Ding, China
- Ravindra Goonetilleke, Hong Kong
- Akihiko Goto, Japan
- Hiroyuki Hamada, Japan
- Michael Harry, UK
- Genett Jimenez-Delgado, Colombia
- Mohamed Fateh Karoui, USA
- Thorsten Kuebler, USA
- Noriaki Kuwahara, Japan
- Byung Cheol Lee, USA

- Kang Li, USA
- Masahide Nakamura, Japan
- Thaneswer Patel, India
- Caterina Rizzi, Italy
- Juan A. Sánchez-Margallo, Spain
- Deep Seth, India
- Meng-Dar Shieh, Taiwan
- Beatriz Sousa Santos, Portugal
- Leonor Teixeira, Portugal
- Renran Tian, USA
- Dugan Um, USA
- Kuan Yew Wong, Malaysia
- S. Xiong, South Korea
- James Yang, USA
- Zhi Zheng, USA
- Rachel Zuanon, Brazil

The full list with the Program Board Chairs and the members of the Program Boards of all thematic areas and affiliated conferences is available online at:

http://www.hci.international/board-members-2020.php

HCI International 2021

The 23rd International Conference on Human-Computer Interaction, HCI International 2021 (HCII 2021), will be held jointly with the affiliated conferences in Washington DC, USA, at the Washington Hilton Hotel, July 24–29, 2021. It will cover a broad spectrum of themes related to Human-Computer Interaction (HCI), including theoretical issues, methods, tools, processes, and case studies in HCI design, as well as novel interaction techniques, interfaces, and applications. The proceedings will be published by Springer. More information will be available on the conference website: http://2021.hci.international/.

General Chair
Prof. Constantine Stephanidis
University of Crete and ICS-FORTH
Heraklion, Crete, Greece
Email: general_chair@hcii2021.org

http://2021.hci.international/

Contents – Part II

Addressing Ethical and Societal Challenges

New Research Issues and Approaches in Digital Human Modelling

Contents – Part I

DHM for Aging Support

Modelling Human Communication

Netlogo vs. Julia: Evaluating Different Options for the Simulation of Opinion Dynamics

Laura Burbach$^{(\boxtimes)}$ (iD), Poornima Belavadi (iD), Patrick Halbach (iD), Lilian Kojan (iD), Nils Plettenberg (iD), Johannes Nakayama (iD), Martina Ziefle (iD), and André Calero Valdez (iD)

Human-Computer Interaction Center, RWTH Aachen University, Campus-Boulevard 57, Aachen, Germany
{burbach,belavadi,halbach,kojan,plettenberg,nakayama,
ziefle,calero-valdez}@comm.rwth-aachen.de

Abstract. Analysing complex phenomena, such as the world we live in, or complex interactions, also requires methods that are suitable for considering both the individual aspects of these phenomena and the resulting overall system. As a method well suited for the consideration of complex phenomena, we consider agent-based models in this study. Using two programming languages (Netlogo and Julia) we simulate a simple bounded-rationality opinion formation model with and without backfire effect. We analyzed, which of the languages is better for the creation of agent-based models and found, that both languages have some advantages for the creation of simulations. While Julia is much faster in simulating a model, Netlogo has a nice Interface and is more intuitive to use for non-computer scientists. Thus the choice of the programming language remains always a trade-off and in future more complex models should be considered using both programming languages.

Keywords: Agent-based modeling · Simulation · Julia · Netlogo · Programming languages

1 Introduction

Today, we live in a world, that is more complex than years ago. We are almost always and everywhere on the mobile Internet, using cloud storage or cloud computing and AI technologies such as deep learning. Also, when humans interact with each other or with digitized technology we speak of complex systems. The interaction of humans in such systems, for example in opinion-forming processes, leads to consequences that we cannot yet overlook or understand. An important component of socio-technical complex systems are single individuals that appear as human-in-the-loop [6]. To look at people, their interactions and the resulting overall behaviour, we need suitable methods, such as simulations.

© Springer Nature Switzerland AG 2020
V. G. Duffy (Ed.): HCII 2020, LNCS 12199, pp. 3–19, 2020.
https://doi.org/10.1007/978-3-030-49907-5_1

Simulations make it possible to observe the resulting overall system or the resulting behaviour by representing individual processes, procedures and behaviour. In addition, simulations make it possible to identify tipping points that lead to a different outcome of the overall system.

Agent-based models are a form of simulation. As the name implies, they always consist of agents. In addition to the agents, the environment in which the agents are located and with which they interact is also modelled. However, agents can be designed in different ways, depending on the context to be considered. For example, agents can be more than just people interacting with each other. If, for example, traffic jams are to be considered, cars are used as agents, if it is considered how possible forest fires can be avoided, the agents are trees. The agents differ not only in their form, but also in several other dimensions. For example, the agents can be completely or to a lesser extent autonomous. Their interests and character traits can also be different. For example, they can act selfishly or in favor of the totality of all agents. They can be outgoing or prefer to remain separate. Some agents are able to learn from their experiences or observations. Agents can also be of varying degrees of complexity [8]. Despite the potential complexity of agents and the possibility to model them in very different ways, most agent-based models tended to focus on simple, local rules [10]. Furthermore, there is a view that the simulations are mainly randomly implemented to run on a computer [14].

Various frameworks have been developed for creating agent-based models. The most established language or program of these is Netlogo [27]. But while Netlogo was authored by Uri Wilensky in 1999, the spread of the Internet also resulted in the evolving of different programming languages [6]. Thereby more languages can be used to create agent-based models. So far, it has not been considered which language is actually best suited for creating agent-based models. Therefore, in this study we investigate whether Netlogo or Julia is better suited for creating agent-based models.

2   Related Work

In this study, using agent-based modelling we consider opinion formation processes, thus we look at a complex system. We want to know, whether it is possible to create an agent-based model with the programming language Netlogo and the programming language Julia. We further consider, how the two languages differ, which are the strengths for creating agent-based models of each programming language and which are the disadvantages. Contentwise, we built a bounded rationality model to simulate opinion formation.

Therefore, we explain, which aspects lead to complexity, we introduce the method agent-based modelling and the two programming languages Netlogo and Julia. Besides, we eplain what is known in theory about opinion formation or the spread of information.

2.1   Complexity and How to Model It

When examining opinion-forming processes, we look at a complex system. Such complex systems can be divided into several ontological levels or interacting subsystems on a micro- or macro-level [9] We first have to look at how systems are structurally designed in order to deduce what leads to complexity [6]. Further, complex systems lead to emergent phenomena. These complex systems and emergent phenomena are difficult to understand, because while it is easy to observe the individual system components, the resulting overall system cannot be considered as the sum of its parts. Instead, understanding the system behavior requires more than understanding the individual parts of the system [6].

Complex vs. Complicated. When we look at complex systems, we do not necessarily mean complicated systems. A system consisting of components can initially be both complicated and complex. However, while the term complicated is always related to human understanding, the term complex is not necessarily so. If something is complicated, such as a mathematical differential equation, this means that it is difficult for us humans to understand. To be complex at the same time, the equation would have to contain many small parts. However, it is also possible that an equation consists of few parts and is therefore not complex, but is nevertheless complicated to understand. The two terms therefore both refer to a system consisting of components, but mean different aspects of the system and a system which is complicated does not necessarily have to be complex system and vice versa. A complex system consists of many sub-components, whose interactions make it difficult to predict the behaviour of the system. The number of components as well as the complicated interactions of the parts are considered complex [4, 24]. Another characteristic of complex systems, which is particularly important for our study, is that complex systems are always dynamic. If a system consists of many parts, but does not show dynamics but remains static, it is never complex. It is easy to investigate it comprehensively [6].

Emergence. Typically, we look at individual components of a system. From these subcomponents we then often infer the behavior of the overall system. However, as Aristotle said, the whole is more than the sum of its parts, and it is therefore not really correct to observe only the components and conclude on the overall behavior. However, it is problematic that we can usually observe and understand individual components or individual behavior, but the overall behavior is often more difficult to observe. If the interaction of the individual components results in a system that cannot be described by the sum of the individual components, we speak of emergence.

With agent-based models we can make emergent behavior visible. We can model the individual agents and design them according to individual rules that they follow at the micro level. When the agents interact with each other and with their environment, unpredictable social patterns, i.e. emergence, occur [3].

2.2   Agent-Based Modelling

To analyse complex systems we need a suitable approach, such as simulations, which enable to model the individual parts of a system and thus make the overall behavior visible. For the simulation of complex systems, agent-based models are very well suited [11].

Agent-based models always consist of the agents or individuals and the environment in which the agents reside [2]. They are neither a representation of reality, nor fully realistic or even complete. Instead, they show a simplified reality. Nevertheless, agent-based models show behaviour on an individual level close to reality. By mapping the individual behavior, the behavior of the overall system can then be qualitatively observed [20]. Agent-based models are well suited to replicate data and present the results to non-experts [17]. The use of a method always requires an evaluation of the method. Evaluating agent-based models is not easy. In order to evaluate them, independent replicating and comparing with other model as well as a validation are necessary [20].

The basis of agent-based modeling is the single agent or the individual. This agent is modelled programmatically as a template. In simulation, due agents make their own decisions based on how they perceive the environment in which they are situated. The perceptions of an agent usually determine the behavioral intent of the agent. If the agents are in a social network, as in our model, they influence their neighbours in the next iteration by their behavioural intention or the behaviour they show. To determine the probability of organizational acceptance, we analyze the results of several agent-based simulations.

A simple way to create agent-based models is to use software toolkits developed for the creation of simulations. These include the Netlogo toolkit considered in this study. With the use of such toolkits, it is easy to formulate the behavior of the individual agents. They also usually contain some useful interfaces. The interfaces allow to visualize the simulation states, interact with the simulation parameters and export the simulation results. In addition, they usually contain a batch mode. This is used to run a large number of simulations. Optimization strategies, such as genetic algorithms, help to find the most suitable parameters [7].

To create agent-based models, Netlogo [27] is the language most commonly used. Nevertheless, there are some other programming languages that are also suitable for creating agent-based models and that seem to be partly more intuitive, at least for people with programming experience. Therefore, in this study we compare two programming languages with respect to their suitability for creating agent-based models.

2.3   Opinion Formation and Bounded Rationality

In describing social phenomena, social scientists traditionally have tended to employ causal modeling techniques. That is, phenomena are explained by causally linking different variables. However, when describing phenomena like opinion formation in groups, repeated interactions between people appear to be more influential than static variables [21, 22]. Analytical models for the process of opinion formation therefore focus on group dynamics. They employ agents whose opinion develops over time as they interact with other agents whose opinion may be similar or different from their own. Computer simulations can be used to explore how varying different parameters, like the number of agents or the way agents interact with each other, will affect the distribution of opinions. Hegselmann and Krause [15] give an overview over how different models mathematically describe the process in varying complexities. One distinction between models is how opinion is represented. For continuous opinion dynamics, the assumption is that opinions are one-dimensional in that they can be described as a number. The smaller the difference between two numbers is, the closer are the opinions they represent. Another main distinction between the models is the way in which other agents' opinions influence one agent's own opinion, i. e., the weight which one agent puts on others' opinions. In the easiest case, this weight is modelled as constant, but it might also be modelled as differing, e.g., dependent on the susceptibility of each agent or as dependent on the disparity between two agents' opinions. This last case can be described by so-called bounded confidence models which have been proposed by both Hegselmann and Krause [15] and Nadal [18]. With a bounded confidence model, the agent will only interact with agents whose opinion is relatively close to their own. To put it another way, they will only put weight on similar opinions. The threshold for similarity is defined as the bounds of confidence epsilon which, assuming continous opinion dynamics, represents the maximum difference between the numbers ascribed to the opinions where the other's opinion will still be considered. An extension to this model of bounded confidence is something we call the backfire effect. As described by Jager [16], if an agent interacts with another agent whose opinion is very dissimilar, they will not just ignore that opinion. Instead, they will shift their opinion to be even further away from the other agents' dissimilar opinion. To summarize, for a bounded confidence model with backfire effect, an interaction between two agents has three possible outcomes: 1. If the difference between their opinions is smaller than or equal to a certain confidence interval epsilon, their opinions will converge. 2. If the difference between their opinions is bigger than or equal to a certain backfire threshold (which might be equal to epsilon), their opinions will diverge. 3. If epsilon and the backfire threshold are not equal and the difference between their opinions is between epsilon and the backfire threshold, their opinions will remain unchanged.

3 Method

Using two different programming languages (Netlogo and Julia language), we created two identical agent-based models that simulate opinion formation. Since our primary aim was to find out whether agent-based models could be implemented equally well in the two programming languages, we chose the most basic model of opinion-forming: bounded rationality.

We built the agent based models using the Atom editor of the Julia programming language and version 6.0.4 of the multi-agent programming language

Netlogo, which was developed by Wilensky [27]. For the following analysis of the results we used R Markdown.

3.1   First Steps in Agent-Based Models

While we have previously (see Sect. 2) explained what agent-based models are and what they are used for, we following describe how they are structured programmatically. We start with the most basic components.

An agent-based model usually contains a "setup" and a "go" procedure. The "setup" procedure defines a kind of basic state at the beginning of the simulation. The "go" procedure then specifies what happens in a single step of the simulation.

In Netlogo the "setup" procedure usually looks like in Fig. 1. In Netlogo, procedures always start with "to" and end with "end". Clear-all makes the world go back to its initial, empty state. For example, if colors were assigned to the spots where the agents are located, they will now turn black again. Create-turtles creates the specified number of turtles, here 100. The turtles usually start at the origin, i.e. in the middle of patch 0.0. The code in the square brackets after create-turtles here indicates that the turtles start at a random x and y coordinate. The square brackets could also be used to create other commands for the agents. Reset-ticks makes sure that the tick counter starts. Once this code is created, the simulation starts in the interface by clicking the "Setup" button. In Julia the setup includes an additional configuration.

Additionally, the agents and their environment are designed before the simulation starts. For example, properties are assigned to the agents and the agents' environment is designed to resemble the reality of what is being observed. In our case, the agents do not have specific properties and the environment is also in its default state.

```
to setup
  clear-all
  create-turtles 100 [ setxy random-xcor random-ycor ]
  reset-ticks
end
```

Fig. 1. Setup procedure in Netlogo

3.2   Bounded Rationality Model

Since our primary goal was to compare the two programming languages with each other, we designed the parameters of the Netlogo model and the Julia model the identical way. Thus, we increased the comparability of the results of both models and reduced the complexity as much as possible. In the beginning of our bounded rationality model, we defined the maximum number of agents, the maximum steps of the simulation, the seed, an epsilon as well as whether a backfire effect takes place or not. The epsilon indicates how different the opinions of two people can be, so that they still include the other person's opinion in their opinion formation. We further defined from the beginning, that each agent has an (floating) opinion between 0 and 1. In each simulation step, every agent compares his opinion with the opinion of an other agent. For example, if Anna compares her opinion with Ralf and the distance between the opinion of Anna and Ralf is smaller than the defined epsilon, then the two converge in their opinions. Additionally we defined in the beginning, whether an backfire effect takes place or not. When the simulation includes the backfire-effect and Ralf's opinion deviates more than the epsilon indicates from Anna's opinion, then the opinion of Anna distances from the opinion of Ralf.

While in Netlogo the parameters for the simulation runs are determined in the Behavior Space (see Fig. 4), in Julia the initial settings are determined in the "main" procedure, what can be seen in Fig. 6.

As can be seen in Fig. 6 and 4, we set the number of agents 100 to 500 in increments of hundreds (100:100:500). We varied the epsilon between 0.1 and 1 in increments of 0.1 and varied between with backfire-effect and without (true/false). We set the maximum number of steps to 100.

Go Procedure. Here we compare the "go" procedures, so what happens in each step of the simulation, of Netlogo and Julia (see Fig. 2 and Fig. 3). Both codes look similar. In Netlogo (see Fig. 3), the procedure starts by addressing the agents (ask turtles). The next line of code says, that the addressed agent gets the opinion of one random other agent. The subsequent lines of code determine what happens to the (new) opinion of the agent. If the other agent's opinion differs less from his own opinion than the epsilon (see above), the agent assumes the average opinion of the two opinions. This means that the opinions of the two agents are added together and divided by two. However, if the opinion of the other agent is further away than the respective (may vary) epsilon indicates, it checks whether the backfire effect exists. If the simulation is set to show that the effect exists, the opinion of the agent is half the distance away from the opinion of the other agent. At the end, the code indicates that the color of the agents depends on the opinion. However, this is only for illustration in the interface. Before the procedure ends, one more "tick" is counted as one time unit.

The "go" procedure in Julia is very similar. One difference is that the procedure is passed a configuration (config) at the beginning. Furthermore, an agent list with the agents in random order is passed.

3.3   What Do We Compare

To find out whether both programming languages are equally suitable to simulate our bounded rationality model, we look at several measurable criteria. These criteria include the outcomes and performance of both models. They further include how many lines of code are necessary to program the simulation.

```
function go(config, rng, agent_list)
    for one_agent in shuffle(rng, agent_list)
        idx = rand(rng, 1:config.agent_count)
        other_agent = agent_list[idx]
        if abs(other_agent.opinion - one_agent.opinion) < config.epsilon
            one_agent.opinion = (other_agent.opinion + one_agent.opinion) / 2
        else
            if config.backfire
                if one_agent.opinion < other_agent.opinion
                    one_agent.opinion = one_agent.opinion -  abs(other_agent.opinion - one_agent.opinion)/2
                else
                    one_agent.opinion = one_agent.opinion + abs(other_agent.opinion - one_agent.opinion)/2
                end
                if one_agent.opinion < 0
                    one_agent.opinion = 0
                end
                if one_agent.opinion > 1
                    one_agent.opinion = 1
                end

            end
        end
    end
    agent_list
end
```

Fig. 2. Go procedure in Julia

```
to go
  ask turtles [
    ; get the opinion of one random other turtle
    let otheropinion [opinion] of one-of other turtles

    ; is opinion in range
    ifelse abs ( opinion - otheropinion ) < epsilon [
      ;then take average opinion
      set opinion ((opinion + otheropinion )/ 2)
    ]
    [ ; do we have backfire
      if backfire [
        ; shift away half the distance
        ifelse (opinion < otheropinion) [
          set opinion opinion - ( abs ( otheropinion - opinion ) / 2 )
        ] [
          set opinion opinion + ( abs ( otheropinion - opinion ) / 2 )
        ]

        if opinion < 0 [set opinion 0]
        if opinion > 1 [set opinion 1]
      ]
    ]
    ; set color to red range
    set color 11 + opinion * 8
  ]
  tick
end
```

Fig. 3. Go procedure in Netlogo

Another aspect, that we take into consideration, is, if learning Julia and Netlogo is equally difficult. For this aspect we consider both computer scientists who are familiar with other programming languages and a person who has no previous experience with programming languages. We further compare the explorability and scalability of both languages.

4 Results

Before we present the results of our bounded rationality model, we reflect on the extent to which the two languages Julia and Netlogo are suitable for developing agent-based models and how easy it is to get started with the two languages.

4.1 Getting Started with both Languages

Both Julia and Netlogo are languages that address both researchers and begin-ners. Netlogo is derived from Logo a language that is aimed at children to lern programming. The core aim of Netlogo is agent-based modeling and it has several primites for this purpose. Julia is aimed at scientists that require both perfor-mance and understandable code. The core aim of Julia is to make code fast, reusable and easy to understand. This quick introduction by no means covers the breadth of both of these languages, it aims to provide a high-level overview.

Netlogo. Netlogo as a modelling language for agent-based modeling is very well suited for beginners wanting to use agent-based modeling. It comes with a rich variety of example models that users can explore and provides a graphical user interface and a graphical user interface toolkit to create models that even non-experts can use. Thus, Netlogo is visually appealing and the interface enables users to create and test agent-based models and also simplifies the initial creation of a model. Figure 5 shows the Interface of our simulation. Netlogo also provides methods for inspecting the model (reporters and visualizations) and for exploring the impact of model parameters on system behavior (i.e. the *behavior space* feature, which allows the user to run any number (usually several hundred) of simulations). The latter allows turning of the GUI for faster simulations (see Fig. 4).

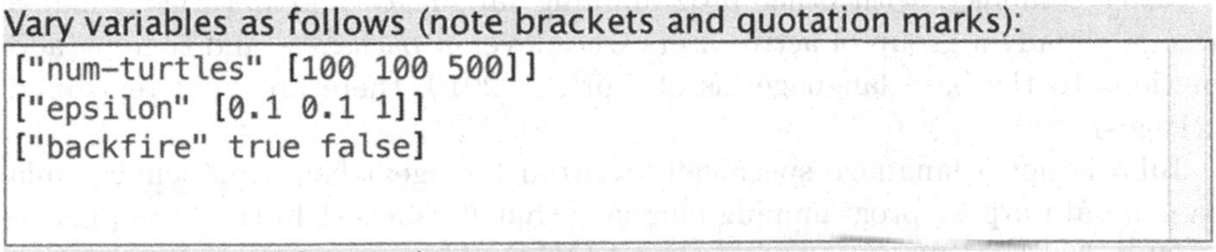

```
Vary variables as follows (note brackets and quotation marks):
["num-turtles" [100 100 500]]
["epsilon" [0.1 0.1 1]]
["backfire" true false]
```

Fig. 4. Behavior space in Netlogo

Netlogo provides immediate visual feedback for the user of an agent-based model and has easy to understand primitives that allow modelling of agent behavior, agent interactions, and agent-environment interactions. It provides an API for extensions, to allow other researchers to complement the functionality of Netlogo.

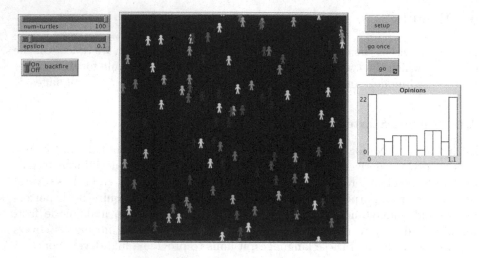

Fig. 5. Interface of our bounded rationality model in Netlogo

Overall, it is very easy to start using Netlogo. However, creating complex models requires understanding of usage contexts in the language. People coming to Netlogo with a computer science background may find some of the language concepts unintuitive and clunky. Several of the authors of this paper have found Netlogo syntax to be confusing and unnecessary simplistic.

Julia. Julia was initially introduced by a group of computer scientists and mathematicians at MIT under the direction of Alan Edelman. Compared to other programming languages Julia is considered fast, easy to learn and use and it is open source. Further advantages of Julia compared to other programming languages are that it supports parallelization or practical functional programming and can be easily combined with other programming languages and libraries. Finally, there is already a group of active users who develop packages (and thereby add functions to the base language; as of April 6, 2019, there are 1774 registered packages).

Julia is not a language specifically written for agent-based modeling. Julia is a general purpose programming language that uses a just-in-time compiler to generate low level machine code (using LLVM). This means there is no native support for typical agent-based modeling tasks. There is a library for agent-based modeling called `agents`. However, our intention here was to compare the programming language itself without the use of a library. It is unclear whether the library is going to be maintained in the future, whereas Julia's support is not likely to expire soon.

This means the user has to design all tools for agent-based modeling themselves. However, this is not necessarily very hard. It depends on the complexity of the model. When this barrier has been overcome, writing a model becomes easier. The language is very similar to python.

```
function main()
    # create config objects
    agent_counts = 100:100:500
    epsilons = 0.1:0.1:1
    max_steps = [100]
    replications = 1:50
    my_config = generateBatchConfig(agent_counts,
                                    epsilons,
                                    max_steps,
                                    replications)
    startandsave(my_config, "results.csv")
```

Fig. 6. Main procedure in Julia

4.2 Comparison of Agent-Based Modeling Results of Julia and Netlogo

Following, we present some exemplarily results of our bounded rationality model. We also show, if the model created with Netlogo showed the same or different results as the model created with Julia. Based on these results, we compare the two considered programming languages and show their advantages and disadvantages.

Opinion Change of Agents. Following we consider, how the opinion of the agents changed during the simulation steps of the bounded rationality model with and without backfire effect. At this point we do not distinguish between the two programming languages used.

We use four examples (see Fig. 7) to illustrate how the agents change their opinion during the simulation and how different the opinions look at the end of the simulation. As can be seen at the top left of Fig. 7, one possible outcome is

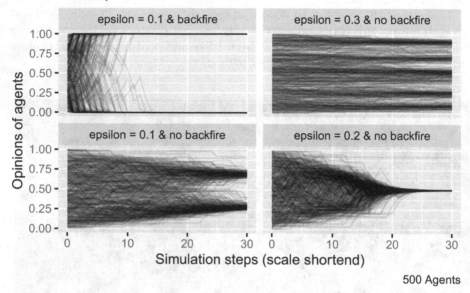

Fig. 7. Four exemplarily examples

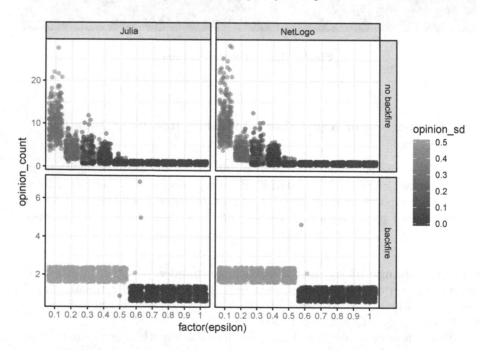

Fig. 8. How language, epsilon and backfire influence the opinion count

Table 1. Comparison of the ten most different settings for both languages

Epsilon	Backfire	agent_count	t-value	p-value	Degrees of freedom
0.3	FALSE	200	−2.245263	0.0269995	97.95147
0.1	TRUE	200	2.103480	0.0386304	78.40132
0.4	FALSE	200	1.989794	0.0494162	97.43888
0.3	FALSE	400	−1.606152	0.1115634	94.89243
0.1	FALSE	200	1.601283	0.1126316	95.08476
0.1	TRUE	100	−1.564258	0.1221526	71.82311
0.2	FALSE	200	1.412877	0.1609382	95.62983
0.5	FALSE	300	1.416342	0.1630015	49.00000
0.4	FALSE	100	1.392850	0.1669769	93.25748
0.1	TRUE	300	−1.301375	0.1965824	86.58427

that the opinions of the agents diverge completely and only two extreme opinions are formed. After less than 15 simulation steps, every agent has either opinion 0.00 or opinion 1.00. In this example, the epsilon is low and the backfire effect takes place.

In comparison to this example, in the third example (bottom left) no backfire effect takes place. In both examples, the epsilon is 0.1. Comparing the two examples, it becomes clear that the backfire effect increases the divergence of opinions. While in the first example two clear opinions quickly establish, in the third example there are more different opinions for a longer time. After 20 simulation steps, two groups of agents form whose opinions are similar to each other. Nevertheless, even after 30 simulation steps, these agents still have similar opinions, but not one uniform opinion.

In example 4 (bottom right), also no backfire takes place. Here, the different opinions converge to a consensus of opinion. After around 20 simulation steps each agent has the opinion 0.5.

In contrast, in example 2 (top right) no majority opinion develops, but several groups with the same opinions form. In this example, the epsilon is higher than in the other examples, which leads the agents to accept opinions that differ more from their own than in the other examples.

Influence of Programming Language, Epsilon and Backfire on Opinion Count. After we looked at the opinion formation of the agents itself, we now consider, whether the epsilon, if the backfire effect takes place or not and the programming language has an influence on the existence of different opinions. To look at the influence of the enumerated factors, we consider (see Fig. 8) how many different opinions exist (y-axis). We further consider the standard deviations of the opinions (color) to analyse how different the opinions are.

As Fig. 8 shows, if the epsilon is higher than 0.55, practically all agents have only one opinion (sd = 0.0), regardless of whether the backfire effect takes place or not and which programming language is used. When the epsilon is lower than 0.55 and the backfire effect takes place, there are two opinions among the agents that diverge to the two extremes of opinion (sd = 0.5). In comparison, when the epsilon is lower than 0.55 and no backfire effect takes place, the agents have more different opinions, but the standard deviations of the opinions are lower (less bright) than in the simulations with backfire effect. The lower the epsilon is, the higher is the amount of opinions. Comparing the two programming languages, the amount of different opinions is a bit higher when NetLogo is used, but the difference is small. Overall, the two programming languages showed almost the same qualitative results. As Table 1 shows, the quantitative comparison of both languages showed, that except of three simulation runs, the t.test wasn't significant. Thus the languages showed the same results.

4.3   Comparison of Julia and Netlogo After Our Bounded Rationality Simulation

When comparing both programming languages to create an agent-based model that simulates the bounded rationality model, Julia proved to be a faster language. The whole simulation took only 82.23 s, whereas the Netlogo simulation took 36 min. While the model calculation in Julia is much faster, Netlogo required less than half the lines of code. To write the bounded rationality model in Julia 97 lines of code were necessary, in Netlogo only 44 lines of code were necessary.

When we consider how difficult it is to learn the two programming languages, we also have to take into account the previous knowledge of the users. Thus Netlogo proved to be a language that is easier to learn for people without programming skills. In contrast, people with previous programming skills reported, that it is easier to learn Julia, because it is more similar to other already used programming languages (for example Python).

An advantageous feature of Netlogo, is that the platform contains an easy to use, clear and attractive interface. These interface makes it easier to get started with and learn the language for people without previous programming experience. The interface offers the user direct feedback, as the simulation runs visibly if he has written the code correctly and also immediately reports back error messages if the code is wrong. In addition, the interface allows the user to try out and change various things in the process.

Also, the fact that there is already a large library of existing agent-based models in Netlogo, since the language is used exclusively for this method, makes it easier to use, since existing models can be built upon or users can orient themselves on them.

In addition to the interface, the Logo programming language, which Netlogo uses, is also easy to use because there is only a manageable number of structurally different commands and users can quickly get a feel for which procedures and functions always need to be set when creating agent-based models.

5   Discussion

In our study, no language turned out to be the perfect programming language for creating agent-based models, but the choice of language seems to be a trade-off between various advantages and disadvantages and also between different potential users and use cases.

For people who have never used a programming language before and are not supported by people with previous programming experience, the entrance to the Netlogo language is certainly easier than to the Julia language. Likewise, starting with Julia is easier for people with programming experience, because they already know, how the language is probably organized. It can be assumed that modelers who are already very familiar with the language they use also develop more complex simulations than simulation based on simple rules [10]. So less effort in learning a language can certainly increase the complexity of the models.

One other aspect, that could be taken into account, is the time, that is needed to run the simulation. Here Julia turned out to be much faster. But, in many research areas or for many research questions it does not really matter, whether the language is really fast. One aspect, that is probably more important is, that very big simulations in Netlogo require high computing power and that the computers sometimes crash, making it impossible to calculate the model In this case Julia makes it possible to calculate the simulation without any problems.

Of course, we have only focused on one very simple bounded rationality model, so that we would have to create further simulations with both languages to be able to make statements about the generality.

Historically, the basis for analytical opinion dynamics models is given by psychological research and philosophical theories about social influence (e.g., [13,23]). And simulations based on those models have frequently proven to reliably enough reproduce real-life phenomena [22]. However, as Flache et al. [12] argue, there is a lack of recent empirical studies reassessing and replicating the assumptions underlying those models, let alone studies examining the size of epsilon in real-life interactions. In future research, finding a way to link analytical opinion dynamics models with contemporary empirical psychological findings would be desirable.

6   Conclusion and Outlook

The results of our research have shown that, although Netlogo has been established for a longer time, both programming languages are well-suited to create agent-based models. Comparing the two languages, we could not find one perfect language, but each language is the better choice for creating an agent-based model in some aspects. The decision for a programming language depends on different trade-offs (previous experience vs. support; time to create the model vs. time used for simulation run; nice interface vs. higher functionality). In the end, however, it does not make sense to decide in favor of one language against the other, but to take advantage of both languages and thus use Netlogo for prototyping and Julia for larger simulations based on these prototypes.

With this study we compared Julia and Netlogo to create a very simple bounded rationality model. In the future, we would like to extend this comparison by using both languages for more complex simulations. We further plan to pursue with studies, that combine both languages.

Acknowledgements. This research was supported by the Digital Society research program funded by the Ministry of Culture and Science of the German State of North Rhine-Westphalia.

We used the following packages to create this document: `knitr` [28], `tidyverse` [25], `rmdformats` [1], `scales` [26], `psych` [19], `rmdtemplates` [5].

References

1. Barnier, J.: rmdformats: HTML output formats and templates for 'rmark-down' documents. R package version 0.3.6 (2019). https://CRAN.R-project.org/package=rmdformats
2. Bonabeau, E.: Agent-based modeling: methods and techniques for simulating human systems. Proc. Nat. Acad. Sci. U.S.A. **99**(Suppl 3), 7280–7287 (2002). https://doi.org/10.1073/pnas.082080899
3. Bruch, E., Atwell, J.: Agent-based models in empirical social research. Sociol. Methods Res. **44**(2), 186–221 (2015). https://doi.org/10.1177/0049124113506405
4. Byrne, D.: Complexity Theory and the Social Sciences. Routledge, London (1999). https://doi.org/10.4324/9780203003916
5. Valdez, A.C.: rmdtemplates: rmdtemplates - an opinionated collection of rmark-down templates. R package version 0.4.0.0000 (2020). https://github.com/statisticsforsocialscience/rmd_templates
6. Calero Valdez, A., Ziefle, M.: Human factors in the age of algorithms. understanding the human-in-the-loop using agent-based modeling. In: Meiselwitz, G. (ed.) SCSM 2018. LNCS, vol. 10914, pp. 357–371. Springer, Cham (2018). https://doi.org/10.1007/978-3-319-91485-5_27. ISBN 978-3-319-91485-5
7. Valdez, A.C., Ziefle, M.: Predicting acceptance of novel technology from social network data-an agent-based simulation-approach. In: Proceedings of the International Conference on Competitive Manufacturing (2019)
8. Conte, R., Paolucci, M.: On agent based modelling and computational social science. SSRN Electron. J. (2011). https://doi.org/10.2139/ssrn.1876517
9. Conte, R., et al.: Manifesto of computational social science. Eur. Phys. J.-Spec. Top. **214**, 325 (2012). https://doi.org/10.1140/epjst/e2012-01697-8
10. Epstein, J.: Generative social science: studies in agent-based computational models, January 2006
11. Epstein, J.M.: Generative Social Science: Studies in Agent-Based Computational Modeling. Princeton Studies in Complexity. Princeton University Press, Princeton (2007). ISBN 0-691-12547-3
12. Flache, A., et al.: Models of social influence: towards the next frontiers. JASSS **20**(4), 2 (2017). https://doi.org/10.18564/jasss.3521. ISSN 1460-7425
13. French, J.R.P.: A formal theory of social power. Psychol. Rev. **63**(3), 181–194 (1956). https://doi.org/10.1037/h0046123. ISSN 0033-295X

14. Gilbert, N., Troitzsch, K.G.: Simulation for The Social Scientist, 2nd edn. Open University Press, Buckingham (2005)
15. Hegselmann, R., Krause, U.: Opinion dynamics and bounded confidence: models, analysis and simulation. JASSS **5**(3), 3–33 (2002). ISSN 1460-7425
16. Jager, W.: Uniformity, bipolarization and pluriformity captured as generic stylized behavior with an agent-based simulation model of attitude change. Technical report, pp. 295–303 (2004)
17. Kiesling, E., et al.: Agent-based simulation of innovation diffusion: a review. CEJOR **20**, 183–230 (2012). https://doi.org/10.1007/s10100-011-0210-y
18. Nadal, J.-P.: Meet, discuss, and segregate!. Complexity **7**(3), 55–63 (2002)
19. Revelle, W.: psych: procedures for psychological, psychometric, and personality research. R package version 1.8.12 (2019). https://CRAN.R-project.org/package=psych
20. Rouchier, J., et al.: Progress in model-to-model analysis. J. Artif. Soc. Soc. Simul. **11**(2), 8 (2008)
21. Smith, E.R., Conrey, F.R.: Agent-based modeling: a new approach for theory building in social psychology. Pers. Soc. Psychol. Rev. **11**(1), 87–104 (2007). https://doi.org/10.1177/1088868306294789. ISSN 1088-8683. Official journal of the Society for Personality and Social Psychology, Inc. www.ncbi.nlm.nih.gov/pubmed/18453457
22. Vespignani, A.: Modelling dynamical processes in complex sociotechnical systems. Nat. Phys. **8**(1), 32–39 (2012). https://doi.org/10.1038/nphys2160. ISSN 1745-2473
23. Wagner, C.: Consensus through respect: a model of rational group decision-making. Philos. Stud. **34**(4), 335–349 (1978). https://doi.org/10.1007/BF00364701. ISSN 0031-8116
24. Waldrop, M.M., Gleick, J.: Complexity: The Emerging Science at the Edge of Order and Chaos. Viking Info, London (1992)
25. Wickham, H.: Tidyverse: easily install and load the 'Tidyverse'. R package version 1.3.0 (2019). https://CRAN.R-project.org/package=tidyverse
26. Wickham, H., Seidel, D.: Scales: scale functions for visualization. R package version 1.1.0 (2019). https://CRAN.R-project.org/package=scales
27. Wilensky, U.: Center for connected learning and computer based modeling. Northwestern University (1999). http://ccl.northwestern.edu/netlogo
28. Xie, Y.: knitr: a general-purpose package for dynamic report generation in R. R package version 1.28 (2020). https://CRAN.Rproject.org/package=knitr

Investigating Key Factors for Social Network Evolution and Opinion Dynamics in an Agent-Based Simulation

Patrick Halbach[(⊠)][iD], Laura Burbach[iD], Poornima Belavadi[iD],
Johannes Nakayama[iD], Nils Plettenberg[iD], Martina Ziefle[iD],
and André Calero Valdez[iD]

Human-Computer Interaction Center, RWTH Aachen University,
Campus Boulevard 57, 52076 Aachen, Germany
{halbach,burbach,belavadi,nakayama,plettenberg,
ziefle,calero-valdez}@comm.rwth-aachen.de

Abstract. In recent years social media platforms have experienced increasing attention of researchers due to their capabilities of providing information and spreading opinions of individuals, thus establishing a new environment for opinion formation on a societal level. To gain a better understanding of the occurring opinion dynamics, the interactions between the users and the content that has been shared in those environments has to be investigated. With our work, we want to shed light on the part played by the underlying network structure as information spread relies directly on it and every user of social media is affected by it. Therefore, we analyzed the role of network properties and dealing with friendships in such networks using an agent-based model. Our results reveal the capability of such models for investigating the influence of these factors on opinion dynamics and encourage further investigation in this field of research.

Keywords: Opinion dynamics · Social networks analysis ·
Agent-based modelling · Network evolution

1 Introduction

In the past decade, the evolution of the internet and social media platforms raised new forms of social networks that changed our interpersonal communication and the methods of information procurement considerably [14]. It has become very easy to connect to existing friends online, making new friends and exchange information with them, for example, using platforms like Facebook or Twitter. Looking at the formation of political opinions in our digital society it becomes evident that such social media platforms do also play an important role in that process as those social networks facilitate information and opinion sharing tremendously. Through Facebook, for example, it is now very easy to voice the own opinion, even with just liking or sharing posts of others [25].

© Springer Nature Switzerland AG 2020
V. G. Duffy (Ed.): HCII 2020, LNCS 12199, pp. 20–39, 2020.
https://doi.org/10.1007/978-3-030-49907-5_2

One problem that arises through social media platforms is that certain behaviors and heuristics of humans like selective exposure and spirals of silence can interfere with an independent opinion formation process as individuals tend to surround themselves with like-minded others [37] and opinion minorities are harder to perceive in such environments. As a consequence, echo chambers in social networks may lead to reducing the tolerance of other opinions and reinforcing the own political stance, thus hampering important democratical processes like consensus formation and acceptance of other opinions [19].

On the other side, social media can also provide an opportunity to enhance political information and participation among citizens as those platforms can encourage discussions and opinion exchange among individuals who would not meet in the real world. Besides providing a public discourse and revealing more diverse political opinions that would not have been voiced offline, social networks like Facebook or Twitter can also help with promoting offline political events and actual political participation. However, current research shows that the potential for this has not been exhausted yet [5].

Through analyzing online social networks and their users' interactions it is possible to understand how certain political campaigns may influence the public discourse and the opinion formation of social media users [21]. But besides passively analyzing the influence of social networks, it is also important to actively develop approaches for facilitating an independent political opinion exchange online which can be done through adjusting the mechanisms of information spread, friendship maintenance and providing further clues for credibility evaluation of particular posts.

For gathering better knowledge about the effects that occur in such social networks, it is necessary to develop simulation models that allow for replicating the reality and also testing imaginable assumptions about the effect of individual behaviors on the overall system.

Online social networks consist of human beings who are very different from each other in terms of behavior, information reception, networking and lots of other factors due to their particular personality. Thus, it seems rather impossible to create an equation-based model that would aggregate all individuals' behavior into one singular kind of acting. Agent-based modeling (ABM), in contrast, provides a toolbox for modeling the desired behavior bottom-up, starting at an individual's or rather agent's called behavior space. A particular agent can hold its own beliefs and will act in the simulation according to them, while she is still interdependent with other agents. Through their adaptivity and the dependency on the past, agents' behaviors in sum lead to so-called emergent behavior. This means that the overall system behavior evoked by bottom-up modeling is harder to describe by a formula that summarizes all individual behavior [20].

Therefore, we decided to implement an agent-based model that consists of an environment and behavior space comparable to realistic social media platforms. Our study contributes to the existing research on opinion dynamics in social networks by combining existing theories about opinion dynamics in agent-based systems with topologies and mechanisms of real-world social media platforms. It serves as a first insight into modeling such systems and reveals the interplay of particular mechanisms and behaviors of the network members with the actual network structure.

2 Related Work

Our work implements the state of the art knowledge about how opinion formation happens and how friendship networks evolve in online environments. This section supplies the prerequisites for creating such a simulation model by looking into the dynamics that occur, indicating how they can be modeled and investigating how the surrounding network can be replicated appropriately.

2.1 Opinion Dynamics in Social Media

In their initial purpose, social media services as Facebook and Twitter were created to open up an online space for interacting with current friends and finding new ones. Nowadays, those services provide far more features as news media entered these environments and people started to not only share their everyday activities and cat photos, but also are voicing their opinions and perceiving the reactions of others.

It has been shown that social media platforms expose their users to a larger range of diverging opinions and information that may or may not fit their initial beliefs than other media could do [1]. While this increased exposure could be suspected as a positive influence on the opinion formation, this type of media also shows more vulnerability for misleading the public discourse on certain topics like it got evident for events as the Brexit [12] or most recently the spread of wrong information about the coronavirus [23].

Furthermore, it is crucial to consider the imbalance of activity of social media users. As Romero et al. found, the majority of users passively consume content on social media platforms and rarely take part in interactions, while only a little part of the users utilize those platforms to actively contribute new content and spread their opinions which transforms them into secondary gatekeepers of information spread [29,32]. Those individuals are also referred to as opinion leaders [6]. Besides a higher intention to share news and other information via social media [31], opinion leaders also get apparent through their prominent position in social networks as they show more ties to other users and a higher influence on information spread [15].

This serves as motivation to take a closer look at the underlying network structure of social media platforms as the structure impacts both active and passive users equally. Looking at the influence of network dynamics, Szymanski et al. revealed an effect on the formation of political opinions among multicultural societies. They found that both sociocultural factors and network dynamics steer the opinion formation of an individual as the initial ties a certain individual holds keep influencing her opinion formation permanently. These initial ties evolve due to cultural factors, ethnicity, and gender [33].

Azzimonti et al. showed that the vulnerability of a social network to the propagation of misinformation and polarization depends on its structure and the features that are provided to the users. They investigated multiple factors that could lead to opinion polarization and spread of misinformation in an agent-based network and showed that particular network characteristics and the behavior of the central agent can foster those two effects. Higher clustering, for example, increases polarization while it does not affect the spread of misinformation. Regarding centrality it is the other way round: if potential spreaders of misinformation occupy positions in the network with high follower count, the dissemination of misinformation is facilitated whereas the polarization is not significantly promoted [2].

In addition to the deception that is initiated through particular users, the algorithms that are used by social media platforms for presenting relevant content can also lead to misguided perceptions of the opinion climate [26]. To reveal the true effect of such algorithms it is inevitable to precisely analyze their interaction with the users [8].

2.2 Modelling Opinion Dynamics

After shedding light on the role of social media platforms on providing social ties and their importance for information and opinion spread it is also central for our research approach to understand, how opinion dynamics can be modeled. Therefore, we take a closer look at research that deals with the operationalization of opinion on the one hand, and the modeling of social networks in simulation environments on the other hand.

It is necessary to transform the opinion of a social network member into a value that allows for comparing it to others based on mathematical operations. Only in this way we can implement mechanisms for the interaction and mutual influence of opinions inside the simulated network community.

The initial idea for turning opinion into a concrete value derives from the objective to measure promoting factors in the process of consensus finding. For this Degroot [11] replicated the beliefs into subjective probability distributions which allowed to perform the required calculations that are modeling the opinion formation.

Another approach for modeling opinion dynamics is to build an agent-based model that directly allows for manipulating various factors in the process of opinion formation.

Deffuant et al. developed such a model and implemented a bounded confidence approach. Their work shows how a fixed threshold in which opinion change occurs alters the overall opinion distribution in a simulation. They chose to opinion is modeled on a one-dimensional, continuous scale from 0 to 1. Besides the condition that the agents talk to each other randomly and each conversation is considered for a possible opinion change, they also applied a network model for regulating communication partners within the agents. Using square lattices as underlying topology, the agents were restricted to only talking to four others directly adjacent to them. In comparison with a model that uses complete mixing of agents, the network version shows that consensus is no longer found for a major group of agents but rather depends on the connectedness of agent clusters, especially for low opinion thresholds [10].

The research of Weisbuch et al. continues the evaluation of network influence on a bounded confidence model by comparing the original fully mixed mode of Deffuant et al. with a model that incorporates scale-free networks as limiting environments for the agent communication. They also found that a scale-free network structure does not have a radical influence on opinion dynamics. Most prominent, the use of scale-free networks leads to far more isolated agents and the role of the most-connected node provides useful information. It could be shown that such supernodes were most influential compared to all other nodes and processed themselves also a significant opinion change during the clustering process. With decreasing density, differences to the standard mixed variant get more visible. Further motivation for investigating the effect of Barabási-Albert networks is given by the research of Stauffer et al. who also differentiated between directed and undirected networks. They discovered that especially for small $\epsilon <$ 0.4 for the bounded confidence intervals the opinions of the simulated agents show stronger deviations from each other. For $\epsilon > 0.4$ their agents always end up finding a consensus. Studies of Fortunato et al. show equal indications that for $\epsilon < 0.5$, an opinion dynamics model based on the approach of Deffuant et al. always leads to the formation of a consensus, independent of the underlying network structure [34].

Later on, Hegselmann and Krause extended the complexity of the bounded confidence approach by implementing dependencies on symmetry and individual agent properties for the confidence value. Looking at the continuous scale of opinions, the threshold for bounded confidence therewith can adapt to the actual position of an agent on this scale and the direction of potential consensus finding. Besides, agents can also hold now individual confidence which allows for implementing different types of agent personalities [17].

2.3 Modelling Structures of Online Social Networks

Several approaches were made to incorporate network structures that are close to real social networks. The previously mentioned study of Deffuant et al. showed a comparison of fully connected agents and a square-lattice topology [10]. Further research shows the importance of an accurate model of the network topology as all examined interactions in such simulations are influenced by the underlying structure [28]. The review of Mastroeni shows three prominent approaches for dealing with the interaction of individuals in an agent-based simulation model: Pairwise interaction (Every agent only talks to one other agent in a certain time step), any-to-any interaction (Every agent talks to every other agent within a time step), and closest neighbors approach (An agent talks only to other agents that are in her neighborhood) [22]. We decided on the last approach as it allows for implementing a network and certain dynamics that are similar to those in existing social media platforms.

In the following, we will describe how we implemented the desired opinion and network dynamics and show how we analyzed the results of our simulation models.

3   Method

We chose the programming language Julia to conduct our research. With the LightGraphs package, this language provides performant network simulation and the required network generators for our agent-based model. We also implemented random seeds so that the performed batch runs can be repeated with reaching the same results as in our analysis.

In our research, we focused on the variation of limited parameters for answering our research questions:

- Size of the network: How do network and opinion dynamics interplay with the size of a social network?
- Adding friends: What is the difference between randomly making friends in the network and choosing only from the friends of existing friends?
- Removing friends: How does the threshold for accepting opinion differences interfere with the overall opinion and network dynamics? The distribution of opinions throughout the agents was not varied but uniformly distributed, because their variation would have blurred the effect of the examined parameters on the network evolution.

To analyze the effect of our parameters, we chose different approaches of social network analysis and evaluated the resulting networks and their nodes regarding their degree distribution, centrality, community structure, and the opinion dynamics.

3.1   The Network Model

We designed a network in which agents interact with each other through publishing posts to their followers and receiving content through their followees. Currently, most of the popular social networks allow for unidirectional relationships therefore we chose a directed network for our simulation. The different edges represent the direction of information spread: outgoing edges from agent x show to which agents the posts of agent x will be sent while incoming edges show from which agents the agent x receives posts.

The initial network is created by using the Barabási Albert Network generator of the LightGraphs package in Julia. We decided on the Barabási Albert topology as it provides an artificial network structure that is similar to real-world social networks [38]. This generator allows defining the size of the network and an initial average edge count per agent that follows a power-law distribution. Through following a preferential attachment algorithm, the degree distribution of the nodes sticks to the power law, including very few nodes with high degrees and a long tail of nodes with rather low degrees [3].

After creating the network, the agents are generated with the following attributes:

- Opinion $[-1, 1]$: The Main attribute to change their network of incoming edges (followees). Initially, the opinion is uniformly distributed over all agents.
- Perceived Public Opinion $[-1, 1]$: The mean opinion a particular agent perceives in its neighborhood through seeing the posts of in-neighbors. If the absolute distance between the public and its own opinion is within a defined threshold, the agent's opinion converges towards the public opinion. If not, the agent's position will move into the opposite direction of the perceived opinion (therewith increasing the distance). If an agent ends up having no neighbors, the perceived public opinion mirrors its own opinion.
- The inclination to Interact $[0, Inf]$: The willingness of agents to share posts. A distribution function sets 80% of the agents to passive receivers who rarely share a post. Very few agents have a higher inclination to interact than 1 and share multiple posts per simulation step. After its initial generation, this attribute is fixed.
- Feed (Array of max. 15 posts): Storage of received posts. The feed of agent x contains all shared posts from agents who are in-neighbors of agent x.

The perceived public opinion is the only factor that has an influence on an agent's opinion and is driven by the posts that are visible to this agent. The most important attributes of a post are:

- Opinion $[-1, 1]$: A post's opinion is generated from the opinion of the agent who publishes it. Its opinion is randomly varied by applying a random addition between $[-0.1, 0.1]$.
- Weight: The weight of a post represents the influence of an agent as it is equal to the count of outgoing edges of the posting agent. Posts with high weights are perceived as more important and influential through the receiving agents compared to posts that have been published from agents with low outdegree.

3.2   The Simulation Architecture

A simulation consists of an initiating phase that creates the required initial network and agents with their properties, the main simulation phase where the agents interact and time steps are performed and a data saving phase. Every simulation timestep follows the same order of actions. First, the agent list is shuffled to ensure that the order in which the agents perform their interactions don't have an impact on the simulation outcomes. Following, the actions of a certain agent in a simulation step are described:

1. *Update the feed:* The posts that were received in the previous step get sorted by their weight and the weight of all posts in the feed is reduced by the factor 0.5 to provide higher visibility to newer posts. The feed is limited to the 15 highest-weighted posts, all other posts are dropped and not further considered for calculation of the perceived public opinion.

2. *Update perceived public opinion:* The updated feed is used to calculate the perceived public opinion. The opinion of posts with higher weights have a higher influence on the calculation. If the feed of the agent is empty, the perceived public opinion mirrors the opinion of the agent.
3. *Update the opinion:* With the perceived public opinion an agent now updates its own opinion. If the absolute distance between public opinion and own opinion is inside a defined threshold, the agent approaches the public opinion by a factor of 0.05. If the absolute distance lies outside the range, the agent moves into the opposing direction and therewith increases the distance what we call the "backfire effect".
4. *Drop ingoing edges:* Regarding its updated opinion, an agent checks if the current posts in his feed are in an accepted absolute distance to the own opinion. If not, the agent also checks the real opinion of the source agent and if this opinion is also outside the accepted range, the agent drops the incoming edge so that it won't receive further posts of the former followee. In one step, an agent can only drop a tenth of his current number (rounded up) of ingoing edges so that a realistic behavior is maintained.
5. *Add ingoing edges:* After disconnecting from agents that are outside of the accepted opinion range, an agent adds new ingoing edges if his in-neighbors count is below the desired value. All agents try to maintain an indegree that equals a tenth of the network size. Adding edges is based on the configuration either done by selecting candidates from the neighbors of the agent's in-neighbors without regarding the opinion or selecting candidates randomly from the whole network that lie inside a defined absolute distance from the own opinion. In the third configuration, both approaches are combined. From the selected candidates, an agent always chooses the one with the highest outdegree first and creates a new directed edge towards itself. This process is continued until the number of new in-neighbors is reached or the list of candidates is empty.
6. *Publish posts:* When the network maintenance is finished, an agent starts to publish posts concerning its inclination to interact. A post is generated through multiplying the own opinion with a randomly chosen factor in $[-0.1, 0.1]$ and setting the post-weight equals to the own current outdegree. After generating the post it is shared with all feeds of the current agent's out-neighbors.

The actions described above are performed by every agent during a simulation step. After all agents are finished, their current states and network measures are logged for analysis. After all steps are done, the simulation object is saved containing the initial and final state, intermediate states at each 10% of the simulation, agent and post logs and the configuration of the certain run.

3.3 Implementation of Opinion Dynamics

As shown in the previous section there are several ways to model the dynamics in opinion formation. We decided to implement a variant of the bounded confidence model proposed by Hegsemlann et al. that relies on an initially randomly generated social network. When in a certain threshold, agents approach towards the perceived public opinion regarding the outdegree of the other agents who influence them. Outside this threshold, a backfire effect is triggered that leads the agent to reinforce her own opinion by increasing the distance between her own and the perceived public opinion. As a result, the agent will tend to disconnect from others who are too far apart in their opinion and thus again reducing the distance between the public and their own opinion.

3.4 Network Analysis

For an appropriate analysis of the resulting social networks, we investigated various measures to evaluate effects on the distribution of degrees, centrality and community structure. Our chosen measures comprise the following:

- The density of the networks, the standard deviation of degrees for ingoing and outgoing edges, the ratio of outdegree to indegree for the analysis of degree distribution
- Closeness betweenness, and eigenvector centrality for the understanding of centrality features
- Clustering coefficient and community detection through label propagation for gaining insights on the community structure

We looked on multiple measures to detect the effect of network structure and the investigated factors on opinion dynamics in the network:

- Standard deviations of opinions
- Opinion Change Delta Mean (Opinion Change from initial to the final opinion of an agent)
- Difference between an individual's opinion and its perceived public opinion

Besides calculating the means of all aforementioned measures we also investigated them for the most important node in the networks in particular.

The measures were all calculated from the final state of the simulation runs and averaged over all repetitions of the same run so that we can calculate confidence intervals for the outcomes of the simulation runs.

4 Results

We performed a total of 13 different simulation runs that cover the following variations of factor configuration:

- Network Size in 100, 200, 300, 400, 500 Agents
- Add friends Method as Neighbors, hybrid and random
- Unfriend Threshold of 0.4, 0.6, 0.8, 1.0, 1.2

This allows us to examine subsequently the influence of the factor levels separately. Each distinct simulation configuration was repeated 100 times to eliminate effects that are due to the usage of random number generators in the simulations. The results that are reported in the following are always averaged over the repetitions of a particular configuration run.

The influence of the factors was evaluated with various measures that can be classified into the following facets:

1) Degree Distribution
2) Centrality Measures
3) Community Measures
4) Opinion Dynamics
5) Supernode properties

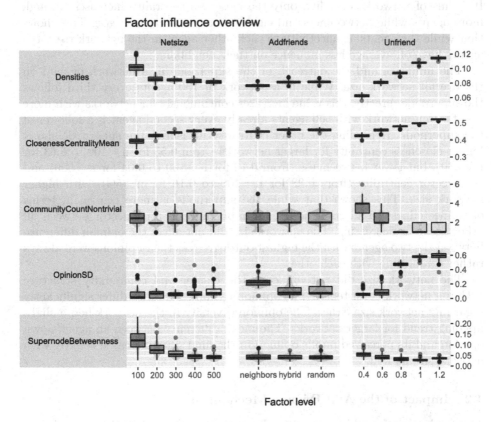

Fig. 1. Overview of the factor influences on exemplary measures of the analyzed facets.

Figure 1 shows the influence of each factor on one representative measure of those facets. As can be seen, the network size did not affect the community structure and opinion dynamics significantly. In comparison, the add friends method had additional on the opinion dynamics and only the unfriend threshold showed an influence on all facets. Subsequently, the particular effects are examined more detailed and separately per factor.

4.1 Impact of Network Size

In our simulation, the size of a social network is especially influential for the deviation of network parameters and opinions throughout the members of a network (see Table 1). While the density of a network decreases significantly from 10.3% in a network of 100 agents to 8.6% for n = 200 and further on to 8.2% for n = 500, the standard deviations of outdegree and indegree increase (outdegree from 5.48 for n = 100 up to 28.09 for n = 500, indegree from 5.18 for n = 100 up to 23.13 for n = 500) which shows that the preferential attachment algorithm overruns the pursuit of each agent to connect to one-tenth of the network members. In terms of network centrality, only the closeness centrality increases through more agents while betweenness and eigenvector centrality decrease. This shows that while the agents' connectivity to each other agent in the network rises, the agents have on average less influence on their neighbors.

The influence and the outreach of the supernode in a network depend on the overall network size. While in a network of 100 agents every third follows the supernode directly, this value increases continuously for networks with more agents. In a network with 500 agents already every second agent is a follower of the supernode. Regarding the other centrality measures, the supernode shows higher closeness centrality for larger networks (from 0.55 for n = 100 to 0.63 for n = 500), but lower betweenness (from 0.12 for n = 100 to 0.04 for n = 500) and eigenvector centrality (from 0.28 for n = 100 to 0.16 for n = 500) with higher network size. This shows that while the supernode is more central in terms of connectedness to all other nodes, its importance as a connector between all other agents is decreasing. The network size did not affect the opinion difference between the two agents with the highest outdegrees as their opinions were always rather conforming with each other.

The network size did not influence the cluster and community structure within a network consistently. The opinion dynamics did not differ significantly regarding network size either. The opinion diversity in the network had a slight upgoing trend for larger networks. The mean difference between an agent's own opinion and its perceived public opinion in the final state increased slightly with network size as well.

4.2 Impact of the Add Friends Mechanism

The mechanism for adding new friends shows an influence on the network and the opinion distribution in it (see Table 2). When picking new friends only from friends of current friends, the density of a network stays with 7.7% lower than for picking randomly from all agents in the network concerning the opinion difference (8.2%) and for a hybrid approach of both methods (8.2%). While the standard deviations of outdegree and indegree for each agent to not differ

Table 1. Influence of the network size.

Network size	100	200	300	400	500
Densities	0.103	0.086	0.085	0.084	0.082
OutdegreeSD	5.483701	11.163	16.946	22.654	28.092
IndegreeSD	5.182528	9.722809	14.309	18.885	23.130
OutdegreeIndegreeRatioMean	0.503	0.495	0.493	0.491	0.491
ClosenessCentralityMean	0.396	0.430	0.448	0.455	0.461
BetweennessCentralityMean	0.016	0.007	0.004	0.003	0.002
EigenCentralityMean	0.082	0.055	0.045	0.038	0.034
ClustCoeff	0.069	0.056	0.056	0.056	0.055
CommunityCount	3.010	3.020	3.090	3.420	2.960
OpinionSD	0.062	0.065	0.063	0.082	0.105
OpChangeDeltaMean	0.484	0.498	0.498	0.493	0.487
PublOwnOpinionDiff	0.020	0.021	0.021	0.023	0.026
SupernodeOutdegree	32.83	75.74	121.670	161.250	210.860
SupernodeCloseness	0.551	0.609	0.625	0.625	0.633
SupernodeBetweenness	0.126	0.082	0.060	0.047	0.043
SupernodeEigen	0.283	0.238	0.205	0.178	0.164
Supernode1st2ndOpdiff	0.023	0.007	0.009	0.009	0.032

significantly between the different approaches, the mean ratio between outdegree and indegree per agent is less balanced when agents only choose from neighbors of neighbors (0.48) compared to random and hybrid approaches (both 0.49).

The least influence of the add friends mechanism can be perceived in terms of network centrality of each agent. Only the closeness centrality is slightly higher for the random and hybrid approach (0.45 for neighborhood and 0.46 for random and hybrid approach), while betweenness and eigenvector centrality do not show significant changes. Concerning clustering and community structure, the clustering coefficient increases slightly by using the random approach (0.055 compared to 0.052 for the neighborhood approach) while the number of communities is higher for networks where agents only pick neighbors of neighbors (6.41 compared to 3.47 for the random approach).

The node with the highest influence and outreach in the network is not affected by the add friends mechanism. The opinion difference between the two nodes with the highest outdegree shows more extreme outliers for the random add friends method but no significant difference to the other approaches. The opinion distribution, on the opposite, is significantly higher if the agents only connect to others that are already in their indirect neighborhood. The sum of opinion changes per agent is slightly higher when agents pick their new friends randomly and according to the opinion difference (0.40 for random and 0.44 for neighborhood approaches). Looking at the distance between perceived public and own opinion in the final state, those two values are significantly closer to each other when the random or hybrid approach for choosing new friends is used (0.03 for random and hybrid approach and 0.04 for neighborhood approach).

Table 2. Influence of the addfriends method.

Addfriends method	Neighbors	Hybrid	Random
Densities	0.077	0.082	0.082
OutdegreeSD	29.148	28.074	28.230
IndegreeSD	24.148	23.102	23.263
OutdegreeIndegreeRatioMean	0.483	0.491	0.491
ClosenessCentralityMean	0.451	0.461	0.460
BetweennessCentralityMean	0.002	0.002	0.002
EigenCentralityMean	0.034	0.034	0.034
ClustCoeff	0.052	0.055	0.055
CommunityCount	6.410	3.820	3.470
OpinionSD	0.226	0.106	0.110
OpChangeDeltaMean	0.442	0.488	0.489
PublOwnOpinionDiff	0.041	0.026	0.026
SupernodeOutdegree	206.700	209.100	207.850
SupernodeCloseness	0.626	0.631	0.630
SupernodeBetweenness	0.043	0.042	0.041
SupernodeEigen	0.165	0.165	0.163
SupernodeOpinion	−0.019	−0.007	0.000
Supernode1st2ndOpdiff	0.090	0.028	0.047

4.3 Impact of Unfriend Threshold

The threshold of an agent to accept diverging opinions (in the following abbreviated as ut) was influential for both the network structure and the opinion distribution in a network. If the agents in a network are more tolerant in keeping friendships, the density of the network increases significantly from 6.3% for $ut = 0.4$ to 11.5% for $ut = 1.2$ and with it also the variety of outdegrees and indegrees within the network members. The ratio between outdegree and indegree gets more balanced for networks of agents with higher opinion tolerance (0.48 for $ut = 0.4$, 0.50 for $ut = 1.2$).

The centrality of each agent in the network changes with the unfriend threshold as closeness and eigenvector centrality increase with higher tolerance of friends with diverging opinions. The betweenness, in contrast, decreases with a rising threshold. The clustering and community measures show that while clustering increases through higher unfriend thresholds, the number of separate communities detected through label propagation decreases.

The role of the agent with the highest follower count also depends on the unfriend threshold (see Table 3). While outdegree and closeness centrality stay rather equal for a threshold from 0.4 to 1.0, in a network with an unfriend threshold of 1.2, both values increase significantly. So the supernode profits only in terms of post reach when every agent is very tolerant with keeping fellowships that bear a high opinion difference. The betweenness and eigenvector centrality decrease continuously with rising unfriend threshold, but this trend seems to turn around at least for the eigenvector centrality with an unfriend threshold of 1.2. Comparing the opinion of the most important and second most important agent we observe a significantly higher difference for unfriend thresholds of 0.8 and 1.2 whereas for the lower and higher thresholds the opinions of them are close to each other.

With changing the unfriend threshold it is possible to subsequently influence the opinion distribution within the network. While in networks with low thresholds the standard deviation of opinions is below 0.1 on average, this measure rises notably up to 0.5 for a network with an unfriend threshold of 0.6 and even continues with higher thresholds to 0.6 for a threshold of 1.2. Meanwhile, the mean delta between the initial and the final opinion of all agents in the networks shows the opposite trend. While the opinion change is with 0.5 rather large for thresholds below or equal to 0.6, it falls below 0.3 for networks with a larger threshold. The least opinion change occurs for a threshold of 1.0 while with 1.2 the opinion change starts to increase again. With rising unfriend threshold also the distance between perceived public and own opinion increases significantly.

5 Discussion

Our work revealed several results that call for further investigation. Subsequently, we will discuss the results concerning other research and look into the lessons learned from our initial approach and possible further steps.

As we could show, the overall model configuration was capable of simulating the opinion dynamics in a social network and suitable to perform experiments regarding specific factors of the network size and behavior. The programming language Julia proved robust as a simulation environment and provided all necessary flexibility to implement our approach as well as enough performance to run several configurations and repetitions in a reasonable time.

With changing the overall agent count in the network, we wanted to observe how a higher availability of possible friends in a network and the strengthening of supernodes through the preferential attachment mechanism will change the structure and dynamics in the network. The obtained results indicate that through increasing the network size, the agents grow closer together although the overall network density decreases significantly. This counterintuitive result can be explained with the significant influence growth of the supernode in the network. We interpret the absent influence of network size on all measures of

Table 3. Influence of the unfriend threshold.

Unfriend threshold	0.4	0.6	0.8	1.0	1.2
Densities	0.063	0.082	0.094	0.108	0.115
OutdegreeSD	26.693	27.921	29.209	31.545	36.109
IndegreeSD	19.050	23.133	26.923	30.335	35.134
OutdegreeIndegreeRatioMean	0.479	0.491	0.496	0.498	0.498
ClosenessCentralityMean	0.426	0.460	0.482	0.499	0.521
BetweennessCentralityMean	0.003	0.002	0.002	0.002	0.002
EigenCentralityMean	0.031	0.034	0.036	0.038	0.038
ClustCoeff	0.051	0.055	0.055	0.058	0.060
CommunityCount	6.700	3.200	1.170	1.350	1.290
OpinionSD	0.070	0.096	0.470	0.582	0.589
OpChangeDeltaMean	0.496	0.487	0.256	0.215	0.274
PublOwnOpinionDiff	0.021	0.025	0.120	0.170	0.184
SupernodeOutdegree	208.030	205.920	201.590	206.360	244.780
SupernodeCloseness	0.629	0.628	0.624	0.631	0.663
SupernodeBetweenness	0.054	0.041	0.033	0.029	0.037
SupernodeEigen	0.183	0.164	0.152	0.139	0.148
Supernode1st2ndOpdiff	0.005	0.027	0.252	0.362	0.085

opinion dynamics except for the higher deviation of opinions in larger networks as confirmation for the robustness of our implementation.

Looking at the other two factors we were able to establish significant influences on both network and opinion dynamics. While the unfriend threshold depicts the effects of direct individual behavior of the agents, the add friends mechanism can be seen as indirect individual behavior as a certain platform could provide recommendations for new friends in various ways and therewith lead the user to establish new connections more locally (through looking into neighbors of neighbors) or more globally (through looking randomly in the whole network). Being limited to the local environment naturally leads to lower network densities as the number of agents who hold similar opinions decreases. As a consequence, the opinion deviation increases and so does the difference between the own opinion and the perceived public opinion. The higher delta of opinion change in networks with random or hybrid add friends mechanisms compared to the other mechanism can be reasoned with the effect of bounded confidence: if agents act in an environment that is closer to their own opinion, they will more likely approach to the opinions of the others and the higher density of networks with randomly chosen friends allows for more opinion fluctuation. The restriction to local neighbors, on the other hand, leads more often to local environments where the public perceived opinion is too distant from their own opinion and alternatively the backfire effect is triggered.

The unfriend threshold showed the most diverse influence on the measured network and opinion dynamics. Inherently, the density of a network increases when its members are less rigorous with cutting unsuitable friendship ties. Also, the effects on centrality and clustering of the network seem rather obvious and the decrease of opinion change delta orthogonal to the rise of the distance between public and own opinion shows again the incidence of the bounded confidence dynamics. More interesting, however, is the sharp change of measures for unfriend thresholds of 0.6 and 0.8. Previous research suggests that members of online social networks tend to unfriend other individuals due to offensive or counter-attitudinal posts but it shows simultaneously that a large share of users is rather lazy in cutting their weak ties [18]. John et al. also found that cutting ties because of political posts happens more often around individuals who hold stronger political inclinations and with the reason to increase homogeneity in their Facebook Newsfeeds. For less politically interested individuals the primary motivation in cutting those ties lay in reducing the number of political posts in their feed.

With our initial approach, we were able to target proof of concept for an agent-based model that provides more closeness to reality through implementing certain dynamics of real-world social media platforms like Facebook and Twitter. Concurrently, our results motivate for further investigation of the examined factors and inclusion of further dynamics into the network model. Like other research showed it is difficult to set a limit on fitting the model to real-world dynamics as almost every effect that occurs can be implemented with more or less complexity into a certain simulation environment. Han et al. for example considered more precisely the personality of agents and focused specifically on the effect of adding "stubborn" agents to a simulation. For simulations with a higher share of agents who stick stubbornly to their opinion, they found that the number of opinion clusters decreased [16].

As Dunbar et al. found, people tend to interact on social media platforms within certain communicational layers [13]. That means that our connections to other individuals hold similar connotations to those in the offline world and that we would differentiate between our interactions with friends, colleagues and more distant acquaintances. For introducing such dynamics into simulation models Salehi et al. showed an approach through varying additional trust levels for the friendship connections of the agents [30]. Along with the implementation of more complex friendships connections, we will also strive to incorporate more features of social networks like the function to share a post from the individual's news feed into her friendship network.

Another important question while simulating opinion dynamics is how one assumes a simulation state to be final or converged. While in cases with consensus formation the answer seems trivial, other cases with unstable opinion distributions in the network might hardly get into a stable final state. Meng et al. found that the convergence time of models operating under the bounded confidence approach of Deffuant et al. strongly depends on the underlying network structure. Also, they stated that there is a critical border for the bounded confidence of $\epsilon = 0.5$ for certain network topologies. When this border is crossed, the convergence time of simulation runs increases significantly [24]. Hence, for advancing our approach in the future it will be also inevitable to investigate the convergence behavior of our simulation.

The last consideration has to be given to the modeling of the network structure. As we aim to simulate the opinion dynamics in real social networks it is also crucial to run our models on suitable network structures that are capable of replicating the real-world conditions. An extensive analysis of the friendship relations in Facebook of Wilson et al. shows that the actual structure of the social graph shows similarities and a power-law distribution of degrees like in Barabási-Albert networks. Nevertheless, fitting of the model parameters is required to facilitate the generation of a realistic artificial network and additional factors as network growth have to be taken into account [38].

In conclusion, there is still a lot do be done for simulating the opinion dynamics on social media platforms as realistic as possible. Nevertheless, this process is worth tackling all the obstacles as it will facilitate the understanding of opinion formation in online social networks and help with designing social media platforms in a way so that they actually will support an independent and democratic opinion formation in online environments. As shown by De et al., the prediction of opinion dynamics in social media platforms is a solvable problem and will be of high value for reaching this goal ultimately [9].

Acknowledgements. This research was supported by the Digital Society research program funded by the Ministry of Culture and Science of the German State of North Rhine-Westphalia. We would further like to thank the authors of the packages we have used. We used the following packages to create this document: `knitr` [39], `tidyverse` [35], `rmdformats` [4], `scales` [36], `psych` [27], `rmdtemplates` [7].

References

1. Anspach, N.M.: The new personal influence: how our Facebook friends influence the news we read. Polit. Commun. **34**(4), 590–606 (2017). https://doi.org/10.1080/10584609.2017.1316329. https://www.tandfonline.com/doi/full/10.1080/10584609.2017.1316329. ISSN 1058-4609, 1091-7675
2. Azzimonti, M., Fernandes, M.: Social media networks, fake news, and polarization. Working paper 24462. National Bureau of Economic Research (2018). https://doi.org/10.3386/w24462. http://www.nber.org/papers/w24462
3. Barabási, A.L., Albert, R.: Emergence of scaling in random networks. Science **286**(5439), 509–512 (1999). https://doi.org/10.1126/science.286.5439.509. arXiv:cond-mat/9910332. ISSN 0036-8075
4. Barnier, J.: rmdformats: HTML output formats and templates for 'rmarkdown' documents. R package version 0.3.6 (2019). https://CRAN.R-project.org/package=rmdformats
5. Bode, L.: Political news in the news feed: learning politics from social media. Mass Commun. Soc. **19**(1), 24–48 (2016). https://doi.org/10.1080/15205436.2015.1045149. http://www.tandfonline.com/doi/full/10.1080/15205436.2015.1045149. ISSN 1520-5436

6. Burt, R.S.: The social capital of opinion leaders. Ann. Am. Acad. Polit. Soc. Sci. **566**(1), 37–54 (1999). https://doi.org/10.1177/000271629956600104. http://journals.sagepub.com/doi/10.1177/000271629956600104. ISSN 0002-7162
7. Valdez, A.C.: rmdtemplates: rmdtemplates - an opinionated collection of rmark- down templates. R package version 0.4.0.0000 (2020). https://github.com/ statisticsforsocialscience/rmd_templates
8. Calero Valdez, A., Ziefle, M.: Human factors in the age of algorithms. understand- ing the human-in-the-loop using agent-based modeling. In: Meiselwitz, G. (ed.) SCSM 2018. LNCS, vol. 10914, pp. 357–371. Springer, Cham (2018). https://doi. org/10.1007/978-3-319-91485-5_27. ISBN 978-3-319-91484-8
9. De, A., et al.: Learning and forecasting opinion dynamics in social networks. In: Advances in Neural Information Processing Systems, pp. 397–405. Neural Infor- mation Processing Systems Foundation (2016). arXiv: 1506.05474
10. Deffuant, G., et al.: Mixing beliefs among interacting agents. Adv. Complex Syst. **03**(01n04), 87–98 (2000). https://doi.org/10.1142/s0219525900000078. ISSN 0219- 5259
11. Degroot, M.H.: Reaching a consensus. J. Am. Stat. Assoc. **69**(345), 118–121 (1974). https://doi.org/10.1080/01621459.1974.10480137. ISSN 1537-274X
12. Del Vicario, M., et al.: Mapping social dynamics on Facebook: the brexit debate. Soc. Netw. **50**, 6–16 (2017). https://doi.org/10.1016/j.socnet.2017.02.002. https://linkinghub.elsevier.com/retrieve/pii/S0378873316304166. ISSN 0378-8733
13. Dunbar, R.I.M., et al.: The structure of online social networks mirrors those in the offline world. Soc. Netw. **43**, 39–47 (2015). https://doi.org/10.1016/j.socnet.2015. 04.005. ISSN 0378-8733
14. Fang, I.: A History of Mass Communication, 1st edn, p. 288. Routledge, New York (1997). https://doi.org/10.4324/9780080508160. https://www.taylorfrancis.com/ books/9781136046827. ISBN 9780080508160
15. Halberstam, Y., Knight, B.: Homophily, group size, and the diffusion of political information in social networks: evidence from Twitter. J. Public Econ. **143**, 73– 88 (2016). https://doi.org/10.1016/j.jpubeco.2016.08.011. http://www.nber.org/ papers/w20681.pdf. ISSN 0047-2727
16. Han, W., Huang, C., Yang, J.: Opinion clusters in a modified Hegselmann-Krause model with heterogeneous bounded confidences and stubbornness. Phys. A Stat. Mech. Appl. **531**, 121791 (2019). https://doi.org/10.1016/j.physa.2019.121791. ISSN 0378-4371
17. Hegselmann, R., Krause, U.: Opinion dynamics and bounded confidence: models, analysis and simulation. JASSS **5**(3), 3–33 (2002). ISSN 1460-7425
18. John, N.A., Dvir-Gvirsman, S.: I don't like you any more: Facebook unfriending by Israelis during the Israel-Gaza conflict of 2014. J. Commun. **65**(6), 953–974 (2015). https://doi.org/10.1111/jcom.12188. https://academic.oup.com/joc/article/65/6/ 953-974/4082326. ISSN 1460-2466
19. Lee, S., et al.: Understanding the majority opinion formation process in online environments: an exploratory approach to Facebook. Inf. Process. Manag. **54**(6), 1115–1128 (2018). https://doi.org/10.1016/j.ipm.2018.08.002. https:// linkinghub.elsevier.com/retrieve/pii/S0306457317307367. ISSN 0306-4573
20. Macy, M.W., Willer, R.: From factors to actors: computational sociology and agent- based modeling. Ann. Rev. Sociol. **28**(1), 143–166 (2002). https://doi.org/10.1146/ annurev.soc.28.110601.141117. ISSN 0360-0572
21. Marozzo, F., Bessi, A.: Analyzing polarization of social media users and news sites during political campaigns. Soci. Netw. Anal. Min. **8**(1), 1–13 (2017). https://doi. org/10.1007/s13278-017-0479-5

22. Mastroeni, L., Vellucci, P., Naldi, M.: Agent-based models for opinion formation: a bibliographic survey. IEEE Access **7**, 58836–58848 (2019). https://doi.org/10.1109/ACCESS.2019.2913787. ISSN 2169-3536

23. McCloskey, B., Heymann, D.L.: SARS to novel coronavirus - old lessons and new lessons. Epidemiol. Infecti. **148**, e22 (2020). https://doi.org/10.1017/S0950268820000254. http://www.ncbi.nlm.nih.gov/pubmed/32019614. ISSN 1469-4409

24. Meng, X.F., Van Gorder, R.A., Porter, M.A.: Opinion formation and distribution in a bounded-confidence model on various networks. Phys. Rev. E **97**(2), 022312 (2018). https://doi.org/10.1103/PhysRevE.97.022312. http://arxiv.org/abs/1701.02070 arXiv: 1701.02070. ISSN 2470-0053

25. Neubaum, G., Krämer, N.C.: Opinion climates in social media: blending mass and interpersonal communication. Hum. Commun. Res. **43**(4), 464–476 (2017). https://doi.org/10.1111/hcre.12118. https://academic.oup.com/hcr/article/43/4/464-476/4670704. ISSN 0360-3989

26. Nguyen, T.T., et al.: Exploring the filter bubble: the effect of using recommender systems on content diversity. In: Proceedings of the 23rd International Conference on World Wide Web - WWW 2014, pp. 677–686. ACM Press, New York (2014). https://doi.org/10.1145/2566486.2568012. http://dl.acm.org/citation.cfm?doid=2566486.2568012. ISBN 9781450327442

27. Revelle, W.: psych: procedures for psychological, psychometric, and personality research. R package version 1.8.12 (2019). https://CRAN.R-project.org/package=psych

28. Rolfe, M.: Social networks and agent-based modelling. In: Analytical Sociology: Actions and Networks. Wiley Blackwell, Chichester, pp. 233–260, May 2014. https://doi.org/10.1002/9781118762707.ch09. ISBN 9781118762707

29. Romero, D.M., Galuba, W., Asur, S., Huberman, B.A.: Influence and passivity in social media. In: Gunopulos, D., Hofmann, T., Malerba, D., Vazirgiannis, M. (eds.) ECML PKDD 2011. LNCS (LNAI), vol. 6913, pp. 18–33. Springer, Heidelberg (2011). https://doi.org/10.1007/978-3-642-23808-6_2. ISBN 978-3-642-23807-9

30. Salehi, S., Taghiyareh, F.: Introducing a more realistic model for opinion formation considering instability in social structure. Int. J. Mod. Phys. C **27**(11) (2016). https://doi.org/10.1142/S0129183116501369. ISSN 0129-1831

31. Schäfer, M.S., Taddicken, M.: Mediatized opinion leaders: new patterns of opinion leadership in new media environments? Int. J. Commun. **9**, 22 (2015)

32. Singer, J.B.: User-generated visibility: secondary gatekeeping in a shared media space. New Media Soc. **16**(1), 55–73 (2014). https://doi.org/10.1177/1461444813477833. http://journals.sagepub.com/doi/10.1177/1461444813477833. ISSN 1461-4448, 1461-7315

33. Szymanski, B.K., et al.: The spread of opinions in societies, pp. 61–84, September 2016. https://doi.org/10.1201/9781315369587-5

34. Weisbuch, G.: Bounded confidence and social networks. Eur. Phys. J. B **38**(2), 339–343 (2004). https://doi.org/10.1140/epjb/e2004-00126-9

35. Wickham, H.: Tidyverse: easily install and load the 'Tidyverse'. R package version 1.3.0 (2019). https://CRAN.R-project.org/package=tidyverse

36. Wickham, H., Seidel, D.: Scales: scale functions for visualization. R package version 1.1.0 (2019). https://CRAN.R-project.org/package=scales

37. Williams, H.T.P., et al.: Network analysis reveals open forums and echo chambers in social media discussions of climate change. Glob. Environ. Change **32**, 126–138 (2015). https://doi.org/10.1016/J.GLOENVCHA.2015.03.006. https://www.sciencedirect.com/science/article/pii/S0959378015000369?via%7B%5C%25%7D3Dihub. ISSN 0959-3780
38. Wilson, C., et al.: User interactions in social networks and their implications. In: Proceedings of the Fourth ACM European Conference on Computer systems - EuroSys 2009, p. 205. ACM Press (2009). https://doi.org/10.1145/1519065.1519089. http://portal.acm.org/citation.cfm?doid=1519065.1519089. ISBN 978-1-60558-482-9
39. Xie, Y.: knitr: a general-purpose package for dynamic report generation in R. R package version 1.28 (2020). https://CRAN.Rproject.org/package=knitr

Sign Language to Speech Converter Using Raspberry-Pi

Sravya Koppuravuri[1], Sukumar Sai Pondari[2], and Deep Seth[1(✉)]

[1] Mahindra Ecole Centrale, 1A Survey Number: 62, Bahadurpally, Hyderabad 500043,
Telangana, India
ksravya2299@gmail.com, sethdeep12@gmail.com
[2] VSigma IT Labs Pvt. Ltd., Vittal Rao Nagar, Madhapur, Hyderabad 500081, Telangana, India
saipsukumar@gmail.com

Abstract. Communication between the speaking and the non-speaking community has always been a difficult task. Millions of people in India suffer from the hearing or speaking impairment. This project provides a solution for these people to communicate with everybody else without any problem. It is an IoT based project, which converts hand gestures into synthesized textual format. The device consists of a glove with flex sensors all over the fingers to understand the orientation of the hand. When hands and fingers moved, words and numbers detected according to the movement. A bluetooth speaker attached to a Raspberry Pi that converts this text to speech. The device needs to be tested on a number of subjects for standardization of gestures. In current work only one hand is used for a gesture to speech conversion.

Keywords: Bio robotics · Sign language · Speech recognition · Sign language translation · Cognitive robotics

1 Introduction

Humans communicate with each other by expressing their thoughts and ideas and the best way to do so is through "speech" but some people deprived of this necessity. The only way by which the deaf and dumb people communicate is through sign language [1]. Sign languages (also known as signed languages) are languages that use the visual-manual modality to convey meaning. Sign languages are full-fledged natural languages with their own grammar and lexicon [2]. Wherever communities of deaf people exist, sign languages have developed as handy means of communication and they form the core of local deaf cultures. Although sign language is used primarily by the deaf and hard of hearing, it is also used by hearing individuals, such as those unable to physically speak. The sign language used in India is the Indian Sign Language. As per Census 2011, in India, out of the 121 Cr population, about 2.68 Cr persons are 'disabled' which is 2.21% of the total population. Out of this 2.68 Cr population, 19% of them are impaired from hearing. In an era where 'inclusive development' is being emphasised as the right path towards sustainable development, focussed initiatives for the welfare of disabled

V. G. Duffy (Ed.): HCII 2020, LNCS 12199, pp. 40–51, 2020.
https://doi.org/10.1007/978-3-030-49907-5_3

persons are essential. This emphasises the need for strengthening disability statistics in the Country [3]. Lot of work has been done over the past couple of years to uplift the hearing-impaired people. Post-independence, State Government and Municipalities have started special schools for the deaf in many states. But, the number of schools has remained inadequate compared to the number of children between the age group of 0–14 years [4]. Even though measures have been taken by the Government and the NGO's to uplift the deaf and dumb community, there is not much work done to bridge the communication gap that exists between the non-speaking people and the speaking people.

Google has introduced a wearable wristband which will detect the gestures and is connected to their mobile device for communication, but it is approved only as theoretically not implemented as such. TOSHIBA is also trying to develop a robot-like sign language interpreter which is used for communication. There are various android applications that are released to provide the communication facility to the mute people [5]. Real time conversion of sign languages using desk and wearable computer-based video has also been done for the communication of mute people [6]. There are also works related to the real time recognition of sign languages in videos as well [7]. Our model proposes a glove-based system that will help translate the gestures into speech. This data glove consists of flex sensors over the fingers that detect the hand orientation. The data which is obtained from the data glove is then communicated to the Raspberry pi using a Wi-Fi module and then decoded to translate the gesture into speech. A Bluetooth speaker is used to say the gesture out loud. Our device has been interfaced with the Indian Sign Language. ISL is predominantly used in India, Pakistan and Bangladesh. It uses both hands to communicate. We have come up with this device in the hope that the deaf and dumb community can be benefitted from it (Fig. 1).

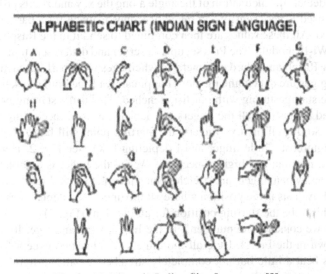

Fig. 1. Alphabets in Indian Sign Language [8]

2 Objective

The project is aimed to overcome the communication barrier between the non-speaking and speaking community through the data glove that converts sign language to speech. Data gloves consist of sensors to recognize any gesture and then converted to speech. In this paper the aim is to convert gestures from one hand to speech. The scope of this project as of now is to depict numbers in the Indian Sign Language from 1–9 in the form of audio output.

3 Methodology

Our system has five flex sensors, a Wi-Fi module and an accelerometer attached at the backside of the glove. Flex sensors work on the principle of variable resistance whose terminal resistance increases when the resistor is bent. It is used to sense changes in linearity [9]. The resistance of the strip is foldable and a range of resistances are produced depending on the bent angle. these analog values are converted into digital values using analog to digital converters. The device used to convert these analog values into digital values is an Arduino Pro mini. These values are then classified as high, medium or low depending on the orientation of the hand. It is depicted high when the finger is completely stretched out and low when the finger is completely bent. These values along with the accelerometer values are combined and sent to the raspberry pi over Wi-Fi. The accelerometer used in this device is a 3-axis Gyroscope, 3-axis Accelerometer and Digital Motion Processor, all in small package. The 3-axis gyroscope detect the rotational velocity along the x, y and z-axis. When the hand is rotated about any of these axes, Coriolis Effect causes a vibration that is detected in the device. The 3-axis accelerometer detects the inclination of the angle along the x, y and z-axis [10]. Since the accelerometer used is very sensitive, a range of values is given for a particular gesture to be recognised. All these values are then combined to send it to the Raspberry Pi over Wi-Fi using a Wi-Fi module. The Pi is set up as a server and data is sent to it. This data is processed in the Raspbian. If the data generated when a gesture is performed matches with the pre-existing gesture data in the memory the pi using a Bluetooth speaker announces the gesture. We start gesturing with our fist clenched. This is the starting point. All the fingers clenched means that all the fingers are depicted as low. (according to the logic we are using). So, for all the five fingers, the starting point will be [$l/l/l/l/l$] (leftmost - thumb and rightmost - little finger and l depicting low). See Fig. 2. Here l, m, and n represent low, medium and high respectively. When the finger is completely bent, it represents low and when fingers are stretched then it depicts high. Figure 2: The fingers is clenched tightly. This is the position where all the fingers are depicted as low and we are assuming this to be the starting position for all the signs (Fig. 3).

Now when we consider the number 7 in the Indian sign language. It is depicted a posture as shown in the Fig. 4. Here all the fingers are clenched except for the index finger which is bent a little but not completely stretched. From the figure we can see that all the fingers are clenched except for the index finger which is neither completely clenched or completely stretched out. Therefore, according to the logic, we are using, the thumb, middle, ring and the little fingers should all be depicted low and the index

Fig. 2. The fingers is clenched tightly.

```
[b'l', b'l', b'l', b'l', b'l', b'']
[b'l', b'l', b'l', b'l', b'l', b'']
[b'l', b'l', b'l', b'l', b'l', b'']
[b'l', b'l', b'l', b'l', b'l', b'']
[b'l', b'l', b'l', b'l', b'l', b'']
[b'l', b'l', b'l', b'l', b'l', b'']
[b'l', b'l', b'l', b'l', b'l', b'']
[b'l', b'l', b'l', b'l', b'l', b'']
[b'l', b'l', b'l', b'l', b'l', b'']
[b'l', b'l', b'l', b'l', b'l', b'']
[b'l', b'l', b'l', b'l', b'l', b'']
[b'l', b'l', b'l', b'l', b'l', b'']
[b'l', b'l', b'l', b'l', b'l', b'']
[b'l', b'l', b'l', b'l', b'l', b'']
[b'l', b'l', b'l', b'l', b'l', b'']
```

Shell

Fig. 3. This shows how each finger is depicted as low when the first is clenched.

finger should be depicted as medium. This means that the pattern which we are looking at is ideally [l/m/l/l/l/l]. but because of the sensitivity of the flex sensors, the flex sensor reading of the thumb finger sometimes shows m and sometimes shows low. So, in our database we have put [l/m/l/l/l] and [m/m/l/l/l] as number 7. The same has been done for other numbers as well so that they can be identified accurately. When we are depicting the number 7, the fingers are clenched in the beginning and the index finger is raised a little.

The reading for the index finger changes from low to medium and the remaining fingers remain at low. This pattern [l/m/l/l/l] matches with our database of numbers which are predefined and the number 7 is depicted. All the numbers from 1–9 are depicted this way. The data from the flex sensors and the accelerometer is sent to the raspberry pi for processing using socket programming.

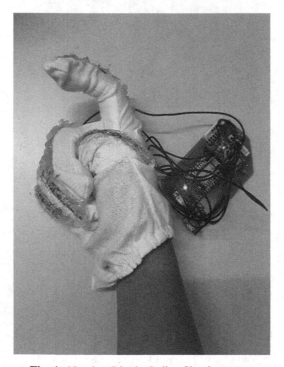

Fig. 4. Number 7 in the Indian Sign language.

The same has been done for other numbers as well so that they can be identified accurately. When we are depicting the number 7, the fingers are clenched in the beginning and the index finger is raised a little. The reading for the index finger changes from low to medium and the remaining fingers remain at low. This pattern [l/m/l/l/l] matches with our database of numbers which are predefined and the number 7 is depicted. All the numbers from 1–9 are depicted this way. The data from the flex sensors and the accelerometer is sent to the raspberry pi for processing using socket programming. A server client scenario is established and the data is sent. The data of the signs is stored in the form of arrays. Each array contains five sub arrays for the five fingers. In each of the sub array, there are three values (Fig. 5).

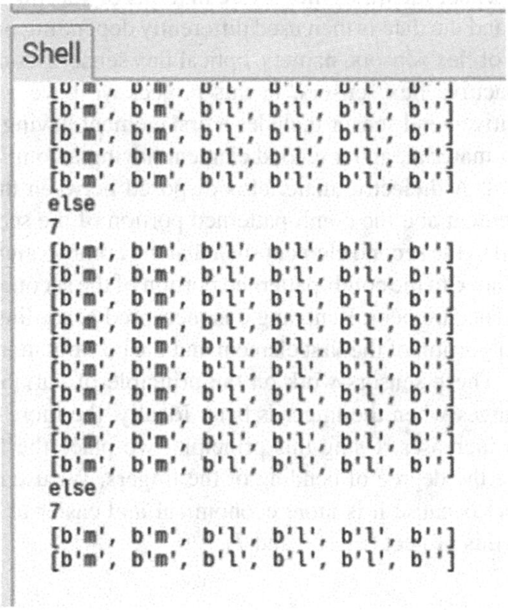

```
Shell
  [b'm', b'm', b'l', b'l', b'l', b'']
  [b'm', b'm', b'l', b'l', b'l', b'']
  [b'm', b'm', b'l', b'l', b'l', b'']
  [b'm', b'm', b'l', b'l', b'l', b'']
  [b'm', b'm', b'l', b'l', b'l', b'']
  else
  7
  [b'm', b'm', b'l', b'l', b'l', b'']
  [b'm', b'm', b'l', b'l', b'l', b'']
  [b'm', b'm', b'l', b'l', b'l', b'']
  [b'm', b'm', b'l', b'l', b'l', b'']
  [b'm', b'm', b'l', b'l', b'l', b'']
  [b'm', b'm', b'l', b'l', b'l', b'']
  [b'm', b'm', b'l', b'l', b'l', b'']
  [b'm', b'm', b'l', b'l', b'l', b'']
  [b'm', b'm', b'l', b'l', b'l', b'']
  else
  7
  [b'm', b'm', b'l', b'l', b'l', b'']
  [b'm', b'm', b'l', b'l', b'l', b'']
```

Fig. 5. This shows how the index finger is depicted as m to communicate the number 7

There are three values in the sub array for the three levels-low, medium and high. Again, to depict the number 7, the way in which it is stored is [[1, 0, 0], [1, 1, 0], [1, 0, 0], [1, 0, 0], [1, 0, 0]]. The zeroth indexed element in the sub array is for low and the first and the second indexed element are medium and high respectively. The zeroth element of the zeroth sub array depicts that the thumb finger is at low. The first element of the first sub array depicts that the index finger is at medium and similarly from looking at the rest of the sub arrays we understand that the middle, ring and the little finger are at low. Due to the sensitivity of the flex sensors we have assumed [[1, 0, 0], [1, 1, 0], [1, 0, 0], [1, 0, 0], [1, 0, 0]] and [[1, 1, 0], [1, 1, 0], [1, 0, 0], [1, 0, 0], [1, 0, 0]] as 7 for accuracy. The starting point for any gesture again is [[1, 0, 0], [1, 0, 0], [1, 0, 0], [1, 0, 0], [1, 0, 0]] - when all the fingers are at low. To depict number 7, the value of the index finger becomes medium which means that the first element of the first sub array changes from 0 to 1. It is programmed in such a way that when the resistance value of a particular finger generated corresponds to medium, the value changes from 0 to 1.

4 Hardware Components

The hardware components used in this project are the flex sensors, a Wi-Fi module and an accelerometer.

Flex Sensors. Flex sensor has multiple applications like most sensors. Even though it is widely used as a goniometer in rehabilitation research, its applications can be seen in different fields like, human machine interfaces, geology and musical instruments. In each application, the sensor identifies the flexure in terms of varying resistance that can be recorded digitally and the data is then used differently depending on application [11]. There are three types of flex sensors, namely, optical flex sensors, conductive ink-based flex sensors and capacitive flex sensors. In this project we have used the capacitive flex sensors. A capacitive bend sensor includes a first element having a comb-patterned portion of conducting material, and a second element having a comb-patterned portion of conducting material. A dielectric material is disposed between the comb-patterned portion of the first element and the comb-patterned portion of the second element. The first element is bonded to the second element such that the comb-patterned portion of the first element slides relative to the comb-patterned portion of the second element when the first and second elements are bent. Bend angle is measured according to the alignment of the comb-patterned portion of the first element and the comb-patterned portion of the second element [12]. These sensors work on the principle of variable resistance. The resistance of this changes when the finger is bent. Ideally, the more the finger is bent, the resistance of this increases. Using this principle, we place the flex sensors along the fingers to measure the degree of bending of the fingers. We use the capacitive flex sensors for this project because it is more economical and easier to interface with the other devices used in this project (Figs. 6 and 7).

Fig. 6. Capacitive flex sensor which is used in the device [11]

Accelerometer. The Accelerometer used in this project is an integrated 6-axis Motion Tracking device that combines a 3-axis gyroscope, 3-axis accelerometer, and a Digital Motion Processor™ (DMP) all in a small $4 \times 4 \times 0.9$ mm package. The accelerometer features three 16-bit analog-to-digital converters (ADCs) for digitizing the gyroscope outputs and three 16-bit ADCs for digitizing the accelerometer outputs. For precision tracking of both fast and slow motions, the parts feature a user-programmable gyroscope full scale range of ±250, ±500, ±1000, and $\pm2000°$/s (dps) and a user-programmable

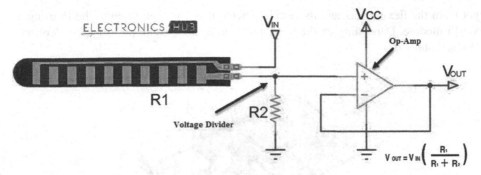

Fig. 7. Interfacing Arduino with a flex sensor

accelerometer full-scale range of ±2 g, ±4 g, ±8 g, and ±16 g. [13] the Accelerometer in this project is used to measure the movement of the hand and its alignment. The data from this is collected and depending on the data, a symbol or movement is depicted (Fig. 8).

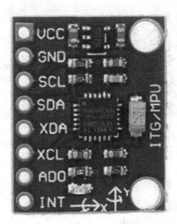

Fig. 8. 3-axes accelerometer and a 3-axes gyroscope

Raspberry-Pi. The model of Raspberry Pi used in this project is a Raspberry Pi model 4 model B. it is a Quad core 64-bit ARM-Cortex A72 running at 1.5 GHz with a 2 GB RAM and it supports dual HDMI display output up to 4Kp60. We can interface this Raspberry Pi with Bluetooth and Wi-Fi. This microcontroller also consists of 2x USB2 ports 2x USB3 ports 1x Gigabit Ethernet port (supports PoE with add-on PoE HAT) 1x Raspberry Pi camera port (2-lane MIPI CSI) 1x Raspberry Pi display port (2-lane MIPI DSI). There are about 28 user General Purpose Input Output Pins supporting various interface options which are UART, SPI, I2C and so on. The software for this microcontroller includes ARMv8 Instruction Set [14]. The Raspberry Pi is used to gather information which we get from the flex sensors and the accelerometer. It is communicated to the Pi using a Wi-Fi module. Depending on the hand movements, the gesture performed is depicted (Figs. 9 and 10).

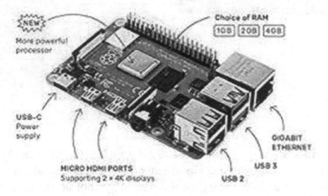

Fig. 9. Raspberry Pi 4

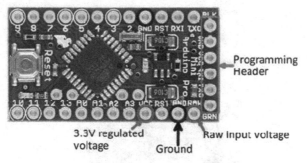

Fig. 10. Arduino Pro Mini

Arduino. The device used to convert the analog values coming from the flex sensors to digital values is the Arduino pro mini. This device has been used as opposed to Arduino uno since it is compact and can fit into the hand easily. The Arduino pro mini operates at 3.3 V as opposed to Arduino Uno which operates at 3.3 V as well as 5 V. The Pro Mini 3.3 V runs at 8 MHz. the resonator on the Pro mini is slower to ensure safe operation of the ATmega. Pro mini's pins surround three of the four sides. The pins on the short side are used for programming. The pins on the other two sides are an assortment of GPIO and power pins [15].

5   Results and Discussion

This project mainly aimed at easing the problems faced by the deaf and dumb society. Developing technology like this enables people with disabilities to participate fully in all activities without any problem. In the case of the deaf and dumb people, the problem arises when their thoughts or ideas cannot be conveyed to other people due to limitation of sign language understanding to public. This project aims at overcoming this communication barrier. The flex sensors used in this project are the 4.5″ in. capacitive flex sensors. The 4.5″ flex sensors are used for the index, middle and the ring fingers. The 2.2″ flex sensors are used for the little finger and the thumb fingers since they are shorter. But since the 2.2″ flex sensors are not producing accurately; it is better to use the longer flex sensors on the thumb and the little finger as well. The longer ones were used so that the sensor can cover the Metacarpophalangeal (MCP) joints and Proximal Interphalangeal (PIP) joints [16]. Since the accelerometer is not enough to perfect the hand orientation, a 3-axis accelerometer gyroscope is used. The data received communicated using a Wi-Fi module since it has a longer communication range when compared to bluetooth. As of now we are not using any Machine Learning or Deep Learning processes to predict the signs. We are performing the gestures which are already pre-existing in the database. We have used a Raspberry-Pi in this project because we were initially wanting to perform only few of the signs and to decode those few gestures a Raspberry pi was sufficient. The next step of this project is to couple both the hands and perform a greater number of gestures.

6   Conclusion and Perspective

We have done this project in the hope that many people can benefit from our work. The gesture glove device work well to generate instructions in the form of number and some texts. In future, we would like to interface our project with deep learning and machine learning concepts to make it more efficient. A set of machine learning algorithms are deployed on raspberry Pi which analyse the output from sensors, reduce the noise in the data using templates of hand movements. The machine generates the text to the corresponding hand movement using LSTM algorithm. The text is converted to speech using a TTS (Text to Speech) module. The workload on raspberry is divided using threading concept. The device to raspberry communication is asynchronous. We would also like to use touch sensors of some sort because there are a lot of gestures in the Indian Sign Language that have the same hand orientation but different positioning of the hand. For example, the letter 'I' and a 'woman' do not have much difference in the gesture. Both are depicted by stretching the index finger completely while the remaining fingers are kept clenched. So, to depict such gestures with such subtle differences, touch sensors or a greater number of accelerometers should be used to get the positioning right.

In Fig. 11 and Fig. 12, we can see how a "woman" and the letter "I" respectively. From the figures we can see the subtle differences in the gestures. With the model we have right now, it is difficult to differentiate between them. Our future goal is to come up with a method that can differentiate between them and identify the gestures accurately. One method through which such subtle gestures can be identified accurately is by incorporating touch sensors that triggers different values when different parts of the body are touched. Another way is to use more number of accelerometers to get the positioning accurately. This problem may also be solved by using Machine Learning or Deep Learning techniques to predict the gesture depending on the context of the situation

Fig. 11. In Indian sign language, a "women". Sign is depicted by touching the index finger to the index nose [17].

Fig. 12. The letter "I" in the Indian language is shown by stretching out finger and touching it to cheek [18]

Acknowledgement. We would like to thank Mr. Anand for providing infrastructure and devices to do this project in VSigma IT Labs Pvt. Ltd, Madhapur, Hyderabad. We would also like to thank Mr. Sai P Sukumar for participating throughout the project.

References

1. Lokhande, P., Prajapati, R., Pansare, S.: Data gloves for sign language recognition system. IJCA (1), 11–14 (2015). Proceedings on National Conference on Emerging Trends in Advanced Communication Technologies NCETACT 2015
2. Sandler, W., Lillo-Martin, D.: Sign Language and Linguistic Universals. Cambridge University Press, Cambridge (2006)

3. Social Statistics Division: Disabled persons in india: a statistical profile. Government of India (2016). http://mospi.nic.in/sites/default/files/publication_reports/Disabled_persons_in_India_2016.pdf. Accessed 29 Jan 2019
4. Hearing Impairment, Rehab Council (2000). http://www.rehabcouncil.nic.in/writereaddata/HI-2-2000.pdf
5. Abraham, A., Article, R.V.: Real time conversion of sign language to speech and prediction of gestures using Artificial Neural Network. Procedia Comput. Sci. **143**, 587–594 (2018)
6. Starner, T., Weaver, J., Pentland, A.: Real-time American sign language recognition using desk and wearable computer based video. IEEE Trans. Pattern Anal. Mach. Intell. **20**(12), 1371–1375 (1998)
7. Bauer, B., Hienz, H., Kraiss, K.: Video-based continuous sign language recognition using statistical methods. In: Proceedings of the 15th International Conference on Pattern Recognition, ICPR-2000, pp. 463–466 (2000)
8. Bharath Academy. https://www.bharathacademy.org/2018/04/03/indian-sign-language/. Accessed 29 Jan 2019
9. Components101. https://components101.com/sensors/flex-sensor-working-circuit-datasheet. Accessed 20 Dec 2019
10. Electronicwings. https://www.electronicwings.com/sensors-modules/mpu6050-gyroscope-accelerometer-temperature-sensor-module. Accessed 25 Dec 2019
11. Teach me micro. https://www.teachmemicro.com/use-flex-sensor/. Accessed 20 Jan 2020
12. Electronicshub. https://www.electronicshub.org/interfacing-flex-sensor-with-arduino/. Accessed 31 Jan 2020
13. Inven sense document number: PS-MPU-6000A-00 revision: 3.4, 19 August 2013
14. Datasheet Raspberry Pi 4 model B, 26 June 2019
15. Arduino Pro mini 328-5 V/16Mhz datasheet (2019)
16. El-Naggar, A., Reichardt, D.: Analyzing hand therapy success in a web-based therapy system. In: Mensch & Computer Workshopband (2016)
17. Snippet from the video "Learn Indian Sign Language - BASIC 25 Words Part - 1", Bumperclapent (2019)
18. Snippet from the video "Alphabets in Indian Sign Language". Digital Arts Academy for the Deaf LLP (2019)

Identification of Target Speech Utterances from Real Public Conversation

Naoto Kosaka and Yumi Wakita[✉]

Osaka Institute of Technology, Osaka, Japan
yumi.wakita@oit.ac.com

Abstract. We are developing a conversation support system that can estimate the smooth progress of human-to-human conversation. When the system senses there has been little progress in the conversation, it attempts to provide a topic to lead a smoother discussion and good atmosphere. The conversation atmosphere is estimated using the fundamental frequency (F0) and sound power (SP). In its practical use, the following problems occur:

1. Ambient noises, especially nonstationary speech signals of a person behind the target speaker, decrease the conversation-atmosphere estimation rate. It is difficult to cancel this speech noise, even when using current noise cancelling methods.
2. Laughter utterances in which acoustic characteristics are quite different from usual speech utterances are often seen in daily conversation, which causes a decrease in the conversation-atmosphere estimation performance.

In this paper, we propose an identification method for target speech utterances from ambient speech noises or laughter utterances using the standard deviation value of SP and Mel-Frequency Cepstral Coefficients (MFCC).

Keywords: Conversation support system · Ambient speech cancelling · Laughter utterance identification

1 Introduction

Recently, with the spread of network devices, such as personal computers and smartphones, various pieces of information can be easily obtained, and the opportunity to obtain information by talking with people has decreased. The number of people who are living alone and are reclusive is increasing, and the lack of communication between humans has become a big problem.

The creation of some communities has been promoted to support the communication between the elderly, especially disaster-stricken elderly people. However, it is not easy to provide communication support to people who once missed the opportunity for interaction with others. When they are not confident in communicating with others or they have a negative impression of the community themselves, it is difficult to get people

© Springer Nature Switzerland AG 2020
V. G. Duffy (Ed.): HCII 2020, LNCS 12199, pp. 52–63, 2020.
https://doi.org/10.1007/978-3-030-49907-5_4

to immediately participate in communication support activities. Therefore, a different approach to solving this problem is necessary.

Many robots that communicate with humans have been developed for elderly persons [1–3]. They are effective at being interested in conversation; however, they have a problem in that the user becomes tired of their conversation for reasons such as lack of conversational flexibility and adaptability. It would be difficult to change their topics, expressions, utterance timings, or talking speeds according to the situation of the user and the conversation atmosphere. We have already proposed a conversation support system for the public community [4]. The system can understand whether or not the human-to-human communication proceeds smoothly. When sensing there has been little progress during the conversation, the system attempts to provide a topic to lead a smoother discussion and good atmosphere. We have already confirmed that the fundamental frequency (F0) and sound power (SP) values for each utterance are effective in estimating the conversation atmosphere using a free conversation database recorded in a recording studio. Figure 1 shows the structure of the conversation smoothness estimation process. The system extracts F0 values from input utterances and calculated the standard deviation of the F0 values (SD-F0). When the SD-F0 values of some utterances in the conversation are detected to be under the threshold value, the system decides that the conversation is not progressing smoothly and provides a new topic to liven up the conversation. However, the system was evaluated using conversations recorded in a studio, and we have not solved the problems of conversation support in real-world use.

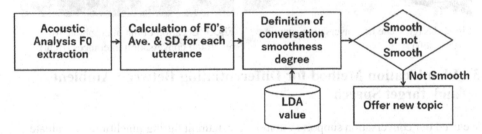

Fig. 1 Conventional process of a conversion support system

We think that if we use our system in a real restaurant or lounge, the following fatal problems will occur and decrease the estimation performance:

1. Ambient noise decreases the estimation performance. In particular, it would be difficult to exclude nonstationary noise, such as a person's speech from behind the target speaker, even when we use current noise cancelling methods.
2. Non-language utterances (e.g., laughter, cough, and clicking tongue) are often included in daily conversation more than in the conversations recorded in studios. The error rate of conversation atmosphere estimation increases when using real daily conversation because the F0 characteristics are different from those of normal speech.

In this paper, we describe an identification method for target normal speech utterances from ambient speech utterances and laughter utterances, which are frequently included in daily conversation.

2 Our Conversation Support System

The left side of Fig. 2 shows a scene of use of our conversation support system listening to a conversation between two speakers and estimating whether the conversation is progressing smoothly. The plush-doll on the table is our conversation support system. The two right pictures in Fig. 3 show the microphone for recording speech. The microphone is a small directional condenser microphone. Several microphones are placed just in front of the chairs on the sides of the table. Furthermore, it is desirable that the position of the microphone is adjustable according to the sitting positions of the speakers. In such locations, even if the microphone is installed near the user, background conversations of other people are frequently inputted.

Fig. 2 Usage scene of conversation support system (left)

Fig. 3 Location of the microphone for recording conversation utterances (right)

3 Identification Method for Differentiating Between Ambient and Target Speech

We used our conversation support system in a restaurant during lunchtime to evaluate it for practical use. The system regarded signals as target utterances when the power level of signals exceeded the threshold. Over a three-minute period, over seventy utterances were extracted as target voices. However, the rate of target speech extraction was only 65%. The extracted utterances included several inputs from people sitting at the neighboring table and employees of the restaurant. It is necessary to distinguish between the speech of ambient speakers and the target speaker.

To exclude background speech, several sound source separation methods have been proposed using microphone-arrays [5, 6]. There are also several identification methods for the separation of sound sources based on the use of a single microphone, such as binary masking using a Bayesian network and non-negative matrix factorization [7, 8]. These methods are effective for separating target sounds from background noise. However, the associated system tends to be complex, and the separation of target sound sources from nonstationary noise, such as ambient speech, is typically insufficient.

We use the standard deviation values of SP (SD-SP) for each utterance to identify the target speaker located near a microphone. In previous our paper [9], we found that the SD-SP of each utterance when speakers talk near the microphone tends to be larger than that when speakers talk far from the microphone. However, we confirmed this using only male speakers. In this paper, we report the experience results using both males and females.

3.1 Free Conversation Recording in a Restaurant Environment

To analyze the difference between the acoustic characteristics of speech originating near a microphone and that originating far from a microphone, we recorded several conversations in an experimental room.

To reproduce the acoustic environment of a restaurant, two loudspeakers were placed behind the speaker and noises from actual restaurants were played. We asked a speaker and a partner to talk to each other freely amidst this noise. The partner stood behind the microphone, and its position was fixed. One speaker (Speaker1) stood at two different positions: one was 30 cm from the microphone and the other (Speaker2) was 120 cm from it. We recorded the speaker's utterances for each spot. When the speaker's distance is 30 cm from the microphone, the system regards the speaker as the target, whereas when the distance is 120 cm, the system does not regard the speaker as the target due to environmental noise. The former is the conversation that should be accepted by the system, and the latter is the conversation that should be excluded.

Table 1 lists the recording conditions. Figure 4 shows the experimental layout used to record the conversations.

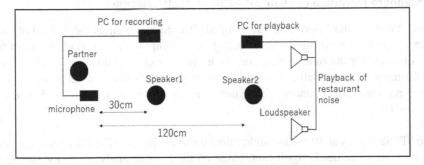

Fig. 4 Schematic diagram of experimental layout

3.2 Acoustic Analysis and Extraction of Each Utterance

We extracted the speaker's utterances from the recorded conversation. The threshold level was decided using Eq. (1), and only parts above the threshold level are extracted as utterance parts.

$$Threshold\ level = (Average\ of\ ambient\ sound\ power) + 5\ dB \qquad (1)$$

We calculated the F0 values and SP values of each utterance as acoustic parameters. The analysis conditions and specifications are listed in Table 2.

Table 1. Conversation recording conditions

Speakers	4 males and 2 females
Conversation period	2–4 min/conversation
Conversation condition	Free dyadic conversation
Distance between microphone and speaker	30 cm/120 cm
Ambient sound	Sound recorded in a restaurant
SP value of the ambient sounds at location of each speaker	120 cm: 59.3 dB 30 cm: 56.7 dB
S/N values at the location of microphone Signal: each speaker's sound Noise: ambient sound	120 cm: 4.2 dB 30 cm: 13.3 dB

Table 2. Parameter extraction details

Sampling frequency [Hz]	16000
Frame length [ms]	128
Frame shift width [ms]	10

3.3 Standard Deviation of F0 or SP Value of Each Utterance

We calculated standard deviation values of SP (SD-SP) as well as the SD-F0 of each utterance. Their relationship is shown in Fig. 5. A comparison was made between the values obtained for utterances originating near the microphone (distance of 30 cm) and those for utterances originating far from the microphone (distance of 120 cm). The line in Fig. 5 represents the boundary calculated using the LDA method. Figure 5 indicates the following:

- The SD-SP values at 30 cm are higher than those at 120 cm. The difference between the two sets of values is significant, based on the F-value analysis (confidence level of 95%). The tendency of the relationship is independent of male and female.
- The difference in the SD-F0 values between the 30 cm and 120 cm cases is small, and the difference is not significant based on the F-value analysis.

We confirmed that the SD-SP values at 30 cm were higher than those at 120 cm as follows:

(1) The SD-SP values for each utterance decrease as the distance between the microphone and the loudspeaker is increased.
(2) The SD-SP values of loud utterances tend to be smaller than those of normal utterances.

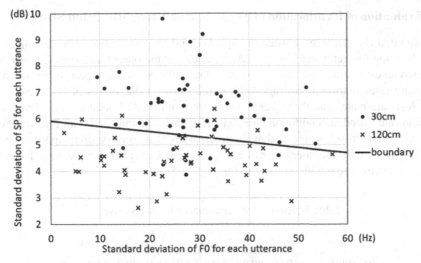

Fig. 5 Relationship of the standard deviation between F0 and SP

To clarify the reason why the SD-SP values of loud utterances are smaller than that of normal utterances, we compared the changes in the time axis of SP values between loud utterances and normal utterances. We recorded two kinds of utterances. One was the normal utterance recorded in the room without noise, and the other was the loud utterance spoken while listening to the restaurant's noises with headphones

Figure 6 shows examples of the two kinds of utterances. The left figure shows an example of a loud utterance's SP, and the right figure shows an example of a normal utterance's SP. The dotted lines in these figures represent the threshold levels when each utterance is spoken in a noisy restaurant. When comparing the shapes of the changes on the time axis of SP values, the flat part indicated dotted circle is found only in the upper threshold of the loud utterance for the Lombard effect. In a normal utterance, the shape of the SP has a tendency to change constantly. This is the reason the SD-SP of the loud utterance is smaller than that of the normal utterance.

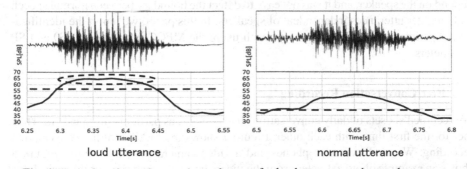

loud utterance   normal utterance

Fig. 6 Examples of waveform and sound power for loud utterance and normal utterance

3.4 Evaluation of Identification of Target Speech Using SD-SP and SD-F0

We estimated the distance between the speaker and the microphone for each speaker using the support vector machine (SVM) function for the other three speakers, and we evaluated an estimation performance by calculating the recall rates, precision rates, and F-measure rates (harmonic average value). Table 3 lists the values of each rate. The talker A–D are males and the talker E and F are females. Although the recall rate and precision rate varied depending on the speaker, the average rate across all four speakers was 80.5%. This result suggests that the realization of a conversation support system that can extract only the utterances of a target speaker near a microphone is feasible, even in an environment with ambient noise.

Table 3. Estkmation performance of each speaker

Person	A	B	C	D	E	F	Average
Recall [%]	90.0	80.0	70.0	90.0	60.0	70.0	76.7
Precision [%]	81.8	88.9	87.5	100.0	75.0	77.8	85.2
F-measure [%]	85.7	84.2	77.8	94.7	66.7	73.7	80.5

4 Differentiation Between Laughter Utterances and Normal Speech Utterances

Daily conversation includes several non-language utterances, such as laughter, coughing, and tongue clicking. The rates of non-language utterances in the free conversation database are 19%. The utterances of the elderly include many types of non-language utterances, but 83% of utterances are "laughter". We have already proposed an identification method between laughter utterances and normal speech utterances using the standard deviations of F0 values for each utterance [8]. However, the identification performance was not high. The F0 values and SP values characteristic of laughter utterances depend on the speaker, and it was not easy to detect the boundary between normal speech and laughter utterances independent of speakers. In this paper, we report the identification experiment results for laughter speech using the MFCC in addition to F0 and SP parameters.

4.1 Free Conversation Recording

We recorded six sets of daily conversations by six males as participating speakers. They met for the first time with each other. Figure 7 shows the location of the conversation recording. We used two microphones and a video camera for this purpose. Figure 8 shows an example photo extracted from the video data. The conditions of the recordings are listed in Table 4.

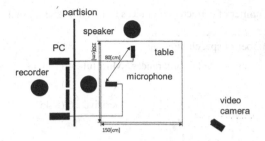

Fig. 7 Location of recording conversation

Fig. 8 Example photo extracted from the video data

Table 4. Conditions of conversation: estimation performance of each speaker

Speakers	6 males
Ages	62–82 yours old
Number of conversations	6 conversations
Conversation periods	Three minutes/conversation
Conversation condition	Free dyadic conversation

4.2 Laughter Utterance Extraction

We extracted both normal speech utterances and laugher utterances from the recording data. The laughter utterances were classified into three types according to social function in Tanaka's paper [10]. Table 5 indicates the number of utterances for each type of extracted utterance.

Table 5. Number of extracted utterances of laughter and normal speech

Number of speech utterances		81
Number of laughter utterances	Mirthful	45 (63.38%)
	Polite	20 (28.17%)
	Derisive	6 (8.45%)

4.3 Acoustic Analysis Conditions

We calculated the F0, SP, and MFCC values of both normal speech and laughter utterances shown in Table 5 as acoustic parameters, and the standard deviations of these parameters were calculated. In a practical noisy environment, the threshold should be set above the SP of noise, and only the part of the input signal over the threshold is regarded as utterances. In the experiment, we calculated the average SP value of each utterance and regarded it as a threshold. We calculated the acoustic parameters of only the utterance parts above the threshold. The analysis conditions and specifications are listed in Table 6.

Table 6. Parameter extraction details

Sampling frequency [Hz]	16000
Frame length [ms]	128
Frame shift width [ms]	10
MFCC dimension [dimension]	8

4.4 Normal Speech Identification from Laughter Utterances by SVM

We confirmed the identification performance between the normal speech and laughter utterances using F0, SP, and MFCC. We used an SVM for identification. In particular, to confirm the effectiveness of MFCC, we compared the performance using only F0 and SP with that using F0, SP, and MFCC. Tables 7 and 8 show the identification performances in terms of recall, precision, F-measure, and accuracy of normal speech extraction from the database shown in Table 4.

To improve the conversation-atmosphere estimation performance, it is important that all extracted utterances are normal speech utterances. When the "True Positive (TP)", "True Negative (TN)", "False Positive (FP)", and "False Negative (FN)" are counted on the side of normal speech utterances, the accuracy rate is defined by Eq. (2).

$$Accuracy = (TP + FN) / (TP + FP + FN + TN) \qquad (2)$$

Tables 7 and 8 show the following:

Table 7. Identification rates of each speaker using F0, SP, and MFCC

Person	A	B	C	D	E	F	Average
Recall [%]	77.78	63.64	50.00	88.24	52.94	80.00	68.77
Precision [%]	70.00	77.78	66.67	78.95	75.00	70.59	**73.16**
F-measure [%]	73.68	70.00	57.14	83.33	62.07	75.00	70.20
Accuracy [%]	68.75	73.91	55.00	81.25	60.71	75.76	**69.23**

Table 8. Identification rates of each speaker using F0 and SP

Person	A	B	C	D	E	F	Average
Recall [%]	77.78	63.64	75.00	88.24	58.82	80.00	73.91
Precision [%]	77.78	53.85	64.29	60.00	71.43	50.00	**62.89**
F-measure [%]	77.78	58.33	69.23	71.43	64.52	61.54	67.14
Accuracy [%]	75.00	86.52	60.00	62.50	60.71	54.55	**61.55**

- The accuracy rate was approximately 69.23%. When using MFCC parameters in addition to F0 and PS, the accuracy rate increases compared to using only F0 and PS (from 61.55% to 69.23%).
- For our conversation atmosphere estimation, a high precision rate is desirable. The precision rate was improved by approximately 10% by using MFCC (from 62.89% to 73.16%).
- The performance depends on the speaker. In particular, the accuracy rates are decreased for speakers B and C. However, the differences in the accuracy tend to decrease when using MFCC.

4.5 Discussion

For the conversation atmosphere estimation, all extracted utterances should be normal speech utterances without laughter utterances, and the precision rates are important. As a result, the precision rates were 73.16%. This is insufficient for identification performance. However, if we extract all the utterances as normal speech, the precision rate is 53.29% (number of normal speech utterances/number of all utterances shown in Table 5). The results suggest that the precision rate would be improved drastically. In addition, the MFCC parameters are quite effective in improving the precision rates.

To clarify the reason for the effectiveness of MFCC, we compared the standard deviation of MFCC (SD-MFCC) values between the normal speech utterances and laughter utterances.

Figure 9 shows the comparison results between normal and laughter utterances using SD-MFCC values of the 2nd dimension values and the 4th dimension values. The SVM method was used for identification. The curved line in Fig. 9 indicates the boundary between normal speech and laughter by SVM.

This figure indicates that the area plotted by the MFCC values of laughter utterances is small. Almost all values of both the 2nd dimension and 4th dimension are plotted within the SVM boundary. However, the area in the case of normal speech is wide. The results indicate that it is difficult to separate both areas, but it is possible to decide the area plotting only normal speech utterances. The results suggest that MFCC values are only useful for extracting normal speech utterances.

The identification performance shown in Fig. 9 depends on the speaker. In the future, it is necessary to develop a speaker adaptation method to improve its performance.

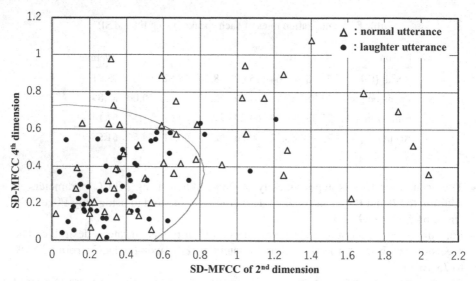

Fig. 9 Comparison between normal and laughter utterances using SD-MFCC values (the 2nd dimension and the 4th dimension).

5   Conclusion

We studied an identification method of target speech utterance to use a conversation support system in a lounge environment. We found that the standard deviation of the SP values is effective for identifying the target speech utterance from ambient speech. As a result of an identification experiment using the SVM method, although the recall rate and precision rate varied depending on the speaker, the average rate across all six speakers was 80.5%. We also confirmed the identification performance between normal speech and laughter utterances using F0, SP, and MFCC. The identification rate of normal speech utterances was 73.1% as the precision rate.

These results indicate that these acoustic characteristics would be effective in conversation atmosphere estimation and suggest that our conversation support system could be useful in practical scenarios.

Acknowledgment. This work is supported by JSPS KAKENHI Grant Number 19K04934.

References

1. Heerink, M., Kröse, B., Evers, V., Wielinga, B.: The influence of social presence on acceptance of a companion robot by older people. J. Phys. Agents **2**(2), 33–40 (2008)
2. Shiomi, M., Iio, T., Kamei, K., Sharma, C., Hagita, N.: Effectiveness of social behaviors for autonomous wheelchair robot to support elderly people in Japan. PloS One **10**(5), e012803 (2015)
3. Robinson, H., MacDonald, B., Broadbent, E.: The role of healthcare robots for older people at home: a review. Int. J. Soc. Robot. **6**(4), 575–591 (2014). https://doi.org/10.1007/s12369-014-0242-2
4. Wakita, Y., Yoshida, Y., Nakamura, M.: Influence of personal characteristics on nonverbal information for estimating communication smoothness. In: Kurosu, M. (ed.) HCI 2016. LNCS, vol. 9733, pp. 148–157. Springer, Cham (2016). https://doi.org/10.1007/978-3-319-39513-5_14
5. Benesty, J., Chen, J., Huang, Y.: Microphone Array Signal Processing: Springer Topics in Signal Processing. Springer, Heidelberg (2008). https://doi.org/10.1007/978-3-540-78612-2
6. Chakraborty, R., Nadeu, C., Butko, T.: Detection and positioning of overlapped sounds in a room environment. In: Proceedings of Interspeech 2012, Portland, USA (2012)
7. Itakura, K., et al.: Bayesian multichannel audio source separation based on integrated source and spatial models. IEEE/ACM TASLP **26**(4), 831–846 (2018)
8. Lee, D.D., Seung, H.S.: Algorithms for non-negative matrix factorization. In: Proceedings of the NIPS 2000, pp. 556–562 (2000)
9. Kosaka, N., Kido, K., Wakita, Y.: A simple identification method for differentiating between ambient and target speech. In: Proceedings of 2019 IEEE 8th Global Conference on Consumer Electronics (GCCE), Osaka, Japan, 15–18 October 2019, pp. 860–863 (2019)
10. Tanaka, H., Campbell, N.: Classification of social laughter in natural conversational speech. Comput. Speech Lang. **28**(1), 314–325 (2014)

IMotions' Automatic Facial Recognition & Text-Based Content Analysis of Basic Emotions & Empathy in the Application of the Interactive Neurocommunicative Technique LNCBT (Line & Numbered Concordant Basic Text)

Jorge Mora-Fernandez[1,2,6(✉)], Azizudin Khan[3], Fernando Estévez[4,6], Felipe Webster[5,6], María Isabel Fárez[6], and Felipe Torres[6]

[1] Arthur C. Clarke Center for Human Imagination, University of California San Diego, USA & Laboratory of Digital Culture & Hypermedia Museography-Research Group Museum I+D+C, Universidad Complutense de Madrid, Madrid, Spain
j2morafernandez@ucsd.edu, multiculturalvideos@gmail.com, jorge.mora@unach.edu.ec, jorge.mora@ucuenca.edu.ec

[2] Research Group UNACH IAMNCEDC R+D+C+I/MANICECDE I+D+C+i, Interactive Arts & Media, Narrative Convergences & Edutainment in Digital Communications & Cultures R+D+C+I (Research+Development+Creation+Innovation), Universidad Nacional de Chimborazo, Riobamba, Ecuador

[3] Psychophysiology Laboratory, Department of Humanities and Social Sciences, Indian Institute of Technology Bombay, Powai, Mumbai 400 076, Maharashtra, India
khanaziz@iitb.ac.in

[4] School of Medicine, Universidad de Cuenca, Cuenca, Azuay, Ecuador
fernando.estevez@ucuenca.edu.ec

[5] School of Psychology, Universidad de Cuenca, Cuenca, Azuay, Ecuador
felipe.webster@ucuenca.edu.ec

[6] Research Interinstitucional Group NEUROSINAPSIS I+D+i, Univesidad de Cuenca, Cuenca, Ecuador
maria.farezp@ucuenca.ec, felipe_t@hotmail.es

Abstract. This research paper focuses on the effectiveness of the Line Numbered Concordant Basic Text (LNCBT) of Narcotics Anonymous as an interactive neurocommunicative and gamificated technique to generate empathic emotions through its process and application. The LNCBT is studied as an effective educational, neurocommunicational and behavioral change technique for recovery from addictions. Firstly, it was analyzed through Facial Action Coding System (FACS) using the iMotions Software. Secondly, the FACS results were also contrasted with text-based content analysis to confirm the relationship between empathic emotions and the prose contained in the LNCBT, which the subjects selected through an interactive communicative and game-based learning process: writing the numbers of their favorite sentences that they related with and sharing about them. The analyzed data suggest that LNCBT technique activates emotional empathy, including the ability of identifying through written text and verbal and nonverbal expressions. Results confirmed multiple complex emotional flow from recognizing negative emotions, at the beginning, to more positive emotions, at the end of

© Springer Nature Switzerland AG 2020
V. G. Duffy (Ed.): HCII 2020, LNCS 12199, pp. 64–80, 2020.
https://doi.org/10.1007/978-3-030-49907-5_5

the technique. From middle time of the technique to the last moments the research observed more balanced emotional states, once the negative experiences were recognized and shared at the beginning. At the end of the experience joy predominates (75%–85% of time) while emotions like anger or disgust tend to diminish. Finally, the text-based content analysis method found data that also suggests that the subjects, during the completion of the LNCBT technique, felt a positive emotional flow towards empathy, a collective, nonjudgmental and shared balance emotional state. The results suggest that the interactive neurocommunicative technique of LNCBT therapeutically supports recovery from the addictive process, from the isolated self-centered obsessive and compulsive emotional state towards a more empathic collective state.

Keywords: Neurocommunications · Social brain · Connective intelligence · Empathic imagination · Narcotics anonymous · Recovery from addictions · Interactive communications · LNCBT · FACS · iMotions · Empathy and emotion · Gamification · Automatic facial emotion recognition · Emotional Text-based content · Behavior change techniques

1 Introduction

The Line Numbered Concordant Basic Text (LNCBT) of Narcotics Anonymous is studied as an effective educational, interactive neurocommunicational and behavioral change technique for recovery from addictions. In the present research empathy is analyzed, based on the emotions found automatically through software in the faces of individuals that are part of addiction recovery groups based on the 12 Step technique. Specifically, for this study, audiovisual recordings have been made during the use of the tool of LNCBT technique, to be analyzed by the IMotions software.

It is intended to find what emotions appear in the most important moments at the presence of empathy, and the tendency of these emotions to appear at a global level through the process of the tool.

It started by using the observation of facial expressions because it is a less intrusive method than electroencephalography (EEG) or Functional Magnetic Resonance Images (FMRI). Also, it is considered an important tool of behavior measuring for the study of emotions, cognitive processes and social interactions [1]. Also, it is used in different areas like job interviews and personalized marketing of products [2].

Addictions have a neurobiological basis and the mesocortical-limbic system anatomic substrate is the most important in relation to the addiction behavior [3].

Currently, addiction studies include, apart from associated chemical substances, some of them of behavioral character, known as non-chemical addictions or toxic [4]. Most of them are included on the list of the denominated behavioral addictions by the DSM V [5].

The pharmacological treatment for addictions by itself is not enough, because it is centered on reducing symptoms of depression, anxiety, concern, and sleep difficulties; in previous studies it has been proved that non-pharmacological techniques as group therapies, cognitive-behavioral and motivations help to reinforce social behaviors that modulate the addict brain [3, 6–10], allowing the person to maintain a lifestyle without drug consume and engendering abstinence [9] that is why it is interesting to study how the 12 steps technique, LNCBT is able to generate empathy which can be recognized and analyzed with software.

2 Materials and Methods

2.1 Emotions

They are actions that respond to external stimulus, perceived or remembered [11]. According to P. Ekman it is possible to find 7 terms that represent families of related emotions: joy, sadness, anger, disgust, fear, mean, and surprise [12]. Each basic emotion has a distinctive facial expression and for most of them have evidence of different physiological responses, changes in the voice and cognitive phenomena evidence as concentrating attention in the emotion stimulus [12–14]. Based on the knowledge about basic emotions it is possible to build up first signs of more complex and interesting emotions, mainly for philosophers. Other authors for generating a more general theory about the fundamentals of the basic emotions a distinction between "primary" and "secondary" emotions [15–18].

The "primary" ones are part of the evolutionary heritage that are shared by all healthy humans and related to specific types of stimulus. The "secondary" ones are acquired during the development of each individual and respond to more complex and abstract characteristics and stimulus.

This approximation identifies each emotion with a type of somatic evaluation and is centered on the functions of emotions on the internal cognitive economy of the organism [12, 17].

Also, according to Damasio & Carvalho, the neurophysiological comprehension of feelings can be conducive to the development of more efficient treatments against depression, addiction to substances and untreatable pain [11].

2.2 Facial Expressions Recognition

There are four types of facial signs systems: static, slow, artificial, and fast. The static signals include the size, the shape and the relative localization of the characteristics and the contour of the bone structure that are related to identity and beauty. The slow signals can be wrinkles or dark circles that carry information about age. The artificial signs such as make up, plastic surgery or extra elements as wigs or glasses try to decrease the slow signs of age. The fast signs include the actions produced by muscles, typically called expressions, and the blood flow on the skin temperature and color [19]. It is about this last type of signs in which the following systems described are focused on.

There are several methods to measure recognizable facial actions visually by humans, around 14 techniques according to P. Ekman in a period of 55 years since 1924 [19]. For automatic categorization, three recognition steps are necessary: detection of the face, extraction of the facial expressions, and classification of the expressions. Most of the studies about facial expressions analysis are based on the emotional classification vision of Ekman of facial expressions, even though it does not mean that all the possible facial expressions can be categorized within the 7 basic emotions [20]. There are two important groups of parameters used to represent facial expressions:

- The one developed by Ekman and Friesen in 1977 [21, 26], denominated FACS, (Facial action coding system).
- And another group of parameters of muscular actions called FAPs (Facial animation parameters), part of the MPEG-4 standard, developed in 1998.

The problem of the automatic classification is difficult at first, because the description of the emotions by Ekman is linguistic, not based totally on the action units; second, because the classification of multiple basic emotions must be possible (complex emotions); third, because it must be independent of the physiognomic variability of the individuals; fourth, because of the difficulty of recognizing the context; and fifth, because there is an increase on the psychological research that time measurement is an important factor for the interpretation of facial expressions [20].

According to Bassili [22], a trained human observer can classify correctly faces within the six emotions, apart from content, on average of 87%. The software iMotions presents a proven performance in a subgroup of data CK+ of the Carnegie Mellon University [23] presented on Fig. 1 [24]. Moreover, an interesting conceptual framework for analyzing emotions through face to face communication is developed by Hellmann [25] and the web of the software IMotions [26] includes a large amount of related researches from the last years that used it.

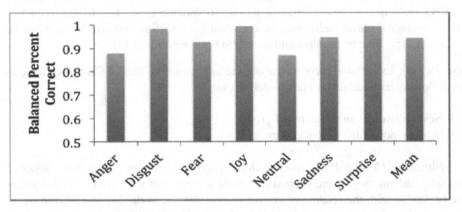

Fig. 1. Performance of iMotions with *CK+*.

For a long time, psychologists and neuropsychologists have discussed if the recognition of faces is by underlying components or by an integral process. While Biederman proposes the theory of recognition by components, under the premise that as well as the oral language is composed by simple phonemes, the vision can be understood as the composition of diverse figures [27]. In that regard, Ekman [28] was a pioneer in studying and classifying the spontaneous expression in the faces generating its FACS system, Facial Action Coding System, which is one of the few agreed system that it is still used in modern research tools such as FACET 2.0 [24] of IMotions . Farah et al. [29] suggest that the face recognition is an integral process that results with more precision to recognize the complete face with each one of the characteristics, therefore the researchers use a holistic focus as a PCA technique (Principal Components Analysis). Until now, there has not been an agreement about this [30], but recent deep learning approaches using convolutional neural networks and recurrent neural networks leads to an integral process [31]. D. Li et al. [32] reported that the fusion of video with electroencephalography outperform the use of each modality separately. Thus, future work with the integration of electroencephalography could improve the emotions recognition.

2.3 Line Numbered Page Concordant

The tool and technique LNCBT, based on the program of 12 Steps for addiction recovery is predicated on the recollection of collective experiences of people around the world in different phases of addiction and recovery. The text is structured through numbered phrases for each chapter. During the application of the technique, an individual reads a phrase and says the number of the next phrase; the process is repeated until the chapter is finished. During the reading the individuals write down the number of the phrases that they identify with by any motive related to their own experiences. Then, everyone has a three-minute period to share about the selected phrases. The main variable that is studied is Empathy and how it is expressed through basic emotions (joy, sadness, fear, anger, disgust, surprise, and mean) [12] that activate by realizing the 3 independent activities of reading, sharing and listening experiences of addiction recovery that the LNCBT technique presents. There is also a sub-variable that refers to the frequency of the numbered phrase selection, the ones that have sentimental content that can be classified as positive or negative and related to basic emotions [33].

Sample. An audiovisual recording about the application of the LNCBT was made to the following individuals for their posterior analysis:

- 9 New Individuals in the recovery group
- 6 Veteran Individuals that attend the group

Within the 15 recordings, apart from the complete analysis of the video, signs of empathy and emotions were studied in 5 main moments of the LNCBT technique: at the beginning with the reading of collective experiences, at the end of the reading, at the beginning of the phrase sharing that made them feel identified, at the middle of the sharing times, and at the end of the sharing times.

The dependent variable, empathy, and the sub-variables, basic emotions, and interactions with the independent variables, reading, sharing and listening there have been identified by being different and significant moments of the technique:

- There is a period around 5 to 12 min for the Reading. In this time, it is observed empathy if there is any annotation of any phrase or expression of facial gestures related with a basic emotion concordant or in relation to the meaning of the text read.
- After that, the participants share experiences in first person statements, using "I" or "we", in turns of 3 min each. It is evident the empathy through the observation of basic expressions during the identification and citation of phrases of the text that called the attention of each participant. Empathy is also evident when the sharing is related with

the words shared by another person, for that expressions like "I feel identified", "me too", "as he said" are considered.

- During the previous periods of time the phases of listening are alternated, so this empathy is observed in basic emotions expressed facially when another person is sharing or reading.

2.4 Keywords Trend

In the five years charted, there are flat and regular search trends shown in Fig. 2 of the technological terms: iMotions and Automatic Facial Emotion Recognition. In other way, the keywords most related to Recovery from Addictions show that Narcotics Anonymous keeps a high trend along the time and a peak in the searches of recovery from addictions at 2017. Interestingly, Neurocommunications and Social Brain, neuroscience related keywords, show peaks at only certain times and it is not clear if there is a periodicity in the Social Brain searches.

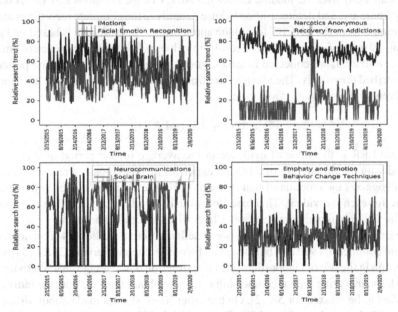

Fig. 2. Search trends. Top left: technical keywords. Top right: recovery keywords. Bottom left: neuroscience keywords. Bottom right: psychology keywords.

Empathy and Emotion and Behavior Change Techniques shows some peaks, but the trends are almost constant along the last five years.

2.5 Data Collection

From the recordings, the time dedicated to reading and sharing are separated. Additionally, time is divided to each activity in three parts: beginning, middle, and end. In this way it is possible to observe the emotional and empathic process of the individuals in different moments of the LNCBT technique. Also, the main moments are extracted on intervals of 10 s, obtaining a sub-recording of 50 s by individual.

Further, for confirming the correlation among the text phrases and the emotions experimented on different moments of the technique applications, the number of the most written phrases at that moment of reading and sharing were collected. A feeling analysis of the selected phrases with higher frequency was made. The feeling analysis of the texts can be grouped in four categories: to highlight keywords, lexical affinity, statistical methods, and approximation in a concept level [33]. For the searching of feelings in the text of the LNCBT technique, the lexical affinity has been used because it is more sophisticated than highlighting keywords, because it assigns words with affinity for each emotion.

2.6 Analysis of Empathy and Basic Emotions

The present study uses the module Emotient FACET of the iMotions software, complementary home-use and demonstration license to analyze the complete recordings and the 5 main moments of the LNCBT technique application. This software is based on FACS, including 19 units of action [24]. The results in values related to the evidence of emotion presence, 8 in total, are collected in tables where averages were made in the periods of time described previously. The averages are transformed in a probability value using the Eq. 1 given by the software developer:

$$PP = 1/(1 + 10^{\wedge}(-LRR)) \tag{1}$$

Where LRR is the value of evidence in the average of one period of time and PP is related with the probability of a human expert in facial expression recognition using FACS recognizes the emotion of that moment [24]. The values of evidence depend of a base line for each individual. This base line adjusts by taking a part of the recording in which the individual maintains his or her face with a neutral expression.

The Emotient FACET software has been used in different studies [24–26]; not only in its current commercial version, but also in its former academic version CERT [34] where it is mention in the use of Gabor filters for the extraction of the image characteristics. So, in a work for analyzing video recorded interviews to obtain the base line, the individuals were asked to be relaxed for 5 s [2]. On the other hand, studies made about: discussing answers and washing hands in different meals of different cultures [35], and about evaluating the performance at the moment of talking in front of an audience [36]; use similarly the average of the evidence obtained as a significant data for the results.

Figure 3 shows facial expressions of joy and the corresponding results of iMotions software.

3   Results

In Fig. 4, is plotted the probability of the average obtained at the most significant moments of the technique application. The tendency of the time on different emotions is observed.

Fig. 3. Top. Expressions recognized as Joy in iMotions software from two different subjects. Bottom. Time series of emotion recognition. Joy is in the first row. The vertical bar indicates the current frame.

Joy predominates over the rest of the emotions, followed by disgust. Anger, confusion, and frustration follow a similar temporal tendency, with a maximum value at that moment of the final reading, and a minimal value at the moment of the middle sharing.

Figure 5 plots the probability of the evidence average of the different emotions for a visualization of the tendency in the time. Joy predominates over the rest of the emotions. Surprise and fear share a similar tendency with a maximum in the middle of the reading and a minimum and the beginning of the sharing.

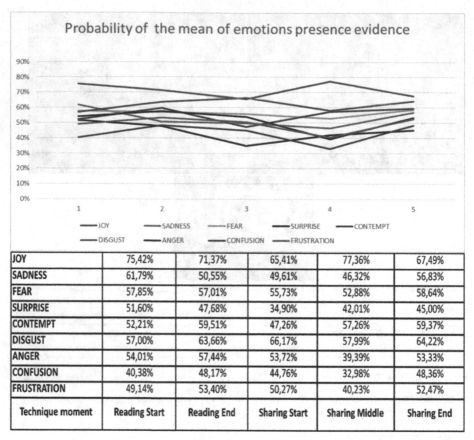

Fig. 4. Top. Temporal tendency of the different emotions' observation. Bottom. Tabulated data of the plot and identification of the LNCBT technique in five moments.

The most selected phrases in the different activities, with their respective frequency are presented on Table 1. For the reading activity the total time of the activity is considered. For the sharing it is considered the division made by the three parts of the beginning, middle, and end.

4 Discussion

During the following discussion the analyzed emotions and sentences are considered individually and in conjunction during the different moments of the techniques. This is because this research considers empathy as a complex emotion, neither positive nor negative in terms of emotions we like and dislike to feel, but as the result of the conjunction of different emotions interacting with each other in a way that they tend to balance. As a result, this emotional balance generates a general balance increment in the positive emotions over the regulation of the strong negative ones. See for instance on Fig. 5 81,74% of Joy in contrast with the following negative emotions of 62,42%

JOY	75,42%	71,37%	65,41%	77,36%	67,49%
SADNESS	61,79%	50,55%	49,61%	46,32%	56,83%
FEAR	57,85%	57,01%	55,73%	52,88%	58,64%
SURPRISE	51,60%	47,68%	34,90%	42,01%	45,00%
CONTEMPT	52,21%	59,51%	47,26%	57,26%	59,37%
DISGUST	57,00%	63,66%	66,17%	57,99%	64,22%
ANGER	54,01%	57,44%	53,72%	39,39%	53,33%
CONFUSION	40,38%	48,17%	44,76%	32,98%	48,36%
FRUSTRATION	49,14%	53,40%	50,27%	40,23%	52,47%
Technique moment	**Reading Start**	**Reading End**	**Sharing Start**	**Sharing Middle**	**Sharing End**

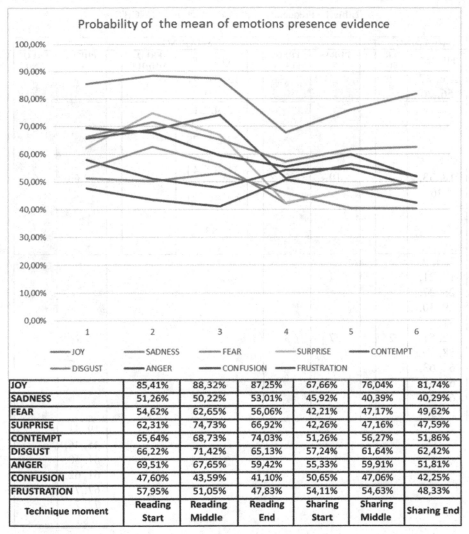

Fig. 5. Top. Temporal tendency of the different emotions' observation. Bottom. Tabulated data of the plot and identification of the LNCBT technique in six moments.

of Disgust, 51% of Anger and Contempt. Joy emotion is reduced at the end in contrast with the beginning of the LNCBT technique from 85,41% to 81,74%, Fig. 5, but it is much higher and suffers less reduction than the second more probable such as Disgust that goes from 66,22% to 62,42%, anger 69.51% to 51.81% or contempt from 65,645 to 51,86%.

The observations of Fig. 4 and Fig. 5 show that joy is the predominant emotion over the others during all the moments of the technique. Joy is the ideal emotion to generate empathy, in terms of the basic save emotion that can motivate the trust to share and release safely other negative emotions with another individual or group.

Table 1. Frequency of phrase selection of LNCBT

READING		SHARING					
PHRASE	FR EQ.	PHRASE	FREQ. START	PHRASE	FREQ. MIDDLE	PHRASE	FREQ. END
2, 6, 37, 56, 76	4	2	8	13, 34, 41, 69	3	85	8
5, 7, 15, 18, 33, 46	3	10	5	2, 4, 21, 23,2 5, 28, 31, 32, 44, 57, 59, 74, 83	2	50,63	6
3, 4, 9, 12, 21, 26, 27, 29, 30, 31, 35, 42, 51, 58, 59, 62, 63, 64, 65, 68, 79, 83	2	27	3			84	5
						19, 41, 45, 46, 51, 60, 61, 62, 67, 71, 72, 75, 83	3

At the beginning of the reading, during the 10 most significant seconds there is a probability of 75.42% while in the average of the moment there is a probability of 85.41%. In the middle of the reading, the average probability that the expressions represent happiness increases and it goes up, Fig. 5, even higher than at the beginning, and at the end of the activity. During the reading the individuals maintain a higher level of probability of being happy than at that moment of sharing. It is curious that sadness, fear, and surprise have similar behaviors of being higher during the reading than during the sharing. The collective concentration that happens in the middle of the collective reading seems to increase emotions generating another empathic moment.

The involution of anger of being the second emotion at the beginning, and being far below in probability than happiness and disgust, in Fig. 4, can be an indication that the individual experiences more confidence and participate with less anger while the shared experience of the technique starts, and in conjunction with others with the same problem, allowing more rational thinking and consciousness in relationship with recognizing him/herself/themselves as a sick person, an addict, in need for help and who is alone facing a collective disease. This is also verified in some another way, with the help of the words found in the LNCBT because the most frequent phrases selected during the beginning of the reading are, according to Table 1, by 4 individuals the sentences numbered: 2, 6, 37; by 3 individuals: 5, 7, 15, 18, 33, 46; and by 2 individuals: 3, 4, 9, 12, 21, 26, 27, 29, 30, 35, 42. Those are phrases that include words such as: *admit, powerless, can't, no power, addiction, convince, inability, disappointed, frustrated, open, recovery, psychiatrist, hospital, physical- mental and spiritual pain*. The meaning and context of these words can be easily associated with feelings of impotence and reject, or disgust, to addiction that the individuals experiment at that moment of being aware of the disgusting consequences of the active addiction.

At the end of the reading the sentences most frequently selected are 4 times the phrases numbered: 56, 76; by 3 individuals: 46 and by 2 individuals: 51, 58, 59, 62, 63, 64, 65, 68, 79, and 83. These phrases include words as: *family, power, admit, fixed, recovery, triumph, change, clean, learn; related to the emotion of happiness, and words such as: impotent, drugs, addiction, rendition, what we don't like, disappointed, frustrated, rejected, abandoned, rescued from insanity, depravation, and death* that have the ability of generating rejection or contempt, an emotion that increases in % of probability at the middle moment of sharing on both Fig. 4 and 5. If the final moment of the reading is considered, Fig. 5, including how the increment of contempt can be a way to balance the reduction of the disgust emotion, this could also mean that there is more acceptance for the text content at the end, less rejection but still feeling contempt when they recognize they are addicts. Then, we could observe how the shared reading can also help to break denial in certain degree, decreasing the disgust of something exterior, the experiences read on the text, and taking it more as contempt, like a more personal problem, with feelings of shame or worthlessness but more personal, a despicable problem that is happening to them. With all, it can be observed that the empathic communication happens also within the expressions of negative feelings. Although it is a complex process, it is still useful to have a communication technique that transforms the individuals from an emotional attitude of disassociation of the addiction problem towards a more embodied problem attitude that the self-contempt emotion generates, since it is a more inward personal emotional experience that disgust.

Taking those observations of the emotions during the reading period and contrasting with other emotional fluctuations, for instance how the joy and surprise increase in the middle of the reading in contrast of the sadness and anger decrement, Fig. 5, it could be affirmed that reading of the LNCBT, and the identification with the experiences contained on it, generate a higher relief and acceptance of the sickness. This happens also through the modulation of the emotions for instance by reducing at the end of the reading the surprise and fear, Fig. 5. On the other hand, an increment of acceptance and conscience about addiction could be indicated through the increament of contempt and the reduction of disgust and anger, Fig. 5. Anger and disgust together can denote also a type of emotional rejection to the technique, but if that would be the case then there will be no an increment and prevalence of the feelings of happiness during the technique.

The beginning of the sharing is where the less probabilities of finding happiness are observed. From these data it can be inferred that at the moment of the sharing start there is logically a fear of being exposed, as it is seen in Fig. 4; nevertheless, in a global way, fear is lower than the % found during the reading. The joy is logically at its least lcvcl since it is a moment of breaking the ice to start sharing more intimate moments. It can be inferred that the reading section of the technique prepares the individual reducing its fear toward the sharing section of the technique, at that moment they have been sharing the reading dynamic of reading a line at a time in turns like if it would be a shared game where everybody participate equally. Moreover, the most selected phrases at this beginning of the sharing are number 2 by 8 individuals: 10 by 5 individuals; 27 by 3 individuals; 5, 6, 28, 61, and 71 by 2 individuals. In these phrases there are words such as: *powerless, unmanageable life, inability, control is impossible, that are related with fe*ar. There are also included words as *denial, substitution, pretenses, justifications, distrust of others, guilt, embarrassment, dereliction, degradation, isolation, and loss of control* that evoke memories in which they may recognize themselves in the experiences of the text and others sharing, generating a little bit of confusion before continuing the more deeply empathic process.

During the middle of sharing, it is observed the biggest rise of joy emotion, from 65,41% to 77,36% on Fig. 4 and from 67,66% to 76,04% on Fig. 5. This can easily have been accomplished because is the part of the technique where people come from being introduced and encouraged to the new idea of sharing in first person *I* or *We* statements and share the lines they feel related with, to the moment where they observe that they selected similar lines and have similar experiences in the recovery process from addiction. In the moments observed in the middle of the sharing the most selected phrases by the individuals were 13, 34, 41, and 69 by 3 individuals; 2, 4, 21, 23, 25, 28, 31, 32, 44, 57, 59, 74, and 83 by 2 individuals. Phrases that include words as: *against our will, change completely our way of thinking, destroying our life, surrender, and talent for manipulating the truth*, words that can generate anger or disgust, that increase also in contrast with the beginning of the sharing moment of the technique, from 55,33% to 59,99%, and from 57,24% to 61,64% respectively as seen in Fig. 5. There are also included words such as: *benefits, work, family, being accepted by society, program; the ones that have a link with the social relationships that can help the physical, mental and emotional isolation of addiction*, provoking happiness in the individuals.

Finally, at the end of the sharing it can be observed how joy is the emotion with the highest percentage, 67,49% in Fig. 4 and 81,74% in Fig. 5, although it is lower than at the beginning, probably higher because the tendency of humans to please when we first meet, it could be said that is a more authentic and empathic joy, since it is the result of having shared intimate negative experiences of the consequences of addiction. The most selected phrases are 85 by 8 individuals; 50 and 63 by 6 individuals; 85 by 5 individuals; 64, 77, and 81 by 4 individuals; 27, 28, 53, 57, 59, 73, and 76 by 3 individuals. These phrases contain the words: *hope, freedom, and expressions as "where we go," "break our chains,"* and *"we accept life as it is"* that evokes happiness on the individuals. In contrast there are words such as: *consuming and redemption*, and expressions like: *admit our full defeat, ask for help and the power of become someone that we didn't want to be,* that are related to disgust, contempt and anger of the individuals at the moment of recognizing their impotence of healing themselves from addiction. However and over all, the interactive communication technique of the LNCBT serves its purpose of breaking the denial that the disease of addiction generates and open the emotional and intellectual perspectives for addressing it through generating an empathic environment to motivate the end isolation, main characteristic of this disease, and to motivate a behavior change through collectively sharing experiences of what works and does not for recovering from addiction.

This practice of reading, annotating and sharing true experiences about the consequences of drug usage and recovery from addiction activates what we call the *Empathic Imagination (EI)*. This *EI* is based on envisioning the other recovering addict's experience as one's own experience. *Empathic Imagination* acts as a mental bridge of compassionate communication that breaks the self-centered isolation of addiction. It allows the brain to imagine the other person's experience similar to oneself, through the mechanism of comparing, imagining, and changing the names of specific narrative elements, such as: places, times, characters or actions, involved in that experience. Paradoxically, *Empathic Imagination* is based in the trust that builds up from sharing truthful and personal histories. *EI* transforms the me into we in a way that the isolation of the self-centered addiction is broken. This type of imagination focuses and serves to connect people mentally and emotionally within visualized and felt common experiences, which may share different narratives elements but that contain similar feelings, resolutions and life lessons.

All these observations make us face a foundational concept, sustained by the theory of the connective intelligence, suggested by De Kerchove and Rowland [37] and later refined by Soberón [38] in their publications, where they make reference to the "new media" (the great net or web), suggesting the existence of a connective intelligence as a tool that can be established a the basis for the collective evolution, or the social homeostasis as described more recently by Damasio [11, 16, 39]. The complexity of the disease of addiction [40] requires also complex but effective solutions and tools to motivate its recovery. From the actual research an observation emerges and calls attention the final findings, in which the sharing in different moments, focused on a common problem and solution from addiction, can allow through that empathic shared and collective process the improvement of the individuals. Retroactively, they also share their experience for the common good of the group so they can keep remembering to practice what they learned that really works and to avoid what does not.

5   Conclusions

After having contrasted and compared the data, during the discussion section, to observe the tendencies of each emotion and between emotions, in the different moments of LNCBT, it can be inferred that the LNCBT technique serves to develop empathic communications related with the recovery from addictions. All emotions tend to decrease from the beginning of the experience towards the end in Fig. 5. The joy prevails as the higher % emotional response during the LNCBT technique. The negative emotions tend to balance and decrease from the beginning much more than joy. Joy has a decrease on percentage of 85,41% (beginning) −81,74% (end) = 3,67%, in Fig. 5. In contrast Anger has decrease from 69,51% (beginning) − 51,81% (end) = 17.7% in Fig. 5. At the end of the application of the technique, Fig. 5 shows how Joy manifest 81,74% probability in contrast with the negative emotions such as Anger 51,81%, Disgust 62,42%, Contempt 51,86%.

With all, the data collected and the observation discussed it can be concluded that the interactive communication technique LNCBT generates empathy, understood as described at the beginning of the Sect. 4, a complex emotional state of mind generated by the conjunction of basic emotions that tend to balance the emotional states decreasing in general the negative arc of the emotions (anger, disgust, contempt, frustration...) and letting the positive arc of the emotion (joy) to rise over all the emotional complex experience.

As seen during the discussion the contrast between Figs. 4 and 5 results contains coincidences between them, but also indicate that the most significant moments, where empathy is presumed by the interaction of the participants, are not necessarily an adequate sample of the global emotional evolution during the technique development. In other words, emotions at the moments of higher empathy of the LNCBT technique do not exactly correspond in its totals to emotions found during its development.

Finally, it is necessary to underline that more research projects need to be developed around the different interactive communication techniques used in 12 Step programs for recovery from different addictions, and specifically of the LNCBT technique from Narcotics Anonymous, in order to firmly confirm these results and conclusions. The next researches could include bigger groups and control groups and could use complementary research methodologies, from the most social classic such as: one's questionnaires, personal interviews and group discussion; to the most interdisciplinary and personalized such as: fMRI, EEG... It will be also important to have personalized follows up to observe the maintenance of "clean time" and the quality of live and recovery that the people persistently using the recovery techniques have through time.

Acknowledgements. This work was supported by the Prometheus Project, SENESCYT, secretary of Higher Education, Science, Technology & Innovation of the Republic of Ecudor, by the DIUC, Direction of Research of the University of Cuenca, through the Research Group NEUROSYNAPSIS I+D+i, School of Medicine, Universidad de Cuenca, and Research Group UNACH IAMNCEDC R+D+C+I/MANICECDE I+D+C+I, Interactive Arts & Media, Narrative Convergences & Edutainment in Digital Communications & Cultures R+D+C+I (Research+Development+Creation+Innovation), Vice-chancellor of Research, Universidad Nacional de Chimborazo, Ecuador. It also counted with the precious collaboration of the Arthur C. Clarke Center for Human Imagination, University of California San Diego, USA, and Laboratory of Digital Culture & Hypermedia Museography-Research Group Museum I+D+C, Universidad Complutense de Madrid, Spain.

References

1. Stewart, M., Hager, J., Ekman, P., Sejnowski, T.: Measuring facial expressions by computer image analysis. Psychophysiology **44**, 253–263 (1999)

2. Chen, L., Yoon, S.Y., Leong, C.W., Martin, M., Ma, M.: An initial analysis of structured video interviews by using multimodal emotion detection. In: Proceedings of the 2014 Workshop on Emoion Representation and Modelling in Human-Computer-Interaction-Systems, pp. 1–6. ACM (2014)
3. Velásquez-Martínez, M.C., Ortiz, J.G.: Abuso de drogras, generalidades neurobiológicas y terapéuticas. Actualidades en Psicología **28**(17), 21–25 (2014)
4. Blas, E.S.: Adicciones psicológicas y los nuevos problemas de salud. Revista Cultura, pp. 111–145 (2014)
5. American Psychiatric Association Diagnostic and Statistical Manual of Mental Disorders, (DSM-5), 5th edn. American Psychiatric Association, Washington (2013)
6. Robbins, T.W., Everitt, B.J.: Limbic-striatal memory systems and drug addiction. Neurobiol. Learn. Mem. **78**(3) 625–636 (2002)
7. Belujon, P., Grace, A.A.: Hippocampus, amygdala, and stress: interacting systems that affect susceptibility to addiction. Ann. N.Y. Acad. Sci. 1216, 114–121 (2011)
8. Ding, W.N., et al.: Trait impulsivity and impaired prefrontal impulse inhibition function in adolescents with Internet gaming addiction revealed by a Go/No-Go fMRI study. Behav. Brain Funct. **10**(1), 1 (2014)
9. NIDA. Principios de tratamientos para la drogadicción: Una guía basada en las investigaciones (2010). https://www.drugabuse.gov/es/publicaciones/principios-de-tratamientos-para-la-dro gadiccion. Accessed 16 Apr 2006
10. Strang, J., et al.: Opioid use disorder. Nat. Rev. Dis. Primers **6**(1), 1–28 (2020)
11. Damasio, A., Carvalho, G.: The nature of feelings: evolutionary and neurobilogical origins. Neurosciences **14**, 143–152 (2013)
12. Ekman, P.: Emotions Revealed. Recognizing Faces and Feelings to Improve Communication and Emotional Life. p. 75. Estados Unidos, New York, St Martin's Griffin (2003)
13. Griffiths, P.E.: Basic Emotions, Complex Emotions, Machiavellian Emotions. University of Pittsburgh, Pittsburgh (2003)
14. Ekman, P.: Emotions in the Human Face. Pergamon Press, New York (1972)
15. Charland, L.C.: Emotion as a natural kind: towards a computational foundation for emotion theory. Philos. Psychol. **8**(1), 59–84 (1995)
16. Damasio, A.R.: Descartes Error: Emotion, Reason and the Human Brain. Grosset/Putnam, New York (1994)
17. Damasio, A.: Toward a neurobiology of emotion and feeling: operational concepts and hypotheses. Neuroscientist **1**(1), 19–25 (1995)
18. Prinz, J.: Emotional Perception. Oxford University Press, Oxford
19. Ekman, P.: Methods for measuring facial action. In: Scherer, K.R., Ekman, P. (eds.) Handbook of Methods in Nonverbal Behavior Research, pp. 45–135. Cambridge University Press, New York (1982)
20. Pantic, M., Rothkrantz, J.M.: Automatic analysis of facial expressions: the state of the art. IEEE Trans. Pattern Anal. Mach. Intell. **22**(12), 1424–1445 (2000)
21. Ekman, P., Friesen, W.: Facial Action Coding System: A Technique for the Measurement of Facial Movement. Consulting Psychologists Press, Palo Alto (1978)
22. Bassili, J.: Emotion recognition: the role of facial movement and the relative importance of upper and lower areas of the face. J. Pers. Soc. Psychol. **37**, 2049–2059 (1979)
23. Lucey, P., Cohn, J.F., Kanade, T., Saragih, J., Ambadar, Z., Matthews, I.: The extended Cohn-Kande dataset (CK+): a complete facial expression dataset for action unit and emotion-specified expression. In: Third IEEE Workshop on CVPR for Human Communicative Behavior Analysis (CVPR4HB 2010) (2010)
24. FACET 2.0 Performance Evaluation, Emotient, iMotions software
25. Hellmann, A., Ang, L., Sood, S.: Towards a conceptual framework for analyzing impression management during face-to-face communication. J. Behav. Exp. Financ. **25**, 100265 (2020)

26. Publications using iMotions Facial Expression Recognition. https://iMotions.com/publicati ons/?page=1&category=publications&modalities=facial-expressions. Accessed 19 Feb 2020
27. Biederman, I.: Recognition-by-components: a theory of human image understanding. Psychol. Rev. **94**(2), 115–147 (1987)
28. Ekman, P., Rosenberg, E.L.: What the Face Reveals: Basic and Applied Studies of Sponta- neous Expression Using the Facial Action Coding System (FACS). Oxford University Press, New York (1997)
29. Farah, M.J., Wilson, K.D., Drain, M., Tanaka, J.N.: What is 'special' about facial perception? Psychol. Rev. **105**(3), 482–498 (1998)
30. Bettadapura, V.: Face expression recognition and analysis: the state of the art, Technical report, arXiv preprint:1203.6722 (2012)
31. Ko, B.C.: A brief review of facial emotion recognition based on visual information. Sensors **18**(2), 401 (2018)
32. Li, D., et al.: The fusion of electroencephalography and facial expression for continuous emotion recognition. IEEE Access **7**, 155724–155736 (2019)
33. Poria, S., Cambria, E., Winterstein, G., Huang, G.B.: Sentic patterns: dependency-based rules for concept-level sentiment analysis. Knowl.-Based Syst. **69**, 45–63 (2014)
34. Littlewort, G., et al.: The computer expression recognition toolbox (CERT). In: 2011 IEEE International Conference on Automatic Face & Gesture Recognition and Workshops (FG 2011), pp. 298–305. IEEE (2011)
35. Pellegrino, R., Crandall, P.G., Seo, H.S.: Hand washing and disgust response to handling different food stimuli between two different cultures. Food Res. Int. **76**, 301–308 (2015)
36. Wörtwein, T., Chollet, M., Schauerte, B., Morency, L.P., Stiefelhagen, R., Scherer, S.: Mul- timodal public speaking performance assessment. In: Proceedings of the 2015 ACM on International Conference on Multimodal Interaction, pp. 43–50 (2015)
37. De Kerckhove, D., Rowland, W.: Inteligencias en conexión: hacia una sociedad de la web, Gedisa (1999)
38. Soberón, L.: La inteligencia conectiva en la Red Informática de la Iglesia en América Latina (RIIAL). Signo y pensamiento, XXVIII, 54 (2009)
39. Damasio, A.: Self Comes to Mind. Pantheon Books, p. 26, New York (2010)
40. Ruiz Sánchez, J.M., Pedrero, E.: Neuropsicología de la Adicción. España. Editorial Médica Panamericana (2014)

User Behavior and Awareness of Filter Bubbles in Social Media

Nils Plettenberg(✉), Johannes Nakayama, Poornima Belavadi,
Patrick Halbach, Laura Burbach, André Calero Valdez, and Martina Ziefle

Human-Computer Interaction Center, RWTH Aachen University, Aachen, Germany
{plettenberg,nakayama,belavadi,halbach,burbach,
calero-valdez,ziefle}@comm.rwth-aachen.de

Abstract. To counter information overflow, social media companies employ recommender algorithms that potentially lead to filter bubbles. This leaves users' newsfeed vulnerable to misinformation and might not provide them with a view of the full spectrum of news. There is research on the reaction of users confronted with filter bubbles and tools to avoid them, but it is not much known about the users' awareness of the phenomenon. We conducted a survey about the usage of Facebook's newsfeed with 140 participants from Germany and identified two user groups with k-means clustering. One group consisting of passive Facebook users was not very aware of the issue, while users of the other group, mainly heavy professional Facebook users were more aware and more inclined to apply avoidance strategies. Especially users who were aware of filter bubbles wished for a tool to counter them. We recommend targeting users of the first group to increase awareness and find out more about the way professionals use Facebook to assist them countering the filter bubble and promoting tools that help them do so.

Keywords: Social media · Filter bubbles · User factors · Professional communication

1 Introduction

Social media has become a dominant factor in everyday communication. Facebook alone had a user base of over 2.2 billion users in 2018. This means that besides private and social communication, also professional communication is to a large extent present in social media channels. Social media, in contrast to traditional media channels, is comprised of user-generated content. Anyone can become a broadcaster in social media. The participation of world wide users has led to an amount of information that no individual user can process, thus making the use of algorithms to filter and recommend content to the users inevitable. One class of algorithms, so-called recommender systems, pick items in accordance with previous user choices and those of similar users. While this approach leads to very accurate recommendations from a users perspective, on a societal

© Springer Nature Switzerland AG 2020
V. G. Duffy (Ed.): HCII 2020, LNCS 12199, pp. 81–92, 2020.
https://doi.org/10.1007/978-3-030-49907-5_6

level recommendations can have critical effects on the flow of information. By recommending items that users are likely to interact with, users are also less likely to receive information that is outside their political alignment, their scope of interest, and in contrast to their held beliefs. This causes problems in professional communication when e.g., decision makers need to get information from a full spectrum of sources. However, little is known about the users awareness of filter bubbles and possible avoidance strategies to combat the negative influence of filter bubbles. To identify whether there are different user groups with different degrees of awareness of the phenomenon, we conducted a study that examines demographics, the big 5 personality traits and the reasons to use Facebook influences as well as the awareness of filter bubbles and the use of possible avoidance strategies. With this information, we clustered the users into two groups showing both different motives to use Facebook and awareness of filter bubbles.

2   Related Work

This chapter will briefly describe the terms filter bubbles, echo chambers and the algorithms that are causing them. Furthermore, strategies to avoid them and to increase users' awareness are discussed.

2.1   Filter Bubbles and Echo chambers

The rise of digital and social media lead to an unprecedented amount of information available to individual users. Virtually anyone can spread news via social media, offering users a broad choice [23]. As there is too much information to consume, users need to choose which sources or channels they use to receive their news.

According to the confirmation bias [18], individuals seek or interpret evidence in ways that are partial to existing beliefs, expectations, or a hypothesis at hand. The cognitive dissonance theory describes the psychological stress an individual experiences when it holds two or more beliefs, ideas or values that contradict each other [11]. To avoid this discomfort, people will always try to keep their views consistent. So when they have the choice, users usually select content that is in accordance with their personal beliefs and opinions while trying to avoid content that contradicts them [3,8].

As there is too much content available in social media, it is close to impossible for a single individual to overview all information and select the relevant ones. To help users with this challenge, social media and news websites use reccomender systems to present a personalized selection of all available information to each user, based on their personal history and interests as well as the content similar users were interested in [21].

The term "filter bubble" was introduced by Pariser [19] to describe the personalization in social media and online searches to an extent where users only see content similar to their history, reducing the diversity to a high degree. While in the real world, people are usually confronted with opinions and facts not strictly in concordance with their views, filter algorithms in online media and social networks are much more likely to produce filter bubbles as they try to show users content similar to what they were previously interested in. The algorithms also favor another distinct phenomenon called echo chambers. Filter bubbles are the result of people not being exposed to all relevant information, possibly by accident. An echo chamber is a structure from which other voices have been actively excluded or discredited [17]. While echo chambers might also benefit from recommender algorithms, this paper focuses on filter bubbles, that might occur without the users noticing. However, sometimes there is no clear distinction between echo chambers and filter bubbles in literature, therefore research concerned with echo chambers might be relevant to understand the effect of filter bubbles.

Dubois and Blank [10] examined the effect of political interest and media diversity on true echo chambers and concluded that only a small part of the population might be impacted by them. Similarly, a study on the political polarization on Twitter came to the conclusion that the effect of echo chambers in social media may be overestimated [1]. However, previous research has demonstrated that filter bubbles are present in search engines and social media content [9]. While the effect of recommender systems on personalization was rather moderate in Google News [12], another study found empirical evidence for stronger personalization in Facebook's newsfeed [20]. The existence of filter bubble leaves users' newsfeeds vulnerable to systematic misinformation or competitor attacks on information flow.

2.2 Filter Bubble Awareness and Avoidance strategies

So far, only few research has been conducted on the users' awareness of filter bubbles. This information might be relevant as users who are not aware of the filtering mechanisms might not notice that their results possibly do not have the desired diversity [5]. There is a study on how users react when they are confronted with the issue by Nagulendra and Vassileva [16]; they designed a tool to show how filter bubbles work in online peer-to-peer social networks. The visualization increased users awareness and the understanding of the underlying filter algorithms. However, it is still unclear which users actually are aware of the phenomenon. Identifying user groups might help reaching people in their filter bubble for professional communication.

It is possible to burst through the filter bubble, when users understand the mechanisms of the underlying algorithms [21]. According to Bozdag and Hoven [4], there are several digital tools to combat the filter bubble, some by increasing awareness and others by presenting unbiased results. For example, Munson, Lee, and Resnick [15] developed a tool that tracks users' reading behavior to visualize their biases. According to the authors, this increases awareness of the filter bubble because even users who are familiar with the concept actually do not realize that it might apply to themselves to quite a high degree.

The browser add-on Scoopinion[1] follows a similar approach but visualizes the "media footprint" instead of just biases, so users can actually see how frequently they visit different providers of news. Bobble [28], another browser add-on, compares the personalized Google results of a user to those of users world wide. This way, not only awareness is increased, but users are also shown a broader spectrum of results, giving them the opportunity to actually escape the filter bubble. Confronted with a visual comparison of the content a user consumes vs. the content all users in a system consume, users are more inclined to discover new content outside their bubble [13].

There are several ways for users to decrease personalization. Many websites and services use cookies to identify users, deleting them regularly or using the browser's incognito mode makes it harder to track and identify users [14,21]. However, this is not possible for services that require users to log-in, e.g. Facebook. Here, users would need to actively try to like content from various sources to enforce diversity in their newsfeed as recommender algorithms try to match content the user has liked in the past [24].

While there is already some research on the effects of users' awareness and tools to increase it or even escape the filter bubble to some extent, it is unclear how many users are actually aware of the phenomenon. There is even less research to what degree users are using tools and strategies to combat filter bubbles. Research into user characteristics could help develop counter strategies against filter bubble phenomena adapted to the users individual needs.

3   Method

We conducted a survey study with 149 participants in order to measure both user attributes and awareness of filter bubbles. All items were measured on 6-point Likert scales. We used convenience sampling to establish a sample in an online survey. Nine participants who did not complete the survey were removed from the dataset. Apart from demographics we also extensively measured the users' Facebook usage. As an additional characteristic we measured big five personality traits to investigate whether they have an impact on filter bubble awareness and avoidance.

To measure awareness of filter bubbles we used the items *"I have already heard of the filter bubble theory."*, *"I believe the filter bubble exist."*, *"The filter bubble affects me personally."*, *"I take deliberate action against the filter bubble."*. All these items were summarized to the scale *filter bubble awareness* ($r = .65$).

We further measured whether users employed any methods to counter filter bubble effects. To do this, we suggested some methods that require some understanding of how recommender systems work, for example that internet companies could identify users and their interest by cookies and that this can be prevented by using the incognito mode of a browser. In particular, we used the items *"I delete my browser history and cookies."*, *"I use the incognito function*

---

[1] www.scoopinion.com.

of my browser.", "I click and like different posts to enforce diversity", "I use the 'explore' button in Facebook to get different news.", "I unfollow some of my friends/pages". All of these items were used for the scale *filter bubble avoidance strategies* $(r = .60)$.

3.1 Statistical Methods

Using the data from the survey we conducted a cluster analysis on the social media usage attributes in order to identify patterns in user behavior. We used the elbow-plot to identify the right amount of different clusters and clustered the users based on their reasons to use Facebook with k-means. Using the resulting clusters we tested the members of clusters for differences in characteristics and filter bubble awareness using analysis of variance (ANOVA). The data was normally distributed for all cases where we tested for correlations, thus we used Pearson correlation. To test for differences between the clusters in ordinal data, Wilcoxon signed-rank test was used. We selected $\alpha = .05$ as the significance level. We report means, standard deviations as well as confidence intervals to characterize the resulting user clusters.

4 Results

4.1 Sample Description

The sample was taken from a previous study published by Burbach et al. [6]. The participants in this sample were on average 25.9 years old $(SD = 7)$ and all of them were Facebook users. Exactly 80 participants were female and 61 were male. Education was rather high (83 university degree, 47 Abitur, 11 other) and users were rather open $(M = 4.5, SD = 1.07)$, conscientious $(M = 4.1, SD = 0.88)$, extraverted $(M = 4.14, SD = 1.1)$, and agreeable $(M = 3.81, SD = 0.77)$. Users on average did not score high on neuroticism $(M = 3.23, SD = 1.01)$. 55% of the participants reported that they used Facebook at least once per day. However, 65% felt that they use it less often, 33% that the frequency of their usage remains unchanged and only 2% were using it more. Most users prefer to use their smartphone for Facebook $(M = 4.35, SD = 1.58)$, followed by laptop $(M = 3.08, SD = 1.43)$. Tablets $(M = 1.60, SD = 1.21)$ and desktop computers $(M = 1.63, SD = 1.27)$ were only rarely used.

4.2 Cluster Generation

Cluster analysis was conducted using dendrograms and elbow-plots. These methods help identify how many different clusters yield sufficiently different clusters in the data. As clustering variables we used variables of behavior in individual Facebook use ("professional use", "meeting people", "keeping in touch", "posting", "sharing", "inform others", "express opinion", "passive use").

Both methods indicated that between 2 and 4 clusters yield sufficiently different user groups for a clustering approach. After inspecting usage behaviors for these three cases we decided to rely on two different clusters that are sufficiently different and allow for a meaningful description from the clustering variables.

4.3 Cluster Description

From the two clusters we derived the two cluster definitions using the clustering variables (see Fig. 1). Users in cluster one were generally less active than users in cluster two. This refers to both passive use (reading only ($M = 2.07$, $SD = 1.27$ vs $M = 3.9$, $SD = 1.16$)), active use (sharing ($M = 1.45$, $SD = 0.73$ vs $M = 2.59$, $SD = 1.08$), inform others ($M = 1.26$, $SD = 0.59$ vs $M = 2.51$, $SD = 1.16$), express opinion ($M = 1.09$, $SD = 0.32$ vs $M = 2.1$, $SD = 1.05$) and posting ($M = 1.54$, $SD = 0.88$ vs $M = 2.45$, $SD = 1.02$)), as well as professional use ($M = 1.85$, $SD = 1.28$ vs $M = 3.29$, $SD = 1.5$). In both clusters *keeping in touch* with friends was the highest characterizations of usage behavior, users in both clusters use the social network for that purpose to a similar degree ($M = 4.2$, $SD = 1.4$ vs $M = 4.35$, $SD = 1.22$). Only *passive use* showed similar agreement in cluster 2. Cluster 2 also claimed to have a stronger use of Facebook for meeting new people ($M = 1.51$, $SD = 0.83$ vs $M = 2.1$, $SD = 1.18$).

Cluster 1 had 92 members and cluster 2 had 49. While the number of friends ($p = 0.21$) and groups ($p = 0.97$) did not vary significantly between the two clusters, the Wilcoxon-Mann-Whitney test showed that users in cluster 2 liked more Facebook pages than those in cluster 1 ($p < .001$).

The genders were balanced in the first cluster, in the second one there were only 14 male participants (29%). As the vast majority of the complete sample was highly educated, there were no differences between the clusters in that regard. There were no significant differences between the clusters for any of the Big Five personality traits (openness: $p = 0.108$, extraversion: $p = 0.684$, conscientiousness: $p = 0.194$, agreeableness: $p = 0.552$, neuroticism: $p = 0.616$).

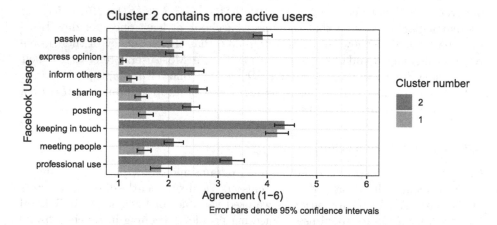

Fig. 1. Differences in users between clusters.

4.4   Awareness of Filter Bubbles

Next, we were interested in determining whether differences exist between both clusters regarding filter bubble awareness and possible avoidance strategies.

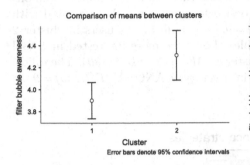
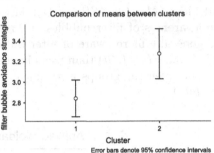

Fig. 2. Differences in users between clusters regarding filter bubble awareness.

Fig. 3. Differences in users between clusters regarding avoidance strategies.

When we look at filter bubble awareness, we see that cluster 1—the passive users—show lower awareness of the phenomenon ($M = 3.9$, $SD = 0.89$ vs $M = 4.31$, $SD = 0.61$). This difference is significant in a one-way ANOVA ($F(1,139) = 8.36$, $p = .004$, see also Fig. 2).

A similar result can be seen for the presence of avoidance strategies regarding filter bubbles. Here, a difference is significant in a one-way ANOVA ($F(1,139) = 8.0$, $p = .005$, see also Fig. 3), showing also more strategies of avoidance in cluster 2 ($M = 2.84$, $SD = 0.87$ vs $M = 3.27$, $SD = 0.85$). There were no significant gender differences for both filter bubble awareness and filter bubble avoidance strategies. Also, the awareness of filter bubbles does not seem to have an influence on whether or not users apply avoidance strategies ($r(139) = .01$, $p = .227$).

4.5   Applied Avoidance strategies

Overall, the participants did not make particularly intensive use of any of the strategies to burst the filter bubble. Users in cluster 2 were generally more inclined to apply avoidance strategies, but there were differences which strategies were used in particular (see also Fig. 4).

The most common strategy was to delete cookies and browser history which was applied by both cluster 1 $M = 3.98$, $SD = 1.46$) and cluster 2 ($M = 4.24$, $SD = 1.33$) rather frequently. Other strategies that were applied by users of both clusters are to unfollow certain friends or pages in order to increase diversity in the Facebook newsfeed (Cluster 1: $M = 3.24$, $SD = 1.61$, Cluster 2: $M = 3.63$, $SD = 1.48$) as well as the use of the browser's incognito mode that does not store any data like cookies and history beyond the current session (Cluster 1: $M = 3.11$, $SD = 1.61$, Cluster 2: $M = 3.24$, $SD = 1.41$). Neither cluster made much use of the explore button in Facebook (Cluster 1: $M = 1.92$, $SD = 1.22$, Cluster 2: $M = 2.35$, $SD = 1.2$). Users in cluster 1 ($M = 1.96$, $SD = 1$) did not deliberately like and click various posts to enforce diversity in their news feed while the second group was more inclined to apply this strategy ($M = 2.9$, $SD = 1.49$)).

Most users wish for a tool to that shows them different topics, opinions and ideas ($M = 4.00$, $SD = 1.28$). The desire for such a tool is associated with the awareness of filter bubbles ($r(139) = 0.19$, $p = .021$). As users in cluster 2 are generally more aware of filter bubbles they were more interested in a tool ($M = 4.44$, $SD = 1.10$) than users in cluster 1 ($M = 3.76$, $SD = 1.30$). The difference between the groups is significant in a one-way ANOVA ($F(1,139) = 9.89$, $p = .002$).

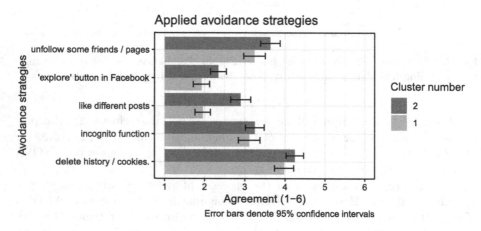

Fig. 4. Differences between clusters in applied avoidance strategies.

5   Discussion

The results presented in the previous section suggest that the awareness of filter bubbles in general is rather high. However, there are severe differences between users, therefore it is worth taking a closer look on how different user types differ in terms of awareness and avoidance strategies in order to burst the filter bubble.

Awareness of filter bubbles is associated with both professional and heavy Facebook use. However, these variables do not correlate with avoidance strategies, therefore it is important to look at all the user factors to understand why people try to avoid the bubble. In order to do so, we identified two types of users that show differences in user behavior on Facebook. These differences relate to both private and professional use of social media. The first type uses Facebook passively to keep in touch for private purposes for the most part. In contrast, the second type does not only use Facebook much more, but also posts, shares and informs others to a much higher degree. Facebook is used professionally by many of these users. The heavy users of the second type seem to be more aware of filter bubble problems in social media and are also more inclined to apply strategies to counter them. Higher awareness alone does not lead to the application of strategies to avoid the bubbles, therefore other user factors in the cluster might play a role. One of them could be the professional use of Facebook, which is much more common in the second group. The professional necessity to get a broader view of the spectrum of opinions on one hand, and the need to reach people from outside their filter bubbles on the other might force users to think about the bubbles and how to overcome problems related to them. Our survey did not cover the nature of the professional Facebook use, but it might be worth looking into for further research for a better understanding why professionals are more aware of the phenomenon.

Some users seem to be familiar with strategies to avoid filter bubbles like the deletion of cookies and browser history. In general though, avoidance strategies are not very common and users seem to be unaware of how to escape the filter bubble phenomenon. Many of them express the wish for a tool helping them do so, especially when they are more aware of the phenomenon. This indicates that even those people who are aware of the problems and like to overcome them in many cases do not have the required knowledge or motivation to do so. Here, communication strategies can be developed that help users understand how the underlying algorithms work in a first step. Making people aware of the issue and its causes might increase the wish for tools to overcome the problem. In fact, research presented in Sect. 2 suggests that users who are confronted with the problem are much more likely to burst their bubble.

In a second step solutions on how to overcome the pitfalls of personalization in social media and web-applications could be promoted. As some of the current mechanisms to counter the filter bubble require some technical knowledge it might be necessary to bundle them in tools that are easy to use for users without technical background. For example, it requires several clicks through some sub-menus to delete cookies and browser history. As this option is not very easy to find and it can be annoying to repeat the process frequently, it could help to promote a browser extension that does it with one click or even automatically. Of course some of the tools that were introduced earlier could provide the user with a broader view of the spectrum of news without requiring any background knowledge. Unfortunately, they usually only work for one specific service like Google or Facebook, so users would need to utilize multiple tools and techniques to effectively combat filter bubbles.

Another improvement that might help users to understand the cause end effects of filter bubbles is transparency of services. For example, Facebook's explore button uses a recommender system that might not increase diversity in content. On the contrary, it recommends content based on the users interest, hence it is very likely that the users only see similar content that affirms their opinions. Software companies might not be willing to disclose information about their algorithms as they are a crucial part of their business model, but there are some third party solutions that demonstrate the way the algorithms work to some extent. Some of them were also mentioned in Sect. 2. As many users of social media and other online services might not be familiar with them, it is important to promote these, especially to professional communicators and decision makers who rely on social media for information gathering.

6   Conclusion

In our exploratory study, we found that many users already know about the filter bubble. The application of the k-means clustering algorithm helped us to identify two different user types. The first type uses Facebook mainly passively and to stay in touch with private contacts, while the second type makes heavier use of Facebook and shares, posts and likes content to a higher degree. The users of the second group also use Facebook for professional reasons. Both the awareness of filter bubbles and the application of avoidance strategies is higher among the heavy, professional users. Higher awareness alone does not encourage users to apply strategies to avoid filter bubbles, so the question opposes why users of the second group are not only more aware, but are also more likely to try to counter the filter bubble. A possible explanation is their professional use of social networks, which requires them to reach people in their bubbles. For further research, it might be interesting to look how they use Facebook in particular to further understand why users try to escape the filter bubble. For the first group, the question remains on how to reach them and increase awareness of the phenomenon.

While not all users might want to burst their filter bubble, especially among those who are aware of it, there are many who would like to have a tool to avoid it. This shows that the current technical solutions to do so are either not sufficient or not known to many users.

We recommend to develop communication strategies to inform those users in the first group about the underlying algorithms of recommendations in social networks and their consequences to increase awareness of filter bubbles among all users, especially the ones who do not use Facebook that much.

In a second step, existing and tools techniques to avoid filter bubbles should be promoted to users. Additionally, it might be necessary to design new user interfaces to simplify the process. More transparent communication on behalf of social networks how their recommender algorithms work could further increase the users' understanding of the problem, but might not be desired by the social networks.

For the private passive users, the question remains whether they really want to burst their filter bubbles. The expression of desire for a tool to do so does not mean that the users would prefer the unbiased presentation of content that includes opposing opinions. For the heavy professional users who actually need a view of the full spectrum of information in order to make decisions, we suggest further research on how they use Facebook in particular. This knowledge might help to develop strategies to communicate effective methods assisting the professional users to get a broader view of social media content.

Acknowledgements. We would further like to thank the authors of the packages we have used. We used the following packages to create this document: `knitr` [27], `tidyverse` [25], `rmdformats` [2], `kableExtra` [29], `scales` [26], `psych` [22], `rmdtemplates` [7].

References

1. Barberá, P., et al.: Tweeting from left to right: Is online political communication more than an echo chamber? Psychol. Sci. **26**(10), 1531–1542 (2015)
2. Barnier, J.: rmdformats: HTML Output Formats and Templates for 'rmarkdown' Documents. R package version 0.3.6 (2019). https://CRAN.R-project.org/package=rmdformats
3. Beam, M.A.: Automating the news: how personalized news recommender system design choices impact news reception. Commun. Res. **41**(8), 1019–1041 (2014)
4. Bozdag, E., van den Hoven, J.: Breaking the filter bubble: democracy and design. Ethics Inf. Technol. **17**(4), 249–265 (2015). https://doi.org/10.1007/s10676-015-9380-y
5. Brauner, P., Calero Valdez, A., Philipsen, R., Ziefle, M.: Defective still deflective – how correctness of decision support systems influences user's performance in production environments. In: Nah, F.-H., Tan, C.-H. (eds.) HCIBGO 2016. LNCS, vol. 9752, pp. 16–27. Springer, Cham (2016). https://doi.org/10.1007/978-3-319-39399-5_2
6. Burbach, L., Halbach, P., Ziefle, M., Calero Valdez, A.: Bubble trouble: strategies against filter bubbles in online social networks. In: Duffy, V.G. (ed.) HCII 2019. LNCS, vol. 11582, pp. 441–456. Springer, Cham (2019). https://doi.org/10.1007/978-3-030-22219-2_33
7. Valdez, A.C.: rmdtemplates: RMD Templates. R package version 0.1.0.0 (2019)
8. Colleoni, E., Rozza, A., Arvidsson, A.: Echo chamber or public sphere? Predicting political orientation and measuring political homophily in Twitter using big data. J. Commun. **64**(2), 317–332 (2014)
9. Dillahunt, T.R., Brooks, C.A., Gulati, S.; Detecting and visualizing filter bubbles in Google and Bing. In: Proceedings of the 33rd Annual ACM Conference Extended Abstracts on Human Factors in Computing Systems, pp. 1851–1856. ACM (2015)
10. Dubois, E., Blank, G.: The echo chamber is overstated: the moderating effect of political interest and diverse media. Inf. Commun. Soc. **21**(5), 729–745 (2018)
11. Festinger, L.: Cognitive dissonance. Sci. Am. **207**(4), 93–106 (1962)
12. Haim, M., Graefe, A., Brosius, H.-B.: Burst of the filter bubble? Effects of personalization on the diversity of Google News. Dig. Journal. **6**(3), 330–343 (2018)
13. Kumar, J., Tintarev, N.: Using visualizations to encourage blind-spot exploration. In: IntRS@ RecSys, pp. 53–60 (2018)
14. Mohan, K.: Web site vistor incentive program in conjunction with promotion of anonymously identifying a user and/or a group. US Patent App. 10/787,990, September 2005
15. Munson, S.A., Lee, S.Y., Resnick, P.: Encouraging reading of diverse political viewpoints with a browser widget. In: Seventh International AAAI Conference on Weblogs and Social Media (2013)
16. Nagulendra, S., Vassileva, J.: Understanding and controlling the filter bubble through interactive visualization: a user study. In: Proceedings of the 25th ACM Conference on Hypertext and Social Media, pp. 107–115. ACM (2014)
17. Nguyen, C.T.: Echo chambers and epistemic bubbles. In: Episteme, pp. 1–21 (2018)

18. Nickerson, R.S.: Confirmation bias: a ubiquitous phenomenon in many guises. Rev. Gen. Psychol. **2**(2), 175–220 (1998)
19. Pariser, E.: The Filter Bubble: What the Internet Is Hiding From You. Penguin (2011)
20. Quattrociocchi, W., Scala, A., Sunstein, C.R.: Echo chambers on Facebook, SSRN 2795110 (2016)
21. Resnick, P., et al.: Bursting your (filter) bubble: strategies for promoting diverse exposure. In: Proceedings of the 2013 Conference on Computer Supported Cooperative Work Companion, pp. 95–100. ACM (2013)
22. Revelle, W.: Psych: Procedures for Psychological, Psychometric, and Personality Research. R package version 1.9.12.31 (2020). https://CRAN.R-project.org/package=psych
23. Van Aelst, P., et al.: Political communication in a high-choice media environment: a challenge for democracy? Ann. Int. Commun. Assoc. **41**(1), 3–27 (2017)
24. Vozalis, E., Margaritis, E.G.: Analysis of recommender systems algorithms. In: The 6th Hellenic European Conference on Computer Mathematics & its Applications, pp. 732–745 (2003)
25. Wickham, H.: Tidyverse: Easily Install and Load the 'Tidyverse'. R package version 1.3.0 (2019). https://CRAN.R-project.org/package=tidyverse
26. Wickham, H., Seidel, D.: Scales: Scale Functions for Visualization. R package version 1.1.0 (2019). https://CRAN.R-project.org/package=scales
27. Xie, Y.: Knitr: A General-Purpose Package for Dynamic Report Generation in R. R package version 1.27 (2020). https://CRAN.Rproject.org/package=knitr
28. Xing, X., Meng, W., Doozan, D., Feamster, N., Lee, W., Snoeren, A.C.: Exposing inconsistent web search results with bobble. In: Faloutsos, M., Kuzmanovic, A. (eds.) PAM 2014. LNCS, vol. 8362, pp. 131–140. Springer, Cham (2014). https://doi.org/10.1007/978-3-319-04918-2_13
29. Zhu, H.: KableExtra: Construct Complex Table with 'kable' and Pipe Syntax. R package version 1.1.0 (2019). https://CRAN.R-project.org/package=kableExtra

Performance Evaluation of Text-Oriented Artificial Chat Operation System (TACOS)

Seiki Tokunaga$^{(\boxtimes)}$, Kazuhiro Tamura, and Mihoko Otake-Matsuura

Center for Advanced Intelligence Project, RIKEN,
Nihonbashi 1-chome Mitsui Building, 15th floor, 1-4-1 Nihonbashi,
Chuo-ku, Tokyo 103-0027, Japan
{seiki.tokunaga,kazuhiro.tamura,mihoko.otake}@riken.jp

Abstract. Many countries are facing aging societies where loneliness and decreased number of communication seriously limit older adults from maintaining a decent quality of life. To tackle this problem, we have designed a chat-bot system to provide more communication chances for older adults, especially those who have fewer opportunities to converse with actual people (e.g., those living alone). With our system, the user converses about a story or topic presented in a photo in a manner and style that are familiar to the user. This approach is based on the original "coimagination method" protocol, which is a group conversation method designed to maintain a balance between listening and speaking with strict rules. Previously, we conducted a preliminary user study with several participants and the prototype system to confirm its working processes, and the initial results indicated that the protocol seemed to work well. However, we did not integrate nor evaluate our system using performance indicators when we conducted the experiment (e.g., how many users can connect to the system at once, etc.). Therefore, in this paper, we explore a dialog system called TACOS (Text-oriented Artificial Chat Operation System), which is an intermediate program that communicates with many applications and a variety of dialog systems. We measure the performance of the system by simulating three essential aspects: the number of virtual users, the frequency of the question data, and the total experiment time. The simulated results show that currently, the system can process the requests of 40 users, where each user asks a question to the system every 5 s during a 5 min period. Our results indicate that the proposed system can effectively process the amount of requests that will be tested in future experiments. In terms of data storage, the proposed system can handle datum quantities from ten thousand to one hundred thousand, and there seems to be no critical performance delay when the emulated client interacts with TACOS.

Keywords: Dialogue system · System performance evaluation · Distributed system

This research was partially supported by JSPS KAKENHI Grant Numbers JP19H01138.

© Springer Nature Switzerland AG 2020
V. G. Duffy (Ed.): HCII 2020, LNCS 12199, pp. 93–104, 2020.
https://doi.org/10.1007/978-3-030-49907-5_7

1   Introduction

In recent years, many societies have started to face rapidly aging populations, and as such, maintaining the quality of life (QoL) of elderly people has become an important concern. Social isolation and loneliness are major problems within older adult populations; to stay mentally and emotionally fit, older adults need to have positive social interactions and communication. Since many social activities require activating cognitive functions, they have the potential to prevent cognitive decline [1]. One research has found that communication with others balances sympathetic nerve activity, leading to more emotional support [7]. Moreover, another research has suggested that older adults sometimes encounter difficulties in communication because of physical and cognitive issues [2]. Such findings reveal the potential value of further research regarding the role of the social environment in protecting against cognitive decline at older age.

To ensure that the QoL of older adults is being maintained, knowing the status of various cognitive functions and the rate of cognitive decline over time are of key importance. Currently, there are several testing methods, such as the Wechsler Memory Scale-Revised and Montreal Cognitive Assessment for Japanese (MoCA-J) methods, which have been applied to healthy older adults. Using the MoCA-J, Suzuki et al. [9] detected the presence of delayed verbal memory through a randomized controlled trial. However, such testing requires a long time to collect sufficient data, and it is also expensive, which can be a burden for older adults and their caregivers. Moreover, long-term testing methods such as these were designed for experimental settings, and they can be difficult to use on a daily basis. Finally, testing is aimed at checking the current status of the participant, so if we would like to carry out cognitive training proactively and sustainably, we need a method that does not burden the older adults and their caregivers.

A wide variety of technologies are being explored that have the potential to provide safe and early detection of cognitive decline for older adults. Tanaka et al. [10] developed a screen-based software agent that could judge with high accuracy whether or not the participant had dementia. Yu et al. [14] proposed assessing cognitive impairment with speech-based prediction methods. Along this line, Otake-Matsuura and her team [5,6] developed a monthly group conversation method system called the coimagination method (CM) that aims to prevent age-related cognitive decline. However, we are aware of no standard method for cognitive training to build resilience against cognitive decline that can be used on a daily basis.

Toward this end, we proposed a dialog-based system that aimed to provide cognitive training for healthy older adults on a daily basis [12]. We designed the system to meet the requirements discussed previously (i.e., not burdening the participant and their caregivers), and some items were added to track the content of the experiment in detail [13]. Previously, we introduced a general model of our system without providing details of the system design, and we did not evaluate its performance. Therefore, in this research, we present the detailed design of our Text-oriented Artificial Chat Operation System (TACOS) and some key

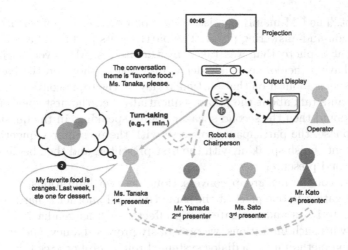

Fig. 1. Overview of conventional coimagination method

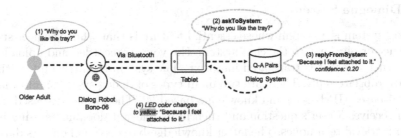

Fig. 2. Overview of one on one dialog system

features, such as user management features and how it manages relationships between users and bots. We then test the system's performance using simulated experiments and show how well the system can handle the message rate from the vast amount of users (e.g., we simulate the requests arising from 40 users at a rate of five requests per second, and we determine the total time to it takes the system to handle these requests). Finally, we discuss how we can improve the performance of TACOS on the basis of the results of the system evaluation.

2 Preliminary

2.1 Coimagination Method

The CM was developed by Otake-Matsuura and her team [5,6], which is a group conversation method designed to prevent the decline of cognitive function through highly structured and managed group conversation. Figure 1 shows an overview of the CM. There are four participants, and the center of photo shows the robot chairperson Bono. The group conversation is almost entirely moderated by the robot. The CM mainly consists of two phases: a topic-conversation phase and a question-and-answering phase. The participants partake in a conversation by looking at a photo that was taken by themselves. Moreover, each conversation can have a theme, i.e., the older adults take a photo on the basis of the theme and speak about it on that particular day. In the topic-conversation phase, the participants talk about the photo sequentially, i.e., the first speaker finishes his/her talk, and then the second speaker begins speaking. In the question-and-answering phase, the participants converse with the presenter sequentially, i.e., the participants finish speaking with the first presenter, and then begin speaking with the second presenter.

However, conducting group conversation has two limitations, one is older adults must gather in one place at the same time and another is hard to manage group characteristics and mitigate group effects, such as gender imbalances et al. To cope with such limitations, we previously proposed a new one on one style coimagination method using a dialog system through a robot (See Fig. 2) [12,13].

2.2   Dialogue System

A dialog system is a system whose essential feature is that when the user speaks a sentence or phrase with the chat system, the voice is recorded and uploaded to the internet where it is translated into text. The system then responds with the most appropriate reply. There are two main types of dialog systems: information retrieval-based (IR-based) and knowledge-based [4]. The former IR-based dialog system receives a user's question and then finds relevant documents using information retrieval techniques. The latter knowledge-based system queries datasets of facts that are stored on the internet. For example, the user may ask the question: "When was Taro Okamoto born?" This phrase is converted into a logical format such as birth-year (Taro Okamoto, ?x) so that the question can be queried easily by the system. Moreover, most dialog systems have confidence values that determine whether the given input value is similar to one in a data set. If a confidence value is near to 1, then the input utterance is very similar to one in the existing data set. Additionally, dialog systems contain some logical separators that are specialized to some topics (e.g., favorite movie and music). To understand this concept, let us consider the following example: Perhaps the user would like to use the dialog system to ask the chat-bot about business travel in the company. In this scenario, the dialog system's workspace will be set to "business travel."

In this research, we focus on IR-based dialog systems because of their simplicity and adaptability for our proposed system.

2.3   System Design Concept

We designed a distributed dialog management system in order to provide one-to-one conversations with an original robot. The most significant difference of our system compared with general dialog systems is that our approach has been adapted to accommodate and facilitate stories spoken by elderly participants using an original conversation-based system called Fonobono Panel introduced by Otake-Matsuura [6]. Our system consists of two main components. The first is a chat-based user interface (UI) for older adults called Native Application of Coimagination-Driven Human-centered Orchestration System (NACHOS). NACHOS was designed to provide a UI that is specialized for displaying photos and providing time management (e.g., 1 min). The second component, NACHOS, was developed so that the user can easily use the inner microphone on the device that was specially adapted for talking and that uses the essential Text-To-Speech (TTS) and Speech-To-Text technologies. We also designed TACOS to serve as the main server program that manages relationships between the user and the dialog system. TACOS also records the dialog with the users as a log. Moreover, we introduced the concept of the "bot," which provides loosely coupled interactions with the dialog system and allows some common data to be extracted.

During operation, the dialog system first learns the data associated with the story in the CM. This requires the dialog system to adapt to a wide variety of dialog topics. A response threshold needs to be set, which allows the dialog system to determine if it has enough confidence to answer a question. For example, currently, some smart speakers may respond with the phrase "I cannot understand you" if the dialog system does not have enough confidence to appropriately reply to the speaker's utterance. To extract common data from various dialog systems, the bot will seek to obtain data via a welcome message, help messages, and user names in order to identify each bot. We designed our distributed system on the basis of the concept of both SOA [8] and Enterprise Integration Patterns [3]; hence, each system has a loosely coupled designed, and individual system has advantage of maintenance.

2.4   Sequence Diagram of Distributed System

Figure 3 shows a diagram of our system's data transmission sequence. First, the user requests authentication with his/her own user_id and password. Once the user is authenticated, their initial screen name is displayed on the tablet (see Fig. 3). On the display, the user can see a photo and the conversation time limit. In our system, authentication is performed by the Fonobono Panel, where NACHOS transfers the authentication request from the user to Fonobono Panel. After authentication, NACHOS receives stories and photos (i.e., data) that originate from the Fonobono Panel (see #7 in Fig. 2). NACHOS then sends a request to TACOS, called a UserBotRelationship, which sets the association between the user and a specific bot. Then, the dialog system is engaged that generates specific stories and photos that are discussed among the older adult users [13]. Hence, the user has an association with a valid configuration in the dialog system; in our system, this means the user has a relationship with the bot, which is relevant to the story. For instance, when the user talks with our system, perhaps about their favorite food, then before the conversation begins, the user establishes a relationship with the food bot via the UserBotRelationship. Each bot has a one-to-one relationship with both a story's topic and the dialog system because the dialog system has learned the conversation topic beforehand, as explained

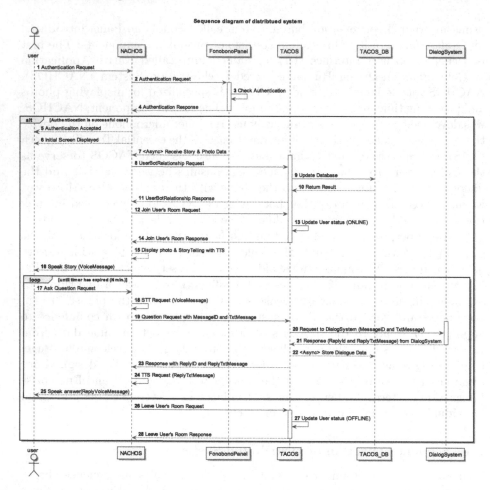

Fig. 3. Sequence diagram of proposed system

in Sect. 2.2. For example, if the topic of conversation is set to "food," then the dialog system will learn about food topics before the conversation is initiated. In a practical sense, due to the internal processing design of the system, TACOS first registers an association with the "FoodBot," and the dialog system learns about the topic of food. Then, NACHOS receive a response to the UserBotRelationship from TACOS. Then, a photo will appear on the screen of NACHOS, which initiates the question-and-answering session with the user. Based on both the conversation topic and the displayed photos, NACHOS participates with the conversation using TTS. Then, NACHOS monitors the question-and-answering time (denoted as "QA-time"), which represents the internal loop diagram shown in Fig. 2. During the QA-time, the users converse with NACHOS using STT technology, where the received data are converted to text format (TxtMessage), which NACHOS then receives, interprets, and responds using TTS. Each

Fig. 4. Screen of NACHOS on the tablet (The left of the figure shows a dialogue plan for the user and the right one shows the chat history for the user.)

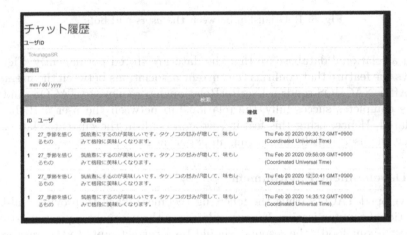

Fig. 5. Chat history feature.

question asked by the user has a unique message identifier (MessageID), and the data format is issued a unix timestamp [11]. In addition, the response from the server to NACHOS also has an identifier with the same format (i.e., a ReplyID). The former MessageID is used by the client program NACHOS, and the latter ReplyID is issued by the server. Hence, the response time between the start of a request and the generated response from the server can be measured. The QA procedure ends once the timer has expired.

3 System Implementation

3.1 Implementation of TACOS

Figures 5 and 6 represent the appearance of TACOS. Figure 5 shows the chat history feature that consists of the user's dialog log. Using this feature, both a researcher and an experiment operator can confirm the results of the chat logs during the experiment. In addition, the questions and answers are recorded as a

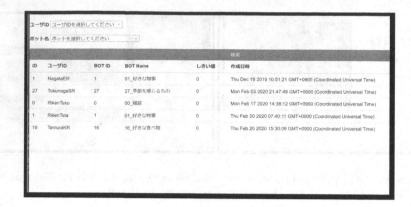

Fig. 6. Relationship between the users and bots.

pair in a relational database, so that the data are stored permanently. Figure 6 displays the feature that confirms the current associations between the users and bots. After NACHOS sends a UserBotRelationship request to TACOS, and the process completes successfully, the relationship between the user and the bot is updated. Hence, using this feature, we can confirm the current relationship between the user and the bot during an experiment.

3.2 Development Environment

We developed TACOS using the following technical stack to provide real-time bidirectional communication. For example, when the user asks a question to some bot (e.g., about food), the response should be a correct reply to the answer. To achieve this requirement, we used Node.js, TypeScript, and SocketIO. Moreover, we adopted a PostgreSQL database because some of the data have relationships with other data (e.g., relationships between the user and bot), and we wanted to store the data consistently. Finally, log data needed to be collected without blocking other processes in NACHOS; hence, our system also adapted the asynchronous messaging system RabbitMQ because of its advantages of traceability and decoupling the program. The following list provides a summary of the languages, databases, etc. used in TACOS:

- Development Language: TypeScript: 3.4.5, Node.js: v10.16.0, JavaScript
- Main Library: Express (Web Framework) & SocketIO (Realtime Engine)
- Database: PostgreSQL 9.2.24
- Messaging Middleware: RabbitMQ 3.7.5.

4 System Evaluation

4.1 Design and Implementation of Testing Script

In this section, we show how we evaluated TACOS from the viewpoint of system performance. It is necessary to conduct cases of large numbers of simultaneous users so that we can confirm whether the system can handle such a load or whether it might crash or produce errors because of the high traffic rate. We evaluated the system from the viewpoint of how it could process transmitted data from many simultaneous clients. When devising the system performance evaluation, we estimated the approximate number of users that could be expected to access the system at any one time (estimated here as 70 to 80). Thus, the server is required to process many requests at the same time. Therefore, our testing script was written to emulate the number of expected users. In addition, during an experiment, the users may ask questions at random intervals during the QA-time period. Hence, when we designed the script, we considered both the frequency of the transmitted data and how long the script should run (i.e., the experiment time). As a result, we designed our testing script to have three parameters, NumberOfUser, FrequencyOfTransmission, and RunTime, as follows:

- Parameter *NumberOfUser*: Set number of clients which simulates the number of connected users.
- Parameter *FrequencyOfTransmission*: Set the frequency of transmitted questions from the users (e.g., one request per 5 s).
- Parameter *RunTime*: Set execution time to run the scripts.

As the first parameter, the NumberOfUser represented the emulated number of virtual users. Hence, with the script, we emulated the system's response and behavior to many virtual users (up to 80). Second, the FrequencyOfTransmission parameter controlled the frequency of the transmitted data sent by the virtual users. Hence, we simulated the system's load as well as how many questions the system received from the participants during regular intervals (in units of seconds). Third, RunTimeparameter represented the total simulated time of the experiment. Using these three parameters, the script emulated NACHOS's procedures (i.e., steps #12(JoinUser's Room request) to #23(Response with ReplyID and ReplyTxtMessage) in Fig.reffig:NACHOS). Based on the above basic requirements, we have implemented the testing script with following programming language.

- Development Language: Node.js: v10.16.0
- Library: socket.io-client: 2.3.0, which is used to communicate with TACOS
- Database: MongoDB: 4.2.2.

4.2 Experiment Condition

Using the testing script described in Sect. 4.1, we conducted a preliminary system performance evaluation to confirm how the main system could process requests from the simulated clients. We set the NumberOfUser parameter to 40 and 80. We formerly conducted a user study to confirm the UI of our dialog system with actual older adults [13]. On the basis of these results, we determined that a participant asks a question about once every 20 s. Thus, we set the FrequencyOfTransmission parameter to 20. Finally, we set the RunTime to 300 s because we plan to conduct an experiment using this 5-min period with actual participants during a future long-term study (e.g., a month or more). We conducted the experiment using the following equipment:

- OS: Windows 10 64 bit professional (16GB memory)
- CPU: Core i7 7th Gen
- Software: Docker version 18.09.1 which mainly focuses on creating containers for database system.

4.3   Experimental Result

As mentioned in the previous section, we set the NumberOfUser to 40 and 80 to emulate the conditions of future experiments that will be run with actual users. During the experiment, FrequencyOfTransmission was set to 20 s and RunTime to 300 s. We then implemented that TACOS to store a question and answer as a single pair. This means that if TACOS has no problem handling the requests, the number of storing datum should be equal to number of transmitted datum. This allowed us to judge whether all requests were processed successfully based on the number of stored datum (Table 1).

Table 1 shows the results of the emulated experiments using the test script. We confirm that the total number of stored datum in the database was equal to the expected number of transmitted datum for both NumberOfUser scenarios (40 and 80 users). This result indicates that TACOS will be able to process the expected requests from clients in our planned future experiments. Moreover, we also measured the delay time arising when NACHOS transmitted data and TACOS produced a response through the dialog system. On the basis of this delay, we evaluated whether the stored number of records affected the response time to a user's question (see Table 2). Although the number of recorded datum increased by factors of 10 to 100,000, no discernable delay was detected. Therefore, based on these results, our future experiment plan seems very feasible from the viewpoint of storing data arising from 40 or 80 users. In addition, we think we can ignore the performance delay when the number of stored records is less than 100,000; however, we may have to revise the system if the number of records exceeds one million.

Table 1. Relationship between NumberOfUser and the amount of stored data.

#NumberOfUser	#stored data
40	600
80	1200

Table 2. Relationships Number of preliminary stored data and response time

#Preliminary stored data	# delay time(milliseconds)
10,000	476
100,000	486

4.4 Limitation

We also explored the limitation of our proposed system. The designed emulating script had a limitation in that the simple frequency of the transmitted data was emulated as burst requests, such as the requests simultaneously arising from 40 users. However, in this study, we did not have to care about it, because we tested the system with the worst-case scenarios. If we would like to emulate the actual random behavior of users, one simple approach would be to add some random intervals before the script emits a pseudo request to TACOS. Moreover, to reproduce the data, we applied fixed-question data as pseudo requests to NACHOS (e.g., "What do you think of this food?") to communicate with TACOS in the testing script. Finally, currently, we only evaluated system from the viewpoint of its performance. However, we also need to evaluate the dialog system, the usability of the system for different users, and how natural the users feel when they use our proposed system. In addition to this, currently we just ignore detailed metrics such as CPU and memory usage and network latency et al. if we have to measure the detailed system performance continuously, we have to measure them.

5 Conclusion

In this paper, we introduced our system called TACOS, and its system performance was tested with a script that emulated expected user scenarios. The script was based on three key parameters: the number of users, the frequency interval of the transmitted data, and the total time taken to run the script. As a result, we confirmed that our system can process the amount of requests from the client program expected during future planned experiments. Our future work is to conduct a long-term experiment to evaluate our system.

References

1. Arnetz, B.B., Eyre, M., Theorell, T.: Social activation of the elderly: a social experiment. Soc. Sci. Med. **16**(19), 1685–1690 (1982). http://www.science direct.com/science/article/pii/0277953682900934
2. Golden, J., et al.: Loneliness, social support networs, mood and wellbeing in community-dwelling elderly. Geriatr. Psychiatry **24**, 694–700 (2009)
3. Hohpe, G., Woolf, B.: Enterprise Integration Patterns: Designing, Building, and Deploying Messaging Solutions. The Addison-Wesley Signature Series. Prentice Hall, Upper Saddle River (2004). http://books.google.com.au/books?id=dH9zp14-1KYC

4. Jurafsky, D., Martin, J.H.: Speech and Language Processing : An Introduction to Natural Language Processing, Computational Linguistics, and Speech Recognition. Pearson Prentice Hall, Upper Saddle River (2009)
5. Otake, M., Kato, M., Takagi, T., Asama, H.: Development of coimagination method towards cognitive enhancement via image based interactive communication. In: The 18th IEEE International Symposium on Robot and Human Interactive Communication, RO-MAN 2009, pp. 835–840, September 2009
6. Otake-Matsuura, M., et al.: Photo-integrated conversation moderated by robots for cognitive health in older adults: a randomized controlled trial medRxiv (2019)
7. Seeman, T.E., Lusignolo, T.M., Albert, M., Berkman, L.: Social relationships, social support, and patterns of cognitive aging in healthy, high-functioning older adults: MacArthur studies of successful aging. Health Psychol. **20**, 243–255 (2001)
8. Srinivasan, L., Treadwell, J.: An overview of service-oriented architecture web services and grid computing, HP Technical report, vol. 2 (2005)
9. Suzuki, H., et al.: Cognitive intervention through a training program for picture book reading in community-dwelling older adults: a randomized controlled trial. BMC Geriatr. **14**(1), 122 (2014). https://doi.org/10.1186/1471-2318-14-122
10. Tanaka, H., et al.: Detecting dementia through interactive computer avatars. IEEE J. Transl. Eng. Health Med. **5**, 1–11 (2017)
11. Unix time. https://en.wikipedia.org/wiki/Unix_time
12. Tokunaga, S., Otake-Matsuura, M.: Design of coimagination support dialogue system with pluggable dialogue system - towards long-term experiment. In: Duffy, V.G. (ed.) HCII 2019. LNCS, vol. 11582, pp. 404–420. Springer, Cham (2019). https://doi.org/10.1007/978-3-030-22219-2_31
13. Tokunaga, S., Seaborn, K., Tamura, K., Otake-Matsuura, M.: Cognitive training for older adults with a dialogue-based, robot-facilitated storytelling system. In: Cardona-Rivera, R.E., Sullivan, A., Young, R.M. (eds.) ICIDS 2019. LNCS, vol. 11869, pp. 405–409. Springer, Cham (2019). https://doi.org/10.1007/978-3-030-33894-7_43
14. Yu, B., Quatieri, T.F., Williamson, J.R., Mundt, J.C.: Cognitive impairment prediction in the elderly based on vocal biomarkers. In: Annual Conference of the International Speech Communication Association- INTERSPEECH 2015, pp. 3734–3738. Dresden (2015)

Modelling Work, Collaboration and the Human Environment

Safety Performance-Based Risk Assessment for Aviation Fuel Supply of Civil Aviation

Mingliang Chen[1,2(✉)], Yuan Zhang[1,2], and Yanqiu Chen[1,2]

[1] China Academy of Civil Aviation Science and Technology, Beijing 100028, China
{chenml,zhangyuan,chenyq}@mail.castc.org.cn
[2] Engineering and Technical Research Center of Civil Aviation Safety Analysis and Prevention of Beijing, Beijing 100028, China

Abstract. With the wide implementation of safety management system in civil aviation industry, the implementation efficiency of safety management system has been paid more and more attentions. Safety performance management is the core of safety management system because of its important role in providing operation data to verify the implementation efficiency. By considering the management mechanisms of safety management system in civil aviation, a big picture of civil aviation safety management is illustrated. In this big picture, the processes of hazard identification, risk assessment, safety control measures, operation monitor and review in the civil aviation operation stage are presented and discussed. A novel operation risk assessment model is proposed to evaluate a certain civil aviation organization with several branches which have a number of departments based on the safety performance indicator system. A case of an aviation fuel company with five branches and twenty-five departments in these branches is studied to verify the flexibility of the proposed model. The assessment results are consistent with the actual operation state of the aviation fuel company.

Keywords: Civil aviation safety management · Risk assessment · Safety performance management · Aviation fuel supply

1 Introduction

As an important part of integrated transportation system, the civil aviation industry plays a significant and irreplaceable role in serving national socio-economic development. Safety is the foundation of civil aviation industry's long-term development. According to Aviation Safety Network, there are a total of 8 fatal airliner (14+ passengers) accidents involving commercial flights, resulting in 234 fatalities from January 1, 2019 to June 30, 2019. The statistics of these fatal accidents is showed in Fig. 1. But the numbers of fatal accidents and fatalities of the five-year average are 6 and 192, respectively. Obviously, the numbers of fatal accidents and fatalities are higher than the five-year average.

Civil Aviation is a very complex and dynamic system. To operate safely, the cooperation of airlines, airports, air traffic controllers, and other service providers is very important. Most of hazards in a certain organization or department can be identified and

© Springer Nature Switzerland AG 2020
V. G. Duffy (Ed.): HCII 2020, LNCS 12199, pp. 107–118, 2020.
https://doi.org/10.1007/978-3-030-49907-5_8

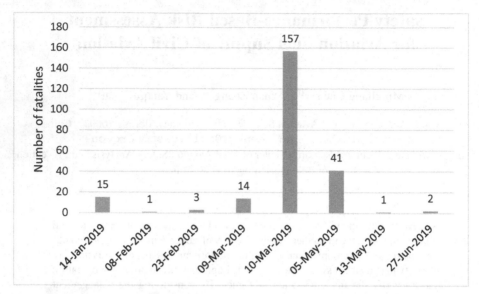

Fig. 1. The statistics of fatal accidents from January 1, 2019 to June 30, 2019 (Data from the Aviation Safety Network)

controlled easily. New hazards continuously emerge at the interfaces between these service providers. These hazards are hard to identify and control. According to the statistics safety data collected through various initiatives, there are a number of serious incidents and general incidents occurred because of poor interface management. The civil aviation safety management is a dynamic and continuous promotion process.

The evolution of civil aviation safety can be summarized as follows: technical era, human factors era, organizational era, and total system era. From the early 1900s, civil aviation emerged as a form of mass transportation. Safety occurrences were identified as related to technical factors and technological failures. Therefore, civil aviation safety endeavours was placed on the investigation and improvement of technical factors. By the early 1970s, human factors were recognized as important and the focus of safety endeavours was extended to human factors. During the mid-1990s, it became clear that organizational factors plays a key role in achieving the effectiveness of safety risk controls. From the beginning of the 21st century, a recognition and emphasis on the role of total civil aviation system emerged [1, 2].

Safety performance management is an important part of safety management system. It has been paid more and more attention because it can verify the effectiveness of risk control measures and test the implementation efficiency of safety management system. In order to present a comprehensive literature review of safety performance-related articles, papers were filtered with keyword as 'safety performance' in the paper title which published from 2008 to 2019 in Elsevier ScienceDirect. The distribution of safety performance-related articles in Elsevier ScienceDirect database is presented in Fig. 2.

According to the search result, we can find that the general trend to increase is well pronounced in the period of 2008-2019.

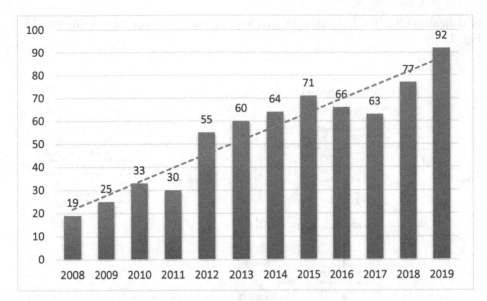

Fig. 2. Distribution of safety performance-related articles in Elsevier ScienceDirect database

With the wide implementation of safety management system in civil aviation industry, safety performance management has been paid more and more attention from academic institutions and civil aviation industry. In the domain of establishing safety performance indicators, a number of research groups adopted different methods to develop safety performance indicators in safety-critical organizations from various perspectives [3–5]. In the domain of classifying safety performance indicators, safety performance indicators have been classified as high-consequence indicators and low-consequence indicators, outcome indicators and process indicators, reactive indicators and proactive indicators, lagging indicators and leading indicators, and so on [6–11]. In the domain of safety management effectiveness, different research groups adopted various methods to evaluate the effectiveness of safety management and performance management for airlines, airports, air traffic controllers, etc. from different dimensions and aspects [12–22]. In the domain of risk management based on safety performance indicators, some research groups established risk assessment model based on safety performance indicator system for different types of organization [10, 11, 23, 24].

The remaining of this paper is organized as follows. The big picture of civil aviation safety management is presented in Sect. 2. Then, Sect. 3 introduces the risk assessment model based on safety performance indicator system. In Sect. 4, a case study of an aviation fuel company is provided to verify the proposed model. Finally, some conclusions are given in the last section.

2 Civil Aviation Safety Management

Safety is typically managed through a risk management cycle which includes the stages of hazard identification, risk evaluation, risk mitigation and risk monitoring [25]. Accidents are prevented by identifying, measuring, analyzing, and adjusting key activities or indicators [26]. The big picture of civil aviation safety management is illustrated in Fig. 3.

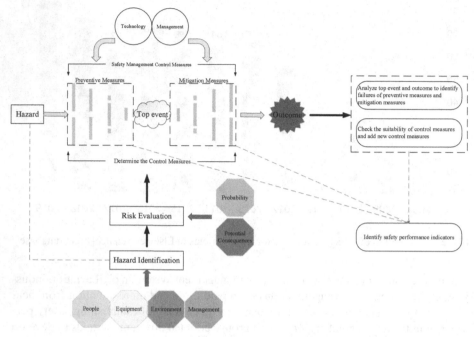

Fig. 3. The big picture of civil aviation safety management

Safety is typically managed through continuous risk management, including hazard identification, risk evaluation, risk mitigation and risk monitoring. According to ICAO, hazard is defined as 'A condition or an object with the potential to cause or contribute to an aircraft incident or accident'. Hazard identification is the first step in the civil aviation safety management process. In the civil aviation industry, there are many hazards from people, equipment, environment, and management. There are two processes to identify hazards: forward analysis process and backward analysis process. Forward analysis process, which from hazard identification to unsafe events, includes: system and job analysis, What-if analysis, event tree analysis (ETA), hazard and operability analysis (HAZOP), etc. Backward analysis process, which from unsafe events to direct or indirect causes, include: Reason model, SHELL model, fault tree analysis (FTA), etc.

For each hazard, there are many possible scenarios that could result in different consequences. Risk evaluation is the process of identifying and measuring risk. In order to carry out risk evaluation, the probability and potential consequence for each scenario should be confirmed. There are many methods proposed to evaluate risk. These methods can be divided into qualitative and quantitative risk evaluation methodologies.

In order to control risk, control measures are used to prevent the occurrence of unsafe events and mitigate the consequence of top events. Control measures should be identified and selected from technology level and management level. Then, the control plan should be developed and implemented. The effectiveness of these control measures should be confirmed to determine whether they continue to provide protection. Control measures can be divided as preventative measures and mitigative measures. Risk should be reduced to the lowest reasonably practicable level by taking preventative measures and mitigative measures. As formalized by professor Trevor Kletz, the five commonly used inherent safety principles include: simplification, substitution, moderation, minimization, and elimination [27]. The control measures that are the most feasible and effective should be selected according to the hierarchy of controls measures: elimination, substitution, engineering measures, administrative measures, and the personal protective equipment.

Once top event occurs, it means that some control measures fail. Then, the investigation should be carried out to identify failures in the control measures. The risk management program should be reviewed to check the design and suitability of control measures.

3   Risk Assessment Model Based on Safety Performance

As mentioned above, safety performance indicators can be classified according to different standards. In this paper, all the identified safety performance indicators in a civil aviation organization are classified as occurrence indicators, foundation indicators, management indicators, and operation indicators. Safety performance indicators used to monitor and measure unsafe events belong to occurrence indicators. Foundation indicators and management indicators refer to the safety performance indicators used to monitor and measure safety foundation status and the implementation of safety management, respectively. Operation indicators refer to the safety performance indicators used to monitor and measure precursor events.

As illustrated in the big picture of civil aviation safety management, risk evaluation process includes the analysis of the likelihood of the consequence occurring and the seriousness of the consequence if it does occur. Risk evaluation process should use whatever safety data and safety information is available. Then, data from the safety performance indicator system can be used to evaluate the probability of the consequence occurring. Statistical value of each safety performance indicator will be collected every month. The statistic value of safety performance indicators should be normalized because the units and data ranges are various. For each safety performance indicator, the range of statistic value will be divided as 'very poor', 'poor', 'average', 'good', and 'very good'. In order to obtain a numerical value in the hundred-mark system, the values representing these five grades are assigned as 100, 80, 60, 40, and 0.

The severity of the consequence if it does occur can be evaluated based on the safety performance indicator system because it includes occurrence indicators, management indicators, foundation indicators, and operation indicators. Heinrich's Law is used as baseline by considering that the severities have small differences even within the same level. According to Heinrich's Law, severity coefficients for different safety performance indicators can be given to represent the differences for occurrence indicators, foundation indicators, management indicators, and operation indicators. Severity scores for different safety performance indicators are assigned based on experts' experience to represent the small difference in the same safety performance indicator classification. Severity coefficients and severity scores for different safety performance indicators are presented in Table 1.

Table 1. Severity coefficients and severity scores for different safety performance indicators

Safety performance indicator		Severity coefficient	Severity score
Occurrence indicator	Accident	1000	[1, 2]
	Serious incident	300	[1, 2]
	General incident	100	[1, 1.5]
Foundation indicator		30	[1, 3]
Management indicator		30	[1, 1.5]
Operation indicator		1	[1, 5]

In some civil aviation organizations, there are a number of branches located in different areas. In these branches, there are some departments to deal with various businesses. In this research, the risk assessment model has three levels: the operation risk of departments, the operation risk of branch, and the operation risk of a civil aviation organization. In the department level, different departments' operation risk should be calculated based on the safety performance indicator system. In the safety performance indicator system, there are a number of occurrence type, foundation type, management type, and operation type of safety performance indicators. In the branch level, all departments' operation risk of this branch will be synthesized as operation risk of the branch. In the civil aviation organization level, all branches' operation risk will be calculated as operation risk of the organization. The risk assessment model based on safety performance is illustrated as Fig. 4.

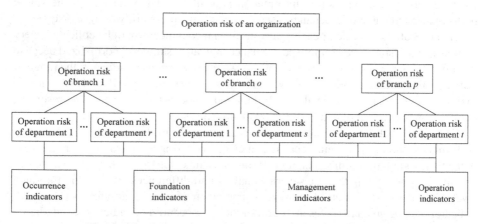

Fig. 4. The risk assessment model based on safety performance

At the department level, safety performance indicator system includes all classifications of safety performance indicators. Statistics values for all these occurrence indicators, foundation indicators, management indicators, and operation indicators can be obtained every month. According to the value assignment criteria mentioned above, there will be a value L_{si} in the hundred-mark system assigned for each safety performance indicator. Then, the operation risk of a certain department can be calculated as:

$$R_d = \sum_{i=1}^{m} S_{ci} \times S_{si} \times L_{si} \tag{1}$$

where, m represents the number of safety performance indicators identified for the department, S_{ci} and S_{si} are the severity coefficient and severity score for the ith safety performance indicator, respectively.

For a certain branch, different departments face different hazards and risks. Then, the weights for different departments are different in the risk evaluation of the branch. The weights for different departments in the branch can be assigned by experts as:

$$w_d = (w_{d1}, w_{d2}, w_{d3}, \ldots, w_{dl}) \tag{2}$$

where, w_{dj} is the weight of the jth department in the branch.

At the branch level, the operation risk can be calculated as:

$$R_b = \sum_{j=1}^{l} w_{dj} \times R_{dj} \tag{3}$$

where, l is the number of departments in the branch, R_{dj} is the operation risk of the jth department in the branch.

For a certain civil aviation organization, the identified hazards and risks for different branch are different. Then, the weights for different branches are different in the risk evaluation of the civil aviation organization. The weights for different branches in the civil aviation organization can be assigned by experts as:

$$w_b = (w_{b1}, w_{b2}, w_{b3}, \ldots, w_{bn}) \tag{4}$$

where, w_{bk} is the weight of the kth branch in the civil aviation organization.

At the civil aviation organization level, the operation risk can be calculated as:

$$R_o = \sum_{k=1}^{n} w_{bk} \times R_{bk} \tag{5}$$

where, n is the number of branches in the civil aviation organization, R_{bk} is the operation risk of the kth branch in the organization.

4 Case Study

Aviation fuel support ability is very important for airport ground support services. Aviation fuel is a kind of dangerous chemical with the characteristics of explosive and easy to produce static electricity. In order to verify the proposed operation risk assessment model, an aviation fuel supply company is used as a case study. There are five branches in this aviation fuel supply company. Each branch has a number of departments. For each department, there are several occurrence indicators, foundation indicators, management indicators, and operation indicators. The numbers of different classifications of safety performance indicators are listed in Table 2.

Table 2. Numbers of safety performance indicators for different branches and departments

Branch	Department	Number of SPIs
Branch A	Emergency command center	16
	Aviation fuel tank farm 1	22
	Aviation fuel tank farm 2	22
	Aviation fueling station 1	18
	Aviation fueling station 2	18
	Equipment maintenance center	20
Branch B	Aviation fuel tank farm	22
	Aviation fueling station	37
	Quality inspection center	10
Branch C	Aviation fuel tank farm	21
	Aviation fueling station	21
	Measuring and testing lab	17
	Q supply station	16
	H supply station	15
	T supply station	20
	Z supply station	21
	CD supply station	20
Branch D	Aviation fueling station	34
	Measuring and testing lab	31
	D supply station	19
	L supply station	13
Branch E	Aviation fueling station	30
	Measuring and testing lab	28
	B supply station	21
	CF supply station	20

As mentioned above, the probabilities and severities of occurrences in different branches and their departments are different. The weights for five branches and their departments are list in Table 3.

Table 3. Weights for different branches and departments

Branch	Weight	Department	Weight
Branch A	0.25	Emergency command center	0.1
		Aviation fuel tank farm 1	0.15
		Aviation fuel tank farm 2	0.15
		Aviation fueling station 1	0.25
		Aviation fueling station 2	0.25
		Equipment maintenance center	0.1
Branch B	0.1	Aviation fuel tank farm	0.3
		Aviation fueling station	0.5
		Quality inspection center	0.2
Branch C	0.25	Aviation fuel tank farm	0.09
		Aviation fueling station	0.14
		Measuring and testing lab	0.07
		Q supply station	0.14
		H supply station	0.14
		T supply station	0.14
		Z supply station	0.14
		CD supply station	0.14
Branch D	0.2	Aviation fueling station	0.2
		Measuring and testing lab	0.14
		D supply station	0.33
		L supply station	0.33
Branch E	0.2	Aviation fueling station	0.2
		Measuring and testing lab	0.14
		B supply station	0.33
		CF supply station	0.33

According to the operation risk assessment model mentioned above, one month's monitoring data of all safety performance indicators is used to calculate the operation risks of the aviation fuel company, five branches, and twenty-five departments. The operation risk assessment results are presented in Table 4.

Based on the collected one month's data of all safety performance indicators, the operation risks of the aviation fuel company, its five branches, and their departments have been assessed. It is found that these operation risk values are in the same magnitude because there is no accident, or incident happened in this month. With the accumulation of collected data of all safety performance indicators, the operation risk trends of the

Table 4. Operation risk for aviation fuel company, branches and departments

Company	Risk	Branch	Risk	Department	Risk
Aviation fuel company	275.57	Branch A	276	Emergency command center	260
				Aviation fuel tank farm 1	320
				Aviation fuel tank farm 2	220
				Aviation fueling station 1	300
				Aviation fueling station 2	280
				Equipment maintenance center	240
		Branch B	274	Aviation fuel tank farm	280
				Aviation fueling station	300
				Quality inspection center	200
		Branch C	267.4	Aviation fuel tank farm	280
				Aviation fueling station	300
				Measuring and testing lab	220
				Q supply station	260
				H supply station	240
				T supply station	280
				Z supply station	260
				CD supply station	280
		Branch D	289.8	Aviation fueling station	320
				Measuring and testing lab	340
				D supply station	280
				L supply station	260
		Branch E	271.8	Aviation fueling station	300
				Measuring and testing lab	240
				B supply station	260
				CF supply station	280

aviation fuel company, its branches, and their departments can be used for decision making.

5 Conclusion

As an important part of safety management system, the implementation of safety performance management can promote the risk management and safety assurance process. In order to assess operation risk of a civil aviation organization, the big picture of civil aviation safety management is illustrated to discuss the risk assessment and risk control process. In this big picture, the sources of safety performance indicators are presented. All identified safety performance indicators have been classified into four classifications: occurrence indicators, operation indicators, management indicators, and foundation indicators. The severity coefficients and severity scores for these four classifications of safety performance indicators have been assigned based on Heinrich's Law and in conjunction with experts' evaluation. A novel operation risk assessment model based on safety performance is proposed. The operation risks of a certain civil aviation organization, its branches, and their departments can be assessed according to the proposed operation risk assessment model. An aviation fuel company with five branches and twenty-five departments is used to illustrate the efficiency and flexibility of the proposed model. The operation risk values for the aviation fuel company, five branches, and twenty-five departments are calculated based on one month's data of all safety performance indicators. The operation risk trends can be given by accumulating of data of all safety performance indicators month by month.

References

1. Chen, M., Rong, M., Chen, Y.: A new safety culture index system for civil aviation organizations. In: Advances in Energy Science and Equipment Engineering II, vol. 1, pp. 815–819 (2017)
2. International Civil Aviation Organization: ICAO Doc 9859 Safety Management Manual, 4th eds. International Civil Aviation Organization, Montreal (2018)
3. Enoma, A., Allen, S.: Developing key performance indicators for airport safety and security. Facilities 25, 296–315 (2007)
4. Reiman, T., Pietikainen, E.: Leading indicators of system safety-monitoring and driving the organizational safety potential. Saf. Sci. 50(10), 1993–2000 (2012)
5. Sultana, S., Andersen, B.S., Haugen, S.: Identifying safety indicators for safety performance measurement using a system engineering approach. Process Saf. Environ. 128, 107–120 (2019)
6. Harms-Ringdahl, L.: Dimensions in safety indicators. Saf. Sci. 47, 481–482 (2009)
7. Hinze, J., Thurman, S.: Leading indicators of construction safety performance. Saf. Sci. 51, 23–28 (2013)
8. Safety Management International Collaboration Group: A system approach to measuring safety performance: the regulator perspective. Technical report, Safety Management International Collaboration Group (2014)
9. Gerede, E., ve Yasar, M.: Evaluation of safety performance indicators of flight training organizations in Turkey. Int. J. Eurasia Soc. Sci. 8(29), 1174–1207 (2017)
10. Chen, M., Luo, M., Sun, H., Chen, Y.: A comprehensive risk evaluation model for airport operation safety. In: The Proceedings of 2018 12th International Conference on Reliability, Maintainability and Safety (ICRMS), pp. 146–149 (2018)
11. Chen, M., Zhang, Y., Chen, Y.: Apron operation risk assessment based on safety performance. J. Civ. Aviat. 2(6), 90–94 (2018)
12. Lu, X., Huang, S.: Airport safety risk evaluation based on modification of quantitative safety management model. Procedia Eng. 43, 238–244 (2012)
13. Kim, S., Oh, S., Suh, J., Yu, K., Yeo, H.: Study on the structure of safety performance indicators for airline companies. In: Proceedings of the Eastern Asia Society for Transportation Studies, pp. 1–17 (2013)

14. McDonald, N., Corrigan, S., Ulfvengren, P., Baranzini, D.: Proactive safety performance for aviation operations. In: Harris, D. (ed.) EPCE 2014. LNCS (LNAI), vol. 8532, pp. 351–362. Springer, Cham (2014). https://doi.org/10.1007/978-3-319-07515-0_36

15. Chang, Y., Shao, P., Chen, H.: Performance evaluation of airport safety management systems in Taiwan. Saf. Sci. **75**, 72–86 (2015)

16. Gander, P., et al.: Effects of sleep/wake history and circadian phase on proposed pilot fatigue safety performance indicators. J. Sleep Res. **24**, 110–119 (2015)

17. Chen, W., Li, J.: Safety performance monitoring and measurement of civil aviation unit. J. Air Transp. Manag. **57**, 228–233 (2016)

18. MacLean, L., Richman, A., MacLean, S.: Benchmarking airports with specific safety performance measures. Transp. Res. A **92**, 349–364 (2016)

19. Panagopoulos, I., Atkin, C., Sikora, I.: Developing a performance indicators lean-sigma framework for measuring aviation system's safety performance. Transp. Res. Procedia **22**, 35–44 (2017)

20. Sun, Y., Luo, M., Chen, Y., Sun, C.: Safety performance evaluation model for airline flying fleets. In: Duffy, V.G. (ed.) DHM 2017. LNCS, vol. 10287, pp. 384–396. Springer, Cham (2017). https://doi.org/10.1007/978-3-319-58466-9_34

21. Sun, Y., Zhang, Y., Zhao, R., Chen, Y.: Safety performance evaluation for civil aviation maintenance department. In: Duffy, Vincent G. (ed.) DHM 2018. LNCS, vol. 10917, pp. 635–646. Springer, Cham (2018). https://doi.org/10.1007/978-3-319-91397-1_52

22. Netjasov, F., Crnogorac, D., Pavlovic, G.: Potential safety occurrences as indicators of air traffic management safety performance: a network based simulation model. Transp. Res. C-Emerg. **102**, 490–508 (2019)

23. Thekdi, S., Aven, T.: An enhanced data-analytic framework for integrating risk management and performance management. Reliab. Eng. Syst. Saf. **156**, 277–287 (2016)

24. Rong, M., Luo, M., Chen, Y.: The research of airport operational risk alerting model. In: Duffy, Vincent G.G. (ed.) DHM 2016. LNCS, vol. 9745, pp. 586–595. Springer, Cham (2016). https://doi.org/10.1007/978-3-319-40247-5_59

25. Boelen, A., Van Aalst, R., Karanikas, N., Kaspers, S., Piric, S., De Boer, R.J.: Effectiveness of risk controls as indicators of safety performance. Aup Adv. **1**(1), 175–189 (2018)

26. Louvar, J.: Guidance for safety performance indicators. Process Saf. Prog. **29**, 387–388 (2010)

27. Gupta, J.P., Edwards, D.W.: Inherently safer design-present and future. Process Saf. Environ. **80**, 115–125 (2002)

Enabling or Stressing? – Smart Information Use Within Industrial Service Operation

Katja Gutsche[⊠] and Carsten Droll

Furtwangen University, Robert-Gerwig Platz 1, 78120 Furtwangen, Germany
Katja.gutsche@hs-furtwangen.de

Abstract. Industrial services as i.e. maintenance are essential for asset-intensive industries. Just as the physical assets become smarter, there is also a change towards digitalization within the workplaces of service technicians. Within service operation, automation scenarios are constantly increasing. No doubt, this will influence the sociotechnical system of service technician, asset and service tools. Research on the effect of digitalized work processes in the field of industrial service are rudimentary, especially its effect on occupational safety and health.

In the context of technological adjustments, the paper focuses on short-term effects on Occupational safety and health (OSH) with special regard towards changes in the mental workload. Under the use of the NASA-TLX the paper sums up the results of an empirical study comparing paper-based vs. Augmented-Reality-based work instructions. How the increase in human-machine interactions work as stressors or enablers seen from the perspective of service technicians will be analyzed.

Keywords: Service technician · AR work instruction · Mental workload

1 Smart Service Operation

1.1 Augmented-Reality

Augmented Reality (AR) is a technical option very much hyped for industrial use. AR is the form of Mixed Reality, where virtual content as computer generated virtual objects or environments is blended into the real world [1, 2]. The user therefore stays connected to the real world which is mandatory for service operation. For industrial service operation AR allows an interactive way of presenting i.e. maintenance information along the service procedure, typically under the use of smartphone, tablet or Head-Mounted-Displays (HMD). It is a new way for equipment manufacturers to deliver maintenance instructions for maintenance specialists and/or equipment users [3]. AR seems a promising tool to ensure a proper, quick and safe maintenance fulfillment and may enrich a service technicians' workplace with modern technique.

However fundamental research on the positive or negative, on the enabling or stressing effects of AR use within service operation is missing. Research of AR-use in typical manufacturing tasks as i.e. show positive effects of AR use [4, 5] But does AR ease the

© Springer Nature Switzerland AG 2020
V. G. Duffy (Ed.): HCII 2020, LNCS 12199, pp. 119–129, 2020.
https://doi.org/10.1007/978-3-030-49907-5_9

work circumstances and therefore supports a safe and healthy workplace and increases performance for service technicians? To find about this, the authors executed a first experimental study comparing differences in workload, performance and operational safety when using paper-based work instructions vs. AR-based work instructions within a maintenance scenario.

1.2 Industrial Service Operation

Industrial services must assure a safe, economic and compliant operation of industrial assets as i.e. paper mills, power plants or trains. As there is an increase of automation and human-computer-interaction in the asset operation, there are comparable changes within the service operation of these assets. Smart technologies as i.e. Head-Mounted-Displays, exoskeletons or smart gloves are promising tools to lower work strains [6]. However, the effects of automation on workplace, OSH and work motivation are even more relevant in the industrial service domain. Due to a low level of repetitive tasks and heterogeneous, highly customized service operation, the human worker will not be completely replaced. Therefore, studying the effects of automation on industrial service technicians is of long-term interest.

Work instructions play an important role for a safe, successful service operation because

- As the variety of problems due to an increase of physical assets (i.e. manufacturing machines) and asset properties (i.e. programming language, functionality) increases the number of customer-driven service tasks for which the technicians has to look for instructions increases.
- Another phenomenon in some regions and industrial service sectors is the employment of low-qualified workers for whom work-instructions are the only way to fulfil the service task.
- Industrial service technicians often have to work in a more hazardous work environment. Safety instructions coming along the work steps are sometimes numerous, must be confirmed by the technician and filed by the employer.

AR offers a smart information providence supporting the service technicians. AR-working instructions give an automated step-by-step guidance depending on the service object and previous working steps. It can be understood as a solution with a low level of automation (LOA) [7, 8]. Through the use of object recognition the technician gets detailed, accurately fitting information helping to fulfil the work routine which the technician confirms and executes. Following Parasuraman and colleagues' (2000), the third LOA (out of 10) is therefore implemented [7].

In comparison, within paper-based work instructions the technician must decide on himself which information is relevant in each working step. There is no situation-adapted automated information providence.

AR-use is a form of human-computer-interaction, where a change in workplace, its procedures and safety issues are to be expected.

1.3 Workload and OSH

Workload is the entirety of all requirements and external conditions at a workplace, which could influence a person physically and/ or psychologically [9]. Workload defines the strain of a task. Both can be understood as synonyms. Within the NASA-TLX the identified components of workload are mental, physical, temporal demand, effort, performance and frustration level [10]. Especially mental workload is of interest in industrial service operation. Heterogeneous work conditions defined trough differences in the assets, the customer requirements and an increase in asset complexity causes mental strain. Temporal demand is as well typical for service operation. In addition, service technicians' workplaces are typically noisier and dustier [11].

Mental workload is seen as the sum of all external parameters influencing the employee mentally [12] and is described as "the degree or percentage of the operator's information processing capacity which is expended in meeting system demands" [13]. Operational features causing mental workload are amongst others

- Lack or overflow of information
- Difficulties in information acquisition
- Conflicting task assignment
- Work discontinuity [14].

Mental workload has a direct input on the task output (Fig. 1.) This is defined by the work quality in relation to the time needed for fulfillment [15]. Service quality is defined by a reliability, assurance, tangibles, empathy and responsiveness [16] and strongly depends on the manpower's capabilities [17]. Therefore service quality incorporates operational safety and health (OSH) as a crucial factor for reliable service operation. OSH can be achieved through (a) good ergonomics, (b) active or passive safety features and (c) personnel qualification and organization. Working instructions have an influence on the personnel qualification and should reduce the effect of the outlined operational features causing mental workload.

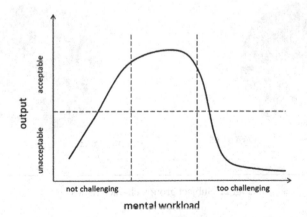

Fig. 1. Output and mental workload [18, 19]

1.4 Hypothesis

If AR has the positive effects on mental load factors and gives automated information on-demand, the following hypothesis are made

H1: AR will cause a significant reduction in the amount of time to complete a service task compared to paper-based work instructions.

H2: The number of errors done by the technician is reduced by using AR compared to paper-based work instructions.

H3: Subjective workload measures indicate a decrease in mental workload for the technicians

H4: The positive effects are appreciated more by younger workers.

H5: Safety instructions are followed better by the use of AR.

2 Study

This study took place January 2020. In total, 20 subjects took part - all of them non-service-technicians in real life. The subjects were grouped in two – paper and AR. The two groups showed the following age and gender characteristics (Fig. 2). Gender and age were selected corresponding to the characteristics in real world, where female technicians are rare [11].

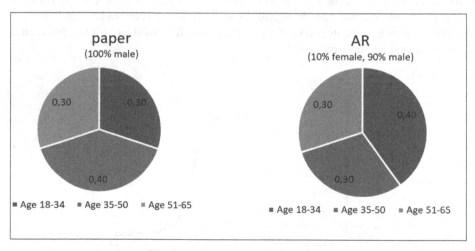

Fig. 2. Subject groups characteristics

The survey included the NASA-TLX by Hart et al. [10], time, quality and safety observations, and demographic variables. The subjects were asked to rate all six demand categories (mental, physical, temporal, effort, performance and frustration) using a 100-point scale. The subjects were then asked to perform pair-wise comparisons to give an individual feedback on which of the load categories of the TLX are more important. The rates of each category and the result of the pair-wise comparisons lead to a mean weighted workload score – the overall task load index.

2.1 Experimental Setting

20 subjects were asked to repair a chain saw whose starter pull cord has been broken (Fig. 3). They were asked to fulfill the task as quick as possible. None of the subjects had ever done this repair before. 10 test persons were asked to fulfil the repair scenario under the help of a printed work-instruction, 10 persons could use the help of an AR-work-instruction installed on the Microsoft Hololens®.

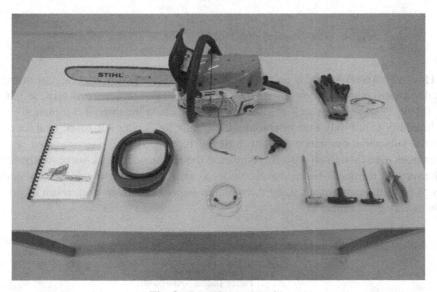

Fig. 3. Experimental setting

7 out of 10 subjects who used the AR-implementation had no experience with AR at all, 3 had low experience. All 10 got a brief introduction in how to use the Hololens® and were asked to go through the gesture control app preinstalled on the Hololens® by Microsoft.

2.2 Findings

Time of Completion. Time of completion is a crucial factor evaluating service output. In general, while service is done, the industrial asset is not available. Unavailability means financial loss due to reduced earnings. Remarkable, the average time of completion using AR-based work instructions is about 35% less compared to subjects using paper-based work instructions (Fig. 4).

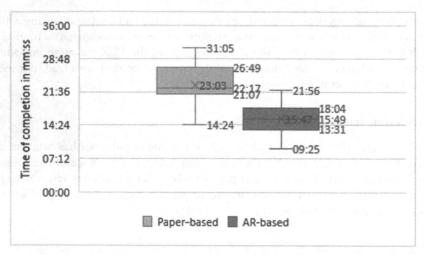

Fig. 4. Effect of instructional medium on time of completion.

However, ANOVAs (using an alpha level of 0, 05) comparing the effect of instructional medium on time of completion showed no statistical significance, F(1,18) = 3,265, p = 0,199. The age has as well no significant influence on the time of completion.

In addition, not only time of completion is a lot less using AR-based instructions, also the subjective evaluation on how well the repair process was completed shows differences even though all subjects completed the maintenance task successfully. 80% of the subjects using AR-based instructions rated their work result as good or very-good, only 50% of the participants using the medium paper rated their work result as good, none as very good (Table 1).

Table 1. Subjective feedback on how well task was fulfilled

	Paper-based	AR-based
Very good	0	2
Good	5	6
Medium	5	3
Bad	0	0
Very bad	0	0

Workload. There is a noticeable difference in mental workload between the two mediums. Descriptive statistics show an average mental workload of 56 when using paper-based instructions compared to 27, 5 (Fig. 5). A one-way ANOVA shows a statistically significant effect of instructional medium on mental workload, F(1,18) = 13,048, p = 0,571. Due to the interference of computer-generated overlaid, animated objects, it is of less cognitive demand to find out about what is meant by the working steps and which parts and tools are needed.

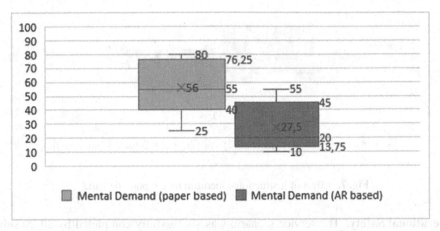

Fig. 5. Effect of instructional medium on mental workload

A one-way ANOVA on the effect of age on mental workload showed no statistical significance. However, Post hoc comparisons showed that there is a statistically significant effect between 'age group < 35' and 'age group > 50' (p = 0,085).

For the overall TLX there is still a difference in favor for the AR-based work instructions (Fig. 6), however this difference is not statistically significant, $F(1,18) = 3,884$, p = 0,875. This is mainly because besides the mental workload there is only a noticeable, but not statistically significant difference in temporal demand (Fig. 7). The other four demand categories are very much independent of the used medium.

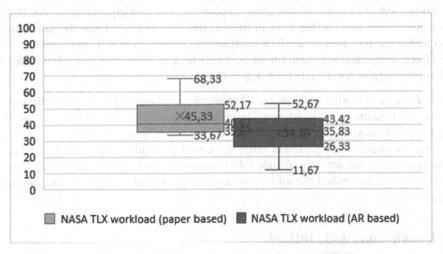

Fig. 6. Effect of instructional medium on overall TLX

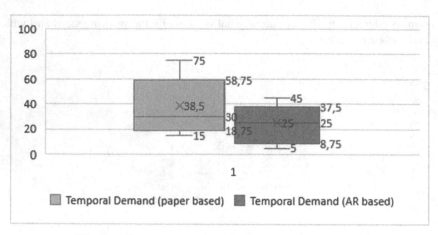

Fig. 7. Effect of instructional medium on temporal demand

Operational Safety. The service scenario was successfully completed by all 20 subjects. However, only during the use of the paper-based instruction most subjects needed help by the instructors (8 out of 10 subjects) as they were unsure in certain steps. As with the chain saw a realistic object was used, the instructors interfered in cases where there was a potential risk to damage the chain saw. In AR computer-generated instructions are overlaid to the real object. This makes it much easier to figure out correct positions, orientations, parts and tools (compare mental workload). None of the subjects got a technical instruction to the chain saw. But the noticeable difference in queries show that the level of safety relevant knowledge is higher after the same time when instructed by AR compared to paper-based work instructed. The findings underline previous research where it is stated that AR applications "are cheaper and more efficient ways to enhance human safety" [20]. AR allows a better safety relevant qualification in shorter period of time for untrained employees. The participants using AR-based work instructions declared the work-instruction much more helpful than the participants who had to use paper-based work instructions. A one-way ANOVA was conducted on the effect of instructional medium on how helpful the instruction was. The effect is statistically significant, $F(1,18) = 6,4$, $p = 0,913$.

Safety Devices. Looking at the usage of protective clothing as passive OSH measurements, no differences could be seen. In both groups 60% of all subjects put on the required safety devices gloves and glasses. AR-use seems to have no influence - neither positive nor negative - on the use of safety devices. This result is unexpected as the AR-work instruction did not only include safety information like in the paper-based work instruction, but also asked the subjects to confirm the information by gesture or voice command.

3   Conclusions and Outlook

AR-based work instruction can be understood as an enabling technology in service operation. Service output defined as the work quality in relation to the time needed for fulfillment is enhanced. Even though paper-based work instructions are well established and standardized, AR offers a big advantage for untrained staff as task-relevant information is overlaid to the physical object. Uncertainty in what and how to do each service step does not arise. Time of completion and mental workload are reduced by AR-based assistance. The self-assessment regarding the task output, a potential motivator, is more positive. However, AR implemented even in the MS Hololens®, as one of the most advanced solution available right now, still has some obstacles hindering the technician in the tool use: (a) the field of view of MS Hololens® 1 is very small – the user finds it difficult to see all animations and the control panel in the field of view at the same time, (b) the weight of the HMD (579 grams) is heavy for long-term use - some subjects felt pain after a short period of time of approximately 20 min.

AR can be a good alternative to the well-established but rather laborious printed handbooks. Looking at the hypothesis, following conclusions can be made from this study:

H1 may be neglected. There is evidence that AR causes a significant reduction in the amount of time to complete a service task compared to paper-based work instructions. However, the effect is not statistically significant. Further research and a bigger sample should be done for verification.

H2 may be neglected. No subject did an error, all completed the repair process successfully. However, the number of queries is significantly higher in the paper-based instructed work. Without the interference by the instructors the number of errors is expected to be much higher in the paper-instructed service operation. For further studies adoption in the scenario should be made.

H3 is confirmed. There is a significant decrease in mental workload for the technicians using AR-based work instructions.

H4 is confirmed. The positive effects are appreciated more by younger workers. The participants younger than 35 had a significant lower mental workload then the ones older than 50 years old.

H5 must be neglected. Safety instructions are not followed better by the use of AR. Even the necessity to confirm safety instructions didn't lead to a higher degree of safety device use. In addition, as all subjects completed the work task successfully, there is no direct effect on OSH by an observed decrease in the number of errors. However, if instruction are understood as a safety tool, AR is much more appreciated then paper-based work instructions.

This study has only looked at the changes from printed to AR-based work instructions. For further research, video instructions as a reasonable, wide-spread option should be included in an evaluation on how smart information use within industrial service operation causes positive and/or negative effects in the technician's workplace.

Further did this study only focus on short-term effects. Long-term effects also with regard to the customer who normally is somehow involved in the service operation has been left aside for this study.

In addition, further research should address possible influences on work motivation coming along with smart information use in service operation. As service performance increases, there might be a positive long-term effect on work motivation leading to many more effects than the ones looked at within this paper.

Notes. As the study is based on a realistic maintenance scenario, the results have to be understood as a comparison between (A) the standardized, well-established medium paper-based work instruction, which was provided by the manufacturer and is so far used for the chain saw maintenance and (B) a prototypic, non-standardized AR-based work instruction whose animated information sequences are based on the paper work instruction.

References

1. Milgram, P., Colquhoun, H.: Mixed Reality-Merging Real and Virtual Worlds. Springer, New York (1999)
2. Barfield, W., Caudell, T.: Basic concepts in wearable computers and augmented reality. In: Barfield, W., Caudell, T. (eds.) Fundamentals of Wearable Computers and Augmented Reality. Lawrence Erlbaum Associates, Publishers, Mahwah (2001)
3. Droll, C., Gutsche, K., Kaesemann, F., Koristka, K.: Mixed reality within maintenance support services – a user-centered design approach. In: eMaintenance, Sweden, Stockholm (2019)
4. Tang, A., Owen, C., Biocca, F., Mou, W.: Comparative effectiveness of augmented reality in object assembly. In: Bellotti, V., Erickson, T., Cockton, G., Korhonen, P. (eds.) Proceedings of the Conference on Human Factors in Computing Systems, CHI 2003, pp. 73–80, Ft. Lauderdale (2003)
5. Blattgerste, J., Strenge, B., Renner, P., Pfeiffer, T., Essig, K.: Comparing conventional and augmented reality instructions for manual assembly tasks. In: PETRA 2017 Proceedings of the 10th International Conference on PErvasive Technologies Related to Assistive Environments, pp. 75–82 (2017)
6. Robelski, S.: Psychische Gesundheit in der Arbeitswelt - Mensch-Maschine-Interaktion. Bundesanstalt für Arbeitsschutz und Arbeitsmedizin (2016)
7. Parasuraman, R., Sheridan, T.B., Wickens, C.D.: A model of types and levels of human interaction with automation. IEEE Trans. Syst. Man Cybern. **30**, 286–297 (2000)
8. Sheridan, T.B.: Adaptive automation, level of automation, allocation authority, supervisory control, and adaptive control: Distinctions and modes of adaptation. IEEE Trans. Syst. Man Cybern. Part A Syst. Hum. **41**(4), 662–667 (2011)
9. Anderson, J.R.: Kognitive Psychologie, 7th edn. Springer, Heidelberg (2013)
10. Hart, S.G., Staveland, L.E..: Development of NASA-TLX (task load index): result of empirical and theoretical research. In: Hancook, P.A., Meshkati, N. (eds.) Human Mental Workload. North Holland Press, Amsterdam (1988)
11. Gutsche, K., Griffith, J.: Automating motivation: a workplace analysis of service technicians and the motivational impact of automated assistance. In: Hara, Y., Karagiannis, D. (eds.) Serviceology for Services, pp. 101–108 Springer (2017). https://doi.org/10.1007/978-3-319-61240-9_10
12. DIN EN ISO 10075-3: Ergonomische Grundlagen bezüglich psychischer Arbeitsbelastung, Beuth, Berlin (2018)
13. Eggemeier, F.T., O'Donnell, R.D.: A conceptual framework for development of a workload assessment methodology: text of remarks made at the 1982 American Psychological Association Annual Meeting. Wright State University, Dayton (1982)
14. Kern, P., Schmauder, M.: Einführung in den Arbeitsschutz, Hanser Verlag (2005)

15. VDI 4006 Part 1: Human Reliability Ergonomic requirements and methods of assessment. Beuth, Berlin (2002)
16. Parasuraman, A., Zeithaml, V., Berry, L.: SERVQUAL: a multiple-item scale for measuring consumer perception of service quality. J. Retail. **64**(1), 12–40 (1988)
17. Gutsche, K.: Sustainable factor input in product-service operation. In: Boucher, X., Brissaud, D. (eds.) 7th Industrial Product-Service Systems Conference, Procedia CIRP 30, pp. 144–148. Elsevier (2015)
18. Schlick, C., Bruder, R., Luczak, H.: Arbeitswissenschaft. Springer, Heidelberg (2010)
19. Johannsen, G.: Mensch-Maschine-Systeme. Springer, Heidelberg (1993). https://doi.org/10.1007/978-3-642-46785-1
20. Agrawal, A., Acharya, G., Balasubramanian, K., Agrawal, N., Chaturvedi, R.: A review on the use of augmented reality to generate safety awareness and enhance emergency response. Int. J. Curr. Eng. Technol. **6**(3), 813–820 (2016)

Improving the Performance in Occupational Health and Safety Management in the Electric Sector: An Integrated Methodology Using Fuzzy Multicriteria Approach

Genett Jimenez-Delgado[1]([✉]), Alexa Senior-Naveda[2], Freddy Marín-Gonzalez[2], Jesus García-Guiliany[3], Lina Fontalvo-Molina[1], Miguel Ruiz-Muñoz[1], Hugo Hernández-Palma[4], and Bertha Santos-Hernandez[5]

[1] Department of Engineering in Industrial Processes, Engineering Faculty, Institucion Universitaria ITSA, Soledad, Atlántico, Colombia
{gjimenez,linapfontalvo,mjruiz}@itsa.edu.co
[2] Faculty of Human and Social Sciences, Universidad de la Costa CUC, Barranquilla, Colombia
{asenior,fmarin}@cuc.edu.co
[3] Faculty of Administration and Business, Universidad Simón Bolívar, Barranquilla, Colombia
jesus.garcia@unisimonbolivar.edu.co
[4] Economic Sciences Faculty, Program, Corporación Universitaria Latinoamericana CUL, Barranquilla, Colombia
hugoghernandezpalma@gmail.com
[5] Department of Business Administration and Marketing, Universidad Tecnologica del Retoño, Aguascalientes, Mexico
bertha.santos@utr.edu.mx

Abstract. The electric sector is fundamental for the economic and social development of society, impacting on essential aspects such as health, education, employment generation, industrial production, and the provision of various services. In addition to the above, the growing trend in energy consumption worldwide could increase, according to expert estimates, up to 40% by 2030, which in turn increases the efforts of the public and private sector to meet increasing demands and increase access to energy services under requirements of reliability and quality. However, the electricity sector presents challenges and complexities, one of which is the reduction of health and safety risks for workers, service users, and other stakeholders. In many countries, this sector is classified as high risk in occupational safety and health, due to its complexity and the impact of accidents and occupational diseases on the health of workers, in infrastructure, in operating costs and competitiveness of the energy sector. Worldwide, there are rigorous regulations for the electricity sector, from local and national government regulations to international standards to guarantee health and safety conditions. However, it is necessary to develop objective and comprehensive methodologies for evaluating occupational safety and health performance that provides solutions for the electricity sector, not only to comply with standards and regulations also as a continuous improvement tool that supports the decision-making processes given the complexity of the industry and the multiple criteria that are taken into account when evaluating and establishing improvement strategies. In scientific

V. G. Duffy (Ed.): HCII 2020, LNCS 12199, pp. 130–158, 2020.
https://doi.org/10.1007/978-3-030-49907-5_10

literature, different studies focus on the analysis of accident statistics, the factors that affect accidents and occupational diseases, and the risk assessment of the sector. Despite these considerations, studies that focus directly on the development of hybrid methodologies for the evaluation and improvement of performance in occupational safety and health in the electrical sector, under multiple criteria and uncertainty are mostly limited. Therefore, this document presents an integrated methodology for improving the performance in occupational health and safety in the electric sector through the application of two techniques of Multi-criteria Decision Methods (MCDM) uses in environments under uncertainly. First, the fuzzy Analytic Hierarchy Process (FAHP) is applied to estimate the initial relative weights of criteria and sub-criteria. The fuzzy set theory is incorporated to represent the uncertainty of decision-makers' preferences. Then, the Decision-making Trial and Evaluation Laboratory (DEMATEL) used for evaluating the interrelations and feedback among criteria and sub-criteria. FAHP and DEMATEL are later combined for calculating the final criteria and sub-criteria weights under vagueness and interdependence. Subsequently, we applied the proposed methodology in a company of the energy sector for diagnosis of performance in OHS to establish improvement proposals, the work path, and implementation costs. Finally, we evaluate the impact of the strategies applied in the improvement of the performance of the company.

Keywords: Fuzzy analytical hierarchy process · Fuzzy AHP · Multicriteria decision making · MCMD · DEMATEL · Occupational health and safety · ISO 45001 · Electric sector · Performance evaluation

1   Introduction

According to the World Bank (2018), the energy sector is a driver of investments, technological development, innovation, and new industries, with an impact on job creation, economic, social growth and the contribution to the Development Goals Sustainable UN 7 - affordable and non-polluting energy, 8 - decent work and economic growth, 9 - industry, innovation and infrastructure, and 11 - Sustainable cities and communities [1]. The energy sector faces new challenges such as a 30% growth in energy demand and, therefore, in the generation, transmission and distribution capabilities of operating companies, the search for new and better sources of energy, the decrease of environmental impacts and occupational health and safety risks for interested parties [2]. Regarding occupational safety and health, it is of high relevance for the competitiveness of the sector due to the complexity in their operations, the regulation, and control of the government, customers, and other stakeholders involved in the energy chain. In this sense, the energy sector is considered as high risk at the Occupational health and safety level, due to the potential risk of accidents and occupational diseases and the seriousness of the damage caused. Given that the circumstances surrounding this type of accident can have an impact on the welfare and health of workers and interested parties, on infrastructure, operational costs and the results of companies in the sector [3].

Following the International Labor Organization, aggregate statistics indicate a general increase in the number of people who died by causes attributable to work from

2.33 million in 2014 to 2.78 million in 2017. In the energy sector, electrical accidents represent a high number of worldwide [4–7]. This situation increases in countries in Africa and Latin America. In Colombia, for example, the energy sector registered for 2017 the fourth-highest accident rate, with an average of 7.33 accidents. Among the leading causes attributable to accidents in the energy sector, there are insecure behaviors [8], deficiencies in training, training, and awareness in safety and self-help culture and shortcomings in the implementation of comprehensive management systems focused on prevention and in the welfare of workers [9–13].

In the literature review, different studies have been carried out to contributes to the analysis, development, and implementation of methodologies and techniques focused on the prevention of accidents and occupational diseases in the energy sector. In this regard, we found different works oriented to analysis of personal factors and consequences of electrical occupational accidents [3], time series analysis of occupational accidents and the assessment of risks applied to the energy and construction industry [14], the longitudinal descriptive study of occupational accidents and their causes [15] as well as the analysis of occupational safety and health in hydroelectric plants [16], photovoltaic industry [17] and energy supply companies [18]. Although several efforts have been made to address this problem, the evidence base is still scant and with scarce information, especially in the develop of integrated multicriteria decision-making methodologies to evaluate and improve the performance in the prevention of accidents and occupational diseases in energy sector, where previous studies have been found in the logistics industry [19].

This paper bridges this gap by extending the multi-criteria decision-making approach adopted in land cargo transportation [19] to improve the performance in Occupational Health and Safety Management in the energy sector. First, the fuzzy Analytic Hierarchy Process (FAHP) is applied to estimate the initial relative weights of criteria and sub-criteria. The fuzzy set theory is incorporated to represent the uncertainty of decision-makers' preferences. Then, the Decision-making Trial and Evaluation Laboratory (DEMATEL) is used for evaluating the interrelations and feedback among criteria and sub-criteria. FAHP and DEMATEL are later combined for calculating the final criteria and sub-criteria weights under vagueness and interdependence. Subsequently, we applied the proposed methodology in a company of the energy sector for diagnosis of performance in OHS to establish improvement proposals, the work path, and implementation costs. Finally, we evaluate the impact of the strategies applied in the improvement of the performance of the company.

A real case study considering four criteria, 23 sub-criteria, six decision-makers, and an instrument for the diagnosis of the occupational health and safety management is presented to validate the proposed approach. The results revealed that the criteria planning (58.9%), improvement (15.0%), and application (14.3%) have the most significant weight in the evaluation of occupational health and safety performance in the context of the energy company. Also, we found strong interrelations among criteria and sub-criteria with an impact on the performance evaluation in the adoption of the OHS management. On the other hand, we evaluated the changes and improvement of the company between the initial diagnosis, and the implementation of the action plans one year later. The outcomes of this evaluation evidenced a significant increase in the level of compliance in occupational health and safety management, going from 14% to 88% compliance, with an impact on the reduction in the indicators of accidents and absenteeism in work company results, increasing its sales by 43.8%. Considering the previous results, this integrated methodology facilitates the decision-making process managers in the energy sector for the improvement in the management of occupational health and safety.

2 Approaches of MCDM for Occupational Health and Safety Performance Evaluation in Electric Sector: A Literature Review

Occupational health and safety (OHS) is a multidisciplinary activity that focuses on the analysis of improving the conditions of workers in their workplaces, to reduce the number of accidents and occupational diseases, increase productivity, the commitment of workers and the competitiveness of companies [20, 21]. The previous implies that companies must adopt different standards and methodologies to manage health and safety in their work environments. Concerning the implementation of standards in OHS, for the electricity sector, it is even more relevant, given their complexity and the high risk that this industry poses in the safety and health of workers, users, and other stakeholders.

One of the critical elements in occupational safety and health management is related to performance evaluation, which according to ISO 45001 [22], is performance related to the effectiveness of the prevention of injuries and deterioration of health for workers and the provision of safe and healthy workplaces. In this sense, performance evaluation includes aspects such as compliance with legal requirements, risk and risk assessment, progress in achieving objectives, goals, and indicators in OHS, and the effectiveness of operational controls.

Concerning the evaluation of performance in OHS, it is in itself a complicated process, where different stakeholders intervene with their needs, expectations, and judgments (workers, managers, clients, government, suppliers, among others) multiple criteria to the time to evaluate, and uncertainty environments that make it difficult to establish the most appropriate actions in the prevention of accidents and occupational diseases. In this sense, there are different qualitative and qualitative methodologies that companies can use to identify gaps in performance, their causes and establish improvement actions, such as the cause-effect or Ishikawa diagram, the 5 W and 2H technique, the time series analyses, the risk assessment matrices, among others. However, multi-criteria decision-making (MCDM) based approaches can help companies in the electricity sector to learn about the evaluation of their performance, in real environments, with multiple criteria, and under uncertainty environments in organizations.

Regarding the object of this research, we found in the literature review evidence of studies oriented to apply the Multicriteria Decision Methods (MCDM) in occupational health and safety management (OHS). In this regard, we found a study that develops a critical state-of-the-art review of OHS risk assessment studies using MCDM-based approaches, includes fuzzy versions of MCDM approaches applied to OHS risk assessment [20]. The results of this study, which analyzed a total of 80 papers cited in high-impact journals, demonstrated the growing trend in the use of MCDM in the evaluation of risks, especially in the use of FAHP-based approaches, with application mainly in the industrial sector. On the other hand, the study identifies that methods such as VIKOR,

PROMETHEE, ELECTRE, and DEMATEL remain superior methods in risk assessment and management due to their flexibility.

Bibliographic research has shown interesting articles written on the application of support systems for decision-making in occupational safety and health (OHS). Still, little has been published on the evaluation of integral performance in the management of OSH and the complex context of the electrical sector, as seen in Table 1, with the studies found related to an assessment in OHS and the MDCM techniques used.

The articles found focus on the application of MCDM techniques for the evaluation of risks, safety and health conditions, the satisfaction of workers concerning the OHS, but few articles focused on the integral assessment of performance in OHS, that consider the international standard ISO 45001. Besides, the main application sectors of MCDM techniques are mining, and construction, and the literature presents a limited development in the application of the MCDM models applied towards performance evaluation in OHS in the electric sector.

At the level of MDCM techniques, the literature review shows that the most used methods are related to the AHP technique and its extensions, such as Fuzzy AHP, Pythagorean Fuzzy AHP, and Intuitionistic Fuzzy AHP. Besides, the AHP methods can be used in combination with other techniques such as TOPSIS, VIKOR, ELECTRE, and DEMATEL, which gives researchers an open field for the use of hybrid MCDM methodologies according to the reality of the industries.

Concerning to the hybrid MCDM approaches, the combination of different methods allows overcoming the limitations of several techniques to obtain better outcomes [35]. Notably, the AHP method has the disadvantage of the phenomenon known as "reversal rank" related to the change of preference or order after an alternative is added or removed [36]. Concerning other methods such as the Technique for Order Preference by Similarity to Ideal Solution" (TOPSIS) do not provide an explicit procedure to allocate the relative importance of criteria and sub-criteria [37]. Due to the considerations mentioned above, it is necessary to apply a hybrid decision-making model that can consider inaccuracy, uncertainty, and lack of consensus in the judgments of the experts regarding the weights of the criteria and sub-criteria and that analyzes the interrelationships between the evaluation factors.

The novelty of the present study is based on the integration of the FAHP, as an extension of the AHP multi-criteria method with the DEMATEL method to evaluate the performance in occupational health and safety in the electric sector to provide a robust framework for evaluation and improvement in OHS. FAHP was chosen due to its capability of calculating the relative importance of criteria and sub-criteria under uncertainly. On the other hand, we proposed the integration of the DEMATEL method to FAHP. DEMATEL is applied to evaluate interrelations be-tween criteria and sub-criteria [38], helping decision-makers identify the interdependencies between decision factors, receiving and dispatching factors, which allows the design of comprehensive improvement plans.

Therefore, this research contributes to the scientific literature and provides a hybrid methodology for overall performance evaluation in occupational health and safety management and provides to managers procedures and techniques to generate a culture of prevention and healthy environments, through strategic alignment, driving the behavior and performance of people towards the achievement of the strategic objectives of electric sector.

Table 1. Performance evaluation in OHS based in MDCM approaches

Authors (Year)	Sector	Application	Objective	MDCM applied/Other
Inan UH, Gul S, and Yılmaz H. (2017) [21]	Mining, construction, ports	OHS performance	It integrates Simo's procedure and the VIKOR technique to build a multi-criteria decision-making model for OHS performance in companies, considering the OHSAS 18001: 2007 standard	Simo's procedure, VIKOR
Adema, A., Çolak, A., Dağdeviren, M. (2018) [23]	Energy sector	Risk evaluation in OHS	It proposes a methodology for the classification of labor risks for the wind turbine production stages	SWOT and Hesitant fuzzy linguistic term
Efe, B., Kurt, M., and Efe, F. (2017) [24]	Textile sector	Risk evaluation in OHS	It provides an integrated IFAHP-IFVIKOR approach for risk evaluation under group decision making	Intuitionistic fuzzy AHP (IFAHP)-intuitionistic fuzzy VIKOR (IFVIKOR)
Badria, A., Nadeaua, S., and Gbodossoub, A. (2012) [25]	Industrial projects	Risk evaluation in OHS	It proposes a risk-factor-based analytical approach for integrating occupational health and safety into project risk evaluation	AHP, risk evaluation
Jiangdong, B., Johansson, J., and Zhang, J. (2017) [26]	Mining	Employee satisfaction in OHS	It provides an analytic method of Evaluation on Employee Satisfaction of mine Occupational Health and Safety Management System based on improved AHP and 2-Tuple Linguistic Information,	Improved AHP 2-tuple linguistic information
Sadoughi et al. (2012) [27]	Government	Evaluation of performance indicators in OHS	It proposes a comprehensive approach for decision-makers to evaluate and prioritize of performance indicators of health, safety, and environment using Fuzzy TOPSIS	Fuzzy AHP
Gul, M., and Ak, M. (2018) [28]	Mining	Risk assessment in OHS	Provide a novelty and comparative methodology to quantify risk classifications in the assessment of occupational health and safety risks	Pythagorean fuzzy analytic hierarchy process (PFAHP), Fuzzy TOPSIS
Hatami-Marbini et al. (2013) [29]	Hazardous Waste Recycling	Safety and health assessment	Propose a multi-criteria decision making (MCDM) model based on an integrated fuzzy approach in the context of Hazardous Waste Recycling (HWR)	Fuzzy logic, ELECTRE

(continued)

Table 1. (*continued*)

Authors (Year)	Sector	Application	Objective	MDCM applied/Other
Ilbahara, E et al. (2018) [30]	Construction	Risk assessment in OHS	Propose a novel approach to risk assessment for occupational health and safety	Pythagorean fuzzy AHP, fuzzy inference system
Koulinas, G et al. (2019) [31]	Construction	Risk assessment in OHS	Propose a risk analysis and assessment in the worksites using the fuzzy-analytical hierarchy process and a quantitative technique	Fuzzy AHP, Proportional Risk Assessment Technique (PRAT)
Sukran Seker, S., and Zavadskas, E. (2017) [32]	Construction	Risk assessment in OHS	Application of Fuzzy DEMATEL Method for Analyzing Occupational Risks on Construction Sites	Fuzzy DEMATEL
Basahel, A., and Taylan, O (2016) [33]	Construction	Safety conditions assessing	Use of Fuzzy AHP and Fuzzy TOPSIS for Assessing Safety Conditions at Worksites	Fuzzy AHP and Fuzzy TOPSIS
Zheng, G., Zhu, N., Tian, Z., Chen, Y., and Sun, B (2012) [34]	Mining	Safety evaluation	Application of a trapezoidal fuzzy AHP method for work safety evaluation and early warning rating of hot and humid environments	Fuzzy AHP

3   Proposed Methodology

The proposed approach aims to evaluate the performance in occupational health and safety management in the electric sector by the integrated methodology using FAHP and DEMATEL. In this regard, the methodology is comprised of four phases (refer to Fig. 1):

- **Phase 1 (Design of the model for performance evaluation OHS FAHP/DEMATEL):** A decision-making group is chosen based on their experience in occupational health and safety in the electric sector. The experts will be invited to be part of the decision-making process through FAHP and DEMATEL techniques. Subsequently, the criteria and sub-criteria are established to set up a decision hierarchy considering the opinion of the expert decision-makers, the literature review, and regulations in occupational health and safety management [19, 35, 38]. Then, the surveys for the application of the FAHP and DEMATEL methods were designed.
- **Phase 2 (FAHP application):** In this step, FAHP is used to estimate the global and local weights of criteria and sub-criteria under uncertainty in the ponderation. In this phase, the experts were invited to perform pairwise comparisons, which are subsequently processed following the FAHP method, as detailed in Sect. 3.1.

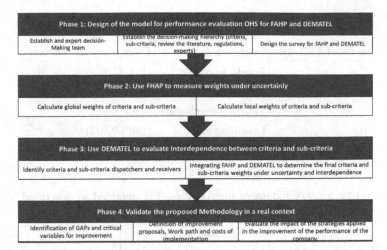

Fig. 1. The methodological approach for evaluating the performance in occupational health and safety management in the electric sector

- **Phase 3 (DEMATEL application):** In this phase, DEMATEL is implemented to determine the interdependence and interrelations between criteria and sub-criteria (described in Sect. 3.2) as well as identify the receivers and dispatchers. Additionally, it is used to assess the strength of each influence relation [35]. Then, FAHP and DEMATEL are combined to obtain the criteria and sub-criteria weights with the basis of interdependence.
- **Phase 4 (Validation of the proposed methodology):** In this step, GAPs and critical variables were identified to improve the performance in OHS management [10, 19, 39]. Subsequently, were defined the improvement proposals, the schedule, and the costs of implementation of strategies. Finally, was evaluated the impact after the implementation of the strategy in the improvement of the performance in OHS, their statistics or accidents, and the revenue of the company.

3.1 Fuzzy Analytic Hierarchy Process (FAHP)

Fuzzy AHP is a derived method of Analytic Hierarchy Process (AHP) proposed by Thomas L. Saaty as combined technique between AHP and fuzzy logic with the purpose of improve the decision-making process due that the AHP method does not consider vagueness of human judgments, the fuzzy logic theory was introduced due to its capability of representing imprecise data [38, 40].

In FAHP, the paired comparisons are represented in a matrix using fuzzy triangular numbers [41] as described below (Refer to Table 2). Considering the findings from the literature review, a reduced AHP scale has been adopted by the decision-makers when making comparisons [38].

The steps of the FAHP algorithm as follows.

- Step 1: Perform pairwise comparisons between criteria/sub-criteria by using the linguistic terms and the corresponding fuzzy triangular numbers established in Table 2.

Table 2. Linguistic terms and their fuzzy triangular numbers

Reduced AHP scale	Definition	Fuzzy triangular number
1	Equally important	[1, 1, 1]
3	More important	[2–4]
5	Much more important	[4–6]
1/3	Less important	[1/4, 1/3, 1/2]
1/5	Much less important	[1/6, 1/5, 1/4]

With this data, a fuzzy judgment matrix $\tilde{A}^k(a_{ij})$ is obtained as described below in Eq. 1:

$$\tilde{A}^K = \begin{bmatrix} \tilde{d}_{11}^k & \tilde{d}_{12}^k & \cdots & \tilde{d}_{1n}^k \\ \tilde{d}_{21}^k & \tilde{d}_{22}^k & \cdots & \tilde{d}_{2n}^k \\ \cdots & \cdots & \cdots & \cdots \\ \tilde{d}_{n1}^k & \tilde{d}_{n2}^k & \cdots & \tilde{d}_{nn}^k \end{bmatrix} \tag{1}$$

$\tilde{d}_{ij}^k$ indicates the *kth* expert's preference of *ith* criterion over *jth* criterion via fuzzy triangular numbers.

– Step 2: In the case of a focus group, the judgments are averaged according to Eq. 2, where K represents the number of experts involved in the decision-making process. Then, the fuzzy judgment matrix is updated, as shown in Eq. 3.

$$\tilde{d}_{ij} = \frac{\sum_{k=1}^{K} \tilde{d}_{ij}^k}{K} \tag{2}$$

$$\tilde{A} = \begin{bmatrix} \tilde{d}_{11} & \cdots & \tilde{d}_{1n} \\ \vdots & \ddots & \vdots \\ \tilde{d}_{n1} & \cdots & \tilde{d}_{nn} \end{bmatrix} \tag{3}$$

– Step 3: Calculate the geometric mean of fuzzy judgment values of each factor by using Eq. 4. Here, $\tilde{r}_i$ denotes triangular numbers.

$$\tilde{r}_i = \left(\prod_{j=1}^{n} \tilde{d}_{ij} \right)^{1/n}, i = 1, 2, \ldots, n \tag{4}$$

– Step 4: Determine the fuzzy weights of each factor ($\tilde{w}_i$) by applying Eq. 5.

$$\tilde{w}_i = \tilde{r}_i \otimes (\tilde{r}_1 \oplus \tilde{r}_2 \oplus \ldots \oplus \tilde{r}_n)^{-1} = (lw_i, mw_i, uw_i) \tag{5}$$

– Step 5: Defuzzify ($\tilde{w}_i$) by performing the Centre of Area method [42] via using Eq. 6. M_i is a non-fuzzy number. Then, normalize M_i via applying Eq. 7.

$$M_i = \frac{lw_i + mw_i + uw_i}{3} \tag{6}$$

$$N_i = \frac{M_i}{\sum_{i=1}^{n} M_i} \tag{7}$$

3.2 Decision Making Trial and Evaluation Laboratory (DEMATEL)

DEMATEL is an MCDM technique applied to identify the complex causal relationships between criteria and sub-criteria involved in a multicriteria decision model [43]. DEMATEL it´s based on the graph theory, and the outcome is a visual representation called impact-digraph map that categorizes the criteria into two groups: dispatchers and receivers [44]. Dispatchers are the criteria or sub-criteria that highly influence other criteria or sub-criteria, while the receivers are the affected criteria or sub-criteria [38]. Additionally, the DEMATEL method indicates the influence degree of each element so that significant interdependencies can be identified [46].

The procedure of DEMATEL method is given as follows [38]:

- Step 1: Make the matrix of direct influence: The decision-makers are asked to make comparisons between criteria/sub-criteria to measure their causal relationship. For this, the experts, based on their personal experience, point out the direct impact that each element i exerts on each of the other elements j using this four-level comparison scale: nonexistent impact (0), low impact (1), medium impact (2), high impact (3) and very high impact (4). With these comparisons, an average n x n matrix called the direct relationship matrix is generated. In this matrix, each element bij represents the average degree to which the criterion/sub-criterion i affect the criterion/sub-criterion j.

- Step 2: Normalize the direct influence matrix: The normalized direct relation matrix N is calculated using Eq. 8–9:

$$N = k \cdot B \tag{8}$$

$$k = min \left(\frac{1}{\max_{1 \le i < n} \sum_{j=1}^{n} |b_{ij}|}, \frac{1}{\max_{1 \le j < n} \sum_{i=1}^{n} |b_{ij}|} \right) i, j \in \{1, 2, 3, \ldots, n\} \tag{9}$$

- Step 3: Obtain the total relation matrix: After normalizing the direct relation matrix N, the total relation matrix S is obtained by implementing Eq. 10, where I is the identity matrix:

$$S = N + N^2 + N^3 + \ldots = \sum_{i=1}^{\infty} N^i = N(I - N)^{-1} \tag{10}$$

- Step 4: Develop a causal diagram: Using the $D + R$ and $D - R$ values, where R_i represents the sum of the $j - th$ column of the matrix S (see Eq. 11–12) and D_i represents the sum of the $i - th$ row of the matrix S (see Eq. 11 and Eq. 13), dispatchers and receivers can be identified. Criteria/Sub-criteria with positive values of D-R, have a strong influence on the other criteria/sub-criteria, and are called dispatchers. The negative values of $D - R$ indicate that the criteria/sub-criteria are very influenced by others (receivers). Besides, the $D + R$ values indicate the degree to which the criteria/sub-criteria i affect or are affected by others.

$$S = [s_{ij}]_{nxn}, i, j \in \{1, 2, 3, \ldots, n\} \tag{11}$$

$$R = \sum_{j=1}^{n} s_{ij} \tag{12}$$

$$D = \sum_{i=1}^{n} s_{ij} \tag{13}$$

- Step 5: Establish the threshold value and obtain impact-digraph map: The threshold value is calculated to identify the significant interrelationships between criteria or sub-criteria (see Eq. 14). If the influence degree of a criterion/sub-criterion in the matrix S is bigger than the threshold value (p), then this criterion/sub-criterion is included in the map of impact digraphs. This graph is done by assigning the data set $(D + R, D - R)$.

$$p = \frac{\sum_{i=1}^{n} \sum_{j=1}^{n} s_{ij}}{n^2} \tag{14}$$

3.3 The FAHP-DEMATEL Method

A combined FAHP-DEMATEL method is suggested to offer more robust results [45]. The mixed technique tackles the drawbacks of FAHP, which is not capable of assessing the feedback and interdependence among decision elements. It is, therefore, necessary to complement it with DEMATEL, which can help occupational health and safety professionals to design short, medium- and long-term plans that improve the performance evaluation in OHS management. The relative weights of factors and sub-factors (w_j) based on interdependence are obtained by multiplying the weights derived from FAHP and the normalized direct relation matrix N (refer to Eq. 15).

$$w_{ij} = \begin{matrix} SC_1 \\ SC_2 \\ SC_3 \\ . \\ . \\ SC_z \end{matrix} \begin{bmatrix} SC_1 & SC_2 & \dots & SC_z \\ n_{11} & n_{12} & \dots & n_{1z} \\ n_{21} & n_{22} & \dots & n_{2z} \\ n_{31} & n_{32} & \dots & n_{3z} \\ . & . & \dots & . \\ . & . & \dots & . \\ n_{z1} & n_{z2} & \dots & n_{zz} \end{bmatrix} * \begin{bmatrix} w_1 \\ w_2 \\ w_3 \\ . \\ . \\ w_z \end{bmatrix} \tag{15}$$

4 Application of the Integrating Proposed Methodology

4.1 Design of the Model for Performance Evaluation FAHP/DEMATEL

In this section, an empirical example is presented to validate the proposed methodology. The case study is illustrated in a medium-sized electric company located in Colombia.

One of the objectives of the company is the improve in the levels of customer satisfaction considering their requirements and needs (e.g., quality, delivery times, price, service), through the active development of services and products, the competence and commitment of its human talent, also fulfilling with the legal regulation in occupational safety and health. The company under study supplies electrical products and performs outsourcing services to improve electrical and telecommunications infrastructure. To support the quality and safety in its operations, the company must adequately identify the regulatory requirements in occupational safety and health, through the design of a decision model that involves different criteria and sub-criteria to evaluate and improve their performance in OHS.

Subsequently, a decision-making team was selected to validate the criteria and sub-criteria through the application of FAHP and DEMATEL techniques for the performance evaluation in occupational health and safety management, given their expertise in these topics and the electric sector. In this regard, four types of experts were found to be meaningful for the decision-making process: three leaders of the company under study, two experts consultors in health and safety management with expertise in the electric sector, and two representatives of academic sector linked to the occupational health and safety in companies. The team of experts for develop of integrated methodology is described below:

- Expert 1 is the General Manager of the company, with more than 10 years of experience in the electric sector.
- Expert 2 is the Leader in OHS department of the company, with more than 5 years of the experience.
- Expert 3 is the Head of the legal department of the company, with more than 5 years of experience in government regulations in OHS.
- Expert 4 is a professional in occupational health and safety with a master's degree in Management Systems and 10 years of experience as a consultant in both private and public organizations in the diagnostic, design implementation and improve health and safety programs in different companies.
- Expert 5 is an Electrical Engineer with a specialization in Automatic Control Systems and more than five years of experience and safety standards in the electric sector.
- Expert 6 is industrial engineering, specialist in occupational health with knowledge and 10 years of experience in health and safety in work, regulations and standards in occupational health and safety management (OHS), risk assessment, and industrial hygiene.
- Expert 7 is an Industrial Engineer and specialist in the application of multivariate methods and multi-criteria models for performance evaluation. The industrial engineer acted as a facilitator to take over the judgment process.

Concerning to hierarchy of the decision-making model is composed of four criteria (C1, C2, C3, and C4) and 23 sub-criteria (S1, S2,..., S23) according to the model developed by Jimenez et al. [19]. These criteria and sub-criteria were determined based on the regulations applicable to the electric sector such as the Decree No 1072 of 2015 (establish the rules in occupational health and safety management for companies) [47], Resolution No 0302 of 2019 (minimum standards in occupational health and safety in organizations) [48], and requirements of the international standard in OHS ISO 45001 [22]. Then, the experts validate these criteria and sub-criteria according to the health and safety regulations, and the literature review presented in order to provide an MCDM model responding to the current needs of the electric sector. Subsequently, the multi-criteria hierarchy was then verified and discussed through different sessions with the expert decision-making team to establish the comprehension of the model and the hierarchy. Finally, the decision model is shown in Fig. 2.

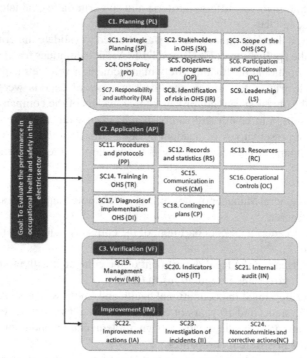

Fig. 2. Multi-criteria decision-making model to evaluate the overall performance in occupational health and safety management in the electric sector

Particularly, the criteria and sub-criteria were labeled and described in Table 3 [19].

4.2 Design of Data Collection Tools for FAHP and DEMATEL

In this step, a data collection instrument was designed for the paired comparisons process performed by the experts (refer to Fig. 3). In this regard, for each pairwise evaluation, the participants answered the following question: According to the goal/criteria, ¿how important is each element on the leftover the item on the right? The experts used Table 1 to represent their responses until finalizing all the factors and sub-factors. Then, via Eqs. 1–7, the weights of criteria and sub-criteria were determined.

On the other hand, we design a survey for the application of the DEMATEL technique (refer to Fig. 4) with the purpose of analyzing the interdependence between factors and sub-factors. Subsequently, it's applying the Eqs. 8–14, to identify the dispatchers and receivers. For each comparison, it was asked: With respect to goal/factor, ¿how much influence each element on the left has over the element on the right? The experts responded by using the 5-point scale shown in Sect. 3.2. The decision process was also repeated to finally calculate D + R and D − R values.

Table 3. Description of criteria

Criterion (C)	Sub-criteria (SC)	Criterion description
C1. Planning (PL)	SC1. Strategic planning (SP) SC2. Stakeholders in OHS (SK) SC3. Scope of the OHS system (SC) SC4. OHS Policy (PO) SC5. Objectives and OHS programs (OP) SC6. Participation and consultation (PC) SC7. Responsibility and authority in OHS (RA) SC8. Identification of risks in OHS (IR) SC9. Leadership (LS)	Planning is defined as the ability of the company to set OHS priorities, objectives, work plans, performance indicators, and resources for the implementation of OHS management, according to stakeholders, risks, current regulations and the context of the organization [19, 22, 47, 48]
C2. Application (AP)	SC10. Procedures and protocols (PP) SC11. Records and statistics (RS) SC12. Resources (RC) SC13. Training in OHS (TR) SC14. Communication in OHS (CM) SC15. Operational Controls (OC) SC16. Diagnosis of implementation OHS (DI) SC17. Contingency plans (CP)	This criterion refers to the aspects that the organization must guarantee to make the management of Occupational Safety and Health operational, such as documentation, procedures, and records, management of accident statistics, resources, training, active communication on OHS issues, initial assessment of OHS compliance, operational controls, and emergency preparedness and response [19, 22, 47, 48]
C3. Verification (VF)	SC18. Management review (MR) SC19. Indicators OHS (IT) SC.20 Internal audits (IN)	Verification in the Health and Safety Management System allows companies to evaluate their performance concerning the OHS, considering their context, processes, and stakeholders. This criterion includes indicators, compliance assessment, internal audits, and management review [19, 22, 47, 48]
C4. Improvement (IM)	SC21. Improvement actions (IA) SC22. Investigation of incidents (II) SC23. Nonconformities and corrective actions (NC)	This criterion assesses the company's ability to improve its performance at OHS taking into account its policy and objectives. [19, 22, 47, 48]

According to your experience with respect to "Improvement" sub-criterion, ¿how important is each sub-criterion on the left concerning the sub-criterion on the right when evaluating the performance in occupational health and safety management in the companies of electric sector?

		1	2	3	4	5		
Improvement actions	is	O	O	O	O	O	Important than	Investigation of incidents
Improvement actions	is	O	O	O	O	O	Important than	Nonconformities and corrective actions
Investigation of incidents	is	O	O	O	O	O	Important than	Nonconformities and corrective actions

① Much less	③ Equally	⑤ Much more
② Less	④ More	

Fig. 3. Data-collection instrument implemented for FAHP judgments

According to your experience with respect to "Improvement" sub-criterion, ¿how much influence each sub-criterion on the left has over the sub-criterion on the right when evaluating the performance in occupational health and safety management in the companies of electric sector?

		0	1	2	3	4		
Improvement actions	has	O	O	O	O	O	Influence over	Investigation of incidents
Improvement actions	has	O	O	O	O	O	Influence over	Nonconformities and corrective actions
Investigation of incidents	has	O	O	O	O	O	Influence over	Nonconformities and corrective actions

(0) Nonexistent impact (1) Low impact (2) Medium impact (3) high impact (4) Very high impact

Fig. 4. Data-collection instrument implemented for DEMATEL comparisons

4.3 Calculating the Relative Weights of Criteria and Sub-criteria Using FAHP

In this phase, by the application of the FAHP method, the local and global weights of criteria and sub-criteria were determined considering the uncertainty and vagueness in the judgments of experts. In this sense, first, the fuzzy matrixes were calculated, taking into account the paired comparisons made by the selected experts. In Tables 4, 5 and 6, the results of the FAHP process for the criteria comparison matrix can be seen as an example, applying Eqs. 1–7 of the methodology detailed in Sect. 3.1. Finally, Table 7 presents the local and global weights of all the criteria and sub-criteria that make up the multi-criteria decision model.

Table 4. Fuzzy reciprocal comparison matrix for criteria

	C1 (PL)	C2 (AP)	C3 (VF)	C4 (IM)
C1 (PL)	[1, 1, 1]	[2.44,3.47,4.49]	[2.69,3.73,4.76]	[2.21,3.23,4.24]
C2 (AP)	[0.22,0.29,0.41]	[1, 1, 1]	[1.22,1.37,1.49]	[1.10,1.17,1.22]
C3 (VF)	[0.21,0.27,0.37]	[0.67,0.73,0.82]	[1, 1, 1]	[0.35,0.42,0.55]
C4 (IM)	[0.24,0.31,0.45]	[0.82,0.85,0.91]	[1.81,2.36,2.85]	[1, 1, 1]

Table 5. Geometric means of fuzzy comparisons for criteria

Criterion	C1 (PL)	C2 (AP)	C3 (VF)	C4 (IM)
Geometric mean of fuzzy comparisons	[2.44,3.47,4.49]	[0.70,0.81,0.97]	[0.55,0.67,0.83]	[0.71,0.85,1.05]

Table 6. Normalized fuzzy priorities for criteria

Fuzzy weight			Non-fuzzy weight	Normalized weight
C1	17.91	20.14	19.70	19.25	0.589
C2	5.11	4.71	4.24	4.69	0.143
C3	4.02	3.86	3.65	3.84	0.118
C4	5.18	4.96	4.62	4.92	0.150
Total			32.70	

The Fig. 5 shows the results of the FAHP technique show. Firstly, the weights of the criteria associated with the evaluation of performance in OHS applied to the electricity sector. Ac-cording these outcomes, "Planning" (GW = 58.9%) is the most relevant factor in this evaluation is "Planning" (GW = 58.9%). This factor presents a difference greater than 40% with respect to the other criteria of the model. On the other hand, the sub-criteria "Application" (GW = 14.3%), "Verification" (GW = 11.8%), and "Improvement" (15.0%), present minor differences in their weights or importance, to evaluate the performance in OHS. These results demonstrate the importance of planning to obtain a satisfactory performance in the assessment of OHS by the design of strategies and plans focused on generating a culture of prevention and safety in work environments. On the other hand, evaluation can allow decision-makers to establish the most appropriate strategies to improve OHS performance, considering the elements of the P-D-C-A (Plan-Do-Check-Act) cycle.

Regarding the sub-criteria, Figs. 6a, 6b, 7a, and 7b show the distribution by the level of importance of the sub-factors for each cluster in the evaluation of performance in OHS. Regarding these results, in the "Planning" cluster, an essential sub-criterion is "Leadership" (23%) and "Strategic Planning" (19.36%). In the "Application" cluster, the sub-criteria "Diagnosis in OHS" and "Operational Control" were identified as the most relevant (20%). For the "Verification" cluster, "Management review" (59.30%) was identified as the most critical sub-criterion, followed by the "Internal Audits" sub-factor (23.06%). In the "Improvement" cluster, the sub-criterion with the highest weight corresponds to "Improvement Actions" (71.68%). All these factors and sub-factors are part of the legal requirements in OHS in correspondence with the ISO 45001 standard, intending to identify opportunities for improvement in OHS performance, define action plans, resources for its execution, and evaluating their impact on the organization in the prevention of accidents and occupational diseases.

Table 7. Local and global weights of criteria and sub-criteria

Cluster	GW	LW
C1. Planning (PL)	**0.589**	
SC1. Strategic management (SP)	0.114	0.194
SC2. Stakeholders (SK)	0.024	0.041
SC3. Scope of OHS (SC)	0.022	0.037
SC4. Policy of OHS (PO)	0.069	0.117
SC5. Objective of OHS (OP)	0.090	0.153
SC6. Participation of workers (PC)	0.036	0.061
SC7. Responsibilities and authority (RA)	0.038	0.065
SC8. Risk management (IR)	0.062	0.106
SC9. Leadership (LS)	0.134	0.227
C2. Application (C2)	**0.143**	
SC10. Procedures and protocols (PP)	0.112	0.083
SC11. Records and statistics in OHS (RS)	0.012	0.084
SC12. Resources for OHS (RC)	0.027	0.187
SC13. Education and Training (TR)	0.015	0.103
SC14. Communication in OHS (CM)	0.007	0.052
SC15. Operational Controls (OC)	0.028	0.198
SC16. Diagnosis in OHS (DI)	0.028	0.198
SC17. Contingency plans (CP)	0.014	0.095
C3. Verification (C3)	**0.118**	
SC18. Management review (MR)	0.070	0.593
SC19. Evaluation of OHS (IT)	0.021	0.176
SC20. Audit od OHS (IN)	0.027	0.231
C4. Improvement (C4)	**0.150**	
SC21. Improvement plans (IA)	0.108	0.717
SC22. Incident investigation (II)	0.030	0.197
SC23. Nonconformities and corrective plans (NC)	0.013	0.086

Finally, we calculated the consistency (refer to Table 8) to guarantee the reliability of the judgments contributed by the expert team. The outcomes evidence that all criteria present adequate consistency values ($CR \leq 0.1$). Therefore, the factors and sub-factors can be then applied consistently to evaluate the performance in occupational health and safety management.

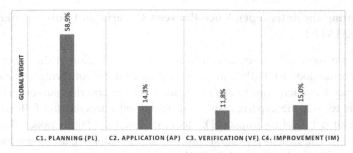

Fig. 5. Global weights of criteria in the performance evaluation in occupational health and safety in companies of electric sector

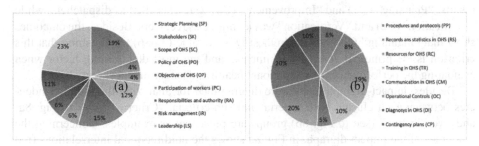

Fig. 6. Local contributions for factors a) Planning b) Application

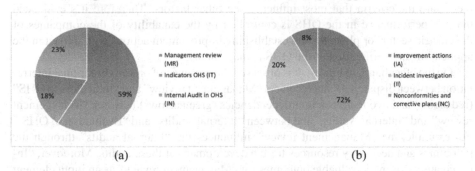

Fig. 7. Local contributions for factors a) Verification b) Improvement

Table 8. Consistency values for FAHP matrices

Cluster	Consistency ratio (CR)
Criteria	0.028
Planning	0.065
Application	0.064
Verification	0.025
Improvement	0.034

4.4 Evaluating the Interdependence Between Criteria and Sub-criteria via DEMATEL

In this step, we applied a survey to collect the paired evaluation of the experts for the DEMATEL technique. To do this, the experts answered the following question: "how much influence has each criterion/sub-criterion over the criterion/sub-criterion on the left?" In this regard, the experts responded, taking into account the following scale: Nonexistent impact (0), Low impact (1), Medium impact (2), High impact (3), and Very high impact (4). The experts repeat this procedure until finishing all the evaluations.

Then, applying the Eq. 8–13 of the DEMATEL technique, the prominence $(D + R)$ and relation (D-R) values are calculated (refer to Table 9). As a result of this process, the dispatchers and receivers were identified, as shown in Table 9. According to these results, "Planning" (C1) and "Improvement" (C4) were classified as dispatchers, while "Application" (C2) and "Verification" was identified as receivers. Besides, the outcomes show that "Planning" (C4) has the highest $D + R$ value (3.686), establishing that this criterion is the principal generator of impacts and the most determining factor when evaluating the performance in occupational health and safety management.

Besides, impact-digraph maps were diagrammed for analyzing the interdependencies between each cluster, both criteria, and sub-criteria. "Criteria" (refer to Fig. 8a) and "Verification" (see to Fig. 8b) groups are presented as examples. Concerning the outcomes of the impact digraph, in Fig. 8a shows the unidirectional interrelations (red arrows) between dispatchers and receivers. In particular, the "Planning" and "Improvement" are the criteria that most influence the other factors. Therefore it´s evidenced that the performance in the OHS is controlled by the capability of the companies of the electric sector for planning and establishing improvement actions with impact in the application and verification of the OHS management.

On the other hand, in Fig. 8b, it is observed the presence of one unidirectional interrelation between dispatchers and receivers "Management review" and "Indicators in OHS" (red arrow) and two feedback interdependencies (green arrows) between "Management review" and "Internal Audits," and between "Internal Audits" and "Evaluation of OHS." For example, the "Management review" influences the "Internal audits" through the guidelines and necessary resources for the development of these audits. Moreover, "Internal audits" provide valuable outcomes for "Management review" as an input element for this process.

4.5 Integration of FAHP and DEMATEL Methods

In this section, FAHP and DEMATEL methods are integrated using Eq. 15 to calculate the global and local weights of criteria and sub-criteria in the performance evaluation of occupational health and safety management taking into account factors such as the uncertainty in the pair comparisons of the judgments and the interdependence between criteria and sub-criteria. The final global and local contributions of criteria and sub-criteria were presented in Table 10. Figure 9 shows the ranking of criteria according to their global contributions.

Concerning the results, "Improvement" (0.292) and "Verification" (0.270) were identified as the most relevant criteria in the performance evaluation of OHS management. However, there is not a big difference (9.7%) between the essential criterion "Improvement" and the last in the ranking "Planning." These outcomes can be explained by the

Table 9. Dispatchers and receivers in the decision-making model

Cluster (Criteria/Sub-criteria)	Prominence (D + R)	Relation (D − R)	Dispatcher	Receiver
C1. Planning (PL)	**3.686**	**1.115**	**X**	
SC1. Strategic management (SP)	0.269	0.048	X	
SC2. Stakeholders (SK)	0.235	−0.020		X
SC3. Scope of OHS (SC)	0.245	−0.008		X
SC4. Policy of OHS (PO)	0.240	−0–002		X
SC5. Objective of OHS (OP)	0.251	−0.017		X
SC6. Participation of workers (PC)	0.255	−0.018		X
SC7. Responsibilities and authority (RA)	0.236	−0.023		X
SC8. Risk management (IR)	0.253	−0.016		X
SC9. Leadership (LS)	0.262	0.056	X	
C2. Application (C2)	**3.065**	**−0.768**		**X**
SC10. Procedures and protocols (PP)	0.247	−0.022		X
SC11. Records and statistics in OHS (RS)	0.252	−0.030		X
SC12. Resources for OHS (RC)	0.073	0.174	X	
SC13. Education and Training (TR)	0.256	−0.036		X
SC14. Communication in OHS (CM)	0.250	−0.050		X
SC15. Operational Controls (OC)	0.281	−0.033		X
SC16. Diagnosis in OHS (DI)	0.274	0.002	X	
SC17. Contingency plans (CP)	0.301	−0.005		X
C3. Verification (C3)	**3.205**	**−0.378**		**X**
SC18. Management review (MR)	0.959	0.174	X	

(*continued*)

Table 9. (*continued*)

Cluster (Criteria/Sub-criteria)	Prominence (D + R)	Relation (D − R)	Dispatcher	Receiver
SC19. Evaluation of OHS (IT)	1.008	−0.125		X
SC20. Audit od OHS (IN)	1.006	−0–049		X
C4. Improvement (C4)	**3.308**	**0.030**	X	
SC21. Improvement plans (IA)	0.973	0.045	X	
SC22. Incident investigation (II)	0.991	−0–027		X
SC23. Nonconformities and corrective plans (NC)	1.035	−0.018		X

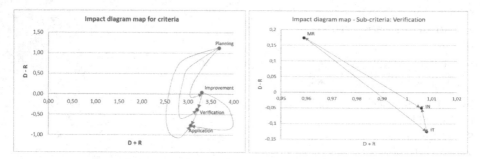

Fig. 8. Impact digraph maps for a) Criteria and b) Improvement (Color figure online)

fact that occupational health and safety management standards regulate all these criteria to guarantee the culture of prevention in the electric sector through adequate performance evaluation in OHS. In this regard, it is crucial to design multi-criteria plans that consider the principles, requirements, and criteria involved in the evaluation process. Thereby, the companies of the electric sector can improve their performance continuously with an impact on the wellness of their workers and stakeholders.

On the other hand, the sub-criteria "Strategic management" (0.025), "Contingency plans" (0.035), "Evaluation of OHS" (0.109) and "Nonconformities and corrective plans" (0.144) were identified as the sub-criteria with the highest global priorities taking into account the integration of FAHP and DEMATEL techniques.

4.6 Validate the Proposed Methodology in a Company of Electric Sector

In this phase, the multi-criteria decision model was applied for the evaluation of the performance in OHS in the electrical sector company described in Sect. 4.1. Table 11 shows the performance obtained by the company, in the first diagnostic evaluation, as in

Table 10. Local and global contributions of criteria and sub-criteria resulting from FAHP-DEMATEL integration

Cluster	GW	LW
C1. Planning (PL)	**0.195**	
SC1. Strategic management (SP)	0.025	0.130
SC2. Stakeholders (SK)	0.020	0.104
SC3. Scope of OHS (SC)	0.022	0.111
SC4. Policy of OHS (PO)	0.020	0.103
SC5. Objective of OHS (OP)	0.020	0.101
SC6. Participation of workers (PC)	0.022	0.115
SC7. Responsibilities and authority (RA)	0.021	0.106
SC8. Risk management (IR)	0.021	0.108
SC9. Leadership (LS)	0.024	0.123
C2. Application (C2)	**0.242**	
SC10. Procedures and protocols (PP)	0.027	0.113
SC11. Records and statistics in OHS (RS)	0.032	0.134
SC12. Resources for OHS (RC)	0.029	0.120
SC13. Education and Training (TR)	0.028	0.114
SC14. Communication in OHS (CM)	0.028	0.115
SC15. Operational Controls (OC)	0.030	0.122
SC16. Diagnosis in OHS (DI)	0.033	0.137
SC17. Contingency plans (CP)	0.035	0.144
C3. Verification (C3)	**0.270**	
SC18. Management review (MR)	0.058	0.213
SC19. Evaluation of OHS (IT)	0.109	0.402
SC20. Audit od OHS (IN)	0.104	0.385
C4. Improvement (C4)	**0.292**	
SC21. Improvement plans (IA)	0.041	0.139
SC22. Incident investigation (II)	0.108	0.370
SC23. Nonconformities and corrective plans (NC)	0.144	0.492

the second evaluation, after implementing the improvement plans. For this, the GAPS or deviations from the maximum value were calculated using the Eq. 16 [39].

$$GAP(\%) - \frac{Score\ obtanied - Score\ max}{Score\ max} \times 100 \qquad (16)$$

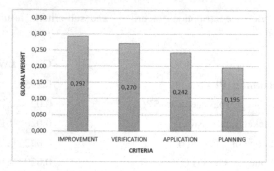

Fig. 9. Ranking of criteria (GW) of FAHP/DEMATEL integration

Table 11. Identification of GAPS and critical variables for improvement of MCDM FAHP-DEMATEL in OHS performance evaluation

Criterion	GW (FAHP/ DEMATEL)	Max Score	Obtained Score (First Evaluation)	Obtained Score (Second Evaluation)	GAP (First Evaluation)	GAP (Second Evaluation)
Planning (C1)	19.6%	4.9	0.1	4.0	98.00%	18.00%
Application (C2)	24.2%	14.5	3.3	12.7	77.50%	12.50%
Verification (C3)	27.0%	1.4	0.0	1.4	100.00%	0.00%
Improvement (C4)	29.2%	2.9	0.0	2.9	100.00%	0.00%
Score	100.0%	23.7	3.4	21.0	85.80%	11.38%
% of Compliance			14.20%	88.62%		

In the first evaluation, it's evidenced that the company has a compliance index of 14% concerning the minimum compliance required by national regulations that are of 86%. According to this evaluation, all evaluation criteria were identified as critical, with GAPS or deviations more significant than 70%.

The results were shared with the company's manager, with whom improvement plans were established according to the company's context and resources. Table 12 shows examples of the improvement plans adopted, and Fig. 10 presents the PERT diagram drawn up with the critical path for the project, which was estimated with an execution time of 42 weeks and an investment of USD 18,000.

On the other hand, we evaluate the effect of the improvement plans both in the evaluation of performance in OHS and in critical indicators for the company. Figure 11 shows the positive evolution in the company's OHS performance, growing from 14.2% to 88.62%, meeting the minimum percentage required established by national regulations in Colombia. The growth mentioned above can be seen in Table 11, where the company meets 100% of the "Verification" and "Improvement" criteria and only presents GAPS of 18% in the "Planning" criterion and 12.5% in the "Application" criterion, which demonstrates the effectiveness of the plans adopted in the performance in OHS.

Table 12. Improvement plans in OHS performance evaluation

No	Improvement plans
1	Define the person responsible for leading OHS management
2	Design of Matrix of Roles and Responsibilities in OHS
3	Design of the policy in OHS
4	Grouping of the emergency brigade
5	Design and implementation of epidemiological surveillance programs to prevent priority risks
6	Design and implementation of safety inspection program
7	Design and implementation of training plans in OHS

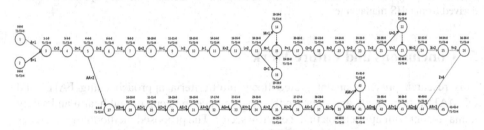

Fig. 10. Scheduling and Critical Route PERT-CPM

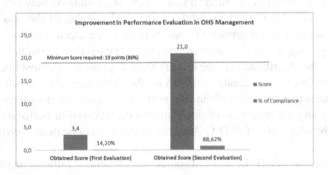

Fig. 11. Improvement in Performance Evaluation in OHS Management

Finally, in Figs. 12a and 12b, the influence of the improvement plans implemented in OHS on critical indicators for the company is observed. In this sense, in Fig. 12a, the 80% reduction in absenteeism from work is evident, as well as the decrease in accidents by 100%, taking into account the data collected between the first and second performance evaluations at OHS. Figure 12b shows the increase in sales derived from improvement in the performance of OHS management, with growth between the first and the second evaluation of 43.83%. The aforementioned outcomes illustrate the positive impact of the assessment of performance in OHS on the well-being of workers, on the productivity of companies, and the competitiveness of the electricity sector.

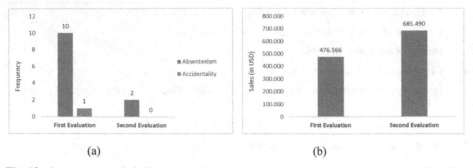

(a)   (b)

Fig. 12. Improvements in indicators a) Absenteeism and accidentality in OHS b) Sales (in USD) derived from OHS management

5   Conclusions and Future Work

This research presents an integrated fuzzy multicriteria approach using FAHP and DEMATEL to evaluate and improve the performance in occupational health and safety management with application in the electric sector. The proposed methodology includes four phases since the design of the MCDM model, the application of FAHP technique to calculate the importance of the criteria and sub-criteria in OHS performance evaluation, the use of DEMATEL method to identify the interrelations between criteria, the integration of FAHP/DEMATEL to establish the final weights of the criteria, and the validation of the proposed approach in a real context in the electric sector.

Concerning the results of this study, it was obtained two critical conclusions. The first conclusion was the identification of the criteria and sub-criteria with most importance and impact in the performance evaluation in OHS for the companies of the electric sector and the second issue is the evaluation of the effects of the proposed methodology considering the importance and interrelations of different criteria involved in performance in OHS that include the elements of P-D-C-A cycle: planning, application, verification, and improvement.

In this sense, the FAHP-DEMATEL outcomes evidence "Improvement" and "Verification" were identified as the most important criteria with global contributions of 0.292 and 0.270, respectively. However, it is necessary to consider the other criteria that composed the performance evaluation due to the little differences in their contributions. Besides, the criteria "Planning" and "Improvement" were identified as the essential criteria in the performance evaluation of OHS management with D + R of 3.686 and 3.308. The managers and leaders should consider these criteria in OHS to design and implement adequate strategies for improving the performance in OHS with impacts in the companies and their stakeholders. Concerning the effects and benefits of the proposed methodology, its evidence that the company obtained an improvement in their OHS performance of 14.2% until 88.62% exceeds the minimum percentage of compliance requirements by national regulations.

In addition, the company decreased critical indicators in OHS, such as absenteeism and the accidents with reductions of 80% and 100%, respectively. On the other hand, the organization under study obtained an increase of 43.83% in their sales that consequence of their improvement in the performance of OHS management. For the considerations mentioned above, the integrated methodology can be helping the companies to generate a culture of prevention in occupational health and safety, taking into account the complexity of the sector, the multiple criteria involved in the evaluation, and the interdependencies between these criteria.

Finally, as future work, the integrated methodology proposed will be extended in other industries. In addition, we propose continue the develop of the approach proposed using different hybrid methods as Fuzzy DEMATEL, TOPSIS, and VIKOR in order to validate and improve the performance of the method.

Acknowledgments. The authors would like to thank the support of the SEINER S.A.S. Company and the Institucion Universitaria ITSA.

References

1. The World Bank, "Understanding Poverty: Energy Overview". https://www.worldbank.org/en/topic/energy/overview
2. El País, "El mundo consumirá un 30% más de energía en 2040 y se aleja de cumplir el Acuerdo de París. https://elpais.com/economia/2017/11/14/actualidad/1510661591_352717.html
3. Castillo, J., Suárez, M., Rubio, J., Aguado, J.: Personal factors and consequences of electrical occupational accidents in the primary, secondary and tertiary sectors. Saf. Sci. **91**, 286–297 (2017)
4. Cawley, J.C., Homce, G.T.: Occupational electrical injuries in the United States, 1992–1998, and recommendations for safety research. J. Saf. Res. **34**, 241–248 (2003)
5. McCann, M., Hunting, L.K., Murawski, J., Chowdhury, R., Welch, L.: Causes of electrical deaths and injuries among construction workers. Am. J. Ind. Med. **43**, 398–406 (2003)
6. Janicak, C.A.: Occupational fatalities due to electrocutions in the construction industry. J. Saf. Res. **39**, 617–621 (2008)
7. Chi, C.F., Lin, Y.Y., Ikhwan, M.: Flow diagram analysis of electrical fatalities in construction industry. Saf. Sci. **50**(5), 1205–1214 (2012)
8. Kotzé, M., Steyn, L.: The role of psychological factors in workplace safety. Ergonomics **56**(12), 1928–1939 (2013)
9. Organización Internacional del Trabajo OIT. La seguridad en cifras: Sugerencias para una cultura general en materia de seguridad en el trabajo. Ginebra (2003). ISBN 92-2-313741-1. http://www.ilo.org/public/english/standards/relm/ilc/ilc90/pdf/rep-vi.pdf
10. Jimenez, G., Novoa, L., Ramos, L., Martinez, J., Alvarino, C.: Diagnosis of initial conditions for the implementation of the integrated management system in the companies of the land cargo transportation in the City of Barranquilla (Colombia). In: Stephanidis, C. (ed.) HCI 2018. CCIS, vol. 852, pp. 282–289. Springer, Cham (2018). https://doi.org/10.1007/978-3-319-92285-0_39
11. Jimenez, G., Zapata, E.: Metodología Integrada para el control estratégico y la mejora continua, basada en el Balanced Scorecard y el Sistema de Gestión de Calidad: aplicación en una organización de servicios en Colombia. In: 51a Asamblea Anual del Consejo Latinoamericano de Escuelas de Administración CLADEA 2016, Medellín, Colombia, pp. 1–20 (2016)

12. Jimenez, G., Hernandez, L., Hernandez, H., Cabas, L., Ferreira, J.: Evaluation of quality management for strategic decision making in companies in the plastic sector of the Colombian Caribbean Region using the TQM diagnostic report and data analysis. In: Stephanidis, C. (ed.) HCI 2018. CCIS, vol. 852, pp. 273–281. Springer, Cham (2018). https://doi.org/10.1007/978-3-319-92285-0_38
13. Jimenez, G.: Procedimientos para el mejoramiento de la calidad y la implantación de la Norma ISO 9001 aplicado al proceso de asesoramiento del Centro de Investigaciones y Desarrollo Empresarial y Regional en una Institucion de Educación Superior basados en la gestión por procesos. In: Congreso de Gestión de la Calidad y Protección Ambiental, GECPA 2014, Habana, Cuba, pp. 1–22 (2014)
14. Marhavilas, P.K., Koulouriotis, D.E., Spartalis, S.H.: Harmonic analysis of occupational-accident time-series as a part of the quantified risk evaluation in worksites: application on electric power industry and construction sector. Reliab. Eng. Syst. Saf. **112**, 8–25 (2013)
15. Rahmani, A., Khadem, M., Madreseh, E., Aghaei, H., Raei, M., Karchani, M.: Descriptive study of occupational accidents and their causes among electricity distribution company workers at an eight-year period in Iran. Saf. Health Work **4**(3), 160–165 (2013)
16. Acakpovi, A., Dzamikumah, L.: An investigation of health and safety measures in a hydroelectric power plant. Saf. Health Work **7**(4), 331–339 (2016)
17. Bakhiyi, B., Labrèche, F., Zayed, J.: The photovoltaic industry on the path to a sustainable future — environmental and occupational health issues. Environ. Int. **73**, 224–234 (2014)
18. Marhavilas, P.K., Koulouriotis, D.E., Mitrakas, C.: On the development of a new hybrid risk assessment process using occupational accidents' data: application on the Greek Public Electric Power Provider. J. Loss Prevent. Process Ind. **24**(5), 671–687 (2011)
19. Jimenez-Delgado, G., Balmaceda-Castro, N., Hernández-Palma, H., de la Hoz-Franco, E., García-Guiliany, J., Martinez-Ventura, J.: An integrated approach of multiple correspondences analysis (MCA) and fuzzy AHP method for occupational health and safety performance evaluation in the land cargo transportation. In: Duffy, V. (ed.) Digital Human Modeling and Applications in Health, Safety, Ergonomics and Risk Management. Human Body and Motion. HCII 2019. LNCS, vol. 11581, pp. 433–457. Springer, Cham (2019). https://doi.org/10.1007/978-3-030-22216-1_32
20. Gul, M.: A review of occupational health and safety risk assessment approaches based on multi-criteria decision-making methods and their fuzzy versions. Hum. Ecol. Risk Assess.: Int. J. (2018). https://doi.org/10.1080/10807039.2018.1424531
21. Inan, U., Gül, S., Yılmaz, H.: A multiple attribute decision model to compare the firms' occupational health and safety management perspectives. Saf. Sci. **91**(106), 221–231 (2017). https://doi.org/10.1016/j.ssci.2016.08.018
22. ISO 45001. Occupational Health and Safety Management Systems (2018)
23. Adema, A., Çolak, A., Dağdeviren, M.: An integrated model using SWOT analysis and Hesitant fuzzy linguistic term set for evaluation occupational safety risks in life cycle of wind turbine. Saf. Sci. **106**, 184–190 (2018)
24. Efe, B., Kurt, M., Efe, F.: An integrated intuitionistic fuzzy set and mathematical programming approach for an occupational health and safety policy. J. Sci. **30**(2), 73–95 (2017)
25. Badria, A., Nadeaua, S., Gbodossoub, A.: Proposal of a risk-factor-based analytical approach for integrating occupational health and safety into project risk evaluation. Accid. Anal. Prevent. **48**, 223–234 (2012)
26. Jiangdong, B., Johansson, J., Zhang, J.: Comprehensive evaluation on employee satisfaction of mine occupational health and safety management system based on improved AHP and 2-tuple linguistic information. Sustainability **2**(133), 1–14 (2017)
27. Sadoughi, S., Yarahmadi, R., Taghdisi, M., Mehrabi, Y.: Evaluating and prioritizing of performance indicators of health, safety, and environment using fuzzy TOPSIS. Afr. J. Bus. Manag. **6**(5), 2026–2033 (2012)

28. Gul, M., Ak, M.: A comparative outline for quantifying risk ratings in occupational health and safety risk assessment. J. Clean. Prod. **196**(20), 653–664 (2018)
29. Hatami-Marbini, A., Tavana, M., Moradi, M., Kangi, F.: A fuzzy group Electre method for safety and health assessment in hazardous waste recycling facilities. Saf. Sci. **51**, 414–426 (2013)
30. Ilbahara, E., Ali Karaşanb, A., Selcuk Cebia, S., Kahraman, C.: A novel approach to risk assessment for occupational health and safety using Pythagorean fuzzy AHP & fuzzy inference system. Saf. Sci. **103**, 124–136 (2018)
31. Koulinas, G., Marhavilas, P., Demesouka, O., Vavatsikos, A., Koulouriotis, D.: Risk analysis and assessment in the work sites using the fuzzy-analytical hierarchy process and a quantitative technique–a case study for the Greek construction sector. Saf. Sci. **112**, 96–104 (2019)
32. Sukran Seker, S., Zavadskas, E.: Application of fuzzy DEMATEL method for analyzing occupational risks on construction sites. Sustainability **9**(11), 2083, 1–19 (2017)
33. Basahel, A., Taylan, O.: Using fuzzy AHP and fuzzy TOPSIS approaches for assessing safety conditions at worksites in construction industry. Int. J. Saf. Secur. Eng. **6**(4), 728–745 (2016)
34. Zheng, G., Zhu, N., Tian, Z., Chen, Y., Sun, B.: Application of a trapezoidal fuzzy AHP method for work safety evaluation and early warning rating of hot and humid environments. Saf. Sci. **50**, 228–239 (2012)
35. Ortiz-Barrios, M., Herrera-Fontalvo, Z., Rúa-Muñoz, J., Ojeda-Gutiérrez, S., De Felice, F., Petrillo, A.: An integrated approach to evaluate the risk of adverse events in hospital sector: from theory to practice. Manag. Decis. (2018). https://doi.org/10.1108/MD-09-2017-0917
36. Maleki, H., Zahir, S.: A comprehensive literature review of the rank reversal phenomenon in the analytic hierarchy process. J. Multi-Criteria Decis. Anal. **20**(3/4), 141–155 (2013)
37. Velasquez, M., Hester, P.T.: An analysis of multi-criteria decision-making methods. Int. J. Oper. Res. **10**(2), 56–66 (2013)
38. Ortiz-Barrios, M.A., Kucukaltan, B., Carvajal-Tinoco, D., Neira-Rodado, D., Jiménez, G.: Strategic hybrid approach for selecting suppliers of high-density polyethylene. J. Multi-Crit. Decis. Anal. **24**, 1–21 (2017). https://doi.org/10.1002/mcda.1617
39. Hernandez, L., Jimenez, G.: Characterization of the current conditions of the ITSA data centers according to standards of the green data centers friendly to the environment. In: Silhavy, R., Senkerik, R., Kominkova Oplatkova, Z., Prokopova, Z., Silhavy, P. (eds.) CSOC 2017. AISC, vol. 574, pp. 329–340. Springer, Cham (2017). https://doi.org/10.1007/978-3-319-57264-2_34
40. Demirel, T., Demirel, N., Kahraman, C.: Fuzzy analytic hierarchy process and its application. In: Kahraman, C. (ed.) Fuzzy Multi-Criteria Decision Making: Theory and Applications with Recent Developments. Springer Optimization and its Applications, vol. 16, pp. 53–83. Springer, Boston (2008). https://doi.org/10.1007/978-0-387-76813-7_3
41. Kusumawardani, R., Agintiara, M.: Application of fuzzy AHP-TOPSIS method for decision making in human resource manager selection process. Procedia Comput. Sci. **72**, 638–646 (2015)
42. Vahidnia, M.H., Alesheikh, A.A., Alimohammadi, A.: Hospital site selection using fuzzy AHP and its derivatives. J. Environ. Manag. **90**(10), 3048–3056 (2009)
43. Shieh, J.I., Wu, H.H., Huang, K.K.: A DEMATEL method in identifying key success factors of hospital service quality. Knowl.-Based Syst. **23**(3), 277–282 (2010)
44. Su, C.M., Horng, D.J., Tseng, M.L., Chiu, A.S., Wu, K.J., Chen, H.P.: Improving sustainable supply chain management using a novel hierarchical grey-DEMATEL approach. J. Cleaner Prod. **134**, 469–481 (2016)
45. Barrios, M.A.O., De Felice, F., Negrete, K.P., Romero, B.A., Arenas, A.Y., Petrillo, A.: An AHP-TOPSIS integrated model for selecting the most appropriate tomography equipment. Int. J. Inf. Technol. Decis. Making **15**(4), 861–885 (2016)

46. Wei, P.L., Huang, J.H., Tzeng, G.H., Wu, S.I.: Causal modeling of web-advertising effects by improving SEM based on DEMATEL technique. Int. J. Inf. Technol. Decis. Making **9**(05), 799–829 (2010)

47. Ministerio del Trabajo: Decreto 1072 de 2015. Por medio del cual se expide el expide el Decreto único reglamentario del sector trabajo, 26 May 2015. http://www.mintrabajo.gov.co/documents/20147/0/DUR+Sector+Trabajo+Actualizado+a+15+de+abril++de+2016.pdf/a32b1dcf-7a4e-8a37-ac16-c121928719c8

48. Ministerio del Trabajo. Resolución 0312 de 2019. Por la cual se definen los estándares mínimos del Sistema de Gestión de la Seguridad y Salud en el Trabajo SG-SST, 13 February 2019. http://www.mintrabajo.gov.co/documents/20147/0/DUR+Sector+Trabajo+Actualizado+a+15+de+abril++de+2016.pdf/a32b1dcf-7a4e-8a37-ac16-c121928719c8

Fine-Grained Map Coloring Web Service for JavaScript

Tetsuya Nakai[1]([✉]), Sachio Saiki[1], and Masahide Nakamura[1,2]

[1] Graduate School of System Informatics, Kobe University,
1-1 Rokkodai, Nada, Kobe, Japan
`manda@ws.cs.kobe-u.ac.jp`, `sachio@carp.kobe-u.ac.jp`, `masa-n@cs.kobe-u.ac.jp`
[2] Riken AIP, 1-4-1 Nihon-bashi, Chuo-ku, Tokyo 103-0027, Japan

Abstract. In this paper, we focus on data visualization in the smart city. We propose a more feasible and portable technique of fine-grained map visualization for smart city analytics. More specifically, we develop a Web service called FigMap4SC (Fine-Grained Map-coloring Web service for Smart City). FigMap4SC provides a service of coloring fine-grained city maps from them. Existing visualization methods require users to prepare all geographic data and users have to perform many operations. In FigMap4SC, all geographic data and map drawing operations necessary for coloring a city maps are hidden under the service. By preparing only a dataset, users get fine-grained city maps without specialized knowledge. The service can eliminate user's trouble and operation. Moreover, FigMap4SC exposes Web-API, to which external applications can post the dataset. As a result, any applications and scripts of smart city analytics can integrate FigMap4SC to visualize their own analysis results on colored maps. We have implemented a prototype of FigMap4SC, currently covering Kobe city area only. FigMap4SC has been implemented as a Web application with JavaScript, HTML5 and Maps JavaScript API which can show Google Maps on this service easily. This service was used by the Kobe Fire Department staff which tried on smart city. They evaluated that the visualization was quick and the operation was easy.

Keywords: Smart city · Data visualization · GIS · Choropleth map · Web service

1 Introduction

With the development of the ICT systems and IoT technologies, many companies and local governments are acquiring and accumulating a wide variety of data, and utilization for town development is increasing. Some data are open to the general public as open data and people can use it for innovation. By utilizing the data, aiming for a more efficient and sustainable city, which is so-called *smart city* [6], is now a global trend. Especially in developed countries, data-driven approaches to optimize functions of a city as well as improve the quality of life of residents are quite a hot topic, which we call *smart city analytics* in this paper.

© Springer Nature Switzerland AG 2020
V. G. Duffy (Ed.): HCII 2020, LNCS 12199, pp. 159–174, 2020.
https://doi.org/10.1007/978-3-030-49907-5_11

The data used in smart city analytics are *geospatial information*, which typically tied to administrative divisions (i.e., city, ward, town, or block). Therefore, for understanding and the result of analyzing the data, *visualizing data on a map* is useful than a tabular format [3]. In general, people create a *Choropleth Map* [7] in which areas are colored in proportion to a value associated with the administrative division data. Before the smart city, the granularity of the data analysis was basically at a city or ward level. Hence, the visualization with the map was not a big problem, and even feasible by human hands. In the smart city analytics, however, the volume and the resolution of the data are far beyond the conventional ones. Therefore, the visualization with the map manually is extremely difficult.

A straight-forward approach to implement the fine-grained map visualization is to use conventional *Geographic Information Systems (GIS)* [8]. A GIS provides a variety of features for analyzing, visualizing, optimizing any kinds of geographic data. Since a user can do almost everything for a given map, the GIS can be used extensively in the smart city analytics.

However, as the drawback of the powerful and general-purpose features, a GIS requires a user to learn many proprietary operations for preparing datasets (maps, shapes, etc.), creating layouts (positions, layers, etc.), specifying representations (colors, textures, etc.), and so on. Basically, these operations are not essential for the smart city analytics itself.

Moreover, a GIS is typically a stand-alone application, where a user conducts all tasks within it. Therefore, it is difficult for external applications to dynamically integrate the visualization features of the GIS.

Our research goal is to propose a more feasible and portable technique of fine-grained map visualization for smart city analytics. More specifically, we develop a Web service called *FigMap4SC (Fine-Grained Map-coloring Web service for Smart City)*. FigMap4SC provides a service of creating fine-grained choropleth maps from given data. All geographic data such as the based map and the shape of administrative divisions are hidden under the service. A user just provides a dataset, consisting of key-values of a multi-grained address (i.e., city, ward, town, or block) and its associated value (numeric value and/or color code). For the dataset given, FigMap4SC automatically colors a city map by the designated granularity. Note that the input dataset does not rely on any specific systems or methods of smart city analytics. Thus, FigMap4SC can decouple the process of map-based visualization from the process of individual data analysis. Moreover, FigMap4SC exposes Web-API, to which external applications can post the dataset. As a result, any applications and scripts of smart city analytics can integrate FigMap4SC to visualize their own analysis results on colored maps.

We have implemented a prototype of FigMap4SC using Maps JavaScript API, JavaScript, and HTML5, currently covering Kobe city area only. To obtain Kobe city maps with multiple granularities, we extensively used Google Maps and Google Maps JavaScript API [4]. The shapes of Kobe city, wards, towns, and blocks have been borrowed from open data provided by e-Stat [2].

In order to confirm the effectiveness, we asked staff members of the Kobe City Fire Department which is conducting joint research with us to use this web service. They carried out case studies to visualize their rescue dispatch logs with this web service. As a result, we got feedback that FigMap4SC is more efficient and easier in visualizing the dispatch logs than the GIS used in the Kobe City Fire Department.

2 Preliminary

2.1 Data Visualization on a Map with GIS

A Geographic Information System (GIS) [8] is a system that can operate geographic information on a computer. A GIS provides a variety of features for analyzing, visualizing, optimizing any kinds of geographic data [1,5].

A general procedure for creating a choropleth map in GIS is as follows:

1. Prepare and load datasets (maps, shapes, etc.).
2. Provide the data to visualize.
3. Combine the shapes and the provided data.
4. Set some options (posisions, layers, and colors).

2.2 Research Tasks

The GIS has general and powerful features, however, it has the following problems in visualization.

P1: It requires operations that are not essential for smart city analytics

As mentioned in Sect. 2.1, when analysts create a choropleth map with GIS, they need to prepare not only the source data to visualize but also a based map and geographic (shape) data. In addition, combining the shape data and the source data is a complicated task. These tasks are equivalent to the user creating maps from scratch, which is not essential to the original smart city analytics.

P2: Setting visualization expressions is complicated

In order to create an ideal choropleth map, analysts need to experiment with the color and layout of shapes.

P3: It is difficult to link directly with external applications

A GIS is typically stand-alone applications, so external applications cannot dynamically operate the visualization features of the GIS. Hence, analysts need to manually load analyzed data created by external applications and provide them to the GIS.

P4: Cannot reuse map objects

When sharing the created choropleth map with other people, there are two ways, by converting it to an image, or by using GIS-specific data. In the first way, anyone can see it, however, detail shapes and map data is lost, and users cannot reuse them as objects. in the second way, users can reuse them as objects, however, they cannot see or reuse without GIS.

We are currently conducting a joint research study with the Kobe City Fire Department. Staff members of the Kobe City Fire Department aim to optimize ambulance operations. They analyze rescue dispatch logs accumulated over the years and optimize their resources. Until now, they have been trying to visualize data analyzed with Microsoft Excel on a map of Kobe City with their GIS. However, according to the complexity of the operation and the slow response of the system, they could not visualize the analyzed data satisfactory within a limited working time. These are the same issues as P1 to P4 above.

3   FigMap4SC

Our research goal is to propose a more feasible and portable technique of fine-grained map visualization. For that, we develop a Web service called FigMap4SC (Fine-Grained Map-coloring Web service for Smart City).

3.1   System Requirements

For the functions of FigMap4SC, we describe four system requirements corresponding to four issues.

R1: Hiding geographic information and operations
FigMap4SC prepares and manages the map data and geographic information required to create a choropleth map, and hides them from a user. In addition, FigMap4SC processes provided data on behalf of a user. Thereby, the user can create a choropleth map by only providing the data they want to visualize, and concentrate on their analysis works.
R2: Specify flexible visualization options
FigMap4SC allows a user to easily and flexibly specify visualization options (color, value range). Thereby, they can change the color and expression of the shape on the map easily.
R3: Link directly with external applications
FigMap4SC allows external applications to provide analyzed data to FigMap4SC directly and to operate them. Thereby, users can directly link their tools or programs with FigMap4SC for extensive analysis efficiently.
R4: Reuse visualization results
FigMap4SC saves a created choropleth map in this service as an object with a unique ID. A user can call and reuse the object at any time. By sharing the object ID to other people, they can check and reuse the same map without installing a dedicated application.

3.2   Overall Architecture

Figure 1 shows the overall architecture of FigMap4SC. The middle part of the figure surrounded by lines shows the system of FigMap4SC. the left part of the

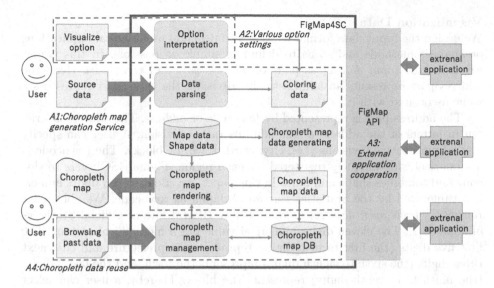

Fig. 1. System architecture

system shows analysts using FigMap4SC, and the right side of the system shows external applications using FigMap4SC. In order to fulfill the requirements R1-R4 described in Sect. 3.1, FigMap4SC is structured based on the following four approaches:

A1: Choropleth map generation service

FigMap4SC creates a choropleth map from the provided data and returns it to a user. The geographic data and operations required to create a choropleth map are included in this service.

A2: Visualization option specification

FigMap4SC accepts options from the user and customizes the colors and value range.

A3: FigMapAPI

This service allows a user to recalled and reused the choropleth maps which FigMap4SC created in the past.

A4: Choropleth map reuse service

This service allows a user to recalled and reused the choropleth maps which FigMap4SC created in the past.

The part enclosed by the dotted line in Fig. 1 and the part that realizes A1-A4 in FigMapAPI are shown. In the following sections, I will explain the input and output of the service first, and then describe the details of each of A1–A4.

3.3 Input Data

We define the input data that the user provides to FigMap4SC.

Visualization Data

We design the input data format so as not to depend on individual applications or analysis methods and so as to define as simple as possible. In this paper, we define the *input dataset* as pairs of *address part* and *value part*. Here, the address part represents an administrative division, the value part represents a value associated with it.

The address part is represented by *towncode* or *address*. The address is written in letters of the address of the administrative division. A user can specify any administrative divisions (i.e., city, ward, town, or block). The towncode is a numerical code uniquely registered for each region. Figmap4SC refers to this code and combines shape and data. In this paper, we adopt eleven digits numerical value used by the Statistics Bureau of Japan as towncode. We obtain *the towncodes from open data* released on e-Stat (Portal Site of Official Statistics of Japan) [2]. The eleven digits numerical value has a hierarchical system. The first five digits (the first to fifth digits) represents the prefecture and city, next three digits (the sixth to eighth digits) represents the town, and the last 3 digits (the ninth to eleventh digits) represents the block. Thereby, a user can select the geographic granularity level to be visualized by the length of towncode In FigMap4SC.

The value part is represented by l *value* or a *color*. The value represents a statistical and numerical value of the area, and a user can specify an integer of a real number. When a user provides a dataset to FigMap4SC, this service automatically creates 10 sections from the given maximum and minimum values and assigns a default color to each section. On the other hand, the color represents the color of the target area. A user specify a color code (#RRGGBB) or a color name (i.e. red, blue, and yellow).

In the address part, a user has to input either towncode or address. If users input both of them, towncode takes precedence. Similarly, in the value part, a user has to input either value or color. If users input both of them, color takes precedence. In addition, each data is allowed to have "description". The description is written in letters, and a user specifies comments.

Table 1. Example of source data format

ID	Address part		Value part	
	Towncode	Address	Value	Color
1	28101001001	Uozaki-Kitamachi 1-chome, Higashinada-Ku	4	#0000FF
2	28101001		40	
3		Higashinada-Ku, Kobe-Shi		Red

Table 1 shows an example of data. For the convenience of explanation, we assign IDs to the data in this example. At ID = 1, both towncode and address exist in the address part and both value and color exist in the value part.

Therefore, FigMap4SC gives priority to the towncode and color pair. Using this pair, the service colors the area of 28101001001 (Uozaki-Kitamachi 1-chome, Higashinada-Ku) in #0000FF (blue). At ID = 2, the towncode is specified by an 8-digit code. The service colors the area of 28101001 (Uozaki-Kitamachi, Higashinada-Ku, Kobe-Shi) in a color corresponding to the value 40. At ID = 3, the address is specified in the ward level, and the service colors the Higashinada-Ku, Kobe-Shi, which area is larger than the others, in red.

Visualization Option

A user can simultaneously provide the data to be visualized and the visualization option used in A2 to FigMap4SC. Users can freely change the colors with the visualization option.

The visualization option is defined by three required attributes, "from", "to" and "color". "from" and "to" are both numeric and define the class division section of the value "[from, to)". "color" represents the color of the target area.

Table 2. Example of option data format

from	to	color
−999	0	White
0	10	Blue
10	20	Yellow
20	30	Red

Table 2 shows examples of visualization options. This example defines four sections. If the value is greater than or equal to −999 and less than 0, paint white. If the value is greater than or equal to 0 and less than 10, paint blue. If the value is greater than or equal to 10 and less than 20, paint yellow. If the value is greater than or equal to 20 and less than 30, paint red. If the value is out of the range, does not color.

3.4   A1: Choropreth Map Generation Service

A1 generates a choropleth map based on the provided data. The center of Fig. 1 shows the structure of A1. A1 consists of master data (shown center cylinder) and three processed (shown rounded rectangles).

Master data has a map and shape of administrative divisions used to show a choropleth map. In FigMap4SC, We use the cloud map service for map master data. This time, we select Google Maps. We get the shape master data by e-Stat and form them. The shapes data is vector data, and have the eleven digits variable-length towncode as a key and arbitrary numbers of longitude and latitude list as the value. By connecting the pairs of longitude and latitude in the list, it represents the boundaries of administrative divisions.

In the *data interpretation process*, FigMap4SC checks the missing data for the provided data and generates "coloring data", which have pairs of administrative divisions and colors. If the visualization option is not specified, the service automatically determines the colors for each value according to the following procedure.

1. Store a default color map consisting of ten colors in the service in advance.
2. Extracts the minimum and maximum value from the provided data set and calculates the difference.
3. Divide the data set into ten class divisions to equal the widths of the data values, and correspond ten colors to each division.
4. Refer to each value and assign the color corresponding to the class division.

In the *coloring map data generation process*, FigMap4SC connects (inner-joins) the coloring data and shape data on towncode, and creates "Choropleth map data" For the connecting, all addressed are converted to the corresponding towncode. The choropleth map data is sent to the choropleth map rendering process and also saved in "Choropleth map database" for other functions.

In the *choropleth map rendering process*, FigMap4SC sends the choropleth map data to the cloud map service and create a choropleth map object. The service displays a Choropleth map on a web browser, and a user can freely enlarge, reduce, and move on their browser.

Accordingly, a user can create a choropleth map from the input data without any data preparation or operation related to map creation.

3.5   A2: Various Option Settings

In A2, FigMap4SC interprets the visualize option user provides and generates "Coloring data" according to the user-defined class division. When a user provides the visualization option, the service gives priority to the user definition.

This allows the users to create a more flexible choropleth map using the desired range and color without any manipulation on the data.

3.6   A3: External Application Cooperation

In A3, FigMap4SC provides a Web-API (we call as FigMapAPI). FigMapAPI allows any external applications to input data directly to FigMap4SC. They can directly input data by specifying query parameters for the URL of FigMap4SC. If users want to provide the data from external application by value, pass the dataset in JSON format to the data parameter. On the other hand, if users want to provide the data by reference, pass the reference URL to the data parameter. The service interprets the data according to the type of the given query parameter and creates a choropleth map through A1 and A2.

Thereby, A3 allows users to call FigMap4SC directly from any program or script without any manual intervention. Hence, users can efficiently visualize data. In addition, the service is not limited to analytics. For example, visualizing the aggregate value of sensors placed in a smart city on a map. The range of services is expanded to dynamic data visualization.

3.7   A4: Choropleth Map Reuse Service

In A4, FigMap4SC calls the past choropleth map data object from the choropleth map database and reuse it. A4 consists of choropleth map database and choropleth map data management. The database stores datasets with unique map IDs as keys and visualization data as values. A user can check the map ID stored in the database via the color map data management. By providing the map ID to the choropleth map data management, it calls the choropleth map object from the database and renders it and show them. By sharing the map ID with other users, they can confirm the same map in different environments. It is also possible to copy, update, and delete the map.

Thereby, a user can reuse a past choropleth map without preparing data again. In addition, anyone who can access Web services can easily share and check the same choropleth map.

4   Implementation

We have implemented a prototype of FigMap4SC, currently covering Kobe city area only.

4.1   Technologies

The technologies for the prototype of FigMap4SC are as follows:

- The shapes of Kobe divisions: World Geodetic System (KML files) by e-Stat
- Borrow and form shape: Python
- Database: MongoDB
- Database access API: Java1.8. Tomcat7.0
- Data process: JavaScript
- Map render: Google Maps JavaScript API
- User interface: HTML5, JavaScript

4.2   Main Screen of FigMap4SC

Figure 2 shows the main screen of FigMap4SC. The left side of the figure shows a data operation part and the right side of the figure shows a map part. In the map part, the service display Google Maps by Maps JavaScript API [4]. A user can perform almost the same operations as the Google Maps web application. Specifically, they can zoom in and zoom out the map, and they can replace an aerial photograph.

In the data operation part, service shows a color bar representing the legend of the data, a form providing the data to visualize, an operating UI for adjusting the visualization result, and a button for saving the visualization result. The color bar displays its color and value based on the class division.

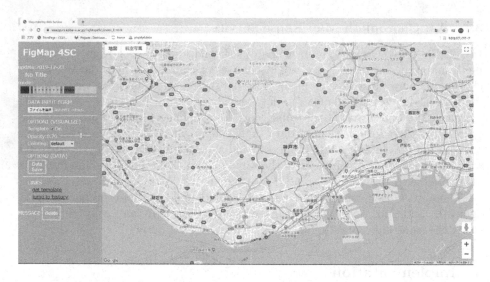

Fig. 2. Main screen of "FigMap4SC"

In this prototype, a user can use the Excel(xlsx) format or JSON format file to visualize. In addition, we prepare an *Excel format template file* so that users can visualize immediately. In this template, there are the address parts of three types of administrative divisions in Kobe city, town, and block that have been entered on three different sheets. Users can easily create visualized data by filling in the value part on the sheet in their desired granularity. A user can also define visualization options in another sheet.

By operating the slider and pull-down menu in the data operation part, a user can partially manipulate the visualization results. By operating the slider, a user can change the transparency of the colors in a choropleth map. In addition, by selecting a different color map from the "Coloring" pull-down menu, a user can change the colors of areas from the default color. When a user gets a satisfactory visualization result, they can save the created choropleth map data object to the database by pressing the DataSave button. By clicking on any area on the map, you can check the information of the area. Since the choropleth map is projected on the Google map, users can zoom in, zoom out, and move the map.

Figure 3 shows the screen of the reusing visualization results of FigMap4SC. The left side of the screen shows a list contains the title and created date of choropleth maps. When a user clicks the title, the service redraws the choropleth map. At the same time, the map ID is copied to the clipboard. By sharing the ID with other users, users can share the same map.

4.3 Direct Integration with External Applications

In this section, we describe the procedure for an external application to provide data directly to FigMap4SC and create a Choropleth map. When the external

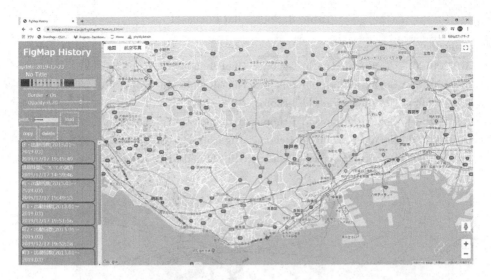

Fig. 3. Past data browseing screen of "FigMap4SC"

application provides its data to FigMap4SC by value, enter the data in JSON format text to the data query parameter, and call the URL of FigMap4SC. On the other hand, when provides by reference, write the JSON format text data to a file with a certain URL, pass the URL to the URL query parameter, and call.

5   Case Study

In order to confirm the effectiveness of FigMap4SC, we conduct a case study to visualize the dispatch logs.

5.1   Case1: Visualization of the Number of Rescue Operations per Year in Block Level

The Kobe City Fire Department records its rescue operations in dispatch logs. For each dispatch log, the date and time of dispatch, the destination address of the ambulance, and the condition of the victim was recorded. By creating a choropleth map about the destination address at the block level, they can find a detailed distribution of emergency demand and regional characteristics. In case1, we count the number of emergency dispatches for each block in 2018 and visualizes by FigMap4SC.

First, we extract the dispatch data from raw data and count them for each block with the external analysis tool (Python) and past the results into an Excel template file. Also, color information is not input because it is automatically assigned by FigMap4SC. Table 3 shows a part of the analysis result.

Figure 4 shows the result of visualization by providing this Excel file into FigMap4SC. Figure 5 shows the result of zooming in around *Higashi-kawasakicho*

Table 3. Source data in case1

towncode	address	value	color
28101001001	Uozaki-Kitamachi 1-chome, Higashinada-Ku, Kobe-Shi	27	
28101001002	Uozaki-Kitamachi 2-chome, Higashinada-Ku, Kobe-Shi	23	
28101001003	Uozaki-Kitamachi 3-chome, Higashinada-Ku, Kobe-Shi	15	
28101001004	Uozaki-Kitamachi 4-chome, Higashinada-Ku, Kobe-Shi	23	
28101002001	Uozaki-Nakamachi 1-chome, Higashinada-Ku, Kobe-Shi	57	
28101002002	Uozaki-Nakamachi 2-chome, Higashinada-Ku, Kobe-Shi	52	

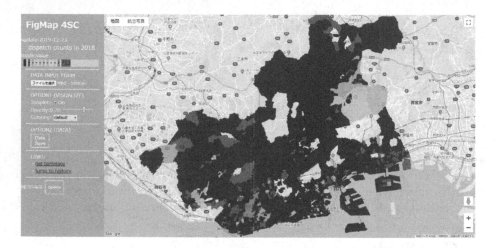

Fig. 4. Visualization of the number of dispatches in 2018

1-chome, Chuo-Ku, Kobe-Shi. The top left of Fig. 4 shows the legend. The number of dispatches decreases as the color of the division approaches blue, and the number of dispatches increases as the color approaches red. Looking at the map part, it can be seen that most of the areas are blue, and the number of dispatches is small. On the other hand, some areas are colored green, yellow, orange, and red, indicating that the number of dispatches is significantly higher than in other areas.

Figure 5 shows the zoomed-up map of the *Chuo-Ku* in the center of the screen in Fig. 4. We can see the difference in the emergency demand at the block level. In this figure, *Higashi-kawasakicho 1-chome* painted in yellow-green had 458 counts, indicating that there was much higher demand than in the surrounding area. We consider that the demand is caused by Kobe Harborland, a large commercial facility. Many people gather to the facility so that there was a lot of emergency demand. In addition, the area near the SN station in the upper right of the figure is colored green. This suggests that rescue operations increase in places where there were heavy traffic of people.

Fig. 5. Detail about the subject area

5.2 Case2: Visualization of Emergency Dispatch Time by FD-CAST

In case2, we provide analyzed data to FigMap4SC with an external application directly and visualize it. We use FD-CAST [9], a developing application in collaboration with the Kobe City Fire Department, as the external application.

FD-CAST (Fire Department Configuration Analysis and Simulation Tool) is a tool that estimates the arrival information of ambulance. At this time, a user can set the **configuration information** such as the location of the fire station and the vehicle formation. This tool is used for the purpose of examining the optimal arrangement and operation of resources.

Figure 6 shows an example of the analysis results on FD-CAST. This figure shows how many meters and minutes it takes ambulances to reach each town in Kobe. The service shows the first to tenth closest ambulances for each area. These values were calculated from **the route on the map**, so please note that different from the actual rescue squad time.

FD-CAST has already implemented the link function with FigMap4SC. By pressing the FigMap button at the top of each column in the table, you can create a choropleth map of the data in that column. Next, we will visualize the distribution of the dispatching time of ambulances from the nearest fire department for each block. Figure 7 shows the result of pressing the figMap button in the first column.

Naturally, areas closer to the fire station are painted blue, and areas farther from the fire station are painted red. Such visualization results can be used for

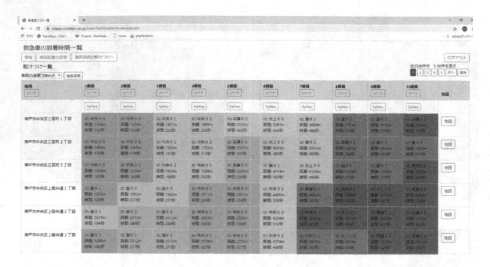

Fig. 6. Screen of "FD-CAST"

future planning such as changing the location of fire stations or establishing new ones.

5.3   Feedbacks from Practitioners

At present, the Kobe Fire Department staffs are using FigMap4SC for their work. In this section, we introduce the advantages and opinions of FigMap4SC from them.

Advantages of FigMap4SC

- Compared with some GIS, the creation of a choropleth map in FigMap4SC is easy and understanding the result speedily.
- Excel files can be used and instantly visualized on a map. Therefore, ready the data to visualize is very easy. In addition, it is good to be able to try various analyzes by trial and error.

This feedbacks show the effectiveness of FigMap4SC, such as clarity of operation and ease of visualization. On the other hand, they raise the following opinions.

Improvements in FigMap4SC

- Some addresses are not displayed on FigMap4SC.
- I want to display multiple analysis results on the same map.

Investigation of the first opinion reveals that they enter some addresses not covered by FigMap4SC. These are old addresses that are not currently used or addressed using different characters and so on. Hence, they did not match the

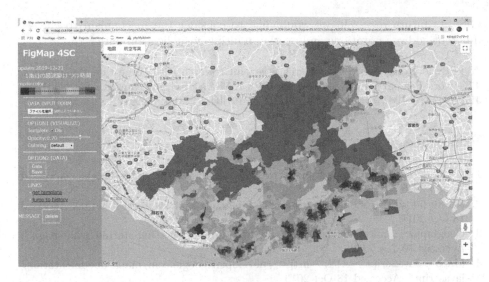

Fig. 7. Visualization of the result FD-CAST analysed

address assumed in FigMap4SC, and they became missing data. In such case, it is necessary to match the given address with the most likely existing address.

The second opinion is not possible with the current implementation. The service can generate only one choropleth map in one visualization. It is technically easy to overlay multiple class maps on the same map, however, the visibility may be low. Hence, the service needs to overlay different analysis results with different expressions for high visibility. For example, the first data is represented by a choropleth map and the second data is represented by pins.

These are future tasks.

6   Conclusion

In this paper, our research goal was to propose a more feasible and portable technique of fine-grained map visualization. In order to achieve this, we proposed FigMap4SC (Fine-Grained Map-coloring Web service for Smart City). The service hides all geographic data and a map under this service. In addition, the service performs the choropleth map generation process automatically and separates the data analysis work from the visualization process. As a result, a user can create a choropleth map easily even if they do not have expertise in geographic information systems. Moreover, the service can directly cooperate with an external application and can share the choropleth map. This enables quick and efficient visualization.

We have implemented a prototype of FigMap4SC, and we conducted a case study to visualize dispatch logs recording by Kobe City Fire Department. From their feedbacks, improvement of operability and trial of efficient analysis were evaluated as the effectiveness of the proposed service Compared with the existing

GIS. As future research, we would like to consider the mechanism to correct different address notations and overlay multiple visualization data.

Acknowledgements. This research is a joint research with Kobe Fire Department. This work was partially supported by JSPS KAKENHI Grant Numbers JP19H01138, JP17H00731, JP18H03242, JP18H03342, JP19H04154, JP19K02973.

References

1. Arcgis—esri japan corporation. https://www.esrij.com/products/arcgis/. Accessed 30 Jan 2020
2. e-Stat: portal site of official statistics of Japan. https://www.e-stat.go.jp/. Accessed 18 Oct 2019
3. Geographic information. https://www.esrij.com/getting-started/what-is-gis/. Accessed 30 Jan 2020
4. Maps JavaScript API. https://developers.google.com/maps/documentation/javascript/. Accessed 18 Oct 2019
5. QGIS project. https://qgis.org/en/site/. Accessed 30 Jan 2020
6. Deakin, M., Al Waer, H.: From intelligent to smart cities. Intell. Build. Int. **3**(3), 140–152 (2011)
7. Kulhavy, K.A.R.W.: Learning and remembering from thematic maps of familiar regions. Educ. Technol. Res. Dev. **46**(1), 19–38 (1998)
8. Maliene, V., Grigonis, V., Palevičius, V., Griffiths, S.: Geographic information system: old principles with new capabilities. Urban Des. Int. **16**(1), 1–6 (2011)
9. Yabuki, N., Saiki, S., Nakamura, M., Oyama, K.: FD-CAST: a tool for analyzing and simulating fire department configurations. In: HCII 2020. LNCS, pp. 199–213. Springer, Heidelberg (2020)

Neural Network Risks Suggested by Optical Illusions

Hiroyuki Nishimoto[✉]

Kochi University, Nankoku, Japan
hiroyuki.nishimoto@kochi-u.ac.jp

Abstract. Although there are various theories about the principle of "optical illusion", many can be explained relatively simply by assuming laws of perspective as a basic theory. Considering the perspective as a brain function cultivated through experience of estimating distance to the target, AI can also see the illusion through learning. Therefore, it is important for safety measures to improve the social environment to eliminate risk factors that are misidentified by AI. Developing the cognitive environment to reduce misperception is not just an issue for AI. Similar problems occur in the elderly. Recognizing that there are signs, fonts, and graphics that the elderly misidentifies, it is time to need the social investment to realize a cognitive barrier-free society that is friendly to the elderly and to AI. It is an urgent issue to build a cognitive barrier-free society for the elderly, just as we realized a barrier-free society for physical ability.

Keywords: Optical illusion · Laws of perspective · Cognitive barrier-free society

1 A Brain Power Acquired by Learning is Reproduced with AI

Although there are various theories about the principle of "optical illusions" [1–8], many can be explained relatively simply by assuming laws of perspective as a basic theory. Considering the perspective as a brain function cultivated through experience of estimating distance to the target, the illusion can be defined as a neural imaging technique of stereoscopically viewing 2D image in perspective. It is that parallel lines appear to meet at infinity.

In addition to the perspective, another brain function works for evoking the illusion, that supplements the part of an object hidden by obstacle by imagination. In the process of our requirement for the complete contour of an object when the obstacles overlap, the layers separated from the 2D image are sorted in the order of obstacle, target, and background. These brain functions help the sense of perspective.

If these 3D contexts work in an integrated manner, it becomes possible to stereoscopically view 2D image. On the other hand, if these contexts are inconsistent, our perception is swing between 2D and 3D contexts, creating a dynamic illusion by movement of our viewpoint. At that time, human image stabilizer works in a direction to cancel the movement of the viewpoint. However, in the oblique coordinate system created by the optical illusion, the movement of the viewpoint on the orthogonal coordinate

V. G. Duffy (Ed.): HCII 2020, LNCS 12199, pp. 175–184, 2020.
https://doi.org/10.1007/978-3-030-49907-5_12

system is distorted. As a result, the movement of the image perpendicular to the actual eye movement is felt as an illusion.

In this way, if the illusion is caused by brain function cultivated through experience, it is considered that AI can see the illusion by learning.

2 Optical Illusions

2.1 The Perspective Cultivated by Experience

In my thought, the perspective is a brain function cultivated through experience of estimating distance to the target (Fig. 1). It is defined as a neural imaging technique of stereoscopically viewing 2D image in perspective. It is that parallel lines appear to meet at infinity (Item 3 in Fig. 1).

In addition to the perspective, another brain function works for evoking the illusion, that supplements the part of an object hidden by obstacle by imagination (Item 1 in Fig. 1).

In the process of our requirement for the complete contour of an object when the obstacles overlap, the image layers separated from the 2D image are sorted in the order of obstacles, target, and background (Item 2 in Fig. 1) These brain functions help the sense of perspective.

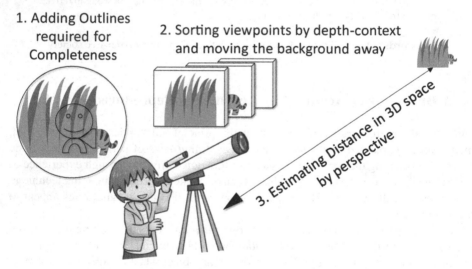

Fig. 1. Illustration of the perspective cultivated by experience

2.2 The Illusion Based on the Perspective

2.2.1 Ebbinghaus Illusion

Ebbinghaus illusion [2] is shown in Fig. 2(a). The two black circles are the same size. However, the upper one appears larger. As shown in Fig. 2(b), it may lead the illusion is based on the perspective.

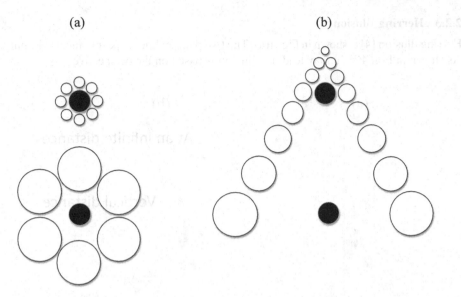

Fig. 2. Ebbinghaus illusion (a) and the supplementary image (b)

2.2.2 Müller-Lyer Illusion

Müller-Lyer illusion [3] is shown in Fig. 3(a). The two horizontal lines are the same length. However, the upper one appears longer. As shown in Fig. 3(b), it may lead the illusion is based on the perspective.

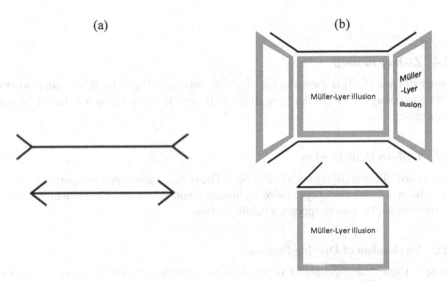

Fig. 3. Müller-Lyer illusion (a) and the supplementary image (b)

2.2.3 Herring Illusion

Herring illusion [4] is shown in Fig. 4(a). The two parallel lines appear to meet at infinity. As shown in Fig. 4(b), it may lead the illusion is based on the perspective.

(a)   (b)

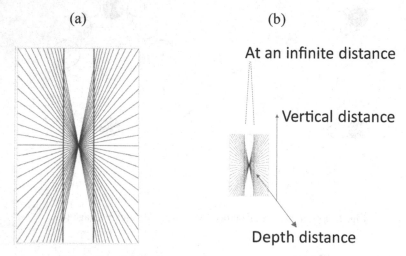

Fig. 4. Herring illusion (a) and the supplementary image (b)

2.2.4 Zöllner Illusion

Zöllner illusion [1, 2] is shown in Fig. 5(a). As shown in Fig. 5(b), this illusion works in the same way as the Müller-Lyer illusion. It may lead the illusion is based on the perspective.

2.2.5 Emboss Drift Illusion

Emboss drift illusion [6] is shown in Fig. 6(a). The center square appears a parallelogram, and drifts in order to cancel eye motion by human image stabilizer. As shown in Fig. 6(b), it shows the center square appears a parallelogram.

2.2.6 Mechanism of Drifting Illusion

Figure 7 shows the mechanism in terms of the drifting illusion by using the vector illustration of human image stabilization effect. This is a hypothesis that the drifting illusion is caused by human image stabilizer.

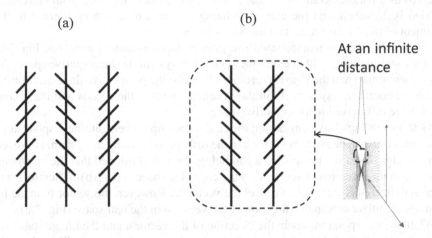

Fig. 5. Zöllner illusion (a) and the supplementary image (b)

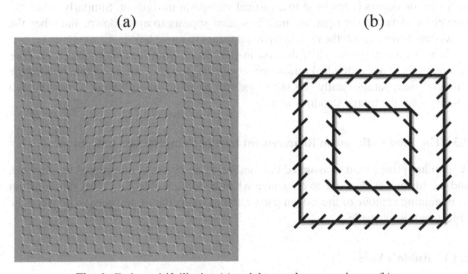

Fig. 6. Emboss drift illusion (a) and the supplementary image (b)

The premise is that, like a camera image stabilizer, our brain has a function to suppress the vibration of the screen image on the retina. In order to reduce the movement of image as much as possible even if the viewpoint moves, our brain stabilizer moves the image in the direction to cancel the movement of the viewpoint. However, since a square is perceived as a parallelogram by optical illusion, the sense in the horizontal or vertical direction is disturbed, and the extra stabilizing acts in a direction orthogonal to the movement of the viewpoint, so that the drift illusion evokes.

Figure 7(a) shows the real space with the orthogonal coordinate system. And Fig. 7(b) shows a cognitive space with the oblique coordinate system. In the cognitive space, the x'-axis (horizontal) and the y'-axis (vertical) tilt due to the perspective illusion, forming the oblique coordinate system. As in the Lorenz transform, the x'-axis and the y'-axis are felt to be orthogonal in the cognitive space.

As shown in Fig. 7(a), considering the case of eye-up movement, the displacement of the viewpoint can be given as vector a in the orthogonal coordinate system. However, by the illusion that a square appears a parallelogram, it is illusioned that the viewpoint is moving in the direction of vector a' in the cognitive space (Fig. 7(b)). Therefore, the image stabilizer acts vector b' to cancel the vector a'. However, the vector b' made by the image stabilizer acts in the direction of the vector b in the real space (Fig. 7(a)).

When the viewpoint moves in the direction of the vector a and the image stabilizer acts in the direction of the vector b, the composite vector c is not zero. This gives the illusion that the middle square is moving to the right. This is the reason that a horizontal drift illusion occurs in response to a vertical viewpoint movement. Similarly, when the viewpoint moves to the right, the middle square appears to move down, and when the viewpoint moves down, the middle square appears to move left.

If you cannot see the drift illusion in this paper, you need to enlarge Fig. 7(a). Although there are individual differences to see the illusion, if it is visible only in the enlarged view, paradoxically, it is suggested that a certain size of image is required as a condition for the image stabilizer to act.

2.3   The Illusion Based on Requirement for the Completeness in Contour

As another principle, it is assumed that outline of an object is interrupted by obstacle, and the illusion evokes due to recognize what the hidden object is. The brain function of imagining contour of the hidden parts clarifies the depth of perspective between the object and the obstacle.

2.3.1   Rubin's Vase

Rubin's vase [7] is shown in Fig. 8(a). A white vase and two black faces appear alternately. However, as shown in Fig. 8(b), the pattern changes a vase-shaped white area to the background.

2.4   The Illusion Based on the Sense of Sorting Image Layers in Perspective

In the process of our requirement for the complete outline of an object when the obstacles overlap, the image layers separated from the 2D image are sorted in the order of obstacles, target, and background.

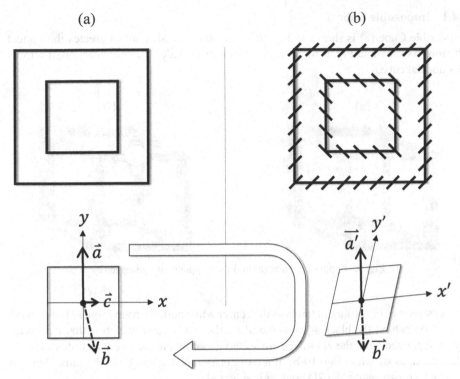

Fig. 7. Vector illustration of image stabilization effect in a drifting illusion

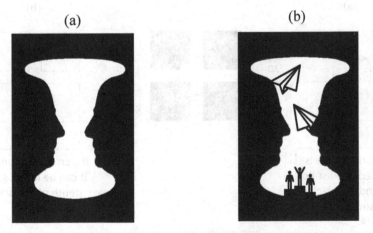

Fig. 8. Rubin's vase (a) and the supplementary image (b)

2.4.1 Impossible Cube

Impossible Cube [8] is shown in Fig. 9(a). Inconsistent 3D context creates the optical illusion. As shown in Fig. 9(b), when the white circle hides the contradiction, it returns to a normal cube.

(a)   (b)

Fig. 9. Impossible cube (a) and the supplementary image (b)

As shown in Fig. 10(a), in terms of the center white part, if a round square is assumed, it must be behind the black squares based on the 3D context, which is that the image layers separated from the 2D image are sorted according to the overlap context. On the other hand, as shown in Fig. 10(b), if a cross is assumed, it can be in the same depth of the black squares when the 2D context is selected.

(a)   (b)

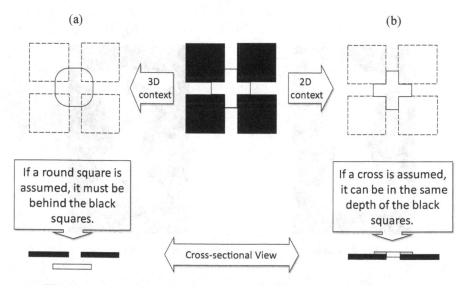

Fig. 10. A round square in the 3D context (a) and a cross in the 2D context (b)

3   Neural Network Risks Suggested by Optical Illusions

As described above, the "optical illusion" is highly likely to be the brain function cultivated through experience in estimating the distance to the target. If the illusion is a brain
function cultivated through experience, AI can also see the illusion through learning.
Optical illusions evoke when it is uncertain whether 2D or 3D context on a perspective drawing. Therefore, AI with a single camera has a higher probability of causing an
optical illusion than with two or more cameras.

When considering the development of autonomous driving with AI, the first illusion
is witnessed as an error that does not converge the correct answer rate during learning
to estimate distance. If this problem is discovered during learning, it is possible to take
safety measures such as increasing the number of cameras. However, after learning
without any solution, AI can endanger the car if it encounters the illusions around the
road. That situation must be avoided.

As shown in the example of Fig. 11, AI is not good at recognizing characters separated by obstacles. Humans can connect the fragments and easily imagine the original
character, but immature AI is not good at restoring them. Therefore, it is important for
safety measures to improve the social environment to eliminate risk factors that are
misidentified by AI, including road signs and the surrounding traffic environment.

Fig. 11. Fragmented numbers

4   Building a Cognitive Barrier-Free Society

Developing a cognitive environment to reduce misperception is not only an issue for
AI. Similar problems occur in the elderly people. For example, it is known that some
elderly cannot correctly read numbers indicated by 7-segment LED display when their
cognitive functions decline. Looking at the number "1" indicated by 7-segment LED
display, some elderly people question "Why are they divided into two sticks?" One of
the reasons is thought that the brain function that connects the two sticks indicating "1"
is weakened.

Recognizing that there are signs, fonts, and graphics that the elderly misidentifies,
it is time to need the social investment to realize a cognitive barrier-free society that is
friendly to the elderly and to AI. It is an urgent issue to build a cognitive barrier-free
society for the elderly, just as we realized a barrier-free society for physical ability.

References

1. Doherty, M.J., et al.: The Ebbinghaus illusion deceives adults but not young children. Dev. Sci. **13**(5), 714–721 (2010)
2. The Illusion Index. https://www.illusionsindex.org/ir/ebbinghaus-illusion/. Accessed 1 Jan 2020
3. The Illusion Index. https://www.illusionsindex.org/ir/mueller-lyer/ Accessed 1 Jan 2020
4. The Illusion Index. https://www.illusionsindex.org/ir/hering-illusion/. Accessed 1 Jan 2020
5. The Illusion Index. https://www.illusionsindex.org/ir/zoellner-illusion/. Accessed 1 Jan 2020
6. Drifting Spines Illusion/Drifting Embosses Illusion. http://www.psy.ritsumei.ac.jp/~akitaoka/togetogedriftillusion.html. Accessed 1 Jan 2020
7. The Illusion Index. https://www.illusionsindex.org/i/rubin-s-vase/. Accessed 1 Jan 2020
8. The Illusion Index. https://www.illusionsindex.org/i/impossible-cube/. Accessed 1 Jan 2020

Approach to Ensure an Optimal Task-Technology Fit Between Industrial Tasks and Modern Information and Communication Technologies

Jan Terhoeven[✉] and Sascha Wischniewski

Federal Institute for Occupational Safety and Health (BAuA), Dortmund, Germany
{terhoeven.janniklas,wischniewski.sascha}@baua.bund.de

Abstract. This article presents the results of industrial field studies and the derivation of an approach to ensure an optimal task-technology fit between industrial tasks and information and communication technologies. Against the background of current developments in the field of information and communication technologies, binocular smart glasses were tested as a work assistance within the scope field studies in electronics manufacturing. It was possible to collect data about the user expectations before using the technology and the user experience after using the technology. Furthermore, a comparison between binocular smart glasses and two alternative technologies was conducted. The results show the importance of a high task-technology fit for the benefit, acceptance and usability of mobile information and communication technologies as work assistance. The study points up the current problem that the introduction of new technologies as work assistance is often technology-driven and only rarely problem- or solution-oriented. This is even more difficult by the fact that there is no structured method to compare technology functions and the characteristics of work tasks for providing indications of a suitable technology for considered use cases.

Keywords: Task-technology fit · Industrial field study · Smart glasses · Usability

1 Introduction

Based on the rapid development of information and communication technologies, digitization is now influencing large parts of the industrial working environment [1]. The integration of cyber-physical systems into the production environment leads to the networking of all elements of work systems, such as machinery, equipment, products and employees via internet. In this way, the increasing complexity and requirements arising from customer orientation and variety of products are considered. It is becoming apparent that the role and tasks of employees will change significantly in the context of an increasing degree of automation [2]. For the required flexibility and responsiveness in industrial production, the employee nevertheless remains a key factor especially due to insufficient creative capabilities of machines [3]. In order to integrate people into the

© Springer Nature Switzerland AG 2020
V. G. Duffy (Ed.): HCII 2020, LNCS 12199, pp. 185–198, 2020.
https://doi.org/10.1007/978-3-030-49907-5_13

networked production systems, modern interfaces between employees and work systems are required in order to do cope with high complexity [1]. New forms of cognitive work assistance can help to deal with the increasing amount and availability of information and to support decision-making processes of employees. These assistance systems should be able to provide employees with context-sensitive information [4].

Currently, more than 80% of employees in Germany already use digital information and communication technologies at work [5]. Driven by the consumer market, these include not only the established technologies of computers and notebooks but also modern display devices such as tablet-pc, smartphones, smartwatches and smart glasses. In increasingly decentralized work systems, these have great advantages due to their mobility. The opinion of the experts interviewed in a lead study on the production work of the future is that employees will increasingly use mobile information and communication technologies as work assistance [3]. However, against the background of expected structural changes in work processes and the wide range of different mobile information and communication technologies, it is not easy to select the appropriate technology for the use as work assistance in existing or future work systems. For this reason, before introducing a new technology, the potential users and the context of use must be analyzed in detail in order to ensure efficient and satisfactory human-system interaction in terms of a high usability [6, 7]. In the following chapters a field study about the user expectations as well as the user experience on binocular smart glasses as work assistance is presented. Furthermore, a pursued approach for developing a method to ensure an optimal task-technology fit between industrial tasks and modern information and communication technologies is described, which was derived from the study results.

2   Field Study About the Use of Smart Glasses in Use Cases in Electronics Manufacturing

One research question is about chances and risks of innovative information and communication technologies in industrial setups. Within the scope of a systematic review [8] it was shown, that only a small number of existing studies describe a potential use of innovative technologies for work applications. Therefore, a field study was conducted to evaluate the use of smart glasses as work assistance within different use cases.

2.1   Use Cases

For the evaluation of smart glasses in an industrial environment, two different use cases – setup machines of surface mounted device (SMD) assembly lines and order picking in the warehouse logistics – were selected. As work assistance, a binocular smart glass technology was implemented in both use cases. In the second use case, the binocular smart glasses were compared to a monocular alternative and a tablet-pc as well. The two use cases are described below.

Setup of Assembly Machines. The first use case is about the setup of SMD assembly lines. The employees get the setup order assigned and displayed on the smart glasses. Additionally there is a tactile feedback by a smartwatch, where the setup order can be accepted via touch input. After this, the storage outsourcing is initiated and the employees get the material. At the assembly line, the employee gets he feeder track to be setup visually highlighted and is able to scan the component reels by smart glasses.

Order Picking in Warehouse Logistics. The second use case was about order picking in a warehouse for small parts. The employees receive the picking order on the smart glasses. They get information about the storage bin, the material number and the required quantity. The storage racks are visually highlighted on the smart glasses for navigation purpose. The process begins by scanning the barcodes of the bin and the material number. After removing material, the picked quantity is confirmed via voice control. Finally, the confirmation of the completed picking process causes the next order to appear.

2.2   Method, Sample and Material

The evaluation of the task-technology fit of smart glasses in different industrial use cases was designed as a pre-post comparison within the two use cases. To compare the expectations against the perception on usability and use of smart glasses as work assistance, for both use cases a between-subject design was chosen. Furthermore, in the second use case (order picking) a comparison of binocular smart glasses, monocular smart glasses and a tablet-pc was conducted by a within-subject design. Therefore, the participants randomly used each technology two times in their usual work task. The expected and perceived usability were surveyed quantitatively via questionnaires based on the design principles for human system interaction according to DIN EN ISO 9241-110 [9]. The expected and perceived usefulness and acceptance were based on the Technology Acceptance Model [10]. Before to the survey, the participants were informed about the different work assistance systems in detail.

In the first use case, $N = 42$ employees took part before using the new technology (pre-test) and $N = 21$ employees took part after using the new technology (post-test). Based on an assumed population of $N = 42$ persons, which are working in this workplace, the subjects represent a sample of 100.0% of the population in the pre-test and 50.0% in the post-test. In the second use case, $N = 17$ employees took part in the pre-test and $N = 12$ employees took part in the post-test. Based on an assumed population of $N = 24$ persons, which are working in this workplace, the subjects represent a sample of 70.8% of the population in the pre-test and 50.0% in the post-test.

Variables regarding the usability were collected by means of an adapted questionnaire based on the Isometrics^S [11], in which each of the seven dialog principles (suitability for the task, learnability, self-descriptiveness, controllability, conformity with user expectations, error tolerance and suitability for individualization) was integrated [9]. Furthermore, there were two questions each about the variables perceived usefulness, perceived ease of use and the affective state as dimension of the user acceptance based on the Technology Acceptance Model [10]. All answers were made by the participants on a 5-point Likert scale (1 = not true, 5 = true).

2.3   Statistical Evaluation

Due to the sample size of each use case, parametric methods were used for the comparison between expectations and perceptions of the users. Dependent on variance homogeneity each variable was compared using an independent two-sample t-test or the Welch's t-test. Error probability for the α-error was set to 5% for all analyses in a two-sided test.

The comparison between the different work assistance technologies in the second use case was analyzed by an one-way ANOVA with repeated measures and a Bonferroni adjustment. Mauchly-test was applied to test for sphericity. In cases of non-sphericity, a Greenhouse-Geisser correction was used in the case of $p < .05$ and $\varepsilon < .75$. As a second step, a pairwise comparison was used as post-hoc test to analyze the different technologies against each other in detail. The error probability for the α-error was set to 5% for all analyses.

2.4 Results

The results of the field study are described below. Primarily the comparison between user expectations and the perceived usefulness regarding the application of binocular smart glasses will be presented. Subsequently the comparison of the three different technologies, which were implemented in the second use case, is described. The aim of the study was to analyze the task-technology fit of innovative information and communication technologies in an industrial environment.

Comparison Between User Expectations and User Experience of Smart Glasses as Work Assistance in the Electronics Manufacturing. The analysis in the first use case by means of the t-test shows as a result, that the mean score of the user experience regarding the perceived usefulness (M = 2.13, SD = .74) was statistically significantly lower than the user expectations (M = 2.90, SD = .84), t(59) = 3.460, p = .001. Similarly, the experience regarding the perceived ease of use (M = 2.92, SD = .77) was statistically significantly lower than user expectations (M = 3.38, SD = .60), t(59) = 2,528, p = .014. The user experience on the seven dimensions of usability as well as the affective state did not differ statistically significantly from the user expectations. However, the results on the suitability for the task show no statistically significant difference, but the user experience (M = 2.74, SD = .81) tends to be lower than the user expectations (M = 3.17, SD = .82), t(59) = 1.900, p = .062.

The results of the statistical evaluation of the comparison between user expectations and user experience in the first use case are shown in Fig. 1.

The analysis in the second use case by means of the t-test shows as a result, that the mean score of the user experience regarding the suitability for the task (M = 3.28, SD = .39) was statistically significantly higher than the user expectations (M = 2.44, SD = 1.26), t(18.94) = 2.490, p = .022. The user experience on the seven dimensions of usability as well as the perceived usefulness, perceived ease of use and affective state did not differ statistically significantly from the user expectations.

The results of the statistical evaluation of the comparison between user expectations and user experience in the second use case are shown in Fig. 2.

Comparison Between Different Work Assistance Technologies in the Second Use Case. Comparing the three different mobile technologies – binocular smart glasses, monocular smart glasses and tablet-pc – used as work assistance, the results of the statistical evaluation show that the technologies differ statistically significantly on all analyzed variables except the suitability for individualization (see Table 1).

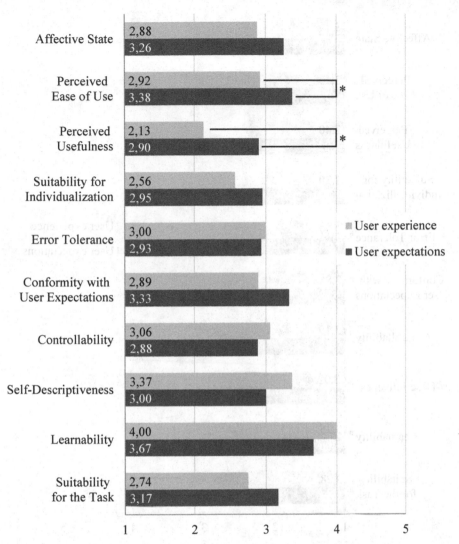

Fig. 1. Comparison of means between user expectation and user experience analyzed by a two-sample t-test; *. The mean difference is significant at the .05 level

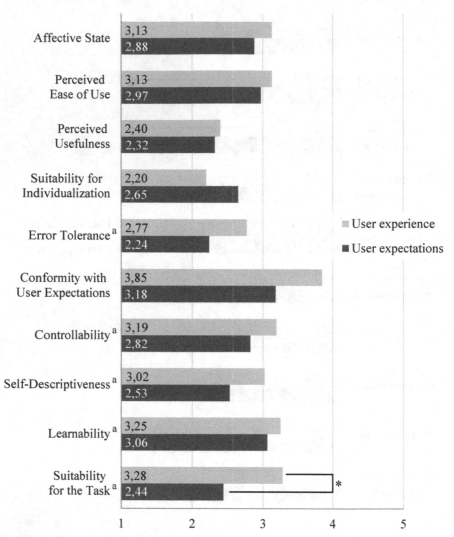

Fig. 2. Comparison of means between user expectation and user experience analyzed by a two-sample t-test; *. The mean difference is significant at the .05 level; a. analyzed by Welch's t-test

Table 1. Results of the one-way ANOVA with repeated measures to compare the different technologies used in the second use case. The mean difference is significant at the .05 level

Variable	MS	df	F	p
Suitability for the task				
Technology	.34	2	7.76	.003
Error	.04	20		
Learnability				
Technology	.90	2	6.50	.007
Error	.14	20		
Self-descriptiveness				
Technology	.30	2	27.99	.000
Error	.01	10		
Controllability				
Technology	.27	2	5.28	.027
Error	.05	10		
Conformity with user expectations				
Technology	.39	2	4.34	.031
Error	.09	16		
Error tolerance				
Technology	.05	2	6.91	.018
Error	.01	8		
Suitability for individualization				
Technology	.08	2	3.52	.080
Error	.02	8		
Perceived usefulness				
Technology	3.20	2	6.22	.008
Error	.51	20		
Perceived ease of use				
Technology	6.09	1.25	6.43	.019
Error	.95	13.77		
Affective state				
Technology	4.40	2	7.64	.003
Error	.58	22		

MS = Mean Square; df = degrees of freedom

Table 2. Pairwise comparison between the different technologies used in the second use case

Variable		MD (I–J)	Std. error	Sig[a]	95% CI	
(I) Technology	(J) Technology				LB	UB
Suitability for the task						
Binocular SG	Monocular SG	−.05	.07	1.000	−.24	.14
	Tablet-PC	−.33*	.09	.012	−.58	−.07
Learnability						
Binocular SG	Monocular SG	−.16	.14	.915	−.57	.26
	Tablet-PC	−.55	.20	.060	−1.13	.02
Self-descriptiveness						
Binocular SG	Monocular SG	−.25*	.04	.005	−.39	−.11
	Tablet-PC	−.45*	.07	.004	−.70	−.20
Controllability						
Binocular SG	Monocular SG	.04	.08	1.000	−.25	.33
	Tablet-PC	−.34	.13	.124	−.79	.10
Conformity with user expectations						
Binocular SG	Monocular SG	−.22	.17	.665	−.73	.29
	Tablet-PC	−.42	.16	.093	−.90	.06
Error tolerance						
Binocular SG	Monocular SG	−.08	.06	.846	−.34	.18
	Tablet-PC	−.20*	.05	.033	−.38	−.02
Suitability for individualization						
Binocular SG	Monocular SG	−.02	.06	1.000	−.27	.22
	Tablet-PC	−.02	.12	.368	−.68	.23
Perceived usefulness						
Binocular SG	Monocular SG	−.66	.32	.200	−1.58	.26
	Tablet-PC	−1.07	.38	.052	−2.15	.01
Perceived ease of use						
Binocular SG	Monocular SG	−.63	.31	.200	−1.49	.24
	Tablet-PC	−1.13	.41	.056	−2.28	.03
Affective state						
Binocular SG	Monocular SG	−.54	.34	.404	−1.49	.40
	Tablet-PC	−1.21*	.33	.011	−2.14	−.27

MD = Mean Difference; CI = Confidence Interval; LB = Lower Bound; UB = Upper Bound; SG = Smart Glasses; a. adjustment for multiple comparisons: Bonferroni; *. The mean difference is significant at the .05 level

With regards to the usability the difference between the technologies was statistically highly significant for the dimension suitability for the task, $F(2, 20) = 7.76$, $p < .01$, as well as for the dimension self-descriptiveness, $F(2, 20) = 6.50$, $p < .01$. Furthermore, the technologies differed statistically highly significantly on the perceived usefulness, $F(2, 20) = 6.22$, $p < .01$, and the affective state, $F(2, 22) = 7.64$, $p < .01$.

Considering the pairwise comparison the results show, that the binocular smart glasses are inferior compared to both alternative technologies – monocular smart glasses and tablet-pc – on all analyzed variables except the controllability, in which the monocular smart glasses are inferior (see Table 2). In detail, the suitability for the task is statistically significantly lower by .33 with the binocular smart glasses compared to the tablet-pc ($p = .012$). The self-descriptiveness is statistically significantly lower by .45 compared to the tablet-pc ($p = .004$) and by .25 compared to the monocular smart glasses ($p = .005$). The error tolerance is statistically significantly lower by .20 and the affective state is statistically significantly lower by 1.21 compared to the tablet-pc ($p = .033$, $p = .011$). Furthermore, the perceived usefulness ($MD = 1.07$) and the perceived ease of use ($MD = 1.13$) show no statistically significant difference, but the tablet-pc tends to perform better than the binocular smart glasses ($p = .052$, $p = .056$).

2.5 Discussion

Within the scope of the field study, it was possible to test binocular smart glasses as an assistance system in real work tasks of the electronics manufacturing. Therefore, in two different use cases data to user expectations as well as user experience was collected regarding the usability, usefulness and acceptance of this technology.

In the first use case – setup of assembly machines – the results show that the user experience tends to be lower than the user expectation on the smart glasses. Especially the experience regarding the perceived usefulness and ease of use was significantly lower than the expectation. A first explanatory approach is a low task-technology fit between binocular smart glasses and the work task. Furthermore, the time for the participants to get used to the technology could be too short.

In the second use case – order picking – the analysis show that the results about user experience tends to be higher than the results to user expectation on the smart glasses. In this use case, the suitability for the task was significantly higher than the expectation. Here, the task-technology fit between binocular smart glasses and the work task seemed to be good. For this reason a second study was initiated, in which the binocular smart glasses were tested against two alternative technologies. The pairwise comparison shows lower values regarding the usability, usefulness and acceptance using the binocular smart glasses compared to monocular smart glasses and a tablet-pc. Especially compared to the tablet-pc, the suitability for the task, self-descriptiveness, error tolerance and affective state was significantly lower with the binocular smart glasses. As a result, on the one hand the binocular smart glasses fit generally to the order picking process, but on the other hand the monocular smart glasses and especially the tablet pc fit still better considering usability, usefulness and acceptance.

In total, the results of the field studies show the importance of a high task-technology fit for an efficient use of modern technologies as work assistance. For this reason, before implementing a new assistance system, it should be ensured that the technology supports indeed the real work task [12].

3 Task-Technology Fit Between Industrial Tasks and Modern Information and Communication Technologies

The results of the field study carried out in electronics manufacturing show the relevance of an optimal task-technology fit. Currently, new assistance technologies are often selected according to their degree of technological innovation and only rarely problem-oriented [13]. For a high user acceptance, however, it is crucial that the introduction of a new technology respective the replacement of an old assistance technology creates added value when a workplace is changed. This can be achieved, for example, by making work easier and processes lean or offering opportunities to extend tasks. In the context of usability engineering, the design of an interactive human-machine system usually involves a defined design process (see Fig. 3) [14].

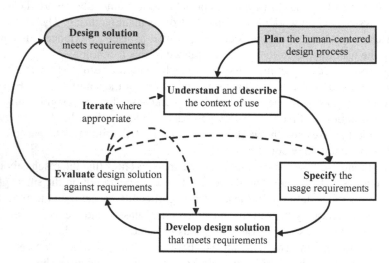

Fig. 3. User-centered design process for interactive systems [15]

In this design process, the following four steps are integrated [15]:

1. Description of the context of use,
2. Analysis of the user,
3. Development of a (first) solution,
4. Evaluation of the design solution.

The design process, however, is based on existing hardware and the implementation is mainly based on software. At this point, there is a risk that the contents of the system are optimally designed and fit the task, but the acceptance of the users is very low due to inauspiciously chosen hardware and therefore no efficient use is possible. Especially in the work context, the selection of suitable hardware plays a central role, since the assistance system must be compatible not only with the user but also with all environmental factors, work processes and the workplace itself in order to exclude potential risks. From the perspective of a human centered work design, starting from the work task, the work system, the potentially applicable technologies and the employees with their individual abilities must be considered [16]. In the following, these four aspects are used to present the process of developing an approach to ensure an optimal task-technology fit between industrial tasks and modern information and communication technologies.

3.1 Work Task

The work task is the central link between hardware and software design. Due to their type, quantity and complexity, the information necessary for the employee to perform the work task specify requirements on aspects of the hardware, e.g. display size, as well as on aspects of the software, e.g. sequencing of information provision or font size [17]. Furthermore, the connections between the work task and other elements of the work system, e.g. the workflow, influences the existing requirements for technology selection. However, these requirements are considered in the context of the work system.

3.2 Work System and Environmental Factors

To examine the work system the REFA work system was used [18]. This includes the following components:

- Input and Output
- Employee
- Work equipment
- Work task
- Work process
- Workplace
- Environmental factors

All components were assigned possible requirements that could be relevant for the selection of the assistance technology by a detailed examination of different work analysis procedures, e.g. Occupational Repetitive Actions Risk Index [19], and standards, e.g. DIN EN ISO 6385 [20]. These include, for example, the type of information as system input, the frequency of work steps in the task, the lighting in the case of environmental influences, or the spatial constraints at the workplace.

3.3 Technology Characteristics

Properties of existing technologies are given and can only be modified to a limited extent. For the examination of a possible use as work assistance, special attention is paid to technology characteristics and functions such as the built-in sensors, possibilities for the network integration, robustness against given environmental influences or compatibility with personal protective equipment. Therefore, the suitability of the superordinate technology type for the work task is of primary importance. After the selection of a suitable technology type, detailed planning concerning the specific model is necessary. Among other things, adaptation possibilities to the user or special requirements regarding the installed sensor technology are relevant.

The analysis carried out considered four types of modern information and communication technologies: smartphone, tablet-pc, smartwatch and smart glasses. For each type, a benchmark of different models was carried out and all possible functionalities per type were aggregated. In this way, the technological possibilities for each technology type could be combined, which can be relevant for the task-technology fit. There are functionalities, which are generally valid, such as the presence of certain communication interfaces, and other characteristics, which vary within the technology type and can be adapted by the model selection, e.g. the display size [21].

3.4 User Requirements

The use of a new technology as a work assistance is primarily based on the work task as well as the information required and existing work system conditions. Basically, the use of a work assistance should be independent of the individual abilities and skills of each employee. An adaptation of the person to the assistance system has to be avoided. If individual differences among employees can influence the use of an assistance system, it is important to enable adaptation possibilities on the side of the technology, which guarantee the usability for every employee. Such individual differences can be, for example, existing visual impairments, which may be relevant when using smart glasses. However, these individual differences do not play a role at the level of technology selection, but at the level of model selection within a technology type.

3.5 Approach to Ensure the Optimal Assistance Technology

In order to develop an approach to ensure an optimal task-technology fit between industrial tasks and modern information and communication technologies, all the aspects and requirements described above are combined. Within the scope of internal expert workshops, those work system requirements that have an indeed influence on the selection of suitable hardware are filtered out. In addition, the functionalities of modern information and communication technologies are identified with which the technologies can meet the identified requirements. For this purpose, the technologies are weighted according to the degree to which they meet the respective requirements with their functionalities.

The approach is developed as a tool in which a responsible person can easily decide, whether the identified requirements are relevant or not relevant for the considered work task. Then, for additional weighting, a pairwise comparison is made between the identified requirements. This weighting feeds into an algorithm, which combines the manual rating with the weighting of the different technology functionalities. Based on this, a proposal is generated as to which technology type is suited to the work task. After the technology selection has been made, additional criteria will be presented, according to which the specific model selection can be made. Furthermore, design recommendations for the consideration of the user's needs will be provided.

4 Conclusion

By means of the described field study conducted in use cases from electronics manufacturing, it was possible to test smart glasses as work assistance. The results show that the user expectations on the technology differ from the indeed perception. While in the first use case – setup of assembly machines – the perceived usefulness and suitability for the task tended to be lower than the user expectations, in the second use case – order picking – it tended to be higher. However, an additional study in the second use case showed with the aid of a pairwise comparison, that the tested binocular smart glasses were inferior to the alternative technologies – monocular smart glasses and tablet-pc. This indicates the importance of ensuring an optimal task-technology fit before implementing a new technology as work assistance.

For the described reasons, an approach for developing a method to ensure an optimal task-technology fit between industrial tasks and modern information and communication technologies was presented. This method tests the suitability of a technology for an existing use case by a structured analysis of the relevant elements of the work system. The matching of the characteristics from the different technologies to the relevant requirements of the work systems takes place automatically by an algorithm with weighted parameters. Individual user requirements and acceptance factors are considered by design recommendations for the specific technology model. The next step is the final definition of the relevant work task requirements by means of an expert workshop. Based on this, the weighting of the technology parameters and the final development of the algorithm follow.

Acknowledgement. The research and development project Glass@Service that forms the basis for this report is funded under project No. 01MD16008B within the scope of the Smart Services World technology program run by the Federal Ministry for Economic Affairs and Energy and is managed by the project management agency at the German Aerospace Center (DLR-PT). The author is responsible for the contents of this publication.

References

1. Bundesministerium für Arbeit und Soziales (BMAS): Weißbuch Arbeiten 4.0. BMAS, Berlin (2017)
2. Bauer, W., Ganschar, O., Gerlach, S., Hämmerle, M., Krause, T., Schlund, S.: Industrie 4.0 – flexiblere und reaktionsfähigere Produktionsarbeit. Ergebnisse der Industrie-4.0-Leitstudie des Fraunhofer IAO. wt Werkstattstechnik online **104**(3), 134–138 (2014)
3. Spath, D., Ganschar, O., Gerlach, S., Hämmerle, M., Krause, T., Schlund, S.: Produktionsarbeit der Zukunft - Industrie 4.0. Fraunhofer Verlag, Stuttgart (2013)
4. Jost, J., Kirks, T., Mättig, B., Sinsel, A., Trapp, T.U.: Der Mensch in der Industrie – Innovative Unterstützung durch Augmented Reality. In: Vogel-Heuser, B., Bauernhansl, T., ten Hompel, M. (eds.) Handbuch Industrie 4.0 Bd.1. SRT, pp. 153–174. Springer, Heidelberg (2017). https://doi.org/10.1007/978-3-662-45279-0_86

5. Grass, K., Weber, E.: EU 4.0 – Die Debatte zu Digitalisierung und Arbeitsmarkt in Europa. IAB-Discussion Paper 39/2016 (2016)
6. Deutsches Institut für Normung (DIN): Ergonomische Anforderungen für Bürotätigkeiten mit Bildschirmgeräten. Teil 11: Anforderungen an die Gebrauchstauglichkeit. EN ISO 9241-11 (1998)
7. Goodhue, D., Thompson, R.: Task-technology fit and individual performance. MIS Q. 19(2), 213–236 (1995)
8. Terhoeven, J., Wischniewski, S.: How to evaluate the usability of smart devices as conceivable work assistance: a systematic review. In: Schlick, C.M., et al. (eds.) Advances in Ergonomic Design of Systems, Products and Processes, pp. 261–274. Springer, Heidelberg (2017). https://doi.org/10.1007/978-3-662-53305-5_19
9. Deutsches Institut für Normung (DIN): Ergonomie der Mensch-System-Interaktion. Teil 110: Grundsätze der Dialoggestaltung. EN ISO 9241-110 (2008)
10. Davis, F.D.: Perceived usefulness, perceived ease of use, and user acceptance of information technology. MIS Q. 13(3), 319–340 (1989)
11. Gediga, G., Hamborg, K.-C.: IsoMetrics: Ein Verfahren zur Evaluation von Software nach ISO 924/10. In: Holling, H., Gediga, G. (eds.) Evaluationsforschung, pp. 195–234. Hogrefe Verlag für Psychologie, Göttingen (1999)
12. Dishaw, M.T., Strong, D.M.: Extending the technology acceptance model with task–technology fit constructs. Inf. Manag. 36(1), 9–21 (1999)
13. Junglas, I., Abraham, C., Watson, R.T.: Task-technology fit for mobile locatable information systems. Decis. Supp. Syst. 45(4), 1046–1057 (2008)
14. Shneiderman, B., Plaisant, C.: Designing the User Interface: Strategies for Effective Human Computer Interaction. Addison Wesley, Boston (2005)
15. Deutsches Institut für Normung (DIN): Ergonomie der Mensch-System-Interaktion. Teil 210: Prozess zur Gestaltung gebrauchstauglicher interaktiver Systeme. EN ISO 9241-110 (2010)
16. Ulich, E.: Arbeitspsychologie, 6th edn. Schäffer-Poeschel, Stuttgart (2005)
17. Renkewitz, H., Kinder, V., Brandt, M., Alexander, T.: Optimal font size for Head-Mounted-Displays in outdoor applications. In: Proceedings of the 2008 IEEE International Conference on Information Visualisation, London, UK, pp. 503–508 (2008)
18. REFA Bundesverband e. V.: Ausgewählte Methoden zur prozessorientierten Arbeitsorganisation. REFA Bundesverband e. V., Darmstadt (2002)
19. Colombini, D., Occhipinti, E., Grieco, A.: Risk Assessment and Management of Repetitive Movements and Exertions of Upper Limbs: Job Analysis, Ocra Risk Index, Prevention Strategies and Design Principles, vol. 2. Elsevier, Amsterdam (2002)
20. Deutsches Institut für Normung (DIN): Grundsätze der Ergonomie für die Gestaltung von Arbeitssystemen. EN ISO 6385 (2016)
21. Zhou, J., Rau, P.-L., Salvendy, G.: Older adults' text entry on smartphones and tablets: investigating effects of display size and input method on acceptance and performance. Int. J. Hum.-Comput. Interact. 30(9), 727–739 (2014)

FD-CAST: A Tool for Analyzing and Simulating Fire Department Configurations

Naoya Yabuki[1]([✉]), Sachio Saiki[1], and Masahide Nakamura[1,2]

[1] Graduate School of System Informatics Kobe University,
1-1 Rokkodai, Nada, Kobe, Japan
yabuki@ws.cs.kobe-u.ac.jp, sachio@carp.kobe-u.ac.jp, masa-n@cs.kobe-u.ac.jp
[2] Riken AIP, 1-4-1 Nihon-bashi, Chuo-ku, Tokyo 103-0027, Japan

Abstract. The fire department configuration, which determines the number and the locations of fire stations as well as the formation of fire trucks, is a key element to achieve efficient fire fighting operations under limited resources. In this paper, we develop a tool, called FD-CAST, which visualizes estimated arrival information of fire trucks for given fire department configuration. FD-CAST first computes the distance and time between every pair of a fire station and a town block, based on the configuration and geographic information. Then, assuming that a fire occurs at a town block, FD-CAST derives a designated set of fire trucks to be dispatched and their estimated time of arrival. The result is visualized in a table and a choropleth map. A user can also simulate various situations by modifying the configuration information. We have implemented a prototype of FD-CAST, and conducted case studies with practical examples. Through feedback from fire officers, we confirm the effectiveness of FD-CAST for analyzing the fire department configuration problem.

Keywords: Smart city · Data visualization · Fire department · Web application

1 Introduction

Recent years, many fire departments in Japan are collecting digital records of every dispatch of fire trucks and ambulances with ICT systems. The large-scale dispatch logs are supposed to be used for various data-driven approaches to predict the demands and optimize their resource operations. For example, the Fire and Disaster Prevention Science Center are showing the distribution of firefighting demands, and the current fulfillment of the demands for some fire departments [2].

The Kobe City Fire Department (KCFD) has also started a similar data-driven trial. The objective is to see how much extent the configuration of the fire departments (i.e., locations of fire stations and the arrangement of fire trucks

© Springer Nature Switzerland AG 2020
V. G. Duffy (Ed.): HCII 2020, LNCS 12199, pp. 199–213, 2020.
https://doi.org/10.1007/978-3-030-49907-5_14

in each station) can suffice the demand from every town block within the Kobe city. More specifically, the KCFD wants to know the answer for the following question:

Question Q1: "When a fire occurs in a town block B, can the designated set F of fire trucks arrive at B within allowable time T?" If the answer of Q1 is negative for some B's, the KCFD also like to know what the better configuration is, which is characterized by the following question. **Question Q2:** "When the configuration is changed, how will the answer of Q1 be updated?" The configuration changes in Q2 include updating the arrangement of fire trucks in a station, moving a station to another place, and creating a new fire station.

The goal of this research is to allow the staffs of the fire department to conduct the analysis for Questions Q1 and Q2 without special expertise of data mining. To achieve the goal, we develop an application, called **FD-CAST (Fire Department Configuration Analysis and Simulation Tool)**. FD-CAST is developed based on the following Requirements R1 and R2, corresponding Q1 and Q2, respectively.

Requirement R1 (Visualization): For every town block B, the application derives a list of fire trucks of all types, each of which arrives at B earliest among those with the same type. Every element of the list should contain the ID of the fire truck, the distance from the fire station, and the estimated time for arrival (**arrival time**). The list should be visualized so as to facilitate the analysis of Questions Q1.

Requirement R2 (Simulation): Every user of the application can change the fire department configuration to address Question Q2. The allowable changes are to add, move, or delete the fire trucks among the fire stations. Similarly, the application allows to add, move, or delete any fire station. For a new configuration, the user can visualize the result as specified in P1.

To satisfy these requirements, we develop FD-CAST based on the following steps:

Step 1 (Preparing Configuration Data): We prepared the data which is essential for FD-CAST. The data includes "fire station", "fire truck", "town block" and "distance along road".

Step 2 (Visualizing Arrival of Fire Trucks): FD-CAST compute where each type of fire truck arrives from and how long it takes, when a fire occured in each town block B.[1]

Step 3 (Simulating New Configration): We develop a feature that allows each staff to independently edit the fire department configuration and re-execute visualization.

In this paper, we implemented the proposed FD-CAST prototype as a Web application and performed a case study. Specifically, we had rough understanding

---

[1] The rushing distance and time are calculated from geographical information and the average speed of the vehicle, and do not match actual dispatch data.

of the current situation of the water discharge vehicle arrival to all town block and simulated improvement measures by relocating the water discharge vehicles. We also analyzed the effects of establishing a new fire station from the perspective of arrival. In addition, the KCFD stuff actually used FD-CAST for their work and they sent us feedback. The results showed that FD-CAST was a useful tool for answering questions Q1 and Q2.

2   Preiliminaries

2.1   Fire Department Data

In recent years, the fire departments of each municipality have introduced the latest ICT system to improve the efficiency of fire and emergency services. Representative data recorded and managed by such ICT systems include dispatch data, fire statioin data, vehicle data, and so on. The dispatch data records details of emergency and fire dispatches at the fire department, and data items include dispatch date and time, disaster type, dispatched vehicle number, arrival date and time, and so on. The type of disaster represents the type and duty of the corresponding disaster, such as fire, emergency, rescue, flood, and alert. Fire station data is data about the fire department, including the name and address of fire stations under the jurisdiction of the fire department. Vehicle data is data of fire and ambulance vehicles owned by the Fire Department, including data such as vehicle numbers, assigned fire departments, vehicle types, and concurrent vehicles. Concurrent vehicle refers to a group of vehicles operated by the same unit that also serves multiple duties Therefore, while one of the concurrent vehicles is dispatched, the other vehicle cannot be dispatched.

2.2   Fire Department Configuration Issues

In this paper, the problem of the local government's fire department deciding where and how many fire stations to set up in the area and how many vehicles to place at each fire station is referred to as **the fire department's configuration problem**. Configuration issues is directly related to the possibility of quick and efficient fire fighting when a fire occurs. Therefore, it is necessary to consider a better composition of the fire department in anticipation of the current situation and the future situation.

In the case of Kobe City, there are 28 fire stations in 9 wards, and a total of 130 fire trucks and ambulances are operating on a daily basis. Table 1 shows the number of fire stations and fire trucks by vehicle type located in each ward. Each row in the table indicates the number of fire stations and fire trucks in each ward. Numbers in parentheses indicate the number of vehicles that can be dispatched at the same time, and are due to restrictions on concurrent vehicles. Considering the municipal finances, it is not easy to increase units and vehicles. The proposition is how to find an efficient configuration within a limited range of resources.

Table 1. Number of fire stations and fire trucks by vehicle type in Kobe

Ward	Station	Command	Rescue	Water discharge	Ambulance	Ladder	Total
Higashinada	4	1	1	9(6)	4	2(1)	17
Nada	2	1	1	3(2)	3	0	8
Chuo	3	1	2	5(3)	4	2(1)	14
Hyogo	2	1	1	3(2)	2	0	7
Nagata	2	1	1	3(2)	3	2(1)	10
Suma	3	1	1	5(3)	3	0	10
Tarumi	4	1	1	7(5)	4	2(1)	15
Nishi	3	1	1	6(3)	4	1	13
Kita	5	2	2	11(6)	5	3(2)	23
Total	28	10	11	52	32	12	117

2.3 Evaluation and Improvement of Configuration Based on Data

When a fire occurs in a area, it is necessary that a group of appropriate fire vehicles arrive to the scene according to the type and scale of the fire and extinguish the fire. For example, there is an *ideal* criterion "four water discharge vehicles can arrive within 8 min in the case of general building fire". Of course, depending on the location of the fire and the configuration of the fire department, these criteria may or may not be met. Therefore, it is the greatest concern for the fire department to understand "How many minutes can a specified set of vehicles arrive at a town block", which is the question Q1 described in Sect. 1.

The KCFD sets various standards and **evaluates** the configuration of the Fire Department based on data, and is making efforts to **improve** it. However, at present, the staff are analyzing data using general-purpose tools such as Excel and GIS (Geographic Information System), and it takes a lot of time to evaluate the current configuration. Furthermore, it is currently impossible to try and evaluate various configurations by simulation, which corresponds to the question Q2 described in Sect. 1.

2.4 FigMap4SC: Fine-Grained Map Coloring Web Service for Smart City Analytics

Our research group is developing a Web service **FigMap4SC** that colors maps based on given data and creates choropleth map [3]. If the user gives a data set with the address (city, ward, town or block) in the area as a key and the value associated with it as a value, FigMap4SC automatically creates a choropleth map with the specified granularity. In addition, we published the Web-API, and external applications can input data directly to FigMap4SC without human intervention. By using FigMap4SC, any external application can easily visualize its analysis results on a map. In this study, we also use FigMap4SC as a means to visualize the fire truck arival time on a map.

3 FD-CAST: Fire Department Configuration Analysis and Simulation Tool

3.1 Requirement

In this study, we will develop a fire department configuration analysis and simulation tool **FD-CAST** to solve the problems described in the previous section. FD-CAST is developed based on requirements R1 (visualization) and R2 (simulation) described in Sect. 1.

3.2 System Architecture

Figure 1 shows the system architecture of FD-CAST. FD-CAST is developed as a client-server type Web application. The left side of the figure shows the functions on the client side. Users can visualize the arrival and change the configuration using a Web browser. It also has a user management function so that multiple users can independently change the configuration and simulate arrival. The right side of the figure shows the functions and data on the server side. The following sections explain these details.

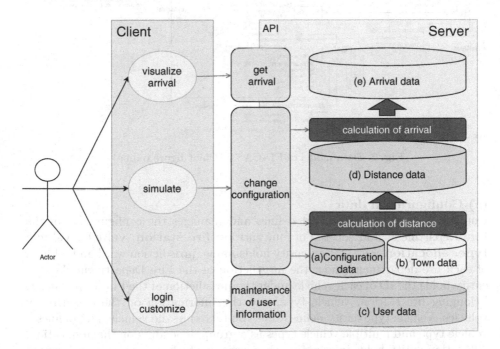

Fig. 1. System architecture of FD-CAST

3.3   Data Preparation

We prepare the data required to implement FD-CAST. As shown in Fig. 1, FD-CAST consists of three types of master data ((a) **Configuration data, (b) Town data, (c) User data**) and two types of derived data ((d) **Distance data, (e) Arival data**). Figure 2 shows the ER diagram that defines the data model of FD-CAST. This ER diagram is based on the notation shown in [4]. Squares represent entities, — represents parent-child relationships, and —... represent reference relationships. Below the data item of each entity, an instance is illustrated.

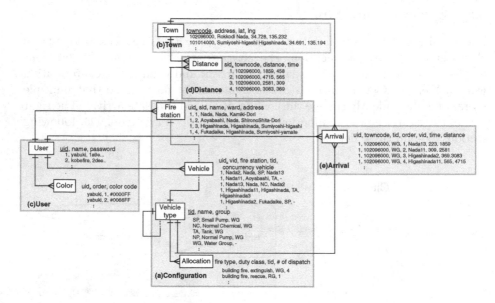

Fig. 2. Data model of FD-CAST (Color figure online)

(a) Configuration data

Configuration data is data that defines and manages the configuration of the Fire Department, and consists of four entities: **fire station, vehicle, vehicle type, allocation**. Fire station entity holds name, jurisdiction ward and address of each fire department under the jurisdiction of the Fire Department. Vehicle entity holds the ID of each vehicle under the jurisdiction of the Fire Department, belonging fire station, vehicle type, and the information on the concurrency vehicles. Vehicle type entity defines the type (class) of the vehicle, and defines a vehicle type and multiple vehicle types as a group depending on the application. Allocation entity holds information that assigns which car type (group) should be dispatched to which fire type/duty class and how many vehicles should be dispatched. For the fire department and vehicles, the user ID is included in the primary key so that FD-CAST users can freely add and change them. This time, the composition data is created based on the data provided by KCFD.

(b) Town data

Town data is composed of a **town** entity that hold the addresses of all the town blocks managed by the local government and the latitude and longitude of the center point. In the case of Kobe City, there are 3,326 town-blocks in nine wards, each identified by a nine-digit address code (towncode) This town data was created by obtaining the list of towns in all Kobe city [1] from the open data catalog of Kobe city, and obtaining its latitude and longitude using Yahoo GeoCoding API [5].

(c) User data

User data is data that manages user information of FD-CAST, and consists of two entities **user, color**. User entity holds the user ID, name, and password. Color entity defines a user-defined color scale for visualization. User data is created by the user registration function of FD-CAST.

(d) Distance data

Distance data consists of a **distance** entity that manage the distance from the fire station to the town block. Each instance holds the distance (m) and the estimated time (sec) of one fire department and one town block. The value of the distance is derived from the address of the fire department and the coordinates of the town block based on geographic information. The estimated time is calculated by dividing the distance by the average speed of the vehicle. This time, using Google Direction API, we found a route along all pairs of 28 fire stations in Kobe × 3,326 town block, and created distance data using the length as the distance. In addition, FD-CAST users can freely set the average vehicle speed, and the default value is 30 km/h.

(e) Arrival data

Arival data consists of a **arrival** entity that holds which vehicle can arrive to each town block in how long time. The primary key is composed of [user ID, town code, vehicle type, order]. We assume that each user independently manages the arrival information and the vehicles arriving at each town in order of vehicle type and arrival time. The attributes of each instance hold the ID of the arriving vehicle, the estimated time, and the distance from the fire station. Arrival data is calculated by FD-CAST according to the procedure described in the next section.

3.4 Visualization of Arrival

When a fire occurs in each town block B, FD-CAST calculate for each type of fire truck which fire truck arrives from where and how long by the following procedure. In the following, the entities in Fig. 2 are abbreviated as [name].

1) Obtain the vehicle type τ and the number of dispatch n required for the specified fire type/duty from [allocation].
2) Got all vehicle types $tau_1, \tau_2, \ldots, \tau_k$ belonging to τ from [vehicle type]
3) Find all vehicles $v_1, v_2, \ldots, v_s$ whose vehicle type is $\tau_1, \tau_2, \ldots, \tau_k$ from [vehicle].

4) Refers to the [distance] using the fire station s_i to which each v_i belongs and the current town block B as keys, and calculates the distance δ_i and the estimated time t_i from s_i to B.

5) Sort $v_1, v_2, \ldots, v_s$ in ascending order by estimated time, and the first n vehicles $v_{f1}, v_{f2}, \ldots, v_{fn}$ are selected as arrival vehicles for the vehicle type τ in town block B. At this time, if a concurrency vehicle is included, the vehicle is excluded and the next vehicle in the order is moved up and selected.

6) For $1 \leq j \leq n$, register $(B, \tau, j, v_{fj}, \delta_{fj}, t_{fj})$ in [arrival].

For example, we will calculate the arrival information required for a fire extinguishing mission for a building fire in Rokkodai, Nada, Kobe, with reference to the instance of Fig. 2. From [allocation], we can see that four Water Group (WG) are required. From the [vehicle type], WG includes four types: small pump, normal chemical, tank, and normal pump. Vehicles in WG such as Nada2 and Nada13 are listed from [vehicle]. From [fire station] and [distance], we find the distance and estimated time between the fire station to which each vehicle belongs and Rokkodai, Nada, and sort them in ascending order. At this time, Nada2 is excluded because it is a concurrency vehicle of Nada13. As a result, four vehicles, Nada13, Nada11, Higashinada2, and Higashinada17, are selected.

After the arrival data for all town blocks is created by the above procedure, they are listed in a table format and visualized. At this time, each row of the table shows the town block, and each column shows the arrival information for each vehicle type. Each cell in the table displays the vehicle ID, the distance from the fire station to the town block and the estimated time.

In addition, color-coding the cells according to the estimated time helps us to understand the data. By default, the shorter the time is, the more blue it is, and the longer it is, the more red it is. This color scale can be customized to the user's preferred color scheme, and the settings are managed by color entities. In addition, we can analyze the arrival data in detail by sorting by the attribute of each column, and searching and narrowing down by the value of the address and the arrival time.

Moreover, by linking with FigMap4SC (see Sect. 2.4), we can visualize arrival data on a map. By passing the pair of the address of each town and the color code assigned to the cell to the Web-API of FigMap4SC, we can visualize the arrival information calculated from the current configuration on the choropleth map. Therefore we can see at a glance which town block it takes time to rush to geographically.

3.5   Change of Configuration and Simulation

To respond to request R2, FD-CAST allows each user to independently change the configuration data. Specifically, it is allowed to add, update, and delete data of [fire station] and [vehicle] in the configuration data of Fig. 2. For vehicle data, it is also possible to set the vehicle to undispatchable. This allows you to set up a new fire station in the area, move vehicles under the control of one fire station to another fire station, and try out various fire station configurations. Since [vehicle

Table 2. Used technology

Client	JavaScript, HTML5
Server	PHP5, Python (generate data)
Database	MySQL
Web server	Apache 2.4.37
Library	Google Maps API, Direction API, phpoffice

type] and [allocation] are commonly used by fire departments nationwide, these changes are not permitted at present.

When the user changes the configuration data, FD-CAST calculates the distance and arrival again, and derives the distance data and installation data based on the new configuration data (see Fig. 1). Users can view and confirm the updated data by visualizing the arrival of Sect. 3.4.

The user can simulate and evaluate various configurations of fire departments by repeatedly executing the above configuration change and visualization processes.

3.6   Login and Customize User

FD-CAST manages user information so that multiple users can independently analyze and simulate configuration information. Users can create a new user account by registering their login ID and password in FD-CAST. When a new user is created, FD-CAST creates its own [fire station], [vehicle], [distance], [arrival] tables and loads the default data. It also creates a [color] table and a default color scale. By creating a dedicated table for each user, users can change configuration information, simulate, and customize visualization without affecting other users.

4   Implementation

Based on the data model and functions described in Sect. 3, we implemented a prototype of FD-CAST.

4.1   Used Technology

Table 2 shows the technology used to implement the prototype. We implemented FD-CAST as a Web application, and programmed using HTML5 and JavaScript on the client side and PHP on the server side. Python was used to generate the distance data. The database used MySQL, the Web Server used Apache 2.4.37, and the library used Google Maps API, Directions API, and phpoffice.

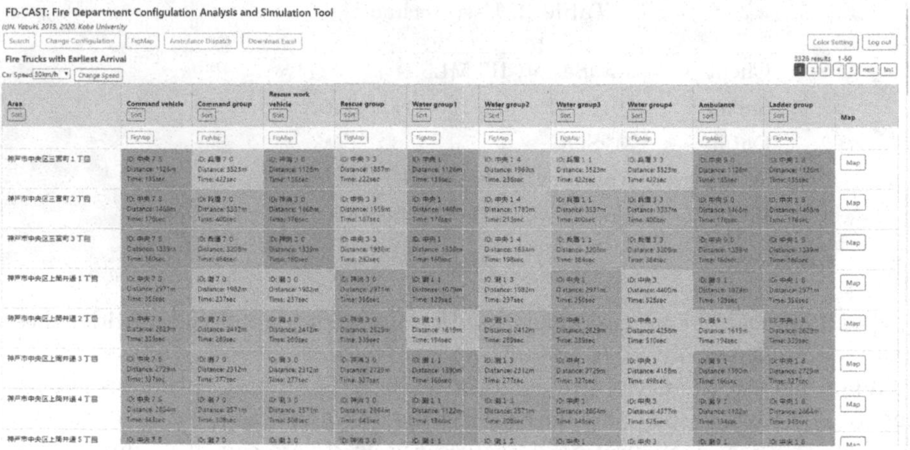

Fig. 3. Arrival visualization screen (Color figure online)

4.2 Arrival Visualization Screen

Figure 3 shows the arrival visualization screen. As described in Sect. 3.4, each row in the table represents a town block, and each column shows the arrival information of the vehicle type at that town block. For example, looking at the first row and fifth column of the table, we can see the first water discharge vehicle that can arrive at 1, Sannomiya, Chuo, Kobe is "Chuo 13".

Each cell in the table is color-coded according to the arrival time of each vehicle. By default, the cells are displayed in blue for fast and red for slow. You can change the average speed of the vehicle from the pull-down list in the upper left. In addition, there are buttons for sorting data by the value of each column and buttons for searching.

Figure 4 shows a display example in map format. This figure visualizes the time it takes for the water discharge vehicle to arrive in the entire area of Kobe City. The same color as the visualization in the table format is used, areas where the arrival time is short are displayed in blue, and long areas are displayed in red.

4.3 Configuration Change Screen

Figure 6 shows the prototype vehicle configuration change screen. As defined in Fig. 2, each fire truck has vehicle number (ID), belonging fire station, vehicle type, and concurrency vehicle, and these are displayed on the list screen. By pressing the "Edit" button, the screen changes to the edit screen, and among these information, it is possible to change information other than vehicle number. The changed information is stored in the database. Users can also add a new vehicle by clicking the "Add" button, or change the vehicle to undispatchable by using the "Unable" button. If you want to search for a specific vehicle, you

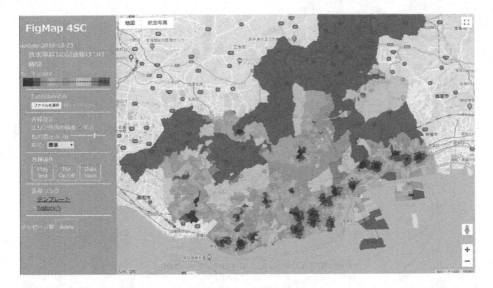

Fig. 4. Visualization of arrival on the map in cooperation with FigMap4SC (Color figure online)

can go to the search screen by pressing the "search" button on the upper left, and you can also search and display only vehicles that meet specific conditions. With these functions, it is possible to simulate the configuration of a virtual fire station that cannot be tried at actual sites.

4.4 Color Scale Setting Screen

FD-CAST performs color coding according to arrival time when visualizing arrival information in tabular format. This color is defined by a color scale that assigns 11 different colors to each segment in units of 60 s from 0 s to 600 s and 600 s or more. Figure 6 shows the default color scale. On this screen, users can change the color of each section to their favorite color and change the appearance of the visualization result. They can set a visualization method suitable for analysis, for example, by defining the color scale according to the standard of interest, such as coloring only the area of 8 min or more by turning colorless within 480 s and red for 480 s or more.

5 Case Study

In order to confirm the effectiveness of FD-CAST, we conducted a case study using realistic examples.

Case 1: Current Situation of Water Discharge Vehicle Arrival and Relocation The rapid arrival of the water discharge vehicle is an important

Fig. 5. Configuration change screen

Fig. 6. Color scale setting screen (Color figure online)

factor in minimizing the spread of fire (see Sect. 2.3). We use FD-CAST to visualize how long a water truck can arrive each town block in Kobe. Figure 7 shows the estimated time of arrival of the second water discharge vehicle at each town street calculated by FD-CAST on a map using FigMap4SC. The central southern city where many fire stations are located is colored in cold colors, and it shows that two water trucks arrive immediately in this area. On the other hand, the northern and western areas, which are far from the fire department, are colored in warm colors, and it shows that it takes time to arrive.

Next, we moved one water discharge vehicle from a fire station in the city to a fire station in the north, and visualized the arrival again. Figure 8 shows the arrival times of the two water discharge vehicles after the configuration change. The × and ○ marks in the figure indicate the locations of the fire station in the city and the fire station in the north, respectively. Comparing Fig. 7 and Fig. 8, this change in configuration significantly decreased the arrival time in some parts of the northern region without sacrificing the rushing time in the city.

Case 2: Establish New Fire Station. Currently, the KCFD is planning to establish a new fire station in Nishi Ward. Therefore, we simulated the arrival time of two water discharge vehicle if a new fire station was established at the construction site. Specifically, we established a new fire station at the address in western Kobe, and a water discharge vehicle is added there. Figure 9 shows visualization of the arrival times of two water discharge vehicles if a new fire

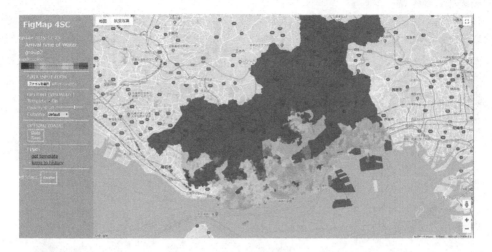

Fig. 7. Estimated arrival time of two water discharge vehicle (Color figure online)

station was established. The circles in the figure indicate the locations of the established fire stations. Compared to Fig. 7, the arrival time around the new fire station is shorter.

5.1 Feedback from Staff Members

The developed prototype of FD-CAST is currently used at the KCFD. We got feedback about its benefits and improvements from staff members using the system. We introduce some of the feedback below.

- It is convenient because we can easily check and visualize the arrival to each town
- It is good to be able to simulate the effects of vehicle configuration and new or changed fire departments that cannot be easily tested at actual sites.
- Why is the rush time significantly different from the actual result in some areas?
- Can FD-CAST automatically determine the optimal configuration by calculation?

The first and second feedbacks show that FD-CAST has contributed to the analysis and investigation of the fire department's configuration problems in actual sites. The third comment is due to the fact that the route calculated by the Google Direction API used to calculate the distance was significantly different from the route that the fire truck actually ran. We want to improve it by reviewing API options. The fourth comment is equivalent to solving an optimization problem, and is a feature that is not supported by current FD-CAST. We want to make it a future work.

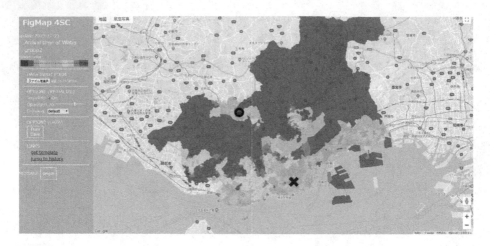

Fig. 8. Estimated arrival time of two water discharge vehicle (after configuration change) (Color figure online)

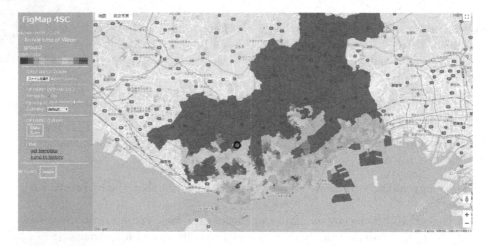

Fig. 9. Estimated arrival time of two water discharge vehicle (after establishing) (Color figure online)

6   Conclusion

In this study, we proposed FD-CAST, a tool to support the analysis and simulation of the configuration of the fire department. For a given configuration, FD-CAST calculates the arrival of fire trucks to each town block, and visualizes it in a tabular form or on a map. In addition, we implemented a prototype of FD-CAST and performed a case study using realistic examples. As future tasks, we plan to study the optimization of the calculation of the distance when changing the position of the fire department and the method of automatically calculating the better configuration.

Acknowledgments. This study is conducted as part of a joint study with the Kobe City Fire Department. This research was partially supported by JSPS KAKENHI Grant Numbers JP19H01138, JP17H00731, JP18H03242, JP18H03342, JP19H04154, JP19K02973.

References

1. Kobe city list. https://www.city.kobe.lg.jp/a53715/kurashi/registration/jukyo/ichiran.html
2. Fire, G., Center, D.P.S.: Business such as appropriate placement of firefighting power. https://www.isad.or.jp/to_fire_department/proper_placement/
3. Nakai, T., Saiki, S., Nakamura, M. July 2020, to be appeared
4. Watanabe, T.: Data Modeling for Production Management and Cost Management System. Japan Business Publisher Co., Chiyoda City (2002)
5. YOLP(map): Yahoo! geocoder api - yahoo! developer network. https://developer.yahoo.co.jp/webapi/map/openlocalplatform/v1/geocoder.html

Addressing Ethical and Societal Challenges

Embedding Ethics in Human Factors Design and Evaluation Methodologies

Joan Cahill[✉] [iD]

Trinity College Dublin, Dublin, Ireland
cahilljo@tcd.ie

Abstract. Methodologies are required to enable the active translation of ethical issues pertaining to the human and social dimensions of new technologies, in a manner that considers the diversity of practices across research and innovation and commercial research projects. This paper presents a new methodology for embedding ethics assessment in human machine interaction (HMI)/human factors (HF) design and evaluation activities.

Keywords: Human factors · Ethics · Impact assessment · Responsible research & innovation · Societal impact · Emerging technologies

1 Introduction

Human activity should not compromise the long-term balance between the economic, environmental and social pillars [1]. The evaluation of impact is a necessary part of all research and innovation (R&I) and attempts to improve the relationship between science and society. This follows a 'perspective oriented to humane and social values' [2] and recommendations from the European Union (EU) in relation to undertaking 'responsible research and innovation (RRI)' [3] and the involvement of societal actors in R&I [4]. New technologies have the potential to deliver benefits. However, such technologies are inherently uncertain. As stated by Capurro (2009), technology designers must examine the ethical implications of things which may not yet exist, or things which may have impacts we cannot predict [5]. In so doing, they must deal with uncertainty. This includes the 'uncertainty of future products, uses and consequences, and associated ethical issues that will result from an emerging technology' [6].

In asking what technology is and how it might be designed, we ask questions about who we are (identity) and what it means to be human [7]. As stated by Heidegger [1977], we examine the nature of existence and human autonomy [7]. Such ideas have led to the concept of 'ontological design' which addresses how the design of technology changes our human and social reality [8]. As such, we are designed by our designing and by that which we have designed [9].

Design/technology teams exercise choice in relation to what is valued and advancing technology that improves the human condition (and not worsens it). As researchers we need methods to assess and practice ethics, to ensure that new technologies positively contribute to human wellbeing and have positive impacts across the triple bottom

© Springer Nature Switzerland AG 2020
V. G. Duffy (Ed.): HCII 2020, LNCS 12199, pp. 217–227, 2020.
https://doi.org/10.1007/978-3-030-49907-5_15

line. In an ideal world, R&I teams are multi-disciplinary and include ethicists. Further, stakeholder evaluation underpins the generation of an evidence map and proposed solutions. However, this is not always the case. Methodologies are required to enable the active translation of ethical issues pertaining to the human and social dimensions of new technologies, in a manner that considers the diversity of practices across R&I and commercial research projects. To this end, this paper presents a new methodology for embedding ethics assessment in human machine interaction (HMI)/human factors (HF) design and evaluation activities.

2   Background

2.1   Underlying Concepts

Human Factors refers to 'the practice of designing products, systems, or processes to take proper account of the interaction between them and the people who use them' [10]. Ethics concerns the moral principles that govern a person's behavior or how an activity is conducted. As researchers, we must distinguish research ethics (i.e. the normative aspects of engaging in scientific research) and the ethics of technological innovation and its impacts at different levels. 'Digital ethics' or information ethics deals with the impact of digital information and communication technologies (ICT) on society and the environment. Data ethics is defined as a branch of ethics that evaluates data practices with the potential to adversely impact on people and society [11].

2.2   The Practice of Ethics in R&I

A recent systematic review indicates that the practice of ethics in R&I is a relatively new topic [12]. While academic discussion on specific practices commenced in the 1990s, this research has gained considerable momentum in the last ten years [12]. According to Reijers et al. (2017), health technologies is the most represented in the literature, followed by the fields of information systems research and computer science [12].

Specific ethics approaches in R&I can take many forms. Reijers et al. (2017) categorize the different methods in relation to their application in the technology development lifecycle – distinguishing (1) ex ante methods, dealing with emerging technologies (2) intra methods, dealing with technology design and (3) ex post methods, dealing with ethical analysis of existing technologies [12]. Research evidence can include information from horizon scanning and participatory foresight activities, literature reviews, and field research with stakeholders [13]. Specific stakeholder evaluation research (i.e. empirical research) may take different formulations. Stakeholders may engage directly or indirectly with R&I teams. Researchers and stakeholders may engage with ethical challenges in a collaborative workshop. Or, research may be undertaken with stakeholders and later examined by research and design teams in a structured format. This format may follow specific conceptual frameworks and assessment approaches. Several key frameworks for ethical assessment have emerged. This includes (but is not limited to): ontological design [9], anticipatory technology ethics/foresight approach [13], value sensitive design [14], ethical impact assessment [15], the ETICA approach

[16], and the techno-ethical scenarios approach [17]. Brey (2017) classifies five sets of ethical impact assessment approaches. This includes generic approaches, anticipatory/foresight approaches, risk assessment approaches, experimental approaches and participatory/deliberative ethics approaches [13]. Increasing, researchers are combining approaches. For example, Cotton (2014) combines participatory/deliberative ethics approaches and stakeholder approaches [18].

2.3 Ethics Canvases

Ethics canvases or visual tools which support the ethics assessment approach are not being used in commercial and research projects. In principle, these canvases allow non-ethicists such as Designers, Human Factors Researchers, Engineers, and Computer Scientists to engage in ethical issues pertaining to the emerging technology product. Examples of such canvases include the 'Research Impacts Canvas' (RIC) [19], The Ethical Matrix [20], The Digital Product Ethics Canvas and Impacts Canvas [21], The Humans & Machines Ethics Canvas's [22], The Online Ethics Canvas [23], and the Data Ethics Canvas [24]. Some canvases focus on ethics and impact in a general sense, while others address specific themes. For example, the Online Ethics Canvas addresses the impact of new technology on human behavior and activity at individual and societal levels [23]. The Data Ethics Canvas considers ethical issues related to data privacy, data use and data quality [24].

3 Human Factors and Ethics Canvas

3.1 Rationale

Critically, human factors and ethical issues must be explored in an integrated way. Although valuable, the existing ethics canvases require further emphasis on framing the problem, specifying the psychosocial dimensions and impacts of new technologies and addressing specific stakeholder/end user requirements and impacts. Further, ethical issues need to be managed in terms of design decisions. These decisions need to be agreed and documented.

The 'Human Factors & Ethics Canvas' introduced by Cahill (2019) [25] reflects an integration of ethics and HF methods, particularly around the collection of evidence using stakeholder evaluation methods [26, 27] personae-based design [28], scenario-based design approaches [29]. Further, it makes use of ethical theories/perspectives that are used in relation to the analysis of technology innovation in relation to the analysis of benefit versus harm including Consequentialism, Deontology & Principlism [30].

3.2 Procedure

The HFEC can be used at any stage of the design process. As such, it spans the classification of methods proposed by Reijers et al. [12]. Overall, it combines anticipatory/foresight approaches and participatory/deliberative ethics approaches. In line with stakeholder evaluation approaches, the canvas can be evaluated using the 'community of practice' [27]. That is, using internal stakeholders (project team) and external stakeholders (relevant ends users/stakeholders and legitimate other parties who may be impacted by the technology). At a minimum, core internal stakeholders/core team members (including an ethicist {if available}, the HF lead, the design lead and the product owner/manager) are involved in completing the canvas. If the project team includes an ethicist, then they should take the role of the 'HFEC' coordinator - recording relevant information in the HFEC. Otherwise, this can be done by the HF lead or another designated member of the project team.

As indicated in Fig. 1, the HFEC is divided into seven stages or sections. For more, please see Appendix A. Stage 0 records project information. Stage 1 is all about framing the problem. Stage 2 involves understanding how the technology fits to the problem, defining stakeholder goals and needs and the specification of expected benefits for different stakeholders. This is followed by several more detailed examinations of core themes. These are: benefits, outcomes and impact (stage 3), personae and scenario (stage 4), data ethics (stage 5) and implementation (stage 6). The final stage (stage 7) presents the outcomes of the preceding analysis. An analysis of literature review data and information from team problem solving sessions can be used to populate the HFEC. However, it is best to complete Stage 3 and 4 either using stakeholder evaluation approaches (either direct engagement of stakeholders in ethical assessment or following the analysis of field research with stakeholders). In addition, Stage 6 can only be completed following implementation and evaluation of the proposed technologies. Ideally, this might occur in a field setting. However, information from simulation studies can also be used.

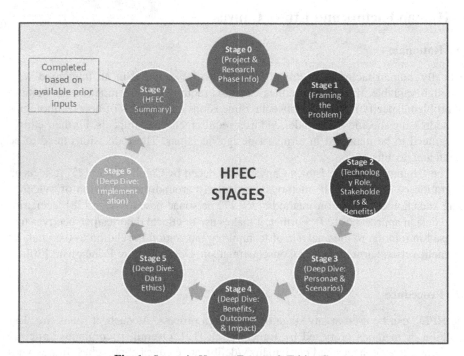

Fig. 1. Stages in Human Factors & Ethics Canvas

4 Discussion

As illustrated in the ethics canvas, there is much convergence between the analysis of new technology both from an ethics and human factors perspective (for example, addressing stakeholder need, expected benefits and outcomes, and impact [intended and unintended] – both at an individual and societal level). Ethical principles need to be both articulated and then embedded in the design concept. Personae/scenarios are useful in relation to considering and documenting the needs/perspectives of different stakeholders and adjudicating between conflicting goals/principles. Moreover, the translation of system objectives in relation to wellbeing and human benefit objectives (and associated metrics) ensures that wellbeing and human benefit are both a reference point and a design outcome.

As highlighted by Brey (2017), the ethics of emerging technologies 'harbors the promise of early intervention when a technology is still malleable and there is still much room for choice in its development and social embedding' [13]. However, researchers have a limited range of empirical data to use. As the technologies are not in use, there are 'significant uncertainties regarding future developments and impacts' (Brey 2017). Some theorists present philosophical objections to speculation about future impacts [31, 32]. For example, Nordmann (2007) contends that speculation about the future should be rejected as researchers cannot gain sufficient knowledge about the future to stipulate procedures for action or guidance in R&I processes [32]. Others argue that the available theories and methods do not provide adequate theoretical grounding in terms of how values might be embedded in design solutions [33]. In addition, VSD and related approaches must address the difference between designer's intentions and user practice [34].

5 Conclusion

Assessing the ethical implications of things which may not yet exist, or things which may have impacts we cannot predict, is very difficult. However, this should not be barrier to posing important questions and ensuring that these questions are addressed as part of the design process. Thinking about both potential positive, negative consequences and unintended consequences enables designers to build in protections into the design concept. Overall, it is argued that the specification of an ethics canvas as part of a broader human factors design approach ensures that ethical issues are considered.

Appendix A: Human Factors and Ethics Canvas (HFEC)

Stage 0 (Project Information and Research Summary)

See Table 1.

Table 1. HFEC: Stage 0 (Project Information & Research Summary)

#	0: Project Information & Research Summary
1	Date
2	Project Name
3	Product Owner
4	HF & Ethics Coordinator
5	HF & Ethics Canvas Version No.
6	Prior HFEC Iterations
7	Research & Innovation Phase
8	Summary of Research Completed & Key Sources of Information/Evidence .

Stage 1 (Formulating the Problem and Framing the Question)

See Table 2.

Table 2. HFEC: Stage 1 (Formulating the Problem & Framing the Question)

#	1: Formulating the problem and framing the question
1	What is the problem that the proposed technology will address?
2	Who is it a problem for? Key stakeholders? Who effect (directly and indirectly?)
3	Setting & Environment?
4	Causes of the problem?
5	Ethical codes that apply in this setting?
6	Ethics embedded in the problem definition?
7	Ethics & Impact of Problem. Individual Level. Societal level. Ethics of acting/not acting?
8	Summary of ethical issues to be addressed?
9	Summary of relevant ethics principles and frameworks?
10	Ethics & Key KPI?

Stage 2 (Understanding Technology and Fit to Problem/Stakeholder Needs & Expected Benefits)

See Table 3.

Table 3. HFEC: Stage 2 (Understanding Technology & Fit to Problem/Stakeholder Needs & Expected Benefits)

#	2: Understanding Technology & Fit to Problem/Stakeholder Needs & Expected Benefits
1	What is the technology? How does tech address the problem? What part of the problem does it address?
2	Who is it a problem for? Key stakeholders? Whom effect (directly and indirectly?)
3	What is the goal/objective? Intended purpose/function?
4	Setting & Environment?
5	Direct users of technology? Goals? Needs? Expected Benefits?
6	Other stakeholders impacted by technology? Goals? Needs? Expected Benefits?

Stage 3 (Deep Dive: Benefits, Outcomes and Impact)

See Table 4.

Table 4. HFEC: Stage 3 (Deep Dive: Benefits, Outcomes & Impact)

#	3: Deep Dive: Benefits, Outcomes & Impact		
1	Overall benefits and outcomes: key stakeholders? Expected positive impacts?			
2	Expected Impact for key stakeholders (psycho-social themes). Individual level? Societal Level?	(A) Human role in the system	(B) Human Identity	(C) Lived experience, wellbeing, quality of life
		(D) Social Interaction & Relationships	(E) Activity & Behavior	(F) Attitudes & Values
3	What could go wrong? Potential failures? Potential negative impacts? Psychosocial? Environmental?			
4	Unintended consequences			
5	Unknowns			

Stage 4 (Deep Dive: Personae and Scenarios)

See Table 5.

Table 5. HFEC: Stage 4 (Deep Dive: Personae & Scenarios)

#	4: Deep Dive: Personae & Scenarios
1	Example Scenario
2	Example Personae
3	How is it expected to work?
4	What does success look like? Benefits for whom? Expected positive outcomes and for whom?
5	What could go wrong? Potential failures? Potential negative impacts?
6	Unintended consequences?
7	Unknowns?
8	Design Decisions & Safeguards

Stage 5 (Deep Dive: Data Ethics)

See Table 6.

Table 6. HFEC: Stage 5 (Deep Dive: Data Ethics)

#	5: Deep Dive: Data Ethics
1	Ethical issues relevant to data collection? What data? Why collecting? Potential for bias in data collection?
2	Ethical issues relevant to data, model & algorithms? Potential for harm and risk?
3	Ethical issues relevant to data use & predictions (i.e. application of model/algorithms)?
4	Ethical issues relevant to data sharing?
5	Design Decisions & Safeguards

Stage 6 (Implementation)

See Table 7.

Table 7. HFEC: Stage 6 (Implementation)

#	6: Implementation
1	Implementation Approach
2	Implementation Enablers
3	Implementation Barriers
4	Systems Perspective: Addressing Ethics as part of Implementation. People. Process. Technology. Culture. Training & Education
5	Design Decisions & Safeguards

Stage 7 (Human Factors and Ethics Summary)

See Table 8.

Table 8. HFEC: Stage 7 (Human Factors & Ethics Summary)

#	7: Human Factors & Ethics Summary
1	Key stakeholders? Who is this technology designed for?
2	What does success look like? Success for whom?
3	Human/Societal Vision & Technology Role/Purpose
4	Summary of Key Ethical Issues to be Addressed?
5	Ethical Principles Underlying Technology Design
6	Design Approach: Balancing Benefits & Harm How managing ethics issues? How increasing potential positive impacts? How preventing risk/harm? How managing potential negative impacts and unintended consequences? How addressing unknowns?
7	Data Ethics Summary
8	Implementation Summary
9	Ethics & Key KPI

References

1. Elkington, J.: Cannibals with forks: the triple bottom line of 21st century business, ISBN 9780865713925. OCLC 963459936. Capstone, Oxford (1999)

2. Stephanidis, C.C., et al.: Seven HCI grand challenges. Int. J. Hum.– Comput. Interact. **35**(14), 1229–1269 (2019). https://doi.org/10.1080/10447318.2019.1619259

3. European Commission: Ethics for researchers. http://ec.europa.eu/research/science-society/document_library/pdf_06/ethics-forresearchers_en.pdf. Accessed 13 Feb 2020

4. Geoghegan-Quinn, M.: Responsible Research & Innovation. European Union Publications Office, Brussels (2014)

5. Capurro, R.: Digital ethics. In: The Academy of Korean Studies (ed.): Civilization and Peace. Academy of Korean Studies 2010, Korea, pp. 203–214 (2009)

6. Sollie, P.: Ethics, technology development and uncertainty: an outline for any future ethics of technology. J. Inf. Commun. Ethics Soc. **5**(4), 293–306 (2007)

7. Heidegger, M.: The Question Concerning Technology, and Other Essays, 6th edn. Harper & Row, New York (1977)

8. Winograd, T., Flores, F.: Understanding Computers and Cognition: A New Foundation for Design. Ablex Publishing Corporation, Norwood (1986)

9. Fry, T.: Becoming Human by Design. Berg Publishers, Oxford (2012)

10. International Standards Organisation (ISO): Standard 6385 (2020). https://www.iso.org/standard/63785.html

11. Open Data Institute (ODI): The Data Ethics Canvas (2020). https://theodi.org/article/data-ethics-canvas/

12. Reijers, W., et al.: Methods for practising ethics in research and innovation: a literature review, critical analysis and recommendations. Sci. Eng. Ethics **24**(5), 1437–1481 (2017). https://doi.org/10.1007/s11948-017-9961-8

13. Brey, P.: Ethics of emerging technologies. In: Hansson, S.O. (ed.) Methods for the Ethics of Technology. Rowman and Littlefield International, Lanham (2017)

14. Friedman, B., David, G.: Value Sensitive Design: Shaping Technology with Moral Imagination. MIT Press, Cambridge (2019)

15. Wright, D., Mordini, E.: Privacy and ethical impact assessment. In: Wright, D., De Hert, P. (eds.) Privacy Impact Assessment Law, Governance and Technology Series, vol. 6. Springer, Dordrecht (2012). https://doi.org/10.1007/978-94-007-2543-0_19

16. Stahl, B., Heersmink, R., Goujon, P., Flick, C., Van den Hoven, J., Wakunuma, K.: Identifying the ethics of emerging information and communication technologies: an essay on issues, concepts and method. Int. J. Technoeth. **1**(4), 20–38 (2010)

17. Boenink, M., Swierstra, T., Stemerding, D.: Anticipating the interaction between technology and morality: a scenario study of experimenting with humans in bionanotechnology. Stud. Ethics Law Technol. **4**(2), 1–38 (2010)

18. Cotton, M.: Ethics and Technology Assessment: A Participatory Approach. Springer, Berlin (2014). https://doi.org/10.1007/978-3-642-45088-4

19. Fecher, B., Kobsda, C.: Research Impacts Canvas (RIC). https://elephantinthelab.org/meet-the-research-impact-canvas-a-structured-guide-for-planning-your-science-communication-activities/. Accessed 13 Feb 2020

20. Forsberg, E.M.: The ethical matrix—a tool for ethical assessments of biotechnology. Glob. Bioeth. **17**(1), 167–172 (2004). https://doi.org/10.1080/11287462.2004.10800856

21. Gerlach, R. The Digital Product Ethics Canvas. https://www.threebility.com/post/the-digital-product-ethics-canvas. Accessed 13 Feb 2020

22. Vaish, P.: Humans & machines ethics canvas (2020). https://adataanalyst.com/wp-content/uploads/2016/09/ETHICS_Canvas_2.pdf

23. Adapt Centre for Digital Content Technologies. The Data Ethics Canvas. https://ethicscanvas.org/. Accessed 13 Feb 2020

24. Cahill, J.: Human factors & ethics canvas: a white paper. https://www.tcd.ie/cihs/projects/hfaecanvas.php. Accessed 13 Feb 2020

25. Cousins, J.B., Whitmore, E., Shulha, L.: Arguments for a common set of principles for collaborative inquiry in evaluation. Am. J. Eval. **34**, 7–22 (2013)
26. Wenger, E.: Communities of Practice: Learning, Meaning, and Identity. Cambridge University Press, Cambridge (1998)
27. Pruitt, J., Grudin, J.: Personas: practice and theory. In: Proceedings of the 2003 Conference on Designing for User Experiences (DUX 2003), pp. 1–15. ACM, New York (2003). https://doi.org/10.1145/997078.997089
28. Carroll, J.M.: Scenario-Based Design: Envisioning Work and Technology in System Development. Wiley, New York (1995)
29. Beever, J., Brightman, Andrew O.: Reflexive principlism as an effective approach for developing ethical reasoning in engineering. Sci. Eng. Ethics **22**(1), 275–291 (2015). https://doi.org/10.1007/s11948-015-9633-5
30. Markus, M.L., Mentzer, K.: Foresight for a responsible future with ICT. Inf. Syst. Front. **16**, 353–368 (2014). https://doi.org/10.1007/s10796-013-9479-9
31. Nordmann, A.: If and then: a critique of speculative nanoethics. NanoEthics **1**(1), 31–46 (2007). https://doi.org/10.1007/s11569-007-0007-6
32. Poel, I.: Translating values into design requirements. In: Michelfelder, Diane P., McCarthy, N., Goldberg, David E. (eds.) Philosophy and Engineering: Reflections on Practice, Principles and Process. PET, vol. 15, pp. 253–266. Springer, Dordrecht (2013). https://doi.org/10.1007/978-94-007-7762-0_20
33. Van den Hoven, J., Manders-Huits, N.: Value-sensitive design. In: Kyrre, J., Olsen, B., Hendricks, V.F. (eds.) A Companion to the Philosophy of Technology. Blackwell Publishing, Malden (2009). https://doi.org/10.1002/9781444310795.ch1
34. Albrechtslund, A.: Ethics and technology design. Ethics Inf. Technol. **9**(1), 63–72 (2007). https://doi.org/10.1007/s10676-006-9129-8

Systematic Literature Review on the Effect of Human Error in Environmental Pollution

Gavin A. Duffy[1,2(✉)] and Vincent G. Duffy[2(✉)]

[1] West Lafayette Jr-Sr High School, West Lafayette, IN 47906, USA
gaduffy@purdue.edu
[2] Purdue University, West Lafayette, IN 47906, USA
duffy@purdue.edu

Abstract. This report is a systematic literature review of the relationship between human error and pollution, to take account of unintentional contributions to environmental pollution. To examine this relation, a systematic literature review of articles, including the keywords "human error" and "pollution" was conducted. The keywords were searched in the Web of Science and Google Scholar (using Harzing's Publish or Perish) databases, then exporting the metadata into VOSviewer to create cluster diagrams or keywords and co-citation analyses. Next, a few articles were selected: four articles from various databases, including Google Scholar, SpringerLink, and ResearchGate, two chapters from the *Handbook of Human Factors and Ergonomics, Fourth Edition* by Salvendy, and three more articles derived from the co-citation analysis. The articles were compiled into Mendeley and then exported into MAXQDA to create a word cloud exhibiting some keywords within the nine articles. Next, the AuthorMapper program from Springer was used to find the current and most relevant contributions to the area of human error and pollution as well as the most relevant keywords for an extended lexical search within the chosen nine articles. Then MAXQDA was used to perform an extended lexical search to find the usage of the keywords and the key points within the articles. Overall, the main keywords of risk management, human factors in accident causation, accident causation, failure, automation, and regulation showed a high relevance within multiple of the chosen articles. Also, from the Springer AuthorMapper, the contributions were not highly concentrated from any specific author, country, or institution, but were varied with an increasing trend of articles being written in this topic area.

Keywords: Human error · Pollution · Environmental pollution · Regulation · Risk management · Human factors · Systematic literature review

1 Introduction and Background

Since the increase in environmental pollutants as a result of industry, the concern for the effects of pollution has increased correspondingly. This mounting concern has resulted in the foundation of countless organizations such as the United States Environmental Protection Agency (EPA), World Wildlife Fund, and Greenpeace, all since 1970, just to name a few. Many studies since the 1970s have been focused on not only the effects but also what causes the release of environmental pollutants. However, others have been concerned with the mitigation of current pollutants in the environment and how to reduce the release of more in the future.

Though it is commonly perceived that the only possible causes of pollution stem from intentional actions taken without regard for their effects in the environment, like careless waste management practices, excessive carbon emissions from factories and transportation, and intentional littering. However, intuitively, that cannot be the case. Examples like the oil rig malfunctions of the Deepwater Horizon oil spill in 2010 are unintentional yet can prove just as dangerous and damaging if not more so than intentional pollution (Lehto and Cook 2012; Sharit 2012). In any case like this, there is likely the factor of human error as the outcome was the result of some mistake along the way from the design of a product to the operation of a facility, resulting in a failure which causes damaging outcomes.

2 Problem Statement

While many are researching the state of the intentional release of pollutants into the environment, it is also necessary to account for the unintentional causes of pollution that feed their way into the environment all the same. For this reason, it is essential to do an analysis of the state of research regarding human error and related pollution as a cause of it.

3 Procedure

Beginning with a key word search of "pollution" and "human error" in Google Scholar, SpringerLink, and ResearchGate, four articles that displayed a relevant abstract were chosen for more in-depth analysis. Next, the same search keywords were used to obtain metadata in Web of Science, including article title, author, abstract, keywords, and references, was exported to VOSviewer, where a cluster diagram of key terms and co-citations were formulated. Next, using Harzing Publish or Perish (through Google Scholar) metadata from 940 articles, including title, authors, and keywords, another cluster diagram of key terms was formulated.

From the cluster diagrams, the key terms with the greatest number of occurrences were chosen. Within nine chosen articles, using MAXQDA, a lexical search was conducted to find all of the places within the article where each term was mentioned in order to glean the essence of each section of the article where one of the key terms was used. Also, within MAXQDA, a word cloud was generated to search for the most frequently used words within the nine articles.

Some practitioners may consider issues related to pollution mitigation as overlapping with environmental management and sustainability, while human error may be considered to be overlapping with ergonomics. Additional information related to ergonomics and sustainability can be found in a systematic review of ergonomics and sustainability that was published in the journal *Ergonomics* (Radjiyev et al. 2015). Some methods for improving sustainability through usability were also reported during the *Int. Conference on Design, User Experience and Usability* (Duffy 2014).

4   Results and Discussion

From the initial keyword search in Google Scholar, SpringerLink, and ResearchGate, four articles "Implementing a sea pollution and safety management system in the navigation companies" by Gasparotti, C. et al., "The impact of human errors on the estimation of uncertainty of measurements in water monitoring" by Kmiecik (2018), "Temporal and spatial variation characteristics of air pollution and prevention and control measures: Evidence from Anhui Province, China" by Kuai, S. and Yin, C., and "Wind, waves, tides, and human error? – Influences on litter abundance and composition on German North Sea coastlines: An exploratory analysis" by Schöneich-Argent et al. (2019). These four articles were uploaded to Mendeley to manage references.

Next, the search in Web of Science was conducted to formulate the cluster diagrams. Though it was initially thought that the Web of Science search would provide a more comprehensive and representative cluster diagram than, because the metadata would include more information, the minimum occurrence for the keywords even within both the abstracts and titles together had to be set to three in order to form any central point (see Fig. 1). This is likely because the total number of articles that could be found using the keywords "pollution" and "human error" was only 34, so despite the extra exported data, there were not enough articles to be picky about the number of times a word appeared.

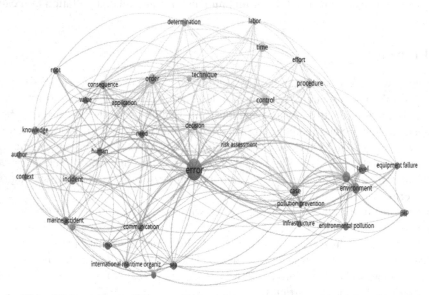

Fig. 1. Web of Science Cluster Diagram of title and abstracts data from 34 articles with a minimum of three occurrences per keyword shows a much more evenly spread diagram in comparison with the Harzing search cluster diagram; however, there is still an evident focus on human factors through the green and yellow strings (*Web of Science*, n.d.; *VOSviewer*, n.d.). (Color figure online)

By comparison, the Harzing search was able to find 940 articles, from which it took only the authors, titles, and keywords. However, there were far more occurrences of each key term, so the minimum number of occurrences was set up to 18, which gave a far more interesting representation of the available literature through Google Scholar (see Fig. 2).

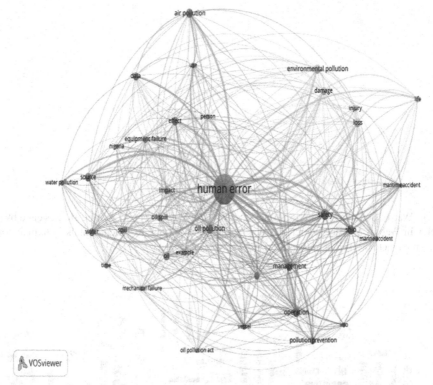

Fig. 2. VOSviewer Cluster Diagram of Harzing keyword search with a yield of 940 articles and a minimum number of key word occurrences of 18 demonstrates a central idea of human error surrounded by causes and effects like various types of pollution and equipment/mechanical failure (*Harzing's Publish or Perish*, n.d.; *VOSviewer*, n.d.).

Also, from the metadata exported from Web of Science, a co-citation analysis was run, which discovered the articles "Human and organisational factors in maritime accidents: Analysis of collisions at sea using the HFACS" by Chauvin, C. et al., "Safety in shipping: The human element" by Hetherington, C. et al., and *Human error* by Reason, J. Each of these articles was cited four times within the 34 articles found within Web of Science. Then through database searches, these three articles, except for the book *Human Error* by Reason (1990), were found and stored in Mendeley for reference management and later use (see Fig. 3).

Next, two related chapters from the *Handbook of Human Factors and Ergonomics, Fourth Edition,* (Salvendy 2012) "Occupational Health and Safety Management" (Lehto 2012) and "Human Error and Reliability Analysis" (Sharit 2012) were chosen as they related to human error and safety management and saved into Mendeley. Then, the four initially selected articles, the two chapters from *Handbook of Human Factors and*

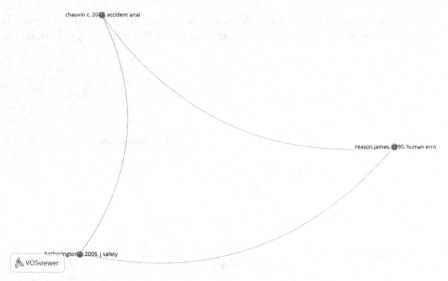

Fig. 3. Web of Science Co-citation Analysis reveals strong ties between three articles cited by 34 articles in Web of Science, which draws a strong relation back to fundamentals in human error and human factors (*Web of Science*, n.d.; *VOSviewer*, n.d.).

Fig. 4. MAXQDA word cloud from nine articles displays a clear emphasis on human factors and secondary results relating to the environment and pollution. The overrepresentation of human factors terms likely is the result of the inclusion of two chapters of the *Handbook of Human Factors and Ergonomics, Fourth Edition* (Salvendy 2012), which did not include much information or vocabulary related to pollution or the environment (*MAXQDA*, n.d.).

Ergonomics, Fourth Edition, and the three articles from the co-citation cluster analysis, except for Reason (1990), were transferred to MAXQDA to create a word cloud that emphasized the most frequently used words from all of the combined literature. In place of Reason (1990), a book review of *Human Error* by Gray et al. (1993) was used to add to the word cloud instead. In order to meaningfully populate the figure, a stop list had to be created to cut out all prepositions and other elements within the word cloud that did not provide any insight into useful terminology for further lexical search (see Fig. 4).

4.1 Leading Global Themes in Human Error and Pollution

Themes of Emphasis Among Leading Authors
Springer's AuthorMapper is reviewed under the search term "pollution" AND "human error." AuthorMapper shows that 1243 articles were published from the year 1979 to the present. However, 1988 is the first year that shows more than 10 related articles. The peak in 2018 and 2019 show 197 and 196, respectively (see Fig. 5).

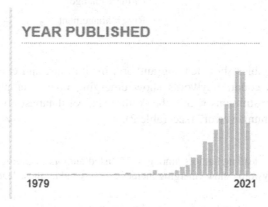

YEAR PUBLISHED

1979   2021

Fig. 5. Trend data from Springer's AuthorMapper shows an increase in the number of articles on the topic search "pollution" and "human error" that lead to a peak of 197 articles published in 2018.

Five 'leading publications' contains 101 out of 1243 listed articles. The articles are distributed among many publications. 1243 related articles are found within 841 different publications. Leading terms among the 1243 articles are shown in Table 1.

In order to further justify this systematic review of "pollution" AND "human error" within the digital human modeling thematic area within HCI International, it may be useful to consider the following. Though not initially apparent, leading terms in keywords among the 1243 articles overlap significantly with the subheading within the digital human modeling area. This theme is titled "Digital Human Modeling & Applications in Health, Safety, Ergonomics & Risk Management. "Safety," "Risk," and "Risk management" are three among the top seven leading terms. These three are listed within the title of our thematic area on Digital Human Modeling (DHM).

Table 1. Table shows leading terms among 1243 articles that contain 4115 authors publishing under 841 different publication titles. 1980 different institutions and 89 different countries are represented. Five of the first seven terms fit well within at least one chapter within the Handbook of Human Factors and Ergonomics. Three among the seven fit directly within the title of this DHM thematic area.

Rank of leading term among keywords	Leading term among keywords in 1243 articles
1	Safety
2	Risk assessment
3	Sustainability
4	Uncertainty
5	Risk
6	Climate change
7	Risk management

The following tables show leading authors, institutions, and countries with years of publication and count. Keywords show emerging themes emphasized by countries, authors, and institutions within the AuthorMapper database for this search topic "pollution" AND "human error" (see Table 2).

Table 2. Table shows leading authors among 4115 listed authors in Springer's AuthorMapper database. Leading keywords show emerging themes emphasized by these leading authors.

Author	Years	Leading keywords	Count
Vinnem, Jan-Erik	2014–2020	Offshore risk assessment, Marine systems risk modeling	10
Atsuji, Shigeo	2016	Unsafety, Cumulative thermal effluent, Sustainability policy	6
Tzafestas, Spyros G.	2010	Human factors in automation, Modeling and simulation	6
Hauptmanns, Ulrich	2015	Process and plant safety, Risk, Engineered systems	5
King, David	2015–2018	Economic crisis, Europe income, Petroleum, Transportation	5

Themes of Emphasis Among Leading Countries. The leading contributions to the topics of human error and pollution, as demonstrated by Tables 3 and 4 as well as Fig. 6, come from a variety of places. The largest number of contributions to this area have come from the United States, followed by the United Kingdom; however, the institutions with the most contributions come from an even more variable set of locations, including Norway and Sweden, which are known for their reasonably strict environmental regulations (see Table 5).

Table 3. A table of leading institutions from Author Mapper (Springer) shows leading institutions among 1980 different institutions that are represented within the 1243 articles. Count information is included. Leading keywords show institutional emphasis.

Institution	Country	Leading keywords	Count
University of Stavanger	Norway	Offshore risk assessment, Lessons learned, Analysis techniques	11
World Maritime University	Sweden	Accident causation, Accidental pollution, Arctic navigation	11
Curtin University	Australia	Human error, Bayesian network, Biomass, Budyko equations	10
Chinese Academy of Sciences	China	Beijing PM2.5, AHP, Air pollution, Chemical constituents	9
University of Copenhagen	Denmark	AI, Anthropocentrism, Bioinformatics, Data Envelopment Analysis (DEA)	8

Table 4. A table of leading countries from Author Mapper (Springer) shows leading institutions among 89 different countries that are represented within the 1243 articles. Count information is included. Leading keywords show emphasis by country.

Country	Leading keywords	Count
United States	Climate change, Petroleum, Automation	270
United Kingdom	Mediterranean Sea, Oil pollution, Regulation, Aerial surveillance	115
India	Emission, Smart city, Machine learning, Recycling, Remote sensing	109
China	Absorbent, Absorption, Aerogel, Cellulose, Hydrophobic, Oil	103
Germany	Bark scorch/Sunburn, Basal burls, Coat shake, Crack causes	75

4.2 Content Analysis

Lexical Search Results

Key terms taken from the cluster analyses, word cloud, and leading global key terms were used to search within the nine chosen articles. For efficiency, the keywords "pollution" and "human error" were not used in the extended lexical search in MAXQDA, as they have many occurrences within the articles. Instead, the following terms were searched.

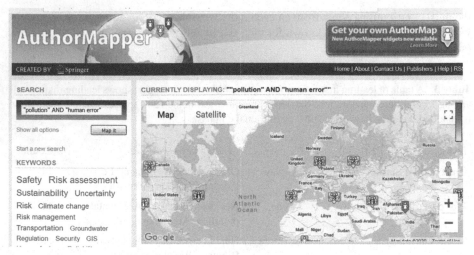

Fig. 6. Clusters within the map from Springer's AuthorMapper show the geographic representation as additional information beyond the table information that highlighted leading countries, including the United States, United Kingdom, India, China, and Germany. Even among a diverse set of publications, authors, and countries, the metadata shown in the list of leading countries helps to confirm is consistent with our intuition countries of what one would expect to be listed among leading countries associated with the "pollution" or environment-related topic.

Also, due to the inability to acquire a digital copy of *Human Error* by Reason, the lexical search was implemented through Google Books, through which samples of the literature were available.

Automation
Reason's book on human error (Reason 1990) is referred to within the co-citation analysis results. However, when considering the topic of automation, Reason refers to prior work of Bainbridge about the ironies of automation (Bainbridge 1987) and Leplat et al. (1987) who co-edited a book about new technology and human error. This book may be of additional interest to the reader interested in the human-automation interaction aspects of pollution prevention. Baxter wrote more recently in 2012, emphasizing the cognitive aspects in an article titled "The Ironies of Automation: Still Going Strong at 30?". Along similar lines, Hetherington et al. (2006) and Sharit (2012) explain how the irony of automation occurs with increases in automation being attributed to increased burden of interaction with the technology. Further describing how it frequently results in increasing cognitive demands and corresponding with increases in human error, especially when the human can least afford the diversion of its attention.

Failure
According to Sharit, performance failure is defined as the outcomes of actions that differ from what was intended or required. To elaborate, Reason states that failure can be considered at three levels of performance, including skill-based, rule-based, and knowledge-based. The interested reader could review Rasmussen's (1983) influential

Table 5. Leading articles over the last five years are shown based on relevance and are listed in table. These are identified from Springer's AuthorMapper and are listed in table with authors, country, and year of publication. It is interesting to note that the leading articles (by relevance) and leading authors are not from countries that are within the original list of leading countries. This further highlights the diversity of contributions and contributors to this research area.

Authors	Title and publication info	Country	Year
Ishak, Ismila Che, Wan Muhammad Hafiz Wan Ab Rani, Shaiful Bakri Ismail, and Norazimah Mazlan	"A Study of Oil Spill at Marine Companies: Factors and Effects." In *Advancement in Emerging Technologies and Engineering Applications*, pp. 1–12. Springer, Singapore	Malaysia	2020
Nakamura, Takahiro, Emiko Kanoshima, Tomofumi Koyama, Hiroshi Nishimura, and Mamoru Ozawa	"Social Disasters and Damages." In *Science of Societal Safety*, pp. 73–86. Springer, Singapore	Japan	2019
De Felice, Fabio, Antonella Petrillo, and Federico Zomparelli	"Human Factors Challenges in Disaster Management Scenario." In *Human Factors and Reliability Engineering for Safety and Security in Critical Infrastructures*, pp. 171–187. Springer, Cham	Italy	2018
Kazmi, Danish, Sadaf Qasim, I. S. H. Harahap, and Syed Baharom	"A probabilistic study for the analysis of the risks of slope failure by applying HEART technique." *Geotechnical and Geological Engineering* 35, no. 6 (2017): 2991–3003	Pakistan, Malaysia	2017
Tavakoli, Mehdi, and Mehdi Nafar	"The Improvement in Human Reliability in Power Grids by Identifying and Assessing the Risk of Failures Caused by Maintenance Operations." *Iranian Journal of Science and Technology, Transactions of Electrical Engineering*: 1–9	Iran	2019

article for additional insight into skill, rule, and knowledge-based performance. Reason highlights potential skill-based failures, including inattention or omissions associated with interruptions. For failures at the rule-based level, Reason refers to a book by Holland et al. (1986) emphasizing processes of inference, learning, and discovery, and a conceptual framework. Reason refers to potential for misapplication of reasonable rules and application of bad rules and suggests redundancy to prevent related adverse outcomes.

Risk Management

Lehto and Cook explain how improvements upon levels of risk must be decided by the management overseeing any kind of operation, based on the most cost-effective ways to implement new control measures. Sharit, however, points out how it is increasingly difficult it is to minimize risks further when reporting incidents is voluntary. This leads to underestimates of the number of incidents and eliminates the opportunity to improve upon near misses where no serious accident has yet occurred, simply because the management is unaware of the issues.

Human Aspects of Risk Management

Reason notes that decision aids can be designed to minimize failures at the plan formation stage. Whereas memory aids can improve performance at the storage and execution stage of a task. For additional insight, Reason also refers to Norman's article (1986) related to cognitive processes and information processing. On the topic of risk management, Reason (1990) refers to Fischhoff's outline of simple behavioral principles in complex system design. The presentation by Fischhoff was referred to by Reason and briefly noted in a book edited by Rasmussen and Batstone in 1989 based on presentations at the World Bank (Fischhoff 1986; Rasmussen and Batstone 1989). Additionally, Reason refers to Fischhoff (1986) on decision making in complex environments that was originally presented as part of an edited book by Hollnagel, Mancini, and Woods (Fischhoff 1986) on intelligent decision support in process environments.

Regulation

In a proactive safety initiative, one would consider human capabilities and limitations as well as design first for reducing potential hazard. However, as a last resort regulation and, in some cases, litigation is effective at bringing about design modifications that reduce the potential hazards. Lehto and Cook (2012) and Sharit (2012) refer to examples where regulation helped to reduce potential hazard and risk. In similar mindsets, Kuai and Yin (2017), Gasparotti et al. (2008), and Chauvin et al. (2013) explain how increases in the number and comprehensiveness of regulations from international and government organizations will help to reduce accidents and pollution emissions. Furthermore, Hetherington et al. (2006) states that among the most common human factors is the failure to comply with regulations, resulting in error. In contrast, Reason (1990) highlights an example where not following the regulation reduced hazard and risk. Ultimately, one may consider that where human factors and design have not already been effective at minimizing hazard and risk, regulation may be needed (see Table 6).

Accident Causation

Among many potential causes, Lehto and Cook (2012) explain that unsafe acts and

Table 6. In reappraisal following review, it is recommended that the following be considered for effective hazard mitigation and human error reduction in the context of pollution.

Steps	Human error reduction	Strategy
1	Consider capabilities and limitations of people in the context of technical aspects	Fit the task to the human- based on human factors-related theory
2	Design out potential hazards	Proactive safety design – engineering and quality improvement
3	Regulate	Administrative and legislative

unsafe conditions cause most accidents. To support, Hetherington (2006) notes that reducing the number of technology failures helps to expose human error's effect on accident causation. Furthermore, Chauvin (2013) references Reason's "Swiss cheese" model on accident causation.

5 Conclusions and Future Work

This systematic review shows an increasing number of research contributions to hazard mitigation incorporating human error and pollution. The co-citation analysis and content analysis show that human factors theories are contributing to pollution-related research for the purposes of minimizing the potential for human error and adverse events. A summary of leading authors, leading countries, and leading publications show a diverse set of contributions, and some of the most relevant articles were found from authors that were not listed among leading authors and were not from leading countries. Articles with the highest relevance did not necessarily originate from leading countries or leading authors. The future looks bright internationally in this area for new projects applying human factors theories in mitigation of human error that could lead to pollution or adverse environmental events.

Additional examples of funded proposals can be found at the National Science Foundation website (www.nsf.gov) using search terms "human error" and "environment". A proposal awarded to Behzad Esmaili at George Mason University is titled "Measuring Attention, Working Memory and Visual Perception to Reduce Risk of Injuries in the Construction Industry". The proposal emphasized the idea that human error, including poor decisions or unsafe actions, are a main causal factor in up to 80% of workplace accidents across a wide variety of industries. The research recognizes our limited capacity for information processing as a major source of error and suggests that better understanding of cognitive processes will yield more effective methods for predicting and reducing the poor decisions that put workers and their environment at risk. A series of eye-tracking experiments is intended to provide an error-detection framework.

The proposal awarded in 2018 has led to a presentation at the Construction Research Congress related to a study of the association of risk perception and risk-taking behaviors (Dao and Hasanzadeh 2018). A similar award was given as a continuing grant to Michael Dodd and Leen-Kiat Soh at University of Nebraska-Lincoln. The project, also emphasizing eye movements and eye-tracking methodologies is a proactive approach to occupational safety and health that has the potential for reducing occupational accidents and preventing injuries or adverse health-related events.

One additional project proposes to measure, predict and improve safety be improving hazards signal detection with augmented virtual environments. The award to Matthew Hallowell and Leaf Van Boven at University of Colorado at Boulder also considers human error in construction. They suggest that skill deficiency could lead to difficulties at recognizing important hazard-related signals. The augmented reality technology, if successful at providing improved hazard signal recognition could lead to reduced human error applicable across various industries. Two recent publications produced as a result of this research emphasized emotional states and their impact on hazard identification skills and situation awareness (Bhandari et al. 2016; Bhandari et al. 2018). The article related to situation awareness emphasizes empirical relationships among hazard recognition, skill, risk perception and risk tolerance.

Projects emphasizing smart services can provide awareness and integration of systems design issues for considering capabilities and limitations of people in the context of human-automation interaction. 'Smart' approaches propose to take sensor data and engineering knowledge to transfer the data into useful services and interventions. One recent proposal "Smart Geoengineering Systems" was recognized among top 100 (Duffy et al. 2019). The proposal, listed alphabetically among top 100, considers whether modern geoengineering methods can be supplemented by systems and smart approaches to provide relief as humanitarian intervention for impact on an increasing number and severity of catastrophic events.

References

AuthorMapper. https://www.authormapper.com/. Accessed 03 Jan 2020

Bainbridge, L.: Ironies of automation: increasing levels of automation can increase, rather than decrease, the problems of supporting the human operator. In: New Technology and Human Error, pp. 276–283. Wiley, Chichester (1987)

Baxter, G., Rooksby, J., Wang, Y., Khajeh-Hosseini, A.: The ironies of automation: still going strong at 30? In: Proceedings of the 30th European Conference on Cognitive Ergonomics, pp. 65–71, August 2012

Bhandari, S., Hallowell, M.R., Van Boven, L., Gruber, J., Welker, KM.: Emotional states and their impact on hazard identification skills. In: Construction Research Congress, p. 2831 (2016). https://doi.org/10.1061/9780784479827.282

Bhandari, S., Hallowell, M.R., Van Boven, L., Golparvar-Fard, M.: What is situational awareness? Empirical relationships among hazard recognition skill, risk perception, and risk tolerance. In: Proceedings of the 2018 Construction Research Congress (2018)

Chauvin, C., Lardjane, S., Morel, G., Clostermann, J.P., Langard, B.: Human and organisational factors in maritime accidents: analysis of collisions at sea using the HFACS. Accid. Anal. Prev. **59**, 26–37 (2013). https://doi.org/10.1016/j.aap.2013.05.006

Dao, B., Hasanzadeh, S.: The association between risk perception and the risk-taking behaviors of construction workers. In: Construction Research Congress (2018)

Duffy, V.G.: Improving sustainability through usability. In: Marcus, A. (ed.) DUXU 2014. LNCS, vol. 8519, pp. 507–519. Springer, Cham (2014). https://doi.org/10.1007/978-3-319-07635-5_49

Duffy, V.G., Hirleman, E.D., Groll, E., Laskin, A. Wang, F.: Smart geoengineering systems, NSF 2026 Idea Machine (2019). (https://www.nsf.gov/news/special_reports/nsf2026ideamachine/index.jsp listed alphabetically in tab among top 100)

Fischhoff, B.: Decision making in complex systems. In: Hollnagel, E., Mancini, G., Woods, D.D. (eds.) Intelligent Decision Support in Process Environments. NATO ASI Series (Series F: Computer and Systems Sciences), vol. 21, pp. 61–85. Springer, Heidelberg (1986). https://doi.org/10.1007/978-3-642-50329-0_5

Gasparotti, C., Georgescu, L., Voiculescu, M.: Implementing a sea pollution and safety management system in the navigation companies. Environ. Eng. Manag. J. **7**(6), 725–729 (2008). https://doi.org/10.30638/eemj.2008.097

Google Scholar. https://scholar.google.com/. Accessed 03 Jan 2020

Gray, W.D., Sabnani, H., Kirschenbaum, S.: Review of the book human error. Int. J. Man-Mach. Stud. **39**, 1056–1057 (1993)

Harzing's Publish or Perish. https://harzing.com/resources/publish-or-perish. Accessed 03 Jan 2020

Hetherington, C., Flin, R., Mearns, K.: Safety in shipping: the human element. J. Saf. Res. **37**(4), 401–411 (2006). https://doi.org/10.1016/j.jsr.2006.04.007

Holland, J.H., Holyoak, K.J., Nisbett, R.E., Thagard, P.R.: Induction. Processes of Inference, Learning, and Discovery (1986)

Kmiecik, E.: The impact of human errors on the estimation of uncertainty of measurements in water monitoring. In: Boring, R.L. (ed.) AHFE 2017. AISC, vol. 589, pp. 162–172. Springer, Cham (2018). https://doi.org/10.1007/978-3-319-60645-3_16

Kuai, S., Yin, C.: Temporal and spatial variation characteristics of air pollution and prevention and control measures: evidence from Anhui Province China. Nat. Environ. Pollut. Technol. **16**(2), 499–504 (2017)

Lehto, M.R., Cook, B.T.: Occupational health and safety management. In: Salvendy, G. (ed.) Handbook of Human Factors and Ergonomics, 4th edn, pp. 701–733. Wiley, Hoboken (2012)

Leplat, J., Duncan, K., Rasmussen, J. (eds.): New Technology and Human Error. Wiley, Hoboken (1987)

MAXQDA. https://www.maxqda.com/. Accessed 03 Jan 2020

Mendeley. https://www.mendeley.com/?interaction_required=true. Accessed 03 Jan 2020

Rasmussen, J.: Skills, rules, and knowledge; signals, signs, and symbols, and other distinctions in human performance models. IEEE Trans. Syst. Man Cybern. **3**, 257–266 (1983)

Rasmussen, J., Batstone, R.: Why do complex organizational systems fail? World Bank Policy Planning and Research Staff, Environment Department (1989)

Radjiyev, A., Qiu, H., Xiong, S., Nam, K.: Ergonomics and sustainable development in the past two decades (1992–2011): research trends and how ergonomics can contribute to sustainable development. Appl. Ergon. **46**, 67–75 (2015)

Reason, J.: Human Error. Cambridge University Press, Cambridge (1990)

ResearchGate. https://www.researchgate.net/. Accessed 03 Jan 2020

Salvendy, G. (ed.): Handbook of Human Factors and Ergonomics. Wiley (2012)

Schöneich-Argent, R.I., et al.: Wind, waves, tides, and human error? – Influences on litter abundance and composition on German North Sea coastlines: an exploratory analysis. Mar. Pollut. Bull. **146**(June), 155–172 (2019). https://doi.org/10.1016/j.marpolbul.2019.05.062

Sharit, J.: Human error and reliability analysis. In: Salvendy, G. (ed.) Handbook of Human Factors and Ergonomics, 4th edn, pp. 734–796. Wiley, Hoboken (2012)

SpringerLink (n.d.). https://link.springer.com. Accessed 03 Jan 2020

VOSviewer. https://www.vosviewer.com/. Accessed 03 Jan 2020

Web of Science. https://apps.webofknowledge.com. Accessed 03 Jan 2020

Data Mining Methodology in Support of a Systematic Review of Human Aspects of Cybersecurity

Brendan M. Duffy[1,2(✉)] and Vincent G. Duffy[1(✉)]

[1] Purdue University, West Lafayette, IN 47907, USA
{duffy45,duffy}@purdue.edu
[2] West Lafayette High School, West Lafayette, USA

Abstract. Cybersecurity is an evolving field in the area of human-computer inter-actions (HCI), but human factors is a relevant area to consider when approaching cybersecurity. This report illustrates the findings of a systematic literature review of current publications on the emerging trends of human factors in cybersecurity. Analyses of content and bibliometrics were accomplished by using tools such as VOS Viewer, MAXQDA, Harzing, and AuthorMapper to establish the findings of emerging trends in the field. This report includes a step-by-step procedure for conducting the content analyses in each tool. The areas of human factors and cybersecurity are examined based on the data of the content analyses. A key find-ing is that human factors theory emerged from content analysis, and can be a basis for future research.

Keywords: Cybersecurity · Human factors · Bibliometric analysis

1 Introduction and Background

1.1 Cybersecurity and Human Factors

Cybersecurity is a field for protecting computers, all internet-capable systems, networks, servers, cloud data, and physical data from malicious software (malware) or cyber-attacks. The other field is Human Factors, which was concisely explained by The Human Factors and Ergonomics Society. The way they put it was, "Ergonomics and human fac-tors use knowledge of human abilities and limitations to design systems, organizations, jobs, machines, tools, and consumer products for safe, efficient, and comfortable human use".

Cybersecurity began with the advent of internet development when users discov-ered flaws in system design. Cybersecurity was not being implemented until users with malicious intent began to take advantage of systems, due to a lack of protection against its usage for unintended purposes. In essence, the first notable case of a user exploiting system vulnerabilities and halt all internet processes with a worm.

The worm effectively incapacitated the functionality of the internet in 1988. The worm was created by Robert T. Morris, a Cornell student at the time. He created the

© Springer Nature Switzerland AG 2020
V. G. Duffy (Ed.): HCII 2020, LNCS 12199, pp. 242–253, 2020.
https://doi.org/10.1007/978-3-030-49907-5_17

worm to demonstrate the lack of security on computer networks. In turn, he was dismissed from Cornell and sentenced to three years of probation and was fined USD 10,050 (US. v R.T.Morris). Later on, he became a professor at MIT and was tenured in 2006 (MIT 2006). He was elected into the National Academy of Engineering in 2019 (NAE 2019). His work sparked an outbreak of worms and viruses, shortly after he had become notorious. These occurrences became the driving motivation for antivirus protection.

The heart of the issue was Human Factors because the companies did not consider all of the human processes of their systems. Their oversight caused human error and ill-intent to damage systems and other users. Human factors has been an emerging area in design since World War II-era because technological advances caused aircrafts to become more challenging to operate than the experienced pilots could manage. The military prompted engineers to design a more human-friendly system, which resulted in a lower fatality rate in combat, due to the improvement in design, based on human limitation.

1.2 Overview of Plan for Bibliometric Analysis and Systematic Review

A trend graph of papers involving both Human Factors and Cybersecurity was created with data Google Scholar. Metadata was retrieved from Google Scholar in Harzing. Then metadata was imported from the leading articles into VOS Viewer. Cluster analysis was completed using leading terms from each cluster. A co-citation analysis to find core articles was created with the reference data from the Web of Science in VOS Viewer. Content analysis was conducted on the core articles, based on the co-citation analysis. Leading articles from Google Scholar, ResearchGate, and Springerlink were used for a word cloud and lexical search in MAXQDA.

2 Purpose of Study

The objective of this study is to conduct a systematic literature review of papers on the topic of Human Factors in Cybersecurity. The review sought to summarize key aspects of new research in this emerging area and identify human factors that are forming the basis for further research on the topic of cybersecurity.

3 Research Methodology

3.1 Data Collection

To collect the data for the analyses, a keyword search was conducted in the two databases: Web of Science, and Google Scholar. There tends to be a higher volume of articles and papers in Google Scholar. The data from Web of Science includes title, abstract, authors, keywords, cited references, and source, although it has fewer articles and papers to analyze. Co-citation analyses require the reference data, which can only be extracted with computer assistance in the Web of Science database. The software, "Harzing's Publish or Perish" can extract bibliometric data from several databases, but is limited to 1000 articles from a search, and includes only the title, keywords, author, and source.

Because the search encompasses a vast summation of articles, it is the best method for collecting the essential keywords of the article sample. Google Scholar was used for the Harzing data extraction. The search terms that were used in the Web of Science and Harzing were, "cybersecurity AND "human factors" " and the search yielded 48 articles in the Web of Science, and was restricted to 1000 articles in Harzing (*Harzing's Publish or Perish*, n.d.). AuthorMapper has the Springer database of articles for the search terms.

3.2 Trend Analysis

The trend analysis is based on the results of the Web of Science data collection. Web of Science is equipped with a few tools for the analysis within the database, so those tools were used to analyze the trend data. All years were represented up to February 2020, and it shows the upward momentum of production in the literature on the topic.

Figure 1 shows the trend for articles involving both cybersecurity and human factors. The first listed publication was in 2014 in the Web of Science, and it shows a steady growth in the literature pool within the database from 2014 to 2020. The number of publications in the first two months of the year suggests that this year will have more publications than in 2019. It is especially important to consider the last 4 years when the number of publications per year stayed at a constant value, indicates that the field will grow from the plateau, or researchers will lose interest in the topic. The data from AuthorMapper gives a clearer picture (Fig. 2) AuthorMapper.

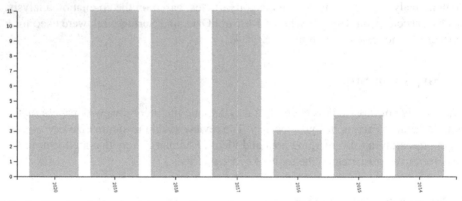

Fig. 1. Trend analysis of articles on cybersecurity and human factors (Web of Science, n.d.) The highest count on Y-axis is 11. X-axis starts with 2020 on the left and continues down to 2014.

It is clear, based on the trend analysis, that human factors in cybersecurity is a growing topic of research. The figure from AuthorMapper is very reassuring for the conclusion that the research is in an emerging area, especially after analyzing the graphs and seeing a jump in the volume of publications from 2018 to 2019, which was not represented in the Web of Science diagram.

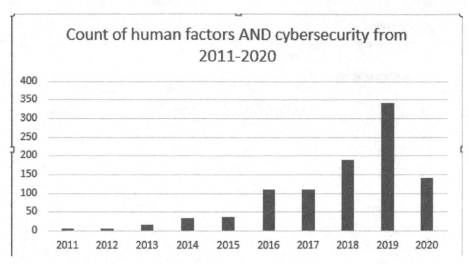

Fig. 2. Trend analysis of articles on cybersecurity and human factors (AuthorMapper, n.d.)

4 Results

4.1 Content Analysis Based on Leading Terms

The bibliometric data from Harzing, which included terms from titles and keywords, was used in VOS Viewer for cluster analysis on the most frequently used and related terms. The process included creating a map based on text data from the Harzing extraction, and setting the parameters for the terms to be selected. The parameter was to have greater than or equal to ten occurrences out of the 2121 terms. From 980 articles in Google Scholar ranging from 2002–2020, 18 terms met the parameters, and all terms were included in the cluster analysis. The clusters are colored based on the average year of occurrence, with the color spectrum key at the bottom right. See Fig. 3.

Table 1 shows the rate of occurrences from the 980 articles from the 19 years. Logically, the top two results are the terms that were searched for initially. Nevertheless, the term that was surprising to find on the list, with the seventh-highest occurrences, was AHFE (Applied Human Factors and Ergonomics). International conference was also on the list, which indicates that the greatest quantity publications on the topic were from the AHFE International Conference. The list of sources from AuthorMapper also supported this assessment with 131 publications in the conference book.

To understand more about AHFE as a leading term in the GoogleScholar search from Harzing, Springer's AuthorMapper is reviewed in more detail under the search term "human factors" AND cybersecurity. AuthorMapper shows that "Advances in Human Factors in Cybersecurity" (from AHFE Conference) is the leading publication in terms of number of articles included as of early 2019. As 'leading publication,' it contains 131 out of 1002 listed articles. It is 1st among 543 publications listed. The following tables show leading authors, years of publication, keywords showing emerging themes emphasized by authors and institutions as well as a count of articles contained in the database on this search topic see Table 2.

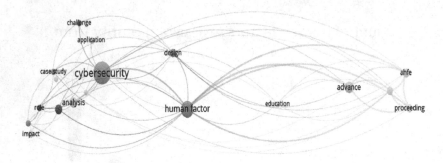

Fig. 3. This figure shows leading terms from cluster analysis in VOS Viewer (Visualization of Similarities). The map is based on metadata captured in Harzing from a search of "human factors" AND "cybersecurity" capturing 980 articles listed within Google Scholar from 2002–2020.

Table 1. Table of leading terms 2002–2020

Term	Occurrences	Relevance
Cybersecurity	236	0.73
Human factor	125	0.09
Advance	56	0.20
Security	44	1.04
Analysis	44	0.94
Design	33	0.05
Ahfe	32	0.33
Proceeding	30	0.33
International conference	29	0.31
Impact	22	1.75
Cyber security	20	1.47
Application	20	1.18
Challenge	19	1.79
Role	19	1.33
Case study	18	1.68
Education	17	0.07
Human	16	1.00
Cybersecurity education	15	3.72

Using the Harzing data from Google Scholar, another cluster map was created for Fig. 4 by the same process as Fig. 3, although with the data from 1000 articles uses the timeframe of 2015–2020. It had several new terms in the map; however the most notable was security. On the other hand, the size and relevance of the AHFE point increased, which indicates that the conference is still emphasizing the importance of research on this emerging area see Table 3.

4.2 Co-citation Analysis

The co-citation analysis is the frequency in which two documents appear together in the reference section of another article (Fahimnia et al. 2015). The articles in the co-citation analysis were taken from two sets of data in the Web of Science database. In the criteria of the search, the parameters were set to only acknowledge articles with three or more co-cited references. The first set of data from 2012–2020 yielded 15 results. The second

Table 2. The table shows leading authors among 2256 listed authors in the AuthorMapper database. Leading keywords show emerging themes emphasized by these leading authors.

Author	Years	Leading keywords	Count
Linkov, Igor	2013–2019	Resilience, Risk, Security, Counterfeiting, Cybernetworks	8
Gonzalez, Cleotilde	2013–2020	Deception, Honeypots, Attack, Behavioral cybersecurity	6
Still, Jeremiah D.	2016–2020	Authentication (graphical and alphanumeric), Cybersecurity, Distorted images	6
Dutt, Varun	2016–2020	Deception, Honeypots, Attack, Behavioral cybersecurity	5
Helkala, Kirsi	2016–2019	Performance, Cognitive ability, Human factors, Socio-technical system	5

Table 3. A table of leading institutions from AuthorMapper shows three countries are represented. Count information is included. Leading keywords show institutional emphasis.

Institution	Country	Leading keywords	Count
University of Oxford	U.K.	Artificial intelligence, Human factors, Privacy, Security, Smart cities	15
Carnegie Mellon University	USA	Deception, Honeypots, Attack, Behavioral cybersecurity, Calibration	14
University of Maryland	USA	Password authentication, Personal data availability, Secondary authentication, User behavior, Anticipatory ethics	11
Old Dominion University	USA	Authentication, Cybersecurity, Graphical authentication, Agent based modeling and simulation	10
Norwegian University of Science & Technology	Norway	Cyber, Cyber security, Human factors, IoT, Security	8

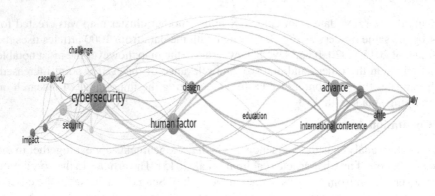

Fig. 4. This figure shows leading terms from cluster analysis in VOS Viewer. The map is based on metadata captured in Harzing from a search of "human factors" AND "cybersecurity" capturing 1000 articles listed within Google Scholar from 2015–2020.

Fig. 5. Co-citation analysis of 48 WoS articles from 2012–2020 and 44 WoS articles from 2015–2020 in VOS Viewer

set of data also yielded 15 results and created an identical cluster map of the co-citation analysis. See Fig. 5 see Table 4.

Dutt is in this co-citation analysis and the table of leading authors in the cybersecurity and human factors field. Rassmussen, Vicente, Flach, and Burns have a foundation in

Table 4. The author, title, publication information, and years from the cluster analysis in Fig. 5.

Authors	Title and Publication Info	Year
Brady, A., N. Naikar, and A. Treadwell	"Organisational storytelling with work domain analysis: Case study of air power doctrine and strategy narrative." In *MODSIM*	2013
Burns, C. M. and Hajdukiewicz JR	Ecological Interface Design, CRC Press	2004, 2017
Vicente, Kim J.	Cognitive work analysis: Toward safe, productive, and healthy computer-based work. CRC Press	1999
Rasmussen, Jens, Annelise Mark Pejtersen, and Len P. Goodstein	Cognitive systems engineering. Wiley	1994
Conti, Greg	Security data visualization: graphical techniques for network analysis. No Starch Press	2007
Bennett, Kevin B., and John M. Flach	Display and interface design: Subtle science, exact art. CRC Press	2011
Dutt, Varun, Young-Suk Ahn, and Cleotilde Gonzalez	"Cyber situation awareness: modeling detection of cyber attacks with instance-based learning theory." *Human Factors* 55, no. 3, 605–618	2013
Pattinson, Malcolm, Cate Jerram, Kathryn Parsons, Agata McCormac, and Marcus Butavicius	"Why do some people manage phishing emails better than others?". *Information Management & Computer Security* 20, no. 1: 18–28	2012

Human Factors and Ergonomics. This is further support that authors in the cybersecurity field are impacted by the literature of human factors.

4.3 Content Analysis from MAXQDA

A set of core articles was collected from the extensive collection that was used for bibliometric analysis. They were selected from ResearchGate, Springerlink, IHF Cyber (an Integrated Human Factors Cybersecurity company), and Google Scholar. The co-citation analysis and additional reading lead to the selection of the core articles.

Word Cloud. Articles were imported into MAXQDA to generate a word cloud. The top terms were a combination of human factors terms and cybersecurity terms. The term in the map that stood out in the diagram was "Wickens". Wickens is one of the authors in the *Handbook of Human Factors and Ergonomics*. (Salvendy 1990). His name (word) in the cloud was relatively large, due to the number of times that it appeared within the core articles. See Fig. 6.

Extended Lexical Search. The MAXQDA software is also capable of other literature analyses, such as an extended literature search. In this section of the content analysis, select terms are outlined from among common themes of leading authors or leading terms in the word cloud from maxQDA, the VOS Viewer analysis highlighting leading items within the clusters, and the co-citation analysis within VOS Viewer. Two main categories for the selected terms are "cybersecurity" and "human factors" see Table 5.

Ecological Interface Design: The article (book) in the co-citation analysis by Burns, "Ecological interface design", prompted an extended literature (lexical) search. The

Fig. 6. The Word Cloud for key terms in the core articles (#2–4, 8, 9 13, 15, 22 in the reference section) within the MAXQDA software (project) from the 150 leading terms

Table 5. This table summarizes the terms shown in more detail as part of the content analysis.

Human factors	Cybersecurity
Ecological interface design	Honeypots
Information processing	Risk
Systems design	Privacy

interface design yielded links back to the *Handbook of Human Factors and Ergonomics* (Salvendy, 1990; 2012) and. This connection to the co-citation analysis supports the claim that Human Factors is central to research in human factors with cybersecurity.

Information Processing: Information processing appears in the reference section several times in Moallem's HCI and Cybersecurity Handbook (Moallem 2019). It also appeared in the *Handbook of Human Factors and Ergonomics* (Wickens and Carswell 2012). That section emphasizes capabilities and limitations of people and summarizes how information is selected (attention), processed (perceived) and comprehended (memory aspects).

Systems Design: Systems design is an integral part of the industrial engineering process. When creating a system to protect against a vast array of attacking capabilities, the designer needs to consult knowledgeable sources on systems design. Systems design was found in the *Handbook of Human Factors and Ergonomics* (Salvendy 1990) in chapter 2 (Czaja and Nair 2012). Emphasis is given to the human factors aspects concerned with interaction of humans with other elements of the system. Beyond the physical aspects, the behavioral aspects are of greater interest in cybersecurity.

Risk: Risk is selected among areas of emphasis of leading author, Igor Linkov, also shown in the table of leading authors from AuthorMapper. Risk relevant to the design process of all cybersecurity technologies. One related article emphasizes comparative risk assessment, recent developments and applications (Linkov et el. 2006). A human factors model that directly relates to the risk assessment is emphasized in Reason's research. James Reason's Swiss Cheese model models a defense against failure with a statistical calculation for the probability of failure, based on the layers of defense with assumptions that one layer may be breached while the next may not (Reason 2006). Redundancy, resilience and human reliability arise as terminologies for further consideration of risk and risk analysis.

Honeypots: This term honeypot is useful as an example that shows how human factors theory can be used in support of cybersecurity. A honeypot is a cybersecurity item that deceives a cyber-attacker into targeting it. When the honeypot is targeted for the attack, it is assumed to have highly sought data and whatnot. Then the attacker is quarantined and loses access to the system. It uses human limitations and desires to tempt the attacker to fall into the trap. The term honeypot is selected among areas of emphasis of leading author Varun Dutt, shown in the table of leading authors from AuthorMapper. The work of Dutt is also referred to among leading articles in the co-citation analysis. That article from the co-citation analysis was published in the Human factors journal (Dutt et al. 2013).

Privacy: Privacy is a leading term in the word cloud and is sometimes considered together with security and trust. Some researchers have emphasized privacy compliance as well as privacy-preserving and privacy-increasing technologies (Moallem 2019). Cybersecurity and protection of privacy, many times, are considered together. The idea of proactive security measures for prevention is preferred to the consequences of loss of reputation and the administrative requirements to notify after a breach of security or privacy.

5 Conclusions and Future Work

Cybersecurity is a rapidly changing field, which involves solving high tech problems with logical defenses. Human factors is steadily gaining recognition in research for cybersecurity systems. Due to the results of the co-citation analysis, it is clear that many of the leading authors recognize the importance of human factors in systems design. The trend analysis shows the increasing awareness and number of publications on the topic, which will help cybersecurity continue to grow and flourish.

Examples of recent funded work from the National Science Foundation in the USA highlight aspects of human-automation interaction and consider practical applications of privacy and security. The proposal awarded to Patricia Delucia and James Yang of Texas Tech in 2016 is titled Translational Research in Psychological Sciences. The work emphasizes research experience for undergraduates and expects both scientific and societal benefits including applications in cyber-security. Their proposal is intended to support training for a growing demand for human factors professionals.

The research award of DeLucia and Yang is intended to advance research with implications for behavior intended to reduce traffic crashes, improve patient safety and inform human-robot interaction in the context of social robots. One article that was produced as a result of the research so far addresses robots that take on human characteristics. Research related to anthropomorphism may be of interest to the reader as part of future work related to cybersecurity and human factors. Anthropomorphism is the term for computing and/or automation that takes on human characteristics. The publication related to the theoretical and practical implications for anthropomorphism research was published in an ACM/IEEE conference on human-robot interaction in 2018 (Jones 2018). Additional information about related projects can be found at NSF.gov using the keywords "cyber security" and "human factors" in search.

References

AuthorMapper. https://www.authormapper.com/. Accessed 03 Jan 2020

Czaja, S.J., Sankaran, N.N.: Human factors engineering and systems design. In: Salvendy, G. (ed.) Handbook of Human Factors and Ergonomics, 4th edn, Chap. 2, pp. 38–54. Wiley, New Jersey (2012)

Dutt, V., Ahn, Y.-S., Gonzalez, C.: Cyber situation awareness: modeling detection of cyber attacks with instance-based learning theory. Hum. Factors 55(3), 605–618 (2013)

Fahimnia, B., Sarkis, J., Davarzani, H.: Green supply chain management: a review and bibliometric analysis, 23 January 2015. https://www.sciencedirect.com/science/article/abs/pii/S09255273 15000067

Google Scholar. https://scholar.google.com/. Accessed 03 Jan 2020

Jones, K.S., Niichel, M.K., Armstrong, M.E.: Robots exhibit human characteristics: theoretical and practical implications for anthropomorphism research. In: Proceedings of the 2018 ACM/IEEE International Conference on Human-Robot Interaction, p. 137 (2018)

Harzing's Publish or Perish. https://harzing.com/resources/publish-or-perish. Accessed 03 Jan 2020

IHF Cyber: Cyber Security : A Human Factors Dichotomy. N.p. Print

Linkov, I., Satterstrom, F.K., Kiker, G., Batchelor, C., Bridges, T., Ferguson, E.: From comparative risk assessment to multi-criteria decision analysis and adaptive management: recent developments and applications. Environ. Int. 32(8), 1072–1093 (2006)

MAXQDA. https://www.maxqda.com/. Accessed 03 Jan 2020

Mendeley. https://www.mendeley.com/?interaction_required=true. Accessed 03 Jan 2020

MIT: 23 faculty members awarded tenure, 25 October 2006. http://news.mit.edu/2006/tenure-1025

Moallem, A. (ed.): Human-Computer Interaction and Cybersecurity Handbook. CRC Press, Boca Raton (2019)

NAE: Professor Robert Morris (2019). https://www.nae.edu/204131/Professor-Robert-Morris

Reason, J., Hollnagel, E., Paries, J.: Revisiting the Swiss cheese model of accidents. J. Clin. Eng. 27(4), 110–115 (2006)

ResearchGate. https://www.researchgate.net/. Accessed 03 Jan 2020

SpringerLink. https://link.springer.com. Accessed 03 Jan 2020
United States v. Robert Tappan Morris, 928 F.2d 504. https://www.courtlistener.com/opinion/557
   785/united-states-v-robert-tappan-morris/
VOSviewer. https://www.vosviewer.com/. Accessed 03 Jan 2020
Web of Science. https://apps.webofknowledge.com. Accessed 03 Jan 2020
Wickens, C.D., Carswell, C.M.: Chapter 5 information processing 2 three approaches to informa-
   tion. In: Salvendy, G. (Ed.) Handbook of Human Factors and Ergonomics, 4th Edn, pp. 117–151
   Wiley: New Jersey (2012)

Ensuring Trust in and Acceptance of Digitalization and Automation: Contributions of Human Factors and Ethics

Monika Eigenstetter[✉]

Niederrhein University of Applied Sciences, 4705 Krefeld, Germany
monika.eigenstetter@hs-niederrhein.de

Abstract. Acceptance of and trust in automation and digitalization refer to the design of technology that is based not only on human factors and ergonomics but also on the human information processing and ethical evaluation of the human being. Highest demands should be placed on a human-centered design approach and in an ongoing evaluation of the violation of basic human rights as privacy rights and non-discrimination in order to maintain trust and control in the socio-technical system. Two theoretical models and their shortcomings will be presented (1) trust in technology and (2) acceptance of technology. A basic overview on human factors will be given, security and ethical problems named. It is concluded that trust in and acceptance of digitalization and automation can only be ensured if the risks of the complex technologies are appropriately addressed, and the users are informed and trained in their use. The companies are required to answer the questions summarized in a heuristic summary at the end of the contribution.

Keywords: Technique acceptance · Trust in technology · Accountability · Human factors · Ethics

1 New Challenges of Digitalization and Automation

Automation and digitalization are concepts, which cannot be separated and are essential for high added value and efficiency (Soule et al. 2016). A broad range of examples is available. Companies use automated systems to roughly classify documents and information they receive from customers. Digitalization, based on 'Artificial Intelligence', is used to monitor and evaluate employee behavior and to initiate actions, such as prolonging and termination contracts. In health care digitalization helps to classify diseases; in aviation digital procedures control flight path, altitude and speed. Semi-autonomous vehicles are on the road, and in production, engineering disciplines are working on the implementation of industry 4.0. Surveillance technologies are installed in public places, classifying behavior and informing police or security services.

With the advent of automated facial recognition, there is now a great deal of resistance among the population, as they do not want to accept an omniscient technology in public space. And even though total surveillance is rejected in public, people use technologies from private providers that are comparably attentive. Technologies as WhatsApp®,

© Springer Nature Switzerland AG 2020
V. G. Duffy (Ed.): HCII 2020, LNCS 12199, pp. 254–266, 2020.
https://doi.org/10.1007/978-3-030-49907-5_18

Alexa® or Google® were established in very short time, although it is known they may not fulfil important aspects of data security legally required in several countries and are only partly trustworthy. Research machines e.g. are accused to be biased and to violate human rights. But all these technologies are convenient and thus accepted.

Because the processes of digitalization based on machine learning are progressing, people in general miss an understanding of how software and machines select, classify and model information they use, and how this is used for decision making. Artificial Intelligence (AI) uses different approaches, for example supervised and non-supervised types of classification. Sometimes the information is aggregated in different layers and form pattern in a way, that even experts are not able to follow the decisions. Deep learning causes concerns, whether the human will control machines or whether the human will be controlled (Anderson et al. 2018).

In contrast to high-reliability organizations such as aviation or nuclear industry in general are, the users of the many emerging digitalized systems of every day technologies will not be trained systematically and repeatedly for the systems they use. This can be easily demonstrated when lending a car from a car rental company. Implemented assistance systems are usually not explained, and sometimes the cockpit and the features are very unique and not self-descriptive. The same is true for several other digital devices implemented in production. Decision makers, who implement digital systems, may not have the knowledge that over- or undercompliance to technologies can be risky, or that there may be some unintended consequences, when users are losing essential decision skills in interaction with technology.

Quite often, there is a lack of awareness or even ignorance about the inherent ethical problems of technology like discrimination or privacy issues. The large amount of data processed in the context of digitization and automation can be misused and manipulated. This was experienced in the Cambridge Analytica Scandal. In other cases, automation enables or limits the scope of human decision making and action, and create a loss of control and safety. How fatal this may be, could be observed in the recent scandal of Boeing. A lack of transparency of the technology in combination with unethical behaviour of the management was present in both cases. So, questions arise: How to make transparent technologies model decisions and actions? How can erroneous decision models of technologies be recognized and corrected? How can the users of the technologies gain a valid understanding of the opportunities and risks of the used technologies, so that trust and acceptance of that technology are justified?

The introduction of new technologies, especially of AI in companies and in the public should include risk assessments to avoid unintended consequences and deviations. A short checklist for an evaluation of technology related to the basic concepts of trust and acceptance in technology will be developed, including aspects from human factors research on automation and from ethical guidelines, which have been developed due to new possibilities and hazards potentially caused by AI. The main goal of this contribution is to raise awareness to potential risks by digitalization.

2 Acceptance of and Trust in Technology

2.1 Technology Acceptance

Technology Acceptance can be described as acceptance ranging from active opposition to consent and commitment to technology. Model from other research describe acceptance as a process based on specified conditions. Venkatesh et al. (2003) introduced the Unified Theory of Acceptance and Use of Technology UTAUT as a process model characterized by several facets: Influencing factors of an intended use and a subsequent actual usage of a technology are

- performance expectancy which is described as expected benefit,
- effort expectancy which means the simplicity or ease of use,
- social influences, meaning how relevant others or peers are in evaluating a system,
- and facilitating condition, which include contextual aids and support to use the technology.

Part of the UTAUT model are also characteristics of the individual such as experience and voluntary use, which may be an important contributor to acceptance. UTAUT and some other models such as TAM (Davis et al. 1989) are often used to assess technologies, which are used in E-Commerce or in the workplace, by questioning users with a survey. An enhanced model (UTAUT II by Venkatesh et al. 2012) includes also factors such as hedonic motivation, which can be related to user experience, closely related to usability. But user experience goes beyond usability and emphasizes aesthetic and emotional qualities as well as the fun of using specific technology (Thielsch and Moshagen 2010). The intention to use a technology maybe given because many others are using it, or it may happen because of the joy of use or because the personal benefit of use exceeds possible disadvantages.

2.2 Trust in Technology

Many people do not understand the functionality of their digital agents and tools. Nevertheless, users rely on them in order to reach their intended goals. A typical example of trust is the use of a navigation device, which can be used to reach a destination. Trust in technology is defined as "the attitude that an agent will help achieve an individual's goals in a situation characterized by uncertainty and vulnerability" (Lee and See 2004, p. 54). Trust is an acceptance of vulnerability in relying on a subject (human) or an object (technology) in a situation which is not fully controlled. Hoff and Bashir (2014) use the definition of Lee and See, introducing a comprehensive model of 'trust in automation', based on research results in human-machine-interaction (see below).

During interactions with a specific technical system, initially, users usually rely on that system without specific knowledge, but after continuous interaction they develop a mental model of that system. This means, there is an initial trust in technology before the initial interaction, and ongoing development of trust is based on experiences with that technical system. Although some factors of trust in technology are based partly on the person himself, e.g. age, gender and experience with digitalization or automatization in general, trust is mainly a quality, which is depending on features and performance of the technical system and on the situation, in which the system is used (situational trust):

Design features describe aspects as appearance, ease of use, transparency and feedback on the input. Control results from the possibility of intervening in the system and take over the functions. These characteristics are essential and quite similar to criteria of usability (ISO 9241-11: 2018). One additional feature is described as 'politeness in communication', and means i.e.: How are users guided to take the next step in the system? Another additional feature is related to appearance and includes for example anthropomorphism. Trust may be generated, because in the system uses the voice of a man instead of a woman.

System performance includes factors like system reliability, validity and the perceived usefulness. Operational safety is based on the accuracy of error messages: timing, difficulty and types of error. The predictability of a system enhances trust. In addition, dependability is related to trust.

The development of trust depends on the extent to which users are able to understand the performance of the technical system and how it is varying in different situations. A lack of understanding leads to deviations from appropriate interactions with the technical system (Hoff and Bashir 2014).

2.3 Comparison of the Concepts

Technology acceptance can be distinguished from trust in technology. It may well be that someone trusts certain technologies, c.g. in the reliability of a company's device. But since the company's product is not needed or alternatives are available that are more convenient and familiar, the technology is not used. For example, order vending machines in cinemas, although designed to be convenient, are still rather unpopular in comparison to human-operated checkouts. Other technologies such as WhatsApp®, instead, have become established over very short time, although it is known that WhatsApp® the protection of data is not sufficiently guaranteed, and thus is not trustworthy.

Common to both models is the reference to 'ease of use', which can be easily related to the dimensions of usability (ISO 9241-11: 2018), a concept which is well known and established in the context of work design and human computer interaction. But in contrast to usability, trust is based on ergonomics and human factors, i.e. an extensive research in human-machine-interaction. This is including the understanding of human information processing and related safety and security issues explained below.

Both concepts, 'trust' and 'acceptance', include affective (e.g. appearance or hedonic motivation) and cognitive evaluations (e.g. assessment of reliability or benefits). But only the model of trust is based on typical and sometimes contra-intuitive experiences of complex technologies in high-reliability organizations. These organizations have a long history of automation and digitization and normally know how to avoid technical failures (for an overview of human factors and automation see Lee and Seppelt 2012).

Both concepts are useful and valuable in research, but they are not sufficient for an evaluation of further development of digitalization, which should also ensure data security and avoid severe judgement biases concerning human rights. In order to maintain trust and control in socio-technical systems, especially if they include AI, new demands must be placed in the evaluation of technology.

3 Dealing with Artificial Intelligence

3.1 Known Safety Risks of Automation

In automation, the human being is often regarded as 'human error'. Therefore, the human is quite often treated as a residual in socio-technical systems. AI is a powerful tool to put the human 'out of the loop'. If, however, the human being is not adequately addressed in the socio-technical system, there is a risk of loss of competence and other 'ironies in automation' (Brainbridge 1983; Endsley 2017; Lee and Seppelt 2012; Lüdtke 2015).

Errors generated by automation are well-known to many users of navigation devices. Sometimes the updates are too late on a device or the GPS signal is lost, so that new one-way streets or street tours are displayed incorrectly. On the highways, sometimes navigation systems indicate a necessary lane change too late, which then leads to some risky driving maneuvers.

Too little confidence in automation can occur if, for example, the navigation system frequently reports a traffic jam when there is no traffic jam. This can happen, if the sensors are too sensitive for detecting possible critical states of the traffic. This situation leads to many so called 'false alarms' without an actual error or critical condition being present. Repeated experience with false alarms quickly leads users to ignore some or all of the given alarms (Lee and Seppelt 2012). If a navigation system suggests alternative routes too often, even if traffic jams would disappear quickly, the drivers loose confidence in the reliability of the device. Automation or software often suggests changes in a route without sufficient information. Then, it is not understandable which consequences a proposed route change involves. This may also affect the trust and acceptance of the users.

Overcompliance in automation has a different effect. There are countless examples in which users have been completely misled by the navigation systems. (Search term on the Internet: Blind trust navigation). Digitalization may lead to a loss of competences (Lee and Seppelt 2012): Young adults have lost the skills how to read maps due to navigation systems available everywhere. Loss of skills due to automation and digitization, often smiled at and used as material for anecdotes, can lead to serious quality and safety problems in the context of production or health care services.

Technology changes behavior, as seen in risk compensation. When a socio-technical system is perceived as very safe, people tend to behave riskier (Lee and Seppelt 2012; Wilde 1988). For example, when the trust in good brakes and technical safety systems such as ABS and EPS is high, this tends to make drivers show riskier behavior.

Lüdtke (2015) sums up:

- The consideration of the human being as the 'essential source of error' leads to the fact that engineering disciplines try to remove it to a large extent from the socio-technical system. Since, however, the developer of a machine or a software is a human being himself, there is a great risk that errors in the design process may arise. Failures in design, e.g. a lack of usability will then lead to incorrect operations.
- Activities that cannot be automated easily and cost-effectively are still taken over by people. These activities are, among other things, the more demanding and complex tasks that remain with humans, e.g. visual control activities.

- It is common to replace people with automated systems, but in an emergency case, responsibility is given back to them. Humans then are required to correct errors and take control, although most of the time, the user has been taken 'out of the loop'.

Onnasch et al. (2014) are speaking of a 'lumber jack effect' and demonstrate in their metanalysis: the higher the level of automation, the more dangerous are the consequences of a failure of the technology. A vivid example of a near catastrophe in this respect is the capsizing of the Viking Sky cruise ship, reported by Eliot (2019).

Clear and intuitively designed displays are required to allow operators or users of the system to react quickly and appropriately in the event of a system break-down. Another important conclusion of the work of Onnasch et al. (2014) is the necessary separation of information gathering and decision making. If people are deprived of the decision for an action, they lose quite fast the ability to control a system and the upcoming situation: "the distinction between situation and action support is critically important" (p. 485). And Lüdtke (2015, p. 127) points out: It is forgotten, that "the most reliable automation systems require the greatest amount of training" (translated by the author).

3.2 Mental Work Load

Today there are already many fully automated systems that only need to be monitored by humans; e.g. automated passport controls in air traffic or plant monitoring in the chemical industry. The operator can keep an eye on 'the big picture' via cameras, display panels and control consoles. Here, constant attention can lead to a 'drop in alertness', reduced vigilance and a monotonous experience. The human is not equipped for surveillance of environments, which give similar signals in high repetition or have slow changes (Landry 2009)

Technical systems often require an exact sequence of steps, and if incorrect inputs result, the user will not reach his destination. This creates 'stress' for customers and employees. However, while customers can usually choose a supplier with better designed systems, the work environment often does not provide choices for employees. Active action diminishes. The creative parts of the work are increasingly lost and people see themselves as externally controlled under technical system.

Mental hazards, i.e. negative effects on health of those affected, arise, for example, from too much or too little demands at work (Landry 2009). On the one hand, too few demanding activities are accompanied by feelings of monotony and reduced reaction times. On the other hand, too much information stresses due to digital systems and corresponds with fatigue. A typical problem is alarm fatigue, often described in health care systems (Wilken et al. 2017) or poor alarm management causing alarm floods in control centers and production (Laumonier et al. 2017).

Long- term high time pressure, frequent disturbances and interruptions at work, feelings of monotonous activities or a lack of recreational opportunities can impair health. In order to ensure the safety, health and well-being of employees at the workplace, technical systems must be adapted to the physical and mental abilities of humans.

3.3 Risks of IT Security

Industry 4.0 is characterized by interaction with many partners. Digital business and production processes can only work on the basis of trust in data security and data protection (BMWi 2016). The recent case of thousands of Alexa® voice files having fallen in wrong hands revealed some of the problems. Companies thus have to ensure:

- Confidentiality of data (protection against disclosure of data)
- Data integrity: completeness and immutability of data
- Availability of data at the required time

Security measures prevent a company from being harmed by third parties, be it through industrial espionage. sabotage or data theft of employees within a company. In addition, there are many risks that can arise simply through carelessness and error-prone processes. Particularly in highly networked systems, there are many weak points that have to be specifically assessed for risks. Examples from the news are hospitals, energy suppliers, universities and many other organizations. Every year, 68% of companies are targeted by data theft, industrial espionage and sabotage attacks. At total of EUR 43 billion damage in 2017 in Germany was announced by the IT industry association Bitkom in 2018.

Two areas of IT or cyber security must be considered: Data protection (personal data) and information security (production or service-related data). Customers rely on their data being secure with the companies they buy from. Risks resulting from manipulation of production-related data, e.g. failure of control systems have to be recognized (BMWi 2016). Since functional safety can be impaired, security and safety should be considered together in the sense of risk management, also in order to consider possible conflicts of interest between safety and security (Weber 2018).

In addition to technical measures, some non-technical precautions should be taken that affect the rights of customers and employees for data protection. Knowledge of encryption and pseudonymization of data or organizational precautions restricting access to data must be available inside a company (BMWi 2016).

This is especially important, because most security threats are caused from the members of the own company and their careless behavior as clicking on bad links. It should be also mentioned, that the majority of companies that have been victims of espionage, sabotage or data theft have identified the perpetrators inside their group. Piko and Bertram (2018) point out that many security problems are characterized by ethical and responsibility deficiencies. A corporate climate that focuses on 'making a profit at any price' favors harmful behavior by employees. Risk factors for contraproductive work behavior, damaging the organizations, is an ethical climate that promotes egoism within the organization and a lack of care orientation for employees (Eigenstetter et al. 2007).

3.4 Ethical Risks

Some ethical problems are on the horizon for which comprehensive solutions are not yet available. AI can make decisions that are not compatible with the principles of equality treatment. Amazon® took an algorithm off the net in October, 2018 because it led to discrimination against women in personnel selection processes: The training material was mainly based on men's files, which is why the algorithm favored men.

A correction, when the error was discovered, did not lead to any significant improvement (Reuters). When the airline 'Air Berlin' went bankrupt, ticket prices of the airline 'Lufthansa' rose: According to Lufthansa, the software made an autonomous decision (Misselhorn 2018). The 'error' lies in the development of the software.

Another problem that can occur in the context of AI is the lack of supervisory control by people. Human thinking is well capable of making linear predictions for the future from the past. However, data and IT develop exponentially as processor performance doubles every 12–24 months (Moore's Law). Who can ultimately understand what is happening inside the algorithms? If technology acts 'autonomously' based on deep learning, many problems may not even be recognized by the developers, because the problems can occur with a large time delay, so that a causal connection is not visible (Misselhorn 2018).

In addition to the lack of attribution of responsibility and accountability due to the lack of transparency of the technical system, the 'problem of many hands' already exists in the development phase: Who—in development teams—is responsible for errors? Misselhorn (2018, p. 129) also fears that moral concepts will be adapted to what is feasible, i.e. 'what can be programmed'.

4 Selected Ethical Guidelines for Artificial Intelligence

In the last three years many different organizations try to address the occurring legal and ethical problems with AI Guidelines. The German Non-Governmental Organization Algorithm Watch built up a Global Inventory of AI Ethics Guidelines and concludes, that the many different guidelines focus on the "similar principles on transparency, equality/non-discrimination, accountability and safety" and that the majority of the guidelines include a voluntary self-commitment of institutions or organizations (Algorithm Watch, without year). Three differing guidelines are selected, a Framework addressing human rights by Amnesty International and Access New (2018), a legal framework of federal and state data protection supervisory authorities of Germany (DSK 2019), and a German association of 2,700 companies in the digital economy, named Bitcom e.V. (2018a, b).

Amnesty international and Access New (2018) declared in the Toronto Declaration the right to equality and non-discrimination in machine learning systems. Their goal is the protection of human rights and the assurance of accountability when human rights are violated. They rely mainly on the protection from discrimination, promotion of inclusion, diversity, and equality. This guideline points out, that technology based on AI changes power structures. AI can be used to suppress people and to marginalize groups. Access of all humans to the positive aspects of AI should be confirmed by the governments. Government and private sector actors have to build up processes for human rights due diligence. They have to identify the potential of discriminatory risks, they should implement measures to prevent and reduce discrimination. Government has the duty to supervise the activities of the private actors and to prosecute violations. The concept for companies is similar to other approaches in human rights protection. Companies should follow a typical management approach which is similar to a compliance management.

The federal and state data protection supervisory authorities of Germany formulated seven binding criteria to ensure privacy rights (DSK 2019). These are:

- AI must not turn people into objects
- AI may only be used for constitutionally legitimate purposes
- AI must be transparent, comprehensible and explainable
- AI must avoid discrimination
- AI has to guarantee the principle of data minimization
- AI needs accountability
- AI needs technical and organizational standards.

Monitoring and evaluation of errors and biases related to the specialized context of applications has to be assured.

Bitkom e.V. (2018b) gives advices for processes within the organizations that document a responsible usage of AI. This includes actions, that ensure transparency during the development process so that AI decisions become understandable. Companies should ensure also transparency for the external users. Organizational actors are encouraged for a systematic involvement of stakeholders. They should give users relevant, understandable and easily accessible information of automated decisions. Companies should ensure, that the technology contributes to the benefit of all. Data quality must be guaranteed: reliable and valid data are a necessary basis for responsible AI. For the avoidance of a possible machine bias, the technology must officially be tested regularly and, in case required, adjusted. In responsible decision-making processes, e.g. in medicine, the final decision competence should remain with responsible human actors until control quality of AI reaches a level accepted by all stakeholders.

5   Assessing and Managing the New Technologies – A Heuristic Approach

AI creates a complexity in the technical systems that requires special know-how in order to assess the multitude of arising risks adequately and to ensure acceptance and trust in AI technologies by all stakeholders. The integration of new technologies in organizations and society, requires acceptance and cooperation of many different stakeholders. How can trust be established between all participants in flexible network structures, e.g. between customers and organization, or employees and organization, citizens and government? This is, what developers and organizations should have in mind: Automation and digitalization are still too often introduced under the primacy of what is technically feasible and in order to improve the overall efficiency of a company or a socio-technical system (Misselhorn 2018). But trust and acceptance in the ongoing digitalization process will only be ensured if typical design errors in automation and digitalization are avoided, and reliability, safety, security and ethics of the ubiquitous technologies are ensured. Public expectancies of legal and social responsibilities in a democratic society have to be met.

The complexity of the challenge points to the fact that only a human-centered view of the world enables value-adding ideas (Brynjolfsson and MacAfee 2014). The active participation of stakeholders is therefore a key success factor. Promising approaches are those represented in participative design and human-centered design. Participative design goes beyond human-centered design. It legitimizes users to evaluate their projects and tasks in terms of objectives and implementation and to design them in an accompanying manner. Since technology influences the future of people and thus the reality of life as well as personality, individuals who (must) use technology should be granted far-reaching rights of co-design (Robertson and Simonson 2013).

Dealing with AI and complex technologies requires a holistic approach. The use of technologies must be accompanied by management structures that address social responsibility in relation to risks. There are developed management approaches in the area of high reliability organizations, which should be systematically combined with accountable and ethical management approaches, so that the 'licence to operate' will be given by authorities, customers, employees and the civic population when using complex AI-technologies. ISO 26000, the Management Guideline for Corporate Responsibility, calls for a management approach based on the principles of accountability, transparency, ethical behaviour, respect of the stakeholder requests, respect of the legislation and law, respect of international codes of conduct, and respect of human rights.

In addition, however, it must be remembered that some unforeseeable errors and problems may occur in conjunction with AI technologies. In a case of failure of technology, the decision makers then will be held accountable and have to give answers to their stakeholders. Dekker and Breakey (2016) developed a just culture approach in such cases of failures. Just Culture asks how trust can be restored and how the needs of the injured party can be adequately addressed in the event of damage or injury.

Only with a profound assessment of the risks of a given technology and a description, how selected accompanying management approaches address them—based on human factors research, security requirements, and possible human rights violation—safe, secure, non-discriminatory and inclusive technological systems in action can be developed. Questions that developers, marketers, sellers and purchasers of AI should ask themselves are summarized in the following heuristic compilation. This compilation is based on the overviews given above, the ethical guidelines which are introduced, and the idea of the just culture approach.

Transparency of the Technical System

- How is it ensured that the AI decisions are comprehensible, correctable and adaptable to the developer?
- Which processes exist, to ensure, that developers are held accountable?

Integration of the stakeholders

- How are the requirements of usability and user participation in the new technologies met?
- How is it ensured that performance of the technical system corresponds to the user's understanding?

- What processes are in place to ensure that the functioning of AI is communicated to users in a manner so that they know what AI can and cannot do with the (personal) data?
- Which processes exist, to communicate in a fair and honest way to stakeholders, in case that AI fails?
- Which processes exist, to restore trust and acceptance in case, that AI fails?

Safety Concerns

- How is it ensured and verified that the technology can be used safely by the user so that there is no over-compliance or under-compliance?
- How is it ensured that alarms and messages of the system do not overstrain users or lead to reactance?
- How is it ensured that unintended effects, e.g. a loss of competence, among users are effectively counteracted?
- How are AI errors systematically recorded, evaluated and eliminated so that reliable technology can be guaranteed?

Security Concerns

- How can users be informed in a simple way about how the personal rights and data protection are guaranteed?
- Which technical and organizational processes in the own organization are in place to prevent unauthorized access to the technical system from inside and outside?
- What additional safeguards are in place in the processes, e.g. via encryption or pseudonymisation of data, so that misuse is as unlikely as possible even in the event of data leakage?
- How are AI errors systematically recorded, evaluated and eliminated so that reliable technology can be guaranteed?

Ethical Values and Human Rights

- How can users be informed in a simple way, that the technology is free of discrimination and ensures the right of equal treatment and inclusion?
- How is it ensured that AI reaches the largest possible group of users and is not only beneficial to the provider/developer?
- How is data quality ensured so that, for example, a machine bias is not generated during development using incomplete data sets (e.g. avoidance of a male bias)?
- Which processes exist, that mitigate violation of human rights like discrimination through AI?
- Which processes are in place to involve vulnerable groups in a machine bias with human rights violations and to compensate them if necessary?
- Which processes are viable ensured, to address accountability, when AI is failing?

The checklist should serve as an initial self-check for decision makers in companies. The potential of new technologies can only be applied, if non-intended possible consequences and deviations are proactively addressed in a comprehensive risk management. Accompanying monitoring should make deviations in the technology quickly recognizable and should enable rapid modifications. Reporting structures and a continuous stakeholder dialogue ensure the necessary transparency. Acceptance of the diverse potential of AI and trust in the technical solutions based on AI can only arise, if people learn to deal with the risks appropriately: during development, in business operations and then in the appropriate use of the technologies.

References

Algorithm Watch: AI Ethics Guidelines Global Inventory. https://algorithmwatch.org/en/project/ai-ethics-guidelines-global-inventory/. Accessed 31 Jan 2020

Amnesty International and Access New: The Toronto Declaration: Protecting the right to equality and non-discrimination in machine learning systems (2018). https://www.accessnow.org/cms/assets/uploads/2018/08/The-Toronto-Declaration_ENG_08-2018.pdf. Accessed 31 Jan 2020

Anderson, J. Rainie, L., Luchsinger, A.: Artificial intelligence and the future of humans. Pew Research Center (2018). http://www.springer.com/lncs. Accessed 31 Jan 2020

BDI Cybersecurity: The backbone of a successful digital transformation (2019). https://english.bdi.eu/article/news/cybersecurity/. Accessed 31 Jan 2020

Bitcom e.V (2018a). https://www.bitkom.org/Presse/Presseinformation/Attacken-auf-deutsche-Industrie-verursachten-43-Milliarden-Euro-Schaden.html. Accessed 31 Dec 2018

Bitcom e.V.: Empfehlungen für den verantwortlichen Einsatz von KI und automatisierten Entscheidungen - corporate digital responsibility and decision making (2018b). https://www.bitkom.org/Bitkom/Publikationen/Empfehlungen-fuer-den-verantwortlichen-Einsatz-von-KI-und-automatisierten-Entscheidungen-Corporate-Digital-Responsibility-and-Decision-Making (2018b).html. Accessed 31 Jan 2020

BMWi: Federal Ministry for Economic Affairs and Energy: IT security in Industrie 4.0. First steps towards secure production. Plattform Industrie 4.0 (2016). https://www.plattform-i40.de/PI40/Redaktion/EN/Downloads/Publikation/it-security-in-i40.pdf?__blob=publicationFile&v=5. Accessed 31 Dec 2020

Brainbridge, L.: Ironies of automation. Automatica 19(6), 775–779 (1983)

Brynjolfsson, E., MacAfee, A.: The Second Machine Age. Work, Progress, and Prosperity in a Time of Brilliant Technology. Plassen, New York (2014)

Davis, F., Bagozzi, P., Warshaw, P.: User acceptance of computer technology - a comparison of two theoretical models. Manag. Sci. 35(8), 982–1003 (1989)

Dekker, S.A., Breakey, H.: 'Just culture:' improving safety by achieving substantive, procedural and restorative justice. Saf. Sci. 85, 187–193 (2016)

DSK: Datenschutzkonferenz: Entschließung der 97. Konferenz der unabhängigen Datenschutzaufsichtsbehörden des Bundes und der Länder, Hambacher Erklärung zur Künstlichen Intelligenz Hambacher Schloss, 3 April 2019. https://www.datenschutz.rlp.de/fileadmin/lfdi/Konferenzdokumente/Datenschutz/DSK/Entschliessungen/097_Hambacher_Erklaerung.pdf. Accessed 31 Jan 2020

Eigenstetter, M., Dobiasch, S., Trimpop, R.: Commitment and counterproductive work behavior as correlates of ethical climate in organizations. Monatsschrift für Kriminologie und Strafrechtsreform 90(2/3), 224–244 (2007)

Eliot, L.: Human in-the-loop vs. Out-of-the-loop in AI systems: the case of AI self-driving cars (2019). https://www.aitrends.com/ai-insider/human-in-the-loop-vs-out-of-the-loop-in-ai-systems-the-case-of-ai-self-driving-cars/. Accessed 31 Jan 2020

Endsley, M.: From here to autonomy: lessons learned from human-automation research. Hum. Factors **59**(1), 5–27 (2017). https://doi.org/10.1177/0018720816681350

Hoff, K., Bashir, M.: Trust in automation: integrating empirical evidence on factors that Influence trust. Hum. Factors **57**(3), 407–434 (2014)

ISO 9241-11:2018: Ergonomics of human-system interaction—Part 11: Usability: Definitions and concepts (2018). https://www.iso.org

Landry, S.: Flight deck automation. In: Nof, S.Y. (ed.) Springer Handbook of Automation, pp. 1215–1237. Springer, Heidelberg (2009). https://doi.org/10.1007/978-3-540-78831-7_68

Laumonier, Y., Faure J.-M., Lesage J.-J., Sabot, H.: Towards alarm flood reduction. In: 2017 22nd IEEE International Conference on Emerging Technologies and Factory Automation (ETFA) (2017)

Lee, J., See, K.: Trust in automation: designing for appropriate reliance. Hum. Factors **46**, 50–80 (2004)

Lee, J., Seppelt, B.: Human factors and ergonomics in automation design. In: Salvendy, G. (ed.) Handbook of Human Factors, pp. 1615–1642. Wiley, New York (2012)

Lüdtke, Andreas: Wege aus der Ironie in Richtung ernsthafter Automatisierung. In: Botthof, Alfons, Hartmann, E.A. (eds.) Zukunft der Arbeit in Industrie 4.0, pp. 125–146. Springer, Heidelberg (2015). https://doi.org/10.1007/978-3-662-45915-7_13

Misselhorn, C.: Grundfragen der Maschinenethik. Reclam, Stuttgart (2018)

Moshagen, M., Thielsch, M.T.: Facets of visual aesthetics. Int. J. Hum Comput Stud. **68**(10), 689–709 (2010)

Onnasch, L., Wickens, C., Li, H., Manzey, D.: Human performance consequences of stages and levels of automation. An integrated meta-analysis. Hum. Factors **56**(3), 476–488 (2014)

Piko, T., Bertram, A.: Current intelligence: expertise über Ethik und Sicherheit als nachrichten-dienstliches Produkt. In: Eigenstetter, M., Darlington, S., Klingels, F. (Hrsg.) Verantwortlich Denken und Handeln in komplexen Umwelten. Hintergründe, Herausforderungen, Gestal-tungsmöglichkeiten, pp. 201–212. Verlag für Polizeiwissenschaft, Frankfurt a. M (2018)

Reuters. Amazon scraps secret AI recruiting tool that showed bias against women (2018/10/19). https://www.reuters.com/article/us-amazon-com-jobs-automation-insight/amazon-scraps-sec ret-ai-recruiting-tool-that-showed-bias-against-women-idUSKCN1MK08G. Accessed 31 Jan 2020

Robertson, T., Simonson, J.: Participatory design: an introduction. In: Simonosen, J., Roberston, T. (Hrsg.) Routledge International Handbook of Participatory Design, pp. 1–17. Routledge, New York (2013)

Soule, D., Puram, A., Westerman, G., Boennet, D.: Becoming a digital organization. The journey to digital dexterity. MIT Center für Digital Business. Working Paper #301 (2016). https://pap ers.ssrn.com/sol3/papers.cfm?abstract_id=2697688. Accessed 01 Apr 2017

Venkatesh, V., Morris, M., Davis, G., Davis, F.: User acceptance of information technology: toward a unified view. MIS Q. **27**(3), 425–478 (2003)

Venkatesh, V., Thong, J., Xu, X.: Consumer acceptance and use of information technology: extending the unified theory of acceptance and use of technology. MIS Q. **36**(1), 157–178 (2012)

Weber, A.: Security und safety: Schnittstellen und Zielkonflikte. In: Eigenstetter, M. Darling-ton, S., Klingels, F. (Hrsg.), Verantwortlich Denken und Handeln in komplexen Umwel-ten. Hintergründe, Herausforderungen, Gestaltungsmöglichkeiten, pp. 102–116. Verlag für Polizeiwissenschaft, Frankfurt a. M (2018)

Wilde, G.: Risk homeostasis theory and traffic accidents: propositions, deductions and discussion of dissension in recent reactions. Ergonomics **31**, 441–468 (1988)

Wilken, M., Hüske-Kraus, D., Klausen, A., Koch, C., Schlauch, W., Röhrig, R.: Alarm fatigue: causes and effects. Stud. Health Technol. Inform. **243**, 107–111 (2017)

Regulated Body-Sharing Virtual Trips for Pleasure and Business

Reem Elkhouly[1,2]($\boxtimes$) (iD), Shin Fukui[3,4] (iD), and Emi Tamaki[1,3,5] (iD)

[1] Faculty of Science and Engineering, Waseda University, Tokyo, Japan
`reem_elkhouly@f-eng.tanta.edu.eg`
[2] Faculty of Engineering, Tanta University, Tanta, Egypt
[3] JST Presto, Japan Science and Technology Agency, Tokyo, Japan
[4] Faculty of Human Sciences, Waseda University, Saitama, Japan
[5] Research Department, H2L, Inc., Tokyo, Japan

Abstract. Nowadays, people believe that not only the remote body operation by one direction control (Tele-existence) but also the remote body sharing by mutual control (*Body-Sharing*) will increase within few upcoming years. In the future, users -including elderly and disabled- can work and enjoy sightseeing using remote body sharing. Meanwhile, when many users deeply concentrate to act through remote bodies, their conscious is transferred to a remote place. As more users get immersed in the *Body-Sharing*, the number of unconscious users increases in arbitrary areas, leaving these areas unsafe. We aim to avoid the hazard resulting from high rates of unconscious users. In this research, the outcomes of five proposed rules that organize the unconscious users' rate are revealed. These rules are (I) Time Limit Rule "limiting the *Body-Sharing* time of each user per day", (II) Visitors Limit Rule "limiting the number of simultaneous remote *Body-Sharing* visitors into an area", (III) Departures Limit Rule "limiting the number of allowed *Body-Sharing* users to depart from an area simultaneously", (IV) Increase Charm Level Rule "granting larger budgets to the least attractive places", and (V) Decrease Charm Level Rule "deducting budgets assigned to the most attractive places". On the other hand, unconscious users rates are monitored when no rule (i.e. free *Body-Sharing*) is applied as a baseline for evaluation. In order to anticipate users' popular *Body-Sharing* destinations, we use a sigmoid function for decision making whether or not he or she travels. The attractiveness levels of different areas are set using the statistical data provided by the Japanese government. With the sigmoid probability function for decision making, the attractiveness of probable destinations, the five proposed rules, and the organization of unconscious users rate are simulated. The inhabitants of the Japanese 47 prefectures are the study case; a total population of 126.9 million according to the announced statistics in 2016. Rules I and II were found, by simulation, effective to suppress depopulation/overpopulation areas compared to free *Body-Sharing*. We realized that like the widely adopted parental rule that limits the time spent online daily by children, applying the Time Limit Rule on the unconscious users' rate organization outperformed other rules.

Keywords: Body-sharing · AR/VR immersion · Safety regulations

© Springer Nature Switzerland AG 2020
V. G. Duffy (Ed.): HCII 2020, LNCS 12199, pp. 267–279, 2020.
https://doi.org/10.1007/978-3-030-49907-5_19

1 Introduction and Background

Due to recent device development, the implementation environment for Telexistence has been rapidly established in HCI research [23]. Telexistence, proposed by Tachi et al. [22], is a concept of technology that enables a human being to perceive various sense at a place different from the place where he or she exists physically, or to interact with the remote environment [21]. This concept includes teleoperation of robot, and such an operation realizes utilizing virtual reality (VR) techniques and robotics recently [2].

These technologies makes it possible to have a travel experience without any physical relocation [1]. Potter et al. [18] suggested that there is a great potential for the use of VR in nature-based tourism for the provision of both information and education. Mirk and Hlavacs [13] demonstrated the feasibility of virtual tourism via UAVs. Quadcopters were used to provide tactile stimulation in VR by Knierim et al. [7]. Furthermore, there is a possibility that movement of consciousness, Body-Sharing, will spread in the research and development of VR, Augmented Reality (AR) and Mixed Reality (MR) [5]. By Body-Sharing we mean to share the same body with two or more people by mutual sharing of sensations accompanying it. The "body" mentioned here does not only refer to a human body but also the body of a robot or the body of a virtual character inside VR, AR, and MR.

New technologies often come with new challenges that we have never considered. Multiple studies proved that the user immersion in VR using developed HMD trades off his awareness of the real environment [3,10,16]. Therefore, when the users of Body-Sharing operate remote robots and people, they intentionally give up their perception of the surrounding circumference. Regardless of their physical location, users are conscious at the place where the remotely shared robot or human bodies exist [15]. Where consciousness in this context does not only refer to thoughts and sensation, but also to feelings and emotions. We speculate that, by the time when Body-Sharing becomes globally adopted, the whole world will be classified by users into "popular" and "unpopular" districts. Consciousness migration from unpopular neighborhoods to popular destinations, which attract many users, is expected. It is important to note that unconscious people, whose majority exist in unpopular districts, are unable to sense physical dangers around them (i.e. robbery breakage into their homes). Since, their senses to the real world is blocked and their mental awareness is absorbed to the virtual world in which referred to as the perceptual and psychological immersion [12,25]. "Smartphone zombie" is an example for a common consciousness problem that even happens in familiar places. In this case, a smartphone user pays all his attention and concentrates deeply into the screen. Nowadays, many traffic accidents are induced by unconscious walking or driving individuals [27]. Body-Sharing user is even more vulnerable to physical environment unconsciousness problems due to VR headset developed technology [11,17]. Preventative measures would include applying regulations to avoid technology over-usage that may result in undesirable side effects.

Due to the development of tele-existence technology where a user operates a robot at a remote place and the proposal of remote operation as a virtual character in AR [4], consequences should be thoroughly investigated. A previous research [24] showed that, although Body-Sharing user has the advantage of being able to move to remote locations instantly, he cannot concentrate on his personal safety while operating Body-Sharing. For example, when the user remotely shares visual and auditory information using an HMD (Head Mounted Display), the user's surrounding visual, auditory and somatic sensation information may be completely blocked. Therefore, even if a disaster (i.e. fire) or a crime (i.e. robbery) occurs around the user, he may not be capable of reacting instantly which exposes him to dangers.

Therefore, in this research, we conducted a simulation of conscious-population density-change when people virtually travel via Body-Sharing under the assumption of this technology becomes cheap enough to be acquitted by anyone. The population can be classified as a "Mass of Individuals" of the mass crowd simulation's subcategories as defined in [26]. This simulation was designed to deduce an effective regulating usage rule to avoid unsafe conscious depopulation. While illustrating the effect of individual travel-motivation characteristic on the crowd behavior. Taking Japan as a preliminary case study, we simulated the flow of consciousness at the prefecture scale. Our aim of this research is to elaborate a convenient regulation that would guarantee to minimize the possibility of physical accident occurrence when Body-Sharing technology is widely used. The danger that we address is a conscious density shrinkage within an area via Body-Sharing, however, the physical population density remains the same. We assume several regulating rules for Body-Sharing and compared the ability of these rules to control the changes in the density of consciousness.

2 System Configuration

The primary purpose of this simulation is to come up with a candidate rule for Body-Sharing organization by authorities in the future. This rule should guarantee that the rates of unconscious Body-Sharing users within a particular area are kept below critical limits. Because high rates of unconscious Body-Sharing users could introduce core safety and security threats. On the other hand, it should also keep popular destinations from being overcrowded with visitors to avoid resources consumption. In this section, we discuss how the individual behavior is predicted and how the three different proposed rules are tested and evaluated.

2.1 Data and Models

In order to simulate the behavior of people who are going to use Body-Sharing technology to visit remote places for work or sightseeing, we used statistical data provided by the Japanese government [19] about the prefectures' information and population as well as tourism statistics. Through our research, we developed a simulation framework, then this framework was implemented in C++, where prefectures, persons, and robots are implemented as classes. In the following sections, we describe the simulation framework design, the data usage, and the probabilities of connecting and travel-motives respectively.

Design. The simulation framework contains multiple classes that describe the proposed environment of the suggested body-Sharing regulating rules. The class "Prefecture" is an abstraction of the Japanese prefectures. It is defined by an ID along with the name. Each prefecture is the place where a part of the Japanese population resides. So, the number of population of a prefecture is used as an attribute. The prefecture attractiveness, that depends on the popularity of a prefecture's sight-seeing, is a key parameter to estimate the number of visitors. For the purpose of testing different rules, a limit for visitors and leavers can be set.

As we are interested in the individual behavior that may lead to safety hazards when applied over the whole population, a "Person" class is introduced. A person is identified by an ID and resides in one prefecture. According to a model that will be described later in this paper, a person will decide to visit another prefecture. If the rule allows him to do so, his record of this day visits will be incremented. This record will be used later as a factor of approving his following Body-Sharing requests. Furthermore, every person is assigned a happiness level generated using the decision making sigmoid probability function explained previously. This happiness level along with the attractiveness of the prefecture are used to select Body-Sharing destinations. Other attributes and classes that do not affect the understanding of the simulation are used for simplifying the programming model.

Data Usage. First, we used the data of Japanese prefectures population to generate a representation for individuals living all over Japan [19]. Later, this representation mimics the individual behavior and aggregates into a broad simulation to show the probable hazards due to lack of conscious people at specific times. Second, we used the data of Japanese prefectures received tourists per year to set an indicator of each prefecture attractiveness [19]. The higher the attractiveness level of a prefecture, the more the Body-Sharing visiting requests a prefecture will receive. Finally, a happiness measure based on the decision making probability sigmoid function is integrated to control the body sharing users activity destination selection process. This decision will be affected by the aforementioned parameters namely prefecture attractiveness level, attractiveness level variation over day time periods, and the decision making sigmoid probability function. The latter is discussed thoroughly in the next section.

Probability of Being Connected. We assume that a person is more likely to use Body-Sharing in case he is off-work. Thus, the probability of requesting a trip through Body-Sharing is strongly coupled with the probability of being on holiday. We calculated this probability as the percentage of the mean person's holidays in Japan. That includes 2-day weekend per week, 21 days of national holiday per year, 5-day new year vacation, and another 5-day summer vacation. A connected person is a candidate for traveling either within his/her own or to another prefecture. Meanwhile, the strength of travel motivation should be estimated then checked against the selected regulating rule.

Probability of Being Travel-Motivated. In this study, we assumed a person who is connected makes a decision to travel through Body-Sharing based on a decision making sigmoid probability function. We adopted a sigmoid curve as the probability function for decision making [20]. Within this simulation, when a person is connected, he/she is at an arbitrary specified level of happiness. A travel destination is chosen arbitrarily among all prefectures including his home one. Each prefecture has a charm level which is calculated based on annual tourism data provided by the government. The travel motivation is driven by how large is the proposed destination charm level compared to the candidate traveler happiness level. This relation can be described using Eq. (1), where:

1. α determines people's attitude to travel with Body-Sharing ($0 < \alpha \leq 1$).
2. β represents the sensitivity towards the difference between the destination's CharmLevel compared to Happiness.
3. D_j denotes charm level of prefecture j.
4. H_i expresses happiness level of person i.

$$p = \frac{\alpha}{1 + \exp(-\beta * (D_j - H_i))} \tag{1}$$

α and β are positive constants. We fixed $\alpha = 1$ and $\beta = 0.1$ throughout this study.

2.2 Rules

Like any new technology, it is expected that governments will try to formulate the body sharing usage by inhabitants when the Body-Sharing spreads beyond limited VR passionate societies. Despite the uniqueness of the goal, multiple strategies may be conducted. Five distinctive rules are thought of when considering regulating the body sharing to maintain the rates of unconscious users within safe margins.

Time Limit Rule. The first rule that will come up to anybody's mind is to limit the time allowed for every individual to use Body-Sharing system. This rule is currently used by parents to control how much time their children spend using electronic devices or watching TV. Also, the same rule is usually adopted by authorities to ensure equal allowance of shared resources for every citizen. A request from a user of Body-Sharing will be approved if and only if he did not exceed a defined limit of total unconscious body sharing time on that day.

Visitors Limit Rule. A simpler rule that is also derived from our daily life would be to limit the accepted number of visitors by each prefecture. It is similar to offering a limited number of tickets for a performance; whenever the tickets are sold out, no extra spectators are allowed in. A request from a user of Body-Sharing will be rejected if the desired destination is already crowded, but it can be approved if resubmitted by the same user for other destinations. Again, we argue that although this rule will prevent popular destination from getting crowded, it will not prevent high rates of unconscious users somewhere else.

Departures Limit Rule. Although it is not the first rule that someone would think of, it is the most directly related to the purpose of setting a rule in the first place. If the authorities want to keep the rate of unconscious Body-Sharing users under a specific threshold, they should set a limit on how much users from the same area can use Body-Sharing simultaneously. Hence, a request from a user of Body-Sharing will be approved as long as the rate of unconscious users at his area is within the safe boundaries. Obviously, this rule needs tailoring many fine-grained evaluation factors so that it can prevent Body-Sharing starvation. In other words, every user should be granted a time portion of Body-Sharing without any unreasonable latency that may let him wait forever. However, this rule does not control the number of visitors to a popular district which may cause overpopulation.

Increase Charm Level Rule. It is not unfamiliar to think of developing the least attractive prefectures. By granting those poor charm prefectures larger shares of the development budget, they will acquire more attractiveness. Pushing up the charm level of a prefecture would consequently guarantee higher numbers of visitors along with lower numbers of leavers. Hence, the rate of conscious people in these areas can be kept within safe margins.

Decrease Charm Level Rule. One of the factors that make conscious rates inconsistent is that some cities are extremely charming. They have a lot of astonishing sightseeing and breathtaking life-styles. On the contrary to the previous rule, charm level deduction may help to avoid awareness leakage from less charming areas towards such fascinating destinations. Governments may try doing so by decreasing these cities shares of the development budget.

It is worth mentioning that we evaluated each rule separately, so, some results may show unexpected indications. However, if the results were interpreted in terms of the efficiency of preventing both over-population and de-population, but not only one of them, the results then may become less surprising.

3   Results

As a result of running the simulation that is described previously, significant differences are recognized in rules outcomes. To illustrate, each suggested rule is compared to no-rule by F-test.

Table 1. F test to compare two variances (Degree of Freedom = 46).

Rule	F-value	P-value	Ratio of variances
I	<0.001	<0.001	<0.001
II	0.040	<0.001	0.040
III	0.527	0.032	0.527
IV	0.942	0.841	0.942
V	1.150	0.638	1.150

The F-test results including F-value, p-value and the Ratio of Variances are shown in Table 1. The ratio of variances indicates the effect of each rule on the suppression of de-/over-population. The smaller the ratio of variance, the higher the rule effect on de-/over-population avoidance. According to the values from the table, Rules (I) and (II) are effective to suppress de-/over-population areas compared to no-rule (free Body-Sharing).

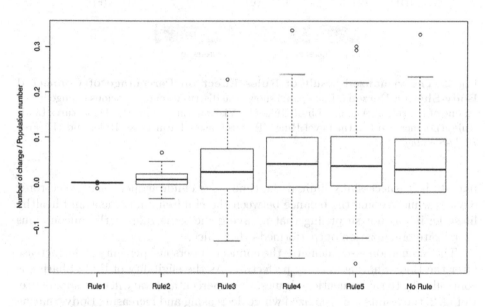

Fig. 1. The box-plots of the de-/over-population rate for each rule (Number of change divided by physical population).

Figure 1 shows the overall change in population by adding or subtracting virtual population of Body-Sharing users to/from the real population of every prefecture. The vertical axis shows the de-/over-population rate (Number of change/Population number). "Number of change" is the change of conscious population after Body-Sharing. "Population number" is the physical population. We can see that Rule (I) is the most effective among the five rules. Because

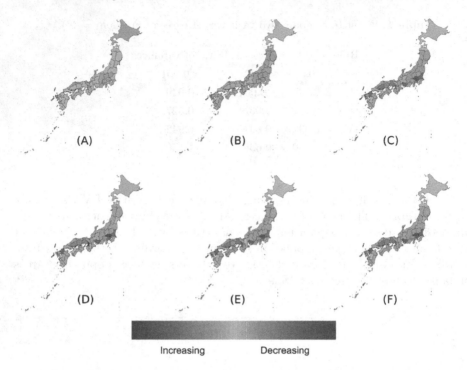

Increasing   Decreasing

Fig. 2. The visualized result of Rules Effect on Percentage of Connected Body-Sharing Persons. Each panel shows the distribution of conscious change based on one of the rules; (A) Time Limit Rule, (B) Visitors Limit Rule (C) Departures Limit Rule, (D) Increase Charm Level Rule, (E) Decrease Charm Level Rule, and (F) Free *Body-Sharing*.

parents have successfully limited the time their children spent using electronic devices while keeping the balance between the children amusement and healthy lifestyle; it was not surprising that applying the same rule on the unconscious users' rate organization outperformed other rules.

The Simulation also calculates the connected persons' percentage de/increase after the Body-Sharing in every prefecture. As the eligibility of Body-Sharing is controlled by the aforementioned rules, these percentages vary in correspondence. In Fig. 2, the results are visualized where decreasing and increasing Body-Sharing existence percentages are represented in red and green respectively. The higher the percentage of change the darker the color that is used to fill the prefecture in the map.

Table 2 shows the top 5 and the lowest 5 prefectures of the conscious density after Body-sharing with no regulation (Rule VI) and charm levels. As shown Table 2, Osaka has the highest conscious population and also it has the highest charm level. However, the prefecture in which the conscious population increased second, Yamanashi prefecture, does not have the second largest charm level. The prefecture with the second highest charm level was Shizuoka prefecture, the third was Tokyo. Shizuoka's consciousness population increase was the fourth from the top, but Tokyo was fifth from the end. Therefore, the high charm level does not cause an increase in the conscious population. Likewise, charm levels of the lowest 5 prefectures are not necessarily low. There is a tendency for the prefectures with large conscious depopulation to have large physical population in the first place. This keeps the total population, physical plus virtual, within a close range to the original physical population.

Table 2. The change in conscious-density and the charm level for the top and lowest 5 prefectures in case of free *Body-Sharing*.

Top 5 conscious density change			
Prefecture	Change (%)	Charm level	Population
Osaka	11.16	100.0	8833000
Yamanashi	03.04	22.08	830000
Nagano	02.88	45.01	2088000
Shizuoka	02.46	54.74	3688000
Tottori	02.17	06.96	570000
Lowest 5 conscious density change			
Prefecture	Change (%)	Charm level	Population
Tokyo	0.56	52.10	13624000
Ibaraki	0.42	07.93	2905000
Fukuoka	0.36	15.89	5104000
Aichi	0.32	22.99	7507000
Saitama	0.14	05.18	7289000

In order to show how many people are moving their consciousness and contributing to the increase of the conscious population elsewhere, the proportion of contribution of change in consciousness was calculated from Tokyo, having the largest real population, and Tottori, having the smallest real population. Osaka and Tokushima were chosen as examples of the travel destination. Osaka has the highest charm level and Tokushima has the least charm level. As shown in Table 3, the contribution from Tokyo is always larger than that from Tottori regardless of rules and travel destination. Focusing on the contribution from Tokyo, the increase of the conscious population to Osaka is highly suppressed by Rule I whereas Rule III, V, and VI have a high contribution of conscious change. In contrast, the contribution from Tottori to Osaka remains quite small regardless of regulation rules.

4 Discussion

Our results clearly showed that the "Time Limit Rule" has a noticeable efficacy to avoid the conscious depopulation whereas the regulations that manipulate the

Table 3. The number of visitors from specified prefectures normalized to the physical population of the destination. Tokyo and Tottori have the highest and least population respectively. Osaka and Tokushima have the highest and the least charm-level respectively.

Visitors home	Tokyo		Tottori	
Destination	Osaka	Tokushima	Osaka	Tokushima
Rule I	0.0002	0.0020	<0.0001	0.0003
Rule II	0.0022	0.0028	0.0001	0.0004
Rule III	0.0099	0.0106	0.0004	0.0015
Rule IV	0.0035	0.0144	0.0003	0.0021
Rule V	0.0111	0.0204	0.0005	0.0026
Rule VI (Free)	0.0109	0.0140	0.0005	0.0023

attractiveness of travel destinations, "Increase Charm Level Rule" and "Decrease Charm Level Rule", have almost no effect. Although there is a charm level bias that considers the budget for a target place as a measure of promotion, our result demonstrated this method has a very slight effect. Because charm-manipulation of top- or lowest-ranked prefecture does not change the people's eager behavior to visit the well known attractive prefecture. Therefore, the effect will not appear unless the manipulation removes the gap between the attractiveness levels of the various destinations.

Our simulation reflects the effect of the actual population of an area and the happiness level of the people there on the virtual Body-Sharing behavior. Moreover, the virtual Body-Sharing trips' options of people who live in a place with a large population greatly affect the result. In Japan, Tokyo has the highest population and people there tend to go travel where the charm level is higher than the happiness level of a person living in Tokyo. This makes the bi-polarization of the conscious population and leads to make Osaka having the biggest conscious population.

The conscious depopulation easily occurs at the prefecture which has a large population and people living there does not have a high happiness level. As shown in Table 3, the contribution to the increase of the conscious population of Osaka from Tokyo is significantly larger than that of Tottori which has the smallest population, especially there is a remarkable difference in Rule III, V and VI. On the other hand, the difference between rules is not large between Tokyo and Tottori about contribution to the increase in conscious population to Tokushima with the lowest charm level. That is why "Visitors limit rule" and "leavers limit rule" could not work for avoiding conscious depopulation by those mechanisms.

Simple updates can make our simulation applicable to other studies as well. For example, we can simulate the workers' shortage for some jobs in the labor market. When some business sectors start to hire more employees and to pay high salaries, more young people turn out to these professions. Gradually, other business sectors start to suffer labor decline [8]. Similarly, we can simulate students insufficiency in some college majors. The majority of university students may prefer to study some college majors while they voluntarily relinquish other majors for various reasons [14]. Another example of a phenomenon that we can simulate is the over-fishing for some species that may become depleted [6].

5   Conclusion and Future Work

As any service that is adopted by a large number of users, regulations should be applied to the Body-Sharing in the future. Because using Body-Sharing free by a large number of immersed users may lead to either dangerous behavior in some districts due to depopulation or over-utilizing resources in others due to overpopulation. We propose a simulation of the behaviour of Japanese people when using Body-Sharing. Then, we tested five different rules that regulating authorities may apply. We found that "Time Limit Rule" was the most efficient in limiting the change in conscious users density among five rules of regulation tested in this study. While "Visitors Limit Rule" and "Departures Limit Rule" were less effective. "Increase Charm Level Rule" and "Decrease Charm Level Rule" were inefficient in the change-control.

As a future work, we will study the profitability of using different rules for different prefectures instead of generalizing one rule for all prefectures. Also, we will expand our simulation in two directions. First, by the help of researchers from other fields such as economics, we can formulate more complicated Body-Sharing regulating rules and include them in our simulation. Moreover, considering other significant parameters would help to tailor a realistic model for our simulation. Right now, our research is concerned with the prefecture population and attractiveness, but, parameters like area, the standard of living, crime-rate,... etc. should be considered as well. Second, we will expand the simulation to a global scale with many challenges come from the diversity of countries and their cultures. On the other hand, monitoring the behavior of small groups of real persons when interacting with Body-Sharing under the different suggested rules is considered to verify the simulated system observations that we encountered in this study. Collecting feedback from users about their experience using this technology and the options that they make will help establishing a consistent argument. In the future, monitoring the social behavior of large groups nationwide will be vital.

Acknowledgments. We would like to acknowledge MapChart [9] for the beautiful map figures that we generated by their free tool.

References

1. Collaboration for creating new services using bodysharing technology and 5G (2019). https://www.nttdocomo.co.jp/binary/pdf/info/news_release/topics_190109_00.pdf

2. Fernando, C.L., et al.: Design of TELESAR v for transferring bodily consciousness in telexistence. In: 2012 IEEE/RSJ International Conference on Intelligent Robots and Systems, pp. 5112–5118, October 2012. https://doi.org/10.1109/IROS.2012.6385814

3. Han, S., Kim, J.: A study on immersion of hand interaction for mobile platform virtual reality contents. Symmetry **9**(2), 22 (2017). https://doi.org/10.3390/sym9020022. https://www.mdpi.com/2073-8994/9/2/22

4. Hedayati, H., Walker, M., Szafir, D.: Improving collocated robot teleoperation with augmented reality. In: Proceedings of the 2018 ACM/IEEE International Conference on Human-Robot Interaction, HRI 2018, pp. 78–86. ACM, New York (2018). https://doi.org/10.1145/3171221.3171251

5. Herbelin, B., Salomon, R., Serino, A., Blanke, O.: Neural mechanisms of bodily self-consciousness and the experience of presence in virtual reality. In: Human Computer Confluence, pp. 80–96 (2016). http://infoscience.epfl.ch/record/220684

6. Jackson, J.B., et al.: Historical overfishing and the recent collapse of coastal ecosystems. Science **293**(5530), 629–637 (2001)

7. Knierim, P., et al.: Tactile drones - providing immersive tactile feedback in virtual reality through quadcopters. In: Proceedings of the 2017 CHI Conference Extended Abstracts on Human Factors in Computing Systems, CHI EA 2017, pp. 433–436. Association for Computing Machinery, New York (2017). https://doi.org/10.1145/3027063.3050426

8. Livingstone, D.W.: The Education-Jobs Gap: Underemployment Or Economic Democracy?. Routledge, Abingdon (2018)

9. MapChart. https://mapchart.net

10. Martins, H., Oakley, I., Ventura, R.: Design and evaluation of a head-mounted display for immersive 3D teleoperation of field robots. Robotica **33**(10), 2166–2185 (2015). https://doi.org/10.1017/S026357471400126X

11. McGill, M., Boland, D., Murray-Smith, R., Brewster, S.: A dose of reality: overcoming usability challenges in VR head-mounted displays. In: Proceedings of the 33rd Annual ACM Conference on Human Factors in Computing Systems, CHI 2015, pp. 2143–2152. ACM, New York (2015). https://doi.org/10.1145/2702123.2702382

12. McMahan, A.: Immersion, engagement and presence. In: The Video Game Theory Reader, pp. 67–86 (2003)

13. Mirk, D., Hlavacs, H.: Virtual tourism with drones: experiments and lag compensation. In: Proceedings of the First Workshop on Micro Aerial Vehicle Networks, Systems, and Applications for Civilian Use, DroNet 2015, pp. 45–50. ACM, New York (2015). https://doi.org/10.1145/2750675.2750681

14. Montmarquette, C., Cannings, K., Mahseredjian, S.: How do young people choose college majors? Econo. Educ. Rev. **21**(6), 543–556 (2002). https://doi.org/10.1016/S0272-7757(01)00054-1

15. Oh, C.S., Bailenson, J.N., Welch, G.F.: A systematic review of social presence: definition, antecedents, and implications. Front. Robot. AI **5**, 114 (2018). https://doi.org/10.3389/frobt.2018.00114

16. Oprean, D., Simpson, M., Klippel, A.: Collaborating remotely: an evaluation of immersive capabilities on spatial experiences and team membership. Int. J. Digit. Earth **11**(4), 420–436 (2018). https://doi.org/10.1080/17538947.2017.1381191

17. Pohl, H., Murray-Smith, R.: Focused and casual interactions: allowing users to vary their level of engagement. In: Proceedings of the SIGCHI Conference on Human Factors in Computing Systems, CHI 2013, pp. 2223–2232. ACM, New York (2013). https://doi.org/10.1145/2470654.2481307

18. Potter, L.E., Carter, L., Coghlan, A.: Virtual reality and nature based tourism: an opportunity for operators and visitors. In: Proceedings of the 28th Australian Conference on Computer-Human Interaction, OzCHI 2016, pp. 652–654. ACM, New York (2016). https://doi.org/10.1145/3010915.3011854
19. RESAS. https://resas.go.jp/#/13/13101
20. Satake, A., Yoh, I.: Coupled ecological and social dynamics in a forested landscape: the deviation of individual decisions from the social optimum. Ecol. Res. **21**(3), 370–379 (2006). https://doi.org/10.1007/s11284-006-0167-9
21. Tachi, S.: Telexistence: enabling humans to be virtually ubiquitous. IEEE Comput. Graph. Appl. **36**(1), 8–14 (2016). https://doi.org/10.1109/MCG.2016.6
22. Tachi, S., Tanie, K., Komoriya, K., Kaneko, M.: Tele-existence (i): design and evaluation of a visual display with sensation of presence. In: Proceedings of RoManSy 1984: The Fifth CISM-IFToMM Symposium, p. 206–215 (1984)
23. Tachi, S.: Telexistence. In: Brunnett, G., Coquillart, S., van Liere, R., Welch, G., Váša, L. (eds.) Virtual Realities. LNCS, vol. 8844, pp. 229–259. Springer, Cham (2015). https://doi.org/10.1007/978-3-319-17043-5_13
24. Tamaki, E.: Presentation method of somatosensory stimulation in VR environment. J. Soc. Biomech. Jpn **43**(1), 3–9 (2019). https://ci.nii.ac.jp/naid/40021832106/
25. Tamborini, R., Skalski, P.: The role of presence in the experience of electronic games. Playing Video Games: Motiv. Responses Conseq. **28**, 225–240 (2006)
26. Templeton, A., Drury, J., Philippides, A.: From mindless masses to small groups: conceptualizing collective behavior in crowd modeling. Rev. Gen. Psychol. **19**(3), 215–229 (2015)
27. Yoshiki, S., Tatsumi, H., Tsutsumi, K., Miyazaki, T., Fujiki, T.: Effects of smartphone use on behavior while walking. Urban Reg. Planning Rev. **4**, 138–150 (2017)

Development and Evaluation of a Research Framework for Measuring the Reliance on Automation in Situations of Risk and Moral Dilemma

Gian Luca Liehner[✉], Philipp Brauner, Anne Kathrin Schaar, and Martina Ziefle

Human-Computer Interaction Center, RWTH Aachen University, Campus Boulevard 57, 52074 Aachen, Germany
{Liehner,Brauner,Schaar,Ziefle}@comm.rwth-aachen.de

Abstract. Digitalization is changing the working world of tomorrow and complex decisions are increasingly being made by hybrid teams of people and automated decision support systems. The interaction of user, task, and interface plays a decisive role, but is insufficiently studied, especially in the context of decision making under uncertainty, risk, and moral dilemmas. In this article, we present a web-based research framework for exploring this factor space with empirical user studies. The framework builds on a combination of tools for linking a user model, with the outcome of game-based decision scenarios, and the participants' evaluations. To validate the framework, we conducted a user study with N = 64 participants and found that the system responded sensitively to factors from each of the three areas user, task, and interface. Consequently, the framework facilitates the systematic investigation of the factor space, the identification and quantification of relevant factors and the description of interactions between the factors. A systematic understanding of these factors is necessary for the development of future joint cognitive systems and Decision Support Systems.

Keywords: Moral machines · User modeling · Trust in automation · Industrial internet · Human factors · Risk perception · Decision support systems · Moral dilemma

1 Introduction

From a simple automated ticket machine to fully automated production factories, automation pushed itself into nearly every domain of our society. Automation can be encountered in all up-and-coming technological sectors, such as robotics, medicine, shipping, manufacturing, or process control. Tasks that were in the past reserved to human operators are now increasingly taken over by machines. As such, [1] defined automation as '*the execution by a machine agent (usually a computer) of a function that was previously carried out by a human*' (p. 231). Because humans by their nature can be unreliable and inefficient, automation attempts to counteract these shortcomings through its near-perfect accuracy and clockwork-like functioning. In addition to that, automation can assist us

© Springer Nature Switzerland AG 2020
V. G. Duffy (Ed.): HCII 2020, LNCS 12199, pp. 280–295, 2020.
https://doi.org/10.1007/978-3-030-49907-5_20

in tasks that have to be performed in difficult and unsafe environments or in those that operators grew tired of executing themselves on account of their repetitive nature. The ever-increasing use of automation leads to an overall increase in productivity, efficiency, reliability, flexibility, and sustainability in a series of different sectors.

Yet, not all tasks can be automated with perfect accuracy and thus the use of automation gives rise to situations of risk and uncertainty. Especially in situations where human lives are at risk, automation is receiving more responsibility and agency consequently raising the difficult question of morality. This is particularly prominent within the rise of the Industrial Internet and Industry 4.0 in which workers work hand in hand with automated robots, decision aids, and decision support systems and must take a decision about whether to rely on automation or opt for manual execution.

May that as it be, for automation to be beneficial, its seamless integration into our work process is crucial. Its successful adoption depends on the willingness to use automated technologies. Research in the acceptance of automation technologies has shown that among other factors, trust plays a decisive role in the willingness to use automated systems [2, 3]. If a technology is not trusted in the first place it will—with a high likelihood—not be used. Thus, the investigation of trust in automation can uncover valuable insights on the successful collaboration between operators and automated systems.

Trust is a multidimensional and complex construct that is difficult to measure and representing it in terms of a mathematical framework is a challenging task. What's more is that trust is not directly observable, making it even more difficult to investigate.

In order to tackle the challenge of measuring trust, current measurement tools need to be improved to assess trust more accurately and reflect upon trust more dynamically. Therefore, the presented work aims at developing and evaluating a research framework for accurately measuring trust in automated systems. [4] suggest that high-fidelity prototypes are needed to map real-life situations in which automation is utilized.

The proposed research framework attempts at mapping the above-mentioned factors in an all-encompassing web-based survey tool in the form of a decision task in which participants have to decide whether to automate a given task. In differently shaped situations and with the variation of a series of factors, the reliance on automated systems—which is often used as a proxy measure of trust [9]—is captured. Mapping real-life situations in which decisions have to be made on the reliance on automated systems using an interactive tool could help to better understand decision-making processes in situations of uncertainty and moral dilemma and provide a better understanding of the role of trust in automation.

In order to systematically address the challenges described here, this paper first concentrates on how complex the construct trust is, which related factors are also relevant in the context of automation, and which challenges arise when starting to measure trust in automation (see Sect. 2.1). Section 2.2 then presents the approach of game-based learning in order to open space for a possible research design. The theoretical considerations made are afterwards applied in Sect. 3 by showing how the research framework on which the study is based was designed. Section 4 illustrates how this framework was validated through a concrete empirical study and presents corresponding research questions, the chosen method, and results. The paper is closed by a discussion of the results, with a focus on a critical examination of the applicability of the presented framework and its transfer to a research agenda (see Sect. 5).

2 Related Work

This chapter provides an insight into the construct trust (in automation), its measurement, and related factors (see Sect. 2.1). In addition, the game-based learning approach is presented to show the advantages of this approach for the investigation of trust (see Sect. 2.2).

2.1 Trust, Trust Factors and Measuring Trust

The construct of trust has been studied within various disciplines (e.g., sociology, psychology or philosophy) and hence a multitude of different definitions have been proposed over the last decades resulting in a few key aspects. For trust to emerge in the first place, two elements are of essential importance: a *trustee* that transmits information and a *trustor* that acts upon the received information [5]. Another key aspect is the possibility that the trustee is not able to successfully fulfil the trustor's expectations and therefore create a situation of *uncertainty* [6]. It is exactly in those situations where the trustor will challenge the trustee to ascertain the amount of trust that can be given [7]. As a result, trust can be viewed as a mediator between a trustor and a trustee in a situation of uncertainty, risk or vulnerability, during which trust can build, solidify, increase or decrease according to the outcome of the situation. Still, trust is not solely a mediator between people but can likewise promote reliance on machines as well as the intention to use and accept them [4].

Trust in machines, and more specifically in automation is dependent on large array of factors. With automation becoming increasingly more complex, human operators are experiencing more and more difficulties in understanding underlying operating principles of automated systems and therefore predict their behavior [8]. Adding to that, at this stage automated systems are not able to perform error-free operations, thus creating situations of uncertainty in which operators are dependent on the reliability of the machine [9]. In a meta-analysis by [10], trust factors are divided into 3 categories: *system factors*, *human factors* and *environmental factors*. While system factors are directly related to the performance and the characteristics of the automated agents, human factors refer to personal traits, beliefs, values, and attributes of a human operator. Environmental factors, on the other hand, are characterized by the physical environment, the type of task, and the domain specificity of the automation. Research in trust factors over the last years has shown that all three factors can influence trust to a certain degree and deserve to be included into the research of trust in automation [11].

To analyze the impact of trust factors, one has to measure trust itself. Due to its multilayered nature and the fact that it is not directly observable, measuring trust is however a challenging endeavor. In fact, developing validated and standardized measures of trust has come short over the last years, as most measures were developed for individual studies. Two methods are currently used to measure trust in automation. First, *subjective measures* of trust are collected by directly asking participants of studies through questionnaires to rate their perceived level of trust [12]. Nonetheless, these measures are only related to perceived trust and might differ from participants actual levels of trust. The second method of assessing trust relies on *behavioral measures* of trust [12]. For instance, [9] identify reliance as behavioral result of trusting automation and can therefore be employed as a proxy for measuring trust in automation [12]. However, it must be taken into account that people might *use automation*, but that *without necessarily trusting automation.*

Next, we propose game-based simulation environments to study behavioral reliance on automation.

2.2 Game-Based Learning

The approach of game-based learning could be useful for a systematic investigation of trust and trust related aspect. Following [13] a *"[...] game is a system in which players engage in an artificial conflict, defined by rules, that result in a quantifiable outcome"* (p. 80). Consequently, games and game-based environments combine several aspects that are useful in the context of our research: First, games build on an *artificial conflict* that players engage in. Players get involved in a specific situation, but after play the situation is resolved, and actions are without consequences in the real world. Second, this conflict is based on arbitrary but well-defined *rules*. These rules can be changed during and through the experiment. Thus, the game serves as a laboratory to study how the rules effect behavior and evaluation. Third, games have a *quantifiable outcome* (such as game money, points, or a designated winner) that can be linked to the parameters from within (rule set) or outside the game environment (user factors and evaluations). Last but not least, games are perceived as *motivating* and can thus increase the willingness to participate in an experiment, reduce the drop-off rate during the investigation, and increase the quality of the collected data.

Based on these benefits game-based learning environments and serious games are usually used to change attitudes or behavior [14, 15]. But game-based environments have previously also been used to study human behavior, decision making, and trust in automated systems [16]. A prominent example from system dynamics research is the Beer Distribution Game that illustrates Forrester's "Bullwhip" effect of exaggerating variance along supply chains [17]. The effect has been, for example, replicated by [18, 19]. Furthermore, Brauner et al. used a complex business simulation game to study how people interact with correct and broken automation, and which factors influence compliance with malfunctioning automation [20]. Key results were twofold: On the one hand, trust is an essential driver in compliance with correct decision support. On the other hand, high perceived usability is important to mitigate compliance with malfunctioning systems.

Transferring both aspects (benefits of games) and prior knowledge from using serious games as an experimental setting in research (e.g., Beer Game) leads to the assumption that this approach could be also beneficial for exploring trust in automation in situations of risk and moral dilemma. The question of morality has recently been explored by Awad et al. in their *Moral Machine* experiment who examined the social perception of moral decisions made by automated machines in the context of automated driving [21]. While their approach mainly was based on classical conjoint analyses, the game-based approach presented in this study could lead to valuable insights on ethical principles in relation to trust in automation that could have been overlooked in previous studies. Within the next section one approach for a game-based research framework for investigating the reliance on automation in situations of risk and moral dilemma is presented (see Sect. 3).

3 Development of an Experimental Research Framework

As measuring trust in the field is for ethical and monetary reasons a rather difficult task, real-life situations needed to be modeled into an experimental framework which allowed to alter a given set of mapped factors over time and measure their impact on the reliance on automation. To measure the behavioral reliance on automation we designed a game-based approach. The designed approach was formulated as a decision-task between the automation of a given task or the manual execution (*automation mode* and *manual mode*). This method has been repeatedly used to study the reliance on automation in relation to a given set of manipulated experimental variables [22–26].

The following two subsections present the challenge of modelling real-life decisions via a game-based approach (Sect. 3.1) and the technical requirements and implementations considered in this context (Sect. 3.2).

3.1 Modelling Real Life Decisions in a Game-Based Approach

To be able to accurately model real-life decision-making processes, the various situations were represented through *microworlds*, which allow for the minimization of the complexity of real-world systems by solely preserving the most essential elements, and therefore allowing for a more controlled experimental environment [27, 28]. Augmenting microworlds with a game-based approach allows for the creation of artificial conflicts which engage players into explicitly shaped situations defined by a specific set of factors. These factors can be presented to players (in experimental terms *participants*) in a series of different modalities depending on the specific research questions. For instance, if investigating the effect of risk on trust in automation, various risk levels can be represented by a graphical representation (e.g., dangerous goods on the shop floor of a factory) displayed to the player.

The conceptualization of the decision task was achieved through an iterative development process which included the analysis of previous literature on the topic, heuristics and the execution of pre-tests. Throughout this process, it became apparent that decision makers needed to be provided with all the relevant information in relation to the task at hand in order to be able to take an informed decision. In other words, factors needed to be modeled in a way that are understandable by the decision maker and provide information that could be included into the decision-making process to evaluate the outcome of a given situation. While this might seem like a trivial point, information assessment is a complex process that is not perceived equally by every person and therefore deserves to be given attention when developing decision tasks. More importantly, the outcome of a situation and thus the consequences of a decision needed to be directly linked to the decision made by the decision maker and made observable to be able to accurately evaluate the taken decision. Without being able to observe the consequences of one's actions, adjusting the decision-making process becomes a nearly impossible task for the decision maker. Additionally, for players to be willing to engage in the game repeatedly, they needed to receive some sort of reward for their performance. This can, for example, be achieved by awarding points or virtual monetary value as a result of a 'right' decision. Lastly, the decision task should be formulated in such a way that a variation in taken decisions should occur throughout the experiment. If the manipulation of the experimental factors does not result in a variation in the type of decision, effects are only difficult to discover.

Figure 1 illustrates the general concept of our framework and possible outcomes of studies conducted with the framework: It links the outcome of experimentally controlled decision tasks (e.g., complexity, decision aids, moral dilemma, ...) with survey-based user-models (e.g., disposition to trust, risk-seeking, self-efficacy, ...) and the participants' task evaluations (e.g., trust in automation, perceived risk, ...). Thus, the framework facilitates the identification of user and task factors relevant for task performance and task evaluation, develops models that predict performance for given tasks, weights the importance of multiple factors on performance and evaluation, and evaluates whether users behave similarly under the same conditions or can be divided into different user segments.

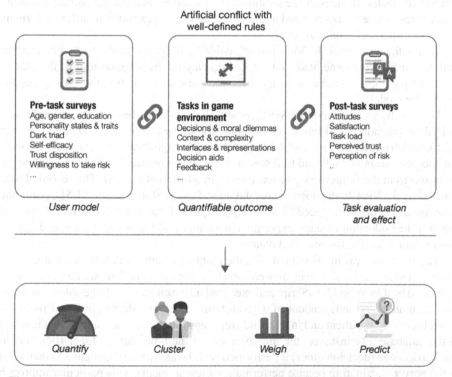

Fig. 1. Design of a game-based research framework; potential factors worth investigating.

3.2 Technical Implementation and Requirements

The developed framework was implemented as a web-service to be accessible across platforms from anywhere in the world (and of course also locally under strictly controlled laboratory environments). This design decision allows on the one hand to investigate cultural and regional effects by distributing the framework to different parts of the world and on the other hand for a seamless integration with commonly used survey tools which can be utilized to assess demographic data, personal preferences and perception of a particular decision task.

For the experimental framework to be reusable, modularizable and customizable for different research matters, the implementation is based on the common Model-View-Controller (MVC) design pattern [29].

The Model implements the core of the framework, in which the constant and manipulated factors as well as their respective levels can be registered. For instance, the factor *reliability of an automated agent* could be registered in the model and assigned with the levels *high, medium* and *low* reliability. Based on the registered factors and levels, a full-factorial set of decision tasks (or trials) is generated. Factors can furthermore be defined as either *within-block* (or block factor) or *between-block* factors to allow for the insertion of post-block questionnaires including subjective measures in relation to a given block factor. Besides the generation of trials, the decision of the participant along with the respective factors is saved to the model and can be exported in different formats (e.g.,.*csv, .sql, .json, .xml, .xls*, etc.).

Within the framework the View is responsible for the retrieval of a randomly selected trial drawn from the generated trial set and displaying the selected trial to the player. Once the participant reaches a decision for the presented situation the view saves the trial to the model.

Ultimately, a variation of the MVC pattern (Model-View-Template) was implement in Python (version 3.7.4) based on the open-source web framework Django (version 2.2.5), which allows for a high scalability and ensures high levels of security on the web. For the generation of trials and trial sets, a series of classes were defined, which can be extracted from the framework and reused within a different context. The recorded data is saved by the View to the open-source database PostgreSQL (version 11.5). Again, the database can easily be replaced by a MySQL, SQLite, Oracle or Microsoft SQL Server. Besides the collection of data, experimental factors and levels can be set as database entities and related to the recorded data.

The front-end was implemented with the front-end framework UIkit (version 3.3.1) which provides fast and powerful web-interface components. The user interaction is supported by jQuery and JavaScript and executed on the client side. To be able to measure data accurately and independent of a given bandwidth, trial data is first and foremost saved locally on the client and in a second step transmitted to the server where it is saved to the database. For instance, the measurement of the time elapsed for participants to reach a decision (decision times) is performed with JavaScript on the client and then send to the server (facilitating precise performance measurement). This particular approach was followed for the entirety of the framework, ensuring an accurate measurement of data in independence of bandwidth. Similar to the model, the front-end can easily be substituted by another front-end framework (e.g., Bootstrap) and therefore offer the possibility to display experimental factors in a variety of different visual and textual representations. Moreover, the developed framework was provided in two languages— German and English—but can be extended to further languages following the i18n internationalization and localization approach. Lastly, the framework was made available as a web-service on the university's server and secured by an SSL certificate for an extra layer of security.

The source code repository of the framework can be found on https://git.rwth-aac hen.de/CommScience/decision-task-framework.

The advantage of the MVC (or MVT, see Fig. 2) design pattern approach lies in the interchangeability of the various components. For example, the graphical representation can easily be adapted to the researchers needs while keeping the model and controller. In this way, the framework can, for instance, be transferred to a desktop or mobile application. Similarly, the database can easily be substituted offering the possibility of different approaches to data collection. The implementation as an independent web-service on the other hand provides a cross-platform access to the service and an easy integration with commonly used survey tools and other services. As such, data retrieved in the developed framework can seamlessly be integrated into accompanying pre or post-task questionnaires.

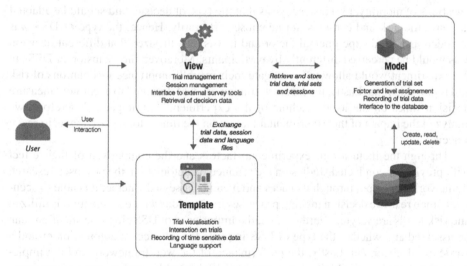

Fig. 2. Illustration of the framework's software architecture.

4 Validation Study

4.1 Goals and Hypotheses

To validate our approach, we conceptualized an experiment to study if (moral) decision making relates to user factors, the factors from within the game-environment, the factors from the automated agent and the later evaluations of the participants. To be able to validate the newly developed research framework, a series of experimental factors were selected and their effect on the reliance on automation was measured. As one of the most investigated trust factors, the *reliability* of the automated agent was chosen as a system factor to be included in the experiment. This factor was selected for the purpose of comparability to previous studies that showed the significant impact of reliability on the trust in automated agents [24, 30–33]. It was therefore hypothesized that the reliability would significantly influence the reliance on automation. Additionally, due to the shift in responsibility of automation taking over more and more task especially in environments of high risk and moral dilemma, the factor of *risk* was included as a second experimental factor to be manipulated during the experiment. While [34] previously included risk in their study on the effect of situational risk on the reliance on trust in automation, their result appeared somewhat inconclusive and seem to deserve further attention. Furthermore Awad et al. in their *Moral Machine* experiment refrained from include the notion of trust in automation or for that matter a level of uncertainty in their experiment [21]. It was here hypothesized that the level of risk for a situation that included the use of automation would affect the reliance on a specific automated agent. Adding to that, in recent years decision support systems have increasingly been utilized to assist operators with decision tasks in situation that could be risky or raise questions of morality. [35] also suggests that the type of decision aid should be adapted to a specific task and can thus not be choses arbitrarily. Hence, the type of DSS was included as a third experimental factor and it was hypothesized that different decision aids would be perceived differently by participants. Moreover, the inclusion of DSSs in the experiment would allow to investigate their overall importance in situations of risk and moral dilemma. Lastly, the research framework was designed to accurately measure decision times on the local machine of the experiment's participants. Therefore, we analyzed the impact of the experimental factors on the time it took participants to reach a decision.

Through the inclusion of experimental factors and the comparison of their effect with previously conducted studies on the reliance on automation, the proposed research framework can be put through its paces and it can be assessed whether it is able to accurately map real-life decision making processes in situations where automation is utilized and risk levels are varying. Furthermore, the importance of DSSs in those situations can be assessed and whether the type of DSS impacts the reliance on automation or/and a particular decision aid. Lastly, the performance of the web-framework and the implementation based on the MVC design pattern is validated by evaluating the framework on its integrability with other commonly used online survey tools and its accuracy to measure relevant data on the various decision tasks (e.g., decision times).

4.2 Method

The decision task for the validation experiment was set in a warehouse in accordance with the increased use of automation in the Industrial Internet and Industry 4.0.

Decision Task: The task of the participants was to decide between the manual or the automated collection of a package within the warehouse. The automation mode was presented to the participant to save on manual labor and therefore save personal cost maximizing the company's profit. Nevertheless, this variant would be less safe, as the automated agent would not always be 100% reliable and could potentially damage dangerous goods or endanger the safety of staff members and hence compromise revenue and reputation of the company operating the warehouse. On the other hand, the manual option was presented as 100% reliable, but less beneficial for the company as personnel costs would have to be deducted from the revenue.

Reliability: In addition to the choice between the two modes, the various manipulated factors were visually presented to the participants. Following common practice derived from the literature on the effect of reliability on automation reliance, reliability levels were subdivided into *low* (60%), *medium* (80%) and *high* (100%) reliability. These levels were visually represented as the previous experience of the vehicle in errors by mileage.

Levels of Risk: The levels of risk were divided into the four following categories: *no risk, property risk, personal risk* and *property and personal risk*. The condition property risk was defined by the potential damage to foreign property and illustrated by positioning barrels containing valuable goods in the warehouse. In contrast, the personal risk condition was characterized by the possible injury of the body, mind, and/or emotions of another human being and visually represented by positioning workers—that the automated delivery vehicle could potentially collide with—on the floor of the warehouse. The no risk condition solely included damage to the automated vehicle.

Type of Support: Lastly, two types of DSSs (*engineer* and *artificial intelligence*) were presented to the participant providing them with a recommendation on a specific course of action. After their decision, participants received feedback whether the automated delivery was successful and were remunerated accordingly.

Study Design: The validation experiment was divided into five distinct phases: *Phase 1* was a pre-experiment questionnaire in which participants were asked about demographic data and personality traits. Additionally, the disposition to trust in automation was assessed on a 3-item-scale ($\alpha = .76$). In *Phase 2* a detailed explanation of the decision task was provided to the participants trough an explanation wizard. *Phase 3* gave participants the opportunity to undergo three randomly selected training trials to accustom themselves with the task. The core of the experiment (*Phase 4*) consisted of a 3 (reliability) × 4 (risk level) × 2 (decision support system) within-subjects full-factorial design resulting in a total of 24 trials (decision tasks) per participant. For this phase, the decision and decision times (time between presenting the decision tasks and the participant's decision), were measured for each trial. Based on the full-factorial design, a pool of counterbalanced trials was generated for each participant and divided into 2 subsets resulting from the factor decision support system that was set as a between-block factor. After each set, a post-set questionnaire (*Phase 5*) asked participants to evaluate their performance and about their perception of the executed task. For instance, participants were asked to estimate to which extent (in %) they complied with the recommendation of the decision support system or relied on the previous experience of the automated agent.

Sample: The experimental framework was hosted on the server of the university and the access link was distributed online. A total of 64 people took part in the experiment (gender balanced 32 male and 32 female). The mean age was 43.5 ($SD = 18.1$) with a minimum of 20 and a maximum of 80 years. The dispositional trust in automation reached a mean score of 4.11 ($SD = 0.67$) on the self-developed measure (range from 1 to 6).

4.3 Results

In a first step, descriptive statistics are reported for every response variable. Secondly, inferential statistics are presented regarding the differences in means between the various factor levels and the relationship between explanatory and response variables. Differences in means are evaluated by conducting repeated measures analysis of variance (RM-ANOVA) with effect sizes reported as η^2. If the assumption of sphericity (Mauchly's W) was not met, Greenhouse-Geiser corrections are considered. In case of significant results of RM-ANOVA, a Tukey HSD post-hoc test is conducted. The relationship between explanatory and response variables is analyzed by Pearson's product-moment correlation coefficient r. The level of significance for rejecting the null-hypothesis was set to $\alpha = .05$ according to conventional practice.

The overall reliance on the automation reached a mean of 49.99% ($SD = 20.24$) while the average median decision time was recorded at 6.93 s ($SD = 3.32$). Analysis of the post-task questionnaire revealed an average subjective compliance with the DSS of 53.06% ($SD = 25.53$).

System Factors: First, the impact of system factors was analyzed: To investigate the effect of the various reliability levels on the reliance on automation, RM-ANOVA was conducted. The results show a significant effect of reliability on the reliance on automation ($F(1.82, 114.78) = 88.2, p < .001, \eta^2 = .38$). Post-hoc comparisons (Tukey HSD) indicated pair-wise significant differences for all reliability conditions ($p < .001$). The highest reliance score was obtained in the high reliability (100%) condition reaching a mean of 77.85% ($SD = 18.12$), followed by the medium reliability condition (80%) with an average score of 44.75% ($SD = 28.56$). The lowest reliance score was recorded for the low reliability condition with 27.34% ($SD = 24.08$). The analysis of differences in means between decision times in dependence of reliability levels shows significant results ($F(1.88, 118.56) = 88.2, p = .003, \eta^2 = .025$). Post-hoc comparison reveals significant differences between the high reliability condition and the other two conditions. While in the high reliability condition decision times were as fast as 6.40 s ($SD = 3.58$), for the medium and low condition decision times were measured with an average median time of 7.80 ($SD = 4.68$) and 7.71 ($SD = 3.74$) seconds respectively. Regarding the compliance with the DSS, subjective compliance with an engineer and the artificial intelligence was not significantly different, as indicated by a paired t-test ($p > .05$). Nevertheless, the compliance with the engineer was 52.58% ($SD = 27.93$) while the compliance with the artificial intelligence reached 51.79% ($SD = 28.81$).

Human Factors: In a second step, the relationship between human factors and the reliance on the automation was investigated. The conducted correlation analyses revealed that the disposition to trust automated agents is positively correlated to the reliance on automation within the experiment ($r(62) = 0.25, p = .049$). Furthermore a positive correlation between the reliance on the previous experience of the vehicle and the disposition to trust in automation was found ($r(60) = 0.40, p = .001$).

Environmental Factors: Lastly, the effect of the level of risk included in a given situation was analyzed. RM-ANOVA was performed to compare the reliance on automation in dependence on the particular level of risk. The results show significant differences between the various levels ($F(2.17, 136.67) = 36.3, p < .001, \eta^2 = .209$). Post-hoc comparison showed significant differences in reliance between the personal risk ($M = 35.12$, $SD = 24.93$) and the property risk ($M = 67.03, SD = 28.91$) condition. Further significant differences were found between the *no risk* ($M = 60.63, SD = 26.91$) condition and the property and personal risk condition ($M = 36.98$ $SD = 29.01$). In addition to that, significant differences were found between the *no risk* and property risk condition, as well as between the personal and property and personal risk condition ($p < .001$). Similarly, to the analysis of decision times for the various reliability levels, differences between the decision times in dependence of the different risk levels were examined. RM-ANOVA did however not show any significant differences between the various risk levels regarding decision times ($F(2.59, 163.08) = 1.72, p = .172, \eta^2 < .001$)

4.4 Discussion

The result of the experimental study indicate that the manipulation of investigated factors is affecting the measured response variables such as the reliance on automation or decision times. This finding shows that the developed framework can be used to quantify and accurately measure the impact of trust influencing factors in the context of trust in automation. As such, effects of system, human, and environmental factors could be determined in the present study. In a first line, similar to previously conducted studies (e.g., [24, 30]) a stepwise decrease in reliability of an automated agent leads to a gradual decrease in reliance on automation. In addition to this, decision times for the various reliability conditions could be accurately measured and compared. The results indicate that yet again the modeled factor reliability would influence the recorded decision times significantly.

In a similar way, the factor risk that was included in the experiment to model situation of uncertainty and moral dilemma proved to affect the reliance on the automated agents, indicating that such a factor can successfully be mapped by the proposed framework. Nevertheless, differences in reliance in dependence of the risk level seem at first sight difficult to interpret and therefore deserve further investigation.

While the factor risk and reliability lead to variations in the reliance on automation, altering the decision support system did not seem to have any effect on the compliance with a particular decision aid. Nonetheless, the compliance on a specific DSS was solely evaluated by the means of subjective measures of trust that merley captured the perceived compliance of participants. Further research should look into complementing subjective measures with behavioral measures of compliance to attain a more accurate result.

Lastly, by coupling the developed framework with online survey tools, a relation between human factors and the behavioral reliance on automation could be uncovered.

For instance, the result show that the dispositional trust in automation measured before the actual decision task can be related to the reliance on automation measured during the task. The same applies for the reliance on the previous experience of the vehicle, which was measured in a post task questionnaire.

In summary, the findings of the experiment reveal that the proposed framework is able to accurately map real-life situation and precisely measure the variation of modeled factors derived from these situations. More precisely it allows to map situation of risk and moral dilemma onto a set of factors and measure their effect on the reliance on automation. Finally, the framework can easily be integrated with commonly used survey tools allowing for the investigation of demographics or personality traits of participants in relation to the variables measured in the decision task.

5   Discussion and Research Agenda

5.1   Conclusion

The developed research framework allows a precise study of human decision making in complex decision tasks. The system facilitates (1) the generation of a quantified user model, (2) a systematic variation of system, interface, and environmental factors, (3) defined performance outcomes (e.g., money or points), (4) an exact recording of time and performed actions as baseline for evaluations, and (5) an assessment of the decision tasks by the participants. The use of a game environment for conducting studies promises a higher motivation among the participants and thus higher data quality and lower drop-out rate [36]. The combination of these aspects creates a unique and versatile research environment that allows the systematic variation of user, interface, and system factors to study their effect on attitudes and behavior. The experimental sandbox is not isolated but can be linked to other tools and services, such as additional (online) questionnaires or tests. Thus, the individual decision tasks and the observed behavior can be linked with user factors (such as personality states and traits, attitudes, believes, …) and the evaluation of the tasks (perceived difficult and pressure, satisfaction, autonomy, fatigue, …). According to this, the influence of individual factors, their interaction, or the temporal course can be precisely recorded, examined and weighted, yielding a holistic view on trust influencing factors in complex automation-supported decision tasks.

5.2   Research Roadmap

Numerous research questions unfold from the versatile possibilities of this research environment, which can only be roughly outlined here: Overall goal should be the systematic mapping of the factor space (people, interface, context) on decision behavior, evaluation, and long-term impact in form of a complete cartography.

First, it allows the systematic exploration of how the various system factors influence decision making and its evaluation. E.g., What effect does an increase in property or personal risk have on decision-making behavior, satisfaction with decisions made, or the need for decision support? What effect do wrong decisions have on employee satisfaction? If and which decision biases can be observed in these complex environments?

Second, the framework facilitates the systematic exploration which interface and design factors are contributing to a trustful interaction between people and technology. Research questions include, for example, how suitable decision aids support decision making, if smart information visualization, explainable AI, or decision aids change decision behavior or mitigate decision biases, or if they reduce decision uncertainty.

Third, how do user factors, such as cognitive ability or personality states and traits influence decision making? Do risk seekers face moral decision-making situations differently? Which personality traits favor good decisions? Which personality traits support good handling of uncertainty?

Fourth, the environment can also be used for personnel selection providing clues as to which candidate is particularly rational and analytical in dealing with critical situations and who is particularly sensitive to moral conflicts?

Fifth, the environment can also be used to sensitize (future) employees to such decision conflicts, to train them to act right, and to show them how they can better learn to deal with uncertainty.

Sixth and lastly, the sandbox can also support self-reflection on (moral) decision making. How would you decide in these situations? Would you trade profit for security?

In summary, this framework contributes towards a weighted map of influencing factors in human-computer collaboration, which can inform designers and implementors of tomorrows' technology of an Industrial Internet and automated technology as a whole. Further studies using this framework can therefore contribute towards trusted interfaces and automated decision aids.

Acknowledgements. This research was funded by the German Research Foundation (DFG) within the Cluster of Excellence "Internet of Production" (EXC 2023, 390621612). We thank all participants for their dedicated support!

References

1. Parasuraman, R., Riley, V.: Humans and automation: use, misuse, disuse, abuse. Hum. Factors J. Hum. Factors Ergon. Soc. **39**, 230–253 (1997)
2. Ghazizadeh, M., Lee, J.D., Boyle, L.N.: Extending the technology acceptance model to assess automation. Cogn. Technol. Work **14**, 39–49 (2012). https://doi.org/10.1007/s10111-011-0194-3
3. Ghazizadeh, M., Peng, Y., Lee, J.D., Boyle, L.N.: Augmenting the technology acceptance model with trust: commercial drivers' attitudes towards monitoring and feedback. In: Proceedings of Human Factors Ergonomics Society, pp. 2286–2290 (2012). https://doi.org/10.1177/1071181312561481
4. Masalonis, A.J., Parasuraman, R.: Trust as a construct for evaluation of automated aids: past and future theory and research. In: Proceedings of Human Factors Ergonomics Society Annual Meeting, vol. 43, pp. 184–187 (1999). https://doi.org/10.1177/154193129904300312
5. Hancock, P.A., Billings, D.R., Schaefer, K.E.: Can you trust your robot? Ergon. Des. **19**, 24–29 (2011). https://doi.org/10.1177/1064804611415045
6. Hoff, K.A., Bashir, M.: Trust in automation: integrating empirical evidence on factors that influence trust. Hum. Factors **57**, 407–434 (2015). https://doi.org/10.1177/0018720814547570

7. Rempel, J.K., Holmes, J.G., Zanna, M.P.: Trust in close relationships. J. Pers. Soc. Psychol. **49**, 95–112 (1985). https://doi.org/10.1037/0022-3514.49.1.95

8. Hoffman, R.R., Johnson, M., Bradshaw, J.M., Underbrink, A.: Trust in automation. IEEE Intell. Syst. **28**, 84–88 (2013). https://doi.org/10.1109/MIS.2013.24

9. Lee, J.D., See, K.A.: Trust in automation: designing for appropriate reliance. Hum. Factors **46**, 50–80 (2004). https://doi.org/10.1518/hfes.46.1.50_30392

10. Hancock, P.A., Billings, D.R., Schaefer, K.E., Chen, J.Y.C., De Visser, E.J., Parasuraman, R.: A meta-analysis of factors affecting trust in human-robot interaction. Hum. Factors **53**, 517–527 (2011). https://doi.org/10.1177/0018720811417254

11. Schaefer, K.E., Chen, J.Y.C., Szalma, J.L., Hancock, P.A.: A meta-analysis of factors influencing the development of trust in automation: implications for understanding autonomy in future systems. Hum. Factors **58**, 377–400 (2016). https://doi.org/10.1177/0018720816663 4228

12. French, B., Duenser, A., Heathcote, A.: Trust in automation - A literature Review (2018)

13. Salen, K., Zimmerman, E.: Rules of Play: Game Design Fundamentals. MIT Press, Massachusetts (2003)

14. Woo, J.C.: Digital game-based learning supports student motivation, cognitive success, and performance outcomes. Educ. Technol. Soc. **17**, 291–307 (2014)

15. Deshpande, A.A., Huang, S.H.: Simulation games in engineering education: A state-of-the-art review. Comput. Appl. Eng. Educ. **19**, 399–410 (2011). https://doi.org/10.1002/cae.20323

16. Lamb, R.L., Annetta, L., Firestone, J., Etopio, E.: A meta-analysis with examination of moderators of student cognition, affect, and learning outcomes while using serious educational games, serious games, and simulations. Comput. Hum. Behav. **80**, 158–167 (2018). https://doi.org/10.1016/j.chb.2017.10.040

17. Sterman, J.D.: Modeling managerial behavior: misperceptions of feedback in a dynamic decision making experiment. Manag. Sci. **35**, 321–339 (1989). https://doi.org/10.1287/mnsc.35.3.321

18. Sarkar, S., Kumar, S.: Demonstrating the effect of supply chain disruptions through an online beer distribution game. Decis. Sci. J. Innov. Educ. **14**, 25–35 (2016)

19. Brauner, P., Runge, S., Groten, M., Schuh, G., Ziefle, M.: Human factors in supply chain management. In: Yamamoto, S. (ed.) HIMI 2013. LNCS, vol. 8018, pp. 423–432. Springer, Heidelberg (2013). https://doi.org/10.1007/978-3-642-39226-9_46

20. Brauner, P., Philipsen, R., Valdez, A.C., Ziefle, M., Philipsen, R.: What happens when decision support systems fail?—The importance of usability on performance in erroneous systems. Behav. Inf. Technol. **38**, 1225–1242 (2019). https://doi.org/10.1080/0144929X.2019.1581258

21. Awad, E., et al.: The moral machine experiment. Nature **563**, 59–64 (2018). https://doi.org/10.1038/s41586-018-0637-6

22. Muir, B.M., Moray, N.: Trust in automation. Part ii. Experimental studies of trust and human intervention in a process control simulation. Ergonomics **39**, 429–460 (1996). https://doi.org/10.1080/00140139608964474

23. de Vries, P., Midden, C., Bouwhuis, D.: The effects of errors on system trust, self-confidence, and the allocation of control in route planning. Int. J. Hum Comput Stud. **58**, 719–735 (2003). https://doi.org/10.1016/S1071-5819(03)00039-9

24. Desai, M., et al.: Effects of changing reliability on trust of robot systems. In: HRI 2012 - Proceedings of the 7th Annual ACM/IEEE International Conference on Human-Robot Interaction, pp. 73–80 (2012). https://doi.org/10.1145/2157689.2157702

25. Merritt, S.M., Ilgen, D.R.: Not all trust is created equal: dispositional and history-based trust in human-automation interactions. Hum. Factors **50**, 194–210 (2008). https://doi.org/10.1518/001872008X288574

26. Sanchez, J., Rogers, W.A., Fisk, A.D., Rovira, E.: Understanding reliance on automation: Effects of error type, error distribution, age and experience. Theor. Issues Ergon. Sci. **15**, 134–160 (2014). https://doi.org/10.1080/1463922X.2011.611269
27. Brehmer, B., Dörner, D.: Experiments with computer-simulated microworlds: escaping both the narrow straits of the laboratory and the deep blue sea of the field study. Comput. Hum. Behav. **9**, 171–184 (1993). https://doi.org/10.1016/0747-5632(93)90005-D
28. Papert, S.: Mindstorms: Children, Computers, and Powerful Ideas. Basic Books, Inc., New York (1980)
29. Gamma, E., Helm, R., Johnson, R., Vlissides, J.: Design Patterns: Elements of Reusable Object-Oriented Software. Addison-Wesley Professional, Boston (1995)
30. Chavaillaz, A., Wastell, D., Sauer, J.: System reliability, performance and trust in adaptable automation. Appl. Ergon. **52**, 333–342 (2016). https://doi.org/10.1016/j.apergo.2015.07.012
31. Rovira, E., McGarry, K., Parasuraman, R.: Effects of imperfect automation on decision making in a simulated command and control task. Hum. Factors **49**, 76–87 (2007). https://doi.org/10.1518/001872007779598082
32. Wang, L., Jamieson, G.A., Hollands, J.G.: Trust and reliance on an automated combat identification system. Hum. Factors **51**, 281–291 (2009). https://doi.org/10.1177/0018720809338842
33. Parasuraman, R., Miller, C.A.: Trust and etiquette in high-criticality automated systems. Commun. ACM **47**, 51–55 (2004). https://doi.org/10.1145/975817.975844
34. Perkins, L., Miller, J.E., Hashemi, A., Burns, G.: Designing for human-centered systems: situational risk as a factor of trust in automation. In: Proceedings of Human Factors Ergonomics Society Annual Meeting, vol. 54, pp. 2130–2134 (2012). https://doi.org/10.1177/1541931210005402502
35. Power, D.J.: Decision Support Systems: Concepts and Resources for Managers. Greenwood Publishing Group, Westport (2002)
36. Bogost, I.: Persuasive Games: The Expressive Power of Videogames. The MIT Press, Cambridge (2007)

Threat or Opportunity – Analysis of the Impact of Artificial Intelligence on Future Employment

Fenglian Wang[✉], Mingqing Hu, and Min Zhu

School of Management Engineering, Anhui Polytechnic University, Wuhu 241000, Anhui,
People's Republic of China
fenglian880611@126.com

Abstract. As the main force of the future development of science and technology, artificial intelligence technology has become the direction of many countries, enterprises and researchers. However, the technological progress represented by artificial intelligence has brought tremendous changes to the labor market, and also has a significant impact on the employment and income distribution of workers. In this paper, we use the methods of text survey, questionnaire survey and in-depth interview to explore the impact of AI on future employment. Specifically, this paper takes the most representative second and third tier cities as the research objects, and uses multiple linear regression analysis technology to study the understanding of the practitioners on the artificial intelligence technology; the acceptance of the practitioners on the artificial intelligence; the reasons why the artificial intelligence technology may cause the difficulty of the employment situation; the new employment opportunities that the artificial intelligence may produce; the strategies to deal with the impact of the artificial intelligence Some suggestions. This paper studies the impact of AI on future employment, and puts forward corresponding suggestions and countermeasures from the government, enterprises, universities and individuals.

Keywords: Artificial · Intelligence · Employment · Threat · Opportunity

1 Introduction

Artificial intelligence is the simulation of the information process of human consciousness and thinking. Artificial intelligence is not human intelligence, but it is possible to think like a human being and to surpass human intelligence. Robot is a form of artificial intelligence, an automatic machine capable of imitating certain human activities. Generally can achieve walking and operating tools, such as moving as, can be used to replace people in the environment can not adapt to work. Modern robots are equipped with electronic computers, through programming, can have a certain level of artificial intelligence, such as recognition of language and images, and make appropriate reaction, etc.

In 2016, the intelligent program AlphaGo defeated the world's top go player, causing a world-class sensation. After that, artificial intelligence began to attract more and

© Springer Nature Switzerland AG 2020
V. G. Duffy (Ed.): HCII 2020, LNCS 12199, pp. 296–308, 2020.
https://doi.org/10.1007/978-3-030-49907-5_21

more people's attention, and our life was gradually surrounded by a variety of artificial intelligence products. Such as smart home, voice input method and so on. Unbanked appears, lets the bank teller even the lobby manager begin to worry; The emergence of unmanned supermarket, let the collector, guide shopkeepers lost their jobs; And the recent series of reports on unmanned driving and product development, is more push artificial intelligence to the top of the wave. According to a study by Oxford University, jobs are now available in the United States forty-seven percent will be replaced by AI robots, compared with 77% in China [1].

The application of artificial intelligence technology can be subdivided into: deep learning, computer vision, intelligent robots, virtual personal assistant, natural language processing-speech recognition, natural language processing-universal, real-time speech translation, situational awareness computing, gesture control, automatic recognition of visual content, recommendation engine, etc. [2]. The existing artificial intelligence products mainly involve perception and cognition. Perceptive artificial intelligence technologies such as Siri, Google assistant and other familiar language recognition technologies, as well as image recognition technologies used by driverless cars to recognize pedestrians, have developed rapidly in recent years, and people's acceptance and use frequency have also increased rapidly. Meet class technology research and development of artificial intelligence is the cognition of things and ability to solve problems, on the one hand, such as network security company to use the intelligent agent to detect malicious code and prevent money laundering, insurance company claim for compensation process automation, and the use of artificial intelligence technology aided Banks credit decisions, the cycle work, such as the industry known as ZhiYun million called intelligent voice robot, etc. In the past, some emerging technologies were limited in their use across industries due to the limitations of specific fields and industries. Whereas in the past advances in technology were mainly about improving the ability to perform assigned tasks, today's AI is about giving machines the ability to respond and adapt to optimize their output. Through the combination of Internet of things, robotics and other technologies, artificial intelligence can construct an integrated information physical world. However, AI technology is different in that it has strong universality, involves a wide range of industries and has a greater impact on people's employment [3].

More and more mature artificial intelligence technology is the pursuit of maximum liberation of human repeated work, improve efficiency, make human life more convenient and comfortable, but also to create more beneficial value for enterprises. However, at the same time, it will also affect the employment and work of many people, and some labor jobs with complicated operation even face the dangerous situation of being replaced by artificial intelligence [4]. The world bank's world development report 2016 predicts: "in the future, as technology advances, traditional labor positions will be largely replaced. Osborne and Frey identified 702 occupations based on the likelihood that AI will replace jobs, and estimated that 47% of jobs will be at risk of being replaced by AI products within the next 20 years" [5]. Artificial intelligence is bound to replace complicated manual operations to the greatest extent, replacing many traditional labor jobs, but in this process will also be accompanied by many new employment opportunities. Because the development and application of artificial intelligence cannot be separated from related talents, the cultivation of talents also needs to have relevant institutions to implement.

Therefore, current education needs to cultivate and improve students' data literacy and computational thinking, so that students can read and use data, communicate and interpret through data analysis, master a certain degree of artificial intelligence application ability, and become talents adapting to the era of artificial intelligence [6, 7].

Artificial intelligence has become a welcome new member of all walks of life because of its high accuracy rate, high work efficiency and other advantages [8]. But is artificial intelligence really accepted in all fields and expected to grow rapidly? In order to understand the future of employment challenges brought by the artificial intelligence and sensitivity to employment, improving people's crisis consciousness, this paper takes the most representative of second - and third-tier cities as an example, through the analysis of the acceptance of part of the group of artificial intelligence and artificial intelligence product penetration and its use in the field of people want to see, for under the high speed development of artificial intelligence, the practitioner groups to adapt to the future work environment, grasp the competitive advice [9].

2 Overview of Research Status

2.1 The Development Status of Artificial Intelligence in China

With the development of artificial intelligence in China's mobile Internet, smart home and other fields, China's artificial intelligence industry will continue to grow at a high speed. According to the analysis report on market foresight and investment strategy planning of China's AI industry 2018–2023 by qianzhan industry research institute, the scale of China's AI market increased from 4.86 billion yuan to 13.52 billion yuan from 2014 to 2017, with an average annual compound growth rate of over 40%. Among them, the scale of artificial intelligence industry in China reached 9.56 billion yuan in 2016, a year-on-year growth of 37.9%. In 2017, China's AI industry reached 13.52 billion yuan, up 41.42% year-on-year. China's artificial intelligence industry has entered a new stage of development. At present, the basic conditions of artificial intelligence industry have been met. With the increasing maturity of deep learning algorithms and the accelerated growth of data resources, artificial intelligence technology is expected to continue to improve, and machine vision, natural voice processing and other artificial intelligence technology will usher in new opportunities for development.

In April 2018, the Ministry of Education issued the institutions of higher learning in artificial intelligence innovation action plan, to implement the State Council on the notice issued by a new generation of artificial intelligence development planning, guide the institutions of higher learning aimed at the world technological frontier, constantly improve the field of artificial intelligence science and technology innovation, personnel training and international cooperation and communication ability, for the development of China's new generation of artificial intelligence to provide strategic support. On the afternoon of March 29, 2019, the ministry of education announced the latest results of the archival filing and examination of undergraduate programs in colleges and universities in 2018. Artificial intelligence, a highly popular major, has been added to the list of newly approved undergraduate majors, and 35 universities across the country have received the first batch of construction qualifications. Universities have officially entered the field of artificial intelligence.

In employment: Artificial intelligence & Has become a major trend in the future. In the era of mobile Internet, the emergence of "Internet +" has brought a significant impact on economic development. With the development of dedicated artificial intelligence, as a huge collection of high and new technologies, "Artificial intelligence +" as a new economic format has begun to sprout, and more and more industries have begun to embrace artificial intelligence. And with the promotion on the Internet and the rapid development of artificial intelligence, let workers in all walks of life began to worry. And some workers think its development will bring many job opportunities.

2.2 Selected Topic Reason

First of all, recently, the word artificial intelligence in the unmanned driving and smart home in the development of a wave. Because of its high accuracy rate and high work efficiency, artificial intelligence has become a welcome new member of all walks of life. There are often discussions about its impact on employment, but few people analyze the impact of artificial intelligence on employment in the future from the perspective of people's acceptance of artificial intelligence and expected field.

But is artificial intelligence really accepted in all fields and expected to grow rapidly? Whether the factors such as people's acceptance degree and expectation will cause the change of people's employment sensitivity and the development direction of artificial intelligence, this paper takes the most representative second and third-tier cities as an example, puts forward the research problems and carries out a more detailed study.

3 Survey Objects and Survey Methods

3.1 Investigation Methods

The survey methods adopted in this survey mainly include: copywriting survey method, questionnaire survey method and in-depth interview method.

Before the formal implementation of the research, the research team had a certain understanding of artificial intelligence and its development status in the form of literature review, so as to facilitate the comprehensiveness of the research framework developed later. After that, a preliminary pre-survey was conducted in the form of issuing network questionnaires on a large social networking platform. The revised and improved questionnaires provided a guarantee for accurate data analysis. In terms of data processing, the research team mainly used SPSS25.0 to process the data, and then used descriptive statistical analysis, principal component analysis, factor analysis, variance analysis, multiple linear regression analysis and other methods to analyze the data. Through scientific data analysis methods to classify the data, so as to make a reasonable analysis of the results of the survey.

3.2 Survey Content

Information and survey content. The basic information includes the gender, age, education background, occupation and city of the respondents. The contents of the survey include the understanding of artificial intelligence, the acceptance of artificial intelligence, the causes of employment difficulties caused by artificial intelligence, and the possible opportunities of artificial intelligence in employment, to carry out systematic investigation and analysis.

3.3 Scope of Investigation

Wuhu city is a major city in the national development plan of the Yangtze river delta city cluster, a core city of the wanjiang city belt demonstration zone for undertaking industrial transfer, and an important member of hefei Wuhu bengbu national independent innovation demonstration zone, south anhui international cultural tourism demonstration zone, hefei metropolitan area and G60 science and innovation corridor. In 2015, it was listed as a "first-tier" third-tier city.

Third-tier cities most of the larger cities and non-agricultural population of most of the city center in more than 1 million people, urban infrastructure, commercial facilities and traffic facilities is relatively perfect, the inhabitants have certain consumption ability, the living standards of residents in general is relatively rich, the city has a pillar industry, industrial structure is relatively reasonable, the large enterprises of some industries have a certain appeal, but the city's comprehensive competitiveness remains to be further improved. Generally, most of them are economically more developed cities in the eastern region, sub-centers and regional centers or economically strong cities in the central region, and provincial capitals in the western region. So Wuhu city as the main survey area is based on scientific evidence, but also more in line with the general situation of the country.

Survey scope: Wuhu city as an example of third-tier cities, other areas (first, second, fourth and fifth tier cities and townships, counties and towns) as a supplement.

3.4 Survey Form

This survey adopts the offline face-to-face in-depth survey method and the online network questionnaire method. This survey actually distributed 800 questionnaires, including 300 online questionnaires and 500 paper questionnaires. Recovered 779 copies. There were 721 valid questionnaires.

3.5 Objects of Investigation

The offline respondents of this survey are college students and residents of Wuhu city. The online respondents were of all ages outside Wuhu.

3.6 Research Contents

- **Part 1** Practitioners' understanding of AI technology;
- **Part 2** Practitioners' acceptance of artificial intelligence;
- **Part 3** The possible causes of employment difficulties caused by artificial intelligence technology;
- **Part 4** The new employment opportunities that artificial intelligence may generate;
- **Part 5** Suggestions and strategies to cope with the popularization of artificial intelligence.

4 Empirical Model Construction and Multiple Linear Regression

Based on the research purpose of this project, a model (1) was established to test the impact of artificial intelligence on the industry:

$$cj_i = \beta_0 + \beta_1 ljcd + \beta_2 xb + \beta_3 nl + \beta_4 xl + \beta_5 zy + \beta_6 cs + \varepsilon \qquad (1)$$

In model (1), cji for impact area of artificial intelligence (including cj1 professional technology, cj2 for traditional manufacturing, cj3 for services, cj4 for administrative institutions, cj5 for education, cj6 for arts, cj7 for finance and business, cj8 for military, cj9 for other), LJCD is the general knowledge of artificial intelligence, xb, nl, xl, zy, cs respectively of respondents said the sex, age, education, occupation, city characteristics.

Table 1 report model (1) the results of the multivariate linear regression model, the regression results, the masses for artificial intelligence to meet and understand the positive influence and impact on traditional manufacturing (cj2), service (cj3), administrative institutions (cj4), education (cj5) (cj7), finance and commerce, and other fields, especially the impact on the traditional manufacturing industry (cj2) and the most significant impact (t0.01 = 7.08). That is, among the people surveyed, the general opinion is that artificial intelligence has a stronger impact on traditional manufacturing, service industry and white collar jobs that are more complicated and regular.

Further, we built a model (2) to study the impact of AI literacy on graduates' skills:

$$jn_i = \beta_0 + \beta_1 ljcd + \beta_2 xb + \beta_3 nl + \beta_4 xl + \beta_5 xy + \beta_6 cs + \varepsilon \qquad (2)$$

In model (2) the jni for graduates should have the skills (which is suitable for computer operation skills, jn1 jn2 for software development skills, jn3 for mechanical manufacturing skills, skills, jn5 jn4 for automatic control and intelligent control for other skills), LJCD is the general knowledge of artificial intelligence, xb, nl, xl, zy, cs respectively of respondents said the sex, age, education, occupation, city characteristics.

Table 1. Multiple regression analysis

	(1)	(2)	(3)	(4)	(5)	(6)	(7)	(8)	(9)
	cj1	cj2	cj3	cj4	cj5	cj6	cj7	cj8	cj9
ljcd	-0.042**	0.152***	0.073***	0.064***	0.039**	0.027	0.167***	-0.114***	-0.011
	(-2.04)	(7.08)	(3.70)	(3.03)	(2.09)	(1.58)	(9.43)	(-4.23)	(-1.45)
xb	-0.086***	-0.023	0.030	-0.036	0.021	-0.033	0.015	-0.084**	-0.015
	(-2.61)	(-0.69)	(0.94)	(-1.07)	(0.73)	(-1.22)	(0.53)	(-1.98)	(-1.25)
nl	0.035*	0.094***	-0.042**	0.105***	-0.027	0.041**	0.019	0.042	-0.003
	(1.67)	(4.36)	(-2.11)	(4.93)	(-1.46)	(2.36)	(1.04)	(1.53)	(-0.43)
xl	-0.065***	0.067***	0.063***	0.117***	-0.010	0.066***	-0.014	-0.078***	0.004
	(-3.13)	(3.14)	(3.20)	(5.57)	(-0.52)	(3.83)	(-0.79)	(-2.91)	(0.58)
zy	-0.023***	0.028***	0.015***	0.014***	0.012***	0.003	0.010***	-0.021***	0.005***
	(-5.23)	(6.20)	(3.77)	(3.17)	(3.00)	(0.86)	(2.78)	(-3.74)	(3.42)
cs	-0.097***	-0.003	0.164***	-0.016	0.011	0.038	0.065**	-0.156***	-0.003
	(-3.15)	(-0.11)	(5.60)	(-0.51)	(0.39)	(1.50)	(2.49)	(-3.93)	(-0.23)
Constant term	1.456***	-0.591***	-0.562***	-0.570***	0.036	-0.310***	-0.542***	1.729***	0.034
	(10.48)	(-4.14)	(-4.26)	(-4.08)	(0.29)	(-2.72)	(-4.60)	(9.65)	(0.66)
Sample size	721	721	721	721	721	721	721	721	721
R2	0.124	0.170	0.133	0.125	0.039	0.048	0.131	0.115	0.031
Adjuste dR2	0.116	0.163	0.126	0.118	0.031	0.040	0.124	0.108	0.023
The F value	16.806	24.348	18.269	17.026	4.882	6.027	17.930	15.467	3.844

Note: the value in brackets is t value; ***, **, and *mean significant at 1%, 5%, and 10% levels, respectively.

Table 2 reported the results of the model (2) multiple linear regression model, the regression results, the general knowledge of artificial intelligence degrees for graduates in software development, mechanical manufacture, automatic control and intelligent control has significant positive influence on expertise, among them, for graduates in the aspect of software development skill is the most significant (t0.01 = 8.85).

Table 2. Requirements for graduates' skills in artificial intelligence

	(1)	(2)	(3)	(4)	(5)
	jn1	jn2	jn3	jn4	jn5
ljcd	−0.027	0.186***	0.054**	0.157***	−0.226***
	(−1.62)	(8.85)	(2.49)	(7.39)	(−11.32)
xb	−0.033	0.004	0.026	0.010	−0.020
	(−1.24)	(0.13)	(0.75)	(0.29)	(−0.64)
nl	0.015	−0.027	0.078***	0.038*	0.032
	(0.89)	(−1.29)	(3.57)	(1.75)	(1.56)
xl	−0.028*	−0.025	0.169***	−0.049**	−0.019
	(−1.66)	(−1.17)	(7.80)	(−2.31)	(−0.93)
zy	−0.003	0.015***	0.014***	0.017***	−0.026***
	(−1.00)	(3.42)	(3.14)	(3.92)	(−6.18)
cs	−0.056**	0.139***	0.063**	0.148***	−0.139***
	(−2.27)	(4.48)	(1.98)	(4.74)	(−4.70)
Constant term	1.181***	−0.447***	−0.810***	−0.528***	1.610***
	(10.64)	(−3.19)	(−5.62)	(−3.74)	(12.09)
Sample size	721	721	721	721	721
R2	0.025	0.151	0.151	0.110	0.264
Adjuste dR2	0.016	0.144	0.144	0.102	0.258
The F value	3.013	21.221	21.222	14.651	42.687

Note: the value in brackets is t value; ***, **, and *mean significant at 1%, 5%, and 10% levels, respectively.

5   Analysis of Survey Results

5.1   People with Different Educational Backgrounds

P(significance) = 0.000 < 0.05, so it can be considered statistically that there is a significant difference between the samples, that is, there is a difference in understanding of artificial intelligence due to different educational backgrounds. Using multi-element cross analysis, in bachelor degree and above 70.2% of people think that although artificial intelligence can bring impact to employment, but on whether or not they will seize the opportunity to feel more optimistic, compared with university college degree and higher than that of 49.7% of the population, namely the degree is the most of the impact of the development of artificial intelligence can keep an optimistic attitude.

5.2 The Degree of Understanding of Artificial Intelligence

In our survey, respondents who do not understand artificial intelligence at all only account for 0.7% of the total sample, indicating that the vast majority of people have at least heard about artificial intelligence; But know about artificial intelligence is, general understanding of artificial intelligence, the artificial intelligence (ai) do not know much about these three options accounted for 14.3%, 49.9% and 29.3% respectively, which exceeds ninety percent of the respondents are product or concept of artificial intelligence of artificial intelligence have certain contact and understanding, and there is no understanding, still in the state in which a little knowledge; Only 5.8% had a deep understanding of artificial intelligence.

5.3 The Direction of the Development of Artificial Intelligence Technology Attitude

Think of the existing artificial intelligence products bring great convenience to human life, looking forward to the more faster development, the number of 55.6%, that of artificial intelligence development too fast, 13.3% want to limit its development, think that artificial intelligence can be a threat to humans, want to stop 28.3% of artificial intelligence research. Combine the following question: "what attitude do you hold towards AI that is stronger than your own thinking ability?" In the results, 47.6% of the total number agree, 35.8% of the total number dislike, and 16.6% of the total number are hard to say. From these two questions, it is not difficult to find that the number of people who agree with and oppose artificial intelligence is more than 1:1. In other words, among the people surveyed, those who can accept and approve artificial intelligence still account for the majority. But the people who don't accept artificial intelligence, or those who don't accept strong artificial intelligence actually account for 30%; A few remain on the sidelines.

5.4 Views on Artificial Intelligence as a Potential Competitor

Among them, those who are worried about being eliminated from the society account for 29.7%, those who believe that competent people live there and have confidence in facing possible difficulties account for 56.9%, and those who believe that they hope so that human beings can enjoy the benefits take the rest account for 11.9%. It can be seen that in the face of the pressure brought by the technological reform represented by artificial intelligence, more than half of the people still hold an optimistic attitude.

5.5   Views on the Future Impact of Artificial Intelligence

6.5% think it will definitely. 51.7% said it was very likely. Some 34.4% were unsure. Nearly 6% said it was likely to have no impact. A minority of 1.4% said no. This may depend on the different jobs of different groups of people. Therefore, we have done the multiple linear regression analysis above, and the result is that the traditional manufacturing industry will be affected the most, and the traditional manufacturing industry will also show more stress. In the results of the multiple linear regression analysis of model (1), it can also be seen that respondents generally believe that artificial intelligence has a stronger impact on traditional manufacturing industry, service industry and white collar jobs with high complexity and regularity.

5.6   The Influence on the Skills of Practitioners

In the questionnaire design, we found some skills needed for the research and development of artificial intelligence products: computer operation technology, software development technology, mechanical manufacturing, automatic control and intelligent control skills. According to the option statistics after recall and the multiple linear regression analysis of model (2), more than 80% of the respondents believe that they need to master computer operation technology and software development technology. It can be seen that the rapid development of artificial intelligence and more and more applications at present also put forward higher requirements for practitioners to master skills, an excellent practitioner must pay attention to the training of professional skills, in order to have more competitiveness, invincible in the society.

6   Suggestions for Investigation

It can be concluded from the investigation and analysis that the development of artificial intelligence is needed by The Times. In China's developing country background, artificial intelligence will bring more uncertainty, we need to look at the rise of artificial intelligence dialectically. We should not only see the substitution effect of artificial intelligence on traditional jobs, but also recognize the high-end employment opportunities that artificial intelligence can bring to job seekers and practitioners. In the process of emerging technologies represented by artificial intelligence shaping all walks of life, how to reduce the negative impact of artificial intelligence on practitioners? It needs the joint response of government, enterprises, universities and individuals.

6.1   To Government

The government needs to actively develop new industries, explore new jobs brought by emerging technologies and expand employment channels; We should establish a supportive system for reemployment, encourage continuing education, and strengthen vocational education and job-transfer training. At the same time for the government to plan and guide the development of artificial intelligence, grasp the development trend of artificial intelligence, step by step, to safely reduce the artificial intelligence development jobs substitution effect, weakening the emerging technology development too quickly may lead to polarization, fundamentally to avoid the unemployed surge and produce too much of the gap between rich and poor could spark social risk problem [10, 11].

6.2 To Enterprises

In the face of the irreversible impact of artificial intelligence, enterprises must actively respond to and adapt to The Times. Learn relevant knowledge, learn from excellent enterprises at home and abroad, and pay attention to cooperate with government policies. While reducing the impact brought by emerging technologies for the whole society, as an employer, it is also beneficial for the enterprise to prepare in advance for future impacts and even benefit from them.

(i)   The personnel department of the enterprise needs to actively adapt to the changes of The Times, reposition its own posts and tasks, realize the integration and transformation of posts according to the intelligent system provided by AI, and improve the efficiency of human resource management. Take its essence, go to its dross, make full use of artificial intelligence system; At the same time, the innovation consciousness of employees should not be neglected to make up for the defects of artificial intelligence and reduce the negative impact of artificial intelligence [12].

(ii) When receiving new employees, the enterprise should formulate a training plan for employees, urge them to improve their abilities, and establish the idea of how to deal with the possible negative effects and improve their competitiveness in the era of artificial intelligence as soon as possible; Besides, it also provides regular and quantitative quality training, and urges employees to pay attention to the improvement of their working ability after work.

6.3 To Colleges and Universities

Colleges and universities are the bridge for the majority of practitioners before they enter the society. While shouldering the responsibility of cultivating a batch and a batch of high-quality practitioners, they also need to face the impact brought by artificial intelligence and other new technologies. And as the first line of college students' employability training, how to ensure that the professional theoretical knowledge imparts conforms to the current trend of The Times? How to make students in the artificial intelligence under the impact of the employment environment to establish a correct view of employment, employment view? And how to properly deal with the negative impact of "artificial intelligence + education" on the traditional education system? These are the problems that colleges and universities should solve nowadays [13].

(i)   A correct understanding of "artificial intelligence + education": faced with the participation of new technologies in traditional education, colleges and universities should maintain a positive and good attitude. Starting from the perspective that the participation of artificial intelligence can improve the quality of teaching, the application of artificial intelligence can strengthen students' interaction in class and practice after class. It is the knowledge and practice of artificial intelligence before the prospective practitioner steps into the society, as well as the implementation of the deep knowledge of professional knowledge.

(ii) Attach importance to professional ethics education for college students: colleges and universities should actively build employment guidance teams, set up courses related to career planning and competition practice, and jointly guide students to set up correct career choice and employment concepts through the combination of classroom, practice and network platform; Attach importance to the cultivation of students' professional ethics. For the young people who are just entering the society, they do not have rich practical experience. Therefore, the way to identify the candidates will be more inclined to their professional ethics. Therefore, a good professional ethics is the most important brick knocking on the door of the enterprise, the high level of professional ethics is the enterprise really dare to use employees [14].

6.4 To Individual

Practitioners are the first major subject facing the impact of emerging technologies such as artificial intelligence. In our research, it can also be seen that the impact of new technologies has different intensity on various posts, and many practitioners can also see the opportunities brought by artificial intelligence. Therefore, practitioners need to improve their competitiveness, pay attention to the trend of The Times, and actively deal with the possible crisis.

(i)   Strengthen the study of professional theoretical knowledge, pay attention to participate in practical activities, and attach importance to the cultivation of comprehensive ability.

(ii) In order to integrate into the rapid progress of modern society as soon as possible, a positive spirit of innovation and a sense of competition are essential. Under the conditions suitable for the development of enterprises, practitioners should be good at breaking the conventional rules and finding their own way.

(iii) Prepare for lifelong learning, pay attention to market development and change, adjust learning direction, and keep growing.

(iv) Make career development plans with a purpose and a plan to improve the chances of employment success; It also ensures that it is possible to gain skills from the job and be prepared for the impact of the new technological revolution.

Acknowledgments. We wish to thank Xinlei Zhou, Zhiyi He, Xinfeng Lin for sending out questionnaire and some commissions for the research assistance. This study is supported by National Social Science Fund of China(16BGL201), Key Project of humanities and social sciences in Anhui Province(SK2018A0111) and General Project of philosophy and social science in Anhui Province(AHSKY2019D022).

References

1. Li, Z.: Application of artificial intelligence in computer network technology. Electron. Technol. Softw. Eng. (10), 8 (2018)

2. Zhao, B., Du, Y.: How does artificial intelligence affect your career choice?. Study Abroad (14), 12–14 (2018)
3. Wang, T.: Impact of artificial intelligence on employment. J. Jiamusi Vocational College (07), 287–288+290 (2019)
4. Li, Z., Bao, Z.: "Cloud management": a new model of social governance in the era of big data. Tianjin Soc. Sci. (03), 62–67 (2015)
5. National Science and Technology Council: Preparing for the future of artificial intelligence [OL]
6. Zhao, C.: Research on the two-way impact of artificial intelligence development on labor employment. Coop. Econ. Technol. (15), 120–121 (2019)
7. Huang, X.: Philosophical reflection on the upsurge of artificial intelligence. J. Shanghai Normal Univ. (Philos. Soc. Sci. Ed.) 47(04), 34–42 (2008)
8. Tao, X., Chen, S.: "Out of control" and "doing nothing": towards a partner type of man-machine relationship. J. Beijing Univ. Sci. Technol. (Soc. Sci. Ed.), (5), 70–77 (2019). [2019-10-21]
9. Jia, K., Jiang, Y.: Three basic problems of AI governance: technical logic, risk challenge and public policy choice. China Adm. (10), 40–45 (2017)
10. Guo, H., Qu, F., Zhan, P.: Research on information sharing service model and its application in smart city. J. Intell. 36(04), 118–124 (2017)
11. He, Z.: Government adaptation and transformation in the era of artificial intelligence. Adm. Manage. Reform (08), 53–59 (2016)
12. Deng, J., Zhang, M., Zhu, L., Wang, M., Zhang, J.: Social network analysis of collaborative innovation system of social governance. China Sci. Technol. Forum (04), 18–24 (2016)
13. Frank, M.R., et al.: Toward understanding the impact of artificial intelligence on labor. Proc. Nat. Acad. Sci. U.S.A. 116(14), 6531–6539 (2019)
14. Agrawal, A., Gans, J.S., Goldfarb, A.: Artificial intelligence: the ambiguous labor market impact of automating prediction. J. Econ. Perspect. 33(2), 31–49 (2019)

New Research Issues and Approaches in Digital Human Modelling

The Difficulties in Usability Testing of 3-Dimensional Software Applying Eye-Tracking Methodology – Presented via Two Case Studies of Evaluation of Digital Human Modelling Software

Mária Babicsné-Horváth[(⊠)] and Károly Hercegfi

Department of Ergonomics and Psychology, Budapest University of Technology and Economics,
Magyar Tudosok Krt. 2, Budapest 1117, Hungary
{bhorvathmaria,hercegfi}@erg.bme.hu

Abstract. Eye-tracking based usability testing methods today are very accepted by researchers. These methods are ones of the most commons in human-computer interaction. There are various types of applications of these methods in software or web usability area, however, there is a difficulty during usability tests with the 3D environment. The problem is occurred when the participant wants to rotate, zoom or move the 3D space. In these cases, the gaze plots, the heatmaps, or the statistics of Area of Interests (AOI) cannot be used regarding the 3D workspace. The data on the menu bar is interpretable, however, on the 3D environment hardly or not at all. In our research, we tested ViveLab and Jack Digital Human Modelling (DHM) software knowing the mentioned problem. Our goal was dual. Firstly, with this usability tests, we wanted to detect the issues in the software. Secondly, we tested the utility of a new methodology which was included the tests. At one point of the usability test, the participants was asked not to move the 3D space, while they had to perform the given tasks. Several methods were used to locate the usability problems of the software. During the tests, we applied eye-tracking method, and after that, each participant was interviewed. Based on the experiences of this research, we can advise future researchers testing similar products. This methodology is useful, and applicable in other related usability tests, and its visualisation techniques for one or more participants are interpretable.

Keywords: Usability testing · Eye-tracking · Human factors and ergonomics (HFE) · ViveLab · Jack · 3D environment

1 Introduction

Eye-tracking based usability testing methods today are very accepted tools among researchers. These method are ones of the most commons in Human-Computer Interaction (HCI). There are various types of applications of these methods in software or web

© Springer Nature Switzerland AG 2020
V. G. Duffy (Ed.): HCII 2020, LNCS 12199, pp. 311–321, 2020.
https://doi.org/10.1007/978-3-030-49907-5_22

usability area [1], however, we have discovered a gap in these researches. The visuali-sation techniques of the eye-tracking device are useful, and in the 2D environment, it is interpretable [2], but in a 3D environment, researchers cannot use them completely. The problem occurs when the participant wants to rotate, zoom or move the 3D space. In this case, the gaze plots, the heatmaps or the statistics of Area of Interests (AOI) cannot be used regarding the 3D workspace (the huge inner area of the screen). The data on the menu bar is interpretable, however, on the 3D environment hardly or not at all. A recent research on a video game from the University of Aveiro, Portugal shows the same problem [3]. In one of our previous studies, we tested a human model-based software for ergonomics, and we encountered the same problem, where the data of the aggregated heatmaps and gaze plots were not interpretable [4].

In our present research, we tested ViveLab and Jack Digital Human Modelling (DHM) software knowing the mentioned problem. Our goal was dual. On the one hand, with this usability tests, we wanted to detect the problems of the software. On the other hand, we tested the utility of a new methodology included in the tests. At one point of the usability test, the participants were asked not to move the 3D space, while they had to perform the given tasks.

2   Methods and Tools

We used several techniques to locate the usability problems of the software. Before the usability tests, the participants were asked about a few basic questions to relieve tension. During the experiment, we apply the eye-tracking methodology, and after that, the moderator interviewed each participant.

2.1   Eye-Tracking as a Usability Testing Technique

The final goal of a usability test is the appraisal of a service or product. To reach this goal, researchers have to make a seties of test sessions with representative users. During the examination, participants usually try to perform specific tasks while observers are watching, listening to them and making notes. In most cases, the analyst also works with audio and video recordings. The aim is to identify usability issues, collect qualitative and quantitative data related to it, and determine the product/service satisfaction of the participant [5].

Eye-tracking methodology in ergonomics, especially in HCI is a known tool for mea-suring usability or user experience [4, 6]. Various types of research were made in the field of web design [7–9], and other HCI fields [10–15]. This methodology, e.g. in usability testing, can give us additional information about the users' behaviour [16]. Combining the conventional usability test techniques (observation, video recording, event recording, etc.) with eye-tracking methods, we can gain more data, and its visualisation techniques can support us to interpret these data in a relatively efficient way.

In our research, we used a monitor based eye-tracking device (Tobii T120). The cameras built in the monitor further to record the participants' movements, gestures, and facial expressions, are able to determine the gaze. The system also records the computer screen, and as a result, we can get a video with the eye movements, heatmaps [17], AOI (Area of Interest) statistics [11], and gaze plot diagrams [18].

2.2 Tested Software

In this research, two DHM software were tested: ViveLab and Jack.

ViveLab

ViveLab is a DHM-based software for ergonomic analysis. The software was released in 2015. The software is cloud-based, which is one of its main advantages. It means the shared model spaces (so-called "virtual labs" or only "labs") can be available from all countries, only a utility software, Citrix Receiver must be installed. Everyone can register on the webpage and get a one-h trial license.

After login, we can create labs, and work with coworkers in the same lab at the same time. The built-in human model has a database of accurate body dimensions. We can adjust the percentile, age, somatotype, and acceleration of our human mannequin. The parameter of acceleration means we can adjust the birth year of the human, since, over the decades, the later they are born, the higher they will be. There is an opportunity for import xsens motion capture file, and we can create our animation manually as well. The software includes three implemented risk assessment methods (RULA, OWAS, NASA-OBI), two implemented standards (ISO 11226, EN 1005-4), and two other analysis techniques (reachability zone, spaghetti diagram). After analysing the human motion and postures, we can generate risk assessment documents and ask for statistics.

Jack

Jack software was developed at the University of Pennsylvania in the 1980s and 90s. It was primarily designed for the NASA's space shuttle program as an ergonomic risk assessment tool, and later attracted the interest in the naval and armed forces in the United States. It was primarily used to simulate military actions, and at the Air Force for maintenance work. Nowadays, the Jack software and brand belong to the Siemens corporataion as a component of the Siemens PLM (Product Lifecycle Management) software, and it is one of the oldest and most widely used software for ergonomics.

Jack's virtual environment allows us to import CAD models. Information such as distance from two points or access zones can be displayed. The human models are detailed and biomechanically accurate, and the body sizes are from valid anthropometric data, ANSUR 88. The limits of movement and the limits of strength correspond to NASA's research results. Motion capture allows us to incorporate the movement of a real person into the human model. It can also generate reports based on exact results. Analysis as reachability zones, RULA, OWAS and other tools are also available in Jack.

2.3 Participants

We defined a partly similar user profile regarding our previous experiences. We recruited the participants in accordance of it: University students, graduates, and university teachers were the participants, nevertheless, we were focusing on their experience on ergonomic risk assessment and anthropometry as well as other CAD software.

Eight persons participated, one student, six graduates and one teacher. Regarding our previous experiences, two participants were proficient in the field of industrial ergonomics, six participants were practiced in CAD modelling, and three are continually using it in their job. According the selection rules, the participants required to be unfamiliar with the software.

3 The Protocol of the Usability Tests

First, the calibration of the Tobii T120 eye-tracker was made. After that, the participants had to complete the given tasks. In each session, the sequence of the two software was randomly chosen. (However, we paid attention to the equal number of the users testing with each order). Eventually, four participants started the tasks with ViveLab, and four started with Jack. Therefore, the effect of the learnability was not always the same.

Before the usability tests, few adjustments were made. We created eight separated virtual lab in ViveLab for the eight participants. A CAD model of a roller conveyor was added, and a viewpoint was defined (with the same view) in every lab. We also created a rectangular solid representing the roller conveyor in Jack, which was necessary due to methodological considerations.

The protocol of the tests was the following. After the calibration of the eye-tracker, the participants have to complete the given tasks.

- Open ViveLab/Jack.
- Try how you can move, rotate the 3D space and zoom.
- Create a human model and set the given parameters.
- Find the viewpoint named "Viewpoint 1" and insert the camera. (We asked the participants not to move the camera for the next two tasks.)
- Create a 10 cm × 10 cm × 10 cm cube (illustrating the workpiece).
- Adjust the colour/transparency of the cube. (After this task, the participants were allowed to move the camera.)
- Adjust the position of the man and the cube without moving the roller bar.
- Turn on the RULA (Rapid Upper Limb Assessment) Risk Assessment Panel. The task is over when they read aloud what point the posture has got.
- Make an animation in which the human lifts the cube, raises it closer to the eye (as visual inspection).
- Play the animation from start to finish.
- Turn on the RULA (Rapid Upper Limb Assessment) Risk Assessment Panel, and check the score of the body posture when the human lifts the cube.

We shortened the task list after the pilot test. The first task time was one and a half h, which is tiring for the participants. The average of current task times is 45 min.

Searching in the menus was the main point of the test. We tried to avoid the change of views by giving the tasks step by step, in a view from which the task can be performed. Also, we asked the participants not to modify it during two tasks. With this little part of the test, we can evaluate heatmaps and gaze plots with the help of the eye-tracking methodology.

4 Results

4.1 Results Regarding the Two Software

As the results of the tests, we have identified many usability problems regarding the software. We gained two types of data: qualitative and quantitative. The qualitative data came from eye-tracking visualisation techniques (heatmaps, gaze plots). The quantitative data came from the task completion time. The usability problems were listed and explained in our previous article [19], however, a summary can be read here.

The first task (Move, Rotate and Zoom in the 3D Space) was the easiest, however, in Jack, only one participant could complete it without help. In ViveLab, this task was easier because the participants needed to use only the mouse.

The Creating Human Model and Changing the Properties tasks were also simple, but in ViveLab, they did not understand the icons at first. After creating a human model, they had to change their properties. It was a more laborious task in Jack because there are two panels: Properties panel and a Human Scale panel. The percentile type can be adjusted in the Human Scale panel. Seven of the eight participants looked for this function in the Properties panel at first.

Finding the RULA panel was easy, however, in ViveLab, to get the score of the body posture, they had to click on the human model even if there were only one. This step wasn't highlighted enough. Based on the scan path data, we can conclude that they looked at the right place relatively soon; however, they originally did not recognise its importance.

Creating Animation was the hardest task in both software. To complete one part of the simulation in Jack, three clicks to Next buttons and one to the Done button were required, which was an unexpected long sequence. In ViveLab, most of the participants needed help.

Overall the interface of ViveLab was more understandable for the participants, however, the Animation and Simulation panel was better in Jack probably because it has a more sophisticated task builder.

4.2 Results Regarding the Methodology

Create a 10 cm x 10 cm x 10 cm cube (illustrating the workpiece) and Adjust the colour/transparency of the cube were two easy tasks, while the participants were asked not to move the camera. (Moving the camera means moving, rotating, and zooming in the 3D space). The easiness of these tasks was crucial for testing the methodology. In this part of the usability test, the particular usability problems of the software were less important for us. Also, we would like to choose a task which can be completed without moving the camera.

Methodological problems of research to solve

Only one participant forgot not to rotate, zoom or translate the virtual space, but the moderator intervened, and the task could continue.

To complete the second task, the participants had to right-click on the cube and select the particular option (see Fig. 1). The cube was on the same place for all participants, at

least there was no task which said move the cube. However, there was another solution
in both Jack and ViveLab. In ViveLab, the user can also click on the model tree on the
left side. In Jack, the user can also open a window and set multiple options for the model
(see Fig. 2).

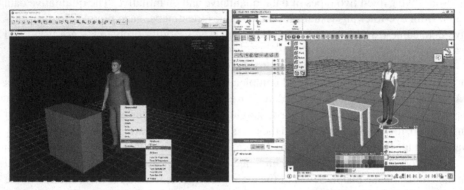

Fig. 1. Adjust the colour/transparency of the cube – the same type of solutions in Jack (left) and
ViveLab (right).

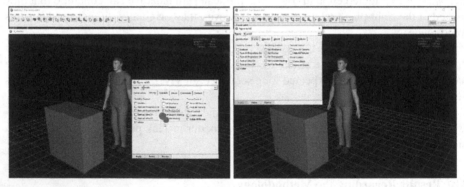

Fig. 2. Adjust the colour/transparency of the cube – identical solutions in Jack with different
window positions.

Furthermore, even if the solution was the same, the popup window or the context
menu could appeared in different positions for most of the participants. An example
for Jack on Fig. 2. In these cases, the aggregated heatmaps are not interpretable for all
participants. However, careful manual summarizing of individual heatmaps (or other
visualisations) of each participants can give right results.

In ViveLab, another unexpected problem has occurred, which influenced the outcome. On the right side of the screen, there is the panel bar which can be closed. There
was no task to close the panel; however, many participants closed it to see the other parts
better. The task can be completed in both cases but Fig. 3 shows the context menus is in
different positions.

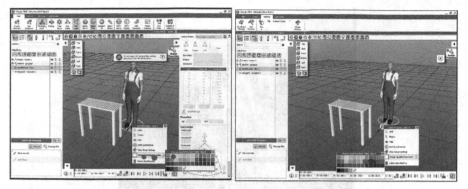

Fig. 3. Adjust the colour of the cube – identical solutions in ViveLab, with the right panel (left screenshot) and without the right panel (right screenshot).

This last problem was not only an issue for the second task. In the first task, the settings panel of the cube were appeared in different places as well, and the whole environment is translated (see Fig. 4).

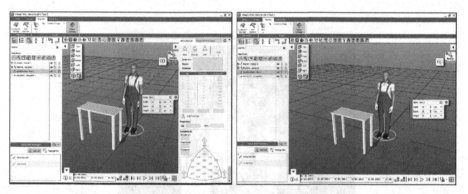

Fig. 4. Setting the dimensions of the cube – identical solutions in ViveLab, with the right panel (left screenshot) and without the right panel (right screenshot).

Interpretable Aggregated Heatmaps

Although many unexpected problems have occurred, all of them can be corrected with some more instruction (or with posterior corrections during analysis). Despite the previous issues, we can create aggregated and individual heatmaps, which will be presented below.

Creating the cube in Jack can be solved in one way. The participants had to click on the menu bar and use the right buttons. In this case, all participant have the same picture in front of them, so we could create an aggregated heatmap for all participants (see Fig. 5). This is a good result, but the searched area is not actually in the 3D space.

Changing the transparency of the cube in Jack was the second task. In this case, the participants had to click on the 3D space area and use a context menu. Because of this

Fig. 5. Creating a cube in Jack, aggregated heatmap for all participants.

task could be completed in two ways, (we were interested in this one,) the aggregated heatmap could be created only for four participants (see Fig. 6). This is also a good result for us, and with further development of the test, the problem can be bypassed.

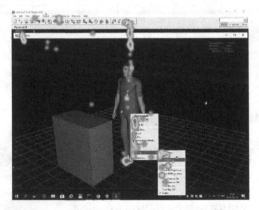

Fig. 6. Changing the transparency of the cube in Jack, aggregated heatmap for four participants.

The similar task in ViveLab was to change the colour of the cube. The participants could complete the task in two ways. The users can click directly on the cube or the model tree on the left side. There was more than one participant who completed each way, so we could create two aggregated heatmap with data of two participants per ways (See Fig. 7).

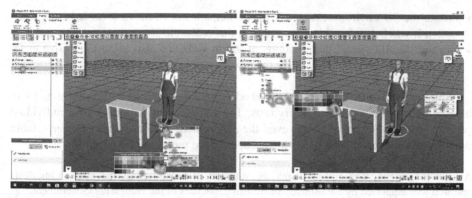

Fig. 7. Adjust the colour of the cube, identical solutions in ViveLab, clicking on the cube (left) or clicking on the model tree (right) – aggregated heatmaps for two participants (left) and other two participants (right).

5 Discussion and Conclusion

In conclusion, our usability research was useful for both purposes. We could conclude the software and the methodology as well. Regarding the software, many suggestions can be made. Not all function was tested, but our goal was to test the user interface differences between the two software. Based on the task completion time, which was, on average, 45 min, the complexity of the task was correct.

The problem of the eye-tracking methodology in a 3D environment is solvable, but with compromises. The biggest problem while using eye-tracking is that the most sophisticated, aggregated visualisations, such as aggregated heatmaps can only be used in restricted situations, so they are not always suitable for modelling natural user behaviour. Zoom in and out, dimension change and rotation make it difficult to evaluate, however, makes it easier for users to complete the task. Despite when the participants were asked not to move the 3D space, they could open context menus on different places, so, in same cases, the aggregated heatmaps and gaze plots would not be interpretable.

With this research, we intend to give suggestions for other researchers how to complete similar usability tests with sufficient results. Our suggestions, which conclude the original ideas and the findings, are the following:

- Give precise tasks. In ViveLab, one task was to adjust the colour of the created cube. We did not give a specific colour, because the palette is broad and there are many different hues, and we were not interested in this part. However, in this case, the heatmaps are less interpretable.
- Avoid possible differences. Give instructions for most cases. After adjusting the human model, the participants did not need the panel on the right side. With one instruction (close the panel), all participant would see the same picture, and more aggregated heatmap can be created.
- Watch out for the popup windows. We can not give a solution for the problem of the popup windows in different positions, but the moderator can ask the participants not to move these windows for the better result.

- Freeze the 3D environment or ask the participant not to move it (at least for some tasks). It was helpful and indispensable in this research.
- Beyond the 3D space, the positions of the models are also important. Give exact instructions on whether they move the model or not.

Summarizing this research, this methodology is considered to be useful and can be applied in other similar usability tests. The visualisation techniques for individual participants are interpretable, however, the aggregated visualisations are interpretable only in special cases. Further tests are needed for the more precise picture.

Acknowledgement. The authors thank the valuable contributions of the participants. This research was supported by the Ministry of Human Capacities of the Hungarian Government.

References

1. Kim, E., Tang, L. (Rebecca)., Meusel, C., Gupta, M.: Optimization of menu-labeling formats to drive healthy dining: an eye tracking study. Int. J. Hosp. Manag. **70**, 37–48 (2018). https://doi.org/10.1016/j.ijhm.2017.10.020
2. Jowers, I., Prats, M., McKay, A., Garner, S.: Evaluating an eye tracking interface for a two-dimensional sketch editor. CAD Comput. Aided Des. **45**, 923–936 (2013). https://doi.org/10.1016/j.cad.2013.01.006
3. Almeida, S., Mealha, Ó., Veloso, A.: Video game scenery analysis with eye tracking. Entertain. Comput. **14**, 1–13 (2016). https://doi.org/10.1016/j.entcom.2015.12.001
4. Babicsné Horváth, M., Hercegfi, K., Fergencs, T.: Comparison of Digital Human Model-Based Ergonomic Software Using Eye-Tracking Methodology – Presenting Pilot Usability Tests (2019). https://doi.org/10.1007/978-3-030-22216-1_2
5. Riihiaho, S.: Usability Testing. In: The Wiley Handbook of Human Computer Interaction Set, pp. 255–275. Wiley Blackwell (2017). https://doi.org/10.1002/9781118976005.ch14
6. Poole, A., Ball, L.: Eye tracking in human-computer interaction and usability research: current status and future prospects. In: Encyclopedia of Human-Computer Interaction (2006). https://doi.org/10.4018/978-1-59140-562-7
7. Romano Bergstrom, J.C., Olmsted-Hawala, E.L., Jans, M.E.: Age-related differences in eye tracking and usability performance: website usability for older adults. Int. J. Hum. Comput. Interact. **29**, 541–548 (2013). https://doi.org/10.1080/10447318.2012.728493
8. Herendy, C.: How to Research People's First Impressions of Websites? Eye-Tracking as a Usability Inspection Method and Online Focus Group Research BT - Software Services for e-Business and e-Society (2009)
9. Herendy, C.: How to learn about users and understand their needs? User experience, mental models and research at public administration websites. Soc. Tyrim. Soc. Res. **41**, 5–17 (2018)
10. Michalski, R.: Information presentation compatibility in a simple digital control panel design: eye-tracking study. Int. J. Occup. Saf. Ergon. **24**, 395–405 (2018). https://doi.org/10.1080/10803548.2017.1317469
11. Józsa, E., Hámornik, B.P.: Find the difference! eye tracking study on information seeking behavior using an online game. J. Eye Track. Vis. Cogn. Emot. **2**, 27–35 (2012)
12. Tóth, A., Szabó, B.: A pilot research on sport application's usability and feedback mechanics. In: 9th IEEE International Conference on Cognitive Infocommunications, CogInfoCom 2018 – Proceedings, pp. 75–80. IEEE (2019). https://doi.org/10.1109/coginfocom.2018.8639870

13. Katona, J., Kovari, A.: The evaluation of BCI and PEBL-based attention tests. Acta Polytech. Hungarica. **15**, 225–249 (2018). https://doi.org/10.12700/aph.15.3.2018.3.13
14. Ujbanyi, T., Katona, J., Sziladi, G., Kovari, A.: Eye-tracking analysis of computer networks exam question besides different skilled groups. In: 2016 7th IEEE International Conference on Cognitive Infocommunications (CogInfoCom), pp. 277–282 (2016). https://doi.org/10.1109/coginfocom.2016.7804561
15. Prantner, C.K.: The evaluation of the results of an eye tracking based usability tests of the so called instructor's portal framework (http://tanitlap.ektf.hu/csernaiz). In: 2015 6th IEEE International Conference on Cognitive Infocommunications (CogInfoCom), pp. 459–465 (2015). https://doi.org/10.1109/coginfocom.2015.7390637
16. Wang, J., Antonenko, P., Celepkolu, M., Jimenez, Y., Fieldman, E., Fieldman, A.: Exploring relationships between eye tracking and traditional usability testing data. Int. J. Hum. Comput. Interact. 1–12 (2018). https://doi.org/10.1080/10447318.2018.1464776
17. Tula, A.D., Kurauchi, A., Coutinho, F., Morimoto, C.: Heatmap explorer: an interactive gaze data visualization tool for the evaluation of computer interfaces. In: Proceedings of the 15th Brazilian Symposium Human Factors Computing Systems, pp. 24:1–24:9 (2016). https://doi.org/10.1145/3033701.3033725
18. Räihä, K., Aula, A., Majaranta, P., Rantala, H.: Static visualization of temporal eye-tracking data. In: Costabile, M.F., Paternò, F. (eds.) INTERACT 2005, vol. 3585, pp. 946–949. Springer, Heidelberg (2005). https://doi.org/10.1007/11555261_76
19. Babicsné-Horváth, M., Hercegfi, K.: Early results of a usability evaluation of two digital human model -based ergonomic software applying eye-tracking methodology: comparison of the usability of vivelab and jack software. In: Proceedings of the 10th IEEE International Conference on Cognitive Infocommunications : CogInfoCom 2019, pp. 205–210 (2019)

Sensory Design in Games: Beyond Visual-Based Experiences

Priscilla Maria Cardoso Garone[1]([⊠]), Sérgio Nesteriuk[2],
and Gisela Belluzzo de Campos[2]

[1] Universidade Federal do Espírito Santo, Vitória, Brazil
prigarone@gmail.com
[2] Universidade Anhembi Morumbi, Sao Paulo, Brazil

Abstract. To play is often known as a voluntary process in a temporary sphere with a unique disposition. In contemporaneity, games are a promising field for application and study, since they are sociocultural products with great impacts on the economy and in technology. Throughout the history of the development of this medium, the sensory experience included the perceptual channels of vision, hearing, and cognition to solve problems. Therefore, this study presents the theme through a systematic literature review and describes several applications and approaches that accentuate and diversify the user's sensory experience. The main contribution of the study is to elucidate and illustrate the multisensory experiences that involve the use of the kinesthetic system (voice and body) and the haptic system (smell and taste). Moreover, visual experiences have been enhanced through augmented reality, virtual reality, and 3-D visualization. The results and discussion note the particularities of this media and aspects for the feasibility of future applications. It is hoped that this research will pave the way for future work involving case studies of games that allow for aesthetic experiences beyond solely visual experiences to deepen the sensitivity analysis and the process of generating meaning as well as emotional, and cognitive responses.

Keywords: Games · Design · Experience

1 Introduction

From a social point of view, games are extremely important for the development of man and culture, as play activities have been present since ancient times. Games satisfy natural impulses for playfulness, pleasure and spontaneous effort. They are stimulating activities that develop motor, psychological, and/or intellectual abilities. By being present in everyday life, play influences and is influenced by society and culture. It also promotes the development of certain technologies and areas of knowledge.

One of these areas is game design; as understood by (Schell 2008), game design is the act of deciding what a game should be. Even if alone, the game is just an artifact. Thus, the game designer is responsible for designing the experience made possible by the game when people play it. The goal of the game designer is to design the gameplay

© Springer Nature Switzerland AG 2020
V. G. Duffy (Ed.): HCII 2020, LNCS 12199, pp. 322–333, 2020.
https://doi.org/10.1007/978-3-030-49907-5_23

by conceiving and elaborating rules and structures that result in an experience for players (Salen and Zimmerman 2004, 19).

Technological expansion permeates game design, transforming data processing, the representation of sounds and images, players' experiences, and the designer's own thinking and design. Games are not just visual and interaction is possible in many ways. The discussion of the aesthetic experience in games goes beyond visuals and game devices. They are often designed and improved to enhance and stimulate our senses through new ways of interaction.

In this paper, devices and applications regarding the sensory experience in games beyond just visual will be presented using a systematic review of literature and examples to illustrate the discussions. The objective of this study is to present the theme of sensory experience in games as being beyond visual. This will be accomplished through a systematic literature review and case studies on applications that aim to accentuate and diversify the user experience.

This study was driven by the question: "How do games' interfaces, input, and output devices allow for interactions that provide a sensory experience beyond just visual?". Literature searching included books and journal articles in the field of game design and aesthetic experience. A keywords search was used for the terms "game aesthetics" or "games aesthetics" or "aesthetics in games" or "aesthetic experience" and "games". The contributions found were filtered and 29 studies were included and classified into 5 categories (Fig. 1):

- **Game design and aesthetics**: studies concerning aesthetics in game design can be found in (Schell 2008); (Salen and Zimmerman 2004); (Zichermann and Cunningham 2011) and (Marache-Francisco and Brangier 2015).
- **Player aesthetic experience**: research about player aesthetic experience and immersion (Sommerseth 2009).
- **Game aesthetics:** contributions about aesthetics in videogames devices and playability (Niedenthal 2008); (Kirkpatrick 2009) and (Gouveia 2010).
- **Sensory aesthetic experience in games**: works about aesthetics experience in computer games as a sensory phenomenon (Jeong, Biocca, and Bohil 2012), (Friedman 2014), (Kim and Sung 2015) and (Wang et al. 2015).
- **Aesthetic experience rather than visual in games**: studies presenting new or discussing old application or device in which visual is not the main interaction input or output (Newman 2002); (Hekkert 2006); (Gaudy et al. 2006); (Neumark et al. 2010); (Luz 2010); (Juul 2010); (Zuanon and Lima 2011); (Medeiros Filho et al. 2013); (Tobin 2013); (Johnson, Wyeth, and Sweetser 2014); (Ng et al. 2015); (Linowes 2015); (Leblanc and Chaput 2016); (Chen et al. 2016) and (McGregor et al. 2016).

The main contribution of the study is to elucidate and illustrate the multisensory experiences that involve the use of the kinesthetic system (voice and body) and the haptic system (smell and taste). In this sense, this research is distinguished from the others by bringing together these applications and devices in which the sensory experience is not driven only through visual input or output devices and proposes a comparison and discussion of the interaction mechanisms for player experience beyond visual in games.

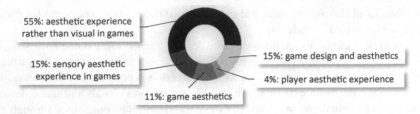

55%: aesthetic experience rather than visual in games

15%: sensory aesthetic experience in games

11%: game aesthetics

15%: game design and aesthetics

4%: player aesthetic experience

Fig. 1. Classification results and research trends of publications about game aesthetics.

2   Sensory Experience in Games: Beyond Visual

Regarding the understanding of a player's experience and immersion, (Sommerseth 2009, 1) argues that art in games cannot be restricted to visual media. Therefore, it is appropriate to consider other qualities of computer games, such as interactivity. These qualities are intrinsic to the gameplay experience and central to an understanding of computer games, as related to the notion of choice, control, and effort. The author noted that games present users not only with a visual environment to experience but also with a fictional world to explore. Hence, it is essential to understand and provide new ways to fulfill this task through sensory stimulation and sensory-perceptual systems.

(Niedenthal 2009, 2) summarized the three most common understandings of game aesthetics in the literature. The first refers to the sensory phenomena in the game (visual, aural, haptic, and embodied). The second refers to those aspects of digital games that are shared with other art forms. The third is that an expression of the game is experienced as pleasure, emotion, sociability, and form-giving. The author alleged that the term "aesthetics" needs to be critically reexamined within a game studies context and noted the need for understanding games as tools for sensory and embodied play, creative activity, and an aesthetic experience.

(Kirkpatrick 2009, 135) discussed the role of video game controller in-game aesthetics, as it marks the difference between watching a screen and interacting with an input device. The author emphasized that good play is about feeling, exploring, and altering the field of tension. To do so, while playing a game, we do not look at our hands with the controller or think about its syntax. The controller keeps the player physically attached to the game and involves a physical tension for the player. As we play, the less attention we pay to the controller and its syntax, the more connected we are with the game experience.

(Gouveia 2010, 19) explained that an aesthetic experience in games incorporates sensory and cognitive aspects through playability. The author argued that the magic circle[1] creates an emotional and aesthetic experience for entertainment in which performance has its place.

According to (Zichermann and Cunningham 2011, 36), one of the most well-known game design frameworks is MDA (mechanics, dynamics and aesthetics). While mechanics define the game's functionality, dynamics are the player's interaction with and

---

[1] The magic circle is an expression used by (Huizinga 2016, 10) as a temporary space for play; it is closed shape, maintained in secrecy, and guided by rules and laws.

response to the mechanics, and the aesthetics are the player's emotional response to the mechanics and dynamics. The sensory-motor dimension of a game uses multimodal coding (visual, audio and haptic) for aesthetics and communication, as was explained by (Marache-Francisco and Brangier 2015, 11).

Other studies about games and their sensory and aesthetic experience can be found in (Niedenthal 2008), (Jeong et al. 2012), (Friedman 2014), (Kim and Sung 2015), (Wang et al. 2015), and (Wang et al. 2016).

2.1 Vibration: A Data Output System Beyond the Audiovisual

(Newman 2002, 416) explained the importance of the insertion and popularization of a vibration system in video game controllers. The author noted that the controller for the Nintendo 64 console had an opening to insert the *Rumble Pak* accessory, which allows users to feel vibrations during play. According to the Nintendo company website[2], the *Rumble Pak* was released in 1997 as a feedback device that can be embedded in the control and allows the player to feel a tremor. For example, the player feels the vibration when his avatar collides with some in-game object.

Following the trend, Sega and Sony launched vibration systems for their console controllers (the *Dreamcast's Vibration Pack* and the *PlayStation's DualShock* controller). Although the vibration of a video game controller can be seen as a way to reinforce the audiovisual stimuli and validate its role as a haptic device, (Newman 2002, 415) argued that, by incorporating tactile output, video game designers recognize and reinforce the connection between the player and controller, breaking the apparent supremacy of audiovisual outputs.

2.2 Touch, Voice, Blow: An Input System in Addition to the Buttons

To expand the possibilities of interaction and visualization, in 2004 Nintendo developed the Nintendo DS (abbreviation for dual screen) portable console (Tobin 2013, 15). The system uses a lower touch-sensitive screen that can be accessed through the use of a Stylus accessory (pen). The top screen works in combination with the lower screen as an information display screen but not as an additional input device.

According to (Tobin 2013, 54), all types of video games require some kind of bodily involvement. Cases such as the use of the mouth to blow the Nintendo DS's microphone are out of what has become conventional interaction of the body with the game interface. In some games, the uses of the microphone are mimetic, as in the case of blowing and extinguishing candles.

With respect to the use of the voice to interact with games, as cited by (Neumark et al. 2010, 291), in 2000 Nintendo released the title Hey You Pikachu! for the Nintendo 64 console. This was one of the first games to employ the use of voice as an input element for data and control in a video game through the use of the Nintendo 64 VRU (voice recognition unit).

---

[2] Nintendo Buyer's Guide: Rumble Pak. Retrieved from: https://www.nintendo.com/consumer/buyers_guide.jsp.

2.3 Body and Performance: A Kinesthetic and Mimetic Input System

(Medeiros Filho, Calado, and Neves 2013, 331) explained that the Nintendo Wii console introduced an innovative control method. It utilized a system (based on movement and captured by accelerometers) that allowed the system to reach a new audience. (Luz 2010, 87) clarified that the console and the Wii Remote controller work with motion recognition, acceleration, and targeting. The author reported that, when announcing the console, developers promised an innovative control method, stating that "it is not about what you play but how you play." The author also ratified that this concept assured Nintendo the innovation that differentiated it from the consoles of their competitors Microsoft and Sony.

According to (Juul 2010, 107), the success of the Nintendo Wii console was because the controllers allowed for the imitation of real actions in games. The author asserted that this made mimetic interface games easier to learn than traditional video games. For example, these games encouraged the player to imagine that the Wii controller was a "real" tennis racket that he swings to hit the ball and not a controller button pushed in order to do so. The author argued that traditional gaming forces the player to imagine their bodily presence in the gaming world while mimetic interface games allow them to play from the perspective of the physical presence of the player in the real world. (Luz 2010, 88) explained that this type of interaction uses movements that include muscular memory that act in conjunction with cognitive visual abilities to make the sensory and immersive experience friendlier and more spontaneous.

(Johnson et al. 2014, 503) confirmed that, with the advent of the Nintendo Wii console, the Sony's accessories PlayStation Move and PlayStation Eye, and the XBOX console's accessory Kinect, active games that require physical activity have become increasingly popular. While PlayStation Move and Nintendo Wii gameplay require the player to hold a controller, the XBOX Kinect has a camera that identifies the player's movement in a three-dimensional space without having to manipulate a controller.

2.4 3-D and Augmented Reality: Enlargement of the Visual System

Regarding the expansion of the visual experience, we highlight the Nintendo 3DS console that was released in 2011. The console aims to visualize 3-D images without the need for special 3-D glasses2. The console also allows for the capture of 3-D photos and videos with the attached cameras and can view images in augmented reality.

According to (Ng et al. 2015, 56), augmented reality (AR) is a version of reality with enhancements created by the use of technology to overlay digital information onto an image viewed through a device. Usually, the reality is recorded through a camera and then elements are added through software. The authors mentioned the Nintendo 3DS console as a popular example of augmented reality, since it comes with cards that are recognized by the software and can show three-dimensional models that are superimposed on the device screen.

2.5 Augmented Reality, Ubiquity, and Walking

(Leblanc and Chaput 2016, 1) reported that there is an urgent need to elaborate new strategies to motivate people to get out and move more due to increased sedentary lifestyles. In this sense, the free-to-play smartphone game Pokémon Go uses augmented reality and georeferencing to offer outdoor fun with physical activity.

Pokémon Go encourages physical activity by having players walk around in search of Pokémon and use their smartphones to "catch" them. The application uses gamification[3] to motivate players to walk to increase their chances of finding new Pokémon and accelerate the in-game "egg incubation" process. The gamification of physical activity can cause people to integrate gaming into their daily lives which, according to the authors, is an effective method of disease prevention and health maintenance.

2.6 Virtual Reality: Broaden the Visual and Immersive Experience

Virtual reality (VR) is a device-aided computer-generated simulation of a three-dimensional environment that seems real to the person who experiences it (Linowes 2015, 3). The author clarified that virtual reality currently involves the use of a head-mounted display that allows interaction simply by moving the head and using manual controls or motion sensors. The goal is to achieve a strong sense of being present in the virtual environment through the impression of visualizing an environment or image not bound by a screen. The Oculus Rift and the PlayStation VR are examples of these kinds of devices.

Regarding augmented haptic gaming, one example is the SoEs (Sword of Elements) project, presented by (Chen et al. 2016, 71). It is based on annexing reality that uses real physical objects and haptic retargeting. This provides a prop-based feedback that coincides with the virtual object to allow the user to have the tactile sensation simulated through a wearable interface, such as the wind of a flying arrow or the heat of iron of a weaponsmith.

Another initiative that can be cited is the FeelReal project, which consisted of the development of a helmet and a mask for virtual reality experiences. It allows the user to explore virtual environments through the involvement of other senses beyond sight and sound. With a 3-D audio system for better immersion and a high-resolution display equivalent to the best smartphones, the mask has micro-coolers and micro-heaters that allow the user to feel cold and hot wind, motors with adjustable vibration levels, an ultrasonic ionization system that produces water mist, a removable cartridge with seven odors, and a microphone.

This project stands out as an interesting proposal for the insertion of olfactory perception into gaming experiences. According to (Hekkert 2006, 163), smell is a rich source for associations and serves our ability to memorize past places and events.

2.7 Neuroscience: Emotion as an Element of Play

The results of a design and neuroscience research project by (Zuanon and Lima 2011, 1) referred to the project titled NeuroBodyGame, a wearable computer that allowed the user to play a game using neurological and physiological signals. The game and wireless wearable interface react to the user's emotions during the interaction

---

[3] (Kapp 2012, 1) defined gamification as the use of game elements and game-thinking to engage people, motivate action, and promote learning.

The authors explained that the device uses the concept of affective computing in which machines are able to recognize, communicate and react to user's emotional state using bio-interfaces, which provide interaction conditions from the biological conditions of the user. Thereby, an organic interaction between the user and game is promoted through the use of wearable interfaces that will change according to the user's thoughts and emotions at the moment of interaction. In NeuroBodyGame, two biosensors were used as input channels to capture physiological information. The wearable computer interpreted data and reacted by changing its colors and providing vibrations. Thus, the wearable interface allowed the player's physiological conditions to be influential elements of the game, thereby favoring unique experiences for each user.

3   Discussion

The study focused on the following questions: How do games' interfaces, input, and output devices allow for interactions that provide a sensory experience beyond just visual? Other than visual, what kinds of perception are required and developed in the applications presented?

Table 1 contrasts the sensory possibilities provided by the output devices of the previously presented applications. The applications that most provide sensory possibilities for the output devices are as follows. The Oculus Rift and PlayStation VR expand the possibilities of visual perception with virtual reality, 3-D images, and 3-D audio. Additionally, the FeelReal project presents the same characteristics of the Oculus Rift and PS VR and enables sensory experiences through smell, the haptic system through the perception of temperature, and tactile perception of vibration.

Table 1. Output of game devices and their sensory potentialities.

Sensory potentialities	Game devices
Visual (3-D)	FeelReal Nintendo 3DS Oculus Rift PlayStation VR
Visual (AR)	Nintendo DS Nintendo 3DS Pokémon Go
Visual (VR)	FeelReal Helmet Oculus Rift PlayStation VR
Aural (3-D)	FeelReal Helmet Oculus Rift PlayStation VR

(*continued*)

Table 1. (*continued*)

Sensory potentialities	Game devices
Haptic (vibration)	DC Vibration Pak FeelReal Helmet N64 Rumble Pak NeuroBodyGame PS DualShock PS Move Pokémon Go SoEs Wii Controller
Haptic (kinesthetic)	PlayStation Move Wii Controller XBOX Kinect
Haptic (temperature)	FeelReal Helmet SoEs
Olfactory	FeelReal Helmet

Table 2 compares the game devices and applications and considers the aspects of the output devices that stimulate multisensory experiences, the input mechanisms, and the response evoked by sensory stimulation through which the player interacts with the game.

Table 2. Comparison between outputs beyond visual and aural, inputs, and response evoked by game devices and applications.

Device/application	Output	Input	Response evoked
PS DualShock N64 Rumble Pak DC Vibration Pak	Haptic (vibration)	Button controller	Attention and feedback
Wii Controller PlayStation Move	Haptic (vibration and kinesthetic)	Button controller with space and movement recognition	Movement; bodily kinesthetic intelligence; attention and feedback
XBOX Kinect	Haptic (kinesthetic)	Kinesthetic, space and movement recognition	Movement; bodily kinesthetic intelligence; attention and feedback
Nintendo 64 VRU	–	Microphone	Linguistic intelligence, attention and feedback

(*continued*)

Table 2. (*continued*)

Device/application	Output	Input	Response evoked
Nintendo DS Nintendo 3DS	Visual (two screens, 3-D, and augmented reality with N3DS)	Touch screen, stylus pen, microphone, buttons	Linguistic intelligence, attention and feedback
NeuroBodyGame	Haptic (vibration)	Wearable interface	Attention and feedback
SoEs	Haptic (temperature and vibration)	Wearable interface	Attention and feedback
Pokémon Go	Haptic (vibration and kinesthetic); visual (augmented reality)	Touch screen	Movement, ubiquity, attention and feedback
FeelReal Helmet	Haptic (temperature e vibration); visual (virtual reality); aural (3-D audio); olfactory	Button controller and microphone	Spatial intelligence, immersion by visual isolation in a virtual environment, 3-D audio, smells, haptic system, attention and feedback
PlayStation VR Oculus Rift	Visual (virtual reality) and aural (3-D audio with earphone)	Button controller and microphone	Spatial intelligence, immersion by visual isolation in a virtual environment, 3-D audio, attention and feedback

With input mechanisms, we emphasize the presence of a microphone in many devices and applications that allow for voice interaction and the exercise of linguistic intelligence[4], outside of the presence of button controllers. Among the possibilities that stand out, we underline the touch screen and *Stylus* accessory of Nintendo DS and 3DS consoles and the interactions through movement in devices such as the Wii controller, *PlayStation Move*, and XBOX *Kinect*.

Among the responses evoked by the sensory stimulation through the output systems, we highlight the possibilities with the Wii controller, *PlayStation Move*, and XBOX *Kinect* devices. They require movement and bodily kinesthetic intelligence[5] and the requested attention and feedback provided by any vibrations of the controller (in the case of Wii and PlayStation devices). The N64 Voice Recognition Unit and the Nintendo DS and 3DS evoke the usage of linguistic intelligence with the use of voice.

---

[4] (Gardner 2006, 13) explained linguistic intelligence as the verbal ability to address written and spoken words and sensibility to sounds, meaning and word rhythm, involving interpretation and explanation through communication and language.

[5] Bodily kinesthetic intelligence was defined by (Gardner 2006, 10) as the capacity to control the movements of the body and address objects ably, with dexterity, agility coordination, and body balance.

The *FeelReal Helmet*, *PlayStation VR* and *Oculus Rift* Head-Mounted Displays require spatial intelligence[6] and provide greater immersion due to visual isolation in a virtual environment and 3-D audio.

4 Limitations and Future Directions

The study attempted to demonstrate examples of applications and devices that allow a multisensory approach to gaming. However, vision is still the main receptor and preceptor for the gaming experience, and therefore the technology of its devices is based on that specific paradigm.

While the existing literature cited act as an important contributor to the immersion in games, little research has explored this topic. It is relevant to mention Kinect games, which uses movements and haptic devices to interact (Vaisshali and Swaminathan 2015) and audio games, which are games that are accessible to the blind, in which the communication process depends on sounds rather than on a specific language (Gaudy, Natkin, and Archambault 2006, 263). In this kind of game, the information output is sonorous rather than visual-graphic. In general, the menu options, rules, and other auxiliary elements for gameplay are described by a narrator, and the constant presence of sounds guide the player throughout the experience. Some of the existing initiatives are projects of web portals, such as *Audio Games*[7] and *Blind Fold Games*[8], which provide a series of free-to-play sound-based games for users who are blind or visually impaired.

It is still a challenge to design games that consider the particularities and limitations of users with some deficiency, especially visual deficiencies. It is necessary that design, along with other areas, such as Ophthalmology, interact to discuss the subject in its complexity to propose inclusive solutions. The absence of sound, haptic perception, smell, or taste can reduce the experience but does not make it infeasible. Designers have the responsibility to ensure access to entertainment through assistive technology and inclusive design. Therefore, investing in research and games that stimulate other senses beyond sight is an act for inclusive design and explores the potential of the medium.

During the research, the only initiative found involving taste in games was *Pixelate*[9], a project that gamifies the act of eating and challenges the player to consider what he eats. However, it is relevant to note that taste, while present and relevant to the experience of the gamification of eating, has little to no role in the game. Actions are validated not by taste but by a special fork that identifies food.

It is important to note that little variety has been observed in the exploration of touch, especially in the use of motors that produce vibrations in controllers and wearable devices. The smell sense was reported in the *FeelReal* project, and this is believed to be a trigger for expanding the possibilities for output devices that aim to provide sensory experiences beyond the existing widespread audiovisual.

---

[6] According to (Gardner 2006, 13), spatial intelligence is the ability to think imaginatively, elaborating a mental model of a spatial world and being capable of actively using this model.

[7] Welcome at AudioGames.net! Retrieved from: http://www.audiogames.net/.

[8] Marty's Blindfold Games: Audio games for the visually impaired community. Retrieved from: https://blog.objectiveed.com/.

[9] Pixelate. Retrieved from: http://sureskumar.com/?p=589/.

Regarding wearable interfaces, other initiatives were found, in addition to Neuro-BodyGame, such as the $ARAIG^{10}$ project that uses special clothes to allow the user to feel vibrations and impacts. As noted by (McGregor et al. 2016, 92), this interface can be used as a way to enhance resilience and tactical training as a serious game. The VUE VR^{11} project allows for more interaction with virtual reality through a special treadmill and tennis shoes. The project cited in this research, *NeuroBodyGame*, captures brain signals as an input device for gaming, and it is an important step for design and neuroscience. Notwithstanding these initiatives, these kinds of applications are still scarce and need to be expanded.

This research analyzed the sensorial dimension of games. It is hoped that this research will pave the way for future work involving case studies of games that allow for aesthetic experiences beyond solely visual experiences to deepen the sensitivity analysis and the process of generating meaning as well as emotional, and cognitive responses.

Acknowledgement. We are grateful to the Anhembi Morumbi University for funding the technical editing and language translation services.

References

Chen, Y.-S., Han, P.-H., Hsiao, J.-C., Hung, Y.-P.: SoEs: attachable augmented haptic on gaming controller for immersive interaction. In: UIST 2016 Adjunct - Proceedings of the 29th Annual Symposium on User Interface Software and Technology, pp. 71–72 (2016)

Friedman, A.: The role of visual design in game design. Games Culture **10**(3), 291–305 (2014)

Gardner, H.: Multiple Intelligences: New Horizons in Theory and Practice. Basic Books, New York (2006)

Gaudy, T., Natkin, S., Archambault, D.: Playing audiogames without instructions for use? To do without an instruction leaflet or without language itself. In: Proceedings of CGAMES 2006 - 9th International Conference on Computer Games: Artificial Intelligence and Mobile Systems, pp. 263–268 (2006)

Gouveia, P.: Artes e Jogos Digitais: estética e design da experiência lúdica. Arts and digital games: aesthetics and design of a ludic experience. Edições Universitárias Lusófonas, Lisboa (2010)

Hekkert, P.: Design aesthetics: principles of pleasure in design. Psychol. Sci. **48**(2), 157–172 (2006)

Huizinga, J.: Homo Ludens: A Study of the Play-Element in Culture. Beacon Press, Boston (2016)

Jeong, E.J., Biocca, F.A., Bohil, C.J.: Sensory realism and mediated aggression in video games. Comput. Hum. Behav. **28**(5), 1840–1848 (2012)

Johnson, D., Wyeth, P., Sweetser, P.: Creating good lives through computer games. In: Huppert, F.A., Cooper, C.L. (eds.) Wellbeing: A Complete Reference Guide, Interventions and Policies to Enhance Wellbeing, vol. VI. Wiley Blackwell, Malden (2014)

Juul, J.: A Casual Revolution: Reinventing Video Games and Their Players. The MIT Press, Cambridge (2010)

Kapp, K.M.: The Gamification of Learning and Instruction: Game Based Methods and Strategies for Training and Education. Pfeiffer, San Francisco (2012)

Kim, T., Sung, J.: The aesthetic view of digital games: following the concept of Heidegger's art theory. Int. J. Appl. Eng. Res. **10**(18), 39005–39007 (2015)

---

[10] ARAIG: as real as it gets. Retrieved from: http://araig.com/.

[11] VUE VR: About. Retrieved from: https://twitter.com/vuetechnologie/.

Kirkpatrick, G.: Controller, hand, screen: aesthetic form in the computer game. Games Culture 4(2), 127–143 (2009)

Leblanc, A.G., Chaput, J.-P., Chaput. Pokémon Go: a game changer for the physical inactivity crisis? Preventive medicine, pp. 0091–7435. ScienceDirect (Elsevier B.V.) (2016)

Linowes, J.: Unity Virtual Reality Projects: Explore the World of Virtual Reality by Building Immersive and Fun VR Projects Using Unity 3D. Packt Publishing, Birmingham (2015)

Luz, A.R.: Vídeo Games: História, Linguagem e Expressão Gráfica. Video Games: History, Language and Graphic Expression. Blucher, São Paulo (2010)

Marache-Francisco, C., Brangier, E.: The gamification experience: UXD with a gamification background. In: Information Resources Management Association (USA). Gamification: Concepts, Methodologies, Tools, and Applications, vol. 1. Information Science Reference Hershey PA (2015)

McGregor, C., Bonnis, B., Stanfield, B., Stanfield, M.: Design of the ARAIG haptic garment for enhanced resilience assessment and development in tactical training serious games. In: IEEE International Conference on Consumer Electronics. Berlin (2016)

Medeiros Filho, M., Calado, F., Neves, A.M.M.: Jogabilidade assimétrica: Uma análise do Nintendo Wii U. Asymmetric gameplay: an analysis of Nintendo Wii U. In: Proceedings of the XII Brazilian Symposium on Games and Digital Entertainment (SBGames 2013), Arts and Design Track. Editora Mackenzie, São Paulo (2013)

Neumark, N., Gibson, R., Leeuwen, T. (eds.): Voice: Vocal Aesthetics in Digital Arts and Media. The MIT Press, Cambridge (2010)

Newman, J.: In search of the videogame player: The lives of Mario. New Media Soc. 4(3), 405–422 (2002)

Ng, G., Chow, M., Salgado, A.: Toys and mobile applications: current trends and related privacy issues. In: Hung, P.C.K. (ed.) Mobile Services for Toy Computing, pp. 51–76. Springer, Heidelberg (2015). https://doi.org/10.1007/978-3-319-21323-1_4

Niedenthal, S.: Complicated Shadows: The Aesthetic Significance of Simulated Illumination in Digital Games. Blekinge Technical University (2008)

Niedenthal, S.: What we talk about when we talk about game aesthetics. In: Breaking New Ground: Innovation in Games, Play, Practice and Theory - Proceedings of DiGRA 2009. London; United Kingdom (2009)

Salen, K., Eric, Z.: Rules of Play: Game Design Fundamentals. MIT Press, Cambridge (2004)

Schell, J.: The Art of Game Design: A Book of Lenses. Morgan Kaufmann, Burlington (2008)

Tobin, S.: Portable Play in Everyday Life: The Nintendo DS. Palgrave Macmillan, London (2013)

Sommerseth, H.: Exploring game aesthetics. In: 4th Digital Games Research Association International Conference: Breaking New Ground: Innovation in Games, Play, Practice and Theory, DiGRA 2009, London, United Kingdom (2009)

Vaisshali, S., Swaminathan, P.: Kinect games for visually impaired using real time sensory substitution. Global J. Pure Appl. Math. 11(3), 1475–1482 (2015)

Wang, X., Goh, D.H.-L., Lim, E.-P., Vu, A.W.L.: Aesthetic experience and acceptance of human computation games. In: Allen, R., Hunter, J., Zeng, M. (eds.) ICADL 2015. LNCS, vol. 9469, pp. 264–273. Springer, Heidelberg (2015). https://doi.org/10.1007/978-3-319-27974-9_28

Wang, X., Goh, D.H.-L., Lim, E.-P., Vu, W.L.A.: Understanding the determinants of human computation game acceptance: the effects of aesthetic experience and output quality. Online Inf. Rev. 40(4), 481–496 (2016). Research Collection School of Information Systems

Zichermann, G., Cunningham, C.: Gamification by Design: Implementing Game Mechanics in Web and Mobile Apps. O'Reilly Media Inc., Sebastopol (2011)

Zuanon, R., Lima Jr, G.: NeuroBodyGame: the design of a wearable computer for playing games through brain signals. In: Proceedings of ISEA 2011: International Symposium for Electronic Arts. Istambul, Turkey (2016)

Virtual Reality and Artificial Intelligence in Mobile Computing and Applied Ergonomics: A Bibliometric and Content Analysis

Chidubem Nuela Enebechi[✉] and Vincent G. Duffy[✉]

School of Industrial Engineering, Purdue University, West Lafayette, IN 47907, USA
{cenebech,duffy}@purdue.edu

Abstract. Virtual Reality (VR) is a budding field in the realm of technology, and it also happens to be one of the main sub-topics entwined with the field of Artificial Intelligence (AI). The main idea of VR also revolves around Virtual Environments. Virtual Environments (VE) contribute to the creation of an out of the world experience for users, by allowing them to interact with the digital universe. Applied Ergonomics is a concept that involves designing for people and since VR is becoming a more mainstream technology being incorporated in various facets of people's lives, like mobile computing, it is only imperative that a bibliometric analysis is carried out to show the relationship between VR in mobile computing and applied ergonomics. This paper shows the connection between VR, Human Computer Interaction and ergonomics using software programs like MaxQDA, Harzing, VOSviewer, and Mendeley. The main keywords used in this bibliometric analysis were Virtual Reality, Artificial Intelligence, Human-Computer Interaction, and Ergonomics. These words were continuously repeated in the articles and chapters referenced in this paper.

Keywords: Virtual Reality · Artificial Intelligence · Bibliometric analysis · Human-Computer Interaction · Ergonomics · Content analysis

1 Introduction and Background

1.1 Problem Statement

Technological advancements and innovative concepts in the world of Science Technology, Engineering and Mathematics (STEM), have led to a breakthrough and cutting-edge solution to various projects with AI, most especially the VR realm. The computational power derived from this breakthrough has created additional opportunities that support more human problem-solving opportunities and provide optimum expertise in the field of automation. Since ergonomics also deals with the efficiency of design for humans, it is necessary to show the relationship between new and innovative technologies such as virtual reality to the field of applied ergonomics.

This paper aims to show the link and connection between VR and applied ergonomics through a bibliometric and content analysis. The analysis will be done through software

© Springer Nature Switzerland AG 2020
V. G. Duffy (Ed.): HCII 2020, LNCS 12199, pp. 334–345, 2020.
https://doi.org/10.1007/978-3-030-49907-5_24

programs including Mendeley, MaxQDA and Harzing. The main point of the analysis will be to show the strong correlation between VR and ergonomics using keywords such as Virtual Reality, Artificial Intelligence, Human-Computer Interaction, and Ergonomics.

In order to motivate this systematic review of virtual reality within digital human modeling, it may be useful to consider the following. Though not initially apparent, virtual reality has traditionally been an important part of digital human modeling. And many digital human modeling studies and design initiatives have had ergonomics and human factors as a foundation. Applied ergonomics is also considered in this analysis while digital human modeling methodologies have had ergonomics-related applications across many industries in recent years.

A search of "digital human modeling" at AuthorMapper.com recognizes 1975 articles from the years 2002 to present. Based on analytics within AuthorMapper highlighted on the search page, "Virtual reality" is the next leading term among keywords after "ergonomics" and "human factors". With "virtual reality" as a leading term ahead of "digital human modeling" within the database of related articles on "digital human modeling", it is important to understand the emerging trends associated with virtual reality that are in this analysis and article.

2 Research Methodology

2.1 Trend Data

Figure 1 illustrates a trend graph data done through the report analysis on the Web of Science platform. The graph shows that the terms "Artificial Intelligence" and "Applied

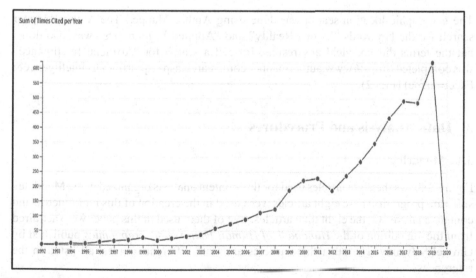

Fig. 1. Trend graph data of keywords "Artificial Intelligence (Virtual reality) and Applied Ergonomics" between the year 1992 up until 2019

Ergonomics" have been cited multiple times in several articles. The term also shows a steady increase in the search of the keywords from the year 2012 up until 2018. These are the peak years that these terms became more acknowledged in the world.

2.2 Author Relationship Table

The author relationship table shown below was created through the search of Harzing. A search was done to see the authors that had more content related to Virtual Reality and Applied Ergonomics. The results from the search are laid out in the Table 1 below. Harzing also enables users to collect metadata that can be used to create an information visualization piece in the form of a linked graph.

Table 1. Author relationship table for key words "Artificial Intelligence" and "Applied Ergonomics"

Name of author	Rank	Publisher
JR Wilson	1	Elsevier
PA Howarth	7	Elsevier
L Gamberini	14	Libertpub.com
VG Duffy	25	Taylorfrancis.com
F Biocca	64	MIT Press

2.3 Geographic Location

The geographic location search was done using Author Mapper. The Author Mapper search for the keywords "Virtual Reality" and "Applied Ergonomics" was also done, but the terms did not yield any results. Instead a search for "Artificial Intelligence" was completed (https://www.authormapper.com/search.aspx?q=artificial+intelligence&Facet=name) (Fig. 2).

3   Data Analysis and Procedures

3.1 Mendeley

Figure 3 shows the eight articles used for this content analysis organized in the Mendeley software program. These eight articles were used in the creation of this bibliometric and content analysis. Of the eight total articles, five of them used in this paper were acquired from the 4th edition of the *Handbook of Human Factors and Ergonomics* published by Gavriel Salvendy. The other three articles are from different sources, all listed in the references.

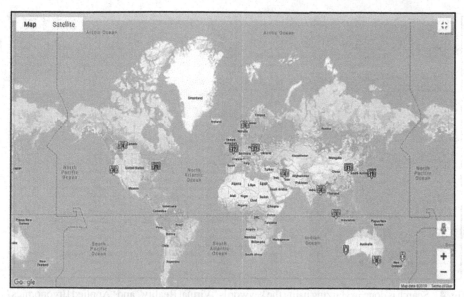

Fig. 2. Geographic locations for the keyword "Artificial Intelligence" generated with Author Mapper (https://www.authormapper.com/)

★	●	▦	Authors	Title	Year	Published In	Added
☆	●	▣	Fahimnia, Behnam; Sarkis, Joseph; Dava...	Green supply chain management: A review and bibliometric analysis	2015	International Journal of ...	Nov 18
☆	●	▣	Duggan, Daniel; Kingsley, Caroline; M...	Exploring Extended Reality as a Simulation Training Tool Through Naturalistic Interacti...	2019		Nov 18
☆	●	▣	Geiger, C; Paelke, V	Structured design of interactive virtual and augmented reality content	2001	Conference Proceeding...	Nov 18
☆	-	▣	Stephanidis, Constantine	Chapter 49 Human Factors in Ambient Intelligence			Nov 18
☆	-	▣	Studies, Case	Chapter 44 Human Factors in Online Communities	2004		Nov 18
☆	-	▣	North, Chris	Visualization Pipeline - Chapter 43 Information Visualization	2005		Nov 18
☆	-	▣	Bennett, Kevin B; Nagy, Allen L; Flach,...	Part 8 Human — Computer Chapter 42 Visual Displays	2012		Nov 18
☆	-	▣	Stanney, Kay M; Cohn, Joseph V	Chapter 36 VIRTUAL ENVIRONMENTS	2012	Handbook of Human Fac...	Nov 18
☆	-	▣	De Crescenzio, Francesca; Frau, Giu...	Design of virtual reality based HMIs (Human Machine Interfaces) of complex systems	2013	Proceedings of the Inter...	Nov 18

Fig. 3. The eight articles used for this content analysis organized in the Mendeley Software. (https://www.mendeley.com/?interaction_required=true)

Harzing

Using the google scholar platform in the Harzing software program, the first search was done.

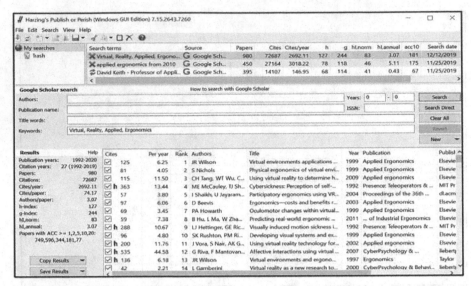

Fig. 4. Search is done in Harzing using the keywords "Virtual Reality" and "Applied Ergonomics" (https://harzing.com/resources/publish-or-perish)

The keywords used were "Virtual Reality" and "Applied Ergonomics". Figure 4 above shows a visual representation of the platform. From the results, there was a total of 980 papers. The search was done for the years 1992–2020. The results yielded a total citation of 72,687 with 74,17 citations per paper.

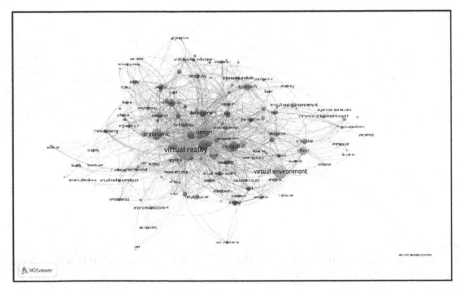

Fig. 5. VOSviewer visualization piece created with metadata from the Harzing search above. (https://www.vosviewer.com/)

3.2 VOS Viewer

Another search was done using the set of keywords, "Artificial Intelligence" and "Applied Ergonomics". More details are provided in the results section.

Metadata from the Harzing Software was used to create an information visualization piece in the form of a graph for the keywords "Virtual Reality" and "Applied Ergonomics".

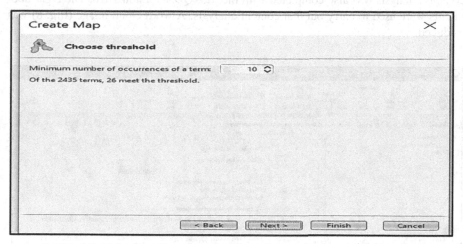

Fig. 6. Minimum occurrence and threshold on VOSviewer. (https://www.vosviewer.com/)

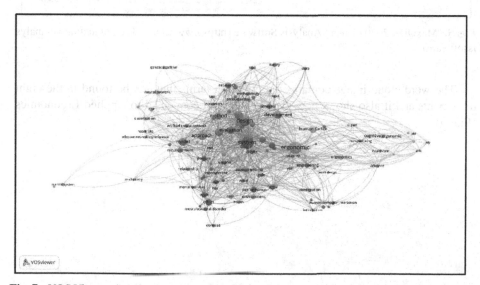

Fig. 7. VOS Viewer visualization piece with additional features selected (https://www.vosviewer.com/)

As indicated in Fig. 6 below, a minimum occurrence of 10 was used for this search, to obtain efficient results. A threshold of 26 was also used. The values used for the occurrence and threshold along with the metadata derived from the search on the Harzing software can be used to replicate the VOSviewer visualization pieces.

3.3 MaxQDA

Content Analysis was also completed with the MaxQDA version 2020. The eight documents were used to carry out that content analysis. A word cloud image (Fig. 8) was produced.

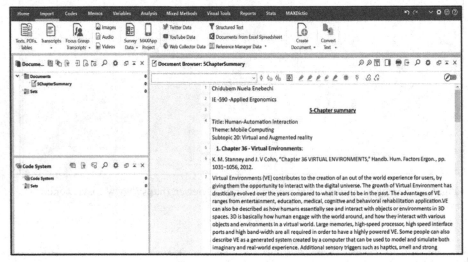

Fig. 8. MaxQDA 2020 Content Analysis Software (https://www.maxqda.com/qualitative-analysissoftware)

The word cloud image contains the common terms that can be found in the eight documents and it also shows how the terms are all connected to Applied Ergonomics (Fig. 9).

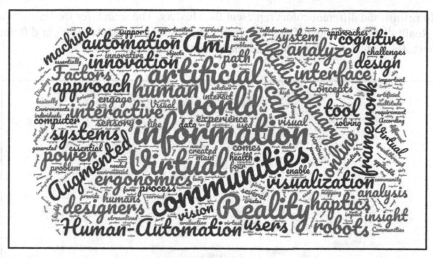

Fig. 9. Bibliometric Analysis with MaxQDA (https://www.maxqda.com/qualitative-analysissoft ware)

4 Co-citation and Further Analysis

A co-citation analysis was carried out on VOS Viewer to show a connection between lead papers and authors in the world of "Virtual Reality" and "Human-Computer Interaction." The results yielded in the analysis are shown in Fig. 10 below.

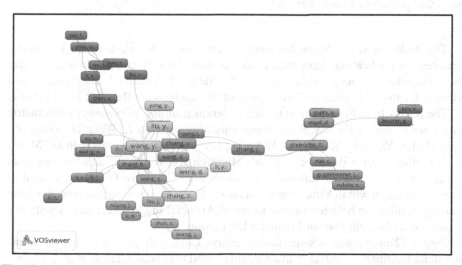

Fig. 10. Co-citation analysis of the terms "Virtual Reality" AND "Human Computer Interaction." (https://www.vosviewer.com/)

In results, the different colors represent the clusters. The search for the terms "Virtual Reality" AND "Human-Computer Interaction" produced a total of eight different clusters. Each cluster contains three-seven nodes that are connected.

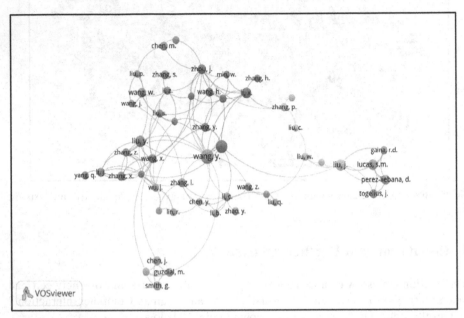

Fig. 11. Co-citation analysis of the terms "Artificial Intelligence" AND Human Computer Interaction. (https://www.vosviewer.com/)

The nodes in each cluster represent a publication. A link between two nodes indicates the publications have been cited together. Another co-citation analysis was also conducted for lead publications in the field of "Artificial Intelligence" and "Human-Computer Interaction". The results of this analysis are shown in Fig. 11 above.

The results from Fig. 11 are not much different from the VOS viewer bibliometric results are shown in Fig. 10. Some popular authors are Guo J., Weng D., Zhang Z., Jiang H., Liu Y., Wang Y, Tarng S., Wang D., Hu Y. with publications such as "Mixed Reality Office System Based on Maslow's Hierarchy of Needs: Towards the long-term immersion in virtual environments" and "Estimating Cognitive Processes Related to Haptic Interaction within Virtual Environments". These are a few publications that have a strong relationship between various facets of Artificial Intelligence, and they show a connection to the term Human-Computer Interaction.

Figure 12 above shows some further analysis that was completed for the terms "Artificial Intelligence" AND "Virtual Reality" AND "Human-Computer Interaction". The results also show a clear connection between authors and their lead publications in their various fields. This result depicts the authors whose publications are strongly entwined with the world of Human-Computer Interaction.

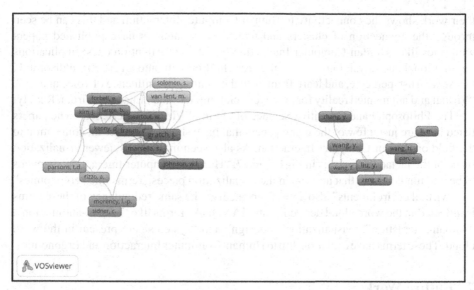

Fig. 12. VOS viewer Co-citation analysis of the terms "Virtual Reality", "Artificial Intelligence" and "Human Computer Interaction. (https://www.vosviewer.com/)

5 Results

While doing searches, the keywords "Cognitive Ergonomics", "Engineering Psychology", "Automation", "Human-Computer Interaction", "Safety Ergonomics", "Contemporary Ergonomic", "Work design" and "Accident Performance" were quite redundant. The regular occurrence of these keywords depicts the fact that there is a correlation between applied ergonomics and AI, especially because VR is a subfield of AI. Therefore, it is safe to say that this was a successful bibliometric and content analysis.

6 Discussion

Terms like "Cognitive Ergonomics" came up on multiple occasions of searches with the keywords "Artificial Intelligence and "Applied Ergonomics". Therefore, there was more emphasis to focus on this keyword. This is unsurprising considering that Cognitive Ergonomics is a field that deals with design systems and the environment, in conjunction with how humans interact with the design system and their cognitive abilities. It can be concluded that the two fields of AI and Applied Ergonomics overlap to birth the world of Cognitive Ergonomics.

According to Fahimnia et al bibliometric review analysis on green supply and chain management, citation analysis is used to examine the degree of connectivity between pairs of nodes/papers a created network (Fahimnia et al. 2015). The analysis results in Figs. 10, 11 and 12 were all connected to Human Computer Interaction and Ergonomics. Authors like Guo J., Weng D., Zhang Z., Jiang H., Liu Y., Wang Y, Tarng S., Wang D., Hu Y., Jyoti V., Lahiri U are shown to appear in different nodes for the various analysis, their work shows the connectivity to Human-Computer Interaction and this can be seen through the connection of clusters and nodes. These authors have published papers with titles like "Human-Computer Interaction based Joint Attention cues: Implications on functional and physiological measures for children with autism spectrum disorder", "How we trust, perceive, and learn from virtual humans: The influence of voice quality", "Virtual and augmented reality for positive social impact" and "Enacting Virtual Reality:

The Philosophy and Cognitive Science of Optimal Virtual Experience". The papers listed here are just a few of the many papers that have shown a significant connection to the field of Human-Computer Interaction. As also seen in the VOSviewer visualization piece of the metadata analysis in Figs. 5 and 7, "Human-Computer Interaction" happens to be a redundant term that appears in the visualization pieces. Terms like "ergonomics" and "virtual environments" also appear repeatedly. The same redundancy of these terms is reflected in the word cloud derived from MAXQDA. Terms like "human-automation", "human-interaction", "visualization", "design" and "systems" are present in the word cloud. These terms have a relationship to Human-Commuter Interaction and Ergonomics.

7 Future Work

As the world keeps expanding so does the innovative technological advancement. Advanced technological innovation in AI and VR have led to groundbreaking solutions and troubleshooting of various problems in different facets of human life. For example, in the medical field, VR has played a huge role in physical therapy for individuals with impaired limbs. AI has also come in very handy in the autonomous driving communities. AI has also been proven to make accurate predictions that provide solutions to propel business organizations forward.

There is also no gainsaying that the application of ergonomics has been effective in ensuring that the design of these advanced technologies is well suited for different objectives in the day-to-day life of a human. However, more research needs to be done in the realm of other areas of ergonomics. For example, Cognitive Ergonomics, which is a subfield of ergonomics whereby human thought processes are replicated to an automated system. Researchers and engineers need to collaborate in the future to create more advanced systems that can replicate the human mind, thoughts, and ideologies.

References

Author Mapper. https://www.authormapper.com/

Bennett, K.B., Nagy, A.L., Flach, J.M.: Visual displays. In: Handbook of Human Factors and Ergonomics, pp. 1179–1208 (2012). Part 8 Human – Computer Interaction, Chapter 42

De Crescenzio, F., Frau, G.: Design of virtual reality based HMIs (human machine interfaces) of complex systems. In: Proceedings of the International Symposium and Workshop on Engineering of Computer Based Systems, pp. 181–186 (2013). https://doi.org/10.1109/ECBS.2013.33

Duggan, D., Kingsley, C., Mazzeo, M., Jenkins, M.: Exploring extended reality as a simulation training tool through naturalistic interactions and enhanced immersion (2019). https://doi.org/10.1007/978-3-030-21565-1_18

Fahimnia, B., et al.: Green supply chain management: a review and bibliometric analysis. Int. J. Prod. Econ. **162**, no. C, 101–114 (2015). https://doi.org/10.1016/j.ijpe.2015.01.003

Geiger, C., Paelke, V.: Structured design of interactive virtual and augmented reality content. In: Conference Proceedings of ..., May 2001. http://citeseerx.ist.psu.edu/viewdoc/download?doi=10.1.1.122.9996&rep=re p1&type=pdf

Harzing. https://harzing.com/resources/publish-or-perish

MaxQDA2020. https://www.maxqda.com/qualitative-analysissoftware?gclid=EAIaIQobChMI r5LLsPiw5gIVGKrsCh2IBglDEAAYASAAEgLy9fD_BwE

Mendeley. https://www.mendeley.com/?interaction_required=true

North, C.: Information visualization. In: Handbook of Human Factors and Ergonomics, pp. 1209–1236 (2012). Part 8 Human – Computer Interaction, Visualization Pipeline - Chapter 43

Stanney, K.M., Joseph, V.C.: Virtual environments. In: Handbook of Human Factors and Ergonomics, pp. 1031–1056 (2012). Part 6 Performance Mondelling, Chapter 36

Stephanidis, C.: Human factors in ambient intelligence. In: Handbook of Human Factors and Ergonomics, pp. 1354–1373 (2012). Part 8 Human – Computer Interaction, Chapter 49

Studies, C.: Human factors in online communities. In: Handbook of Human Factors and Ergonomics, pp. 1237–1249 (2012). Part 8 Human – Computer Interaction, Chapter 44

VOSviewer. https://www.vosviewer.com/

Web of Science. http://login.webofknowledge.com

What Is the State of Smart Glass Research from an OSH Viewpoint? A Literature Review

Daniel Friemert[1]([✉]), Claudia Terschüren[2], Benno Groß[3], Robert Herold[2],
Nicolai Leuthner[1], Christopher Braun[1], Ulrich Hartmann[1], and Volker Harth[2]

[1] University of Applied Sciences Koblenz, Joseph-Rovan-Allee 2, 53424 Remagen, Germany
friemert@hs-koblenz.de
[2] Zentralinstitut für Arbeitsmedizin und Maritime Medizin, Seewartenstraße 10,
20459 Hamburg, Germany
[3] Institut für Arbeitsschutz der Deutschen Gesetzlichen Unfallversicherung, Alte Heerstraße
111, 53757 Sankt Augustin, Germany

Abstract. Data glasses can enable more efficient, mobile and flexible work processes, but at the same time new hazards can arise for employees. A number of questions in the context of safe and healthy work with data glasses and the associated application context have not yet been sufficiently investigated or represented in a normative way. So how can work with data glasses currently be made safe and healthy? The literature review analyzes over 2950 papers in regard to different important OSH viewpoints concerning the new introduction of technology at the workplace.

Keywords: Review · Ergonomics · Occupational · Safety · Health · Smart · Data · Glasses · Stress · Fatigue · Radiation · Efficiency · Eye · Logistics · Picking · Assembly

1 Introduction

Data glasses have been piloted in various areas of the working world for several years and are now also used under real conditions. The areas of application range from logistics, the construction industry and the automotive sector. Because of their design, data glasses are told to have specific advantages over digital work equipment typically used in these areas. Although their functionality is comparable, they must be held in the hand when in use and require the wearer to look away from the work process when recording information.

Three application scenarios for data glasses can currently be identified for operational practice: In intralogistics, employees picking with data glasses (Pick-by-Vision) receive relevant information such as storage location, product details and route guidance through the warehouse via data glasses in their field of vision.

In the assembly and production area, data glasses can be used for training and further education (training on the job), as employees visualize context-based information on the respective work steps via data glasses.

V. G. Duffy (Ed.): HCII 2020, LNCS 12199, pp. 346–364, 2020.
https://doi.org/10.1007/978-3-030-49907-5_25

2 Methods

Our literature review is based on the Cochrane guidelines for scientific reviews, with the exception that our goal was not find the answer to a specific research question, but more to give overview over findings in smart glass research concerning Occupational Safety and Health as a whole. Because of the strong connection between OSH and questions from the medical field papers from this field where also added to this review in specific cases. A group of experts in the field of ergonomics and experts from the field of smart glasses discussed what keywords would yield good results for an overview over the topic. These keywords where then used for a literature search on November 2 using Citavi. The following platforms were included in the search:

• GBV Common Library Network	• BasicBIOSIS (EBSCO)
• Swiss National Library	• MEDLINE Complete (EBSCO)
• Austrian Library Network General Catalogue	• Academic Search Premier (EBSCO)
• German National Library	• Econlit with Full Text (EBSCO)
• PubMed	• INSPEC [EBSCO]
• IEEE Biomedical Engineering Library (OvidSP)	• Psyndex (EBSCO)
• National Library of Medicine	• SocINDEX with Full Text (EBSCO)
• DAHTA database (DIMDI)	• SPORTDiscus with Full Text (EBSCO)
• German Medical Science (DIMDI)	• Scopus (Elsevier)
• EMBASE (Elsevier)	• ScienceDirect (Elsevier)
• LIVIVO, ZB MED, Cologne	

The result was $n_{full} = 2965$ papers including duplicates which were grouped into categories using the keywords used for the search. From these duplicates where removed $n_{dupli} = 1627$ and papers from earlier than the year 2000 ($n_{old} = 101$) where removed resulting in $n_{cleaned} = 1237$ left for title screening. The remaining papers titles were then read by two experts in the field which each gave an advice own their own and in private, if to include the paper into this review on the basis of if the title had anything to do with smart glasses. If the two experts agreed in their advice the paper was included or excluded following this advice. If the experts disagreed the papers title was presented to a small council of five other experts which voted for or against the inclusion. Astonishing for the experts was the fact that very many studies used the terms augmented reality, virtual reality, mixed reality and assisted reality very liberally and without any further definition. This resulted in exclusion of a large portion of the studies ($n_{title\ screen\ exclude} = 1172$) due to their relevance to other kinds of simulated reality rather than to augmented or assisted reality as these glasses are used predominantly in the occupational field of logistics and warehousing. The abstract of the remaining $n_{after\ titlescreen} = 65$ papers was read by the same two experts and the process was repeated in the same manner. The exclusion criteria in this stage was to find out if authors presented results concerning smart glasses which led to an inclusion into the final stage or did a presentation of an ongoing project which lead to an exclusion. The remaining $n_{final} = 22$ papers contained

18 papers and 4 doctoral thesis of which latter is excluded for this paper due to the length of presenting the contents.

Note: For discussing the results of these doctoral thesis please contact us directly.

3   Presentation of the Studies

3.1   Topic: Applications of Smart Glasses

Description of the Studies. In their qualitative review, Damiani et al. [1] examined the application areas of Augmented Reality (AR) and Virtual Reality (VR) technologies in an industrial context. In total they included 39 studies published until 2017 in their article.

In the publication by Moon and Seo [2], a Google Glass application was prototypically implemented to facilitate data access when monitoring safety at construction sites. In this case study, glasses was integrated into a safety management system where the site manager could check the safety status via PCs, mobile phones and Google Glasses.

Berkemeier et al. [3] see an application for glasses in the area of self-service in various industries such as logistics, production and technical customer service.

Borisov et al. [4] report on the use of smart glasses in the final inspection of electronic components in the automotive industry.

In the publication by Niemöller et al. [19], the authors identify various fields of application and related use cases for smart glasses and discuss the challenges involved.

Results. Damiani et al. [1] concluded that the main areas of application for smart glasses are virtual training (22%) and remote maintenance (19%). Other areas of application included product design, logistics, management of production systems and security of production systems. The included studies name easier control of the production line as well as the execution of fault diagnosis, safety and security of production processes and systems, improvement of the planning processes, providing the required information at both operational and corporate level, improvement of the human-machine interaction/cooperation and safer learning of complex processes.

According to Moon and Seo [2], smart glasses are emerging as a new technology to improve construction management. Photography and video filming with smart glasses can also be used to record the construction process.

Niemöller et al. [19] identified the categories management, communication, value added service and quality assurance as well as phase-specific use cases as process groups. These included prioritizing employees on the basis of process metrics, display instructions for action, display inspection plans, document damages, measuring and documenting objects, record stocks automatically, automated control of picking and display and control packing list.

Summary. The analysis of the publications clearly shows that smart glasses are used for different purposes in the most diverse areas e.g. logistics, construction and automotive industry. In principle, almost all available publications focus on easy access to relevant information and its adequate presentation for users. The main focus is therefore on improving the human computer interface and interaction.

3.2 Topic: Acceptance Analyses

Description of the Studies. The factors that determine the acceptance of smart glasses were examined from two perspectives, product characteristics and user intention, in the publication of Basoglu et al. [1] With regard to the product characteristics of smart glasses, the effects of selected design features such as field of view and display technology on acceptance were analyzed in an experimental study. The factors enjoyment, self-efficacy, external and peer influence, risk, attitude, usefulness, ease of use, anxiety, health concern, intention and complexity were identified as decisive for the acceptance of a new technology. The conjoint analysis was used to investigate the product properties. Various product descriptions were developed and presented to the participants for preference evaluation. Different product characteristics and associated evaluation levels were defined for this study to measure usability. A total of eight product alternatives were generated from these product features. The total of 81 participants rated these alternatives as most (1) to least (8) desirable. 122 persons were interviewed to investigate the user intention.

The study by Berkemeier et al. [2], also contains an analysis of the acceptance of smart glasses. In their study on the use of smart glasses in self-service, the research questions concerning acceptance, usability and features for acceptance and usability were investigated. An Android application for the smart glasses Vuzix M100 was developed to perform a simulated maintenance process. The determination of acceptance included the factors expected performance, expected expense, social influence, general conditions, data protection concerns, trust, risk and intended use. The evaluation was based on a seven-level Likert scale. Suitability was measured in point results between 0 and 100. Results from 70 points upwards were rated as good. The sample comprised 29 student subjects. The test persons had no experience with smart glasses.

Koelle et al. [14] report quantitative results from a multi-year study conducted in 2014, 2015 and 2016 to investigate user attitudes towards smart glasses. The forecasts were also evaluated by 51 experts. The research questions were asked towards attitude smart glasses and parameters forming this attitude towards this technology. This study was intended to clarify under which conditions smart glasses can make the step to a technology accepted in society. The Technology Acceptance Model (TAM) used in the study defines the acceptance of new technologies by individuals on the basis of two main factors: usefulness and perceived ease of use. The 118 participants aged between 18 and 58 years (47% female) evaluated 56 scenarios (28 with smart glasses, 28 with smartphones) on the basis of a so-called semantic differential.

Based on expert opinion, the same paper examined whether these negative attitudes towards smart glasses are related to a lack of social acceptance and whether the benefits that can be gained from using smart glasses are able to overcome initial reservations about smart glasses. The main part of the expert survey consisted of two two-stage questions (Q1, Q3 with a 6-stage Likert Scale) and one question (Q2) in which participants were asked to sort improvement criteria according to relevance. 51 experts (15 women) filled out the questionnaire completely.

- Q1: Within the next 10 years: Do you expect smart glasses to be routinely worn by people?

- Q2: What would need to be improved to make smart glasses a tool that people use in their everyday life?
- Q3: To what extent do you believe that social acceptance will be relevant for the success of smart glasses?

In another acceptance study, the authors Kim et al. [13] examined the influence, different HMD types (mono- vs. binocular), different forms of presentation (graphics vs. text) and the duration of information availability (permanent vs. on-demand) towards the subjectively perceived workload, the usefulness of the smart glasses, the eye strain and the work performance and compared the results with a picking method based on conventional paper lists. A total of 16 test persons took part in the study. Those who wore glasses were excluded before the start of the study. During one run, the participants performed four picking and four sub-assembly tasks with the aid of a paper list or smart glasses on a reproduced picking workstation. Subjective parameters to determine the subjective parameters included acceptance analysis, cognitive load, efficiency analysis, efficiency analysis and signs for simulator sickness. To measure the objective parameters, the time taken to complete the tasks and the number of errors in completing the tasks were measured.

In the project Glass@Service, in which smart glasses for industrial use in logistics, assembly and optical quality control are developed and tested, the authors Terhoeven et al. [24] examined the subjectively evaluated usefulness, usability and acceptance of smart glasses. The subjectively expected usability or applicability was measured by means of a quantitative questionnaire and contained constructs for suitability for the task, learnability, self-descriptiveness, controllability, conformity with user expectations, error tolerance and suitability for individualization. The subjective usefulness as well as the user acceptance were evaluated according to the questionnaire "Technology Acceptance Model". A total of 59 test persons participated in the study.

The experimental laboratory study by Wille et al. [28] examined the differences between the use of a so-called Head Mounted Display (HMD) and a tablet display with respect to mental workload, general subjective workload, visual system fatigue and technical affinity of 41 subjects. The technique affinity of the participants was determined using the TA-EG questionnaire. Interviews were conducted with the test persons after the end of the study regarding the use of the HMD and the tablet display.

Borisov et al. [3] developed six different human-machine interfaces (HMIs) in their study in cooperation with a car manufacturer. In phase 1, the workplace was analyzed by field observation and interviews. Phase 2 consisted of a field trial in which the six newly designed devices were tested. In phase 3, two of the six devices were tested with two workers under real working conditions. At the original workplace, the workers used handheld devices that gave instructions via the test program. The devices provided by the car manufacturer were heavy and unwieldy. As a result of the first phase, the authors of the study found a high potential for increasing user-friendliness and user experience. In phase 2, a rating concept was developed which enabled the newly developed interfaces to be evaluated in a realistic study with 67 employees. Different combinations of input and output devices were tested.

Based on the results of phase 1, a so-called Device Score Model (DSM) was also developed. Ergonomics and user interface were examined with questions about hands-free working, weight and size of the devices, amount of eye movement required as well as the interaction flexibility and interaction speed. The performance was determined by analyzing eye-tracking data. The motivation an employee felt while working with the device was queried. In addition, a questionnaire was designed to measure the acceptance of the technology.

In phase 2 the 67 participants worked with the newly developed devices and evaluated them with the DSM. The entire field trial lasted 2.5 weeks and 12 working days. Each employee used two of the six devices in succession. In phase 3, the aim was the direct comparison of two HMIs with a new diagnostic device. Instead of a microphone a smartwatch was used as input device for the smart glasses. The smartphone with additional software options was chosen as the second comparison device. The field experiment was carried out with only two persons. The whole process took about 300 min for each employee.

The acceptance study of Rauschnabel and Ro [21] is based on the modified Technology Acceptance Model. The Microsoft Hololens and Google Glass were used in the study. A survey of 201 randomly selected test persons was conducted in a German shopping mall. The survey included the constructs knowledge of smart glasses, social norms, expectation of simplicity of use, expectations versus benefits in self-expression, expected functionality benefits, attitude towards the sales brands, image of the manufacturers in questions of private data protection, technical innovation, attitude towards smart glasses and intention to use smart glasses.

Results. In the study by Basoglu et al. [1] the following results were obtained regarding the desired product features of smart glasses and the user's intended use. Accordingly, the stand-alone device with a large field of view, speech recognition and touchpad interaction take first place in the selection of eight product alternatives. The evaluation of the web survey showed that "Enjoyment" received the highest score of 3.3 on the Likert scale, which goes up to the numerical value 4. The participants also preferred self-efficacy (3.1) when using smart glasses. They were strongly influenced by their friends, family and neighborhood in their opinions about smart glasses (3.0). Participants were also influenced by news, advertising and promotion (2.9). Some indicated that the use of Smart Glass could pose a risk (2.7). Their attitude towards the use of smart glasses was positive (2.6). Participants agreed that they were easy to use and useful (usability 2.4 and usefulness 2.6). They were a little scared (2.1) when using smart glasses also because of possible health risks (2.0). It also showed that their intention to use smart glasses was not very pronounced (1.9). Finally, participants found that using smart glasses was not a complex task (1.8).

The results of the study by Berkemeier et al. [2] can be summarized in the categories acceptance, serviceability, observations and recommendations. The median values were divided into the following classes: 1–3: rejection, 4: neutral attitude, 5–7: agreement. The results in the acceptance category were expected performance (5), expected expense (6), perceived risk (5), confidence (5), social influence (4), general conditions of use (4), privacy concerns (3) and intended use (2). The serviceability was below average at 60. The authors also conclude some observations and comments. Three participants rubbed their eyes after using smart glasses. Seven users had to close one eye. Ten had to adjust the Smart Glasses during use. Two participants put the smart glasses down in the meantime. Three participants accidentally switched off the smart glasses. Eight participants mentioned problems with information at the edge of the screen.

From this the authors derived recommendations for actions as to ensure increased IT security, implement data economy to reduce the perceived risk, use robust hardware, increase wearing comfort, allow flexible positioning of the display, facilitate navigation to avoid incorrect entries, improving the legibility of information. To better process management they propose to adapt the complexity of the process steps to the state of knowledge and integrate feedback mechanisms for successful actions.

The evaluation of the multi-year study by Koelle et al. [14] did not reveal any significance. The attitude towards smart glasses thus remained stable rather negative. The expert survey also included interesting results. The majority of participants estimated that smart glasses would be routinely worn within the next 10 years (median = 3). Participants appreciated the advantage of hands-free function (n = 5), easy access to information (n = 7) and natural interaction (n = 4). They also mentioned technological and social issues that need to be solved before a wide use of smart glasses becomes possible. Participants expected that smart glasses will be successful in specialized application areas (n = 18).

Factors that hinder the acceptance of smart glasses were according to the expert survey are the lack of use cases and applications, lack of wearing comfort and ergonomic aspects, too high acquisition costs, lack of user-friendliness, social shame, lack of data protection and ethical problems. The answer to question Q2 resulted in this ranking: usefulness, functionality, user-friendliness and lastly compatibility with daily routines.

Kim et al. [13] found that the average values of the Usability Satisfaction Questionnaire were significantly influenced by the availability of information. Thus, the average values for the permanent presentation of information were higher than those for the on-demand presentation. Twelve participants (75%) preferred the graphic-based permanent presentation of information. Six of the twelve respondents preferred binocular smart glasses, five preferred monocular smart glasses, and one respondent indicated no preference regarding the type of smart glasses. Ten respondents (62.5%) indicated that they would least prefer the text-based on-demand information display. Five of the ten respondents rejected monocular smart glasses and the remaining five rejected binocular smart glasses compared to the other type of smart glasses.

Terhoeven et al. [24] came to the several results for the application case "picking" in their Glass@Service project. The expected average values were 3.0 for all questionnaire items. For the dimension "error tolerance" was 0.76 significantly lower as was the average value for the dimension "perceived usefulness" with 0.68. The other dimensions showed no significant differences from the expected average value of 3.0. For the application "fitting of an assembly line" they came to similar results. The average value of the dimension "learnability" was 0.67 significantly higher. The average value of the dimension "conformity with user expectations" was 0.33 significantly higher and the average value for the dimension "perceived ease of use" was 0.38 significantly higher. The remaining averages did not differ significantly from the expected average value of 3.0. In addition, the authors compared the results. The average values of the dimension "suitability for the task" of the use case "picking" were 0.70 significantly lower than the average value of 3.17 of the use case "equipping an assembly line". The average values of the dimension "error tolerance" of the application "picking" were significantly lower by 0.69 than the average value of 2.93 of the application "equipping an assembly line". The average values of the dimension "perceived usefulness" of the application "order picking" were 0.58 significantly lower than the average value of 3.17 of the application "equipping an assembly line". Again, the other average values of the other dimensions did not differ significantly from each other.

The results of the study by Wille et al. [28] regarding affinity for technology and acceptance. A significant interaction between technology affinity and the display type used could be shown. Subjects with a lower affinity for technology showed both generally higher stress values and a lower decrease in stress due to the use of the tablet display than subjects with a higher affinity for technology. 40 of the 41 test persons preferred working with the tablet display to working with the HMD.

In the experimental study by Sedighi et al. [22] the authors come to the conclusion that the rankings were significantly gender dependent with $p = 0.019$; $\eta_p^2 = 0.141$. Women preferred the smartphone and the paper-based system to the same extent. Men preferred the smartphone more than the paper-based system or the smart glasses.

The study by Borisov et al. [3], shows that the smartphone with an overall score of 2.1 is the winner of this comparison. The smart glasses with microphone input perform very well in terms of performance, but the evaluation of the user experience and acceptance of this HMI is rather mediocre. For devices with gestures and voice input, the authors consider the reliability of recognition to be the greatest problem. Performance and error rate were independent of gender, age, gender and work experience. However, well-trained employees were less convinced of the combination of smart glasses.

The results of phase 3 suggest that smartphone again received the best marks. With an overall score of 1.7, it leaves the new diagnostic device (2.8) and smart glasses (3.9) far behind. Smart glasses were rejected mainly because of health concerns and their weight and size. Headaches were reported in some cases. Workers' attitudes towards smart glasses did not change significantly during the field study.

In the survey by Rauschnabel and Ro [21] the authors found significant differences between the sexes with regard to previous knowledge. The attitude of younger age groups towards smart glasses was also significantly better than that of the older participants, but this did not lead to a significantly higher purchase intention.

Summary. The literature research revealed a large number of hits for the topic of acceptance of smart glasses. Many of the studies examined the acceptance of smart glasses in the population [1, 21] and the fewest analyses were carried out with specialists in companies [3] or experts [14]. By large, the authors agree on the methodology used to measure acceptance. Some existing questionnaires were used [24] or modified [21] by adding their own evaluation criteria. But also, web surveys [1] and expert interviews [14, 28] are used. In the synopsis of all results it becomes clear that the topics of data and health protection [3] were critically evaluated. The wearing comfort, which is related to the weight and the fixation of the smart glasses on the head, was also frequently criticized. The users wanted flexible display positioning with high display resolution [14].

As the result of a study, it was recommended to push the graphics-based information [13].

Koelle et al. [14] saw no change in the rather negative attitude towards smart glasses during their multi-year study. A survey conducted among 51 experts showed that a change is expected to increase the acceptance of smart glasses by 2026. The experts identified usefulness, functionality and user-friendliness as the most important factors for long-term acceptance. In none of these studies were smart glasses ranked first during comparison of display types.

Gross et al. [10] compared a tablet with two different types of smart glasses (monocular, binocular). The tablet received the highest score and the binocular smart glasses the lowest.

In the study by Sedighi et al. [22] smart glasses were compared with a smartphone and a paper-based system. The participants of the study preferred the smartphone over the paper-based system or smart glasses. The least preferred display was the smart glasses. Responses were equally divided between the two categories most and least useful. The negative responses in terms of usefulness focused primarily on the design of the smart glasses and not on the quality of the display. In particular, there were complaints that the weight of the glasses was uncomfortable and difficult to balance. With regard to the display, the smart glasses were considered the most useful.

The study by Borisov et al. [3], who were the only ones to examine the acceptance of smart glasses in field tests. The smartphone received the best marks because its lightweight and ergonomic design makes it a suitable tool for use in product control. The authors see a high potential for use of smart glasses in the industrial environment by addressing the health and hygiene issues that inevitably arise when using smart glasses.

3.3 Topic: Eye Strain

Description of the Studies. Gabbard et al. [8] examined in their experimental study the effect of context switching and focal distance switching of the eyes when working with smart glasses. The author showed different combinations of letter on different displays. In addition, the distance between the displays was varied between 0.7 m, 2 m and 6 m. Interviews were conducted after the examination was completed. 24 students participated in the study.

Huckauf et al. [11] conducted three different experiments. The first experiment was intended to answer the question of whether the performance of the test subjects is greater when displayed on only one screen (PC screen or AR display) than when displayed simultaneously two screens. Performance was defined as reaction time and number of errors during the search task to be performed. A 6×6 board with O's and zeros was initially displayed either on a computer screen or the AR display where participants had to find the differences. Five people participated. The second experiment was designed to answer the question of how well the participants perceive information emanating from one medium while they are busy with another medium. The experimental setup was the same as in experiment. Again, five people participated in this experiment. The third experiment was conducted to determine whether the visual system processes the information shown on different displays at the same distance as that shown at different distances. 10 subjects were equipped with both the HMD and an eye tracker. With the help of the eye-tracker the position of the eye axes can be calculated.

In their study, Theis et al. [25] examined the influence of smart glasses in two different configurations (transparent/opaque) on the musculoskeletal system, the visual system, the subjective workload and the work performance in comparison to the use of conventional (wall) displays. 60 participants carried out 3.5 h of assembly work. Muscle activity was investigated by electromyography, vision by eye test, subjective workload and head position/posture based on video recordings.

Results. Gabbard et al. [8] come to conclusions that context switching at a large distance (6 m) from the screens has a significant impact on the number of tasks performed. The context change at long distance (6 m) to the screens has a significant impact on the number of correctly performed tasks. The context change has a significant effect on eye fatigue at all distances. Participants rated the execution of the tasks in the real screen condition as less tiring than in the HMD screen condition. The focal distance switching has a significant influence on the number of tasks performed and on the number of correctly performed tasks. Participants completed more tasks and were more accurate when no focal length change was necessary. In the final interviews 87.5% of the participants reported eye complaints. They also complained of headaches.

Kim et al. [13] found in their study that the average values of the Simulator Sickness Questionnaire were significantly influenced by the interaction between information presentation and information availability. All experimental conditions led to higher average values of the SSQ than the control condition.

The evaluation of the Visual Fatigue Questionnaire in the study by Wille et al. [28] showed a significant increase in visual fatigue over time under all conditions, with a stronger effect when using the HMD.

The three experiments conducted by Huckauf et al. [11] provided that the reaction time for the PC display was significantly shorter than for the AR display. Simultaneous display on both screens resulted in slower reaction times than when displayed on only one screen. The interaction between the display and the type of display was significant. When analyzing experiment 2, the authors concluded that the display used had a significant influence and the change between the displays had a marginal influence on the reaction time of the participants. The reaction time when using the PC display was shorter than when using the AR display. Experiment 3 showed a significant difference in the convergence point of the eyes when displayed on the AR display or the PC screen.

In the study by Theis et al. [25] it was found that the use of the different display types had no significant effect on near vision or television. Also, long-term use (3.5 h) had no significant influence on the sensitivity of the visual field.

Summary. In summary, Gabbard et al. [8] conclude on the basis of the results of their laboratory study that both context and focal length changes of the eyes lead to significantly lower power. The repeated performance of work with the HMD display led to increased discomfort such as eye fatigue and headaches. In the study by Wille et al. the use of HMDs led to increased visual fatigue.

Huckauf et al. [11] found that the convergence point of the eyes differs significantly when displayed on an AR display from that when displayed on a computer screen.

Kim et al. has shown that the form of display (text vs. graphics) has an influence on the development of nausea due to the movement feigned in the eye because of the display being directly in front of the eyes. The findings of this study are in agreement with those of Theis et al. [25] with regard to the influence of the different display types.

It should be noted that these results are based on experiments with a small number of young subjects.

3.4 Topic: Effects on the Musculoskeletal System

Description of the Studies. Friemert et al. [7] examined the aspect of the change in physical stress associated with the use of smart glasses at typical order picking workstation which was reproduced. The information required for the sorting process was presented randomly. It was assigned on a monitor in the first test run and projected onto smart glasses in the second run or vice versa.

Results. The evaluation of the CUELA measurement data collected by Friemert et al. [7] provided temporal joint angle curves that showed significant differences between the two runs, especially in the neck and head area.

The study by Theis et al. [25] could not detect any significant change over time with regard to the muscle activity of any of the muscles except the left splenius capitits.

Summary. Friemert et al. [7] results of the pilot study gave rise to the hypothesis that smart glasses have at least partially a positive influence on posture during order picking when used as an active biofeedback information system. This hypothesis has not yet been tested in a larger field and laboratory study. Theis et al. [25] observed altered head postures and changes in muscle activity in the neck when wearing smart glasses.

3.5 Topic: Radiation Exposure from Electromagnetic Fields

Description of the Studies. The contribution by Choi and Choi [4] proposes a novel miniaturized antenna for smart glasses. The electromagnetic radiation emitted by the antenna, which penetrates into the human body, was determined by simulation calculations and then partially validated by measurements. The calculated SAR value for the proposed antenna was 0.557 W/kg on the left and 0.454 W/kg on the right side of the head. These values did not exceed the Federal Communications Commission (FCC) guidelines of 1.6 W/kg.

The exposure of the user of a Google Glass was also calculated in a publication by Ferreira et al. [6] using numerical-dosimetric simulations for realistic use scenarios. A maximum SAR value of 1.42 W/kg was specified (FCC report), which is below the official threshold of 1.6 W/kg.

The publication of Ferreira et al. [6] presents an assessment of radiation exposure for a user wearing smart glasses with a mobile phone connection. SAR values were calculated for f our different usage scenarios with correspondingly different frequency bands (0.9 GHz, 1.94 GHz, 2.6 GHz and 2.43 GHz).

A voxel model of a head with 5 mm resolution was used for the computer calculations. A model of the Google Glass was imported into the simulation software.

The publication by Pizarro et al. [20] focuses on the computer-based calculation of SAR values in the head caused by Google glasses. Apart from a simple head model, which considers only two different materials (solid & liquid), realistic adult and child head models were used. The model of Google Glass was equipped with two different antennas in this study: a monopole antenna (MONO) and a Planar Inverted F antenna (PIFA).

Likamwa et al. [16] looked at the power management and CPU utilization of the Google Glass prototype for different use cases. To characterize the thermal behavior, they used a surface thermometer and measured the temperature at the point where the Google Glass comes into contact with the temple.

Results. Choi and Choi [4] assume that the miniaturized antenna they propose can be attached to smart glasses.

According to Fereirra et al. [6], most of the energy is absorbed in the head area near the antenna. A comparatively higher energy absorption at the lowest frequency (0.9 GHz) is reported. For the maximum permissible power EIRP (Effective Isotropic Radiated Power) of 0.1 W, a peak SAR value of 1.65 W/kg for 1 g of tissue was calculated. This value is comparable to that in the FCC report (1.42 W/kg averaged over 1 g). However, this value slightly exceeded the limit set by the FCC (1.6 W/kg averaged over 1 g).

The maximum recommended SAR value of 2 W/kg was achieved at a radiation power of 0.152 W for the 0.9 GHz (GSM) band. Since up to 8 GSM time slots are used for data services and an EIRP of 2 W is defined in the standards (at an antenna gain of 0 dB), this resulted in a SAR value that was higher than the maximum recommended; however, this maximum is not reached in normal operation. For the 1.94 GHz (UMTS), 2.43 GHz (Wi-Fi) and 2.6 GHz (LTE) bands, it was found that the SAR values were below the recommended limit.

In the publication by Pizarro et al. [20] the SAR values for the Google Glass in the 2.45 GHz frequency band were simulated at an assumed normalized radiated power of 100mW (0.1 W). The percentages of power absorbed in the head are given below for the three different head models.

The results of the calculations were all above the FCC SAR limit of 1.6 W/Kg (averaged over 1 g of tissue) and almost all above the ICNIRP limit of 2 W/kg (averaged over 10 g of tissue).

Likamwa et al. [16] measured the heating of Google Glass smart glasses (1st gen.) during a video chat. The thermometer shows a rapid temperature rise. After 120 s, the temperature is 39 °C until it reaches a stable 51.9 °C.

Summary. In the publication by Fereirra et al. [6] a Google Glass with mobile phone connection was examined in different frequency bands. This does not correspond to the typical situation at the workplace, as only WLAN and Bluetooth connections are available here. The recommended SAR limit for the human head was only exceeded in the 0.9 GHz (GSM) mobile radio band. There were no exposure problems for UMTS, LTE and Wi-Fi, as the maximum radiated power that meets the SAR requirements is above the maximum permissible radiated power.

In Pizarro et al. [20] the homogenic SAM phantom head model showed the highest SAR values in the simulations compared to the two heterogeneous models for an adult and a child. Some of the calculated SAR values were close to 8 W/kg, i.e. far above the FCC and ICNIRP limits.

Likamwa et al. [16] assume that high temperatures exert stress on the human body. According to the authors, the body's stress-regulating responses lead to reduced well-being and have the potential to cause cardiovascular problems. Blood vessel damage can occur in contact with 38 °C–48 °C warm surfaces and can lead to skin damage.

Almost all authors of the studies cited here emphasize the fact that smart glasses are typically used very close to the head over long periods of time. This should be taken into account when assessing radiation exposure in future studies.

3.6   Topic: Effects on Gait and Posture

Description of the Studies. In the experimental study by Tegtmeier and Wischniewski [23] the use of smart glasses was compared with the use of tablet PCs and clipboards with paper sheets. A total of 36 volunteers had to walk down a 290 m long and 75 cm wide corridor and completed various cognitive, dual tasks. One walk was carried out by each of the participants without equipment. One half of the participants used monocular smart glasses for the dual tasks, the other half received binoculars.

In the experimental study by Sedighi et al. [22] the influence of smart glasses on different parameters describing gait variability in a dual-task setup was investigated. In their study, the authors therefore examined the gait parameters identified as relevant in a typical dual-task scenario. The authors formulate hypothesis concerning gait variability, less negative effects on gait while using smart glasses and changes in sensitivity in gait pattern. The study included 20 participants. They were healthy students who did not wear glasses. The materials used in the study included a treadmill, a seven-camera system for marker tracking, three different information display types. The experiment contained three different cognitive tasks (Stroop test, Object categorization, Boston Naming Test) and a mental arithmetic with increasing degree of difficulty.

Results. Tegtmeier and Wischnewski [23] observed that there were no statistically significant differences between the information options with regard to running errors. However, when using digital media, the participants were able to complete the walking distance faster with the solution of the dual tasks than with the paper version on the clipboard.

Sedighi et al. [22] reported statistically significant results. There were significant major effects of display conditions DC on the standard deviations both at the step time and at the step speed. The standard deviations of the step times increased significantly when the participants used the paper-based system. The comparison of single task and dual task smartphone showed a significant reduction in the standard deviations of the step speed. There was a significant main effect on the sample entropy (SaEn) of the step times. Compared to the single task, SaEn was significantly higher in terms of step times for dual task paper. Compared to the dual task paper, the SaEn value for dual task glass was significantly lower and similar to the value for single task. SaEn (related to stride length) decreased significantly in women in the dual task paper. SaEn (related to step length) was significantly higher in women in the single task condition compared to the value for men. There were significant major effects of display type on almost all cognitive performance test scores (except NASA TLX scores). Smart glasses were perceived as less comfortable than the paper-based system and the smartphone.

Summary. Tegtmeier and Wischniewski [23] conclude on the basis of their study that smart glasses and tablets can improve access to information in production with short texts and adequate walking distances without an increased risk of accidents or a higher subjective load compared to analog information on a clipboard.

Most of the results of the study by Sedighi et al. [22] support their hypothesis that there is an increase in gait variability when using an information display while walking compared to the single-task condition. However, in the area of linear evaluation methods, there was no uniform picture regarding the change in gait variability and the associated risk of falling. On the one hand, an increased step length variability SLV was found in all three dual-task tasks.

The nonlinear analysis (SaEn) gave clear indications of the walking behavior under the different conditions. Higher SaEn values indicate higher complexity and less regularity in the gait pattern. However, the cognitive studies do not support the results on motor variability. In general, participants preferred to use the smartphone and the paper-based system. In contrast, the study shows that the gait was less negatively affected when using smart glasses (hypothesis no. 2). As assumed in hypothesis no. 3, there were differences in the sensitivity of different methods for determining the variability of human gait. All methods of analysis used had different "magnitudes" of effect, which means that these measures had different sensitivities to changes due to different walking conditions. In summary, it can be said that the gait performance is less affected by the smart glasses than with the other two display types.

3.7 Topic: Effects on Visual Attention

Description of the Studies. In five experiments, Lewis and Neider [15] are investigating in a dual-task scenario the impairments caused during a primary visual search by the fading in of secondary information on smart glasses. A visual search paradigm was applied as the main task. In all experiments the main task was to find the letter T (target) in a set of letters L (distractor) on a computer screen. The secondary information was presented as a single word under different experimental conditions simultaneously on a Google Glass. A total of five different experiments were performed from which 2 are presented because of their close relation to OSH.

In experiment 1, the costs for primary task fulfilment, which arise due to the presentation of secondary information, were investigated. At the same time, the perceived relevance of secondary information was manipulated by instructions to the participants. The extent to which secondary task information was processed at all was analyzed with a recognition memory task with surprise effect. Ninety students from the University of Central Florida participated. All participants had normal or corrected visual acuity and normal color vision. Five smart glasses conditions were linked to the secondary task.

In order to establish a baseline and to detect a possible visual occlusion that may occur when wearing smart glasses, there were two conditions in which no secondary information is presented. In experiment 2, the context of secondary information was changed by informing the participants in advance that they had to solve a recognition memory task. It was expected that secondary information would be more disruptive to the main task if the participants were aware that they were being tested on the secondary information. 72 participants without prior knowledge were recruited for experiment 2. All experimental details were similar to those in experiment 1.

Tegtmeier and Wischniewski [23] conducted an experimental study with a total of 36 subjects. Monocular and binocular smart glasses were compared with the use of a tablet and a DIN A4 clipboard as an analogue variant. As they walked, they had to read aloud two-syllable words and name the accompanying background color of the display. In the experiment, numbers and characters had to be announced on desktop computers set up at eight stations along the route, with the additional indication of whether the numbers were greater or less than "1000". Following this task, one of twelve pictograms representing emergencies, warnings or bans was shown on the display for 250 ms (ms). The participants had to announce form, color and content.

Results. Lewis and Neider [15] present the following findings in their study. There were no differences in the correctness of the answers in the conditions, but there was a major effect of smart glasses conditions on response times (RT), indicating that participants took longer to complete the primary search task when secondary information was available. In addition, increased response times were observed in the dual-task conditions compared to both the control condition and the condition where no information was presented. There were no differences between the dual-task conditions. The analysis in the memory task showed no differences between the dual task conditions, which means that the participants processed secondary information independently of given instructions. The results were similar to experiment 1, with no differences in the correctness of the answers between the conditions. When secondary information was presented, the participants took longer to perform the primary search task. Reaction times (RT) differed significantly from those of the control conditions. The search RTs were longer when supposedly useful secondary information was presented on the smart glasses. Memory performance showed no difference between the conditions.

Tegtmeier and Wischniewski [23] observed that the mean error in maintenance task was statistically significantly different, with higher mean errors for smart glasses and tablet use. The number of errors did not differ in the comparison of the use of smart glasses and clipboard, while the number of errors in character recognition was higher for tablet use than for clipboard use.

Summary. Lewis and Neider [15] results are both surprising. Participants were not able to block secondary information presented on the smart glasses, even if they wanted to or were instructed to do so. If the participants were informed that the information on the smart glasses could be useful, the reaction times were increased by about 86%.

Based on their results, the authors Tegtmeier and Wischnewski [23] conclude that reading while walking led to a disadvantageous performance for the two digital media they used.

3.8 Topic: Effects on Workload

Description of the Studies. Three publications were found regarding the workload associated with the use of smart glasses. Two of these studies [25, 28] have already been presented.

In order to determine workplace hazards with a preventive approach, Gross et al. [10] examined the effects of the use of smart glasses on forklifts with regard to cognitive stress. For this purpose, the use of two types of smart glasses and a forklift terminal was investigated. A standardized reaction test procedure, the Detection Response Task (DRT) was used to assess the cognitive load while driving forklift.

For the study, a forklift simulator was used and three different digital display systems were employed: a forklift terminal (tablet: 10.1-inch display with holder on the center console of the forklift simulator) and two different smart glasses (mono-, binocular).

A total of 32 male participants were invited to the study. Prerequisite for participation was a valid forklift license; furthermore, the test persons were not allowed to wear glasses or drive a forklift without glasses. The remaining 23 test persons were between 23 and 53 years old with an average of 40 years.

The primary task was to drive through a virtual warehouse with numbered racking lanes without other road users and to access racks with specific numbers in the driving simulator. Driving errors were recorded for each run. The secondary task was carried out in three consecutive randomized two-minute runs on the three digital display systems used: The test subjects were asked to navigate to the displayed navigation destinations and confirm their arrival on the display. In addition, the degree of workload was increased by constantly reading out numbers (1–10) that appeared on the display system every 5 s. The reaction task was performed with an optical stimulus using the Detection Response Task (DRT). During each run, the test subjects had to react to about 30 stimuli by pressing a button on their index finger. A hit was counted and stored with the corresponding reaction time if a reaction between 100 ms and 2500 ms occurred. In addition to the reaction time, the hit rate was also recorded.

Results. Gross et al. [10] evaluated the three performance parameters. Driving errors occurred in only 21 of 92 complete runs. There was no statistically significant correlation between driving errors and cognitive load. The results for average response times were lower for digital display systems than for runs without additional tasks. But no significant difference in response times or hit rates was found when using one display system compared to another. In the assessment of the workload between the different devices, the analysis showed no significant difference in workload.

The subjects of the study by Theis et al. [25] did not report any significant differences in the subjectively perceived workload when using three different display types.

The evaluation of the NASA TLX in the context of the study by Wille et al. [28] showed a significantly higher subjective workload when using the HMD compared to the tablet display. The increase in perceived stress over time was also significant, but there were no significant differences between the use of the HMD and the tablet display. Furthermore, the Rating Scale of Mental Effort (RSME) showed a significantly higher mental workload when using the HMD compared to the tablet display. A significant increase in mental workload over time and higher stress values were found in the older group of participants.

The study by Sedighi et al. [22] did not reveal any noticeable differences with regard to the three display types, but with regard to user preference and their performance in task solving, differences become clear.

Summary. Gross et al. [10] found that the cognitive load increases significantly when using digital display systems. However, the results of the study do not show significant differences in cognitive load between the three digital display systems investigated. This is consistent with the findings of Sedighi et al. [22] and Theis et al. [25].

Wille et al. [28] found an increased subjective workload compared to a tablet. Regarding the perceived stress, both display types were again found to be similarly stressful.

3.9 Topic: Efficiency Analyses

Description of the Studies. The study by Ishio et al. [12] examined the working efficiency of searching for information using smart glasses. The main interest was the age dependency of a potential increase in efficiency through the use of smart glasses. A specially designed test with visual search tasks was developed and used in a study, that models a part of an assembly process. A total of 142 volunteers participated in the study.

Results. In the experiment by Ishio et al. [12] the search time, the convenience of the search, the degree of fatigue and the correctness of the answers was measured. The analysis focused on the correctness of the answers. In the case of the instructions on paper, the percentage was very similar for all age groups (between 45% and 55% correct answers). In the case of instructions with smart glasses, the percentage of correct answers was higher for all groups. The percentage of correct answers decreased with age.

The study by Kim et al. [13] cited above arrives at the following results with regard to efficiency. Presenting the information as graphics significantly reduced the time needed to perform the task compared to presenting the information as text. The time saving was greater when the information was displayed permanently compared to on-demand display. Graphic-based information presentation led to significantly fewer errors in the execution of tasks compared to text-based information presentation. The presentation of the information had a significant influence on the subscales "Mental Demand", "Performance" and "Effort" of the NASA TLX. Thus, the graphic-based presentation of information led to a decrease in the "Mental Demand", "Performance" and "Effort" subscales by 54.4%, 37.5% and 35% respectively.

Theis et al. [25] came to the conclusion in their study that work performance, measured by the time required for the performance, was significantly influenced by the use of the different display types.

Summary. Scientific publications that examine the efficiency of workflows when using smart glasses are rare. The research resulted in only one publication that dealt exclusively with efficiency analysis. Ishio et al. [12] found a significantly improved work performance when using smart glasses compared to the use of paper. This effect applied to all age groups of the participants, although it decreased with increasing age. Theis et al. [25] came to a different conclusion. When measuring time for a standardized production task, smart glasses performed approximately 15% to 20% worse than a conventional wall projection. The study by Kim et al. [13] clearly indicates that when using smart glasses, graphics-based information presentation is preferable in every respect (including efficiency) to text-based presentation.

References

1. Basoglu, N., Ok, A., Daim, T.: What will it take to adopt smart glasses: a consumer choice based review. Technol. Soc. **50**, 50–56 (2017). https://doi.org/10.1016/j.techsoc.2017.04.005
2. Berkemeier, L., Werning, S., Zobel, B., Ickerott, I., Thomas, O.: Der Kunde als Dienstleister: Akzeptanz und Gebrauchstauglichkeit von smart glasses im self-service. HMD Praxis der Wirtschaftsinformatik **54**(5), 781–794 (2017). https://doi.org/10.1365/s40702-017-0342-1
3. Borisov, N., Weyers, B., Kluge, A.: Designing a human machine interface for quality assurance in car manufacturing: an attempt to address the "functionality versus user experience contradiction" in professional production environments. In: Advances in Human-Computer Interaction (2018). https://doi.org/10.1155/2018/9502692
4. Choi, S., Choi, J.: Miniaturized MIMO antenna with a high isolation for smart glasses. In: IEEE-APS Topical Conference on Antennas and Propagation in Wireless Communications (APWC), pp. 61–63. IEEE, Verona (2017). https://doi.org/10.1109/apwc.2017.8062241
5. Damiani, L., Demartini, M., Guizzi, G., Revetria, R., Tonelli, F.: Augmented and virtual reality applications in industrial systems: a qualitative review towards the industry 4.0 era. In: 16th IFAC Symposium on Information Control Problems in Manufacturing INCOM 2018, vol. 51, pp. 624–630. IFAC PapersOnLine, Bergamo (2018). https://doi.org/10.1016/j.ifacol.2018.08.388
6. Ferreira, M., Oliveira, C., Cardoso, F., Correia, L.: SAR assessment of Google Glasses at cellular wireless frequency bands. In: 10th European Conference on Antennas and Propagation (EuCAP), pp. 1–4. IEEE (2016)
7. Friemert, D., Ellegast, R., Hartmann, U.: Data glasses for picking workplaces. In: Nah, F.H., Tan, C.H. (eds.) HCIBGO 2016. LNCS, vol. 9752, pp. 281–289. Springer, Cham (2016). https://doi.org/10.1007/978-3-319-39399-5_27
8. Gabbard, J., Mehra, D., Swann, J.: Effects of AR display context switching and focal distance switching on human performance. IEEE Trans. Vis. Comput. Graph. (2018). (IEEE, Hrsg.). https://doi.org/10.1109/tvcg.2018.2832633
9. Glockner, H., Jannek, K., Mahn, Mahn, J., Theis, B.: Augmented Reality in Logistics, DHL Research 2014. Abgerufen am 24. Februar 2019 von (2014). http://www.delivering-tomorrow.de/wp-content/uploads/2015/08/dhl-report-augmented-reality-2014.pdf
10. Gross, B., Bretschneider-Hagemes, M., Stefan, A., Rissler, J.: Monitors vs. smart glasses: a study on cognitive workload of digital information systems on forklift trucks. In: Duffy, V. (ed.) DHM 2018. LNCS, vol. 10917, pp. 569–578. Springer, Cham (2018). https://doi.org/10.1007/978-3-319-91397-1_46
11. Huckauf, A., Urbina, M., Böckelmann, I., Schega, L., Mecke, R.: Perceptual issues in optical-see-through displays. In: Proceedings of the 7th Symposium on Applied Perception in Graphics and Visualization, pp. 41–48. ACM, Los Angeles (2010)
12. Ishio, H., Kimura, R., Miyao, M.: Age-dependence of work efficiency enhancement in information seeking by using see-through smart glasses. In: Proceedings of the 12th International Conference on Computer Science and Education (ICCSE), pp. 107–109. Springer, Houston (2017)

13. Kim, S., Nussbaum, M., Gabbard, J.: Influences of augmented reality head-worn display type and user interface design in performance and usability in simulated warehouse order picking. Appl. Ergon. **74**, 186–193 (2019). https://doi.org/10.1016/j.apergo.2018.08.026
14. Koelle, M., El Ali, A., Cobus, V., Heuten, W., Boll, S.: All about acceptability?: Identifying factors for the adoption of data glasses. In: Proceedings of the 2017 CHI Conference on Human Factors in Computing Systems, pp. 295–300. ACM, Denver (2017)
15. Lewis, J., Neider, M.: Through the Google Glass: the impact of heads-up displays on visual attention. Cogn. Res.: Princ. Implic. **1**(13), 1–13 (2016). https://doi.org/10.1186/s41235-016-0015-6
16. LiKamWa, R., Wang, Z., Carroll, A., Lin, F., Zhong, L.: Draining our glass: an energy and heat characterization of Google Glass. In: Proceedings of 5th Asia-Pacific Workshop on Systems, Beijing (2014)
17. Mitrasinovic, S., et al.: Clinical and surgical applications of smart glasses. Technol. Health Care **23**(4), 381–401 (2015). https://doi.org/10.3233/THC-150910
18. Moon, S., Seo, J.: Integration of smart glass technology for information exchange at construction sites. In: Proceedings of the International Symposium on Automation and Robotics in Construction, vol. 32. IAARC Publications (2015)
19. Niemöller, C., et al.: Sind Smart Glasses die Zukunft der Digitalisierung von Arbeitsprozessen? Explorative Fallstudien zukünftiger Einsatzszenarien in der Logistik. Wirtschaftsinformatik, St. Gallen (2017)
20. Pizarro, Y., De Salles, A., Severo, S., Garzon, J., Bueno, S.: Specific absorption rate (SAR) in the head of Google Glasses and Bluetooth users. In: IEEE Latin-America Conference on Communications (LATINCOM), pp. 1–6. IEEE (2014)
21. Rauschnabel, P., Ro, Y.: Augmented reality smart glasses: an investigation of technology acceptance drivers. Int. J. Technol. Mark. **11**(2), 123–148 (2016)
22. Sedighi, A., Ulman, S., Nussbaum, M.: Information presentation through a head-worn display ("smart glasses") has a smaller influence on the temporal structure of gait variability during dual-task gait compared to handheld displays (paper-based system and smartphone). Plos One **13**(4), 1–23 (2018)
23. Tegtmeier, P., Wischniewski, S.: Tablets and smart glasses in modern production environments – a lab study on distracted walking. In: Karwowski, W., Ahram, T. (eds.) IHSI 2018. AISC, vol. 722, pp. 614–619. Springer, Cham (2018). https://doi.org/10.1007/978-3-319-73888-8_95
24. Terhoeven, J., Schiefelbein, F., Wischniewski, S.: User expectations on smart glasses as work assistance in electronics manufacturing. Proc. CIRP **72**, 1028–1032 (2018). https://doi.org/10.1016/j.procir.2018.03.060
25. Theis, S., Mertens, A., Wille, M., Rasche, P., Alexander, T., Schlick, C.: Effects of data glasses on human workload and performance during assembly and disassembly tasks. In: Proceedings 19th Triennial Congress of the IEA, Melbourne (2015)
26. Ubimax: Volkswagen rolls out 3D smart glasses as standard equipment. Abgerufen am 24. Februar 2019 von (2015). https://www.ubimax.com/web2017/en/references/volkswagen-casestudy.html
27. Wei, N., Dougherty, B., Myers, A., Badawy, M.: Using Google Glass in surgical settings: systematic review. JMIR Mhealth Uhealth **6**(3) (2018). https://doi.org/10.2196/mhealth.9409
28. Wille, M., Grauel, B., Adolph, L.: Strain caused by HEAD mounted displays. In: de Waard, D. (Hrsg.) Proceedings of the Human Factors and Ergonomics Society Europe 2013, pp. 267–277 (2014)

A Systematic Literature Review of Game-Based Learning and Safety Management

Sameeran G. Kanade[1]([⊠]) and Vincent G. Duffy[2]

[1] School of Industrial Engineering, Purdue University, West Lafayette, IN 47906, USA
kanade@purdue.edu
[2] Department of Agricultural and Biological Engineering, Purdue University, West Lafayette, IN 47906, USA

Abstract. With the rapid advancement of computer and multimedia technologies, game-based learning has the potential to increase the effectiveness of learning. One of the applications of game-based learning can be safety training. In this study, a systematic literature review of both these topics has been conducted using tools like VOSviewer, MAXQDA, Harzing's Publish or Perish, AuthorMapper and Mendeley. A co-citation analysis was conducted to determine the most important articles in the literature. It was found that there are very few examples of game-based learning being used for safety training. To encourage the use of game-based learning, it is essential to develop a better understanding of the tasks, activities, skills and operations that different kinds of game can offer and examine how these might match desired learning outcomes. Virtual reality (VE) technology is another promising technology that can be used to increase the effectiveness of safety training. Finally, it was concluded that a combination of cognitive, motivational, affective, and sociocultural perspectives is necessary for both game design and game research to fully capture what games have to offer for learning.

Keywords: Game-based learning · Safety management · Training · Bibliometric analysis · Harzing · VOSviewer · MAXQDA · Mendeley · AuthorMapper

1 Introduction

In recent years, various issues of educational games have been widely discussed because of the rapid advancement of computer and multimedia technologies (Sung and Hwang 2013). Game-based learning techniques have the potential to increase the effectiveness of training. The study of gaming communities, from the perspective of education, is still at a nascent stage. Educators could benefit by studying games as a social community because increasingly games have become social activities, especially for the younger generation (Studies 2004). Researchers have indicated that educational games can be an effective way of providing a more interesting learning environment for students to acquire knowledge (Sung and Hwang 2013).

The high rates of accidents in the construction industry are due to factors such as lack of safety in design, poor construction planning, inadequate safety training, worker behavior, and lack of knowledge of site rules (SAEED 2017). In this study, an attempt has been made to explore if any research has been conducted on the role of game-based learning in safety management. In this context, the issue of human-computer interaction (HCI) design becomes even more important. The aim should be to provide access to training material to anyone, from anywhere and at any time, through a variety of platforms and devices (Stephanidis et al. 2012).

2 Purpose of Study

The aim of this study is to conduct a systematic literature review of articles based on game-based learning and see if game-based learning techniques can be applied to safety management in general and safety training in particular. With emerging technologies like virtual reality (VR) and other online training tools, there is an opportunity to reduce costs and increase the effectiveness of safety training. This study tries to find out if efforts in this direction have been made and the level of success achieved during these efforts. Various tools like Harzing's Publish or Perish, VOSviewer and MAXQDA have been used in this study. Mendeley was used to cite the articles and generate a bibliography (*Mendeley*, n.d.).

3 Research Methodology

3.1 Data Collection

Data required to carry out analysis of the literature was collected by conducting keyword search in two different databases – Web of Science and Google scholar. The data acquired from the web of science includes authors, title, source, abstract and cited references. The information related to cited references is necessary for co-citation analysis which has been described later in this paper. The data acquired from Google scholar does not contain cited references. However, it encompasses a wider range of sources which helps get better results for cluster analysis of keywords. "Harzing's Publish or Perish" which is a software tool used to collect data from different databases was used to get metadata from the keyword search conducted in Google scholar. The maximum number of results that this tool can give is 1000. Two separate searches were carried out using the keywords "game based learning" and "safety management". The search conducted in Web of Science core collection yielded 2960 and 7600 results respectively. The search conducted through Harzing's Public or Perish in Google scholar's database for "game based learning" was stopped at 450 results. For "safety management", the search stopped at 1000 results which is the upper limit for Harzing's (*Harzing's Publish or Perish*, n.d.).

3.2 Trend Analysis

Trend analysis is based on the data from the web of science. Web of Science allows the analysis of its data by providing various tools. The data from 2020 was excluded as the year has just begun. This was done to get a better sense of the trend.

Figure 1 shows the trend analysis for game-based learning. It was observed that the first published article was dated June 2001 in the Web of Science database for this particular keyword search. There was a steady rise in the number of articles published after 2006. The number peaked in 2017. A similar trend was noticed when data from Harzing's was analyzed for trend (*Harzing's Publish or Perish*, n.d.). The number peaked in 2015. It is possible that there is a lag in the database and citation updates. It is also possible there is a decline in the number of papers in 2018. One cannot tell with certainty now. However, the upward trend through 2017 is clear.

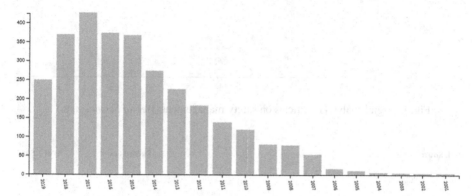

Fig. 1. Trend analysis of articles on game-based learning (*Web of Science*, n.d.)

Field: Source Titles	Record Count	% of 2,937
PROCEEDINGS OF THE EUROPEAN CONFERENCE ON GAMES BASED LEARNING	274	9.329 %
LECTURE NOTES IN COMPUTER SCIENCE	141	4.801 %
INTERNATIONAL JOURNAL OF GAME BASED LEARNING	78	2.656 %
EDULEARN PROCEEDINGS	76	2.588 %
COMPUTERS EDUCATION	73	2.486 %
INTED PROCEEDINGS	54	1.839 %
PROCEEDINGS OF THE 11TH EUROPEAN CONFERENCE ON GAMES BASED LEARNING ECGBL 2017	53	1.805 %
PROCEEDINGS OF THE 12TH EUROPEAN CONFERENCE ON GAMES BASED LEARNING ECGBL 2018	48	1.634 %
PROCEEDINGS OF THE 10TH EUROPEAN CONFERENCE ON GAMES BASED LEARNING	46	1.566 %
PROCEEDINGS OF THE 8TH EUROPEAN CONFERENCE ON GAMES BASED LEARNING ECGBL 2014 VOLS 1 AND 2	46	1.566 %

Fig. 2. Analysis of source titles for game-based learning (*Web of Science*, n.d.)

Top ten sources of titles for game-based learning have been shown in Fig. 2. This analysis was done using tools provided by Web of Science. This figure shows that most of the titles have been sourced from various editions of the proceedings of the European conference on game based learning.

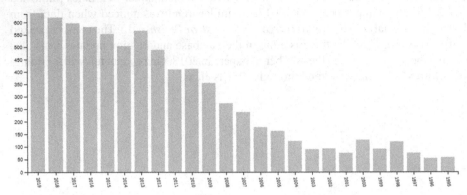

Fig. 3. Trend analysis of articles on safety management (*Web of Science*, n.d.)

Field: Source Titles	Record Count	% of 7,546
SAFETY SCIENCE	431	5.712 %
PROCESS SAFETY PROGRESS	186	2.465 %
PROGRESS IN SAFETY SCIENCE AND TECHNOLOGY SERIES	153	2.028 %
JOURNAL OF LOSS PREVENTION IN THE PROCESS INDUSTRIES	141	1.869 %
APPLIED MECHANICS AND MATERIALS	103	1.365 %
FOOD CONTROL	102	1.352 %
PROCEDIA ENGINEERING	92	1.219 %
ACCIDENT ANALYSIS AND PREVENTION	82	1.087 %
ADVANCED MATERIALS RESEARCH	81	1.073 %
JOURNAL OF CONSTRUCTION ENGINEERING AND MANAGEMENT	59	0.782 %

Fig. 4. Analysis of source titles for safety management (*Web of Science*, n.d.)

Trend analysis of articles on safety management is shown in Fig. 3. It can be seen that there has been a steady rise in the number of articles published since 2004. The higher number of articles published in 2013 indicates a temporary peak bucking the trend because the number of articles published in 2014 is less than in 2013. However, there is a steady increase in the number of articles published after 2013. Overall, the trend indicates that interest in safety management has increased in the last 25 years.

Top ten sources of titles for safety management have been shown in Fig. 4. Unlike game-based learning, the titles for safety management have been sourced from eclectic sources. The sources indicate that research was carried out in various fields like process safety, accident analysis and construction safety.

4   Results

4.1   Co-citation Analysis

"Citation analysis is used to examine the degree of connectivity between pairs of papers" (Fahimnia et al. 2015). VOSviewer was used for co-citation analysis. Pairs of papers which have been cited together form clusters. To determine important papers within them, papers which have been cited the greatest number of times were selected. So, the criteria to select the most important papers was the link strength (the number of times they have been co-cited) and the number of times they have been cited individually. The latest 500 papers in terms of date of publication were considered for this analysis.

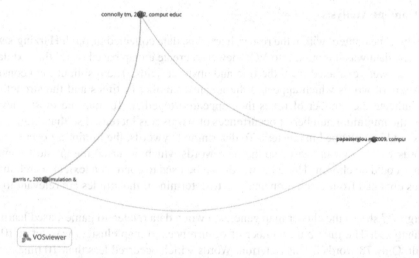

Fig. 5. Co-citation analysis for game-based learning (*VOSviewer*, n.d.).

The data file exported from the Web of Science was imported into VOSviewer. Figure 5 shows a co-citation analysis of game-based learning. For game-based learning, the minimum number of citations of a cited reference was set at 36 to get the top three research papers which were cited the greatest number of times. The top three papers had 55, 40 and 36 citations respectively.

Figure 6 shows the co-citation analysis of safety management. For safety management, the minimum number of citations of a cited reference was set at 17 to get the top three research papers which were cited the greatest number of times. Each of the three papers had 18 citations. Full references associated with the nodes in Figs. 5 and 6 are shown in the reference section.

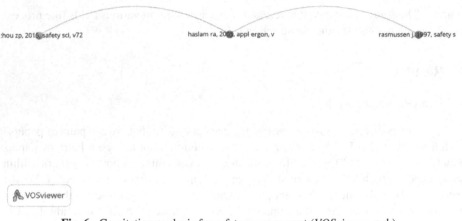

Fig. 6. Co-citation analysis for safety management (*VOSviewer*, n.d.).

4.2 Content Analysis

To analyze the content within the research articles, data collected through Harzing's was used. The data was imported into VOSviewer to create a map based on all the text data. The terms were extracted from the title and abstract fields. The resultant map consists of clusters of words which appeared the greatest number of times and the strength of links indicate the number of times they appeared together. To map the most relevant words, the minimum number of occurrences of words was increased so that around 150 words could be mapped in clusters. To determine keywords, the minimum occurrences of words was further increased so that five words which occurred the greatest number of times could be chosen. These keywords can be used to conduct a lexical search in the articles obtained from co-citation analysis to determine if the articles are relevant to the study.

Figure 7 shows the cluster map generated when data related to game-based learning was analyzed. The minimum number of occurrences to map clusters was set at 10 by default. Only 78 words fit this criterion. Words which occurred less than 10 times were deemed to be irrelevant. Table 1 shows the keywords and the number of times they occurred in the data that was analyzed. The table indicates that except the word "game" which has expectedly occurred the greatest number of times, the rest of the words have occurred fairly close to 150 times.

Figure 8 shows the cluster map generated when data related to safety management was analyzed. The minimum number of occurrences to map clusters was set at 35 resulting in 157 words being mapped. Table 2 shows the keywords and the number of times they occurred in the data that was analyzed. It can be seen that in general, the number of times these words occurred is way more when compared with the number of occurrences of keywords related to game-based learning. This can be attributed to the fact that articles related to safety management have been published for much longer and hence have a greater number of publications compared to game-based learning.

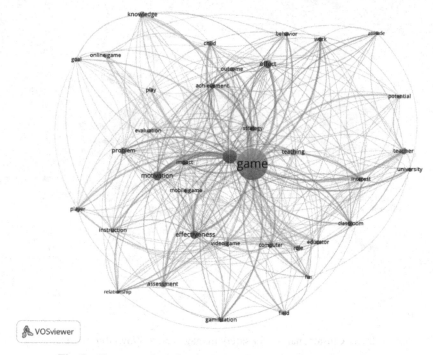

Fig. 7. Cluster analysis for game-based learning (*VOSviewer*, n.d.)

Table 1. Keyword selection for game-based learning (*VOSviewer*, n.d.)

Keyword	Occurrences
Game	913
Learning	184
Digital game	159
Environment	141
Student	140

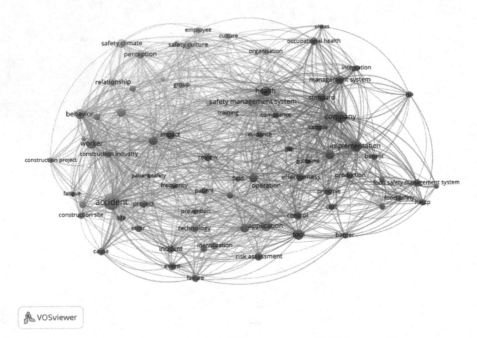

Fig. 8. Cluster analysis for safety management (*VOSviewer*, n.d.)

Table 2. Keyword selection for safety management (*VOSviewer*, n.d.)

Keyword	Occurrences
System	1091
Safety	1002
Risk	412
Safety management	580
Accident	495

4.3 Content Analysis Results from MAXQDA

To get the keywords from all the articles which are referred to in this paper, MAXQDA was used. All the key articles selected through co-citation analysis and other reference papers were imported into MAXQDA and a word cloud was generated. This gives us the overall keywords which are important in the context of this study. The word cloud has been shown in Fig. 9.

Fig. 9. Word cloud from MAXQDA (*MAXQDA*, n.d.)

5   Discussion

5.1 Game-Based Learning

Students' motivation towards games contrasts with their lack of interest in curricular content. To bridge this gap, games that encompass educational objectives and subject matter have the potential to make the learning of academic subjects more learner-centered, easier, more enjoyable, more interesting, and, thus, more effective (Papastergiou, 2009). It was found that simulations were by far the most frequently occurring genre in game-based learning techniques. To encourage the use of games in learning beyond simulations, it is necessary to develop a better understanding of the tasks, activities, skills and operations that different kinds of game can offer and examine how these might match desired learning outcomes (Connolly et al. 2012).

There are some issues which need to be resolved to make game-based learning techniques effective. One of them is the capacity of a particular game to hold the player's attention over a longer period of time. It has been seen that players tend to get addicted to a game until they are "played out" following which they move on to another game. This indicates that simulation games become less effective when they are used over a longer duration of time (Garris et al. 2002).

A considerable amount of work has already been done by educational researchers to make game-based learning techniques good for learning. However, this has not led to widespread adoption of game-based learning techniques in the classroom (Denham et al. 2016).

The trend analysis for game-based learning (in Fig. 1) based on the data from Web of Science showed a decreasing trend in the number of articles being published after 2017. This seemed counter-intuitive and hence to verify this trend, data was obtained by conducting a search in AuthorMapper. The keyword used was "game based learning". The search yielded 4446 results. The results from 2020 were excluded from the trend analysis. The trend analysis cannot be exported directly. The other issue was that the number of results that could be exported was limited to 2000. To get around this, the number of publications for every year were manually entered into Microsoft Excel and trend analysis was obtained which is shown in Fig. 10.

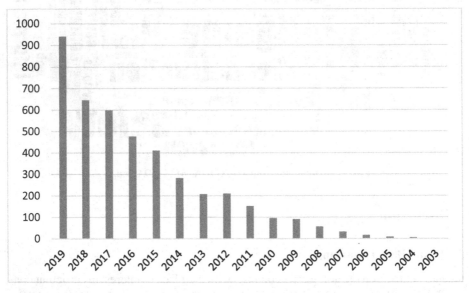

Fig. 10. Trend analysis for game-based learning from AuthorMapper (*AuthorMapper*, n.d.)

It can be seen that the trend shows an increase in the number of articles published year over year. This is contrary to the trend analysis obtained from the Web of Science. One reason for this could be that there is a time lag between the publication of the article and the date it is updated in Web of Science. However, a deeper analysis is needed to ascertain the reason for the trend shown by the data from Web of Science. This analysis is outside of the scope of this study.

5.2 Safety Management

Over the years, accidents and injuries have continued to plague the construction industry notwithstanding the efforts made towards improving safety. Because of this, the number of peer-reviewed papers published, and the range of research topics has been increasing over the years (Zhou et al. 2015). Greater attention needs to be given to the design and selection of tools, equipment and materials (Haslam et al. 2005). Visualization technology has been widely used in construction management research. Some studies show that BIM-based 4D models created during the design process can help site safety planning (Zhou et al. 2013).

Depending on the nature of the hazard, different risk management strategies have evolved. Occupational safety focusses on frequent, but small-scale accidents (Rasmussen Jens 1997). The root cause of worker injuries and illnesses can be addressed through a workplace ergonomics program as part of a larger occupational safety and health program (Lehto et al. 2012). Occupational safety is concerned not only with construction safety but with workplace safety in general. Safety training is an important component of any occupational safety and health program. Hence, an effective safety training program is necessary to improve workplace safety.

6 Conclusion

Despite the optimism that games might be useful in promoting better learning outcomes, the few papers which provide evidence to support this claim present qualitative rather than quantitative analysis (Connolly et al. 2012). As researchers explore innovations in visualization and apply them in new domains, effective information visualization has the potential to improve the usability of information and to increase the generation of valuable insight (North 2012). Although some examples of game-based learning being used for safety training like fire safety training for children were found in literature, there is scope for a lot more research in this area intersecting game-based learning with safety training. It can be concluded that a combination of cognitive, motivational, affective, and sociocultural perspectives is necessary for both game design and game research to fully capture what games have to offer for learning (Plass et al. 2015).

7 Future Work

Apart from game-based learning, another interesting training technique that can be explored is virtual environment (VE) consisting of unique I/O devices, perspectives, and physiological interactions. However, there are certain factors that need to be considered before using VE as a training method. VE simulators are generally less effective for initial training. High fidelity VE training can be used to reinforce acquired knowledge and develop advanced strategic knowledge and tactical skills (Stanney and Cohn 2012). The application of VE in safety training is something which can be explored further.

In one of the studies, a web-based Construction Safety Management Information System (CSMIS) was developed for better management of safety. CSMIS can be utilized for safety education and training. The CSMIS helped the construction managers and workers to understand the possible risk factors better (Park et al. 2015). A virtual environment (VE) training integrated into these types of systems has the potential to increase the effectiveness of safety training.

References

AuthorMapper. (n.d.). https://www.authormapper.com/. Accessed 29 Feb 2020

Connolly, T.M., Boyle, E.A., MacArthur, E., Hainey, T., Boyle, J.M.: A systematic literature review of empirical evidence on computer games and serious games. Comput. Educ. **59**(2), 661–686 (2012). https://doi.org/10.1016/j.compedu.2012.03.004

Stephanidis, C., et al.: Design for all: computer-assisted design of user interface adaptation. In: Handbook of Human Factors and Ergonomics, pp. 1484–1507 (2012)

Denham, A.R., Mayben, R., Boman, T.: Integrating game-based learning initiative: increasing the usage of game-based learning within K-12 classrooms through professional learning groups. TechTrends **60**(1), 70–76 (2016). https://doi.org/10.1007/s11528-015-0019-y

Fahimnia, B., Sarkis, J., Davarzani, H.: Green supply chain management: a review and bibliometric analysis. Int. J. Prod. Econ. **162**, 101–114 (2015). https://doi.org/10.1016/j.ijpe.2015.01.003

Garris, R., Ahlers, R., Driskell, J.E.: Games, motivation, and learning: a research and practice model. Simul. Gaming **33**(4), 441–467 (2002). https://doi.org/10.1177/1046878102238607

Harzing's Publish or Perish. (n.d.). https://harzing.com/resources/publish-or-perish. Accessed 24 Feb 2020

Haslam, R.A., et al.: Contributing factors in construction accidents. Appl. Ergon. **36**(4) 401–415 (2005). https://doi.org/10.1016/j.apergo.2004.12.002

Lehto, M.R., Lafayette, W., Cook, B.T., Engineering, M., Arbor, A.: Management of occupational safety. In: Handbook of Human Factors and Ergonomics, pp. 701–733 (2012)

MAXQDA (n.d.). https://www.maxqda.com/. Accessed 22 Feb 2020

Mendeley (n.d.). https://www.mendeley.com/?interaction_required=true. Accessed 29 Feb 2020

North, C.: Information visualization. In: Handbook of Human Factors and Ergonomics, pp. 1209–1236 (2012)

Papastergiou, M.: Digital game-based learning in high school computer science education: impact on educational effectiveness and student motivation. Comput. Educ. **52**(1), 1–12 (2009). https://doi.org/10.1016/j.compedu.2008.06.004

Park, J., Park, S., Oh, T.: The development of a web-based construction safety management information system to improve risk assessment. KSCE J. Civ. Eng. **19**(3), 528–537 (2015). https://doi.org/10.1007/s12205-014-0664-2

Plass, J.L., Homer, B.D., Kinzer, C.K.: Foundations of game-based learning. Educ. Psychol. **50**(4), 258–283 (2015). https://doi.org/10.1080/00461520.2015.1122533

Jens, R.: Risk management in a dynamic society: a modelling problem. Saf. Sci. **27**(2/3), 183–213 (1997)

Saeed, Y.S.: Safety management in construction projects. Journal Univ. Duhok, **20**(1), 546–560 (2017). https://doi.org/10.26682/sjuod.2017.20.1.48

Stanney, K.M., Cohn, J.V.: Virtual environments. In: Handbook of Human Factors and Ergonomics, pp. 1031–1056 (2012)

Studies, C.: Human factors in online communities. In: Handbook of Human Factors and Ergonomics, pp. 1237–1249 (2004)

Sung, H.Y., Hwang, G.J.: A collaborative game-based learning approach to improving students' learning performance in science courses. Comput. Educ. **63**, 43–51 (2013). https://doi.org/10.1016/j.compedu.2012.11.019

VOSviewer (n.d.). https://www.vosviewer.com/. Accessed 22 Feb 2020

Web of Science (n.d.). https://apps-webofknowledge-com.ezproxy.lib.purdue.edu/WOS_GeneralSearch_input.do?product=WOS&search_mode=GeneralSearch&SID=7EKUw7yEVcCGVrUwOlu&preferencesSaved. Accessed 22 Feb 2020

Zhou, Y., Ding, L.Y., Chen, L.J.: Application of 4D visualization technology for safety management in metro construction. Autom. Constr. **34**, 25–36 (2013). https://doi.org/10.1016/j.autcon.2012.10.011

Zhou, Z., Goh, Y.M., Li, Q.: Overview and analysis of safety management studies in the construction industry. Saf. Sci. **72**, 337–350 (2015). https://doi.org/10.1016/j.ssci.2014.10.006

Integrating Lean Six Sigma and Discrete-Event Simulation for Shortening the Appointment Lead-Time in Gynecobstetrics Departments: A Case Study

Miguel Ortíz-Barrios[1]([envelope]), Sally McClean[2], Genett Jiménez-Delgado[3], and David Enrique Martínez-Sierra[4]

[1] Department of Productivity and Innovation, Universidad de la Costa CUC, Barranquilla, Colombia
mortiz1@cuc.edu.co
[2] School of Computing and Information Engineering, University of Ulster, Coleraine, UK
simcclean@ulster.ac.uk
[3] Department of Industrial Engineering, Corporación Universitaria Reformada CUR, Barranquilla, Colombia
g.jimenez@unireformada.edu.co
[4] Department of Industrial Engineering, Faculty of Engineering, Universidad Simón Bolívar, Barranquilla, Colombia
dmartinez@unisimonbolivar.edu.co

Abstract. Long waiting time to appointment may be a worry for pregnant women, particularly those who need perinatology consultation since it could increase anxiety and, in a worst case scenario, lead to an increase in fetal, infant, and maternal mortality. Treatment costs may also increase since pregnant women with diverse pathologies can develop more severe complications. As a step towards improving this process, we propose a methodological approach to reduce the appointment lead-time in outpatient gynecobstetrics departments. This framework involves combining the Six Sigma method to identify defects in the appointment scheduling process with a discrete-event simulation (DES) to evaluate the potential success of removing such defects in simulation before we resort to changing the real-world healthcare system. To do these, we initially characterize the gynecobstetrics department using a SIPOC diagram. Then, six sigma performance metrics are calculated to evaluate how well the department meets the government target in relation to the appointment lead-time. Afterwards, a cause-and-effect analysis is undertaken to identify potential causes of appointment lead-time variation. These causes are later validated through ANOVA, regression analysis, and DES. Improvement scenarios are next designed and pretested through computer simulation models. Finally, control plans are deployed to maintain the results achieved through the implementation of the DES-Six sigma approach. The aforementioned framework was validated in a public gynecobstetrics outpatient department. The results revealed that mean waiting time decreased from 6.9 days to 4.1 days while variance passed from 2.46 days^2 to 1.53 days^2.

© Springer Nature Switzerland AG 2020
V. G. Duffy (Ed.): HCII 2020, LNCS 12199, pp. 378–389, 2020.
https://doi.org/10.1007/978-3-030-49907-5_27

Keywords: Six sigma · Discrete-event simulation (DES) · Appointment lead time · Gynecology · Healthcare

1   Introduction

Patient waiting time is commonly regarded as a key indicator of healthcare quality of service. For the patients, long waiting times can be viewed as a barrier to obtaining appropriate services, while healthcare professionals can fail to meet important targets and face punitive action. However, waiting time reduction is a complex problem, involving diagnosis, patient prioritisation, monitoring and management of waiting times, in addition to resource management. As such, long appointment lead-time remains a significant challenge across many healthcare specialties leading to delayed diagnosis and treatment as well as increased mortality, morbidity and dissatisfaction. Also, lengthy waits can lead to increased hospitalisation, as well as outpatient and emergency department visits.

Discrete Event Simulation (DES) has been widely used for many years to model healthcare, with previous work providing and evaluating waiting time improvement strategies [1]. For example, a fairly recent study has analysed the appointment scheduling system in an Obstetrics Gynecology Department and developed a simulation-based decision support system [2]. An example of using DES to reduce waiting time in accident and emergency departments can be found, for example, in Nuñez-Perez [3]. Such simulation and analysis of patient flows can contribute to efficient functioning of healthcare systems as well as achievement of key performance targets.

Six Sigma is a well-known Process Improvement technique which tries to improve the quality of a process by identifying and removing the causes of defects, thus minimising process variability. The main approaches utilise an empirical, statistical approach to identify some problem issues, and then try to reduce or eliminate them with a focus on, for example, reducing overall patient waiting time or appointment lead-time. Over recent years, the use of Six Sigma in healthcare has been increasing, but work is still needed to sell the idea to healthcare practitioners, to extract the lessons learned towards sustained improvement and to identify barriers to advancement in healthcare processes. To date, most of the work using Six Sigma in Healthcare applications has focused on the Emergency Department, particularly with regard to reducing patient waiting time. However, there has also been some previous application to Outpatient departments, which are our current focus.

In this paper we concentrate on reducing appointment lead-times in gynecobstetrics outpatient departments, where a long waiting time may be a worry for pregnant women, particularly those who need perinatology consultation because of their high-risk pregnancy [4]. As a result, appointment lead-time can be regarded as a key performance index for gynecobstetrics departments, where lengthy waiting times for an appointment could increase patient anxiety and, in a worst case scenario, lead to an increase in fetal, infant and maternal mortality. Treatment costs also may increase since pregnant women with diverse pathologies can develop more severe complications. As a step towards improving this process, we here propose a methodological approach to reduce the appointment lead-time in outpatient departments of Gynecology and Obstetrics. The framework involves combining Six Sigma methods to identify defects in the appointment process with a discrete-event simulation (DES) aimed at evaluating the potential success of removing such defects in simulation before we resort to changing the real-world healthcare system. Such a hybrid approach has received recent attention in Ahmed et al. [5] which highlights the importance of further work in this area. The novelty of our current research is to develop a methodological tool based on combining DES and Six Sigma for application to the field of Gynecology and Obstetrics; this represents a way of developing and assessing better ways of managing outpatient appointment, especially in time-critical specialties.

Nonetheless, relatively few studies to date have focused on the reduction of appointment lead-time in gynecobstetrics outpatient departments. As such, this paper proposes the application of Six Sigma and Discrete-event Simulation (DES) to evaluate potential improvement strategies aiming at reducing appointment lead-time for such patients. The remainder of this paper is as follows. Section 2 reviews the related reported literature. Section 3 describes the proposed methodology combining Six Sigma and DES whereas Sect. 4 outlines the results of its application in a public gynecobstetrics outpatient department. Lately, conclusions and future work are presented in Sect. 5.

2   Literature Review

Six Sigma has been around for some time but, in healthcare, has been slow to be adopted and integrated into Process Improvement. For example DelliFraine et al. [6], carried out an extensive literature review study in 2010 and suggested that the technique provided relatively new, but popular, quality improvement tools already being used in the health care industry They also stated that earlier research showed that often organisations must undergo a cultural change before obtaining performance improvement through Six Sigma. In a very recent literature review, it is concluded that the number of empirical research articles on Six Sigma in healthcare is still increasing but work is needed to understand how such approaches can be best implemented and sustained [7].

More recently, Six Sigma has been used in healthcare for decreasing the occurrence of diagnostic errors in laboratory medicine [8]. Laboratory diagnostics are an essential part of clinical decision making, which routinely uses error reduction for quality management and as such is well suited to the Six Sigma approach. Another suitable area for Six Sigma is to help reduce the risk of hospital acquired infections in surgery departments [9]. The authors conclude that the approach could be applied, inter alia, for redesign and improvement of a wide range of healthcare processes.

Such healthcare topics have an obvious synergy with Six Sigma as there are underlying errors or other undesirable events that can be mitigated by focusing on and trying to eliminate such unwanted outcomes. However, Six Sigma has also been used for process improvement in Healthcare processes where waiting times may become excessive with associated inefficiencies and patient dissatisfaction. For example, Hynes et al. [10] describe the use of Use of Lean Six Sigma methodology to successfully reduce inpatient waiting time for catheter placement in interventional radiology while Chang et al. [11] describe Six Sigma based interventions to improve waiting times for hospital surgical rooms, particularly with regard to reducing variability in the process.

Discrete Event Simulation (DES) has been widely used in healthcare for many years to model healthcare and predict the likely performance of proposed improvements. As such it is a complementary technique to Six Sigma, providing powerful evaluation tools for such approaches to reducing errors and improving service quality. With regard to our current focus, some previous work has used DES to analyse waiting time improvement strategies in general, and also in particular for outpatients [1]. For example, Aeenparast et al. [12] describe a simulation model to improve the performance of a healthcare facility by providing a strategy for reducing outpatient waiting times by concentrating on healthcare schedules. A more recent example is provided by Jamjoon et al. [2] who analysed the appointment scheduling system in an Obstetrics Gynecology Department using a simulation-based decision support system for the evaluation and optimisation of waiting times and scheduling rules. This model was used to extract some critical factors that underlie patient waiting times and propose approaches to reschedule outpatient appointments thus improving patient waiting times. In general, such DES of patient journeys can make a good contribution to efficient functioning of a healthcare system; this is further described in a recent paper which provides various contexts and also describes some simulation tools [13].

3   The Proposed Methodology

The proposed approach aims to reduce the appointment lead-time in gynecobstetrics departments by the integration of Lean Six Sigma and Discrete-event Simulation (DES). The methodology is comprised of five phases (refer to Fig. 1):

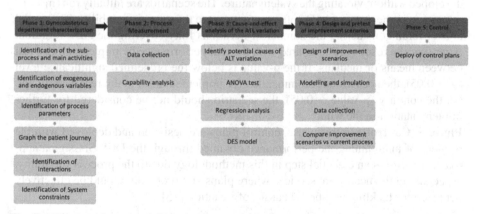

Fig. 1. The five-phase methodology for modelling gynecobstetrics outpatient departments through integration of DES and Six Sigma

- **Phase 1 (Gynecobstetrics department characterization):** To appropriately model the outpatient gynecobstetrics department, it is critical to pinpoint their key sub-processes, the data variables, and the process parameters followed by the identification of endogenous and exogenous variables. This information is later consolidated in a

Supplier-Input-Process-Output-Client (SIPOC) diagram detailing the patient journey, existing interactions, and system constraints. In this step, the health service managers, healthcare professionals, administrative staff, and stakeholders are required to provide the information on the gynecobstetrics healthcare system and work closely to modelers so that realistic and robust DES models can be fully generated [14].

– **Phase 2 (Process Measurement):** In this phase, a capability study is performed on the critical parameter "appointment lead-time (ALT)". In particular, this study denotes how well the gynecobstetrics department complies with the specification defined by the Ministry of Health and Social Protection (Upper specification limit = 8 days). In this regard, capability indices such as sigma level, Ppu, Ppk, and DPMO are estimated to measure the current gap between the process performance and the desired status.

– **Phase 3 (Cause-and-effect analysis):** A cause-and-effect analysis is developed to detect the potential causes of variations in the "appointment lead-time". In this respect, a Fishbone diagram-analyze is implemented considering six domains: materials, human resources, measurement system, patient, methods, and equipment. Then, these causes are validated using the Analysis of Variance (ANOVA) test, regression analysis, and Discrete-event Simulation (DES). In particular, DES is employed to computationally model the behavior of the gynecobstetrics department and analyze its performance under constraints [17].

– **Phase 4 (Design and evaluation of improvement scenarios):** One of the most important advantages of the DES is its capability to represent and evaluate different improvement scenarios targeting reduced appointment lead-times in the gynecobstetrics departments. Such scenarios should be designed with the participation of the healthcare managers to ensure that the proposed initiatives are realistic and can be developed without violating the system nature. The scenarios are initially run ($n_1 = 10$ iterations) in the Arena 14.5® software to measure the system variability. The model is later rerun considering the number of iterations fully covering the ALT variation. After this, the results are compared with the real performance by implementing a test between means or medians. If the p-value is below the predefined significance level ($\alpha = 0.05$), the scenario is recommended for implementation in the real department. On the contrary (p-value > 0.05), the scenario should not be considered for further implementation in the wild.

– **Phase 5 (Control):** In this phase, control plans are designed and deployed with the purpose of maintaining the performance obtained through the DES-Six sigma approach. *Control* is an essential step in this methodology due to the process variability, especially in the healthcare services where plans and protocols should be effectively deployed for tackling the special causes of variation [15].

4   A Case Study in a Public Gynecobstetrics Outpatient Department

The aforedescribed methodology was implemented in a public gynecobstetrics outpatient department from South America. This institution offers consultations in a wide range of specialties including cardiology, internal medicine, gynecobstetrics, and surgery with a special focus on the binomial *mother-child*. Despite the tremendous efforts made by this organization to propel the continuous quality improvement of its outpatient services, there is still too much room for interventions delivering timely gynecobstetrics care to patients. Indeed, the average appointment lead time is 6.9 days/appointment with a standard deviation of 1.6. In the next sub-sections, we will illustrate the step-by-step Six sigma-DES procedure through which reduced ALT and unit operational cost was finally achieved.

4.1 Gynecobstetrics Department Characterization

A 1-year dataset (pregnant women admitted from 1 January until 31 December) containing information regarding the gynecobstetrics appointments was extracted from the Appointment Scheduling software supporting the operations of the department. The patients belong to different age groups ranging from underage to adults (Máx: 43 years old). A SIPOC diagram (refer to Fig. 2) was drawn for characterizing the suppliers, inputs, outputs, and clients relating to the gynecobstetrics outpatient department under study.

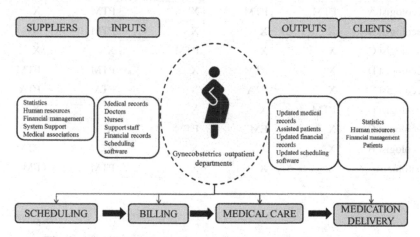

Fig. 2. SIPOC diagram for the gynecobstetrics outpatient department

The key sub-processes (Scheduling, Billing, Medical care, Medication delivery) can be identified in Fig. 2. Moreover, various process parameters were defined: i) time between arrivals for first-seek appointments, ii) time between arrivals for monitoring appointments, iii) time between arrivals for gynecology appointments, iv) time between arrivals for perinatology appointments, v) medical consultation time for first-seek appointments, vi) medical consultation time for monitoring appointments, vii) medical consultation time for gynecology appointments, viii) medical consultation time for perinatology appointments, ix) number of gynecologists, x) number of perinatologists, xi) number of schedulers, xii) number of billing operators, xiii) number of medication deliverers, xiv) scheduling time, xv) billing time, and xvi) medication delivery time.

On a different note, it was determined that the department normally operates from 8:00 to 17:00 (Monday-Friday) although the involved personnel present different shifts (refer to Table 1). In this respect, five shifts were identified: FT1 (8:00–12:00 and 13:00–17:00), FT2 (8:00–13:00 and 14:00–17:00), PTM (8:00–12:00), PTA (13:00–17:00), and EM (8:00–14:00).

Table 1. Personnel shifts in the gynecobstetrics outpatient department under study

	Monday	Tuesday	Wednesday	Thursday	Friday
Scheduler A	FT1	FT1	FT1	FT1	FT1
Scheduler B	FT2	FT2	FT2	FT2	FT2
Billing op1	FT1	FT1	FT1	FT1	FT1
Billing op2	FT2	FT2	FT2	FT2	FT2
Medication del1	FT1	FT1	FT1	FT1	FT1
Gynecologist A	PTM	PTM	X	PTM	X
Gynecologist B	X	X	X	PTM	X
Gynecologist C	X	X	PTM	X	X
Gynecologist D	X	PTM	X	PTM	PTM
Gynecologist E	X	PTA	X	PTA	PTA
Gynecologist F	PTM	X	X	X	X
Gynecologist G	X	EM	PTM	X	X
Gynecologist H	X	X	X	X	PTM
Perinatologist	X	X	X	PTM	EM

4.2 Process Measurement

Initially, the Kolmogorov-Smirnov test supported the normality assumption of ALT (KS = 0.134; p-value > 0.15). A capability analysis (refer to Fig. 3) was later performed using Minitab 19® to verify whether the gynecobstetrics department complies with the upper specification limit (USL = 8 days/appointment). The results revealed that 243466 out of 1 million of pregnant women will have to wait for over 8 days before being assisted by the gynecologist. On the other hand, the Ppu and Ppk (0.23) were found to be lower than the reference value (1.25) and the process is therefore concluded not to be capable to meet the specification. Such finding is also confirmed by the sigma level (1.12) which confirms that there is still much room for improvement in this department regarding the ALT.

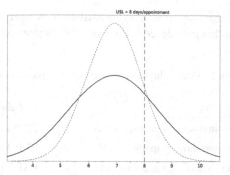

Fig. 3. Current performance of the gynecobstetrics department in terms of appointment lead-time

4.3 Cause-and-Effect Analysis

Considering that the gynecobstetrics department is not capable to meet the specification, the next step is to find the factors increasing the appointment lead time experienced by patients. In this regard, we initially undertook a fishbone diagram to present the main causes of the problem (refer to Fig. 4).

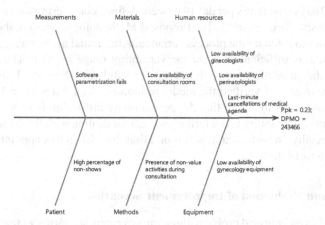

Fig. 4. Fishbone diagram for the appointment lead-time problem

Following this, we decided to perform an ANOVA test to check whether the appointment lead time in perinatology strongly affects the total ATL. In this case, a p-value lower than 0.05 provided enough support for the significance hypothesis. In fact, a regression test revealed that this variable explains approximately 60% of the total ATL. Complementary to this activity, we modeled the process through ARENA 15.0® software. To do these, we firstly evaluated the randomness assumption of the predefined variables through run tests which, in all the cases, were found to confirm the independency nature (p-value > 0.15). We next assessed the homogeneity hypothesis using ANOVA (α = 0.05). In this study, all the variables were found to be homogeneous and one probability distribution is therefore concluded to be enough for representing their behavior. After verifying the homogeneity condition, goodness-of-fit tests were carried out to find the probability distribution that best describes the variable performance (see Table 2).

Table 2. Probability distributions of process variables

Process variable	Probability distribution
Time between arrivals for first-seek appointments	EXPO (0.75) hours
Time between arrivals for monitoring appointments	EXPO (0.81) hours
Time between arrivals for gynecology appointments	EXPO (2.72) hours
Time between arrivals for perinatology appointments	EXPO (0.26) hours
Medical consultation time for first-seek appointments	UNIF (0.75, 1.05) hours
Medical consultation time for monitoring appointments	NORM (0.58, 0.09) hours
Medical consultation time for gynecology appointments	UNIF (1.05, 1.50) hours
Medical consultation time for perinatology appointments	UNIF (0.33, 0.60) hours

The above-cited information was later entered in the simulated model whose replication length (30 days) and hours per day (9 h) were defined considering the current system constraints. As specified in the "3. The Proposed Methodology" section, the model was first run 10 times to estimate the process variance. After initial assessment, 40 iterations were considered as sufficient to cover the variability range of ALT. The ALT values derived from the simulations were then used for validating the virtual model. In this case, a p-value over 0.15 verified the model reliability. On a different tack, the virtual department allowed us to detect that the perinatology utilization is over 100% which reveals that current capability is not further enough for dealing with the current demands in this sub-specialty. In particular, it was found that the ALT in this appointment type is ranging from 6 to 14 days.

4.4 Design and Evaluation of Improvement Scenarios

To tackle the abovementioned problem, three improvement scenarios were established in conjunction with the stakeholders: i) Reorganize the medical agenda of the perinatologist by assigning the tasks performed in emergency room and intensive care unit to other gynecologists, ii) Increase the installed capacity of gynecology by hiring 3 new doctors, and iii) Eliminate reinterrogation tasks during medical consultation.

All these scenarios were designed and simulated for further analysis before implementation in the wild. Table 3 summarizes the results emanating from comparing the proposed scenarios and the current gynecobstetrics department. In this case, all the initiatives were found to be suitable for implementation in the wild (p-value < 0.05). Among these alternatives, strategy i was concluded to be the most beneficial considering the high sigma level variation that may be achieved if executed. After implementation of strategy ii, the results revealed that mean waiting time decreased from 6.9 days to 4.1 days while variance passed from 2.46 days^2 to 1.53 days^2.

Table 3. Summary of improvement strategies results

Strategy	P-value	Sigma level variation	Conclusion
Strategy i	<0.05	6.3	Recommended
Strategy ii	<0.05	4.2	Recommended
Strategy iii	<0.05	1.2	Recommended

4.5 Control

A critical step towards the consolidation of improvements derived from Six sigma implementations is the development of effective control plans. Such plans are expected to
provide a strong basis for launching new six-sigma projects whose starting point not to
be the same as the initial. In such a case, it is important to define suitable control actions
propelling continuous commitment of stakeholders while empowering six-sigma teams
to guide the gynecobstetrics department towards delivering timely care. In consequence,
I chart (refer to Fig. 5) for individuals has been designed for monitoring the ALT behavior regarding its central tendency and variation. In addition, it was necessary to include
the aforedescribed changes in the Quality Management System so that the inherent procedure can be institutionalized, updated, and properly socialized. The control plan also
considers periodical visits of the Six-sigma black belt consultant to monitor the progress
of the process and consequently inform the presence of irregularities if detected.

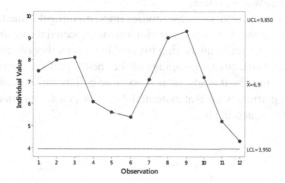

Fig. 5. I chart for appointment lead-time values in the gynecobstetrics department

5 Conclusions

In this document, we have developed a methodological tool based on the combination
of discrete event simulation (DES) and Six Sigma to reduce appointment waiting time
in outpatient gynecology departments. The results revealed that considering the current
system of a public gynecobstetrics department from South America 243.466 of 1 million

pregnant women will have to wait more than 8 days before receiving assistance from the gynecologist. Improving this indicator was critical considering that long waiting times for an appointment could increase patient anxiety and, in the worst case, lead to an increase in the fetus, the infant and maternal mortality. For this purpose, three improvement scenarios were established in conjunction with stakeholders to address the aforementioned problem. All these scenarios were designed and simulated for subsequent analysis before implementation, with the help of Arena 15® software, Minitab 19® and the knowledge provided by health service managers, health professionals, and administrative staff.

When comparing the proposed scenarios, it was found that all the initiatives were adequate for their implementation with a value of $p < 0.05$. Among these alternatives, it was concluded that strategy i is the most beneficial considering the high sigma level variation that can be achieved if executed. After implementing the strategy ii, which contemplated increasing the installed gynecology capacity by hiring 3 new doctors, the results revealed that the average waiting time decreased from 6.9 days to 4.1 days, while the variation passed from 2.46 days to 1.53 days. This indicates a considerable decrease and benefit for the forthcoming pregnant mothers.

On the other hand, after seeing the good results derived from this study, the managers of medical centers should consider the feasibility of implementing the proposed methodology in other healthcare areas where waiting times are crucial. Thereby, changes in the provision of healthcare services can be pretested to analyze their improvement potential and impact on operational costs. This is relevant to avoid errors and cost overruns during implementation in the practical scenario. However, it is necessary to work closely with doctors and other health professionals to ensure that the models being simulated are equivalent to the real-world system.

For future work in the area, new case studies implementing this methodology should be proposed including an additional evaluation on the expected return on investment per scenario. Similarly, it would be interesting to combine this methodology other lean manufacturing tools (i.e. value stream mapping) so that better performance can be achieved at a low investment. Finally, it is advisable to explore collaboration scenarios with other gynecobstetrics departments so that potential benefits can be extended to the entire healthcare system as stated in [16].

References

1. Gunal, M., Pidd, M.: Discrete event simulation for performance modelling in health care: a review of the literature. J. Simul. **4**(1), 42–51 (2010)
2. Jamjoom, A., Abdullah, M., Abulkhair, M., Alghamdi, T., Mogbil, A.: Improving outpatient waiting time using simulation approach. In: UKSim-AMSS 8th European Modelling Symposium, Pisa, Italy, pp. 117–125. IEEE (2014)
3. Nuñez-Perez, N., Ortíz-Barrios, M., McClean, S., Salas-Navarro, K., Jimenez-Delgado, G., Castillo-Zea, A.: Discrete-event simulation to reduce waiting time in accident and emergency departments: a case study in a district general clinic. In: Ochoa, Sergio F., Singh, P., Bravo, J. (eds.) UCAmI 2017. LNCS, vol. 10586, pp. 352–363. Springer, Cham (2017). https://doi.org/10.1007/978-3-319-67585-5_37

4. Ortiz-Barrios, M., Lopez-Meza, P., McClean, S., Polifroni-Avendaño, G.: Discrete-event simulation for performance evaluation and improvement of gynecology outpatient departments: a case study in the public sector. In: Duffy, Vincent G. (ed.) HCII 2019. LNCS, vol. 11582, pp. 101–112. Springer, Cham (2019). https://doi.org/10.1007/978-3-030-22219-2_8
5. Ahmed, A., Page, J., Olsen, J.: Enhancing Six Sigma methodology using simulation techniques: literature review and implications for future research. Int. J. Lean Six Sigma 11(1), 211–232 (2019)
6. DelliFraine, J.L., Langabeer, J.R., Nembhard, I.M.: Assessing the evidence of Six Sigma and Lean in the health care industry. Qual. Manage. Healthc. 19(3), 211–225 (2010)
7. Henrique, D.B., Godinho Filho, M.: A systematic literature review of empirical research in Lean and Six Sigma in healthcare. Total Qual. Manage. Bus. Excellence 31(3–4), 429–449 (2020)
8. Lippi, G., Plebani, M.: A Six-Sigma approach for comparing diagnostic errors in healthcare—where does laboratory medicine stand? Ann. Transl. Med. 6(10), 1–3 (2018)
9. Montella, E., et al.: The application of Lean Six Sigma methodology to reduce the risk of healthcare–associated infections in surgery departments. J. Eval. Clin. Pract. 23(3), 530–539 (2017)
10. Hynes, J.P., et al.: Use of Lean Six Sigma methodology shows reduction of inpatient waiting time for peripherally inserted central catheter placement. Clin. Radiol. 74(9), 733.e5–733.e9 (2019)
11. Chang, D.S., Leu, J.D., Wang, W.S., Chen, Y.C.: Improving waiting time for surgical rooms using workflow and the six-sigma method. Total Qual. Manage. Bus. Excellence 31, 1–18 (2018)
12. Aeenparast, A., Tabibi, S.J., Shahanaghi, K., Aryanejhad, M.B.: Reducing outpatient waiting time: a simulation modeling approach. Iran. Red Crescent Med. J. 15(9), 865–869 (2013)
13. Bean, D.M., Taylor, P., Dobson, R.J.B.: A patient flow simulator for healthcare management education. BMJ Simul. Technol. Enhanced Learn. 5(1), 46–48 (2019)
14. Ortíz-Barrios, M., Jimenez-Delgado, G., De Avila-Villalobos, J.: A computer simulation approach to reduce appointment lead-time in outpatient perinatology departments: a case study in a maternal-child hospital. In: Siuly, S., et al. (eds.) HIS 2017. LNCS, vol. 10594, pp. 32–39. Springer, Cham (2017). https://doi.org/10.1007/978-3-319-69182-4_4
15. Ortiz Barrios, M., Felizzola Jiménez, H.: Reduction of average lead time in outpatient service of obstetrics through six sigma methodology. In: Bravo, J., Hervás, R., Villarreal, V. (eds.) AmIHEALTH 2015. LNCS, vol. 9456, pp. 293–302. Springer, Cham (2015). https://doi.org/10.1007/978-3-319-26508-7_29
16. Ortiz Barrios, M.A., Escorcia Caballero, J., Sánchez Sánchez, F.: A methodology for the creation of integrated service networks in outpatient internal medicine. In: Bravo, J., Hervás, R., Villarreal, V. (eds.) AmIHEALTH 2015. LNCS, vol. 9456, pp. 247–257. Springer, Cham (2015). https://doi.org/10.1007/978-3-319-26508-7_24
17. Izquierdo, N.V., Lezama, O.B.P., Dorta, R.G., Viloria, A., Deras, I., Hernández-Fernández, L.: Fuzzy logic applied to the performance evaluation. Honduran coffee sector case. In: Tan, Y., Shi, Y., Tang, Q. (eds.) ICSI 2018. LNCS, vol. 10942, pp. 164–173. Springer, Cham (2018). https://doi.org/10.1007/978-3-319-93818-9_16

Choosing the Most Suitable Classifier for Supporting Assistive Technology Adoption in People with Parkinson's Disease: A Fuzzy Multi-criteria Approach

Miguel Ortíz-Barrios[1]([✉]), Ian Cleland[2], Mark Donnelly[2], Jonathan Greer[3], Antonella Petrillo[4], Zaury Fernández-Mendoza[5], and Natalia Jaramillo-Rueda[1]

[1] Department of Productivity and Innovation, Universidad de la Costa CUC, Barranquilla, Colombia
{mortiz1,njaramil}@cuc.edu.co
[2] School of Computing and Mathematics, Ulster University, Jordanstown, Northern Ireland, UK
{i.cleland,mp.donnelly}@ulster.ac.uk
[3] School of Computing, Ulster University, Newtownabbey, Co. Antrim BT37 0QB, UK
jonathan.greer1@sky.com
[4] Department of Engineering, University of Napoli "Parthenope", Naples, Italy
antonella.petrillo@uniparthenope.it
[5] Department of Industrial Engineering, Institución Universitaria ITSA, Barranquilla, Colombia
zefernandez@itsa.edu.co

Abstract. Parkinson's disease (PD) is the second most common neurodegenerative disorder which requires a long-term, interdisciplinary disease management. While there remains no cure for Parkinson's disease, treatments are available to help reduce the main symptoms and maintain quality of life for as long as possible. Owing to the global burden faced by chronic conditions such as PD, Assistive technologies (AT's) are becoming an increasingly common prescribed form of treatment. Low adoption is hampering the potential of digital technologies within health and social care. It is then necessary to employ classification algorithms have been developed for differentiating adopters and non-adopters of these technologies; thereby, potential negative effects on people with PD and cost overruns can be further minimized. This paper bridges this gap by extending the Multi-criteria decision-making approach adopted in technology adoption modeling for people with dementia. First, the fuzzy Analytic Hierarchy Process (FAHP) is applied to estimate the initial relative weights of criteria and sub-criteria. Then, the Decision-making Trial and Evaluation Laboratory (DEMATEL) is used for evaluating the interrelations and feedback among criteria and sub-criteria. The Technique for Order of Preferences by Similarity to Ideal Solution (TOPSIS) is finally implemented to rank three classifiers (Lazy IBk – knearest neighbors, Naïve bayes, and J48 decision tree) according to their ability to model technology adoption. A real case study considering is presented to validate the proposed approach.

Keywords: Parkinson's disease (PD) · Technology adoption · Fuzzy Analytic Hierarchy Process (FAHP) · Decision Making Trial and Evaluation Laboratory

© Springer Nature Switzerland AG 2020
V. G. Duffy (Ed.): HCII 2020, LNCS 12199, pp. 390–405, 2020.
https://doi.org/10.1007/978-3-030-49907-5_28

(DEMATEL) · Technique for Order of Preference by Similarity to Ideal Solution
(TOPSIS) · Healthcare

1 Introduction

According to the World Health Organisation, global average life expectancy increased by
5.5 years between 2000 and 2016, the fastest increase since the 1960s [1]. Major factors
contributing to these increases include advances in the economy, healthcare provision,
science, and technology. As people live longer, however, the growing burden of long-
term chronic diseases rapidly impacts upon society's capability to delivery sustainable
care. In 2001, chronic disease was attributed to approximately 60% of the 56.5 million
total reported deaths in the world and approximately 46% of the global burden of disease
[2]. It is anticipated that this burden will increase to 57% by 2020.

One such chronic condition is Parkinson's disease (PD). PD is a degenerative disorder, thought to affect around 1 in 500 people. It impacts the central nervous system
leading to impairments in motor skills and speech. Most people with Parkinson's start
to develop symptoms when they're over 50, although around 1 in 20 people with the
condition first experience symptoms when they're under 40. Symptoms include tremors,
shuffled walks, sudden jerky movements appearing from time to time, continuous chorea,
or akinesia. Coping with movement disorders is reported to be physically exhaustive,
leading to the inability to perform very basic activities such as getting dressed or drinking
from a cup without spilling the water.

While there remains no cure for Parkinson's disease, treatments are available to help
reduce the main symptoms and maintain quality of life for as long as possible. These
may include medication and surgery, however, often incorporation physical and mental
health self-management techniques [3]. Nevertheless, as the condition progresses, the
symptoms of Parkinson's disease can become worse making it increasingly difficult to
carry out everyday activities without assistance. Consequently, investigating methods to
sustain independence and maintain an acceptance quality of life of people living with
PD is crucial. Owing to the global burden faced by chronic conditions such as PD,
Assistive technologies (AT's) are becoming an increasingly common prescribed form of
treatment. Early studies investigating this usage of ATs have hinted at promising benefits,
including a greater level of independence and autonomy for individuals and, importantly,
their caregivers. The effectiveness of any AT, however, is inherently dependent upon the
usability and user acceptance of these ATs, in particular, among those baby boomers
born during the 1950 and 60s for whom technology familiarity is a relatively recent
phenomenon.

Unsurprisingly, this demographic cohort has, therefore, largely been reluctant to
adopt ATs as a sustainable low-cost replacement for human caregivers. Consequently,
low adoption is hampering the potential of digital technologies within health and social
care [4].

It is then necessary to employ classification algorithms have been developed for
differentiating adopters and non-adopters of these technologies; thereby, potential negative effects on people with PD and cost overruns can be further minimized. As several

classifiers have been developed, modelers and practitioners should select the algorithm better responding to the multi-criteria nature of technology adoption in people with PD. Although several efforts have been made to address this problem, the evidence base is still scant and only restricted to performance measures.

This paper bridges this gap by extending the Multi-criteria decision-making approach adopted in technology adoption modeling for people with dementia [5]. First, the fuzzy Analytic Hierarchy Process (FAHP) is applied to estimate the initial relative weights of criteria and sub-criteria. The fuzzy set theory is incorporated to represent the uncertainty of decision-makers' preferences. Then, the Decision-making Trial and Evaluation Laboratory (DEMATEL) is used for evaluating the interrelations and feedback among criteria and sub-criteria. FAHP and DEMATEL are later combined for calculating the final criteria and sub-criteria weights under vagueness and interdependence. The Technique for Order of Preferences by Similarity to Ideal Solution (TOPSIS) is finally implemented to rank three classifiers (Lazy IBk – knearest neighbors, Naïve bayes, and J48 decision tree) according to their ability to model technology adoption. A real case study considering 5 criteria, 16 sub-criteria, 8 decision-makers, and mobile smartphone data from mPower study on Parkinson's disease is presented to validate the proposed approach.

The rest of the paper is organized as follows: Sect. 2 presents problem statement and background trying to respond to the question "Digital Management of Parkinson Disease: Is Technology the Future?"; Sect. 3 develops and explains the methodological approach proposed in the present study; Sects. 4 and 4.1 summarize and discuss the results respectively. Finally, the main contribution and scientific implications are analyzed in Sect. 5.

2   Problem Statement and Background: Digital Management of Parkinson's Disease

Certainly, there is no doubt that in the near and recent future our modern life will be characterized by the use of innovative digital technologies. It is evident and it is hoped that there will be important implications also in the medical field [6].

Thus, it seems intuitive and simple enough to think that the answer to the question *"Digital Management of Parkinson Disease: Is Technology the Future?"* is affirmative.

In fact, with the growing use of digital devices to provide personalized feedback on measures of health, including those worn on the wrist or contained in shoes, it is conceivable that similar tools could be designed to facilitate the continuous monitoring of disease manifestations in patients with PD [7].

The Consumer Electronics Show CES which takes place every year in Las Vegas (United States) is the world's gathering place for all those who thrive on the business of consumer technologies. CES shows new inventions and health technologies every year. Here below are some technologies with the potential to help people with Parkinson's.

ExoBeam Walking Assistive Device for Parkinson's Disease by MedEXO Robotics (Hong Kong) Company Limited helps the users maintain stable gait and balance by 3 types of cues (visual, vibration and sound) to strengthen assistive signals (Fig. 1).

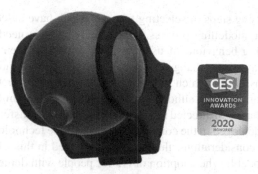

Fig. 1. ExoBeam Walking Assistive Device (CES)

Parkinson's disease can cause problems with the sleep cycle. An "intelligent pillow" has been proposed by ZEEQ. The pillow records natural sleep movements and can also wake up at the ideal time for the sleep cycle (Fig. 2).

Fig. 2. ZEEQ smart pillow (CES)

This research field is being studied by many researchers around the world. Recently, Marxreiter et al. [8] evaluate the use of digital technologies in different age groups of PD patients while Espay et al. analyze an important issue. Despite advances in mobile health technologies, authors point out that the implementation of digital outcome measures is hindered by a lack of consensus on the type and scope of measures [9]. An interesting study was proposed by Amini et al. [10], in which a novel system incorporating the Microsoft Kinect v2 is used to monitor and to improve mobility in people with Parkinson's.

As stated by Cunningham et al. [11] AT can enable a person to carry out a task which otherwise they would be unable to undertake independently. In other words, new technology, digital devices and social media can provide a wealth of help and support for people with Parkinson's.

Relatively simple regression-based models have demonstrated the ability to identify, with high levels of precision, those who are likely to wish to adopt technology based solutions [12]. Refinement of the adoption models have been possible through inclusion of additional processing steps of selecting features which have aided in improving the generalisation of the modelling process. Additionally, models need to be dynamic to facilitate the changing behaviour of users as a result of how their disease may have progressed. This may cause changes in personality, cognition and ability to engage in social interactions, all of which need to be accommodated for from a technology adoption process. For the latter, although many efforts have been undertaken within this domain, little effort has been directed towards development of transferability functions to allow models to be deployed in the context of more than one technology-based solution. Based on the above considerations, the problem addressed in this study is to develop a decision-support model for the adoption of AT for people with dementia.

3   The Proposed Methodology

A six-step methodology (Fig. 3) is proposed to choose the most suitable classifier for supporting assistive technology adoption in people with PD:

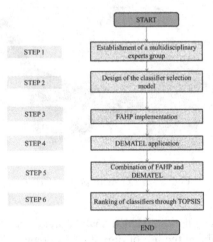

Fig. 3. The proposed methodology for selecting the most suitable classification algorithm supporting the assistive technology adoption in people with PD

Step 1: A decision-making team is chosen considering their expertise for dealing with the global decision. The experts will be involved in the classifier selection process through FAHP and DEMATEL techniques.

Step 2: The criteria and sub-criteria are set considering the decision-makers' opinion and the related reported literature.

Step 3: FAHP is used to estimate the relative priorities of criteria and sub-criteria considering the vagueness of human thought. In this phase, the experts are required to make paired judgments as detailed in [13].

Step 4: DEMATEL is applied to identify the deliverers and receivers as well as the influence strength among criteria/sub-criteria. The decision-makers here analyze the effect of each criterion/sub-criterion on the others by implementing the procedure described in [14].

Step 5: FAHP and DEMATEL are later integrated to compute the final global and local weights as outlined in [15].

Step 6: TOPSIS technique is used for ranking the classification algorithms and identifying the best alternative for underpinning assistive technology adoption in people with PD [16].

4 A Case Study Based on Mobile Smartphone Data

This application uses data from the mPower mobile Parkinson's disease study [17] for evaluating a set of three classification algorithms: Lazy IBK, Naïve Bayes, J48 decision tree. In particular, 74 adopters and 307 non-adopters participated in this study. Each one was asked to perform for activity categories: Memory, Walking, Voice, and Tipping guided by the mPower app. More information about these experiments can be found at [19] where the efforts were only focused on the classification accuracy. The next subsections will present the MCDM model that has been designed for the same problem but considering other criteria and sub-criteria that were not previously incorporated.

4.1 Establishment of a Multidisciplinary Expert Group

This project was discussed in advance with several members from the REMIND Consortium [18] in order to gain a multidisciplinary view of the problem before launching the study. The decision-making procedure was led by an academic researcher who also designed the classifier selection model, introduced experts in the application of FAHP and DEMATEL, collected the resulting data, and established TOPSIS indicators. In total, eight experts related to assistive technology applications in people with PD participated in this process. A short outline of the experts' biography can be found below:

- Seven *academic researchers* with more than 10 years of experience in modeling technology adoption for people with PD. Furthermore, they have performed as consultants of several companies focused on designing technologies alleviating the burden faced by these people and their families when addressing this disease.
- One *commercial director* of a company specialized in smart solutions for quality and certified outcomes. He is also a *European Commission expert* with approximately 30 year of experience in the creation and deployment of IT devices for upgrading healthcare delivery.

4.2 Design of the Classifier Selection Model

The classifier selection model was discussed during two sessions with the experts in order to verify whether it was pertinent and understandable. The final MCDM arrangement is presented in Fig. 4. In this respect, 5 criteria and 16 sub-criteria were considered to rank three classification algorithms (Lazy IBK, Naïve Bayes, J48 decision tree). A short explanation of each criterion is outlined in Table 1.

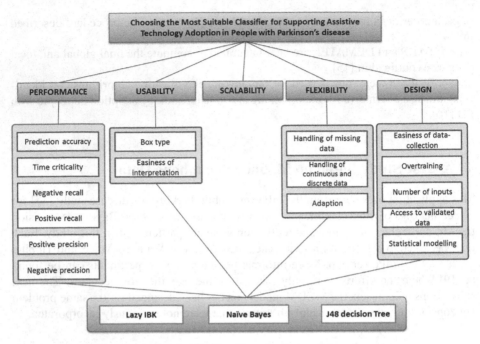

Fig. 4. The classifier selection model

Table 1. Description of criteria

Criterion	Sub-criteria	Criterion description
Performance (C1)	Prediction accuracy (SC1.1) Time criticality (SC1.2) Negative recall (SC1.3) Positive recall (SC1.4) Positive precision (SC1.5) Negative precision (SC1.6)	It is considered as the classifier capability of discriminating between PD adopters and non-adopters
Usability (C2)	Box type (SC2.1) Easiness of interpretation (SC2.2)	It determines how easy the classifier's application is in the clinical scenario
Scalability (C3)	No sub-criteria	It measures the replicability nature of the classifier considering the cost of implementation and PD context
Flexibility (C4)	Handling of missing data (SC4.1) Handling of continuous and discrete data (SC4.2) Adaption (SC4.3)	This criterion evaluates the algorithm response when facing constraints related to the availability of high-quality datasets
Design (C5)	Easiness of data-collection (SC5.1) Overtraining (SC5.2) Number of inputs (SC5.3) Access to validated data (SC5.4) Statistical modelling (SC5.5)	This factor covers aspects related to the classifier parameterization including training, data collection and processing

4.3   FAHP Implementation

A survey was used to collect the paired judgments required as input for the FAHP technique. The experts responded to the following question: "How much important is the criterion/sub-criterion on the left over the criterion/sub-criterion on the right?" Such a question was answered by implementing the reduced as follows: Equally important [1], More important [2–4], Much more important [4–6], Less important [1/4, 1/3, 1/2], and Much less important [1/6, 1/5, 1/4]. The local and global priorities of all decision elements are presented in Table 2.

Table 2. Local and global priorities of criteria and sub-criteria obtained from FAHP

Decision element	Global priority	Local priority
PERFORMANCE (C1)	0.241	
Time criticality (SC1.1)	0.019	0.082
Prediction accuracy (SC1.2)	0.056	0.235
Negative recall (SC1.3)	0.035	0.148
Positive recall (SC1.4)	0.044	0.183
Positive precision (SC1.5)	0.043	0.180
Negative precision (SC1.6)	0.041	0.172
USABILITY (C2)	0.178	
Box type (SC2.1)	0.027	0.155
Easiness of interpretation (SC2.2)	0.150	0.845
SCALABILITY (C3)	0.255	
FLEXIBILITY (C4)	0.228	
Handling of continuous and discrete data (SC4.1)	0.052	0.231
Handling of missing data (SC4.2)	0.145	0.639
Adaption (SC4.3)	0.029	0.130
DESIGN (C5)	0.098	
Overtraining (SC5.1)	0.021	0.224
Easiness of data-collection (SC5.2)	0.019	0.201
Number of inputs (SC5.3)	0.013	0.135
Access to validated data (SC5.4)	0.029	0.302
Statistical modelling (SC5.5)	0.013	0.138

The consistency ratios (CR) were also computed to examine the reliability of judgments provided by the experts (refer to Table 3). Considering that CR is not over 10%, the calculated priorities can be then used for ranking the classification algorithms.

	Consistency Ratio (CR)
Criteria	3.7%
Performance	0.2%
Usability	0.0%
Flexibility	5.6%
Design	1.4%

4.4 DEMATEL Application

A questionnaire was also implemented to gather the paired judgments required in the DEMATEL method. In this case, the decision-makers responded the following question: "how much impact each criterion/sub-criterion over the criterion/sub-criterion on the left?" In this case, the question was answered considering the following scale: No influence (0), Low influence (1), Medium influence (2), High influence (3), and Very high influence (4). This procedure was iterated until finishing all the judgments.

The prominence $(D + R)$ and relation $(D - R)$ values are later generated from these judgments by applying the DEMATEL method (refer to Table 4). The deliverers and dispatchers were also pointed out in Table 4. In this case, *Flexibility* (C4) and *Design* (C5) were categorized as dispatchers; whereas *Performance* (C1), *Usability* (C2), and *Scalability* (C3) were classified as dispatchers. The results show that *Flexibility (C4)* has the greatest $C + R$ value (9.590), denoting that is the main generator of effects and the most influencing criterion when selecting the best classification algorithm.

Also, impact-digraph maps were drawn for analyzing the interrelations within each cluster. "Criteria" (Fig. 5a) and "Usability" (Fig. 5b) clusters are depicted as examples. In particular, Fig. 5a evidences the presence of one-direction interrelations (green arrows) and multiple feedback interactions (red arrows) between dispatchers and receivers. This confirms the high influence that *Flexibility* and *Design* have in the behavior and easy adoption of classifiers in the clinical scenario. The modelers should therefore focus their efforts on these aspects to facilitate the implementation of technology adoption process in people with PD. The same pattern is observed in Fig. 5b where all the relationships are of two-sided nature. For instance, the procedures (models supporting the prediction of mission values) used for *handling the missing data* will depend on the *type of data* (either discrete or continuous) considered in the algorithm; on the other hand, the availability of suitable missing data models how the input data can be processed for increasing the predictive ability of classifiers.

4.5 Combination of FAHP and DEMATEL

Table 5 presents the global and local priorities of criteria and sub-criteria after combining FAHP and DEMATEL techniques. Figure 6 depicts the ranking of criteria based on their global priorities. Based on the results, *Flexibility* and *Design* were found to be the most important criteria with overall weights of 0.235 and 0.260 respectively. Such finding

Table 4. Dispatchers and receivers in the decision-making model

Criterion (C)/sub-criterion (SC)	Prominence (D + R)	Relation (D − R)	Dispatcher	Receiver
PERFORMANCE (C1)	9.017	−1.142		X
Time criticality (SC2)	5.603	−1.153		X
Prediction accuracy (SC1)	7.311	0.733	X	
Negative recall (SC3)	6.261	−0.343		X
Positive recall (SC4)	6.626	0.211	X	
Positive precision (SC5)	6.309	0.219	X	
Negative precision (SC6)	6.299	0.333	X	
USABILITY (C2)	9.234	−1.002		X
Box type (SC7)	35.000	1.000	X	
Easiness of interpretation (SC8)	35.000	−1.000		X
SCALABILITY (C3)	9.049	−0.106		X
FLEXIBILITY (C4)	9.590	1.258	X	
Handling of continuous and discrete data (SC9)	12.665	0.246	X	
Handling of missing data(SC10)	12.533	−0.627		X
Adaption (SC11)	12.531	1.122	X	
DESIGN (C5)	9.555	0.991	X	
Overtraining (SC12)	10.463	−1.940		X
Easiness of data-collection (SC13)	12.508	0.470	X	
Number of inputs (SC14)	12.368	0.775	X	
Access to validated data (SC15)	12.450	1.151	X	
Statistical modelling (SC16)	12.052	−0.456		X

dictates that approximately a half (0.495) of the global importance backs into these aspects. This is of paramount relevance even considering the high prominence related to these criteria (see Sect. 4.4 Demated Application).

On a different note, the top-five sub-criteria with the highest global priorities are as follows: *Box type* (0.139), *Adaption* (0.109), *Handling of continuous and discrete*

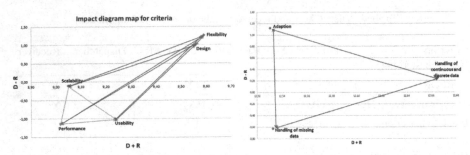

Fig. 5. Impact digraph maps for a) Criteria and b) Usability (Color figure online)

Table 5. Local and global priorities of criteria and sub-criteria resulting from FAHP-DEMATEL approach

Decision element	Global priority	Local priority
PERFORMANCE (C1)	0.169	
Time criticality (SC1.1)	0.021	0.123
Prediction accuracy (SC1.2)	0.034	0.200
Negative recall (SC1.3)	0.027	0.158
Positive recall (SC1.4)	0.030	0.175
Positive precision (SC1.5)	0.028	0.168
Negative precision (SC1.6)	0.030	0.176
USABILITY (C2)	0.162	
Box type (SC2.1)	0.139	0.859
Easiness of interpretation (SC2.2)	0.023	0.141
SCALABILITY (C3)	0.174	
FLEXIBILITY (C4)	0.235	
Handling of continuous and discrete data (SC4.1)	0.092	0.391
Handling of missing data (SC4.2)	0.034	0.144
Adaption (SC4.3)	0.109	0.465
DESIGN (C5)	0.260	
Overtraining (SC5.1)	0.033	0.126
Easiness of data-collection (SC5.2)	0.056	0.217
Number of inputs (SC5.3)	0.063	0.241
Access to validated data (SC5.4)	0.053	0.203
Statistical modelling (SC5.5)	0.055	0.213

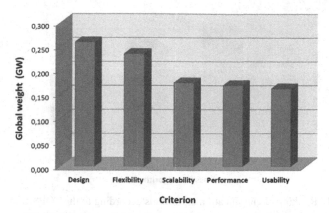

Fig. 6. Ranking of criteria considering their global weights

data (0.092), *Number of inputs* (0.063), and *Easiness of data-collection* (0.056). In particular, white-box classifiers are advisable considering their easiness of interpretation for clinicians and modelers. Moreover, it is also useful to count on algorithms capable of evolving taking into account the ever-changing clinical context of PD and their associated parameters. On the other hand, the ability of handling continuous and discrete data makes classifiers more responsive to the aforementioned context while increasing their discrimination ability between adopters and non-adopters. Lately, two sub-criteria to be carefully considered in the implementation of technology adoption classifiers are *Number of inputs* and *Easiness of data-collection*. First, it is highly recommended to count on algorithms requiring the fewest possible input information to accelerate the classification process in the practical clinical scenario. Regarding the data-collection process, classifier features are expected to be gleaned through simple short questions or extracted from decision support systems of hospital and clinics so that decision-making on the adoption of an assistive technology in a particular PD patient can be further optimized.

4.6   Ranking of Classifiers Through TOPSIS

In this study, the global priorities of criteria and sub-criteria derived from the FAHP-DEMATEL approach were utilized as input for the TOPSIS method. The ranking of classification algorithms illustrated in Fig. 7 was reached by implementing the standard procedure explained in [16]. The results revealed that *Naïve Bayes* achieved the first place with 67.7% while *J48 decision tree* obtained the lowest score (46.8%). Such findings also evidence that there is much room for improvement in the design of optimal, scalable, and easy-to-use classifiers for effectively discriminating between adopters and non-adopters of assistive technology solution focused on people with PD.

   Considering the gap detected between the ideal performance and each of the alternative classifiers (Fig. 8 and 9): *Naïve Bayes* (33.3%), *Lazy IBK* (42.4%), and *J48 decision tree* (53.2%); we decided to analyze the Euclidean distance to the positive ideal solution (PIS) and negative ideal solution (NIS) for providing modelers with an improvement guide underpinning their future interventions. For instance, the cost of the

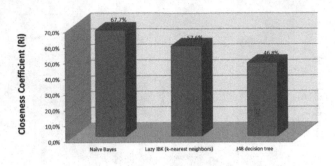

Classifier Algorithm

Fig. 7. Ranking of classification algorithms according to the TOPSIS method

learning process in J48 decision tree is over US$1000 (Euclidean distance = 0.0049882) which diminishes its scalability in the wild. *Prediction accuracy* should be also significantly improved by the modelers. In this case, the highest predictive ability was detected in J48 decision tree (76.98%; Euclidean distance = 0.0000381). Other performance measures like *Negative recall* (0.72; Euclidean distance = 0.0000325), *Positive recall* (0.74; Euclidean distance = 0.0000420), *Positive precision* (0.73; Euclidean distance = 0.0000352), and *Negative precision* (0.73; Euclidean distance = 0.0000412) were also concluded as potential improvement points in *Lazy IBK* since they are still far from the ideal performance ($A^+ = 1$). The rest of gaps can be further appreciated in Fig. 8 and 9.

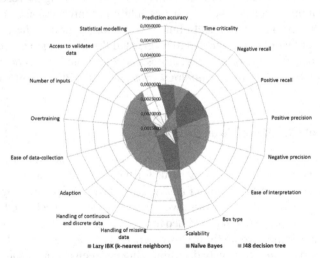

Fig. 8. Spider diagram for Euclidean distances of classifiers to PIS

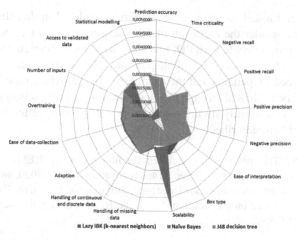

Fig. 9. Spider diagram for Euclidean distances of classifiers to NIS

5 Conclusions

This article presents a combined FAHP-DEMATEL-TOPSIS technique to choose the most suitable classification algorithm for supporting assistive technology adoption in people with PD. The proposed methodology encompasses the design, validation, and implementation phases of these solutions and it therefore tackles the limitations of accuracy-based approaches by incorporating the knowledge-driven angle to technology adoption.

The model here proposed is critical for discriminating PD patients to which assistive solutions may provide support to complete everyday activities while maintaining a certain level of independence and autonomy. This is limited for the capability of users to integrate such solutions into their daily life, the family environment, and individual engagement throughout the adoption process. From the hospital perspective, it is necessary to direct investment and time resources towards PD patients who are likely to adopt the solution in the long term. In this regard, it is important to understand the factors behind the effective implementation of classifiers in the clinical scenario.

Two important issues emerged from this study: i) the identification of the most important and influential criteria in the classifier selection problem which complements the current technology adoption models used by clinicians and researchers and ii) the ranking of alternative classifiers considering several aspects from the technology adoption context including: design, flexibility, scalability, performance, and usability.

In particular, *Flexibility* and *Design* were concluded to be the most relevant criteria with global weights of 0.235 and 0.260 correspondingly. These criteria were also found to be the main generators of effects within the decision-making model with $C + R$ of 9.590 and 9.555. Such aspects must be therefore carefully addressed by modellers when designing classifiers supporting technology adoption in people with PD. Finally, *Naïve Bayes* was found to be most suitable classifier for this particular application with a closeness coefficient 67.7%. Of note, there is, however, a wide room for improvement in aspects related to performance and scalability.

The results are limited to the set of classifiers considered in this study. Therefore, future work may consider the inclusion of other algorithms that can better model the technology adoption in people with PD. It is also advisable to implement this approach in other diseases where assistive technologies may play a vital role for reducing the current burden faced by patients and their families. On a different note, more complex interrelations can be evaluated through the incorporation of fuzzy sets in the DEMATEL method. Ultimately, feasibility studies can be proposed for complementing the classifier selection problem here described.

Acknowledgments. This research has received funding under the REMIND project Marie Sklodowska-Curie EU Framework for Research and Innovation Horizon 2020, under Grant Agreement No. 734355. The authors also acknowledge the contribution of users of the Parkinson mPower app as part of the mPower project developed by Sage Bionetworks and described in Synapse [https://doi.org/10.7303/syn4993293].

References

1. The World Health Organisation, "Global Health Observatory (GHO) data". https://www.who.int/gho/mortality_burden_disease/life_tables/situation_trends_text/en/. Accessed 10 Mar 2020
2. The World Health Organisation: The world health report 2002: reducing risks, promoting healthy life. 1st edn. World Health Organisation, Geneva (2002)
3. NHS Inform: Parkinsons disease in Illnesses, conditions and disorders of the nerves and central nervous system. https://www.nhsinform.scot/illnesses-and-conditions/brain-nerves-and-spinal-cord/parkinsons-disease. Accessed 10 Mar 2020
4. Cook, E.J., et al.: Exploring the factors that influence the decision to adopt and engage with an integrated assistive telehealth and telecare service in Cambridgeshire, UK: a nested qualitative study of patient 'users' and 'non-users'. BMC Health Serv. Res. 16(137), 1–20 (2016)
5. Ortiz-Barrios, M., Nugent, C., Cleland, I., Donnelly, M., Verikas, A.: Selecting the most suitable classification algorithm for supporting assistive technology adoption for people with dementia: a multicriteria framework. J. Multi-Criteria Decis. Anal. 27(1–2), 20–38 (2019)
6. Klucken, J., Krüger, R., Schmidt, P., Bloem, B.R.: Management of Parkinson's disease 20 years from now: towards digital health pathways. J. Parkinson's Dis. 8(Suppl 1), S85–S94 (2018)
7. Hansen, C., Sanchez-Ferro, A., Maetzler, W.: How mobile health technology and electronic health records will change care of patients with Parkinson's disease. J. Parkinson's Dis. 8(Suppl 1), S41–S45 (2018)
8. Marxreiter, F., et al.: The use of digital technology and media in German Parkinson's disease patients. J. Parkinson's Dis. pp. 1–11 (2019, in press)
9. Espay, A.J., et al.: A roadmap for implementation of patient-centered digital outcome measures in Parkinson's disease obtained using mobile health technologies. Mov. Disord. 34(5), 657–663 (2019)
10. Amini, A., Banitsas, K., Young, W.R.: Kinect4FOG: monitoring and improving mobility in people with Parkinson's using a novel system incorporating the Microsoft Kinect v2. Disabil. Rehabil.: Assist. Technol. 14(6), 566–573 (2019)
11. Cunningham, L.M., Nugent, C.D., Finlay, D.D., Moore, G., Craig, D.: A review of assistive technologies for people with Parkinson's disease. Technol. Health Care 17(3), 269–279 (2009)

12. Chaurasia, P., et al.: Modelling assistive technology adoption for people with dementia. J. Biomed. Inform. **63**, 235–248 (2016)
13. Guneri, A.F., Gul, M., Ozgurler, S.: A fuzzy AHP methodology for selection of risk assessment methods in occupational safety. Int. J. Risk Assess. Manag. **18**(3–4), 319–335 (2015)
14. Ortiz-Barrios, M.A., et al.: The analytic decision-making preference model to evaluate the disaster readiness in emergency departments: the ADT model. J. Multi-Criteria Decis. Anal. **24**(5–6), 204–226 (2017)
15. Ortiz-Barrios, M.A., Herrera-Fontalvo, Z., Rúa-Muñoz, J., Ojeda-Gutiérrez, S., De Felice, F., Petrillo, A.: An integrated approach to evaluate the risk of adverse events in hospital sector. Manag. Decis. **56**(10), 2187–2224 (2018)
16. Ak, M.F., Gul, M.: AHP–TOPSIS integration extended with Pythagorean fuzzy sets for information security risk analysis. Complex Intell. Syst. **5**(2), 113–126 (2019). https://doi.org/10.1007/s40747-018-0087-7
17. Bot, B.M., et al.: The mPower study, Parkinson disease mobile data collected using ResearchKit. Sci. Data **3**(1), 1–9 (2016)
18. Ali Hamad, R., Salguero, A.G., Bouguelia, M.R., Espinilla, M., Quero, J.M.: Efficient activity recognition in smart homes using delayed fuzzy temporal windows on binary sensors. IEEE J. Biomed. Health Inform. **24**(2), 387–395 (2019)
19. Greer, J., Cleland, I., McClean, S.: Predicting assistive technology adoption for people with Parkinson's disease using mobile data from a smartphone. In: 13th Conference on Data Science and knowledge Engineering for Sensing Decision Support FLINS 2018, pp. 1273–1280. World Scientific, Belfast (2018)

Identifying the Most Appropriate Classifier for Underpinning Assistive Technology Adoption for People with Dementia: An Integration of Fuzzy AHP and VIKOR Methods

Miguel Ortíz-Barrios[1]([⊠]), Chris Nugent[2], Matias García-Constantino[2], and Genett Jimenez-Delgado[3]

[1] Department of Productivity and Innovation, Universidad de la Costa CUC, Barranquilla, Colombia
mortiz1@cuc.edu.co
[2] School of Computing and Mathematics, Ulster University, Jordanstown, Northern Ireland, UK
{cd.nugent,m.garcia-constantino}@ulster.ac.uk
[3] Industrial Engineering Program, Institución Universitaria ITSA, Barranquilla, Colombia
gjimenez@itsa.edu.co

Abstract. Recently, the number of People with Dementia (PwD) has been rising exponentially across the world. The main symptoms that PwD experience include impairments of reasoning, memory, and thought. Owing to the burden faced by this chronic condition, Assistive Technology-based solutions (ATS) have been prescribed as a form of treatment. Nevertheless, it is widely acknowledged that low adoption rates of ATS have hampered their benefits within a health and social care context. It is then necessary to effectively discriminate between adopters and non-adopters of such solutions to avoid cost implications, improve the life quality of adopters, and find intervention alternatives for non-adopters. Several classifiers have been proposed as advancement towards the personalisation of self-management interventions for dementia in a scalable way. As multiple algorithms have been developed, an important step in technology adoption is to select the most appropriate classification alternative based on different criteria. This paper presents the integration of Fuzzy AHP (FAHP) and VIKOR to address this challenge. First, FAHP was used to calculate the criteria and sub-criteria weights under uncertainty and then VIKOR was implemented to rank the classifiers. A case study considering a mobile-based self-management and reminding solution for PwD is described to validate the proposed approach. The results revealed that *Easiness of interpretation* (GW = 0.192) and *Handling of missing data* (GW = 0.145) were the two most important criteria. Furthermore, SVM (Q_j = 1.0) and AB (Q_j = 0.891) were concluded to be the most suitable classifiers for supporting ATS adoption in PwD.

Keywords: Technology adoption · Dementia · Fuzzy Analytic Hierarchy Process (FAHP) · VIKOR · Healthcare

© Springer Nature Switzerland AG 2020
V. G. Duffy (Ed.): HCII 2020, LNCS 12199, pp. 406–419, 2020.
https://doi.org/10.1007/978-3-030-49907-5_29

1   Introduction

In recent years, the number of People with Dementia (PwD) has been rising exponentially globally, representing a challenge to governments and health services to provide the most adequate and cost-effective care and treatment services. According to Alzheimer's Research UK, as of today, the number of PwD globally is estimated to be 50 million and it is projected to nearly triple by 2050. While it is desired a type of care in which carers look after PwD at most times during their working hours, in many cases the growing number of PwD has outnumbered available carers, resulting in insufficient and sub-optimal care. Technology has been used to alleviate the burden faced by PwD and their carers, and, more importantly, to provide more personalised types of treatment. Assistive Technology-based Solutions (ATS) have been commonly prescribed as a form of non-pharmacological treatment to PwD to help them complete everyday activities whilst maintaining a level of independence, bringing health and social benefits to them. Some of the areas in which ATS provide support include: memory, mobility, indoor and outdoor safety, independence and socialising.

However, it has been acknowledged that low adoption of ATS have hampered their potential benefits over time, and might cause distress and anxiety on PwD. The main causes of low adoption of technology-based solutions to assist PwD may be the result of not being the most adequate for particular individuals. It could be the case, for example, that a certain technology provides support in a particular area but the implementation is not user-friendly enough and/or disliked by the PwD, a scenario that typically results in an early use of the technology that gradually decreases until it is no longer used. In this respect, the personal needs and preferences of PwD have a crucial role in how ATS are adopted and used for a successful treatment that provides the most possible benefits while at the same time being cost-effective. In the context of personalised health interventions, it is necessary to identify the most significant features of potential users in the form of personal profile and individual preferences in order to obtain the most benefits of ATS interventions. These significant features are then used to effectively discriminate adopters and non-adopters of ATS amongst potential users for the purposes of: avoiding cost implications, improving the quality of life of adopters, and finding adequate intervention alternatives for non-adopters. To support the identification of adopters and non-adopters of technology, adoption model studies, also known as classifiers, have been used to provide an insight on how successfully a PwD will adopt a certain ATS based on their input criteria from different domains.

The performance of the classifiers used for adoption model studies is influenced to a great extent by the set of features selected, hence the importance of selecting the best set of features. Several classifiers have been proposed as advancement towards the personalisation of self-management interventions for dementia in a scalable way. It is then important to select the most appropriate classification algorithm to support in the technology adoption task based on the different criteria available. Multicriteria Decision Making (MCDM) methods are used to assign weights to the criteria and to rank the classifiers considered. These methods can be deemed as appropriate tools to support developers, healthcare professionals, and practitioners in the selection of the most suitable classifiers for ATS in PwD. This paper presents an approach that integrates the Fuzzy AHP (FAHP) and VIKOR methods to weight criteria to rank classifiers and to identify the most appropriate one for ATS adoption for PwD. FAHP was first used to calculate the criteria and sub-criteria weights under certainty and then VIKOR was implemented to rank the classifier alternatives. The proposed approach is validated with the case study of a mobile-based self-management and reminding solution for PwD.

The remainder of the paper is organised as follows: Sect. 2 presents the related work in the area of ATS for PwD focusing on the FAHP and VIKOR methods. Section 3 outlines the proposed methodology whereas Sect. 4 describes a case study considering a mobile-based self-management and reminding solution for PwD. Finally, conclusions and future work are presented in Sect. 5.

2 Related Work

There has been extensive work in the literature related to ATS in general [1, 2] and for specific health problems like disabilities [3, 4], visual impairment [5], and dementia [6–8]. The ATS for PwD studies are the ones that are of interest to the work presented. This section provides an insight into recent relevant work in ATS for PwD.

Finding appropriate assistive technology to support PwD can be particularly challenging because of the range of cognitive abilities that impair the adaptation and use from the users. As the prevalence of dementia is expected to increase in the near future, it is necessary to find the most adequate ATS to alleviate the burden of patients and caregivers. Zhang et al. [9] investigated the use of a predictive adoption model for a mobile phone-based video streaming system for PwD, which considered features like users' ability, preferences and living arrangements. In this case, seven classification algorithms were used in models that were evaluated using multiple criteria of model predictive performance, prediction robustness, bias towards two types of errors and usability. Zhang et al. [9] reported that the best predictive model to support the adoption of assistive technology was the one trained using the kNN (k-Nearest Neighbour) classification algorithm, which obtained a prediction accuracy of 0.84 ± 0.0242.

The approach presented by Chaurasia et al. [7] uses cognitive prosthetics, in the form of the Technology Adoption and Usage Tool (TAUT) reminder app, to identify a subset of relevant features that could then be used to improve the accuracy of technology adoption prediction. The data analysis considered 31 features from the Cache County Study on Memory and Aging (CCSMA) that included range of age, gender, education level, and health condition. The findings of Chaurasia et al. [7] are that relevant features can provide an insight on the adoption of ATS by PwD. They reported that while features related to the background of PwD (like job or education level) can have an impact in the user's ability to adopt a technology, other features related to the dementia condition (like genetic markers and comorbidity) could decrease the adoption of assistive technology. The best prediction model was obtained using the kNN classification algorithm, with an average prediction accuracy of 92.48% when tested on 173 participants.

The study presented by Ortiz-Barrios et al. [8] introduced a multi-criteria framework to select the most adequate classification algorithm for supporting the adoption of ATS for PwD. This framework is based on the integration of a five-phase methodology based on the Fuzzy Analytic Hierarchy Process (FAHP) and the Technique for Order of Preference by Similarity to Ideal Solution (TOPSIS): FAHP-TOPSIS. The case study considered was a mobile-based self-management and reminding solution for PwD. FAHP was used to determine the relative weights of criteria (performance, usability, scalability, flexibility and design) and sub-criteria under uncertainty. TOPSIS was used to rank the seven classification algorithms considered. Similarly to the work of Zhang et al. [9], in Ortiz-Barrios et al. [8] the best results were obtained using the kNN classification algorithm to support the adoption of assistive technology, with a closeness coefficient of 0.804. It was found that the most important criterion for classification selection was scalability.

The work presented in this paper extends the multi-criteria framework introduced by Ortiz-Barrios et al. [8] by considering the VIKOR method instead of TOPSIS to rank the classifier alternatives. Interestingly, to the best knowledge of the authors there have not been studies that consider an integrated approach of FAHP and VIKOR to support ATS for PwD, hence the novelty of this study. There are, however, integrated approaches of FAHP and VIKOR that have been used in other areas such as: manufacturing [10], supplier selection [11, 12], and performance evaluation [13]. An integrated FAHP-VIKOR that has been applied and used in other disciplines seems like a promising alternative multi-criteria framework to support the adoption of ATS for PwD.

3 Proposed Methodology

The proposed approach aims to identify the most appropriate classifier for underpinning Assistive Technology Adoption for PwD by integrating the FAHP and VIKOR methods. In this regard, the methodology is comprised of three phases (refer to Fig. 1):

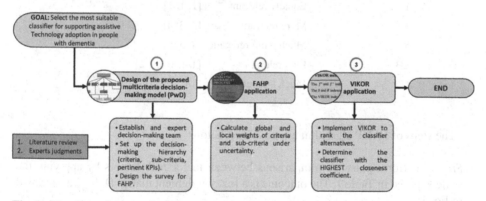

Fig. 1. The three-phase methodology for selecting the most suitable classifier for supporting assistive technology adoption in people with dementia

- *Phase 1 (Design of the proposed multi-criteria decision-making model)*: A decision-making group is chosen based on their experience in the use of supporting assistive technologies. Subsequently, the criteria and sub-criteria are determined with the participation of the decision-making team and the pertinent scientific literature.
- *Phase 2 (FAHP application)*: In this step, FAHP is applied to estimate the global and local weights of criteria and sub-criteria under uncertainty. In this regard, the experts

are invited to perform pairwise comparisons, which are later processed following the FAHP method as detailed in Sect. 3.1.
- *Phase 3 (VIKOR application):* In this phase, VIKOR is developed to rank the classifiers in accordance with their closeness coefficient. The distances from the ideal and worst solution are also incorporated into this study. Finally, we select the classifier that can better support the assistive technology adoption in people with dementia (This is the alternative with the highest closeness coefficient).

3.1 Fuzzy Analytic Hierarchy Process (FAHP)

The Fuzzy Analytic Hierarchy Process (FAHP) proves to be an advantageous methodology for multiple criteria decision-making under uncertainty and has been therefore highly applicable in recent years [14]. FAHP tackles the disadvantages of the AHP technique [15, 16] which cannot represent the vagueness of decision-makers during the pairwise comparison process [17]. In FAHP, the paired comparisons are represented through fuzzy triangular numbers ratios [18, 19]. According to the literature, the representation of fuzzy triangular numbers and their correspondence with the scale of AHP is as follows (refer to Table 1) [16].

Table 1. Correspondence between linguistic terms and fuzzy triangular numbers

Reduced AHP scale	Definition	Fuzzy triangular number
1	Equally relevant	[1, 1, 1]
3	More relevant	[2, 3, 4]
5	Much more relevant	[4, 5, 6]
1/3	Less relevant	[1/4, 1/3, 1/2]
1/5	Much less relevant	[1/6, 1/5, 1/4]

The steps of FAHP algorithm are described below:

- *Step 1:* Perform pairwise comparisons between factors/sub-factors by applying the scale exposed in Table 1. The outcome is a fuzzy judgment matrix $\tilde{D}^k (d_{ij})$ as outlined in Eq. 1:

$$\tilde{D}^K = \begin{bmatrix} \tilde{d}_{11}^k & \tilde{d}_{12}^k & \cdots & \tilde{d}_{1n}^k \\ \tilde{d}_{21}^k & \tilde{d}_{22}^k & \cdots & \tilde{d}_{2n}^k \\ \cdots & \cdots & \cdots & \cdots \\ \tilde{d}_{n1}^k & \tilde{d}_{n2}^k & \cdots & \tilde{d}_{nn}^k \end{bmatrix} \tag{1}$$

$\tilde{d}_{ij}^k$ indicates the fuzzy *kth* expert preference of *ith* criterion with respect to *jth* criterion.
- *Step 2:* In group decision-making, it is necessary to calculate the geometric mean of all comparisons according to Eq. 2. Here, K represents the number of participants in

the decision-making process. The initial fuzzy judgment matrix is now updated taking into account the average judgments of experts (Eq. 3).

$$\tilde{d}_{ij} = \sqrt[K]{\tilde{d}_{ij}^1 * \tilde{d}_{ij}^2 * \cdots * \tilde{d}_{ij}^k} \tag{2}$$

$$\tilde{D} = \begin{bmatrix} \widetilde{d_{11}} & \cdots & \widetilde{d_{1n}} \\ \vdots & \ddots & \vdots \\ \tilde{d}_{n1} & \cdots & \tilde{d}_{nn} \end{bmatrix} \tag{3}$$

- *Step 3:* Calculate the geometric mean of fuzzy comparisons values of each criterion applying Eq. 4. Here, $\tilde{r}_i$ denotes the triangular numbers.

$$\tilde{r}_i = \left(\prod_{j=1}^{n} \tilde{d}_{ij} \right)^{1/n}, \ i = 1, 2, \ldots, n \tag{4}$$

- *Step 4:* Establish the fuzzy weights of each criterion ($\widetilde{w}_i$) using Eq. 5.

$$\widetilde{w}_i = \tilde{r}_i \otimes (\tilde{r}_1 \oplus \tilde{r}_2 \oplus \ldots \oplus \tilde{r}_n)^{-1} = (lw_i, mw_i, uw_i) \tag{5}$$

- *Step 5:* Apply the Centre of Area technique to defuzzify ($\widetilde{w}_i$) using Eq. 6. The outcome of this step is the non-fuzzy number M_i. Then, use Eq. 7 to normalize M_i.

$$M_i = \frac{lw_i + mw_i + uw_i}{3} \tag{6}$$

$$N_i = \frac{M_i}{\sum_{i=1}^{n} M_i} \tag{7}$$

- *Step 6:* Compute the *Consistency Index* (CI) to verify whether the weights of factors and sub-factors are adequate for their use in the classifier selection problem. If CI $\leq$ 0.10, the weights are then concluded as consistent [20]. Otherwise, the experts should review their judgments perform the pairwise comparisons again.

3.2 Vlsekriterijumska Optimizacija I Kompromisno Resenje (VIKOR)

VIKOR is a technique that classifies a set of alternatives taking into account their closeness to the ideal scenario based on predefined decision criteria [21]. VIKOR uses a multi-criteria ranking index describing the closeness of each alternative to the ideal scenario [22]. The VIKOR procedure is detailed as follows:

- *Step 1*: A set of m classification algorithms denoted as P_1, P_2..., P_m is established in the context of the MCDM problem. Each alternative P_i is characterized by a number of decision factors (n) as described in matrix A (Eq. 8). The value of each sub-criterion SC_j is here represented by f_{ij}.

$$A = \begin{array}{c} P_1 \\ P_2 \\ P_3 \\ \vdots \\ P_m \end{array} \begin{bmatrix} SC_1 \ SC_2 \ \ldots \ SC_n \\ f_{11} \ f_{12} \ \cdots \quad f_{1n} \\ f_{21} \ f_{22} \ \cdots \quad f_{2n} \\ f_{31} \ \ f_{32} \ \ \cdots \quad f_{3n} \\ \vdots \quad \vdots \quad \cdots \quad \vdots \\ f_{m1} \ f_{m2} \ \cdots \ f_{mn} \end{bmatrix} \tag{8}$$

- *Step 2:* Define the best (f_j^*) and the worst (f_j^-) values of each sub-criterion using Eqs. 9–10.

$$f_{ij} = \left\{ \begin{array}{ll} max_i f_{ij}, & \text{for benefit criteria} \\ min_i f_{ij}, & \text{for cost criteria} \end{array} \right\}, \quad i = 1, 2, \ldots, m \tag{9}$$

$$f_{ij}^- = \left\{ \begin{array}{ll} max_i f_{ij}, & \text{for benefit criteria} \\ min_i f_{ij}, & \text{for cost criteria} \end{array} \right\}, \quad i = 1, 2, \ldots, m \tag{10}$$

- *Step 3:* Use Eq. 11 and Eq. 12 to calculate the S_i and R_i values respectively. In the aforementioned equations, w_j is the weight of each sub-criterion obtained from the FAHP technique.

$$S_i = \sum_{j=1}^{n} \frac{w_j \left(f_j^* - f_{ij} \right)}{f_j^* - f_j^-}, \tag{11}$$

$$R_i = max_j \left(\frac{w_j \left(f_j^* - f_{ij} \right)}{f_j^* - f_j^-} \right). \tag{12}$$

- *Step 4:* Apply Eq. 14 and Eq. 15 to determine the Q_i values. In the Eq. 13, v represents the weight of the strategy for the maximum group utility [23].

$$Q_i = v \frac{S_i - S^*}{S^- - S^*} + (1 - v) \frac{R_i - R^*}{R^- - R^*} \tag{13}$$

$$S^* = min_i S_i, \quad S^- = max_j S_j, \tag{14}$$

$$R^* = min_i R_i, \quad R^- = max_j R_j, \tag{15}$$

- *Step 5:* Rank the classifiers taking into account the S_i, Q_i and R_i values.
- *Step 6:* Determine a compromise solution ($P^{(1)}$) comprising of the best-classified alternative considering the Q_i ranking and the following conditions:

- Acceptable benefit (As described to Eq. 16 and Eq. 17):

$$Q\left(P^{(2)}\right) - Q\left(P^{(1)}\right) \geq DQ, \tag{16}$$

$$DQ = \frac{1}{(m-1)}. \tag{17}$$

Where $Q\left(P^{(2)}\right)$ is the classifier with the second highest priority in the Q_i ranking. In Eq. 17, m denotes the number of classifiers.

- Acceptable stability in decision making: The classifier or alternative $\left(P^{(1)}\right)$ must be also the best-ranked in in S_i, and R_i rankings.

If one of the above conditions is not complied, select one of these alternatives:

- $\left(P^{(1)}\right)$ y $\left(P^{(2)}\right)$ if there is not an acceptable stability in decision making process.
- $\left(P^{(1)}\right)$, $\left(P^{(2)}\right)$, ..., $\left(P^{(m)}\right)$ if there is not an acceptable advantage. Such an advantage is defined as follows:

$$Q\left(P^{(m)}\right) - Q\left(P^{(1)}\right) < DQ, \tag{18}$$

4 A Case Study of a Mobile-Smartphone Based Video Technology

A mobile-smartphone based video technology has been targeted for validating the proposed FAHP-VIKOR approach. This reminding solution delivers videos assisting PwD to function more independently. In particular, the videos are used as reminders with a range of multimedia formats supporting the Activities of Daily Living (ADLs) performed by PwD. Such technology has progressed at a staggering pace due to its capability of providing users with an interface to book and acknowledge reminders for a large set of everyday tasks. This application is, however, useful in PwD with high adoption likelihood. It is therefore necessary to effectively classify between adopters and non-adopters of such solutions to avoid cost overruns, improve the life quality of adopters, and find intervention alternatives for non-adopters. To do this, five criteria and sixteen sub-criteria were proposed to evaluate seven alternative classifiers (NN, DT, SVM, NB, AB, CART, and KNN). The next sub-sections will illustrate the decision-making process undertaken for the classifier selection problem.

4.1 Establishment of a Multidisciplinary Expert Group

In this case, seven decision-makers were invited to contribute to the design of the multi-criteria decision-making hierarchy supporting the classifier selection problem. In particular, they provided significant input for defining the criteria to be considered into the technology adoption model. Moreover, they supported the implementation of FAHP through which the relative importance of criteria and sub-criteria was properly calculated.

The experts are part of REMIND, a project whose primary aim is to create a multidisciplinary, international, and inter-sectoral network for progressing developments in reminding solutions for PwD that can be implemented in smart environments. Such experts are a Consortium comprised of academic and non-academic partners committed to provide efficacious ATS using computational techniques, behavioral science, and user-centered design techniques.

The decision-makers have been also involved in several projects targeting ATS for assisting PwD. Furthermore, they have enough related experience (>10 years) to deal with the adoption modeling context and can therefore serve as consistent experts when defining criteria and sub-criteria weights. As a result, they have constructed win-to-win relationships between the ATS-related companies and the academic sector, an aspect also evident through different research publications.

4.2 Design of the Classifier Selection Model

After scanning the pertinent scientific literature and summarizing the input information provided by the experts, a decision-making hierarchy comprising of five criteria (Design, Flexibility, Scalability, Performance, and Usability) and sixteen sub-criteria was finally established for selecting the most suitable classifier and subsequently supporting assistive technology adoption in PwD. The list of sub-criteria is as follows:

- Computational time
- Accuracy
- Negative precision
- Positive precision
- Positive recall
- Negative recall
- Scalability potential
- Box type
- Handling of missing data
- Handling of discrete and continuous variables
- Number of input variables
- Cost of training.
- Easiness of interpretation by clinicians.
- Easiness of input data gathering.
- Online learning.
- Access to validated datasets
- Statistical-based processing

Each component of this hierarchy was further explained to the experts so that they can undertake consistent pairwise comparisons on their importance for technology adoption modeling in PwD. This information was also attached to the FAHP surveys for better comprehension on the decision-making process.

4.3 FAHP Implementation

The next step in the proposed approach is the implementation of FAHP method. Initially, the decision-makers were invited to complete questionnaires containing pairwise comparisons between criteria or sub-criteria. Specifically, the following question was stated: *How important is the element on the left column over the element on the right column when selecting the best classifier of ATS adoption in PwD?* The decision-makers responded by using the modified Saaty scale [24] described in Table 1. After collecting all the judgments, we processed the information according to Eqs. 1–7. The final criteria and sub-criteria weights under uncertainty, both global and local, were tabled in Table 2.

Table 2. The final criteria and sub-criteria weights under uncertainty

Criterion/sub-criterion	Global priority	Local priority
PERFORMANCE (F1)	24.1%	
Computational time (SC1)	1.9%	8.2%
Accuracy (SC2)	5.6%	23.5%
Negative recall (SC3)	3.5%	14.8%
Positive recall (SC4)	4.4%	18.3%
Positive precision (SC5)	4.3%	18.0%
Negative precision (SC6)	4.1%	17.2%
USABILITY (F2)	17.8%	
Box type (SC7)	2.7%	15.5%
Easiness of interpretation by clinicians (SC8)	15.0%	84.5%
SCALABILITY POTENTIAL (F3)	25.5%	
FLEXIBILITY (F4)	22.8%	
Handling of discrete and continuous variables (SC9)	5.2%	23.1%
Handling of missing data (SC10)	14.5%	63.9%
Online learning (SC11)	2.9%	13.0%
DESIGN (F5)	9.8%	
Cost of training (SC12)	2.1%	22.4%
Easiness of input data-gathering (SC13)	1.9%	20.1%
Number of input variables (SC14)	1.3%	13.5%
Access to validated datasets (SC15)	2.9%	30.2%
Statistical-based processing (SC16)	1.3%	13.8%

Figure 2 depicts the ranking of classifier selection criteria considering their global weights under uncertainty. While *Scalability* (F3) was ranked first (global weight = 0.26), it is also observed the small difference (0.08) between this criterion and the fourth in the list (*Performance – F1*). Such a finding entails the applications of multidimensional strategies considering the scalability, usability, flexibility, and performance of classification algorithms for improving their suitability upon modelling technology adoption in PwD. Furthermore, the healthcare system is interested in delivering ATS to appropriate patients. Thereby, resource allocation can be optimized while fully complying with delivering new alternatives for better health monitoring and care [25, 26]. Likewise, these results demonstrate the need for developing robust classifiers profile users considering their engagement or lack thereof with the ATS.

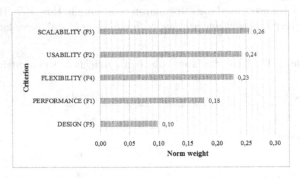

Fig. 2. The ranking of criteria considering global weights

4.4   Ranking of Classifiers Through VIKOR

After estimating the final weights of criteria and sub-criteria under uncertainty, we applied the VIKOR method followed by the analysis of parameters with significant separation from the ideal scenario in each classifier. VIKOR allowed us to obtain a ranking of classifier alternatives considering the S_j and R_j values (Table 3). Figure 3 describes the final ranking produced by VIKOR considering the Q_j ($v = 0.5$) metric.

Table 3. The Sj and Rj values and rankings for each classifier alternative

Classifiers	Sj	Rank	Rj	Rank
NN	0.336	6	0.192	6
DT	0.266	7	0.192	6
SVM	0.722	1	0.255	1
NB	0.367	4	0.255	1
AB	0.623	2	0.255	1
CART	0.357	5	0.255	1
KNN	0.410	3	0.255	1

After this, the compromise solution was defined. As stated in Subsect. 3.2, two conditions have to be evaluated: i) acceptable benefit and ii) acceptable advantage. Despite that SVM achieved the first place in S_j (0.722) and R_j (0.255) rankings, the *acceptable benefit* condition is not satisfied given that $0.109 \leq 0.167$. Therefore, the compromise solution is composed by SVM ($Q_j = 1.0$) and AB ($Q_j = 0.89$). Additionally, the following is a list of some aspects for potential improvement in each classifier:

- AB: Computational time (117.25 s), Negative recall (18.59%)
- KNN: Negative recall (21.25%), Positive recall (25.26%)
- NB: Accuracy (34.9%), Negative recall (23.9%)
- CART: Computational time (467.25 s), Positive recall (13.28%)
- NN: It is not easily interpretable by clinicians and does not handle missing data.
- DT: It is not supported by statistical modeling and is a black-box classifier.

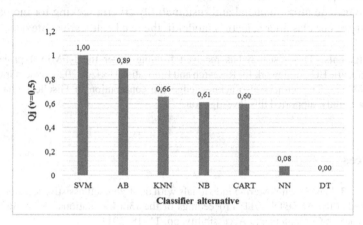

Fig. 3. The ranking of classifiers considering Q_j ($v = 0.5$) values

5 Conclusions

In this paper, we used the FAHP-VIKOR approach for selecting the best classifier algorithm as a support of ATS adoption in PwD. ATS have hinted at promising advantages including an increased degree of autonomy and independence for PwD which alleviates the burden faced by their caregivers and family members. The adoption of these sustainable solutions, however, is restricted by external and internal factors hampering the delivery of effective monitoring and healthcare of dementia patients. It is hence critical to count on classifiers not only discriminating between adopters and non-adopters of these technologies but can be effectively deployed by clinicians in the practical scenario. The use of technology adoption models has then become a pillar for the optimal allocation of resources, the definition of alternative interventions for non-adopters, and the increasing in life expectancy of adopters.

The here described application considered five criteria and sixteen sub-criteria emanating from the experts' opinion and pertinent scientific literature. Three main contributions arise from this intervention: i) the importance of criteria and sub-criteria under uncertainty, ii) the ranking of classifiers and iii) the identification of potential improvement areas for each classifier. First, with the aid of FAHP, *Scalability* (F3) was found to be the most important aspect in classifier selection (global weight = 0.26). Nevertheless, the small gaps detected among the four first criteria calls for multidimensional intervention for improving the appropriateness of classification algorithms when modelling technology adoption in PwD. Second, the compromise solution provided by VIKOR evidenced the suitability of SVM and AB for supporting the adoption of a mobile-smartphone based video solution with Q_j values of 1.0 and 0.89 respectively. Lately, potential improvements were pointed out in reference to the negative recall obtained from various classifiers.

Future studies may consider the inclusion of interactions among criteria and interval-valued indicators supporting a fuzzy version of the VIKOR method. We will also apply the proposed approach in other ATS for further validation in the wild. Finally, it is expected to include more financial and sustainability criteria seeking for increasing the applicability of our classifier selection model in the real healthcare context.

Acknowledgments. This research has received funding under the REMIND project Marie Sklodowska-Curie EU Framework for Research and Innovation Horizon 2020, under Grant Agreement No. 734355. The authors also acknowledge the contribution of Giselle Paola Polifroni Avendaño who fully supported this investigation.

References

1. Hurst, A., Tobias, J.: Empowering individuals with do-it-yourself assistive technology. Paper Presented at the ASSETS 2011: Proceedings of the 13th International ACM SIGACCESS Conference on Computers and Accessibility, pp. 11–18 (2011)
2. Lee, C., Coughlin, J.F.: PERSPECTIVE: older adults' adoption of technology: an integrated approach to identifying determinants and barriers. J. Prod. Innov. Manag. **32**(5), 747–759 (2015)
3. Kintsch, A., DePaula, R.: A framework for the adoption of assistive technology. In: SWAAAC 2002: Supporting Learning Through Assistive Technology, pp. 1–10 (2002)
4. Goodman, G., Tiene, D., Luft, P.: Adoption of assistive technology for computer access among college students with disabilities. Disabil. Rehabil. **24**(1–3), 80–92 (2002)
5. Pal, J., et al.: Agency in assistive technology adoption: visual impairment and smartphone use in bangalore. Paper Presented at the Conference on Human Factors in Computing Systems - Proceedings, pp. 5929–5940 (2017)
6. Cleland, I., et al.: Predicting technology adoption in people with dementia; initial results from the TAUT project. In: Pecchia, L., Chen, L.L., Nugent, C., Bravo, J. (eds.) IWAAL 2014. LNCS, vol. 8868, pp. 266–274. Springer, Cham (2014). https://doi.org/10.1007/978-3-319-13105-4_39
7. Chaurasia, P., et al.: Modelling assistive technology adoption for people with dementia. J. Biomed. Inform. **63**, 235–248 (2016)
8. Ortiz-Barrios, M., Nugent, C., Cleland, I., Donnelly, M., Verikas, A.: Selecting the most suitable classification algorithm for supporting assistive technology adoption for people with dementia: a multicriteria framework. J. Multi-Criteria Decis. Anal. **27**(1–2), 20–38 (2020)
9. Zhang, S., et al.: A predictive model for assistive technology adoption for people with dementia. IEEE J. Biomed. Health Inform. **18**(1), 375–383 (2014)
10. Singh, S., Olugu, E.U., Musa, S.N., Mahat, A.B., Wong, K.Y.: Strategy selection for sustainable manufacturing with integrated AHP-VIKOR method under interval-valued fuzzy environment. Int. J. Adv. Manuf. Technol. **84**(1–4), 547–563 (2016). https://doi.org/10.1007/s00170-015-7553-9

11. Chaghooshi, A.J., Zarchi, M.K.: Using integration of fuzzy AHP-VIKOR for selecting the best strategy in green supply chain management. Glob. J. Manag. Stud. Res. **1**(1), 46–53 (2014)
12. Awasthi, A., Govindan, K., Gold, S.: Multi-tier sustainable global supplier selection using a fuzzy AHP-VIKOR based approach. Int. J. Prod. Econ. **195**, 106–117 (2018)
13. Rezaie, K., Ramiyani, S.S., Nazari-Shirkouhi, S., Badizadeh, A.: Evaluating performance of Iranian cement firms using an integrated fuzzy AHP-VIKOR method. Appl. Math. Model. **38**(21–22), 5033–5046 (2014)
14. Wang, Y., Chin, K.: Fuzzy analytic hierarchy process: a logarithmic fuzzy preference programming methodology. Int. J. Approx. Reason. **52**(4), 541–553 (2011)
15. Saaty, T.L.: Analytic hierarchy process. In: Gass, S.I., Fu, M.C. (eds.) Encyclopedia of Operations Research and Management Science, pp. 52–64. Springer, Boston (2013). https://doi.org/10.1007/978-1-4419-1153-7_31
16. Ortiz-Barrios, M.A., Kucukaltan, B., Carvajal-Tinoco, D., Neira-Rodado, D., Jiménez, G.: Strategic hybrid approach for selecting suppliers of high-density polyethylene. J. Multi-Criteria Decis. Anal. **24**(5–6), 296–316 (2017)
17. Kahraman, C.: Fuzzy Multi-Criteria Decision Making: Theory and Applications with Recent Developments, 1st edn. Springer, Boston (2008). https://doi.org/10.1007/978-0-387-76813-7
18. Kusumawardani, R., Agintiara, M.: Application of fuzzy AHP-TOPSIS method for decision making in human resource manager selection process. Procedia Comput. Sci. **72**, 638–646 (2015)
19. Izquierdo, N.V., et al.: Methodology of application of diffuse mathematics to performance evaluation. Int. J. Control Theory Appl. **9**(44), 201–207 (2016)
20. Kułakowski, K.: Notes on order preservation and consistency in AHP. Eur. J. Oper. Res. **245**(1), 333–337 (2015)
21. Shemshadi, A., Shirazi, H., Toreihi, M., Tarokh, M.J.: A fuzzy VIKOR method for supplier selection based on entropy measure for objective weighting. Expert Syst. Appl. **38**(10), 12160–12167 (2011)
22. Our Yang, Y.P., Shieh, H.M., Leu, J.D., Tzeng, G.H.: A VIKOR-based multiple criteria decision method for improving information security risk. Int. J. Inf. Technol. Decis. Making **8**(2), 267–287 (2009)
23. Sayadi, M., Heydari, M., Shahadah, K.: Extension of VIKOR method for decision making problem with interval numbers. Appl. Math. Model. **33**(5), 2257–2262 (2009)
24. Ortiz-Barrios, M.A., et al.: The analytic decision-making preference model to evaluate the disaster readiness in emergency departments: the ADT model. J. Multi-Criteria Decis. Anal. **24**(5–6), 204–226 (2017)
25. Ortiz, M.A., López-Meza, P.: Using computer simulation to improve patient flow at an outpatient internal medicine department. In: García, C.R., Caballero-Gil, P., Burmester, M., Quesada-Arencibia, A. (eds.) UCAmI 2016. LNCS, vol. 10069, pp. 294–299. Springer, Cham (2016). https://doi.org/10.1007/978-3-319-48746-5_30
26. Ortiz Barrios, M., Felizzola Jiménez, H., Nieto Isaza, S.: Comparative analysis between ANP and ANP-DEMATEL for six sigma project selection process in a healthcare provider. In: Pecchia, L., Chen, L.L., Nugent, C., Bravo, J. (eds.) IWAAL 2014. LNCS, vol. 8868, pp. 413–416. Springer, Cham (2014). https://doi.org/10.1007/978-3-319-13105-4_62

Multi-pose Face Recognition Based on Block Adaptation

Jianguo Shi[✉] and Yuanyuan Zhao

School of Computer and Information, Anhui Polytechnic University, Beijing Central Road. 8,
Wuhu 241000, People's Republic of China
jgshimail@163.com

Abstract. Considering that the SRC algorithm cannot solve the error offset problem between the testing and training samples, we propose one method as the
affine transformation and partition by integrating into the linear reconstruction
model, which were named as block adaptive multi-pose face recognition algorithm (BA-SRC). In this method, we first model the pose change using the affine
transformation model for the face after the human face was blocked. Then we
estimate the initial value of the affine transformation parameter by minimizing
the image block reconstruction error, and then compensate the local area error
caused by pose change, so as to improve the performance of face recognition. The
experiments show that the algorithm proposed in this paper is very robust to pose
change, and has a good recognition result.

Keywords: Block adaptive · Affine transformation · Sparse coding ·
Multi-pose · Face recognition

1 Introduction

Face recognition is a hot issue in pattern recognition and computer vision research,
which is widely used in public safety and information security. Face recognition has
been successfully commercialized under certain conditions. However, the accuracy is
still not satisfactory under non-ideal imaging conditions such as illumination, pose and
object mismatch.

In view of the research on the pose problem in face recognition, the existing method
mainly includes:

A. Method based on 3D. As noted in [1], the face recognition is used as a three-
dimensional object recognition problem, and the model is constructed by drawing the
principal curvature and direction. Another method in [2] using 3D scanning to generate
depth images, aligning images by registration of salient feature points, then using PCA
to reduce dimensionality. Face image is the mapping of 3D face in 2D image, when the
imaging angle of view changes, the position of the 3D face feature point in the 2D face
image will also change, which will lead to the alignment errors. Therefore, pose can be
attributed to imaging angle change problems.

© Springer Nature Switzerland AG 2020
V. G. Duffy (Ed.): HCII 2020, LNCS 12199, pp. 420–428, 2020.
https://doi.org/10.1007/978-3-030-49907-5_30

B. Method based on image matching. In [3], a face recognition scheme based on actual scene is proposed. The face geometry is used to align the image being identified with the template, and the face recognition method is used to identify the face. In [4], the distribution of image features of the same object in different poses was proposed.

C. Method based on pose normalization. In [5], the pixel requirements can be reduced by using multi-scale and multi-directional Gabor filtering, and the interpolation of the face image space is utilized to the greatest extent in another paper [6].

A two-step nonlinear view correction method was proposed, which finally verified the face by directly calculating the similarity for the pose correction.

We propose to model the pose change of the entire face by using the affine transformation. Since the affine transformation model of the image can only describe the pose change of the planar object, using the affine transformation model to describe the pose change of the entire face will reduce the accuracy of the model.

In the process of affine transformation parameter estimation, the existing method is actually linearing the affine transformation model, and gradually approximating the optimal affine transformation parameters by continuously and iteratively updating the affine transformation parameters.

This parameter estimation method is very sensitive to the setting of the initial value of the parameter, which is easily falling into the local optimum. The initial value of the affine transformation parameter is required to be as close as possible to the optimal value. Therefore, the affine transformation model of the image is used to model the pose change of the face image [7], and the optimal affine transformation parameters are estimated by the Lucas-Kanade method [8]. The pose of the test image is corrected based on the parameter, so as to improve the robustness of SRC algorithm when pose changes. A Nearest Subspace Patch Matching algorithm to deal with illumination and pose problems was proposed in [9], which achieved good results.

Based on the above analysis, we propose a block adaptive multi-pose face recognition algorithm (BA-SRC). The main idea is to use the affine transformation model for the face after the block to model the pose transformation. Meanwhile, the initial value of the affine transformation parameter is estimated by minimizing the image block reconstruction error, which compensates for the local error caused by the pose change and improves the performance of the face recognition algorithm.

2   Block Adaptive Multi-pose Face Recognition Algorithm

2.1   Image Blocking and Affine Transformation Model

Given a face image P, the face images are represented by d image segments.

In this respect, the algorithm first aims at d points $(x_i, y_i)(1 \leq i \leq d)$ in the image P as the center point of each image block. A size of $h \times w$ neighborhood $N(x_i, y_i)$ is selected as a face image block around each center point, the pixel value corresponding to the image block is recorded as $P(N(x_i, y_i)) \in R^{h \times w}$. N_i represent the ith image block $N(x_i, y_i)$ for convenience.

In order to model the regional pose change, we use the affine transformation model to establish the geometric transformation relationship of face images from different

Table 1. The SRC Algorithm

The SRC Algorithm
1. Normalize the columns of A to have unit l_2 - norm
2. Code y over A via l_1 - minimization
$\hat{x} = \arg\min \|x\|_1 \quad s.t. \quad \|y - Ax\|_1 < \varepsilon$
3. Compute the residuals
$r_m(y) = \|y - A\delta_m(x)\|_2$
Where $\delta_m(x)$ is the coding coefficient vector associated with class m
4. Output the person of y as
$person(y) = \arg\min_m (r_m)$

perspectives according to the imaging model. We assume that $P0(N_i)$ is the ith image block of the face image under the reference angle of view, $P'(N_i)$ is the corresponding image block in the test image. According to the imaging model, we can use the affine transformation model to describe the geometric transformation relationship between them, which is as follows:

$$P'(N_i) = P_0(T(N_i, t)) \tag{1}$$

Where t is the affine transformation parameter.

2.2 Affine Transformation Parameter Estimation

Suppose that Pjm is the jth registered image of the mth user $(1 \leq j \leq k)$, $P_j^m(N_i, t) \in R^{h \times w}$ is the best matching block corresponding to the ith image block of the test image. $V(P_j^m(T(N_i, t)))$ and $V(P'(N_i))$ respectively represent vectorization of image block pixels. If the user registration image forms a separate subspace partition, the strictly aligned face image can be represented by a linear combination of registered images of the same user. Image segmentation also has this linear relationship. so we have:

$$V(P'(N_i)) \approx \sum_{j=1}^{k} \beta_j V(P_j^m(T(N_i, t))) = A_i^m(t)\beta \tag{2}$$

Where $A_i^m(t)$ represents the best matching block of the mth personal face registration image vector set, $\beta = [\beta_1, \beta_2, \ldots\ldots, \beta_k]$ represents linear fit coefficient. In order to obtain the affine transformation parameter t, we solve the following optimization expression:

$$(t_i^m, \beta_i^m) = \arg\min \|V(P'(N_i)) - A_i^m(t)\beta\|_2^2 \tag{3}$$

First we get the linear representation coefficient β, then get the affine transformation parameter t as follows.

$$\beta = ((A_i^m(t))^T A_i^m(t))^{-1} (A_i^m(t))^T V(P'(N_i)) \tag{4}$$

When given a linear representation coefficient $\beta = [\beta_1,, \beta_2, \ldots\ldots, \beta_k]^T$, we can solve the following optimization problems:

$$t = \arg\min \sum_{X \in N_i} (P'(X) - \sum_{j=1}^{k} \beta_j P_j^m (T(X, t)))^2 \tag{5}$$

According to the initial value of the given affine transformation parameter $t = t_{start}^m$, calculate the update step size of the current estimate Δt, then iteratively update the current estimate $t = t + \Delta t$. Finally, we gradually approximate the optimal estimate by multiple iterations:

$$\Delta t = \arg\min_{\Delta t} \sum_{X \in N_{ii}} (P'(X) - \sum_{j=1}^{k} \beta_j P_j^m (T(X, t + \Delta t)))^2 \tag{6}$$

Experiments have shown that when the image resolution is 100×100, if the change angle of face does not exceed 450, the displacement of the pixel of the face image will exceed no more than 5 pixels. Based on this prior knowledge, given an image partition N_i, within the range of 5 pixels around the center point (x_i, y_i) of the block, the reconstruction error minimization technique can be used to find the registration image block which is most similar to the test image block $P'(N_i)$.

2.3 Classification Based on Sparse Representation Framework

For the ith test image block, after obtaining the affine transformation parameter t_i^m, the image block that best matches the test image block in the R-type registration image is obtained by calculation t_i^m to form a dictionary matrix A. Using the SRC algorithm to calculate the sparse representation coefficient x of the test image block $V(P'(N_i))$ on the dictionary A. Finally, the difference from each type of registered image block and $V(P'(N_i))$ is calculated, then the classification result will be obtained. When the categories of all the blocks in the test image are determined, the category of the entire test image will also be determined.

3 Experimental Results

In order to verify the effectiveness of the proposed algorithm, we choose the Extended Yale B face database as the experimental data set. The Extended Yale B databases contains face images taken by 38 people in 9 poses and 64 lighting conditions. As shown in Fig. 1.

3.1 Parameter Setting

The setting of parameter in the BA-SRC algorithm mainly involves three aspects: the block position, the block size, and the number of blocks.

Table 2. The BA-SRC Algorithm

The BA-SRC Algorithm

Input: Testing image P', $A_m = [P_1^m, \ldots, P_k^m]$, $1 \leq m \leq k$.

Output: Test face Category

1. Let $P'(N_i)$ $(1 \leq i \leq d)$ be testing image block, where d represents the number of blocks.

2. For each $P'(N_i)$ represents the ith test image block do

For mth image do

3. Initialize

Calculating the initial value of affine transformation, $t_i^m = t_{start}^m$;

While $||\Delta t||_2^2 \geq \varepsilon$ do

$t_i^m = t_i^m + \Delta t$

4. Block matching

Obtain the optimal block of signing image and testing image

$A = [A_i^1(t_i^1), A_i^2(t_i^2), \ldots, A_i^R(t_i^R)]$

5. Update the sparse coding coefficients

$\hat{x} = \arg\min_{X,e} ||x||_2 + ||e||_2 \quad s.t. \quad V(I'(S_i)) = Ax + e$

6. Calculating the fitting error

$r_m(V(P'(N_i))) = ||V(P'(N_i)) - A_i^m(t_i^m)\hat{x}_m||_2$, $1 \leq m \leq R$

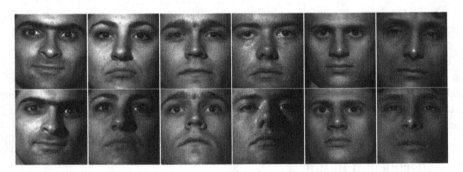

Fig. 1. The example of Extended Yale B databases

A. Block position. The experimental scheme is as follows: the size of the fixed image block is 15×15 and the number of the image blocks is 64, the recognition rate of the image block by grid distribution and random distribution is studied respectively. In the process of studying the recognition rate of the random distributed image block, we do five experiments and average the experimental results to obtain the final recognition rate. When we study the recognition rate of image segmentation according to the grid distribution algorithm, due to the mesh distribution according to the key information of the face, the coverage is relatively fixed, so we only do one experiment. In the experiment,

Fig. 2 is the position distribution when the image block is grid distributed, Fig. 3 is the position distribution when the image block is randomly distributed. Each sign of plus in the figure represents the center point of an image block. The experiment results are shown in Table 1. When the image is divided into grids, all image segments can cover the key information of the entire face as much as possible, so the algorithm obtains a higher recognition rate.

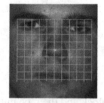

Fig. 2. Grid distribution   **Fig. 3.** Random distribution

Table 3. The relationship between the position of the image block and the recognition rate

Distribution class	Grid distribution	Random distribution
Recognition rate	90.38%	88.23%

B. Block size. The experiment scheme is as follows: the number of fixed image blocks is 64 and distributed according to the grid, then we study the relationship between the image block size and the algorithm recognition rate. The experiment results are shown in Fig. 4. When the image block size is 35×35, the algorithm achieves the best recognition performance. When the image block changes smaller or larger, the recognition rate of the algorithm shows a downward trend. The image block size in this experiment is 35×35.

C. The number of blocks. On the basis of determining the image segmentation position distribution and the image segmentation size, the relationship between the number of image segments and the algorithm recognition performance is further determined. The experiment scheme is as follows: the size of the fixed image block is 15×15 and distributed according to the grid, and then we study the relationship between the number of image blocks and the recognition rate of the algorithm. The experiment results are shown in Fig. 5. When the number of image partitions is relatively small, the algorithm recognition rate increases with the number of image partitions, while the image partition reaches a certain number (more than 60), the algorithm recognition rate is nearly unchanged. In the experiment we set the number of blocks of the image to 64.

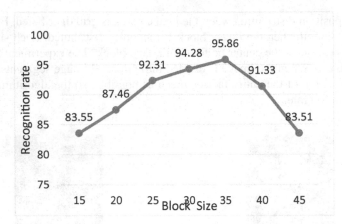

Fig. 4. The relationship between the size of the image block and the recognition rate

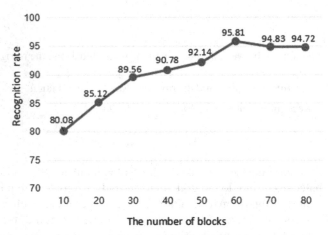

Fig. 5. The relationship between the number of the image block and the recognition rate

4   Experimental Results Analysis

4.1   Performance Comparison on the Extended Yale B Database

In the experiment, we selected the frontal images (1st pose, Pose0) obtained under the first 1, 6, 13, 15 and 19 kinds of illumination conditions as the registration set, and the test images were the 4th (Pose3) and the 7th (Pose6). The face image of the first 28 kinds of lighting conditions under the pose as shown in Fig. 1. Each face image is represented by 64 image blocks, and the center points of each block are arranged in an 8 × 8 grid. Table 2 shows the performance comparison results of the BA-SRC, SRC algorithm and the literature [7] method in the Extended Yale B face database.

It can be seen from Table 2 that the BA-SRC algorithm achieved good recognition results under different poses. When the pose change is relatively large, despite the SRC algorithm, the recognition performance of the literature [7] algorithm drops sharply, and the BA-SRC can still have a good recognition rate. The literature [7] algorithm uses the affine transformation model to model the whole face image pose change, but when the pose changes greatly, the affine transformation model has failed, which results in a sharp decline in its recognition performance. For the BA-SRC method, since the face image is represented by block, each image block is approximated as a plane, even if the face pose changes greatly, the affine transformation model can well model the pose change, so it still gets a higher recognition rate (Table 4).

Table 4. Face recognition rates on the Extended Yale B database

Pose	Pose3 (+10°)	Pose6 (+20°)
SRC	61.93%	23.58%
Algorithm [7]	69.26%	29.76%
BA-SRC	98.28%	94.32%

4.2 Influence of Initial Value Estimation on Performance of BA-SRC Algorithm

Compared with the existing methods, the major improvement of the proposed algorithm is to estimate the initial value of the affine transformation parameters by using the local area reconstruction error minimization technique, which improved the accuracy of the affine transformation parameter estimation. In order to investigate the importance of the initial value estimation of parameters, we compare the recognition performance of BA-SRC algorithm with initial value estimation and no initial value estimation, the results are shown in Table 3. Here BA-SRC indicates that initial value estimation is performed, and BA-SRC-none indicates that initial value estimation is not performed. It can be seen from Table 3 that the recognition performance of the initial value estimation BA-SRC is significantly better than that of the none-BA-SRC without the initial value estimation. As the range of pose change increases, the performance gap between them becomes more obviously (Table 5).

Table 5. Initial estimates on Extended Yale B database.

Pose	Pose3 (+10°)	Pose6 (+20°)
none-BA-SRC	96.86%	91.67%
BA-SRC	98.28%	94.32%

5 Conclusion

Aiming at the problem of face recognition under the condition of pose change, a block adaptive face recognition algorithm (BA-SRC) was proposed. The algorithm improves the robustness to pose change by modeling the pose changes of the blocked face rather than the entire face. By performing effective initial value estimation, the algorithm can avoid falling into local optimal values, moreover, it improved the estimation accuracy of affine transformation parameters, and the recognition performance. The experimental results on the Extended Yale B database show that the BA-SRC algorithm is more robust to pose change and has better recognition performance compared with the existing methods.

References

1. Tanaka, H.T., Ikeda, M., Chiaki, H.: Curvature-based face surface recognition using spherical correlation. In: Proceedings of the IEEE International Conference on Automatic Face and Gesture Recognition, pp. 372–377 (1998)
2. Hesher, C., Srivastava, A., Erlebacher, G.: A novel technique for face recognition using range imaging. In: Proceedings and Its Applications, pp. 201–204 (2003)
3. Beymer, D.: Face recognition under varying pose. In: Proceeding of IEEE Conference on Computer Vision and Pattern Recognition, pp. 756–761 (1994)
4. Pentland, A., Moghaddam, B., Starner, T.: View-based and modular eigenspaces for face recognition algorithm. Image Vis. Comput. **16**(5), 295–306 (1998)
5. Duvdevani-Bar, S., Edelman, S., Howell, A.J., Buxton, H.: A similarity-based method for the generalization of face recognition over pose and expression. In: Proceeding of IEEE Conference on Automatic Face and Gesture Recognition, pp. 118–123 (1998)
6. Lam, K.M., Yan, H.: An analytic-to-holistic approach for face recognition based on a single frontal view. IEEE Trans. Pattern Anal. Mach. Intell. **20**(7), 673–686 (1998)
7. Huang, J.Z., Huang, X.L., Metaxas, D.: Simultaneous image transformation and sparse representation image transformation and sparse representation recovery. In: Proceedings of IEEE Conference on Computer Vision and Pattern Recognition, Anchorage, Alaska, USA, pp. 1–8 (2008)
8. Baker, S., Matthews, I.: Lucas-Kanade 20 years on: a unifying framework. Int. J. Comput. Vis. **56**(3), 221–255 (2004). https://doi.org/10.1023/B:VISI.0000011205.11775.fd
9. Zhou, Z., Ganesh, A., Wright, J., et al.: Nearest subspace patch matching for face recognition under varying pose and illumination. In: Proceedings of the 8th IEEE International Conference on Automatic Face Gesture Recognition, Amsterdam, The Netherlands, pp. 1–8 (2008)

User Preference Toward Appearance of Mobile Input Method Editor Based on Kansei Engineering

Yun Zhang, Yaqin Cao[✉], Yi Ding, and Yujie Zhao

School of Management Engineering, Anhui Polytechnic University, Beijing Central Road. 8,
Wuhu 241000, China
Caoyaqin.2007@163.com

Abstract. This study aimed to research the relationship between input method skin elements, kansei words and users' preferences, optimize the input method skin design and improve users' satisfaction. The input method skin elements are divided into six categories: toolbar, candidate area, shortcut keys, function keys, keyboard background and button background. The twelve most representative element levels were identified. Eight pairs of kansei words were screened to evaluate those element levels. The results show that the toolbar and function keys with unique shapes, the appropriate decorations for the candidate area, the color of the shortcut keys that are consistent with the background, and the use of pictures as the keyboard background conforms to users' preferences, and bringing good user experiences.

Keywords: Input method editor · Kansei words · User preferences · Mobile application

1 Introduction

An mobile input method editor (IME for short) is a mobile app that allows for using numeric keypads on mobile phones to input various characters, such as English, Chinese, Japanese or any other alphabet characters [1]. According to the survey of the big data company Aurora, by June 2018, the amount of input method app users is nearly 700 million. Sogou, iFlytek and Baidu are the only three input method apps with a MAU (monthly active users) of over 100 million. Sogou has a market share of 70%, and the average value of MAU is 455.51 million [2]. Compared with the three apps, the market share, MAU and coverage ratio of other input methods and the competitive advantage are relatively small [3]. With so fierce competition between mobile IME app providers, it is crucial to IME app developers, operators and researchers to explore the determinants that influence a user before installing an mobile IME [4].

According to the existing literature, the previous research focus mainly on the technical level of input method. Zhang [5] carried out a research about the UI design of Sogou. Combined with the principles and methods of UI design, this research studied

© Springer Nature Switzerland AG 2020
V. G. Duffy (Ed.): HCII 2020, LNCS 12199, pp. 429–438, 2020.
https://doi.org/10.1007/978-3-030-49907-5_31

the size and shape of keys that fit in with a user's click patterns, drew the drop point map to calculate the click accuracy, refined the product concept and determined the design style. Then, this study-pointed the design ideas of Sogou: standardization, unity, orientation, habituation, leanness and aesthetics. Finally a new input method is designed according to the idea. Wen [6] evaluated the usability of different types of the pattern lock and full keyboard input method. In the usability evaluation experiment, the text input time, state switching time and error times of four input methods with two kinds of keyboard patterns were recorded, and a two-way analysis of variance that studied how two kinds of keyboard patterns influence user input efficiency was carried out The results showed that pattern lock was most suitable for Chinese characteristics and number, and full keyboard for English. The availability and satisfaction of the method are affected by the conciseness of state switch. Li [7] analyzed the gestures of mobile phones entering Chinese characters to meet the emotional needs of users. It was found that the operation of mobile phones with both hands can improve the efficiency of inputting Chinese characters, and this is also in line with the shortcut symbol key of input method interface in the left hand, which performs relatively simple input tasks. Xu [8] believes that Keyboards, and function keys are located on the right hand, which performs relatively complex input tasks. In addition to the input area, adding decorations to the candidate area, taking the picture as the keyboard back and setting the key background can enrich the content of the input method interface design, and improve the user's pleasure in the use process.

With the development of technology related to IMEs, existing IMEs have similar functions. Guo [9] consider that in order to improve their market competitiveness, users' non-functional requirements, especially the emotional requirements, have received considerable attention from scholars and designer. IMEs should provide customized and personalized products for users to meet their emotional needs [10].

Kansei Engineering, originated in Japan, was proposed to explore the emotional needs of "people" and the design concept of "things" [11]. As a product design tool, Kansei Engineering is used to identify user emotional requirements and find out the relationships between their emotional requirements and product design features [12]. At present, there are seven research methods of kansei engineering [13]: hierarchical analysis, kansei system engineering, mixed kansei engineering system, kansei mathematical model, virtual kansei engineering, collaborative kansei design system, combined kansei engineering and concurrent engineering. Kansei engineering is widely used in automobile industry [14] (Ford, Mazda), construction machinery industry (Komatsu), office equipment (printers), electronic appliances (TV, voice box), cosmetics industry, clothing, websites and so on. For example, used the Kansei Engineering to extract user-centered emotional dimensions, identify the quantitative relationship between emotional dimensions and key design factors, and find a near-optimal design [15]. However, so far as we know, there is no research applied Kansei Engineering to the design of the skin of mobile IME apps. Xu [16] obtained through research: The navigation background color of clothing products of sub-commerce websites should be distinguished from the background color of web pages. Ding [17] found in the study: the shape of the car should be strong and the line should be soft, so as to meet the user's kansei needs.

This research aims to use the Kansei Engineering to extract kansei words of the skin of mobile IME apps, identify the quantitative relationship between kansei words and key design elements of the skin of mobile IME apps. By bridging the literature about mobile IMEs app design and Kansei Engineering, this work extends the broader knowledge of Kansei Engineering. The research found could provide theoretical reference to the design of the skin of mobile IMEs.

2   The Selection of IME Samples and Design Elements

2.1   The Selection of IME Samples

The original samples - 15 skin interfaces of mobile IME apps were retrieved from the mobile system application and APP Store. They were coded according to the 12 design element levels that may affect users' kansei image. Toolbar has unique shape (A1), toolbar has common shape (A2), candidate area has decorations (B1), candidate area has no decorations (B2), shortcut symbol key has the same color with background picture (C1), shortcut symbol key has different color from background picture (C2). Function key has unique shape (D1), function key has common shape (D2), keyboard background is a picture (E1), keyboard background is filled with pure color (E2), button has background (F1), button has no background (F2) [18]. If a skin interface has a design element level, the corresponding code of this element level was set to "1", otherwise, it was set to "0" [19]. The coding results of IME samples were analyzed using the hierarchical clustering analysis by the statistical analysis software SPSS 18.0.

According to the results of the hierarchical clustering analysis [20], it is relatively stable to gather 15 skin interface samples into three categories. Then one representative sample was selected from each classification. Finally, three samples were selected as representative samples. The skin interface of the three representative mobile IME apps is shown in Fig. 1. The layout of the interface can be divided into four areas: the candidate column, the functional area, the background area and the keyboard area.

Fig. 1. The skin interface of the three representative mobile IME apps

2.2   The Selection Representative Design Elements and Their Levels

Six design elements of the skin of mobile IME apps were selected by morphological analysis through expert discussion. Each design elements has two corresponding levels. The six design elements and their levels are shown in Table 1.

Table 1. The six design elements and its levels of the skin interface of mobile IME apps

IME design elements	Element level
Toolbar	Unique shape (A1)
	Common shape (A2)
Candidate area	Decorations (B1)
	No decorations (B2)
Shortcut symbol key	The same color with background picture (C1)
	Different color from background picture (C2)
Function key	Unique shape (D1)
	Common shape (D2)
Keyboard background	Picture (E1)
	Pure color (E2)
Button background	Filled button background (F1)
	Empty button background (F2)

3   The Selection of Kansei Words

In this section, kansei words were obtained through semantic difference questionnaire. After item and factor analysis, kansei words that can be used to evaluate IME is finally determined.

3.1   The Collection of Kansei Words

80 kansei words were selected according to relevant literature, newspaper andwebsites. 24 kansei words were determined after an online survey. An bipolar adjective was assigned to each word to form a pair of kansei words, which are shown in Table 2.

3.2   Kansei Evaluation and Analysis

80 undergraduate students (42 males, 38 females) from Anhui Polytechnic University participated in the kansei evaluation of the skin interface of mobile IME apps. Their age ranged from 21 to 26. They were asked to evaluate the three representative IME samples in a seven-points questionnaire from −3 to 3 composed of 12 bipolar words

Table 2. Primely screened kansei words

No	Kansei words	No	Kansei words	No	Kansei words
B1	Various-Monotonous	B2	Lovely-Disgusting	B3	Warm- Cold
B4	Personal-Common	B5	Novel -Obsolete	B6	Ideal- Realistic
B7	Beautiful-Ugly	B8	Relaxed- Reserved	B9	Joyful- Sad
B10	Delicate-Coarse	B11	Classical-Modern	B12	Fancy- Sober

Data from the questionnaires were analyzed as following

(1) The negative value was transformed to a positive value. In turn, the kansei scores were from 1 to 7 Then, the total score of each subject was calculated. (2) The total score is divided into different groups. The first 27% is the higher group, and the last 27% is the lower group. (3) Independent sample t test was used to analyze the difference between the higher group and the lower group. The kansei words B3 B6, B10 and B12 were deleted according to the results of t test. (4) Factors analysis was used to find the potential common factors of the kansei words. Three factors were obtained according to the results of factors analysis, which is shown in Table 3.

Table 3. Kansei factors and kansei words

IME background	IME interface	IME function	User preference
Relaxed- Reserved (B8)	Lovely-Disgusting (B2)	Personal-Common (B4)	Like-Dislike
Joyful-Sad (B9)	Various-Monotonous (B1)	Novel-Obsolete (B5)	
Classical-Modern (B11)			
Beautiful-Ugly (B7)			

4 Relation Between Design Elements, Kansei Words and User Preference

Partial least squares regression is used to study the relationship between design elements, kansei words and users' preference. The model is built with design elements as independent variables and kansei words as dependent variables.

4.1 Relation Models of Design Elements and Kansei Words

Taking six IME elements as independent variables and the statistical data of eight pairs of kansei words as dependent variables, the partial least square regression is used to

Table 4. Statistical results

Kansei word	Design element	Element level	Element score	Partial correlation coefficient
Various-Monotonous	A	A1	0.082	0.312
		A2	−0.056	
	B	B1	0.073	**0.274**
		B2	−0.051	
	C	C1	−0.047	0.534
		C2	0.098	
	D	D1	0.121	**0.728**
		D2	**−0.113**	
	E	E1	**0.188**	0.615
		E2	0.046	
	F	F1	0.139	0.497
		F2	−0.096	
		F2	0.021	

build the relationship model between design elements and kansei words. Taking "Rich-Monotonous" as an example, the results calculated by MATLAB 2019 are shown in Table 4.

As the Table 4 shows, to the kansei words "Various-Monotonous", "picture in keyboard background (E1)" obtained the largest positive score, which means that the element level made users' feel of various; "Common shape of function key (D2)" got the smallest negative score, which means that the design element level made users feel of monotonous. As for the partial correlation coefficient of each design element, we found that Function key (D)" obtained the highest partial correlation coefficient, which means that the design element has the greatest impact on the user's feeling of "Various-Monotonous". While Candidate area (B)" got the lowest partial correlation coefficient, which means that the design element has the least impact on the user's feeling of "Rich-Monotonous".

Using the same way to get the most typical element levels s of each kansei word, as is shown in Table 5.

According to the partial correlation coefficient of kansei words, the design elements that have the greatest impact on users' kasnei cognition are: Toolbar, Function key, Keyboard background, Keyboard background, Button background, Shortcut key, Function key, Button background.

Table 5. Most typical element level

Kansei word	Vocabulary	IME element	Element level
Relaxed-Reserved	Relaxed	Toolbar	Unique shape
	Reserved	Shortcut key	The same color with background color
Personal-Common	Personal	Function key	Unique shape
	Common	Toolbar	Common shape
Beautiful-Ugly	Beautiful	Keyboard background	Picture
	Ugly	Function key	Common shape
Joyful-Sad	Joyful	Keyboard background	Picture
	Sad	Keyboard background	Pure color
Novel-Obsolete	Novel	Button background	Filled button background
	Obsolete	Keyboard background	Pure color
Classical-Modern	Classical	Candidate area	Decorations
	Modern	Shortcut key	Different color from background picture
Various-Monotonous	Various	Keyboard background	Picture
	Monotonous	Function key	Common shape
Lovely-Disgusting	Lovely	Button background	Filled button background
	Disgusting	Function key	Common shape

4.2 Relation Between User Preference and Design Elements Levels

The kansei word pair "Like-Dislike" was used as the dependent variable. The element levels were used as the independent variables. The results of PLS showed that (E1) got the highest score, that is to say, users prefer using a picture as keyboard background, while common shape of function key (D2) will not be liked. Keyboard background (E) had the highest corresponding partial correlation coefficient, which indicates that it has the greatest impact on user preferences.

4.3 Relation Between Users' Preference and Kansei Words

The kansei word pair "Like-Dislike" was used as the dependent variable, other kansei word pairs were taken as the independent variables. The results of the PLS showed that, the score of "Various" is the highest, indicating that users like various perceptual images. The lowest score of "Ugly" indicated that users did not like ugly skin of IMEs. The "Various-Monotonous" (B1) have the highest partial correlation coefficient, indicating that the word pair have the highest impact on users' preferences.

5 A Case for Appearance of a Mobile IME Satisfying User Preference

According to the analysis in the previous chapter, the skin design elements of input method can be optimized as follows based on the previous design of mobile input method editor. The following is the improved input method interface design (Fig. 2).

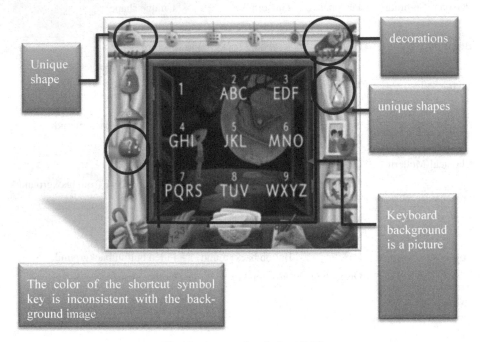

Fig. 2. A case of optimized IME

6 Conclusions and Limitations

This research aims to study the relationship between the skin elements of mobile IMEs, kansei words and users' references. The main conclusions are as follows:

1. Extract six design elements of the input method skin and obtain three input method skin samples. Three representative input skin samples were obtained through cluster analysis.
2. Using semantic difference method and factor analysis, eight pairs of kansei words that can be used to evaluate the input method skin were screened out.
3. Construct a relationship model between the skin elements of mobile IMEs, kansei words and users' references, and optimize the design of the skin of mobile IMEs.

This study extend the research of Kansei Engineering to the interface of mobile IEMs. The results demonstrate that the appearance of IEMs can be design according to users' kansei needs to meet users preference, which can provide suggests for the design of the interface of IEM according to users' kansei needs.

There are at least two limitations of this study. Firstly, participants in this study were university students. Further study should consider a more diversified group. Secondly, the design elements of IEMs were selected according experts' opinion based on morphological analysis, which may be not comprehensive and accurate. A more objective method, such as eye tracking, should be explored to obtain the design elements of IEMs.

Acknowledgments. This work is supported by the National Natural Science Foundation of China (Grant No. 71701003, 71801002, 71802002), Ministry of Education Industry-University Cooperation Collaborative Education Project (Grant no. 201901024006), the Key Project for Natural Science Fund of Colleges in Anhui Province (Grant no. KJ2017A108).

References

1. Beijing Sogou Technology Development Co. Ltd.: Patent application titled "input method, apparatus, and electronic device". Computers, Networks & Communications (2018)
2. Chen, J., Luo, R., Liu, H.: The effect of pinyin input experience on the link between semantic and phonology of Chinese character in digital writing. J. Psycholinguist. Res. **46**, 923–934 (2017). https://doi.org/10.1007/s10936-016-9470-y
3. Judith, O., Yan, M.: Considerations for Chinese text input methods in the design of speech generating devices: a tutorial. Clin. Linguist. Phonetics (2019). https://doi.org/10.1080/026 99206.2019.1652934
4. Kim, H.-W., Park, J.H., Jeong, Y.-S.: An efficient character input scheme with a gyro sensor of smartphone on ubiquitous cluster computing. Cluster Comput. **18**, 147–156 (2015). https://doi.org/10.1007/s10586-014-0382-z
5. Zhang, Y.Y.: Research on the application of Sogou mobile phone input method in UI visual design. Capital Normal University (2014)
6. Wen, T., Li, X., Li, C., Liu, X., Qing, X.G., Yan, H.Y.: Research on the usability evaluation of mobile input method. Chin. J. Ergon. **18**, 27–31 (2012). https://doi.org/10.3969/j.issn.1006-8309.2012.02.007
7. Li, M.L.: Research on web interface optimization design based on perceptual engineering. Northeastern University (2014)
8. Xu, L.: Research on the design of mobile input method interface. Xi'an Polytechnic University (2018)
9. Guo, F., Liu, W.L., Cao, Y.Q., Liu, F.T., Li, M.L.: Optimization Design of a Webpage Based on Kansei Engineering. Hum. Factor Ergon. Manuf. **26**, 110–126 (2016). https://doi.org/10.1002/hfm.20617
10. Barrero, A., Melendi, D., Pañeda, X.G., García, R., Cabrero, S.: An empirical investigation into text input methods for interactive digital television applications. Int. J. Hum.-Comput. Int. **30** (2014). https://doi.org/10.1080/10447318.2013.858461
11. Jindo, T., Nagamachi, M., Matsubara, Y.: A study of image recognition on Kansei engineering. Adv. Hum. Factors/Ergon. **20** (1995). https://doi.org/10.1016/s0921-2647(06)80030-4
12. Llinares, C., Page, A.F.: Kano's model in Kansei engineering to evaluate subjective real estate consumer preferences. Int. J. Ind. Ergon. **41** (2011). https://doi.org/10.1016/j.ergon.2011.01.011
13. Mitsuo, N.: Kansei engineering as a powerful consumer-oriented technology for product development. Appl. Ergon. **33** (2002). https://doi.org/10.1016/s0003-6870(02)00019-4

14. Toshinori, F.J., Yukihiro, M.N., Mitsuo, N.: Evaluation of Kansei engineering system based on virtual reality. Jpn. J. Ergon. **32** (1996).https://doi.org/10.5100/jje.32.supplement_178

15. Kashiwagi, K., Matsubara, Y., Nagamachi, M.: Considerations for applying Kansei engineering to basic design. Jpn. J. Ergon. **28** (1992). https://doi.org/10.5100/jje.28.supplement_324

16. Xu, Z.: Perceptual analysis in the design of human-computer interface. Fine Arts Lit. 138–139 (2014). https://doi.org/10.16585/j.cnki.mswx.2014.01.007

17. Ding, Y.Y.: A study on the relationship between the appearance and the perceptual intention of urban small electric vehicles. Art Des. **2**, 113–115 (2015). https://doi.org/10.16824/j.cnki.issn10082832.2015.07.034

18. Amanda, L.S., Barbsrs, S.C.: Smartphone text input method performance, usability, and preference with younger and older adults. Hum. Factors: J. Hum. Factors Ergon. Soc. **57** (2015). https://doi.org/10.1177/0018720815575644

19. Ryohei, N., Nobuchika, S., Shogo, N.: Study of the input method in the touchpad interface to manipulate AR objects. Trans. Virtual Reality Soc. Jpn. **19** (2014). https://doi.org/10.18974/tvrsj.19.2_265

20. Maji, A., Velaga, N.R., Urie, Y.: Hierarchical clustering analysis framework of mutually exclusive crash causation parameters for regional road safety strategies. Int. J. Inj. Control Saf. Promot. **25** (2018). https://doi.org/10.1080/17457300.2017.1416485

Author Index

Printed in the United States
By Bookmasters